INTERLANGUAGE PHONOLOGY
The Acquisition of a Second Language Sound System

Georgette Ioup

University of New Orleans

Steven H. Weinberger

University of Washington

NEWBURY HOUSE PUBLISHERS, Cambridge

A division of Harper & Row, Publishers, Inc.

New York, Philadelphia, San Francisco, Washington, D.C.
London, Mexico City, São Paulo, Singapore, Sydney

Library of Congress Cataloging-in-Publication Data

Interlanguage phonology.

(Issues in second language research series)
Bibliography: p.
Includes index.
1. Interlanguage (Language learning) 2. Grammar,
Comparative and general—Phonology. 3. Second
language acquisition. I. Ioup, Georgette.
II. Weinberger, Steven H. III. Series.
P53.I519 1987   414   86-21830
ISBN 0-06-632287-1

Production Coordinator/Maeve Cullinane
Copy editor/Dorothy Seymour
Composition/ComCom, A division of Haddon Craftsmen
Printer/McNaughton & Gunn

NEWBURY HOUSE PUBLISHERS
A division of Harper & Row, Publishers, Inc.

Language Science
Language Teaching
Language Learning

CAMBRIDGE, MASSACHUSETTS

Printed in the U.S.A.   First printing: March 1987
   63 22879   2 4 6 8 10 9 7 5 3

SERIES ON

ISSUES IN SECOND LANGUAGE RESEARCH

under the editorship of

Robin C. Scarcella and Michael H. Long

ISSUES IN SECOND LANGUAGE RESEARCH is a series of volumes dealing with empirical issues in second language acquisition research. Each volume gathers significant papers dealing with questions and hypotheses in areas central to second language theory and practice. Papers will be selected from the previously published professional literature as well as from current sources.

OTHER BOOKS IN THIS SERIES

Child-Adult Differences in Second Language Acquisition
   Stephen D. Krashen, Robin C. Scarcella, and Michael H. Long, Editors

Input in Second Language Acquisition
   Susan M. Gass and Carolyn G. Madden, Editors

Language Transfer in Language Learning
   Susan Gass and Larry Selinker, Editors

Research in Second Language Acquisition
   Robin C. Scarcella and Stephen D. Krashen, Editors

Sociolinguistics and Language Acquisition
   Nessa Wolfson and Elliot Judd, Editors

Talking to Learn
   Richard R. Day, Editor

For justice in the Middle East

Contents

v

ACKNOWLEDGMENTS

The editors are grateful to the contributors to this volume who have allowed us to reprint their material. We also thank the publishers of the journals and volumes for their permission to reprint the following articles:

Altenberg, E., and R. Vago. Theoretical implications of an error analysis of second language phonology production. *Language Learning*, 1983, *33*, 427–448.

Anderson, J. The markedness differential hypothesis and syllable structure difficulty. In *Proceedings of the Conference on the Uses of Phonology.* Carbondale: Southern Illinois University, 1983. (This article was adapted for the present volume.)

Beebe, L. Sociolinguistic variation and style shifting in second language acquisition. *Language Learning*, 1980, *30*, 433–447.

Beebe, L. Myths about interlanguage phonology. *Studies in Descriptive Linguistics,* Vol. 13. In Stig Eliasson, (Ed.), *Theoretical Issues in Contrastive Phonology.* Heidelberg: Julius Groos Verlag, 1984, 51–62.

Broselow, E. Non-obvious transfer: On predicting epenthesis errors. In S. Gass and L. Selinker (Eds.), *Language Transfer in Language Learning,* Rowley, MA: Newbury House, 1983, 269–280.

Broselow, E. An investigation of transfer in second language acquisition. In *International Review of Applied Linguistics (IRAL).* 1984, *22,* 253–269.

Dickerson, W. The psycholinguistic unity of language learning and language change. *Language Learning,* 1976, *26,* 215–231.

Eckman, F. Markedness and the contrastive analysis hypothesis. *Language Learning,* 1977, *27,* 315–330.

Eckman, F. On the naturalness of interlanguage phonological rules. *Language Learning,* 1981, *31,* 195–216.

Flege, J. and J. Hillenbrand. Limits on phonetic accuracy in foreign language speech production. *Journal of the Acoustical Society of America,* 1984, *76,* 708–721. © 1984 American Institute of Physics.

Kiparsky, P., and L. Menn. On the acquisition of phonology. In J. MacNamara (Ed.), *Language Learning and Thought.* NY: Academic Press, 1977, 47–78.

Macken, M., and C. Ferguson. Phonological universals in language acquisition. In H. Winitz (Ed.), *Native Language and Foreign Language Acquisition.* NY: New York Academy of Sciences, 1981, 110–129.

Mulford, R., and B. Hecht. The acquisition of a second language phonology: Interaction of transfer and developmental factors. *Applied Psycholinguistics.* NY: Cambridge University Press, 1982, *3,* 313–328.

Neufeld, G. On the acquisition of prosodic and articulatory features in adult language learning. *The Canadian Modern Language Review,* 1978, *34,* 163–174.

Sato, C. Phonological processes in second language acquisition: Another look at interlanguage syllable structure. *Language Learning,* 1984, *34*:4, 43–57. (This article was adapted for the present volume.)

Schmidt, R. Sociolinguistic variation and language transfer in phonology. *Working Papers in Bilingualism.* 1977, *12,* 79–95.

Tarone, E. The phonology of interlanguage. In J. Richards (Ed.), *Understanding Second and Foreign Language Learning.* Rowley, MA: Newbury House, 1978, 15–33.

Tarone, E. Some influences on the syllable structure of interlanguage phonology. *International Review of Applied Linguistics (IRAL.)* 1980, *18,* 139–152.

CONTRIBUTORS TO THIS VOLUME

Evelyn Altenberg
Queens College of the City University of
    New York

Janet Anderson
Iowa State University

Warren Anderson
University of Southeast Missouri

Leslie Beebe
Columbia University Teachers College

Ellen Broselow
State University of New York at
    Stony Brook

Budsaba Budsayamongkon
Southern Illinois University

Wayne Dickerson
University of Illinois

Fred Eckman
University of Wisconsin at Milwaukee

Charles Ferguson
Stanford University

James Flege
University of Alabama at Birmingham

Barbara Hecht
University of California at Los Angeles

James Hillenbrand
Northwestern University

Richard Hurtig
University of Iowa

Georgette Ioup
University of New Orleans

Simin Karimi
University of Washington

Paul Kiparsky
Stanford University

Marlys Macken
Stanford University

Roy Major
Washington State University

Lisa Menn
University of Colorado

Randa Mulford
University of Iceland

Geoffrey Nathan
Southern Illinois University

Gerald Neufeld
University of Ottawa

Catherine Ringen
University of Iowa

Charlene Sato
University of Hawaii

Richard Schmidt
University of Hawaii

Marianne Stølen
University of Washington

Amara Tansomboon
University of Washington

Elaine Tarone
University of Minnesota

Robert Vago
Queens College of the City University of
    New York

Steven Weinberger
University of Washington

INTRODUCTION

Within the past few years there has been a resurgence of interest in the phonological aspects of second language acquisition research. This is due presumably to the fact that phonological theory is currently undergoing revolutionary changes unprecedented in generative phonology. Not only are there new approaches to a characterization of the rule systems that relate underlying representation to phonetic structure, but there are innovative non-linear models, such as metrical and autosegmental phonology, which provide a principled account of phenomena that were previously resistant to an adequate analysis. Because of these new approaches, the constructs of the syllable and the suprasegmental have attained greater significance within phonological theory, and they thus provide the basis for much of the structural description.

The excitement resulting from these advances in generative phonology acutely affected second language research, where interlanguage phonology, long ignored or trivialized, has now become an important area of investigation. Inspired by the recent developments in synchronic and L1 developmental phonology, researchers have applied these insights to the analysis of L2 data with very interesting results, and these endeavors have led to new directions for future exploration. At the same time, L2 data appear to have implications for phonological theory. L2 phenomena provide important evidence to justify and motivate phonological descriptions (cf. Kenstowicz and Kisseberth, 1979, p.154). In essence, we observe a symbiotic relationship developing between phonological theory and L2 phonological research.

Previously, it had been assumed that the investigation of the learner's phonological system would provide no useful insights into the nature of the second language acquisition process, since all phonological errors were believed to be the result of direct transfer of the NL phonology to the IL system in uninteresting ways. Recent investigations have revealed that transfer is not the simplistic process once believed to be the case; moreover, it is just one of several forces at work shaping the form of the L2 phonological system. And these processes appear to interact in rather interesting ways. A principal goal of current work in L2 phonology is to determine the exact nature of these interactions. Other developments currently being investigated include the search for an expanded understanding of developmental sources of phonological problem areas, the universal tendencies in L2 phonology, the role of markedness in shaping the IL phonological rule system, and the variation in phonological development resulting from the interplay of social and psychological factors.

By examining L2 phonology from a number of perspectives, recent research has been able to give new insight into the complexities that define the developmental process. Nevertheless, there remain many unresolved problem areas. First and foremost, our research is not at the stage where it allows an *a priori* prediction of the error types that will occur, given a particular source and target language. Rather, one can analyze only those errors that have already been attested. For example, there is still no explanation for the reason certain source languages produce a [t,d] substitution for English [θ,ð] while others consistently produce a [s,z] substitution. Even more puzzling is the fact that dialects of the same language with essentially the same phonemic inventory of consonants produce different substitution variants. In the earliest work on contrastive phonology, this lack of predictive ability was identified as a major problem for a theory of L2 phonology (cf. Lado, 1957; Richards, 1968). We are no closer now to an adequate solution.

There are other problems that remain unsolved in part because of insufficient investigation. There has been relatively little work done to determine differences in perceptual and articulatory difficulties. For example, is a new segment or contrast in the L2 equally difficult to produce and perceive? With respect to processes that shape IL phonology, while some attention has been focused on the fact that developmental forces similar to those at work in L1 phonology contribute to the interlanguage phonological system, unlike the case of first language acquisition, these processes must interact with transfer processes. What is still unknown is the extent to which the two processes affect each other and the exact nature of this interaction. Also puzzling is the fact that only a certain subset of the developmental processes occurring in the acquisition of a L1 phonology are employed by the second language learner. We find that epenthesis seems to be more prevalent than cluster reduction, especially in word-initial position, common L1 phonological processes such as metathesis and reduplication are seldom witnessed, and certain simplifications of problematic segments are not utilized by L2 learners, who prefer instead to resolve the problem through the transfer of a phonological approximate from the native language. What remains to be made precise in interlanguage phonological research is exactly which developmental processes occur in L2 phonology and why in specific cases transfer is preferred to a L1 learner's simplification strategy.

Ultimately, the major question to be answered is to what extent a new sound system can be acquired by a second language learner. First we will want to determine the point at which the acquisition of a native-like pronunciation is no longer a foregone conclusion. Do all children learning a L2 before puberty achieve accent-free speech? What percentage of teenage learners do? How do youngsters who do acquire a native command differ from their peers who don't, both in the cognitive and the affective domains? Finally, for those learners for whom the acquisition of a native pronunciation cannot be achieved in an untutored learning context, is there any hope? Is the research in L2 phonology leading us in the direction of developing effective methods for teaching accent-free speech to adults? Two articles in the present volume, those in Part Five by Neufeld and by Ioup and Tansomboon, allude to approaches that might lead to more successful pronunciation. There are important research issues that must first be resolved, however, before we can know whether there exist effective techniques to enhance the acquisition of pronunciation.

The present volume aims to consolidate the current work in interlanguage phonology. It brings together both articles that provide a basis for the current work in interlanguage phonology and studies that articulate new directions for future research. The book is organized around six major themes. The first two are intended to provide a theoretical foundation for IL phonological research, and the latter four pertain to particular aspects of L2 phonology. Part One contains articles that focus on the general nature of phonological acquisition, through an assessment of the various models of phonological development and a discussion of acquisition universals. Part Two provides a theoretical background to interlanguage phonological research. The articles in Part Three deal with the segment, those in Part Four focus on the syllable, those in Part Five concern suprasegmentals, and those in Part Six discuss the diverse dimensions of variation in L2 phonological acquisition.

The text is organized in such a way as to be utilized as both a research reference and a classroom text for a course that devotes a significant portion of its time to L2 phonological acquisition. Such a course may be concerned solely with interlanguage phonology, or it may be a course devoted to the general nature of either second language acquisition or phonological development from all perspectives. In a course of the latter type, the instructor will find that the research in this volume allows easy comparison to work in L1 phonology. The articles in each section have been selected and organized to form a coherent grouping, one work often referring to other work within the section and frequently providing a response to an unresolved issue raised in the previous article. The interrelatedness of current research in L2 phonology is a major focus of the book. In every section the articles build upon ideas presented elsewhere in the volume. Contributing authors frequently cite the work of the other authors. Thus it is hoped that a major outcome of the book is the encouragement of research intended to resolve issues currently being raised in the field of interlanguage phonology. Readers will find many potential research endeavors embedded within the studies presented.

REFERENCES

Kenstowicz, M., and C. Kisseberth. 1979. *Generative Phonology.* NY: Academic Press.
Lado, R. 1957. *Linguistics Across Cultures.* Ann Arbor: University of Michigan Press.
Ritchie, W. 1968. On the explanation of phonic interference. *Language Learning, 18:*183–197.

Part One

GENERAL MODELS OF PHONOLOGICAL DEVELOPMENT

The two articles in this section are intended to provide the reader with the theoretical background necessary to understand the current work being done in developmental phonology. The theoretical issues discussed are relevant to both first and second language research and should form a basis for the ideas presented throughout the book. Both articles touch upon the relationship between current theories of developmental phonology and second language acquisition.

The article by Macken and Ferguson develops a cognitive model of phonological acquisition in which the learner is actively engaged in creative processes. Most important, the authors note a current shift away from the earlier deterministic models to a more flexible one that can accommodate variation. This variation is said to be a result of several factors, among them the fact that processes that are universal do not apply uniformly to every segment or syllable; nor do they operate consistently in every child. The course of phonological development is thus seen to be shaped by the interplay of language universals and individual variation.

Kiparsky and Menn also argue for a cognitive approach to phonological acquisition. A major goal of their article is to define the common set of learning

1

principles that operate at every level of phonological acquisition, from the acquisition of the phonetic repertoire and the phonological rule system to the development of complex morphophonemic rules at more advanced stages of learning. The authors demonstrate that the same linguistic problem-solving mechanisms underlie the acquisition of all domains of phonology. They evaluate two current models of phonological acquisition, Jakobson's model based on his hierarchy of distinctive features and Stampe's theory of natural phonology. These are compared to a third model, which they set forth, one that can be described as a cognitive problem-solving approach to acquisition. They illustrate that, using this approach, one is able to provide a more adequate analysis of phonological acquisition data.

1

PHONOLOGICAL UNIVERSALS IN LANGUAGE ACQUISITION*

Marlys A. Macken   **Charles A. Ferguson**

The paradox of human language is that it is at once both fixed and free; universals of structure and process coexist with diversity and change. True universals are so deeply a part of language, so basic to the ways in which we think about language, that—like fish in water—we find it difficult to recognize them, or, when we do, they seem obvious or trivial. Not surprisingly, progress has been slow toward the goal of characterizing human language. In phonology, exceptionless universals include linearity of units that are analyzable into hierarchical structures, rule-governed systems, redundancy, and variation in sounds by context, speaker, and social setting, as well as over time.

Easier to discover are the widespread tendencies of languages to pattern in certain ways. The term "universal" will be used here, as it is often used in linguistics, to describe such cross-language patterns—ones that have a high probability of occurrence but are not without exception, such as Trubetzkoy's

*Some of the research reported here was carried out at the Child Phonology Project of Stanford University, under a series of grants from the National Science Foundation, the National Institutes of Health, the National Institute of Education, and the W.T. Grant Foundation.

typology of vowel systems, Ferguson's universal states and normal tendencies for nasals, and Greenberg's implicational universals for glottalized consonants (Greenberg, Ferguson, & Moravcsik, 1978). In phonology, many such universals derive from universal properties of human articulatory and perceptual systems (Ohala, 1974 and 1980; Lindblom, 1979; Liljencrants & Lindblom, 1972). Yet the hallmark of human language is its range of variation, across particular languages and within the individual. A characterization of the constraints on this variation is as much a part of a theory of human language as is the characterization of the commonly occurring patterns.

The same paradox exists for language development: It too is both fixed and free. The determination of true universals is likewise difficult, the statement of general patterns somewhat easier. And once again, the hallmark is variation, across languages and in the individual. Much research in child phonology is directed toward finding regularities in this variation. The formulation of a theory of acquisition lies in the distant future, and behind us lies a history of the sequential demise of elegant, yet ultimately too simple, acquisitional theories.

We begin this paper by briefly reviewing the major universalist theories, both to provide the necessary framework for the data we discuss and also to emphasize the point that a discussion of "language universals" (developmental and otherwise) entails a particular theoretical position—one that is not uncontroversial. The philosophical debate over language universals goes back centuries. Although the universal status of the phonological properties we gave earlier (as examples of true universals) is widely accepted in the field, not all phonologists are committed to the view that there exists a set of general patterns (e.g., most early American structuralists and the proponents of the British prosodic school). Likewise, in child phonology, debate continues over the existence of a universal developmental sequence.

In the second section, we give a partial typology of phonological processes that are universal in the probabilistic sense and appear to be due to purely linguistic constraints. In addition to summarizing the major findings of a certain body of research, this review serves to exemplify the nature of linguistically oriented work conducted (explicitly or implicitly) within a universalist framework. Accurately reflecting the general state in the field as a whole, this typology is descriptive, not explanatory.

From general patterns, we take up the issue of variation, exploring a single topic—the acquisition of voicing—in search of universals, methodological explanations for variation, and regularities underlying cross-language differences. Just as cross-cultural, anthropological research on Polynesian navigation systems, iKung San hunting practices, and Kpelle class-inclusion concepts has revealed the cultural context of western theories of cognition including that of Piaget (e.g., Super, 1979), cross-linguistic phonological acquisition research has demonstrated that the developmental sequence is affected greatly by both the macro context (the particular language) and the micro context (e.g., the specific input to the child).

In the final section, we turn to variation in the individual child—abstracting away from this linguistic variation to formulate general functional characteristics of the acquisition process that seem to be nonlinguistic in origin: Underlying the linguistic variation are regularities that appear to reflect a general process of rule formation, which we refer to as "regularization." Here, as in the section on voicing, we propose that at least some general patterns underlie variation, and that insight into the developmental process can be gained by a detailed consideration of variation itself. Together these sections exemplify two directions that research must take if the goal of characterizing constraints on variation is to be met. In discussing regulation, we propose two hypotheses that cast a different light on the nature of at least some developmental universals; these hypotheses, with the data that support them, partially constitute the foundation of a more cognitive model of phonological acquisition.

Throughout this paper, the two themes of pattern and diversity are interwoven. The topic of phonological universals is exceedingly complex: The data we obtain from children are diverse, and many central theoretical issues are not yet well understood (and, in fact, not often discussed). Thus it is premature for first language (L1) research to provide answers to questions of importance to second language (L2) research. A more modest goal is, however, attainable: The purpose of this paper is to present a perspective from normal L1 phonological development in the child that will offer clues for research in L2 phonology acquisition.

UNIVERSALIST THEORIES

During the past fifteen years, linguistically oriented research on child phonology has been dominated by three universalist acquisition theories, each related to a particular phonological theory.

In the structuralist tradition, Jakobson's theory formulated several acquisition predictions based on the premise that there is a universal hierarchy of structural laws that determine the inventory of phonemic systems and the relative frequency, combinatorial distribution, and assimilatory power of particular phonemes (Jakobson, 1941). Jakobson's predictions include the following: (a) the order of acquisition of minimal consonant and vowel inventories (e.g., $p > t > m > n$); (b) stops are acquired before nasals, with fricatives next and liquids late; (c) voiceless consonants are acquired before voiced; (d) front consonants are acquired before back; (e) in the early stages, fricatives will be replaced by stops and back consonants by front consonants. Jakobson's theory is by far the most influential of the various universalist models: Several researchers have worked from a Jakobsonian framework (e.g., Moskowitz, 1970 and 1973); and many cross-linguistic data have been interpreted as providing support for its general outline of development (e.g., Velten, 1943, for English; Pačesová, 1968, for Czech; Jeng, 1979, for Chinese).

The universalist/nativist approach to acquisition most often associated with Chomsky, and with it the classic generative phonology paradigm (Chomsky & Halle, 1968) is represented in the works of Smith (e.g., Smith, 1973 and 1975). Smith identifies four universal tendencies: the tendencies toward consonant and vowel harmony, consonant cluster reduction, systemic simplification (mostly deletion and substitution rules), and grammatical simplification (e.g., the use of a single CV[1] syllable for all unstressed syllables). Smith—who is purposely neutral on the nativist issue—views these universal constraints as "part of a universal template which the child has to escape from in order to learn his language."[2]

The third theory is that of Stampe's natural phonology, which emphasizes universal innate natural processes and an associated acquisition theory (Stampe, 1969; Donegan & Stampe, 1979). Stampe's basic assumption is that the phonological system of a language is the residue of a universal system of processes, governed by forces implicit in human articulation and perception. During acquisition, those processes inapplicable to the particular language being learned are constrained by the mechanisms of suppression, limitation, and ordering (e.g., Edwards, 1971). Examples of early processes are unstressed syllable deletion, cluster reduction, de-spirantization (that is, stopping), and depalatalization. A proponent of natural generative phonology (a theory that is based on some aspects from each of the three theories previously mentioned), Hooper (1977) takes a strong position on the similarity between the child's phonological system and the adult's (as do Stampe and Smith).

From the early 1960s (and especially since 1968, the publication date of the English translation of Jakobson), interest and publication in child phonology have increased dramatically. This period of research—largely universalist and linguistic-theory dominated—has made important contributions to the field in at least two ways. First, a great deal of information has been collected on the sounds and substitutions that children produce and, more generally, the set of simplificational processes that characterize the relation between the adult model and the child replica. Second, this research period has produced insight into issues of central importance to universals and generalizations that underlie cross-linguistic differences. The following two sections summarize selected findings within each of these two types of contribution. The first section catalogues and interprets a number of universal tendencies. This typology of rules thus covers a variety of topics. The second section, to clarify several factors affecting the developmental sequence, explores a single topic in greater detail.

Throughout this research period, the universalist theories were examined and evaluated, and each was criticized on various empirical and theoretical grounds (e.g., Olmsted, 1971; Ferguson & Garnica, 1975; Kiparsky & Menn, 1977). For example, several key points of Jakobson's theory were called into question, most importantly its claim that development is uniform across children (cf. counterexamples to the Jakobsonian order of acquisition in Macken, 1980) and the claim that the process of acquisition is one of successive acquisition of phonological oppositions (cf. evidence for the early priority of whole-word contrasts and effects of word position in Ferguson & Farwell, 1975). A second important body of research challenged the empirical assumptions on which Chomsky's hypothesis of an innate "language acquisition device" was based (Levelt, 1975; McCawley, 1977). For example, research has shown that the input to the child is *not* degenerate in quality (e.g., Snow & Ferguson, 1977) and that language acquisition is not independent of cognitive development (Clark, 1973). A third important finding is summed up by Harris (in his 1979 critique of Hooper):

The considerable developmental literature over the last decade suggests that the acquisition process involves a series of successive approximations to adult grammars and that some adjacent stages involve discontinuities that might well be characterized as "radical."[3]

With some notable exceptions, the critiques during this period did not alter substantively the basic premises of the universalist approach. Now, however, a shift is in progress in the field as a whole, toward a new model of acquisition, one that focuses on a new and different type of universals.

This shift is due mainly to the accumulation, over the past several years, of data that cannot be handled within the universalist linguistic models. These data document the existence of significant, widespread individual differences between children acquiring the same language and show that the acquisition process, in certain key aspects, is not, as assumed by the universalist model, a linear progression of unfolding abilities. The emerging model recognizes several types of learning (e.g., accretion and tuning) but emphasizes the cognitive aspects of acquisition (Kiparsky & Menn, 1977; Fey & Gandour, 1979; Ferguson & Macken, 1980). In this view, the child is an active seeker and user of linguistic information who forms hypotheses on the basis of input data, tests and revises these hypotheses, and constructs more complex systems (or "grammars") out of earlier, simpler ones. The shift is away from a deterministic linguistic model toward a flexible model that accommodates variation in development by acknowledging the active role of the child, the diversity of input, and the variety of possible solutions. The contributions of the earlier period of research were to clarify universal tendencies that result from purely linguistic constraints imposed by the nature of human language and human articulatory and perceptual systems. To these universals now is added a set assumed to result from universal cognitive, problem-solving abilities of the human learner—a set that describes how the young child deals with complexity (what Cazden calls universal processing strategies), recognizes patterns, constructs linguistic categories, and organizes categories into systems. It is this new set of proposed universals that is the topic of the last section of this paper.

PHONOLOGICAL PROCESSES AGE 1 YEAR 6 MONTHS TO 4 YEARS

One of the best-attested facts about child language development is the appearance of systematic relationships between adult speech sounds and the corresponding child speech sounds during the period of greatest phonological development, typically between one and a half and four years of age. Children make systematic "errors" in producing speech sounds—i.e., they tend regularly to produce a particular wrong sound in place of the correct adult sound, as when an English-learning child says *t* for *k* in several words (e.g., *tum* for *come*). The relationships between the target sounds and the child's counterpart sounds ("model" and "replica" sounds) are not random but are phonetically systematic, and in current analyses they are regarded as instances of *phonological processes* (PPs) in operation (Oller, 1975). The replacement of *k* by *t* is thus an example of the PP of "fronting," by which a palatal or velar consonant is replaced by a corresponding dental/alveolar one. Ingram (1979) summarizes present knowledge of PPs in children, and his classification is followed here.

In addition to the fact that PPs universally appear in operation at this age, the PP phenomenon has universal significance in that some processes are extremely common across many languages and many children, while others are more likely in particular languages or are favored by particular children. Although the incidence of particular processes cannot be predicted, probability statements of considerable interest can be made. For example, in accordance with the fronting process, it is much more likely that model [k] will be represented by replica [t] than vice versa.

Substitution Processes

The most obvious kind of child PP is the substitution of one segmental sound for another, and such patterns of substitution have been discussed in detail in various places (Jakobson, 1941; Smith, 1973; Leopold, 1939–47). One substitution process, *stopping,* will serve as an example of the type: Fricatives are replaced by stops of the corresponding place of articulation. Thus, in acquiring their first language, many children will at some stage make "errors" in producing such fricatives as [f v s z . . .], replacing them with corresponding stops [p b t d . . .], as in [dɛ] for English *there* or [to] for French [so] *sceau* (bucket) (Ferguson, 1978; Ingram, 1978).

The stopping process is a good example of a fundamental principle accounting for such varied phenomena as the distribution of phoneme types among the world's languages, the processes of language change over time, language acquisition, and language loss. Jakobson and his successors have sought such fundamental principles. In this instance the principle is one of "markedness": Fricatives are more complex articulatorily and more "marked" than stops, and hence their presence in a language or in a child's phonology presupposes the presence of stops in the same system. Any natural human language that has fricative phonemes in its inventory also will have stops but not vice versa; a language typically has more stops than fricatives, and any child who produces fricative consonants also produces stop consonants. Yet in this instance, as in some others, the principle does not carry over directly into sound change: The change of fricative to stop is not nearly as common as stop to fricative in the history of the world's languages (Ferguson, 1978).

Other substitution processes operative in child phonology include fronting, gliding, and vocalization (Ingram, 1979).

Assimilation Processes

Another common type of child PP is one in which sounds in the child's production are assimilated to neighboring sounds in the same word or other unit. Thus the affected sound has a phonetic relation not only to the model sound but also to relevant other sounds that occur near it. For example, if a child regularly says *guck* for *duck,* the initial alveolar /d/ is being assimilated to the velar /k/ later in the word, and the same child may say [d] for adult /d/ in words that do not contain a following velar stop.

Assimilatory processes are the commonest type of PPs in operation in synchronic alterations, and they are also common in child phonology. The example we choose here, however, is *consonant harmony,* the assimilation of consonants at a distance within the same word, a PP quite frequent in child phonology but extremely rare as a process in the world's languages (Drachman, 1978; Vihman, 1980). In a detailed study of thirteen children acquiring six different first languages, this PP affected more than 14 percent of the words in their vocabulary, with more than half the children showing 12 percent or more consonant harmony words (Vihman, 1978). Investigators have noted evidence of a strength hierarchy such that velars and labials are most resistant to assimilation and dentals the most likely to assimilate: [gʌk] is more likely than [dʌt] for adult *duck.* It also has been noted that this hierarchy differs from the order-of-acquisition hierarchies, which provide that velars more often are acquired later than anteriors (labials or dentals) and that the control of the voicing parameter is typically achieved earlier in anteriors than in velars (Macken, 1980, 1979).

Other assimilation processes operative in child phonology include consonant voicing (in voiced surroundings; devoicing in word-final position) and denasalization (Ingram, 1979).

Syllable Structure Processes

One of the most noticeable phonetic relationships between model and replica sounds is children's omission of segments or whole syllables present in the adult item. Such deletion processes are examples of syllable structure PPs, ones that affect the phonetic complexity of the speech chain. Such processes range from simple deletions (e.g., [bɛ] for *bed*) to highly idiosyncratic rearrangements (e.g., [kajan] for *chocolate*) (Priestly, 1977). The sample process chosen here is *consonant cluster reduction:* A sequence of two or more consonants is replaced by a single consonant (e.g., [dɛs] for *dress*) or is eliminated in some other way.

This PP is extremely widespread; it probably appears in the course of L1 acquisition of any language that has consonant clusters, and it is part of a general trend favoring simple CV syllables as against CCV, CVC, and other more complex syllable types. It is possible to identify strong statistical trends that hold across languages. For example, clusters of stop plus liquid (e.g., *tr, kl*) typically progress through liquid deletion to liquid substitution to correct production (e.g., *tain, twain, train*) (Greenlee, 1974). Cluster reduction appears in language phenomena other than L1 acquisition, but the cluster reduction recorded in the history of languages often shows very different trends than in child phonology; e.g., epenthesis, the insertion of a vowel to break up the cluster, is common in language change and borrowing, but not in child phonology (Vihman, 1980). An example of close matching in trends, however, is the treatment of medial clusters of nasal plus stop. In both child phonology and historical change, the most likely outcome is the deletion of the nasal if the stop is voiceless and the deletion of the stop if it is voiced (presumably through an intermediate stage of assimilation, e.g., *nd* → *nn* → *n*) (Greenlee & Ohala, 1980).

Other Processes

As is evident from the example of nasal cluster reduction, many PPs in child language combine assimilatory and syllable structure aspects or do not fit neatly into the classification. As an example of such not readily classifiable processes, we choose *reduplication*—i.e., the transformation of model words into structures of repeated identical or partly identical CV syllables. This PP, or family of PPs, may involve extension of adult monosyllables, e.g., *ball* → [bʌbə], modification of adult reduplication, e.g., *bye-bye* → [dɛdɛ], or of an adult nonreduplication model, e.g., *water* → [wɔwɔ]; it may thoroughly transform an adult word, e.g., *window* → [ŋeːŋeː], or it merely may affect the child's choice of which adult words to produce.

This phenomenon is widespread, attested for many children and many languages. Recently it has been the subject of experimental study, as in Schwartz *et al.* (1980), from which our examples are taken. The extent of operation of this process varies very much from one child to another (Smith, 1973), just as the grammatical, lexical, and discourse uses of reduplication and repetition vary from one language to another. Schwartz et al. have provided evidence that, for some children at least, reduplication plays an important role in the acquisition of polysyllabic words.

Phonological Processes in L2 Acquisition

Phonological processes operate in L2 acquisition in the sense that there are systematic phonetic relationships between the sounds of the target language and those of the learner's interlanguage. Some of the PPs apparent in L2 acquisition are similar to those of child language development and may be interpreted as a kind of reactivation of L1 strategies and processes. Others are transfer processes representing interference from the structure of the learner's L1. Still others cannot be accounted for by either explanation.

Recent studies of *substitution* processes in L2 acquisition emphasize the interaction of developmental and transfer PPs. Mulford and Hecht (1980) explore this interaction in detail in the phonology of a six-year-old Icelandic boy, Steinar, acquiring English. A simple illustration is Steinar's pronunciation of final stops in English: He devoiced them (a common L1 process) and strongly aspirated them (a characteristic of Icelandic). Mulford and Hecht hazard some tentative hypotheses on the interaction, e.g., that "substitutes predicted by both transfer and developmental processes are the ones most likely to appear and to persist." A more interesting hypothesis they offer is that the relative roles of the two kinds of processes differ depending on the part of the phonology involved, along the continuum shown in Table 1.1.

Wode (1977, 1978) proposes other hypotheses about the interaction of the two types of processes: that children acquire the L2 phonology "through the grid of their L1 system" and that the two crucial issues are their developmental stage in the L1 and the matching process by which they identify L2 elements similar to L1 elements, which they substitute for them, and nonsimilar elements, for which they have natural developmental sequences like those of L1 learners. All these hypotheses are steps toward a predictive theory of L1-L2 phonological development, but as their authors acknowledge, they need much more research to confirm or modify.

Assimilation processes in L2 acquisition have not been much studied, although it is very likely that both developmental and transfer processes operate, and that such common L1 assimilation processes as consonant harmony are uncommon in L2 acquisition—one does not expect a foreign learner of English to say [gʌk] for *duck.*

Tarone (1976) studied *syllable structure* processes in L2 acquisition. She analyzed the speech of six subjects learning English, two native speakers each of Cantonese, Korean, and Portuguese. About 20 percent of the syllables at-

TABLE 1.1

Vowels	Liquids	Stops	Fricatives and affricates
Transfer processes predominate			Developmental processes predominate

11

tempted by each speaker had syllable structure errors: consonant deletion, epenthesis, and glottal stop insertion (breaking up a vowel sequence). Attributing the changes to transfer of L1 structure whenever possible, Tarone found a residue of nontransfer errors ranging from 47 percent for one of the Korean speakers to 10 percent for one of the Portuguese speakers. Much of the consonant deletion could be explained as either transfer or developmental, but the amount of epenthesis was much higher than is found in L1 acquisition, and Tarone attributed it to a universal preference for CV syllables that operated independently of transfer and was manifested differently than in L1 phonological development.

Reduplication seems very much tied to the age of the learner and to L1 rather than L2 acquisition. Certainly reduplication strategies rarely are noted in classroom L2 learning by adolescents or adults. Data on reduplication in L2 acquisition by very young children—if this can be separated from simultaneous acquisition of two languages—would bear directly on the sources and functions of reduplication in language acquisition.

In summary, we can say that PPs operate in both L1 and L2 acquisition. Those common in L1 acquisition presumably reflect universal constraints of human speech perception and production systems, coupled with general developmental characteristics apparent also in nonphonological behavior. They are influenced by the phonological structure of the language being acquired and by the characteristics of the particular vocabulary to which the child is exposed. PPs found in L2 acquisition are similar in part to those of L1 acquisition; such similar processes presumably represent either continued operation of the same universal constraints or reactivation of developmental processes in connection with a new acquisition situation. Other PPs found in L2 acquisition are clearly transfer processes that reflect the phonological structure of the L1, and many may combine both sources or at least not provide unequivocal evidence one way or the other. Still other PPs in L2 acquisition are neither developmental nor transfer. They may represent universal or language-specific constraints operating differently than in L1 acquisition, or they may represent language-external factors such as social constraints.

The central question here is the interaction among these different kinds of processes, and future research directed to this question will probably be highly productive.

ACQUISITION OF THE VOICING CONTRAST

The literature on L1 acquisition of voicing in stops is a particularly rich source of information on the acquisition process and the nature of universals. It is extensive, with data from a wide variety of languages and several age groups. Further, it benefits from the development of sophisticated instrumental analysis techniques and a considerable body of knowledge accumulated by phonologists and phoneticians on the distribution and properties of voicing contrasts in languages of the world and their acoustic and articulatory components. As a result, this research clarifies several issues of central importance to both L1 and L2 research: the appropriate units of analysis, research methodology and its consequences, and the interpretation of cross-language differences.

A Universal

Data from a number of languages provide strong support for Jakobson's proposed universal that "so long as stops in child language are not split according to the behavior of the glottis, they are generally produced as voiceless and unaspirated."[4] Macken (1980) provides a general discussion and references on English, Spanish, Cantonese, Garo, Taiwanese, and Hindi. Kewley-Port and Preston (1974) claim that voiceless unaspirated stops are used first because they are articulatorily easier to control than either prevoiced or aspirated stops. Characteristics of the English acquisition process provide some support for this claim, (Macken & Barton, 1980) since they match the kind of rule change identified by Macken for articulatorily based rules as opposed to perceptually based ones (Macken, 1980).

In contrast to this universal, we find either individual or language differences in other aspects of voicing acquisition or insufficient data to make further claims. The age at which the voicing contrast is acquired varies by child and by language: for example, the age at which English-speaking children acquire a voicing contrast in initial stops may vary from under age 1;10[5] to 2;8 (Macken & Barton, 1980; Smith, 1973), while Spanish-speaking children acquire an adultlike phonetic voicing contrast after age 4 (Macken & Barton, 1979). For languages with more than two types of voice in stops, only Srivastava's Hindi study (1974) is available. He reports the following sequence: voiceless unaspirated stops at 1;1, prevoiced at 1;4, voiceless and voiced aspirates at 2;0. With respect to contrast at different places of articulation, the results of Macken and Barton (1979, 1980) indicate differences by language (or by voicing type): The English (aspiration) contrast is acquired in the order dental > labial > velar, while the Spanish (true voicing contrast) appears first at the labial place of articulation.

Issues

Units of analysis   There are several reports of apparent counterexamples to Jakobson's proposed universal. In Velten (1943), for example, we find that Joan acquired the "voiced" stops (by 1;1) before the "voiceless" ones (2;1), while in Contreras and Saporta (1971), the child acquiring Spanish acquired the "voiceless" (1;0–1;2) before the "voiced" stops (1;6). The problem here is with the labels "voiced" and "voiceless."

Phonologically contrastive stops produced at the same place of articulation traditionally are said to differ in "voicing." While this description may be sufficient to describe the phonological contrast, it is not the case that all "voicing" contrasts are the same at the phonetic level. In fact, English "voiced" stops generally are voiceless unaspirated at the phonetic level, comparable to Spanish "voiceless" stops. Given this fact and the results of Macken and Barton (1979, 1980), who use voiceless unaspirated stops (as measured by voice onset time, VOT) as the unit of analysis, it is likely that in the Velten (1943) and Contreras and Saporta (1971) accounts, language-particular labeling practices obscure the underlying similarity of the acquisition process.

Thus the first requirement of L1 and L2 research is the determination of the appropriate phonetic units for analysis, units not subject to conflicting interpretation either within or across languages. For the analysis of voicing acquisition, the appropriate units, measured in terms of VOT, are prevoiced, voiceless unaspirated, and voiceless aspirated (Lisker and Abramson, 1964). Researchers must know the phonetic components of the voicing contrasts under study and should be aware that even the three types given above may differ across languages (Ladefoged, 1978).

Methodology In part, the reported differences within and across languages can be attributed to differences in research methodology (see Wells, 1979). For example, the difference in age of acquisition reported in the studies of Macken and Barton (1980) on the one hand and Smith (1973) on the other is due partly to different criteria used for assigning the point of acquisition and to different means of analysis. A second point of methodological importance is the value of spectrographic analysis. Because Macken and Barton used this technique, they were able to determine an early stage of acquisition wherein the English-speaking children were making statistically significant contrasts between adult voiced and voiceless phonemes and yet where all the children's productions fell within the adult perceptual boundaries for a single phoneme: The children's productions would have been labeled "voiced" by the non-phonetician and were in fact generally transcribed as "voiceless unaspirated" by the researchers. This example demonstrates the problems involved in the imposition of adult categories on child speech and the importance of supplemental instrumental analysis: Without the aid of spectrographic analysis, an important fact about acquisition (i.e., a stage of a "nonadult" contrast) would have been missed (cf. the similar lesson in Williams' study of bilinguals, 1980).

Cross-Language Differences

Two of the above differences demonstrate the importance of a close examination of the sound patterns that occur in the language—specifically, the particular lexicon—being acquired by the child. In contrast to the Hindi child reported in Srivastava (1974), the Spanish children in Macken and Barton (1979) produced prevoiced stops correctly only after age four. These children, however, already had acquired the Spanish "voicing" contrast by age two as a kind of stop-continuant contrast: Voiced stops frequently were produced as glides, while the voiceless stops were nearly always well-formed stops. This language-specific pattern apparently has its roots in the allophony involved in the Spanish voicing system. Second, the differences between the Spanish and English orders of acquisition by place of articulation correlated with differences between the two languages (and in the individual child lexicons) in the distribution of word-initial stop types, i.e., differences between the two languages in the utilization of the voicing contrast (see Macken, 1980 for a more complete discussion). Several studies over the past several years (e.g., Lust, Flynn, Chien, & Clifford, 1980; Peters, 1980) have found similarly that "universality is confounded by the particular data the child is confronted with" (Menyuk, 1979).

In summary, the L1 acquisition process, even for a highly restricted portion of a phonological system (voicing in word-initial stops), is complex. What do these L1 findings suggest for L2 research? First, universals have different etiologies and different implications. If the articulatory ease of voiceless unaspirated stops is not restricted to the speech of very young children (as the distribution of these stops in languages of the world suggests), then the early acquisition of these stops would also be expected during L2 acquisition. Second, L2 research must take full account of (a) the different phonetic components underlying even superficially similar phonological contrasts, (b) the full set of allophonic and morphophonemic rules in the different phonological systems, and (c) perhaps most important, the phonetic and phonological characteristics of the particular input the child receives. Note that a contrastive analysis based solely on segment inventories would have been inadequate to either predict or explain the cross-language differences discussed here for L1 acquisition. Third, the use of spectrographic techniques—especially for the acquisition of voicing in stops—is particularly valuable for the exploration of nonadult contrasts; instrumental techniques can thus be used to look for and investigate characteristics unique to a bilingual system or interlanguage. Such techniques can document phenomena that cannot be detected by the categorically bound perceptual systems of researchers. We realize that these points are not unknown to L2 researchers (Lehtonen & Sajavaara, 1979), but we repeat them here because they are so often neglected by L1 researchers.

REGULARIZATION

The issue of variation has been addressed in two different ways in the preceding two sections. First, to account for the fact that individual children may provide no evidence for the operation of a particular process or, may, in some cases, provide counterevidence, we stated our process universals in terms of statistical probabilities. Second, because we found that there exist some cross-language differences in voicing acquisition, we considered several factors, such as the differential effects of the particular input to the child, that in effect place conditions on the operation of universals.

There remains, however, a substantial residue of variation—individual differences between children acquiring even the same language and in some cases confronted with the same input (Leonard, Newhoff, & Mesalam, 1980). These differences are particularly striking in the earliest stages, where the number of adult-based words a child produces is small, but they are also apparent throughout the developmental process. Yet the diversity itself reveals regularities—regularities that seem to reflect the processing carried out by the child. Two important hypotheses can be derived from these facts:

Hypothesis 1 Phonological acquisition, like other types of linguistic and nonlinguistic learning, involves a process of discovering patterns, via forming, testing, and revising hypotheses—a process we refer to as "regularization."

Hypothesis 2 At least some linguistic universals are not due to the operation of an innate linguistic language acquisition device; rather, they derive from the interaction of the learner and a patterned input.

With the publication of several multisubject longitudinal studies, each documenting widespread individual differences, researchers began to recognize the active role played by the child. This literature continues to grow (e.g., Ferguson & Farwell, 1975; Leonard, Newhoff, & Mesalam, 1980). Since a review of the frequency and diversity of such differences is beyond the scope of this paper, three examples from English will suffice: There is no invariant order of acquisition or set of substitution processes for stops or fricatives (Macken, 1980); early phonotactic patterns are highly varied (e.g., Braine, 1974; Menn, 1976); later rules for polysyllabic words are often idiosyncratic (e.g., Smith, 1973 [page 172]; Priestly, 1977). On the surface, a certain amount of cross-subject difference could be attributed to random variation; however, underlying these differences, there appears to be a general pattern that demands further explanation.

What seems to cut across such linguistic differences is a general similarity in stages prior to final correct production: early piecemeal, unintegrated data, with occasional isolated accuracy on a few forms ("idioms"); experimentation; regularization where several words are produced the same way for the first time; and a period of overgeneralization, sometimes resulting in the loss of the accuracy of previously correct forms ("regression").

Words that show accurate production (in advance of the other words produced by the child in the same period) and then lose their adultlike accuracy have been called "progressive idioms" by Moskowitz (1973). The classic example is Hildegard Leopold's *pretty:* This word, which was this child's first permanent word (at ten months), was produced with near-perfect accuracy for almost a year; it subsequently was changed to [pɪti] and then to [bɪdi], at the times when rules of consonant cluster reduction and voicing (respectively) appeared elsewhere in her system. Leopold reports that nine words during the first two years followed a similar development from early accuracy to later reduction (Leopold, 1939–47, 1: 164–5). It seems that for the child these idioms are unanalyzed wholes. As the child learns to break down whole-word shapes into phonetic components, he or she discovers or invents rules that systematize relations between sounds in different contexts.

That this process of building up a phonological system is not an automatic one but rather an active, constructive one can be seen clearly in "experimentation" episodes and "overgeneralization" data. An example of experimentation is one child's attempts to say *boat,* eight attempts scattered throughout a twenty-minute session: (1) [pɔpʰ kʰ]; (2) [potʰ]; (3) [pʌp‿pʰo̜kʰ]; (4) [pʌkʰ] (two times); (5) [pɔkʰ] (two times); (6) [pɔkʰ kʰ] (two times); (7) [papʰ kʰ]; and (8) [pʌkʰ kʰ] (at age 1;5.30). Subsequent analysis showed that on the three previous sessions, *boat* was produced as [pɔ] or [pɔʔ] (final consonant deletion or substitution), and that in the following five sessions it was produced as [pop] (consonant harmony). The fourth session was unusual in several ways: the final consonant varied between [p] and [k] (with one [t] token), sometimes within the same production; the frequency of *boat* was two to six times greater than in any other session; and the productions of *boat* were interpreted at the time of utterance by the adults present (who were unaware of the developmental significance of the final consonant variation) as deliberate effortful attempts by the child to say this word. Sometime between the fourth and fifth sessions, a regular rule of consonant harmony was established, one that affected several words with final stops.

Data from another child's idiosyncratic acquisition of stop+/r/ clusters provide not only an example of regularization (similar in form to the above child's development of a rule of consonant harmony) but also a particularly striking example of overgeneralization. Initially, this child deleted the /r/ from stop+/r/ clusters (1;6–1;10). Subsequently (1;11), she produced initial /tr/ and /dr/ as [f]. Then beginning at 2;0, this child extended her [f] rule to initial /pr/ and /kr/ clusters: from 2;0 to 2;1 (and later), all four clusters were produced as [f] (the stage of overgeneralization and regression). When this child overgeneralized her [f] rule to /pr/ and /kr/, her previous productions for these clusters "regressed": [f] for /pr/ and /kr/ is less adultlike than were her previous productions of [pʰ] and kʰ] (respectively). These phonetic changes appear to be due to a change in the child's hypothesis about how such clusters should be pronounced. The significance of this example and the other examples does not lie in the specifics of the particular phone that is produced in substitution for, e.g., initial stop+/r/ clusters or final alveolar consonants: Children may and often do differ in the particular substitutions produced for these and other difficult sounds. Rather, what is significant is what the examples suggest about the underlying process—the process of "regularization."

Cognitive Model (Hypothesis 1)

Regularization (particularly its features of overgeneralization and regression) points to the active role of the child and gives evidence of the universal disposition of the child to discover patterns. Moreover, there is a parallelism between this process of rule formation and stages in the acquisition of nonlinguistic knowledge (Karmiloff-Smith & Inhelder, 1974/75) that suggests that both types of learning share the following features: (a) single-item match; (b) gradual recognition of a pattern; (c) period of exploration; (d) construction of a theory, followed by overgeneralization and loss of ability; (e) gradual recognition of regularity of counterexamples; (f) construction of a new theory, distinct from the first; and (g) gradual development of a single unified theory. Further evidence for the active role of the child are data showing children's creativity (such as invented words and the use of segments or rules plausible, given the child or adult system, but incorrect from the adult point of view) (Macken, 1979) and data showing children's selectivity (i.e., children's selection or avoidance of words with a particular sound structure) (Ferguson & Farwell, 1975).

The process of regularization underlying individual differences in phonological development and the parallel between this process and that seen in the acquisition of nonlinguistic knowledge—together with other evidence for the child's active role (creativity and selectivity)—have led child phonologists to posit a more cognitive model of acquisition, one that focuses on the child's organization of phonological data and the nonautomatic, nonlinear nature of the child's progress toward the adult system. This model is discussed in detail in Ferguson and Macken (1980) (see also Kiparsky & Menn, 1977; Fey & Gandour, 1979). In its current stage, the model has several serious defects and requires elaboration and testing. It signals an important new direction, precisely because the data on which it is based are data (individual differences and regularization) that are difficult for linguistic universalist theories to explain.

Universals (Hypothesis 2)

Early diversity and evidence for a cognitive model of regularization suggest that some "linguistic universals" are due to the interaction between the child's ability to categorize and the child's experience with language: Given similar categorization abilities and the broad similarities between the phonological systems of languages of the world, certain regularities will necessarily result. In contrast, only those universals present from the beginning are evidence of innate linguistic universals, and, as we have noted, there seem to be few of these. If we assume that regularization and its components (as described under "Cognitive Model") constitute a set of processing universals relevant to language learning and other nonlinguistic learning, it seems likely that there exists an associated set of purely linguistic universals that would characterize probable outcomes, given particular linguistic inputs and the child's categorization skills and physiological capabilities at particular stages of development.

The two hypotheses we have proposed here on the basis of the accumulated research of the past fifteen years have important implications for L2 acquisition research. First, a model of L2 acquisition will necessarily involve consideration of the L2 learner's stage of cognitive development and prior linguistic knowledge and the context of learning (e.g., the particular input to the child). Second, substantive cross-linguistic similarities of L2 acquisition will be evident primarily in situations where similarities in these factors exist in the L2 situations being compared. Third, probability statements of phonological development do not predict individual cases as exceptionless universals would, and a developmental L2 model based on such probabilities (from L1 research) is correspondingly limited. Finally, a recognition of the child's disposition to recognize patterns (inferred from a consideration of the regularization process) casts doubt on traditional accounts of the motivational force underlying L1 language acquisition (cf. Bowerman, 1982): The learner will try out new hypotheses, revise old ones, and progress toward full knowledge in a series of backward and forward steps largely independently of such pressures as adult correction of errors or child self-correction for communication clarity.

NOTES

1. C = consonant; V = vowel.
2. N.V. Smith, *The Acquisition of Phonology* (Cambridge, England: Cambridge University Press, 1973).
3. J.W. Harris, Some observations on "substantive principles in natural generative phonology," in D.A. Dinnsen (Ed.), *Current Approaches to Phonological Theory.* (Bloomington, IN: Indiana University Press, 1979).
4. R. Jakobson, *Kindersprache, Aphasie und Allgemeine Lautgesetze (Child Language, Aphasia and Phonological Universals,* trans. A.R. Keiler, 1968 (The Hague, the Netherlands: Mouton, 1941).
5. 1;10 means 1 year 10 months.

REFERENCES

Bowerman, M. 1982. Starting to talk worse: clues to language acquisition from children's late speech errors. In S. Strauss (ed.), *U-Shaped Behavior Growth.* NY: Academic Press.
Braine, M.D.S. 1974. On what might constitute a learnable phonology. *Language, 50,* 270–299.
Chomsky, N., and M. Halle. 1968. *The Sound Pattern of English.* NY: Harper & Row.
Clark, E. 1973. Non-linguistic strategies and the acquisition of word meanings. *Cognition, 2,* 161–182.
Contreras, H., and S. Saporta. 1971. Phonological development in the speech of a bilingual child. In J. Akin et al. (Eds.), *Language Behavior, a Book of Readings in Communication,* The Hague, the Netherlands: Mouton.

Donegan, P.J., and D. Stampe. 1979. The study of natural phonology. In D.A. Dinnsen, (Ed.), *Current Approaches to Phonological Theory.* Bloomington, IN: Indiana University Press, 126–173.

Drachman, G. 1978. Child language and language change. In J. Fisiak, (Ed.), *Historical Phonology.* Berlin, Federal Republic of Germany: De Gruyter, 123–144.

Edwards, M.L. 1971. One child's acquisition of English liquids. *Papers and Reports on Child Language Development, 3,* 101–109.

Ferguson, C.A. 1978a. Fricatives in child language acquisition. In V. Honsa & M.J. Hardman-de-Bautista (Eds.), *Papers on Linguistics and Child Language,* The Hague, the Netherlands: Mouton.

Ferguson, C.A. 1978b. Phonological processes. In J.H. Greenberg, et al. (Eds.), *Universals of Human Language.* Stanford, CA: Stanford University Press, *2,* 403–442.

Ferguson, C.A., and C.B. Farwell. 1975. Words and sounds in early language acquisition. *Language, 51,* 419–439.

Ferguson, C.A., and O.K. Garnica. 1975. Theories of phonological development. In E.H. Lenneberg & E. Lenneberg (Eds.), *Foundations of Language Development,* NY: Academic Press, *2,* 153–180.

Ferguson, C.A., and M.A. Macken. 1980. Phonological development in children—play and cognition. *Papers and Reports on Child Language Development, 18,* 133–177. Also in *Children's Language,* K.E. Nelson, ed. NY: Gardner Press, 1983, *4.*

Fey, M., and J. Gandour. 1979. Problem-solving in phonology acquisition. Paper presented at the 54th Annual Meeting of the Linguistics Society of America, December 27–29, Los Angeles, CA.

Greenberg, J.H., C.A. Ferguson, & E.A. Moravcsik, Eds. 1978 *Universals of Human Language.* Stanford, CA: Stanford University Press, *2.*

Greenlee, M. 1974. Interacting processes in the child's acquisition of stop-liquid clusters. *Papers and Reports on Child Language Development, 7,* 85–100.

Greenlee, M., and J. Ohala. 1980. Phonologically motivated parallels between child phonology and historical sound change. *Language Sciences, 2,* 283–308.

Harris, J.W. 1979. Some observations on "substantive principles in natural generative phonology." In D.A. Dinnsen (Ed.), *Current Approaches to Phonolocal Theory.* Bloomington, IN: Indiana University Press, 281–293.

Hooper, J.B. 1977 Substantive evidence for linearity: vowel length and nasality in English. *Papers from the Thirteenth Regional Meeting,* Chicago Linguistics Society, *13,* 152–164.

Ingram, D. 1978. The production of word-initial fricatives and affricates by normal and linguistically deviant children. In A. Carammazza & E.B. Zurif (Eds.), *Language Acquisition & Language Breakdown.* Baltimore, MD: The Johns Hopkins University Press, 63–85.

Ingram, D. 1979. Phonological patterns in the speech of young children. In P. Fletcher & M. Garman (Eds.), *Language Acquisition.* Cambridge, England: Cambridge University Press, 133–148.

Jakobson, R. 1941. *Kindersprache, Aphasie and Allgemeine Lautgesetze.* (*Child Language, Aphasia and Phonological Universals,* A.R. Keiler, Trans. 1968) The Hague, the Netherlands: Mouton.

Jeng, H.H. 1979. The acquisition of Chinese phonology in relation to Jakobson's laws of irreversible solidarity. In *Proceedings, Ninth International Congress of Phonetic Science.* Copenhagen, Denmark: University of Copenhagen, *2,* 155–161.

Karmiloff-Smith, A., and B. Inhelder. 1974–75. If you want to get ahead, get a theory. *Cognition, 3,* 195–212.

Kewley-Port, D., and M.S. Preston. 1974. Early apical stop production: a voice onset time analysis. *Journal of Phonetics, 2,* 195–210.

Kiparsky, P., and L. Menn. 1977. On the acquisition of phonology. In J. Macnamara (Ed.), *Language Learning and Thought.* NY: Academic Press, Inc., 47–78. (Also this volume.)

Ladefoged, P. 1978. Phonetic differences within and between languages. *UCLA Working Papers in Phonetics, 41,* 32–40.

Lehtonen, J., and K. Sajavaara, Eds. 1979. Papers in Contrastic Phonetics. Jyväskylä, Finland: University of Jyväskylä.

Leonard, L., M. Newhoff, & L. Mesalam. 1980. Individual differences in early child phonology. *Journal of Applied Psycholinguistics, 1,* 7–30.

Leopold, W.F. 1939–47. *Speech Development of a Bilingual Child.* 4 volumes. Evanston, IL: Northwestern University Press.

Levelt, W.J.M. 1975. What became of LAD? In *Ut Videam: Contributions to an Understanding of Linguistics, for Pieter Verburg on the Occasion of his 70th Birthday.* Lisse, the Netherlands: Peter de Ridder Press.

Liljencrants, J., and B. Lindblom. 1972. Numerical simulation of vowel quality systems: the role of perceptual contrast. *Language, 48,* 839–862.

Lindblom, B. 1979. Some phonetic null hypotheses for a biological theory of language. In *Proceedings, Ninth International Congress on Phonetic Science.* Copenhagen, Denmark; University of Copenhagen, *2,* 33–40.

Lisker, L., and A.S. Abramson. 1964. A cross-language study of voicing in initial stops: acoustical measurements. *Word, 20,* 384–422.

Lust, B., S. Flynn, Y. Chien, & T. Clifford. 1980. Coordination: the role of syntactic, pragmatic and processing factors in first language acquisition. *Papers and Reports on Child Language Development, 18,* 79–87.

Macken, M.A. 1979. Developmental reorganization of phonology: a hierarchy of basic units of acquisition. *Lingua, 49,* 11–49.

Macken, M.A. 1980a. The acquisition of stop systems: a cross-linguistic perspective. In G. Yeni-Komshian, J.F. Kavanagh, & C.A. Ferguson, (Eds.), *Child Phonology: Perception and Production.* NY: Academic Press, Inc.; 1:143–168.

Macken, M.A. 1980b. The child's lexical representation: the "puzzle-puddle-pickle" evidence. *Journal of Linguistics, 16,* 1–17.

Macken, M.A., and D. Barton. 1979. The acquisition of the voicing contrast in Spanish: a phonetic and phonological study of word-initial stop consonants. *Papers and Reports on Child Language Development, 16,* 42–66.

Macken, M.A., and D. Barton. 1980. A longitudinal study of the acquisition of the voicing contrast in American-English word-initial stops, as measured by voice onset time. *Journal of Child Language, 7,* 41–74.

McCawley, J.D. 1977. Acquisition models as models of acquisition. In R. Shuy, (Ed.), *Studies in Language Variation.* Washington, DC: Georgetown University Press, 51–64.

Menn, L. 1976. Pattern, control and contrast in beginning speech, a case study in the development of word form and word function. Ph.D. Dissertation. Urbana-Champaign, IL: University of Illinois.

Menyuk, P. 1979. Speech sound categorization by children. In *Proceedings, Ninth International Congress of Phonetic Science.* Copenhagen, Denmark: University of Copenhagen, *2,* 176–182.

Moskowitz, B.A. 1970. The two-year-old stage in the acquisition of English phonology. *Language, 46,* 426–441.

Moskowitz, B.A. 1973. Acquisition of phonology and syntax. In K.J.J. Hintakka, J.M.E. Moravcsik, & P. Suppes (Eds.), *Approaches to Natural Language.* Dordrecht, the Netherlands: Reidel Publishing Company, 48–84.

Mulford, R., and B.F. Hecht. 1980. Learning to speak without an accent: acquisition of a second-language phonology. *Papers and Reports on Child Language Development, 18,* 16–74. (Also this volume.)

Ohala, J.J. 1974. Phonetic explanation in phonology. In A. Bruck, et al. (Eds.), *Papers from the Parasession on Natural Phonology.* Chicago: Chicago Linguistics Society, 251–274.

Ohala, J.J. 1980. The application of phonological universals in speech pathology. In N.J. Lass (Ed.), *Speech and Language: Advances in Basic Research and Practice.* NY: Academic Press, Inc., 75–97.

Oller, D.K. 1975. Simplification as the goal of phonological processes in child speech. *Language Learning, 24,* 299–303.

Olmsted, D.L. 1971. *Out of the Mouth of Babes.* The Hague, the Netherlands: Mouton.

Pačesová, J. 1968. *The Development of Vocabulary in the Child.* Brno, Czechoslovakia: J.E. Purkyne.

Peters, A.M. 1980. Language typology and the segmentation problem in early child language acquisition. *Working Papers in Linguistics.* Manoa, HI: University of Hawaii.

Priestly, T.M.S. 1977. One idiosyncratic strategy in the acquisition of phonology. *Journal of Child Language, 4,* 45–66.

Schwartz, R.G., L.B. Leonard, J.J. Wilcox, & M.K. Folger. 1980. Again and again: reduplication in child phonology. *Journal of Child Language, 7,* 75–87.

Smith, N.V. 1973. *The Acquisition of Phonology.* Cambridge, England: Cambridge University Press.

Smith, N.V. 1975. Universal tendencies in the child's acquisition of phonology. In N. O'Connor, (Ed.), *Language, Cognitive Deficits and Retardation,* London, England: Butterworths, 47–65.

Snow, C.E., and C.A. Ferguson, Eds., 1977. *Talking to Children: Language Input and Acquisition.* Cambridge, England: Cambridge University Press.

Srivastava, G.P. 1974. A child's acquisition of Hindi consonants. *Indian Linguistics, 35,* 112–118.

Stampe, D. 1969. The acquisition of phonetic representation. *Papers from the Fifth Regional Meeting,* Chicago Linguistics Society, *5,* 443–454.

Super, C.M. 1979. A cultural perspective on theories of cognitive development. Paper presented at the Society for Research in Child Development Meeting, March 1979, San Francisco, CA. (Expanded version: Anthropological contributions to theories of child development) In C.M. Super & S. Harkness (Eds.). 1980. *Anthropological Perspectives on Child Development.* San Francisco: Jossey-Bass.

Tarone, E. 1976. Some influences on interlanguage phonology. *Working Papers in Bilingualism,* 87–111. (Also this volume.)

Velten, H.V. 1943. The growth of phonemic and lexical patterns in infant language. *Language, 19,* 281–292.

Vihman, M.M. 1978. Consonant harmony: its scope and function in child language. In J.H. Greenberg, et al. (Eds.), *Universals of Human Language,* Stanford, CA: Stanford University Press, *2,* 281–334.

Vihman, M.M. 1980. Sound change and child language. In E.C. Traugott, et al. (Eds.), *Papers from the Fourth International Conference on Historical Linguistics.* Amsterdam, the Netherlands: John Benjamin, 303–320.

Wells, G. 1979. Variation in child language. In P. Fletcher & M. Garman, (Eds.), *Language Acquisition.* Cambridge, England: Cambridge University Press, 377–395.

Williams, L. 1980. Phonetic variation as a function of second-language learning. In G. Yeni-Komshian et al. (Eds.), *Child Phonology.* NY: Academic Press, Inc., *2,* 185–215.

Wode, H. 1977. The L2 acquisition of /r/. *Phonetica, 34,* 200–217.

Wode, H. 1978. The beginnings of non-school room L2 phonological acquisition. *International Review of Applied Linguistics, 16,* 109–125.

2

ON THE ACQUISITION OF PHONOLOGY*

Paul Kiparsky   **Lise Menn**

In acquiring the phonology of a language, the child accomplishes two feats. First, the child must master the phonetic repertoire of the language. Second, the child learns the phonological rules that represent the regularities governing the variation of its words and morphemes. Each accomplishment involves both perceptual and productive ability. Learning the phonetic repertoire of the language involves both learning to pay attention to its relevant acoustic cues and achieving articulatory control over its sounds and sound combinations. Learning the phonological rules involves both the ability to recognize word identity across rule-governed phonological differences and the active internalization of at least some phonological rules for purposes of production, such as those accounting for the inflectional morphology of English, which are learned productively by the primary school stage.

*This work was supported in part by a grant to Paul Kiparsky from the National Institute of Mental Health, 2P01 MH13390-09, and in part by NSF Dissertation Grant NSF SOC 74-22167 to Lise Menn. We thank Charles Ferguson, Dan Kahn, Michael Kenstowicz, and Charles Kisseberth for noticing errors of omission and commission in our first draft. The blame for remaining errors is ours.

The learning of the phonetic repertoire and the later learning of the more abstract phonological regularities are often considered to be quite distinct in nature. It is of course true that the learning tasks that the child faces are very different in the two cases. In the following, we shall argue that the linguistic means by which the child solves these tasks are nevertheless the same. At every stage on the long road from the child's first utterances that attempt to match the segmental phonemes of adult models to the adolescent's learning of the fine details of morphology, the same basic learning principles and the same kinds of internalized linguistic systems come into play.

THE LEARNING OF THE PHONETIC REPERTOIRE

We shall begin by reviewing the well-known theories of Jakobson and Stampe. Both of these view the child's speech as the result of a filtering of the adult speech, where the filter is a reflex of a set of constraints in universal grammar.

On Jakobson's account, there is a universal hierarchy of features arranged in a strict pattern of successive dichotomous branchings. The unfolding of a child's phonemic system is governed by this hierarchy: At any given stage, distinctions corresponding to branches lower than a certain set of nodes on this hierarchy "tree" are not manifested in the child's speech. We may illustrate by considering a portion of the hierarchy set forth in *Kindersprache,* and in Jakobson and Halle (1956). The hierarchy is complicated by the existence of relations among some branches: High vowels, for example, are claimed to show a palatal–velar (front/back) distinction before low vowels do.

For this reason, actual representation of the hierarchy as a tree is confusing, and Jakobson and Halle choose a "decimal" coding of the hierarchy, assigning to each contrast a number sequence chosen so that if dichotomy A presupposes dichotomy B, then the sequence of numbers for A contains the sequence of numbers for B. A portion of the table reads:

Consonants:	dental versus labial	0.1
Vowels:	narrow versus wide	0.11
Narrow vowels:	palatal (front) versus velar (back)	0.111
Wide vowels:	palatal versus velar	0.1111
Consonants:	velo-palatal versus labial and dental (anterior)	0.112
Consonants:	palatal versus velar	0.1121
	[No firm predictions are made about glides or liquids.]	

This embodies such predictions as: The child will not have a phonemic contrast between /k/ and /t/ (0.112) before contrasting low and non-low vowels (0.11), but a phonemic contrast between dentals and labials (0.1) will precede or be simultaneous with any contrast among vowels.

This hierarchy also determines the phonemic systems of the languages of the world: The use by a language of any contrast in the hierarchy presupposes the presence in that language of all those contrasts ordered above it.

Jakobson puts forth no theory of children's perception of words. He remarks that perception is in advance of production, but that at the time production begins the child may still fail to pay attention to certain acoustic cues.

Interpreted as a predictive theory, Jakobson's schema has some odd properties. It seems to make very strong predictions, and has not yet been strictly falsified, so that it has remained widely accepted (McNeill, 1970). Yet careful examination shows that one reason for its durability is that it is very difficult to falsify. The small corpuses that can be gathered, even by diary methods, for children at the early stages of speech are often too small to establish whether the subject has command of certain contrasts. Furthermore, Jakobson's theory is explicitly only a theory of the acquisition of contrast, not a theory of the mastery of phonetic targets.

In assessing the phonetic predictions made by Jakobson's theory, we must keep in mind that he views features not as absolute but as relative properties of phonemes, defined within a network of oppositions, whose phonetic value is thus allowed a certain latitude. For example, contrary to what is sometimes asserted by other authors, Jakobson does not say that the child will have bV before gV (using $b, d, g,$ to stand for labial, dental/alveolar, and velar stops, respectively); what he claims is that there will not be a phonemic opposition bV/gV or dV/gV before the appearance of the opposition bV/dV. In order to falsify this claim, a child must show both the *absence* of a bV/dV opposition and the *presence* of an opposition between gV and the members of the other set. Absence of an opposition like bV/dV can be shown only if the child attempts to say adult words containing labials and words containing dentals and then fails to distinguish those sounds in output. A child may have no dentals, at a time when he or she has both bV and gV, and yet fail to be a counterexample to the Jakobson schema if there is no evidence that labials and dentals are merged (Daniel, described in Menn, 1971). Absence of dentals from the child's output is no evidence of merger if the absence is achieved by the child's not attempting adult words that have dental stops.

To illustrate Jakobson's schema, we construct six hypothetical examples of corpuses. The first corpus would be a perfect example for showing development according to the two predictions (mentioned above): (A) "a phonemic contrast between dentals and labials will precede or be simultaneous with any contrast among vowels"; (B) "the child will not have a phonemic contrast between /g/ and /d/ before contrasting low and non-low vowels." The second hypothetical corpus is one type that is compatible with the Jakobson schema but which might better be approached by some other theory. The third and fourth hypothetical corpuses would falsify prediction A, and the fifth and sixth would falsify prediction B, as shown below:

Good Case, Hypothetical Corpus 1 (hypothetical total output corpus predicted by A and B)

time 1: [pa]   (regardless of the model word)
time 2: [pa], [ta]   dentals versus labials
time 3: [pa], [ta], [ti]   low versus non-low vowels
time 4: [pa], [ta], [ti], [ka]   velar versus labials and dentals

Hypothetical Corpus 2 (does not contradict A or B) (total output corpus)

time 1: *pa* → [pa]   *tea* → [ti]   (complementary distribution)
time 2: *pa* → [pa]   *tea* → [ti]   *cup* → [kʌ] (complementary distribution)

Hypothetical Corpus 3   Hypothetical Corpus 4 (both falsify A)
pa, ball, doll → [ta]   [ta] ~ [pa]   [ti] ~ [pi]
bee, tea → [ti]   (regardless of the model word)
(vowel heights contrast, but dentals do not contrast with labials)

Hypothetical Corpus 5   Hypothetical Corpus 6 (both falsify B)
cat, kiss → [ka]   [ki] ~ [ka]   [ti] ~ [ta]
toy, tea → [ta]   (regardless of the model word)
(vowel heights do not contrast, but velars contrast with dentals)

For testing Jakobson's schema, we depend on evidence from merger of adult contrasts or from free variation in the child's speech. The latter phenomenon is relatively uncommon, and so we rely heavily on the former, a test that requires consideration of both input and output levels of child speech.

Here we face a problem in interpretation of Jakobson, for we must bear in mind that he is concerned almost entirely with the internal phonemic structure of the child's speech, and not with its behavior as a representation of adult language. Jakobson speaks almost exclusively in terms of contrasts "appearing" and "failing to appear" in the child's speech. What exactly do we mean by saying that a contrast *fails to appear?* If we speak of a contrast that fails to appear, it is necessarily defined with respect to something outside the child's speech. We must be defining it either by a universal phonetic description, or by a description of the ambient adult language, or by both. Suppose we refer only to universal phonetics, and suppose we have a child like Jacob Hankamer (Menn, 1976) who has dental and velar stops, but no labials, for a certain period. When Jacob has only *d* and *k,* then it is certainly true that in one sense, the *b/d* contrast "failed to appear" prior to the appear-appearance of the *d/k* contrast. On what grounds do we then claim that such a case fails to test (and falsify) the Jakobson schema? What is the basis for our interpretation of Jakobson? Does it rest on explicit statements by him?

It does not; an intermediate step of reasoning is required which will certainly be obscure to those who have not dealt directly with the small corpuses that can be obtained from even the most intensive diary study of children at the threshold of speech. In a small total corpus, accidental gaps are everywhere. Only recent work unavailable to Jakobson (see Ferguson & Farwell, 1973; also below) has shown that many gaps in a corpus may be nonaccidental and due to phonological selection by the child. Certainly, we do not wish to interpret Jakobson's schema in a fashion that would make it trivially falsifiable by a child who happened not to be interested in naming any objects whose names began with labials at a time when his or her total vocabulary consisted of, say, ten words, such as (a hypothetical example) *hi, no, down, daddy, kitty-cat, nanna, ta-ta, doll, toast, light.* If all gaps are accidental and we wish to avoid trivial falsification, we must require that a putative falsification of the Jakobson schema show that the child in question really does not have the ability to make an output distinction, e.g., between labials and dentals at a time when he or she does make the output distinction between dentals and velars. The only positive evidence that a child cannot maintain a certain distinction is phonemic merger of adult phonemes which do make that distinction.

Let us next consider Stampe's approach, which he calls a theory of "Natural Phonology." Stampe, a generative phonologist, deals explicitly with adult words as forms underlying the child's output forms, relating adult word to child word by a set of rules. His theory is concerned primarily with the properties of these rules, which he considers to be innate. Again we have a filter simplifying adult speech, but it is not a static hierarchy like Jakobson's. It is, rather, a dynamic system consisting of innate rules or "natural processes," each of which reflects some property of the articulators that we might characterize as some "inertia" that must be overcome with effort. The processes are held to apply initially in unordered fashion wherever their structural description is met, and if all the processes apply, essentially all phonemic distinctions are lost.

Some natural processes are context-free replacements and others are context-dependent. Learning adult phonology requires the child to inhibit the application of some of these processes. There are three mechanisms by which this is done: suppression, limitation (context-dependent suppression), and ordering. Processes may, and often do, conflict. For example, there is considered to be a context-free denasalization process (loss of the nasal/oral distinction in favor of the oral phonetic realization) and on the other hand a nasalizing process that appears in the neighborhood of nasal consonants. The possibility of varying resolutions of conflicting processes can account for the wide phonetic range of treatment of adult forms that we find in children, and this is then one source, for natural phonology, of the richness necessary in any adequate theory of child phonology.

In principle, the postulated natural processes are identifiable independently of child language in two main ways. The processes should first of all follow from the structure of the speech mechanism under an adequate theory of phonetics. At present, this is more in the nature of a promissory note. There is as yet no theory that accurately predicts a wide range of phonological facts from physiological or acoustic facts, although phoneticians have been chipping away at it since Sievers, and some success has been achieved in certain subdomains (for two recent attempts, see Lindblom & Liljencrantz, 1972; Ohala, 1974). Second, examination of enough cases of language change and synchronic phonological systems should reveal the recurring operation of the processes. The lack of systematic surveys of phonological processes in the languages of the world which is delaying progress here is now beginning to be remedied (Greenberg, 1970; Bhat, 1973; Bell, 1971; and other contributions to the Stanford Language Universals Project). In the case of segment systems, on which more information is accessible (Trubetzkoy, 1949; Hockett, 1955), some testing of the theory of natural phonology has been done (Miller, 1972).

Contrary to Jakobson, Stampe claims that the input to the child's system —the child's lexical representation—by the time he or she starts to speak is THE adult surface form. Stampe's approach, however, would not lose its essential character if it were modified to allow for incomplete perception of the adult phonetics at the onset of speech.

We may exemplify Stampe's analysis with the derivations from his 1969 paper, as shown in Table 2.1:

"Later, 'candy' became {kǣni}, by ordering (b) after (a)." (Details of representation of nasalized vowels and vowel off-glides are not worked out, being peripheral to the discussion, as is the rule velarizing the initial palatal.) Central to Stampe's position is the resolution, exemplified here, of phonological rules into minimal steps. Above, *nd* is not regarded as being deleted, but as undergoing, in some sense, four separate reductions in strength: *nd* → *nn* → *n* → *ň* → Ø in the course of deletion. The postulated "natural processes" are those that bring about these and similar minimal changes.

We see that in Stampe's theory, the approach to adult competence via suppression, ordering, and limitation of rules corresponds in a certain sense to the elaboration of the feature hierarchy in Jakobson's theory. However, an important difference not made fully explicit by Stampe is that his theory predicts the phonetic outcome of each process: The merger of nasal and oral sounds referred to earlier is not only a loss of opposition but is also specified as a loss of nasality; the output must be oral, not nasal. Jakobson, because of his focus on phonemic contrast, does not deal with such "allophonic" facts.

According to Stampe, then, early phonology is an ever-shrinking system of ordered processes that reduces the forms of adult speech to the child's ever-growing phonetic repertoire. This view allows Stampe to make an interesting connection between child and adult phonology. He draws a sharp distinction within the adult system between *processes* and *rules.* The flapping of *t, d* in American English *matter, madder,* or the devoicing of obstruents in German

TABLE 2.1

		Channing /čǣnɨŋ/	candy /kǣndi/
Rule a.	*nd* → *nn*	—	kǣnni
	degemination	—	kǣni
Rule b.	flapping of *n*	kǣňɨŋ	kǣňi
	flap deletion	kǣɨŋ	kǣi
	desyllabification	{kǣɨ̯ŋ}	{kǣi̯}

Land, Weg are typical processes. Processes, unlike rules, admit no exceptions or morphological conditioning, and they are inevitably extended to foreign words adopted into a language. Typical examples of rules are those that take *k* to *s* or change the vowel in words like *opacity, electricity* (cf. *opaque, electric*). Stampe claims that while the rules of the adult system are learned, the processes are not. The adult processes are, in his theory, simply those of the child's innate processes that are not suppressed by contrary data in the course of language acquisition.

There is a misleading aspect to this formulation, however: The relation between the child's modifications of adult words and the allomorphy found in adult language cannot be so direct. The modifications introduced by children, regardless of whether they are innate, as Stampe holds, or discovered by the experimenting child, as we shall propose, are purely phonetic adjustments. After all, in these very early stages of language acquisition there is no allomorphy, each morpheme having a unique phonetic shape.

In most of the languages of the world, except for the strict isolating languages, the major role of phonological rules is to describe the relations between allomorphs. This is true of those rules that are considered to be "processes" by Stampe as well as of those that he considers "learned rules." Learning such rules involves the conceptual task of discovering allomorphies.

For example, let us suppose that we have a language that devoices final obstruents, as many do. By all available evidence, final-obstruent devoicing is very common among children, regardless of how they start to use it; this rule —or process—is one of the best candidates for a "natural" rule of child phonology and of adult phonology.

It is quite possible that a child learning a language that devoices final obstruents will never learn how to articulate voiced obstruents preceding word boundary; he or she may be spared learning this rule *as an articulatory task.* But the conceptual task of linking up allomorphs remains: $[V_i C_{i+voice} + X]$ will still have to be recognized as containing an allomorph of $[V_i C_{i\Delta voice} \#]$. We have no reason to assume that this conceptual task of decoding the allomorphy is any easier than it would be for the child if the language happened instead to have the opposite, antinatural rule of final-obstruent voicing.

It should be noted that these arguments do not apply where allomorphic variation is uninvolved. In those restricted cases where a rule of the sort that children typically have functions in a language *only* as a redundancy rule (only as a descriptor of surface patterns), and where there is no allomorphy to be decoded, then a language that has that natural rule might be easier for most children to learn than one that had an antinatural redundancy rule. The speakers of a language that has a natural redundancy rule not involving allomorphy may be spoken of in Stampe's fashion as not having suppressed processes of child phonology, but this is a very special case.

Stampe (1969) distinguishes phonological from purely phonetic manifestations of final devoicing (and, by implication, of other rules or processes):

English-speaking children must suppress this process if their pronunciation is to conform to standard, but German children need not, because German permits this devoicing, *hunt/hunde* 'dog/dogs'. As the example shows, the devoicing process governs only the phonetic representation of German words, since the phonological representation of *hunt* is *hund*. In other languages it governs the phonological representations as well, since there is no voicing opposition in morpheme-final obstruents. [p. 445]

But by implication and example, Stampe would not agree with our arguments based on the distinction between cognitive and articulatory learning. From his basic procedure of "factoring" all possible rules of adult phonology into natural steps, in the same fashion as his treatment of *candy* → [kǽi̧] and *Channing* [kǽi̧ŋ] exemplified above, it would seem that he holds precisely the opposite view: that the procedure of abstraction from surface to underlying forms runs most easily along "natural" path increments, and that the *conceptual* task of decoding allomorphy should be easier if the allomorphs are related by a phonetically natural rule like final-obstruent devoicing rather than by an antinatural rule like a hypothetical final-obstruent voicing.

We can construct one sort of possible test concerning the distinction of articulatory from cognitive learning, if Stampe's view on this matter is taken in conjunction with some other tenets of his theory. Let us consider the implications of the following quote from Stampe (1969):

In languages which, for example, lack morpheme-final consonants altogether, the process of final-obstruent devoicing stays in the system but has no overt manifestation. This claim . . . appears to be supported by the pronunciation, in such languages, of foreign words with final voiced obstruents, which, if they are pronounced at all, are characteristically devoiced.

(Stampe has not cited sources for the claim that loanword final consonants, if they are pronounced as such in a language that generally permits no final obstruents, are devoiced, but we will assume, for the sake of the argument, that he is right on this point.)

Let us consider three hypothetical native speakers of, respectively, Japanese, which has no final obstruents, English, which has both voiced and unvoiced final obstruents, and Russian, which has a phonological rule of final obstruent devoicing. Let us have these three persons attempt to learn German without textbook instruction. Since all three speakers have a voicing contrast in their native language, let us assume that they all perceive the phonetic difference between *Tag* [tāk] and *Tage* [tāgə]. They might, however, face problems in the phonetic task of learning to pronounce them and in the cognitive tasks of learning that they contain the same morpheme and learning the devoicing rule by which the allomorphs [tāk] and [tāg] are related. For the Russian, who has essentially the same rule in his or her native language, we would predict, and so would Stampe, that the phonetic task will be automatic and the cognitive task of discovering the allomorphy may be facilitated by transfer of the principle underlying the corresponding allomorphy in Russian: Assuming there is such transfer, on hearing the plural *die Tage,* the Russian would expect the singular to be pronounced [tāk], and on hearing a singular [hunt], he or she would assume that the inflected forms might show up with either /d/ or /t/ at the end of the stem and would be on the outlook for evidence as to which might be the case. For the native speaker of English, who according to Stampe has suppressed the natural process of final-obstruent devoicing, and who according to us may have once invented such a rule as a child but has long since discarded it, both the phonetic and conceptual tasks will be novel and therefore harder than for the Russian speaker.

The differentiating case between our position and Stampe's will be the case of the speaker of Japanese. On Stampe's theory, the Japanese is in the same position as the Russian. Since the Japanese speaker has not suppressed the innate process of final-obstruent devoicing, he or she should find it easier than the English speaker to learn the German rule not only in its phonetic aspect but even in its cognitive aspect; the discovery that [tāgə] and [tāk] contain the same morpheme should pose less of a problem to the native speaker of Japanese than to a native speaker of English. Our conjecture is, on the contrary, that while the Japanese speaker may spontaneously devoice final obstruents like the Russian, he or she is in exactly the same position as the speaker of English when it comes to figuring out German patterns of allomorphy. (Note: This is a hypothetical case to make clear in principle the empirical nature of the disagreement between natural phonology and our discovery-oriented approach to the acquisition of phonology. If it is not the case that final-obstruent devoicing is generally found among speakers of languages without final obstruents when they start to learn a second language with voiced final obstruents, an example to illustrate the same point could be constructed around some other natural process.)

As seen by both Jakobson and Stampe, the early stages of the acquisition of phonology are rather different from the later stages, when morphophonemic relations are being learned. In the later stages the child behaves as an active grammar-constructor. The child is faced with the problem of remembering, producing, and recognizing variant forms of morphemes and solves it by devising a system of rules and underlying representations that represent the general and predictable aspects of this variation.

The pattern of rule learning in children on the schema "special case-overgeneralization-learning of exceptions" is well known from the work of Berko, Anisfeld and Tucker, and Bogoyavlenskiy (reprinted in Ferguson & Slobin, 1973). As a schematic illustration, learning the past tense of *bring* might involve the following stages:

I	*bring ~ brought*	(present and past tense forms of verbs are learned separately in the lexicon)
II	*bring ~ bringed*	(the child learns the regular dental suffix and overgeneralizes it)
III	*bring ~ brought*	(*brought* is relearned as an exception to the general rule)
IV	*bring ~ brang*	(the child learns the ablaut rule $i \rightarrow æ$ and overgeneralizes it)
V	*bring ~ brought*	(*brought* relearned)

(We do not claim, of course, that this whole sequence will occur for this particular word in each child; we claim merely that such a pattern of bracketing out successively finer generalizations is typical.)

It is clear also that the child's speech development cannot be viewed simply as a monotonic approximation to the adult model. Linguistic structure occasionally drags red herrings across the trail of the learner. Consequently, progress may be interrupted by false hypotheses, which include not only over-generalizations but entire rules which must later be discarded. For example, Zwicky (1970) reports his daughter Elizabeth at age 4;6 invariably producing "doubly regular" participles of strong verbs like *aten, gaven, roden, sawn, shooken, tooken,* and *wroten.* According to Zwicky, "six subsequent months of frequent corrections by her parents had no noticeable effect." Elizabeth had devised the two promising but, alas, wrong rules of English:

(A)   The participle has the same stem as the past.
(B)   The strong participle is formed by the suffixation of $-n$.

She applied them conjunctively to produce the doubly marked participles.

Compared to what we know about later acquisition, the picture we get from Jakobson and Stampe of early acquisition seems rather deterministic: There is no "discovery," no experimentation, no devising and testing of hypotheses. The child's problem, in their view, contains a built-in solution—for Jakobson, unwrap the features; for Stampe, get rid of processes.

We shall argue here that, on the contrary, phonology acquisition is a "problem-solving" activity from the earliest stages. The child has a goal—learning to talk—and a subgoal with which we are concerned—saying recognizable words. This is a difficult task, and the child must discover ways to circumvent the difficulties. These discoveries are made through experimentation, guided by the child's innate hypothesis-forming capacity and a complex feedback toward the goal of speaking.

Different children exclude definable classes of output by different means. When we observe such repeated "exclusion," we conclude that these classes of outputs (clusters, certain co-occurrences, the "third position," etc.) represent difficulties to the child, and that the various rules of child phonology (substitutions, deletions, etc.) as well as selective avoidance of some adult words are devices the child finds for dealing with those difficulties. For extensive consideration and exemplification of rules of child phonology, the reader should consult Ingram's (1974) basic article, "Phonological Rules in Young Children." We shall discuss here a few examples of classes of outputs that children are known to avoid and their means to that end. Note that not all children avoid all of these difficulties; we present these as general tendencies rather than as universals.

We take as our first example the "third position" problem. We use this term for a phenomenon reported in a more general case by Ferguson and Farwell (1973) and actually found, although not generally noted as a typical occurrence, in several corpuses: Children learning English who have output control of two of the three principal stop positions often have few or no output words manifesting the remaining one.

If there has been phonemic merger of dentals with velars, and absence of velars (or dentals) results, the child is progressing as predicted by Jakobson. However, in several cases the child gives no evidence of merger but instead selectively avoids input words using one stop position—dentals, for Daniel Menn; labials, for Jacob Hankamer. Substitutions of several kinds, avoidance of different positions, and possibly deletions of disfavored stops are all means toward the end of restricting output words for a period of time to only two stop positions. The same problem is solved by different means in each "third-position-avoiding" child studied. Selective avoidance is a phenomenon of great theoretical interest, as has been noted by Ferguson and Farwell and by Drachman. It requires that the child be aware that some phonetic targets are difficult for him or her and is entirely outside the scope of theories, such as Jakobson's and Stampe's, which are concerned with the child's failure to mark distinctions made by the ambient language.

Similarly, there are several ways of dealing with consonant clusters: deletion of all but one of the phonemes (in a stop-X or X-stop cluster, the one preserved is *not* always the stop), conflation of some of the features of the elements of the cluster (e.g., *sm* > *M, fl* > *w*), insertion of a vowel to break up the cluster, metathesis *(snow > nos),* and so on (see Greenlee, 1974).

The very diversity and "ingenuity" of these devices might indicate that early phonology should be regarded as the result of the child's active "problem-solving" rather than merely of an intrinsic filter acting on the target forms. Stronger evidence for this position comes from the earliest stages of speech. There is first the well-known although imprecise observation that children often manifest a "presystematic" period before they begin the orderly discarding of sounds by information-reducing rules (Nakazima, 1972). We also find what A. Moskowitz has called "phonological idioms," those occasional words children say that transcend their usual output limitations and come much closer to the adult model than would be expected. Phonological idioms are frequently found in the presystematic period. (Actually, the onset of phonemic systematization is probably gradual and not restricted to a "period." This topic is difficult and has not been well studied.) Our claim is that during this "period," the child is inventing rules for simplifying his or her lexical representation of words in order to be able to say them fluently.

One of the examples studied by Moskowitz (1970) is one of Hildegard Leopold's first words, *pretty.* She said it essentially correctly, with the /pr/ cluster and the medial /t/ following it. Yet as the next of her words came in, Hildegard had no consonant clusters, and in fact for months after the acquisition of this word she had no other output words in which there were two different stops (cf. Ferguson & Farwell, 1973). The consonant harmony, consonant deletion, and cluster reduction rules that Hildegard used and that resulted in her restricted output seem not to have been available at the time she acquired *pretty,* and thus not to have been automatic but invented slightly after that time.

Again, consider the general avoidance of sequences $C_1VC_2(V)$ (C_1 not homorganic with C_2) found in many children. The "open-syllable" children, those who prefer CV(CV) canonical form, like Hildegard Leopold, may avoid mixed sequences of consonants by whole-syllable reduplication or by deletion of a final stop in a C_1VC_2 model. The closed-syllable children (Smith, 1973; Menn, 1971) tend to assimilate the stops according to several rule types. Yet in the Daniel Menn corpus, for example, the first twenty-nine words, a few of which were CVC output and many of which were CVC input, showed no consonant harmony, and then consonant harmony quite suddenly appeared, as the cornerstone of the child's system of phonological rules.

Phonological idioms may also occur after phonemic systematization seems established, by what we take to be a process comparable to lexicalization in adult phonology. Jonathan Kiparsky systematically substituted dentals for velars, for example, [ato] *Michael,* [dæts] *catch;* later (at about age 1;8) substitution began to be restricted to initial positions [teyk] *cake,* [tuki] *cookie;* but even then the [t] was retained as an archaism in his rendering of *Michael,* [ato], and persisted even in its improved rendition, [maito].

Significantly, even some of the most plausible natural "processes" may give evidence of having been discovered by a child rather than of being automatic results or inherent constraints on the speech mechanism. Daniel Menn's second and third words were the phonological idioms [hay] *hi* and [hwow] *hello;* at a later stage he added /h/ deletion to his phonology.

As Ferguson and Farwell note, Jakobson's approach cannot (and in general, no "filter" approach can) very well be modified to allow for a stage in which a contrast is controlled followed by a stage in which the same contrast is neutralized, as is the *h:Ø* contrast in this example. (Jakobson himself did not fail to notice such cases; cf. 1968, p. 23.) Taking the more "cognitive" view that we advocate, these are simply the expected cases of apparent regression reflecting the addition of new rules, comparable to morphological regression of the standard *brought → bringed* type.

A further argument for our view is that many of the characteristic rules of child phonology that are used to simplify words for output are not "low-level" rules, such as deletions and contact assimilations. We have mentioned the more sophisticated kind of simplification found when the child uses consonant harmony, as in [gɔg] for *dog,* (Menn, 1973; Stampe, 1969; Smith, 1973) or reduplication, as in [be:be:] for *biscuit* (Waterson, 1971). Such rules increase the redundancy of the articulatory instructions in the word; we may assume that [gɔg] is easier than *dog* in the same way that *101* is easier to type than *103,* for example. Metathesis over intervening vowel ([nos] for *snow*), discussed by Ingram (1973) as being one of the most powerful arguments for the child's preference for a small set of canonical output forms, is sometimes found as a way of avoiding consonant clusters. It is difficult to see how such a rule could arise from the operation of automatic articulatory processes.

A third kind of simplification of this type, found in older children, is achieved by stereotyping the surface inventory by the use of dummy syllables. Here the simplification does not necessarily involve reducing the number of articulatory features that have to be produced per word; instead, the repertoire of output word forms is reduced. Ingram (1973) has discussed such cases in terms of phonological redundancy rules (Stanley, 1967). We may illustrate it by continuing with the analogy used in the preceding paragraph: If we know that all the sequences we will be called upon to type have O as the second character, and we have access to this knowledge while typing, then we have less information that must be kept in mind about each individual sequence while typing. Smith's son used the dummy syllables *ri:* or *ri* for virtually all unstressed initial syllables: *attack* [ri:tæk]; *arrange* [ri:reinz]; *guitar* [ri:'ta]. The child has actually increased the number of articulatory instructions required for the word *attack, arrange,* and he has departed from his normal treatment of velars in *guitar,* but he has sharply decreased his repertoire of pretonic unstressed syllables. Avoidance of clusters by metathesis over vowels, discussed above, and other devices for restricting the output to a few canonical forms also increase the repertoire without necessarily reducing the number of articulatory features that have to be produced per word.

One interesting consequence of a "problem-solving" view of phonology acquisition is that one might expect the child's previous solutions to be extended to new problems. A child's learning could thus show a certain amount of overall patterning attributable to the repeated use of certain strategies for devising rules.

Consider from this point of view the observation of Branigan (1974) that his subject shows a "focus" on the initial segment of a word in two distinct ways: The child uses initial stops to copy from in reduplication, and the word-initial position is the locus of experiments with and mastery of new phonemic distinctions. (A restricted version of this observation is made in Moskowitz, 1970.) For Daniel Menn, we see almost the mirror image of this case; final consonants are the ones he prefers to assimilate to, and word-final position is the place where new or complex phonemes (fricatives, affricates) and consonant clusters make their first appearance.

We suggest that here we see two children who have devised similar strategies, "pay attention to/try to match the beginnings of words" and "pay attention to/try to match the ends of words." If we assume that the child is capable of learning from his successes, we can account for those two "syndromes" by saying, for instance, that Branigan's subject has learned to deal with one problem, say the avoidance of $C_1VC_2(V)$, by focusing on C_1, and that this focusing then guides his attempts to deal with phonetic complexity of other sorts.

A further consequence is that Stampe's distinction between learned rules and innate processes loses its ontogenetic basis, at least in its present form. If we are right, then *all* phonological rules are in some sense acquired. The actual diversity observed among children's phonologies also tends to cast doubt on the idea that some adult phonological processes might be retentions of innate processes operating in child language. We are not aware of any longitudinal studies that bear on this claim. However, it seems to be falsified by children who exhibit no given process even though it is compatible with the target speech (cf. Braine, 1974, for discussion). For example, among his earliest words, Jonathan Kiparsky had a splendid *t* in [ata] *daddy,* contrary to *both* the flapping process and the flap of the adult speech he heard. In fact, the distinction between rules and processes does not emerge altogether clearly in the grammars of the languages, either. Even quite "low-level" rules may have lexical exceptions or morphological and/or syntactic conditioning (in particular, there are analogs to "phonological idioms" in adult language). On the other hand, morphologically conditioned rules can be quite as exceptionless as phonologically conditioned rules. In our view of the acquisition of phonology, there is reason to expect just this to be the case.

The development of the child's perception and classification of phonetic categories is a notoriously difficult area to study. It would be consonant with our general approach to find an element of learning here as well. Although there are some indications that the child must discover how to attend to linguistically relevant distinctions in perception (Edwards, 1974; Garnica, 1973) and how to classify them (Menn, 1973; Halliday, 1973) there is very little that can be said with any confidence on this subject.

In summary, we propose the framework in Figure 2.1. Each of the representations in the three boxes has a different status. A is constituted by the child's hypotheses about the underlying representations of the adult language he or she is learning. B is constituted by the child's perceptions of the phonetic representations of the adult language he or she is learning (to repeat, it is possible and even likely that these are distinct in some respects from the adult phonetic representa-

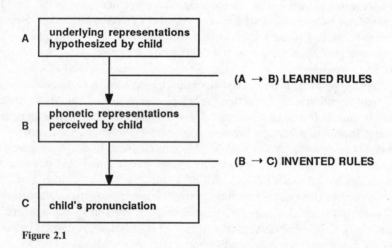

Figure 2.1

tions, although there is little concrete data on this point). And C is the child's ("intended") pronunciation *(Lautabsicht),* which may in turn be different in certain ways from the physical output, as when a purely *physical* limitation (say, a lisp) merges segments that the child may believe he is in fact distinguishing.

In the early stages of language acquisition, A and B coincide, while B and C are maximally distinct. As the child masters more of the phonetics, after the initial period of rule invention, C approaches B and the system of rules (B → C) shrinks. The process normally terminates when C becomes identical with B. Independently, and surely concurrently in part, though continuing well into adolescence, a second learning process goes on. As the child keeps discovering the phonological relationships of his language, A becomes increasingly different from B and the system of rules (A → B) becomes increasingly elaborate. This process terminates when A and A → B develop into the adult lexicon and rule system.

This picture can be compared to Jakobson's only in part, for Jakobson's goals were different. He presented a theory of the child's learning of the *phonemic* system, not of the morphophonemic system. Within this domain, however, a difference between his view and ours is that we differentiate between inherent phonetic limitations and linguistic, "invented" devices for coping with them, whereas for Jakobson there is only an inherent "filter." Therefore, the actual diversity in the child's solutions becomes somewhat problematic for Jakobson, whereas it is expected on our account.

Of course, if we are right about the inventive and diverse character of even the first steps in phonology acquisition, the difficulties of testing some of the best-known predictions of Jakobson's theory, and the need to take into account more than just the acquisition of contrasts, what we take to be Jakobson's central claim may perfectly well still hold true: namely, that whatever implicational laws hold for the languages of the world also hold for each stage in a child's acquisition of phonology. For it is quite possible that these implicational laws (presumably expressed by markedness principles of some sort) establish a hierarchy of features that is only partial but that does hold in both domains. For example, there seems to be no strict hierarchical relation between the major points of consonant articulation either developmentally or cross-linguistically, so that there is neither a single fixed order in which the *p, t, k* series are learned, nor an implicationally fixed distribution (that is, any of the series can show a gap: Hawaiian has *p, k* but no corresponding dental; the velar position can be missing, as is commonly the case for nasals; and labials can also be lacking, either for a particular manner of articulation, or altogether, as in Iroquoian and Tlingit). On the other hand, it may well be true that plain consonants are implied by palatalized, pharyngealized, aspirated, glottalized (and so on) consonants *both* in acquisition and across languages. Work now in progress by Myrl Solberg (at Massachusetts Institute of Technology) on the acquisition of Quechua phonology so far tends to confirm the hypothesis, for features of the latter type. How far this kind of correspondence goes remains a matter for further investigation.

Stampe's idea of the learning of "processes" resembles Jakobson's in that the differentiation between inherent limitations and invented devices is not made, although he does allow for an aspect of "invention" (insufficient, in our view) in the possibility of selecting between different inherent processes by their selective suppression. Stampe's theory is the first to account for both the learning of the phonetic repertoire and of the phonological relations. Our main difference with Stampe in this respect is that we see the two as separate, so that all phonological rules are learned, and there is no basis in language acquisition for any distinction one might wish to draw in the adult system between "rules proper" and "processes" (with the possible exception, noted above, of certain types of redundancy rules—viz., those that are natural and produce no allomorphy).

THE LEARNING OF MORPHOPHONEMICS

The question of how morphophonemics is acquired is complicated from the outset by some basic uncertainties about the nature of what is learned. Generative grammar holds that what is learned is a system of rules of a certain form, which apply to underlying phonological representations in order and whose output is the set of phonetic representations. Contemporary phonological theories fall more or less within this ballpark; in the forefront of ongoing theoretical debate are such questions as whether the types of ordering or the abstractness of underlying phonological representations might be limited in some ways, whether intermediate levels of some sort should be assumed to exist, and where morphology fits in.

Recently, the psychological reality of generative phonology has been questioned on the grounds of experimental results by Ohala (1972) and Krohn, Steinberg, and Kobayashi (1972). They elicited pronunciations of made-up morpheme combinations to see whether speakers would apply to them such morphophonemic rules as trisyllabic laxing and velar softening. They found that in most responses, no changes were made in the stem, and what changes were made were rather heterogeneous and mostly not predicted from the morphophonemic rules. This shows at best that these rules are not fully productive—a fact that could have been discovered more simply by noticing that they do not automatically apply to new words that are formed in English.

However, there seems to be a more fundamental problem with these experiments. Neither Ohala nor Krohn, Steinberg, and Kobayashi included in their experiment the control case of productive rules. As a matter of fact, in the one experiment (of which we are aware) in which this has been tested in adults (Haber, 1975), their performance on English plurals was generally poor. On a Berko-type setup, the percentage of correct responses ranged from 100 percent (on one item /wuwǰ/) to 53 percent (/rowmǝz/). The commonest deviant responses were (1) no change, e.g., /dǝ́piš/ → /dǝ́piš/; (2) devoicing, e.g., /frawg/ → /frawks/; (3) voicing, e.g., /blif/ → /blivz/. Less common were (4)

38

misplaced /əz/, e.g., /blif/ → /blifəz/; (5) internal vowel change, e.g., /fowθ/ → fayθ/. Several other even more exotic formations occurred marginally. It seems clear that errors of this type do not occur, at least in such numbers, in ordinary speech. (Derwing and Baker's [1977] replication of Berko's experiments with adult subjects has now confirmed Haber's results.)

These rather surprising findings cast some doubt on the interpretation of the Ohala and Krohn–Steinberg–Kobayashi experiments and suggest that there may be something about the experimental situation, a "strangeness effect," that causes subjects' performance to deteriorate relative to their normal speech. (Compare the well-known pitfalls in obtaining grammaticality judgments of sentences in isolation—Labov, 1971; Spenser, 1973.) Producing pieces of language out of context—especially, perhaps, single words—may well be a task of a special sort, comparable in its artificiality to that of making love to an arrangement of rubber and electrodes under the watchful eyes of Masters and Johnson, which reportedly also has a negative effect on some subjects' performance. (Our comparison is only in part facetious; there may well be a real effect from the severe feelings of insecurity about language that most people have. More on these and other experimental designs, and on different kinds of "productivity" that they might be used to test, can be found in Kiparsky, 1975.)

Moskowitz's (1973) study on the learning of English vowel shift by children also relies on production tasks. Her subjects "were required to learn two front vowel alternations and then were tested for generalization to a third front vowel alternation as well as two kinds of back vowel alternations, the surface ones and the rule-predicted ones." This paradigm was run three different ways: Under Condition I, subjects were given pairs with two of the three front vowel alternations of the actual English pattern *(sīyp ~ sĕpity, pāyp ~ pĭpity)*. Under Condition II, they were given two kinds of pairs differing in tenseness and diphthongization but no vowel shift *(sēyp ~ sĕpity, pīyp ~ pĭpity)*. Under Condition III, they were given two kinds of pairs with an incorrect vowel shift pattern *(sēyp ~ sĭpity, pīyp ~ pǽpity)*. On the learning of the two given kinds of vowel pairs, she found (for nine–twelve-year-olds) that "Condition I was considerably easier than either II or III. There also seems to be a tendency for III to be easier than II on all three measures—i.e., whether or not the subject learned to criterion, the number of trials completed before the ten criterion trials, and the number of errors made" (p. 241). Correct generalization to the third type of front vowel pair *(ēy ~ ǽ, āy ~ ǽ, and āy ~ ĕ, respectively)* was also highest for Condition I, and somewhat better for III than for II (pp. 242–243). Transfer to back vowels was equally bad for all three groups (p. 244).

Moskowitz (p. 248) sums up that "there is no doubt that these children have knowledge of vowel shift, since the data are almost overwhelming." But "it seems at first mysterious that at an age when children are relatively unfamiliar with much of the relevant vocabulary, they not only are able to manipulate vowel-shift patterns well but also are strongly resistant to other patterns in such an easy task. Likewise it seems mysterious that an incorrect vowel-shift pattern is easier than a phonetically simpler pattern involving no shift"—i.e., that Condition III is easier than Condition II. She concludes, somewhat obscurely, that their competence is derived from their literacy, which may be true but does not follow from her findings (the near-impossibility of varying literacy while holding other cultural/social variables constant should not excuse investigators from caution in claiming that a certain behavior is due to literacy).

Moskowitz's remark about the late acquisition of the relevant vocabulary really applies only to the *context* of trisyllabic laxing, the knowledge of which this experiment did not test in any way. The vowel shift *pattern* itself, whose knowledge was at issue, is of course contained in quite basic vocabulary, notably in the inflectional morphology of verbs: *hide ~ hid, bite ~ bit, feed ~ fed, keep ~ kept,* and so on. It is therefore not so surprising that children know it, and there is certainly no need to invoke spelling as a necessary source of this knowledge. Indeed, the poor performance on the back vowels is evidence against doing so. Spelling should have led the children to respond to *spōwb* with *spɔ̄bity,* for example, since they presumably learn these two values for orthographic *o* just as they learn two values for the other vowels. The fact that the children failed to respond correctly with back vowels could, however, be explained on the assumption that the children know the vowel pairings from the verb morphology, for there are in fact no back vowel verbs like **bāwt ~ *bʌt,* corresponding to *hide ~ hid,* and the pattern [ūw] ~ [ɔ], corresponding to front *feed ~ fed,* is also rare (*shoot ~ shot* is the only example in inflection). Generalization from the front vowels might be difficult because the back vowel inventory is different—there are only two short back vowels, with no ɔ/o contrast. Besides, the orthography hypothesis also fails to predict the difference between Condition II and Condition III.

Moskowitz concludes from the failure of subjects to perform well on Condition II that "the vowel-shift rule is not separable from the rules of tensing and diphthongization" (p. 249). Again, we think that this may well be true but in no way follows from her results. If anything, these tend to suggest just the opposite. For if Moskowitz's line of argument from production tasks to grammatical form is taken seriously, her experiment would actually have to be interpreted as supporting not only the separation of Vowel Shift and Trisyllabic Laxing but even the actual formulation of Vowel Shift in *Sound Pattern of English* (SPE).[1] We hasten to add that in spite of note 1, we do not consider Moskowitz's results as particularly compelling support for the SPE analysis. Our own prejudices, for the record, run somewhere close to hers. We differ from her in being more skeptical about the ability of production tasks to show much of anything, at present, about the form of internalized linguistic knowledge, given the near-total obscurity surrounding the question of whether and how this knowledge is used in speech. It is for this reason that we cannot see these results as support for Moskowitz's final conclusion that the learning process involved in acquiring Vowel Shift is very different from other phonological learning.

The contrary conclusion is in fact indicated by what seems to us the most systematic and exciting work to date on speakers' knowledge of the marginally productive patterns of English derivational morphology: Rosemary Myerson's as yet unpublished doctoral thesis at the Harvard Graduate School of Education. Myerson used production tasks to elicit trisyllabic laxing, palatalization, and stress shift in eight-, eleven-, fourteen-, and seventeen-year-olds. In this task she replicated the Krohn–Steinberg–Kobayashi results. She also probed with a task that proved to be far more sensitive, one that she devised along lines suggested by work on memory by Piaget and Inhelder and work reported by Olson (in Moore, 1973). Myerson's recall task shows that children do learn some of the nonproductive patterns described by SPE as they become adolescents. For the acquisition of derivational morphology a pattern of results emerged that is highly consonant with the pattern we already have of the emergence of inflectional morphology in younger children.

The recall task was to learn word pairs, where each pair consisted of a nonsense stem that was given meaning as a noun, verb, or adjective, and a derivative made with an appropriate member of the set *-ic, -ity, -ion.* For example:

romal, romal + ic
inclort, inclort + ion
grice, grice + ity

All of the derivatives met the structural description of one of the rules in question, but only half the derivatives were presented to the subjects in accordance with the applicable rule; the other half were taught to the subjects with the endings merely "tacked on."

Thus one set of subjects might have seen

romal, [rómʌlɪk]
grice, [grɪ́sɪtiy]
inclort, [ɪnklɔrtiʌn]

while the other might have seen

romal, [románlɪk]
grice, [grájsɪtiy]
inclort, [ɪnklɔršʌn]

It should be noted again that the "tacked on" forms were of the same nature as the subjects' own output on production (Berko-type) tasks.

For the younger children, in recall, the words were either retrieved as taught or had their endings replaced by endings like *-ness, -ty* which produce no allomorphy *(griceness, gricety)* and which are mastered earlier by English-speaking children. However, at age eleven or later, the phonological rules operated in recall: Derivatives like [ɪnklɔrtiʌn] that had been originally learned as preserving the surface phonetic form, and derivatives like [ɪnklɔršʌn] that had been learned as obeying the phonological rule were eventually recalled as if they had been presented according to the phonological rules: [ɪnklɔrtiʌn] was recalled as [ɪnklɔršʌn].

Myerson found that, at ages fourteen and seventeen, certain subjects were able to transcend the rules and to recall the forms exactly as they had been taught, but such subjects also displayed a metalinguistic awareness that forms like [ɪnklɔrtiʌn] were strange.

We see that a recall task, then, taps a level at which some phonological rules operate, even when a production task may not, and that the pattern "special case–overgeneralization–learning of exceptions" emerges for such rules as stress shift and palatalization in English, apparently during early adolescence. The "dips in learning curves" that, as Bever (1970) has noted, are the surface symptoms of a discontinuous leap in the developing system from an initial analysis of low generality to a functionally superior, but (at first) observationally less adequate one, seem thus to occur throughout language acquisition at increasingly fine points of linguistic structure.

This view of language acquisition suggests an interpretation of certain types of analogical change. The commonest cases involve simply the elimination of arbitrary restrictions on rules. For example, *brethren* > *brothers* is the extension of the regular plural rule to a word that has hitherto been an exception to it. In more concrete terms, the exceptional plural of this word began not to be learned by increasing numbers of speakers some hundreds of years ago. (As often happens, the irregular form survived where lexicalized in special uses— e.g., in reference to members of religious or fraternal organizations.)

Of course, this does not answer the question of how innovations of individual speakers become general changes of language. The mechanism of this process has begun to be studied for sound change (Labov et al., 1972); whether analogy spreads the same way is not presently known. There are some considerations that may be relevant in this connection. First, the frequently observed tenacity with which children hang on to their early speech forms against even explicit correction could be a factor (see Kornfeld & Goehl, 1974, p. 216, for a recent example and a tentative explanation for the phenomenon). The extreme case is the occasional retention of stylized baby talk by siblings as a secret language (Applegate, 1961; Forchhammer, 1939). It is also worth noticing that many childhood forms may persist as *optional* variants into adult language, where they become dominant by selection (Haber, 1975). A further factor may be an active favoring by the adult community of analogical forms as "simple." Whatever the mechanisms, they will presumably have to be invoked also to account for the substratum effects long known to historical linguists, whereby features of the original language of immigrant and conquered populations may persist for generations in the new language, even in monolingual speakers.

What we have said so far pertains only to the learning of individual rules. However, a basic insight of modern linguistics is that linguistic regularities are interdependent. In work on generative grammar, substantial evidence has been accumulated that the formal relationships between rules are of the specific type representable by means of ordering. In both syntax and phonology, derivations work by applying the first rule to the input and each successive rule to the output of the preceding one.

There is evidence that rule ordering is required in children's grammars at a rather early stage. The well-known phenomenon of *displaced contrast* must usually be described in these terms. For example, Smith's (1973) son Amahl pronounced *puzzle* as *puddle* but *puddle* as *puggle*. In his speech, therefore, the rules

$$1.\ d \rightarrow g/\_\_l$$
$$2.\ z \rightarrow d/\_\_l$$

had to apply in that order. What is interesting is that the *g* in the child's rendering of *puddle* is retained even though he can pronounce *d* there, as shown by his version of *puzzle* (cf. L. Anderson, 1975).

Applegate (1961) has reported an interesting "sibling dialect" of two brothers, who were four and five and a half years old. According to Applegate, "it was the only language spoken by them, and they used it in communicating with the adults of the community, who spoke English, as well as in communicating with each other and with their playmates." A third brother, then eight and a half years old, who Applegate was told had earlier spoken the same way, "understood the speech of his brothers and served as a translator for them in situations in which they could not communicate effectively with adults." The principal difference between the sibling dialect and the (New England) speech of their parents and community was constituted by two additional rules in the children's speech:

A. The second of two identical stops within a word is replaced by a glottal stop.
E.g., [dayʔ] *died,* [teykiʔ] *taked* 'took,' [dæʔiy diʔit] *daddy did it,* [baʔiy] *Bobby,* [peyʔər] *paper,* [pəʔiy] *puppy,* [keyʔ] *cake,* [kiʔ] *kick,* [beyʔiy] *baby*

B. Fricatives and affricates are replaced by homorganic stops.
E.g., [wakt] *walks* (both third person singular of the verb and plural of the noun), [mænd] *mans* 'men,' [kænd] *cans* 'can'

These two rules applied only in the order given, as shown by two independent facts. *Fact 1:* The *t*'s and *d*'s derived from *s, z, č, ǰ* by Rule B did not become glottal stops by Rule A even if preceded by an identical stop within the same word—[takt] *talks,* [teykt] *takes,* [dagd] *dogs,* [dəd] *does. Fact 2:* The *t*'s and *d*'s derived from *s, z, č, ǰ* by Rule B did not trigger replacement of a following dental by a glottal stop in spite of Rule A—[tuwt] *suit* (contrasting with [tuwʔ] *toot*).

Applegate's observations support the claims to psychological validity of theories countenancing (extrinsic) rule ordering. Theories with only intrinsic ordering (e.g., feeding, see below) cannot express the connection between Fact 1 and Fact 2, and indeed are unable to treat either—that is, cases like [dəd] *does* or those like [tuwt] *suit*—as anything more than exceptions to Rule A. This is of course the standard argument for rule ordering. This argument is elsewhere sometimes countered with the proposal that the relevant regularities are explained sufficiently by the historical chronology of the corresponding sound changes, and that speakers are in reality learning surface forms without apprehending the regularities that depend on ordering. This objection cannot be made here, since the rules and their output are "invented" by the children themselves.

We know of no systematic work on the actual process by which the ordering of phonological rules is learned. However, it is possible to draw some conclusions indirectly, with due caution, from examination of the way ordering functions in synchronic and historical phonology.

There are two sorts of elementary ordering relations between rules.

1. Feeding When a rule A creates potential inputs to another rule B, A and B are in the *feeding relation*. When, in such a case, A is ordered before B (so that B applies to the output of A), we have *feeding order*. If A creates potential inputs to B, but A is ordered after B, then A and B are in *nonfeeding order*. For example, the English rule that simplifies a sequence of consonants with identical place of articulation feeds the "flap" rule that turns *t* and *d* into a voiced flap *D* between a stressed and unstressed syllabic—for example, *gotta, what does (he do?):*

/wat	dəz/	
wat	əz	consonant simplification
waD	əz	flapping

2. Bleeding When a rule A removes potential inputs to another rule B, A and B are in the *bleeding relation*. When A is ordered before B (i.e., B fails to apply in the cases to which A applies), we have *bleeding order*. For example, the (optional) rule that deletes the vowel of certain unstressed auxiliary verbs in English bleeds (and therefore precedes) flapping:

/wat	dəz/	
wat	əz	consonant simplification
wat	z	ə-deletion
(inapplicable)		flapping

While it is convenient to examine the logic of ordering in terms of such pairs of individual rules, an additional important consideration is that each rule forms part of a system in which the ordering relation is, apparently, transitive; that is, rules can be arranged in a single sequence where all necessary pairwise ordering relations are preserved. (This has, however, been contested by S. Anderson, 1974.) We would like to claim that in the case of both the feeding and bleeding relations, the two possible orderings of rules that fall into each relation are asymmetrical from a language learner's point of view. Feeding and bleeding order are preferred ("unmarked") compared to nonfeeding and nonbleeding order. Examination of phonological rule systems shows that instances of bleeding order tend to outnumber instances of nonbleeding order, and instances of feeding order generally outnumber instances of nonfeeding order in a quite dramatic way. The closer we move to the lower end of the sequence of phonological rules, the more pronounced this preference for feeding and bleeding order becomes. In fact, *all* rules of English phrase phonology studied in Selkirk (1972) are in feeding or bleeding order.

There is a historical phenomenon that is probably related to this synchronic observation. Cases of the far from common, but very interesting, type of change where nothing but the order of two rules changes show (unless certain other factors, to be discussed shortly, happen to intervene) a consistent directionality toward feeding and bleeding order. In line with our earlier reasoning, this directionality of reordering is interpretable as the historical reflex of a language acquisition strategy of the following sort: Given no evidence to the contrary, assume that rules apply in the "unmarked" feeding and bleeding orders.

We hypothesize, therefore, that a child who has learned two rules without encountering evidence for their mutual ordering will set up the hypothesis that they apply in unmarked order. This hypothesis should be verifiable by a study of children's mistakes. Where the adult language shows unmarked ordering, the child should not, if we are correct, make mistakes attributable to marked ordering. Suppose, for example, that a child has mastered the rule determining the choice of plural suffixes in English. Let us assume that the underlying form of the suffix is /z/ and that i is inserted before it after "hissing" and "hushing" sounds by the rule:

$$i\text{-insertion:} \quad \emptyset \longrightarrow i/\check{c},\check{j},\check{s},\check{z},s,z + \underline{\quad} z \#.$$

Suppose now the child speaks a dialect in which final dentals are deleted before consonant and word boundary—e.g. *toas'* but *toaster, toasting.* That is, he has the phonological rule

$$t\text{-deletion:} \quad \text{dental} \longrightarrow \emptyset/\underline{\quad}\begin{cases} \text{C} \\ \# \end{cases}$$

Our prediction is that when a child who has never happened to hear the plural form of a word like *test* (or even if he has heard it, has not registered its form) has occasion to use it, he will pronounce it [tesɨz] even if forms like *testing* have caused him to enter it in the lexicon with the underlying representation /test/. The reason is that this form results from the unmarked (in this case, feeding) order. (Subsequent encountering of the "correct" form *tests* might of course then lead the child to reorder the rules.) Plurals like [tesɨz] are in fact reported for Black English (Labov, 1972), where dental-deletion rules of this family exist.

Notice that this prediction is made independently of how the relevant rules are formulated. Suppose that (as is sometimes claimed) the underlying form of the plural suffix is /ɨz/ and the *i* is deleted in the complement of the left-hand context of the insertion rule. (The *t*-deletion rule must be made more complicated in that case, in order to make it apply before the now vocalic plural suffix /ɨz/.) The point to note is that the unmarked ordering of the two rules is still the one that outputs [tesɨz], this time because it is a bleeding order. This invariance under rule reformulation is a general property of ordering asymmetry.

A suggestion for formalizing these ordering asymmetries and at the same time relating them to other phenomena has been to introduce the concept of *opacity* (converse: *transparency*) as a *(quantitative)* property of rules, defined as follows:

A rule (R) of the form

$$A \longrightarrow B/C\_\_D$$

is opaque to the extent that there are phonetic representations of the form

  (i)   A in the environment C__D, or
  (ii) B (not from R) in the environment C__D
(cf. Kiparsky, 1973).

Both cases are quite straightforward. According to (i), a rule is made opaque by forms that look as if they should have undergone it but did not; according to (ii), it is made opaque also by forms that look as if they should not have undergone the rule but did. Transparency is thus related to the concept of recoverability in syntax. The unmarked orders can now be characterized as those that maximize transparency. The marked nonfeeding and nonbleeding orders will always lead to one rule being opaque by (i) and (ii) respectively. The advantage of this formulation is that we can now consider opacity as a general property of rules that may have other sources than marked ordering. For example, all exceptions make a rule opaque by case (i). It now turns out that opaque rules as a class, whatever the source of opacity, have certain properties in common. For example, only opaque rules are known to be lost historically from grammars.

What we have done is essentially to distinguish two sorts of linguistic difficulty: one, complexity, measured, we hope, by the number of symbols in the grammar, the other, opacity, measured as just proposed. As a simple illustration of their independence, let us consider an arbitrary rule P and ask how it might be made harder to learn. One way would be to add more conditioning factors to its structural description. This would increase its complexity but not its opacity. Another way would be to order other rules after it in marked order. This would increase its opacity but not its complexity. A third way would be to mark certain items as exceptions to it. This, the worst case of all, would both make the rule opaque and add complexity to the grammar.

The status of these two sorts of linguistic difficulty is furthermore rather different from two viewpoints, that of the language learner and of the theory we are proposing. Complexity is assigned by the evaluation measure to grammars as abstract objects. Opacity is a property of the relation between the grammar and the data. An opaque rule is not more complex, merely harder to discover. Consequently, we do *not* predict that the rules of early phonology, which are not hypotheses about data but figments of the child, should show the same preference for transparent order. In fact, opaque orders are quite common in this domain. The examples of displaced contrast cited earlier are cases in point.

The preferred ordering among the invented rules may depend on other functional considerations than learnability, however. In general, feeding order reduces contrasts and nonfeeding order preserves them. For example, if the $d \rightarrow g$ and $z \rightarrow d$ rules operate in that order, as they did in Amahl Smith's grammar (see above), the contrast between *puzzle* and *puddle* is preserved (albeit in altered form). The reverse order of application would merge them both as *puggle*. If the child seeks to represent as many adult contrasts as possible given his phonetic resources (something that seems plausible but has admittedly not been demonstrated so far—for discussion, see L. Anderson, 1975), then a useful strategy for deploying rules would be the following: *Put the rules in nonfeeding order if possible.*

In the learning of morphophonemics proper, it may also happen that transparency is at odds with other functional requirements on the grammar (Kisseberth, 1973; Kaye, 1975). One such factor is paradigmatic leveling, probably the best-known type of analogy in both child language and linguistic change. Kazazis (1969) has described a case in the speech of his daughter Marina at age 4;7. Marina was trilingual, and the example concerns her Greek. In this language, the fricatives [x] (back) and [ç] (front) are in complementary distribution; in the cases under consideration, the choice between them is determined by whether the following vowel is back or front. In nonderived environments, Marina pronounces [x] or [ç] with the correct distribution. In the verbal paradigm, however, she generalized [x], for example, third person singular *exete* for adult *eçete*.

A good example of the way in which paradigmatic leveling is connected to bleeding order is Canadian Raising, the change of the diphthongs *ay, aw* to *əy, əw* before voiceless consonants, as in *write* versus *ride*. The rule that does this interacts with another rule that makes *t* voiced intervocalically in words like *eating;* let us denote the output of this rule simply as *d.* In words like *writing,* the *t*-voicing rule has the effect of potentially depriving—bleeding—the raising rule of some of its inputs. If the *t*-voicing rule precedes, *writing* will retain its open *ay,* contrasting with the *əy* of *write:*

System A:		/rayt ɨŋ/	/rayt/
	t-voicing	rayd ɨŋ	—
	Raising	—	rəyt
	Output	[rayd ɨŋ]	[rəyt]

However, if Raising precedes t-voicing, we have instead:

System B:		/rayt ɨŋ/	/rayt/
	Raising	rəyt ɨŋ	rəyt
	t-voicing	rəyd ɨŋ	—
	Output	[rəyd ɨŋ]	[rəyt]

The ordering of System B is opaque, since the output of Raising there appears on the surface in environments in which the rule is inapplicable. Nevertheless, this opacity appears to be offset by the fact that in System B the stem of *write* and similar words appears with a fixed vocalic nucleus. In Canada, System B appears to have ousted System A in the last thirty years (Chambers, 1973). The corresponding directionality of change can be observed in other cases of the same type.

The example is instructive in yet another respect. Notice that if we adopt a very "concrete" analysis, with /ay/ and /əy/ as separate phonemic entities, the change from System A to System B can be represented as a straightforward simplification of the grammar. We should then need, at the stage described above as System A, a lowering rule that changes /əy/ to /ay/ before the voiced segments resulting from t-voicing. The change that took place in the language can then be understood as a loss of this (opaque) lowering rule.

In general, an attentive examination of historical change suggests in many cases that the underlying representations constructed by speakers are shallower than many current phonological theories would have it. In particular, non-derived (morpheme-internal) outputs of sound change seem to be characteristically restructured by speakers in a form that is close to their phonetic form.

However, sometimes we get indications in the child's error pattern of a more "abstract" analysis of a surface form if it is one that looks as though it could have been produced by a rule the child knows. If the rule involved is optional, like flapping and some parts of vowel reduction in English, but of very high probability, we may get "back formations" in which an opposition almost always neutralized on the surface appears because the child fails to apply an optional rule. *Raisins* with [ʌ] instead of [ɨ] in the second syllable and *recorder* (flute) with [t] instead of [d] resulted from such cases where insufficient surface information allowed Stephen Menn to hypothesize the wrong underlying forms (a non-high vowel in *raisin,* /t/ in *recorder*). Drachman and Malikouti-Drachman (1973) present material on the reanalysis of the voiced allophone of /p/ in Modern Greek (occurring after nasals), which suggests that the child's ability to recover the allophony follows his or her acquisition of the voicing rule when it appears productively across the article–noun boundary. We do not yet know what the conditions are under which a child will "dig beneath" the phonetic surface.

Let us summarize our conclusions. The child is faced with two distinct problems in learning phonology: in the early stages, the quasi-physiological problem of his own limited phonetic capabilities, to which the adult output must be fitted; later (though doubtless in part concurrently) the cognitive problem of learning the abstract regularities of the phonological system, whether in order to remember, understand, or speak his language. We have suggested that the *form* of the child's solution to both problems is the same. It is a "cognitive" form that is determined by the child's ability to construct grammars. The child devises a system of underlying representations and general rules, which operate on phonological features, in order to derive the output form. In both systems the rules allow lexical exceptions. In both systems the rules may apply in extrinsic order. The child's speech reveals, in both cases, a highly plastic, active process of acquisition, with many signs of restructuring of underlying representations and addition and discarding of rules. On the other hand, it remains an open question as to what extent, if at all, there is a *substantive* connection between the two systems, in the sense of rules being continued directly from one into the other.

NOTES

1. Vowel shift is there formulated as a *two-part* process:

$$
\begin{bmatrix} + \text{ tense} \\ \\ \text{V} \end{bmatrix}
\rightarrow
\left\{
\begin{array}{l}
[- \alpha \text{ high}] \quad \begin{bmatrix} \alpha \text{ high} \\ - \text{ low} \end{bmatrix} \\
\\
[- \beta \text{ low}] \quad \begin{bmatrix} \beta \text{ low} \\ - \text{ high} \end{bmatrix}
\end{array}
\right\}
\begin{array}{l} \text{(a)} \\ \\ \text{(b)} \end{array}
$$

The Vowel Shift pattern (Condition I in Moskowitz's experiment) is derived as follows:

		/ī/	/ē/	/ǣ/
Underlying forms				
(Trisyllabic Laxing, if applicable)		(ĭ	ĕ	ǽ)
Vowel Shift, if Trisyllabic Laxing has not applied	(a)	ē	ī	ǣ
	(b)	ǣ	ī	ē
Other rules		āy	īy	ēy

Obviously, Moskowitz's findings on Condition I would follow from the assumption that her subjects knew this process, in addition to the Trisyllabic Shortening rule. They would then recognize pairs presented to them *(skīyg ~ skĕgity, kāyč ~ kĭčity)* as instances of these processes, correctly take the third case *(zēyg)* as underlying /zǣg/, and produce *zagity*. To produce the alternation pattern of Condition II *(skēyg ~ skĕgity, kīyč ~ kĭčity, zāyg ~ zăgity)*, subjects would have to either drop both parts of Vowel Shift (entering the stimulus words as underlying /skēg/, etc.) or reorder both parts of Vowel Shift ahead of Trisyllabic Laxing (with underlying /skǣg/, etc.). The alternation pattern of Condition III *(skīyg ~ skăgity, kēyč ~ kĭčity, zāyg ~ zēgity)* is the result of a smaller modification of the grammar. We apply part (b) of Vowel Shift before part (a):

	/ǣ/	/ī/	/ē/
(Trisyllabic Laxing)	(æ̆	ĭ	ĕ)
Vowel Shift (b)	ē	ĭ	ǣ
(a)	ī	ē	ǣ
Other rules	[īy]	[ēy]	[āy]

yielding the pairing of tense and lax vowels in Condition III. Both Moskowitz's principal findings—viz., (1) that Condition I is by far the easiest, and (2) that Condition III is somewhat easier than Condition II—then follow if we assume that her subjects analyzed English vowel alternations literally as in SPE and were trying to accommodate the unfamiliar alternation patterns of Conditions II and III by modifying this analysis. Furthermore, no other hypothesis with which we are familiar accounts for Moskowitz's finding (2)—in particular, her own hypothesis that Vowel Shift and Trisyllabic Laxing are learned together as a single indivisible alternation pattern incorrectly predicts that performance on Conditions II and III should be the same.

REFERENCES

Anderson, L. 1975. Learning your language or another's. Ditto, preliminary version.

Anderson, S. 1974. *The organization of phonology.* NY: Seminar Press.

Anisfeld, M., & G.R. Tucker. 1973. English pluralization rules of six-year-old children. In Ferguson and Slobin (Eds.), *Studies of child language development.* NY: Holt.

Applegate, J. 1961. Phonological rules of a subdialect of English. *Word, 17,* 166–193.

Bell, A. 1971. Some patterns of occurrence and formation of syllable structures. Working Papers in Language Universals, No. 6. Stanford University.

Berko, J. 1959. The child's learning of English morphology. *Word, 14,* 150–167.

Bever, T.G. 1970. The cognitive basis for linguistic structures. In J.R. Hayes (Ed.), *Cognition and language learning.* NY: Wiley.

Bhat, D.N.S. 1973. Retroflexion: An areal feature. Working Papers in Language Universals, No. 13. Stanford University.

Bogoyavlenskiy, D.N. 1973. The acquisition of Russian inflections (translated). In Ferguson & Slobin (Eds.), *Studies of child language development.* NY: Holt.

Braine, M.O.S. 1974. On what might constitute learnable phonology. *Language, 50,* 270–299.

Branigan, G. 1974. Syllabic structure and the acquisition of consonants. Mimeo, Boston University.

Chambers, J.K. 1973. Canadian raising. *Canadian Journal of Linguistics, 18,* 113–125.

Derwing, B. and W. Baker. 1977. The psychological basis for morphological rules. In J. Mac-Namara, (Ed.), *Language learning and thought.* NY: Academic Press.

Drachman, G. 1975. Generative phonology and child language acquisition. In W.V. Dressler and F.V. Mares (Eds.), *Phonologica 1972.* München: Finck, Pp. 235–251.

Drachman, G., & A. Malikouti-Drachman. 1973. Studies in the acquisition of Greek as a native language, I. Ohio State University Working Papers, No. 15.

Edwards, M.L. 1974. Perception and production in child phonology: The testing of four hypotheses. *Papers and reports on child language development, 7,* 68–84. Committee on Linguistics, Stanford University.

Ferguson, C.A., & C. Farwell. 1975. Words and sounds in early language acquisition: English initial consonants in the first 50 words. *Papers and reports in child language development,* 1973, *6,* 160. Committee on Linguistics, Stanford University. (Also *Language, 51,* 419–439.)

Ferguson, C.A., & D.I. Slobin (Eds.). 1973. *Studies of child language development.* NY: Holt.

Forchhammer, E. 1939. Uber einige Fälle von eigentümlichen Sprachbildungen. *Archiv für die gesamte Psychologie, 104,* 395–438.

Garnica, O.K. 1973. The development of phonemic speech perception. In T.E. Moore (Ed.), *Cognitive development and the acquisition of language.* NY: Academic Press.

Greenberg, J. 1970. Some generalizations concerning glottalic consonants, especially implosives. *International journal of American linguistics, 36,* 123–145.

Greenlee, M. 1974. Interacting processes in the child's acquisition of stop-liquid clusters. *Papers and reports on child language development, 7,* 85–100. Committee on Linguistics, Stanford University.

Haber, L. 1975. The muzzy theory. *Papers from the eleventh regional meeting.* Chicago Linguistic Society.

Hockett, C. 1955. *Manual of phonology.* Indiana University Publications in Linguistics.

Ingram, D. 1973. Phonological analysis of a developmentally aphasic child. Mimeo, Institute for Childhood Aphasia, Stanford University.

Ingram, D. 1974. Phonological rules in young children. *Journal of child language, 1,* 49–64.

Jakobson, R. 1968. *Child language, aphasia, and phonological universals.* A. Keiler, Trans. The Hague: Mouton.

Jakobson, R., & M. Halle. 1975. *Fundamentals of language.* The Hague: Mouton, 1956.

Kaye, J. 1975. A functional explanation for rule ordering in phonology. *Papers from the Parasession on Functionalism.* Chicago Linguistic Society.

Kazazis, K. 1969. Possible evidence for (near-) underlying forms in the speech of a child. *Papers from the fifth regional meeting,* Chicago Linguistic Society.

Kiparsky, P. 1973. Phonological representations. In O. Fujimura (Ed.), *Three dimensions of linguistic theory.* Tokyo: TEC Co.

Kiparsky, P. 1975. What are phonological theories about? In D. Cohen and J. Wirth (Eds.), *Testing linguistic hypotheses.* Washington & London: Hemisphere. Pp. 187–210.

Kisseberth, C.W. 1973. *The interaction of phonological rules and the polarity of language.* Mimeo, Indiana University Linguistics Club.

Kornfeld, J., & H. Goehl. 1974. A new twist to an old observation: Kids know more than they say. *Papers from the parasession on natural phonology.* Chicago Linguistic Society, Pp. 210–219.

Krohn, R., D. Steinberg, & L.R. Kobayashi. 1972. The psychological validity of Chomsky and Halle's vowel shift rule. XXth International Congress of Psychology, Tokyo. Abstract Guide, p. 1905.

Labov, W. 1972. *Sociolinguistic patterns.* Philadelphia: University of Pennsylvania Press.

Labov, W., M. Yaeger, & R. Steiner. 1972. *A quantitative study of sound change in progress.* Philadelphia: U.S. Regional Survey.

Leopold, W.F. 1939–1949. *Speech development of a bilingual child.* Evanston, Ill.: Northwestern University Press.

Lindblom, B., & J. Liljencrantz. 1972. Numerical simulation of vowel quality systems: The role of perceptual contrast. *Language, 48,* 839–62.

McNeill, D. 1970. *The acquisition of language.* NY: Harper and Row.

Menn, L. 1971. Phonotactic rules in beginning speech. *Lingua,* 26:225–251.

Menn, L. 1973. Origin and growth of phonological and syntactic rules. *Papers from the ninth regional meeting.* Chicago Linguistic Society.

Menn, L. 1976. Pattern, control, and contrast in beginning speech: A case study in the development of word form and word function. Unpublished doctoral dissertation, University of Illinois.

Miller, P. 1972. Some context-free processes affecting vowels. Ohio State University Working Papers in Linguistics No. 11.

Moore, T.E. (Ed.). 1973. *Cognitive development and the acquisition of language.* NY: Academic Press.

Moskowitz, A. 1970. Acquisition of phonology. Working Paper No. 34, Language-Behavior Research Laboratory, University of California, Berkeley.

Moskowitz, A. 1973. On the status of vowel shift in English. In T.E. Moore (Ed.), *Cognitive development and the acquisition of language.* NY: Academic Press.

Myerson, R. 1975. A developmental study of children's knowledge of complex derived words of English. Mimeo, Harvard Graduate School of Education.

Nakazima, S. 1972. A comparative study of the speech development of Japanese and American children (Part Four)—The beginning of the phonemicization process. *Studia Phonologica.* *6,* 1–37. University of Kyoto.

Ohala, J.J. 1972. On the design of phonological experiments. Paper presented at Linguistics Society of America Winter Meeting, Atlanta.

Ohala, J.J. 1974. Phonetic explanation in phonology. *Papers from the parasession on natural phonology.* Chicago Linguistic Society.

Selkirk, E. 1972. The phrase phonology of English and French. Doctoral dissertation, Massachusetts Institute of Technology.

Shibatani, M. 1973. The role of surface phonetic constraints in generative phonology. *Language, 49,* 87–106.

Skousen, R. 1974. An explanatory theory of morphology. *Papers from the parasession on natural phonology.* Chicago Linguistic Society.

Slobin, D.I. 1973. Cognitive prerequisites for the development of grammar. In Ferguson and Slobin (Eds.), *Studies of child language development.* NY: Holt, 1973.

Smith, N.V. 1973. *The acquisition of phonology: A case study.* Cambridge, England: Cambridge University Press.

Spenser, N.J. 1973. Differences between linguists and nonlinguists in intuitions of grammaticality-acceptability. *Journal of psycholinguistic research, 2,* 83–98.

Stampe, D. 1969. The acquisition of phonetic representation. *Papers from the Fifth Regional Meeting,* Chicago Linguistic Society.

Stampe, D. 1972. What I did on my summer vacation. Manuscript, Ohio State University.

Stanley, R. 1967. Redundancy rules in phonology. *Language, 43,* 393–435.

Troubetzkoy, N.S. 1949. *Principes de phonologie.* (J. Cantineau, Trans.) Paris: Librairie C. Klincksieck.

Velten, H.V. 1943. The growth of phonemic and lexical patterns in infant language. *Language, 19,* 440–449.

Waterson, N. 1971. Child phonology: A prosodic view. *Journal of linguistics, 7,* 179–221.

Zwicky, A.M. 1970. A double regularity in the acquisition of English verb morphology. *Papers in linguistics, 3.*

Part Two

THEORETICAL PERSPECTIVES ON INTERLANGUAGE PHONOLOGY

Part Two contains papers that provide a theoretical perspective on interlanguage phonology. These works have laid the foundations from which later research developed. Eckman contributes two such papers to this section. The first, entitled "Markedness and the Contrastive Analysis Hypothesis," discusses a crucial shortcoming in the original approach to contrastive analysis: its inability to predict the relative difficulty of error types within an interlanguage. He proposes a Markedness Differential Hypothesis that, when incorporated into the CAH, will make it more descriptively adequate. This is one of the earliest and clearest applications of the notion of markedness to IL (interlanguage) phonology. In his second article, Eckman seeks to determine whether an IL phonology contains the same types of rules as are found in natural languages, as well as the extent to which an IL is independent of the TL (target language) and NL (native language). Using data from Mandarin and Spanish learners of English, he does indeed find IL rules that appear to be motivated independently or that seem to be unnatural in terms of a mature native speaker's grammar. He does not discuss the degree to which such rules are natural to L1 acquisition.

Tarone also criticizes a simplistic approach to contrastive phonology. She is one of the first to posit a conjunction of interacting influences shaping the course of the developing interlanguage phonology. These include transfer, over-generalization, avoidance, and L1 acquisition processes. She also notes the importance of describing the variability in the learner's system, and she recommends an analysis of the social and psychological factors that give rise to it.

Dickerson demonstrates that an interlanguage phonology is just as susceptible to sociolinguistic variability as a native language. His work is directed toward the specification of the rule variability found in L2 phonology. This is the first attempt to apply a sociolinguistic model of sound change to the acquisition of a L2 sound system. Dickerson discusses the similarities between the L2 developing grammar and the ongoing linguistic change found in a homogeneous speech community.

The article by Major is a more recent attempt to develop a model of interlanguage phonology. He argues that developmental and transfer processes vary in their degree of influence on the IL phonology in relation to the learner's proficiency. The same determinants, he believes, can also account for the variation witnessed in style shifting. His model of IL phonology is based on three hypotheses:

1. At the early stages of acquisition, interference processes predominate and then decrease over time.
2. Developmental errors are infrequent initially, increase in the intermediate stages, then diminish.
3. Style has the following correlation to proficiency. As the style becomes more formal, there will be fewer interference errors; concurrently, developmental processes increase and then decrease.

3

MARKEDNESS AND THE CONTRASTIVE ANALYSIS HYPOTHESIS

Fred R. Eckman*

INTRODUCTION

The purpose of this paper is to suggest that the main principle behind the Contrastive Analysis Hypothesis (CAH), namely that the comparison of the native and target languages is crucial in predicting the areas of difficulty that a language learner will have, can be maintained as a viable principle of second language acquisition. Moreover, I will argue that if the CAH is revised to incorporate certain principles of universal grammar, it is possible to predict what can be termed the "directionality of difficulty." That is, given these universal principles along with the description of the two languages, A and B, where these languages differ with respect to some phenomenon, say, superficial voice contrasts in obstruents, it is possible to predict whether voice contrasts in language A present more of a problem for a speaker of B learning A than does the lack of a voice contrast in B for a speaker of A learning B.

*I would like to thank D. Dinnsen, H. Gradman, G. Iverson, and G. Sanders for taking the time to discuss this topic with me, and for their comments and suggestions. Of course, any errors or inconsistencies are my own.

In what follows, I shall consider an application of the CAH to a segment of English and German phonology. I shall show where the CAH as presently formulated fails to make the correct predictions when the descriptions of the respective languages are done first within the framework of taxonomic phonemics and second within the standard theory of generative phonology. It will then be demonstrated how, with the incorporation of universal principles, the empirically correct predictions can be made. We shall then show that these same principles can be used to correctly predict the areas of difficulty in an example from syntax.

THE CONTRASTIVE ANALYSIS HYPOTHESIS

In the course of the controversy over the viability of the CAH in the last ten years, two versions of this hypothesis have emerged: The strong form of the CAH is evidenced in the following quotations, taken from Lado (1957).

". . . in the comparison between native and foreign language lies the key to ease or difficulty in foreign language learning. . . ." (p. 1)

"We assume that the student who comes in contact with a foreign language will find some features of it quite easy and others extremely difficult. Those elements that are similar to his native language will be easy for him and those elements that are different will be difficult." (p. 2)

Thus the strong form of the CAH claims that one can predict the errors a language learner will make on the basis of a comparison of descriptions of the native and target language.

However, because it has been found that many of the predictions made by the strong form of the CAH are wrong, a weak version of this hypothesis has emerged. This form of the CAH can be characterized by the following statement, taken from Wardhaugh (1974).

"In contrast to the demands made by the strong version, the weak version requires of the linguist only that he use the best linguistic knowledge available to him in order to account for observed difficulties in second-language learning. It does not require what the strong version requires, the prediction of those difficulties and conversely, of those learning points which do not create any difficulties at all." (p. 181)

From this we can see that the weak version of the CAH makes no predictions whatever as to which errors will be made. In view of this, it seems clear that the weak version of the CAH is not intended as a principle of second language acquisition, since it is not falsifiable. Rather, the weak version appears to be a heuristic which can be followed in analyzing student errors in a second language learning situation. For this reason I shall disregard the weak form of the CAH, and, for the purpose of this paper, shall deal only with the strong form.

With this in mind, let us now consider an application of the CAH to voiced and voiceless obstruents of German and English. Considering these first from the point of view of taxonomic phonemics, we see that Moulton (1962) lists the phonemes of these two languages as in Table 3.1. Moulton points out that there is a distributional difference with respect to these phonemes. While both voiced and voiceless obstruents occur word-initially, -medially and -finally in English, both voiced and voiceless obstruents occur only word-initially and -medially in German. In word-final position, German has only voiceless obstruents. Thus German exhibits voiced-voiceless alternations as in [tak] 'day' and [tagǝ] 'days'.

Given this fact, the CAH would predict that since German and English differ with respect to whether or not voiced obstruents can occur word-finally, this will be an area of difficulty for German speakers learning English, and for English speakers learning German. However, as can be seen from the statements below, taken from Moulton (1962), there is a directionality of difficulty associated with this phenomenon.

"The native speaker of German does not, of course, make any such analytical observation. For him the occurrence of /p/ rather than /b/ in these positions is simply a matter of habit, something which seems entirely natural, even inevitable. This habit is so firmly fixed that when he learns a foreign language, he finds it very difficult to pronounce voice obstruents in one of these positions." (pp. 49–50)

"In English, on the other hand, aside from the few forms like *leaf-leaves, wife-wives,* the shape of the stem is fixed and it is the consonant of the ending which alternates: . . . Fortunately, if the student refuses to let himself be misled by the spelling, the German alteration of voiced and voiceless obstruents is not hard to learn." (p. 50)

Thus from these statements it is clear that it is the German speaker learning English who has more difficulty.

This directionality of difficulty is not predicted by the CAH alone. In order to explain this phenomenon, proponents of the CAH would need an auxiliary hypothesis which claims that it is difficult to learn new contrasts, or new positions of contrast, but that it is not difficult to learn to suppress contrasts. Given this additional assumption, the CAH can correctly predict the facts stated above by Moulton, since a German speaker learning English must learn to make word-final voice contrasts whereas an English speaker learning German must learn to suppress such contrasts.

While this extension of the CAH is sufficient to account for the English German obstruents, it makes the wrong prediction with respect to the degree of difficulty involved in the occurrence of the phoneme /ž/ in French and English. As shown by the data in Table 3.2, in French this phoneme occurs word-initially, -medially and -finally, whereas in English, it occurs only word-medially and -finally. Therefore an English speaker learning French must learn to contrast /ž/ with other phonemes in initial position while a French speaker learning English must learn to suppress this contrast.

Superficially, this situation looks exactly parallel to the situation involving voice contrasts in German and English. German speakers have a voice contrast in some positions and must learn to make this contrast word-finally when they learn English. Likewise, English speakers do contrast /ž/ with other phonemes in some positions, and they must learn to maintain this contrast word-initially in French. However, as Gradman (1971) points out, learning to contrast /ž/ in initial position is not difficult for English speakers learning French. Thus, while the assumption that the CAH can correctly predict areas of difficulty based on learning versus suppressing new contrasts is valid for some cases, it is not valid for others. Given this fact, let us now focus our attention on how these examples would be handled when the descriptions of the languages in question are done within the theory of generative grammar.

Within the framework of generative grammar, the facts concerning the distribution of voiced and voiceless obstruents in German would be accounted for by assuming that words which exhibit a voiced-voiceless alternation contain word-final voiced obstruents in their underlying representation, and that the grammar of German contains the rule demonstrated below. Thus we have the derivations shown in Table 3.3.

Terminal Devoicing (TD)

[-sonorant] → [-voice] /＿#

(Obstruents are voiceless in word-final position)

The rule of Terminal Devoicing is very well suited for German, since it accounts for the observed voice-voiceless alternations and since it states a true generalization about word-final obstruents in German. For English, on the other hand, no such rule is necessary since English maintains a voice contrast in initial, medial and final positions.

Given these two partial analyses, it should now be possible to apply the CAH to these descriptions of German and English to determine the directionality of difficulty. However, if any claim concerning the directionality is made in this case, the prediction is exactly the opposite of that stated above by Moulton (1962). This is true because according to the descriptions, both English and German have underlying voice contrasts in obstruents in initial, medial and final position. However, the grammar of German contains the TD rule described above, whereas the grammar of English contains no such rule. Thus, an English speaker learning German has more to learn (i.e., the TD rule) than a German speaker learning English. Consequently, it should be the English speaker learning German who has the greater difficulty. But as stated in Moulton (1962), this is in fact not the case.

The generative analysis of the distribution of /ž/ in French and English also provides no insight into the directionality of difficulty involved in second language acquisition. Underlying representations in French may have /ž/ in initial, medial, or final position, whereas English underlying representations can

TABLE 3.1

English

```
pb   td   kg
fv   θð   čj
     sz   šž
```

German

```
pb   td   kg
fv   sz   ç
     šž   x
```

TABLE 3.2

	Initial	Medial	Final
French	je [žə] 'I'	bouger [bužé] 'to move'	plage [plaž] 'beach'
English		azure [æžər]	garage [gəraž]

TABLE 3.3

Underlying representation	/tag/	/tagə/	/dek/	/dekə/	/grat/	/gratə/	/grad/	/gradə/	/kalb/	/kalbəs/	/hawz/	/hawzə/
Terminal devoicing	tak	—	—	—	—	—	grat	—	kalp	—	haws	—
Phonetic representation	[tak]	[tagə]	[dek]	[dekə]	[grat]	[gratə]	[grat]	[gradə]	[kalp]	[kalbəs]	[haws]	[hawzə]
Gloss	day	days	deck	decks	edge	edges	degree	degrees	calf	calf's	house	to the house

contain /ž/ in only medial or final positions. Since initial /ž/ in French does not alternate with any other phonemes, no phonological rule is relevant in this case.

In comparing these analyses within the context of the CAH, we see that there is nothing which would lead one to suspect that the contrast between initial /ž/ and other phonemes is something which is easy for English speakers to learn. Thus, apparently, the present formulation of the CAH, even when applied to generative descriptions, can correctly predict neither the areas of difficulty nor the relative degree of difficulty.

THE MARKEDNESS DIFFERENTIAL HYPOTHESIS

Given that the CAH, as presently formulated, is inadequate to account for the facts discussed, let us now attempt to propose an alternative to the CAH. The general thrust of this proposal will be that the assumption embodied in the CAH, namely that it is necessary to compare descriptions of the native and target languages in order to predict the areas of difficulty in second language learning, is valid. However, comparison of the native and target languages is not sufficient. What must be incorporated into the CAH in addition is a notion of "relative degree of difficulty." Moreover, this notion of difficulty must be independent of any given language (i.e., must be universal), and must be valid on grounds which are independent of the facts surrounding second language acquisition. In what follows, we shall attempt to propose such a notion and to test it with respect to the facts presented above.

The proposal which we shall make centers around the notions of typological markedness and implicational relations. Thus we shall propose that the notion of "degree of difficulty" corresponds to the notion "typologically marked," where markedness is defined as below:

Markedness A phenomenon A in some language is more marked than B if the presence of A in a language implies the presence of B; but the presence of B does *not* imply the presence of A.

To take a concrete example, there are languages with only voiceless obstruent phonemes (Korean), and there are languages with both voiced and voiceless obstruent phonemes (English). However, there are apparently no languages with just voiced obstruent phonemes. Therefore, the presence of voiced obstruent phonemes in a language implies the presence of voiceless obstruent phonemes, but not the reverse. According to the definition of markedness, then, voiced obstruent phonemes are more marked than voiceless obstruent phonemes.

Taking an example from syntax, there are languages (e.g., Arabic, Greek, Serbo-Croatian, Persian) which have passive sentences without expressed agents (i.e., sentences like *a* below but do not have passive sentences with expressed agents (i.e., sentences like *b*):

a. The door was closed.
b. The door was closed by the janitor.

There are languages (e.g., English, French, Japanese) which have both types of passive sentences. However, there are apparently no languages which have passives with agents without also having passives without agents. Therefore the presence of passives with agents implies the presence of passives without agents, but the reverse is not true. Thus sentences like *b* above are more marked than sentences like *a*.

Given this definition of markedness, let us propose the following hypothesis:

Markedness Differential Hypothesis (MDH)   The areas of difficulty that a language learner will have can be predicted on the basis of a systematic comparison of the grammars of the native language, the target language and the markedness relations stated in universal grammar, such that,
(a) Those areas of the target language which differ from the native language and are more marked than the native language will be difficult.
(b) The relative degree of difficulty of the areas of the target language which are more marked than the native language will correspond to the relative degree of markedness.
(c) Those areas of the target language which are different from the native language, but are not more marked than the native language will not be difficult.

In order for the facts which were discussed above to be explained by the MDH, it must be the case that (a) the distribution of voiced and voiceless obstruents in English is more marked relative to German; and (b) the distribution of /ž/ in French is not more marked relative to English.

Turning first to the German-English obstruents, that the distribution of these consonants is more marked in English is supported by a recent study by Dinnsen and Eckman (1975). Specifically, it was found that, with respect to the positions in which a voice contrast is maintained, languages can be typologized as in Table 3.4.

From this typology, we see that there is apparently an implicational relationship with respect to where a language maintains a superficial voice

TABLE 3.4

Type	Description	Examples
A	Those which maintain a superficial voice contrast in initial, medial and final positions.	English, Arabic Swedish
B	Those which maintain a superficial voice contrast in initial and medial positions, but fail to maintain this contrast in final position.	German, Polish, Greek, Japanese, Catalan
C	Those which maintain a superficial voice contrast in initial position but fail to maintain this contrast in medial and final positions.	Corsican, Sardinian
D	Those which maintain no voice contrast in initial, medial, or final positions.	Korean

contrast. Thus the presence of a contrast finally implies a contrast medially, which in turn implies a contrast initially. However, the presence of a voice contrast medially does not imply such a contrast finally, and the presence of a contrast initially does not imply a contrast medially or finally. To account for these facts, one can propose the universal hierarchy shown in Figure 3.1.

This hierarchy is to be interpreted in such a way that maintenance of a superficial voice contrast at any position on this hierarchy necessarily implies the maintenance of that contrast at all higher positions on the hierarchy but does not imply such a contrast at lower positions. Thus, for example, according to Figure 3.1 any language which maintains a voice contrast in obstruents word-medially necessarily maintains this contrast word-initially but does not necessarily maintain such a contrast word-finally. Moreover Figure 3.1 excludes the possibility that a language will maintain a voice contrast finally but not medially or initially.

What is inferable from the typology in Table 3.4 and the hierarchy in Figure 3.1 is that the maintenance of a voice contrast word-finally is more marked than the maintenance of a voice contrast word-medially, which, in turn, is more marked than the maintenance of a voice contrast word-initially. This being the case, we see that if the Markedness Differential Hypothesis is now applied to the facts about English and German obstruents, the following two statements are true: (1) The difference between these two languages lies in the maintenance versus non-maintenance of a word-final voice contrast; (2) the position in which English maintains a contrast and German does not maintain a contrast (word-finally) is more marked relative to the positions in which German maintains a voice contrast (word-medially and word-initially). Thus the MDH correctly predicts that the German speaker should have greater difficulty with English word-final contrasts than should an English speaker with the lack of such a contrast in German. That is, the MDH correctly predicts the directionality of difficulty stated in Moulton (1962).

Turning now to the distribution of /ž/ in French and English, we see that the MDH also makes the correct prediction in this case. Given the interpretation that the difference between these two languages is that French has an initial /ž/-/š/ contrast, but English does not, then what is involved is the maintenance versus non-maintenance of a voice contrast in initial position.[1] However, English does maintain a /ž/-/š/ contrast in medial and final positions. Given the hierar-

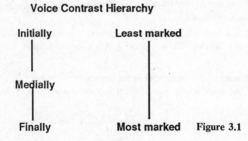

Voice Contrast Hierarchy

Initially   Least marked

Medially

Finally   Most marked   Figure 3.1

chy in Figure 3.1, we see that a voice contrast in initial position is not more marked than a voice contrast in medial and final positions. Therefore, it should not be difficult for an English speaker to learn to contrast /ž/ and /š/ in initial position.

What has been shown so far is that, with respect to the phonological examples discussed, the MDH is capable of explaining certain facts about second language acquisition that the CAH could not explain. We shall now attempt to demonstrate that the MDH is also superior to the CAH when applied to an example from syntax.

Schachter (1974) discussed the difficulties that speakers of some languages have with English relative clauses. Schachter analyzed fifty written compositions of Persian, Arabic, Chinese, and Japanese students studying English at the American Language Institute at the University of Southern California. Half of the compositions from each group were from intermediate level classes and half were from advanced level classes.

In her analysis, Schachter considered the errors which were made from three different aspects of how relative clauses are formed in English as opposed to the other languages in question. These were: (1) position of the relative clause with respect to the head noun phrase; (2) the marking of the relative clause by either an arbitrary subordination marker, for example, *that* in English, or by the insertion of an inflected pronominal particle between the head NP and the clause, for example, *who,* or *whom* in English; and (3) the occurrence of a pronominal reflex marking the position of the relativized NP in the underlying representation of the sentence. English has no such pronominal reflexes, but if it did, the forms below would be examples:

Subj: the boy that *he* came
Dir. Obj: the boy that John hit *him*
Indir. Obj: the boy that I sent a letter to *him*
Obj. Prep: the boy that I sat near *him*

The distribution of the pronominal reflexes in the above languages is shown in Table 3.5. The number and percentage of errors which were made in the compositions by the speakers of the various languages, including an American control group, is shown in Table 3.6.

TABLE 3.5 Pronominal reflexes in five language groups

	Subj.	Dir. obj.	Indir. obj.	Obj. prep.
Persian	(+)	+	+	+
Arabic	(+)	(+)	+	+
Chinese	−	−	+	+
Japanese	−	−	−	(+)
English	−	−	−	−

TABLE 3.6 Relative clause production in five language groups

	Total	Correct	Errors	Percentage of errors
Persian	174	131	43	25
Arabic	154	123	31	20
Chinese	76	67	9	12
Japanese	63	58	5	8
American	173	173	0	0

The number of errors which involved pronominal reflexes which speakers of Persian and Arabic made is shown below (Schachter presents no statistics of this type for Chinese or Japanese speakers):

Errors involving pronominal reflexes
Persian   35
Arabic   12

One interpretation of these facts is that of the languages tested, speakers of Persian have the most difficulty with English relatives; speakers of Arabic have less trouble than Persian speakers, but more than Chinese speakers, who, in turn, have greater difficulty than Japanese speakers.[2] Moreover, from the numbers above we can see that, for Persian and Arabic speakers at least, a large percentage of the errors made involved pronominal reflexes. The question which now arises is whether either the CAH or the MDH can predict this degree of difficulty.

It seems clear that since the relative clauses of Persian, Arabic, Chinese, and Japanese are different in some way from those of English, the CAH predicts only that speakers of these languages should have some difficulty with English relatives. However, there is nothing in the CAH that predicts that Persian speakers should have more difficulty than Arabic speakers, who should have more difficulty than Chinese speakers, and so on. Relative clauses in these languages are similar to English in some respects, but different in others. Thus Persian and Arabic relative clauses follow the head NP, as in English, but Persian and Arabic relative clauses either can contain or must contain pronominal reflexes, which English relatives do not. Likewise Chinese and Japanese relative clauses prohibit pronominal reflexes in some of the same positions as English, but the order of the head NP with respect to its clause in these languages differs from that of English. Consequently, there seems to be no non-arbitrary way of predicting what the difficulties will be or the relative degree of difficulty involved. What remains to be investigated is whether or not the MDH can account for these facts.

In order for the MDH to explain the facts represented in Table 3.6, the differences in relative clauses between English and Persian must be more marked than those between English and Arabic, which, in turn, must be more marked than those between English and Chinese; and finally, the differences between Japanese and English must be the least marked.

Evidence that such a relationship does exist between these languages has been put forth by Keenan and Comrie (1977). Specifically, Keenan and Comrie argue that there is a universal hierarchy of positions, or grammatical functions, out of which an NP may be relativized without leaving a pronominal reflex behind. This hierarchy is shown in Figure 3.2.

The hierarchy in Figure 3.2 is to be interpreted in such a way that if a language can relativize an NP out of a given position on the hierarchy without leaving behind a pronominal reflex, it can necessarily in a similar manner relativize an NP out of all positions higher on the hierarchy, but not necessarily out of lower positions. Thus, for example, if a language can relativize indirect objects without pronominal reflexes that language can also relativize direct objects and subjects but not necessarily objects of prepositions, possessive NPs, or objects of comparative particles. Moreover, this hierarchy predicts that there will be no language which can both relativize possessive NPs without leaving a pronoun behind, and relativize an object of a preposition, leaving a pronoun behind.

Given this information, we see that there is an implicational relationship with respect to the positions or functions out of which a language can relativize an NP without leaving a pronominal reflex. According to this relationship and the definition of markedness stated above, relativization out of the subject position is the least marked and relativization out of the object comparative particle position is the most marked.

Applying the Markedness Differential Hypothesis to these facts, we see that it is possible to explain the relative degree of difficulty represented in Table 3.6. From Table 3.5 we see that English relativizes NPs from all of the positions without leaving pronominal reflexes, whereas Persian can relativize from only one position (subject) without leaving a pronoun behind. Thus a Persian speaker learning English must learn to relativize from five positions without leaving a pronominal reflex. Moreover, according to the Keenan and Comrie hierarchy, all of the positions from which a Persian speaker learning English must learn to relativize without a pronominal reflex are more marked than the position

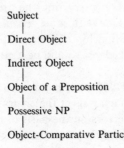

Subject
|
Direct Object
|
Indirect Object
|
Object of a Preposition
|
Possessive NP
|
Object-Comparative Particle   **Figure 3.2**   Noun phrase accessibility hierarchy

from which such relativization is possible in Persian. On the other hand, if we compare Arabic to English, we see that there are four positions (Indirect Object, Object of a Preposition, Possessive NP, and Object of a Comparative Particle) which differ from English with respect to relativization. Therefore an Arabic speaker learning English must learn to relativize an NP without a pronominal reflex out of four positions which are more marked than those in his or her native language. Given this information, the MDH would predict that the Persian speaker would have more difficulty than the Arabic speaker. We see that this prediction is borne out in Table 3.6. The situation is similar when we compare Chinese and Japanese to English. The Chinese speaker should have greater difficulty with English relative clauses than the Japanese speaker but less than the speaker of Arabic. These predictions are also borne out in Table 3.6.

The central claim of the MDH is that given a number of differences between languages, and therefore given also a number of potential areas of difficulty for language learners, only some of these differences will be areas of difficulty, while others will not. In addition, it is claimed that the areas of difficulty are predictable from markedness relations. For example, as mentioned above, there are several other areas besides the leaving behind of pronominal reflexes in which these languages differ from English. However, with respect to these other differences, no systematic implicational relations exist, and therefore the differences in the target language are neither more nor less marked than the native language. Thus the MDH predicts that these should not be areas of difficulty, and Schachter's data bears out this claim; as can be seen from the data above, a substantial portion of the errors made by Persian and Arabic speakers involved pronominal reflexes.

It would be possible to falsify the MDH if it could be shown that the areas of difficulty that a given language learner has are not those areas of the target language which are different from and more marked than the native language; or if it could be shown that there is an area of the target language which is clearly more marked than the native language but that this is not an area of difficulty.

CONCLUSION AND SPECULATIONS

Having argued that the MDH, which incorporates certain markedness relations from universal grammar, is superior to the CAH in predicting the areas of difficulty a language learner will have, let us conclude with some speculations about (a) some of the recent claims about the relationship of first and second language acquisition, and (b) why typological markedness should be a measure of degree of difficulty.

The inadequacy of the strong form of the CAH led many linguists to adopt the weaker version. This, in turn, required only an analysis of the errors made with a view toward possible explanation of these errors on the basis of differences between the languages in question. As work progressed on the analysis of language-learning errors many linguists concluded that a large portion of these errors could be attributed to *intra*lingual rather than *inter*lingual interference. That is, many of these errors were similar to those made by children acquiring the target language as a first language (see, for example, Dulay and Burt [1972] and Bailey, Madden, and Krashen [1974]). To the extent that this is true, it is reasonable to conclude that second language acquisition is the same type of process as first language acquisition. Furthermore, this conclusion is even more attractive given the demise of the strong form of the CAH, which predicts that the errors involved in second language acquisition are due to interlingual interference.

The MDH is a step in the direction of resolving the controversy between whether second language learning errors are due to interlingual or intralingual interference. Jakobson (1940) pointed out that the order of acquisition of contrasts and segments in first language acquisition is parallel to the cross-linguistic implicational relationships that exist with respect to these elements. That is, the order of acquisition parallels what we have termed typological markedness. Given the MDH, which is based on such markedness relationships, there should be a parallel between first and second language acquisition errors. Specifically, those segment types, contrasts, positions of contrasts, sentence types, etc., which are typologically marked, and therefore are acquired later in first language acquisition, are those areas which should be more difficult for second language learners. Thus, for example, Stampe (1969) has pointed out that the maintenance of a superficial voice contrast in word-final obstruents is acquired later by English-speaking children than are medial or initial contrasts. Therefore, at an early stage of acquisition, English-speaking children exhibit the same alternations which motivate a rule like Terminal Devoicing for German, and they make many of the same errors involving voiced and voiceless obstruents as German speakers learning English.

However, the MDH also predicts what has long been either implicitly or explicitly assumed, namely that the errors a language learner makes will be due, to some extent, to that person's native language. Specifically, the errors will be dependent on the native language to the extent that the areas of difference between the native and target language are marked.

Thus second language acquisition will parallel first language acquisition when the second language learner and first language learner must deal with the same areas of the language in question. However, there will be some sentence types, contrasts, segment types, etc. that the second language learner will not have to learn anew because he or she has already learned them by virtue of having learned his or her own native language.

Let me conclude with a brief consideration of why typological markedness is a reasonable measure of degree of difficulty. What seems an uncontroversial position on language universals is that languages, and hence, language universals, are a reflection of the structure of human cognition (Lenneberg, 1967, 374–5). Thus it is the nature of human cognition that no language will have *only* passive sentences *with* agents, but a language may have only passives without agents. Moreover, if one makes the additional assumption that humans learn to do things which are less complex before they learn to do things which are more complex, and, further, that no human being learns to do things which are more complex without also *a fortiori* learning to do related things which are less complex (Sanders 1977), then typological markedness is an accurate reflection of difficulty. If this is the case, then typological markedness should be incorporated into a theory of second language acquisition.

The point of this paper has been to suggest that rather than being abandoned altogether, the CAH should be revised to incorporate a notion of degree of difficulty which corresponds to the notion of typological markedness. While the arguments for this conclusion are based on a limited set of examples, it seems clear nonetheless that this conclusion is a step in the right direction towards shedding some light on the issue of whether first and second language acquisition are identical processes. This alone should make it worthy of further scrutiny.

NOTES

1. It seems reasonable to assume that what is involved here is a voice contrast rather than, say, a stop-fricative contrast, since French does not have palato-alveolar stops or affricates. However, even if it can be shown that a stop-fricative contrast of some sort is involved here, it would not change the markedness relations involved, since the hierarchy in Figure 3.1 appears to hold also with respect to stop-fricative contrasts.

2. Schachter comes to the opposite conclusion, based on her hypothesis that the Chinese and Japanese speakers found English relatives *more* difficult than did the Arabic and Persian speakers, and, therefore, avoided them. While Schachter's hypothesis is intuitively plausible, it seems that it should be testable by some means other than avoidance. For example, under Schachter's hypothesis, it would be reasonable to expect that, if forced to use relative clauses, they would in fact make more errors than the Persian and Arabic speakers. This, however, is an open question.

REFERENCES

Bailey, N., C. Madden, and S. Krashen. 1974. Is there a "natural sequence" in adult second language learning? *Language learning, 24,* 235–44.
Dinnsen, D.A., and F.R. Eckman. 1975. A functional explanation of some phonological typologies. In R. Grossman, et al. (Eds.), *Functionalism.* Chicago: Chicago Linguistic Society.
Dulay, H., and M. Burt. 1974. Errors and strategies in child second language acquisition. *TESOL Quarterly, 8,* 129–36.
Gradman, H. 1970. The contrastive analysis hypothesis: What it is and what it isn't. Ph.D. dissertation, Indiana University.
Gradman, H. 1971. Limitations of contrastive analysis predictions. *Working papers in linguistics, 3,* 11–15.
Jakobson, R. 1940. *Kindersprache, aphasie, und allgemeine lautgesetze.* Translated as *Child language, aphasia, and phonological universals.* The Hague: Mouton, 1968.

Keenan, E., and B. Comrie. 1977. Noun phrase accessibility and universal grammar. *Linguistic Inquiry, 8,* 63–99.

Lado, R. 1957. *Linguistics across cultures.* Ann Arbor, MI: The University of Michigan Press.

Lenneberg, E. 1967. *Biological foundations of language.* NY: John Wiley and Sons.

Moulton, W. 1962. *The sounds of English and German.* Chicago: The University of Chicago Press.

Sanders, G. 1977. A functional explanation of elliptical coordinations. In F. Eckman (Ed.), *Current themes in linguistics.* Washington, DC: Hemisphere Publishing Corporation.

Schachter, J. 1974. An error in error analysis. *Language Learning, 24,* 205–14.

Stampe, D. 1969. The acquisition of phonetic representation. In R. Dinnick, et al. (Eds.), *Papers from the fifth regional meeting,* Chicago Linguistic Society. Chicago: Chicago Linguistic Society.

Wardhaugh, R. 1974. *Topics in applied linguistics.* Rowley, MA: Newbury House.

4

THE PHONOLOGY OF INTERLANGUAGE

Elaine E. Tarone

The phonology of interlanguage is an area which was largely neglected by second language acquisition research until very recently. There seemed to be very little interest in the pronunciation patterns of the speech of second language learners. When Schumann summarized existing second language acquisition research in 1976, he found absolutely no studies on the phonology of interlanguage. Even now, we have only a small amount of phonological data collected from second language learners in reasonably natural speech situations. The reason for the dearth of studies is hard to pin down. Perhaps one reason is the commonly held belief (commonly held even among researchers) that the learner's pronunciation of the sounds of a second language is influenced more strongly by negative transfer from the first language than is the learner's interlanguage grammar. Thus studies of interlanguage phonology would be likely to produce the least amount of interesting data in support of a creative construction of interlanguage theory of second language acquisition. However, as we shall see, the research which *has* been done in this area quite clearly shows that transfer is only a part—and often a small part—of the influence on interlanguage phonology. Another, perhaps more decisive, reason may be a general conviction on the part of second language acquisition researchers, second language teachers, and students, that pronunciation of a second language is simply not very important. This conviction is more difficult to fight, but I think the evidence will show that it too is incorrect. It is essential not only that second language learners should acquire the grammar system and vocabulary, but also that they should be *intelligible* to other speakers of that language; it is clearly possible for a learner to master the syntax of a language but not the phonology. Further, it is my belief that research in this area will shed much light on our understanding of the process of speech perception in general.

Whatever the reasons, however, the studies on interlanguage phonology have been sparse. This chapter will examine the nature of the data and the major issues involved in current research on interlanguage phonology. The two central issues seem to be:

(1) the nature of the processes which shape interlanguage phonology;
(2) the phenomenon of fossilization of interlanguage phonology.

THE PROCESSES SHAPING INTERLANGUAGE PHONOLOGY

In the 1960s, there were quite a few papers written which claimed to be able to predict errors in the pronunciation of second language learners on the basis of a contrastive analysis of the phonologies of the native language (NL) and target language (TL). All learner errors in pronunciation were felt to originate from negative transfer—that is, the learner's attempt to use inappropriate sound patterns of the NL in place of the sound patterns of the TL. A very simplistic contrastive analysis of the NL and the TL might reveal the patterns in Table 4.1:

In example (1) we have a case of *positive transfer:* both the native language and the target language have the phoneme /t/, so we would expect that the learner will have no difficulty with this sound in the target language. In example (2) we have an example of *negative transfer* which we might call *convergence:* where there are two phonemes /f/ and /v/ in the native language, these two sounds are considered variants in the target language of a single phoneme /f/. We would predict few if any problems for the learner in this case, either, since

TABLE 4.1

	Native language	Target language
(1)	/t/	/t/
(2)	/f/ |	/f/
	/v/ |	—
(3)	/l/	⌈ /l/
	—	⌊ /r/

71

the learner does not have to learn to make or hear any new distinctions in the TL. It is example (3), a case of *divergent negative transfer,* which would predict the most difficulty for the learner; where his native language has only one phoneme /l/, the target language has two, /l/ and /r/. These two are likely to be perceived and uttered by the learner as minor variants of the NL phoneme /l/, and the learner would be predicted to have much difficulty in discriminating between them.

It is important to note that few of the early papers on contrastive analysis made any attempt to go beyond anecdotal examples in support of their claim that *all* learner errors in pronunciation could be predicted in this way. The concept seemed to make sense intuitively, and so it was never rigorously tested experimentally.

Those experiments which *were* run to measure empirically the degree of negative NL transfer effects in the learners' pronunciation of TL sounds were all run in more or less artificial experimental situations, presenting TL words and sounds in isolation and examining the learners' ability to perceive or produce the sounds being studied. I will not attempt to summarize all of the early experimental studies here; for a complete summary of these studies see Johansson (1973).

Brière (1966) reports on one of the most thorough of these early experiments. Words containing 14 non-English sounds (from Arabic, French, and Vietnamese languages) were presented on tape as targets for 20 American students. The students repeated the words as they heard them, and their responses were recorded and transcribed. Based on the mean number of correct responses by the subjects, a hierarchy of difficult sounds was established. It is interesting to note that while most of the results of Brière's investigation were predicted by his contrastive analysis, some were not. For example, when /ɡ/ (a voiced uvular fricative), was the target, subjects substituted several American English sounds as predicted—but they also substituted /R/ (a uvular trill), a sound which does not occur in American English. Generally, Brière found that NL and TL sounds which were similar were easy for learners to pronounce; the major exception to this finding was /x/, which, while very different from any American-English (AE) sound, was still easy for the subjects to learn. Also the non-AE sound /t/ (a voiceless nonaspirated fortis dental stop) was significantly easier to learn than the dentalized /tʼ/, very close to AE. Finally, in his contrastive analysis, Brière found it necessary to use the syllable as the prime unit of analysis, showing that the American-English rules for distribution of /ž/ within the syllable affected the students' ability to learn the sound in other syllable positions. Hence, any contrastive analysis had to take the syllable structures of the two languages into account. Thus, Brière's results showed in 1966 that contrastive analysis, as it was commonly being used to predict pronunciation problems for second language learners, was not completely successful in its predictions of learner performance on an experimental task.

Other experimental studies using isolated words and syllables examined the perception of speech sounds by speakers of several languages. Carroll and Sapon (1957–1958), Lotz (1960), and Scholes (1968) had results indicating that negative transfer from the NL was influencing subjects' performance on experimental perception tasks, while Stevens (1969) and Singh and Black (1966) concluded that the subjects' perception of some TL features operated independently of their first language background.

So, even though contrastive analysis was claimed to be able to predict all learner errors in pronunciation, experimental evidence from the 1960s showed that processes other than negative transfer were also at work.

It is important to reiterate that these studies did not look at spontaneous interlanguage (IL) performance—that is, they did not examine the IL speech of second language learners engaged in communication. Indeed, Brière's was the only study which looked primarily at pronunciation rather than perception. All these studies artificially isolated TL words and sounds, and examined the perception and repetition skills of subjects in a fairly limited environment.

The limitations inherent in such a reductionist experimental approach are highlighted in a paper by Nemser (1971). Nemser ran an experiment using Hungarian subjects learning English, and showed that the nature and number of the sound substitutions made by subjects in his study depended on the experimental task used (e.g., transcription of sounds in nonsense syllables, translation from NL to TL, etc.). That is, the method used to gather data on interlanguage phonology influenced the nature of the data gathered. Nemser's results have serious implications for second language acquisition researchers interested in studying phonology. As we shall see later, interlanguage phonology happens to be variable, that is, highly sensitive to shifts in communication situation, speaker mood, etc. Researchers in this area should be aware of this fact. It is this writer's opinion that if researchers' results are to be at all applicable to L2 learner speech and speech perception in the classroom and in the real world, an attempt should be made to gather spontaneous speech data. Certainly researchers should avoid the testing of isolated speech segments in artificial settings.

The earliest study of which I am aware which gathers data at the sentence level is that of Johansson (1973). Johansson reports on a very extensive study which analyzes the segmental interlanguage phonologies of 180 native speakers of nine different languages, who were asked to repeat Swedish (TL) words and sentences which they heard on tape. Johansson's subjects were not engaged in spontaneous communication when her data were collected, and hence, as she herself notes, "it is possible that our results would be different in a different testing situation." She justifies her method of data collection, however, by noting that the repetition of sentences involves the skills of both speech perception and production, and by pointing to first language acquisition studies indicating that sentence repetition tasks elicit better performance in pronunciation than spontaneous speech elicited by the description of pictures (p. 48). A similar position has been taken by researchers using elicited imitation tasks in second language acquisition research. Certainly, the fact that the TL materials were presented at the sentence level is a vast improvement over all the previous experimental studies, and Johansson's careful detailed analysis of the results of her multiple contact study produce a significant contribution to our understanding of second language learner phonology.

Johansson's subjects were 20 native speakers each of nine different languages: American English (AE), Czech, Danish, Finnish, Greek, Hungarian, Polish, Portuguese, and Serbo-Croatian. The subjects' repetitions of Swedish words and sentences were recorded and transcribed; deviations from the Swedish model were recorded in narrow phonetic transcription. The quality and quantity of each of these segmental deviations from the Swedish model were recorded and the results are presented in great detail by language group. After an extensive review of the literature on contrastive analysis and error analysis, with particular reference to phonology, Johansson analyzes her data to determine the extent to which errors seemed to be caused by negative NL transfer and hence were predictable by contrastive analysis. She concludes that "a large number of the substitutions made could have been predicted by contrastive analysis"; however, she also concludes that there were some general common directions for substitution followed by all language groups. There was a general "tendency [in substituting for TL sounds] to move from the extreme higher and lower positions in the articulation area toward the middle height, the tongue's rest position." Further, there were some very real limitations to the power of contrastive analysis to predict the shape of interlanguage phonology:

There is definite evidence for the claim that learners confronted with a new language use not only sounds which occur in L1 and L2 but also other sounds which could not be directly predicted by contrastive analysis.

For example, she found that her subjects seemed to be trying to modify certain sounds away from L1 and toward L2, as when her American-English and German subjects produced [ʉ] for the Swedish [ʉː]. She found examples of overgeneralization, with learners who used "one Swedish sound for another where neither has a counterpart in the speaker's L1"; an example of this type of overgeneralization occurred when native speakers of Czech and Polish used [y] for the Swedish [ʉː]. Finally, Johansson notes that

contrastive analysis provides for no way of determining where differences between languages will not lead to difficulty or where seemingly similar differences lead to various degrees of difficulty.

For example, contrastive analysis could not predict that higher vowels and some long and back vowels would be more difficult for all groups.

Johansson's study is a valuable contribution to our understanding of the relative effect of transfer on segmental interlanguage phonologies. Her data seem to indicate that language transfer does operate to shape certain aspects of the IL phonology, but that other processes, such as overgeneralization and approximation, also operate. In addition, her study repeats Brière's finding that it is not enough to predict that differences between two phonological systems will automatically create learning problems in exact proportion to the degree of difference between them. In some cases, NL and TL sounds which seemed to be very similar were very hard to learn, and in others, NL and TL sounds which seemed to be very different presented no learning problem. Johansson's data suggest that one of the constraints involved in shaping the relative difficulty of the learning of new L2 sounds may have to do with the *intrinsic* difficulty of those L2 sounds, an effect operating independent of the process of negative transfer, but interacting with it. That is, given that higher vowels in Swedish were usually more difficult for all groups, was there an interaction effect such that those learners whose L1s had similar vowels found the Swedish vowels somewhat less difficult than those learners whose NLs had no such similar sounds? It seems to me that a theory of interlanguage phonology would have to take into account any such interaction effects of the several processes which seem to be identified as operating to shape IL phonology.

Wode and Felix have reported recently on the findings of an extensive first and second language acquisition project in Kiel, Germany, which is investigating German L1 children learning English L2 and English L1 children learning German L2. This is a longitudinal study collecting data in real communication situations and analyzing its syntactic, morphological, and phonological characteristics. The Kiel findings on the IL phonologies of children seem to be quite consistent with those of Johansson for adults. Wode (1976) finds evidence that some phonological elements are strongly affected by negative transfer from the NL, while other elements seem to be acquired with no influence from the NL, but rather in the same way that a child would acquire them in a L1 phonology. For German children learning English as a L2, those elements which did evidence negative transfer were

the stressed and unstressed vowels/vocoids, the syllabic and non-syllabic consonants/contoids except /r/ possibly /w/. The acquisition of the latter two, especially /r/, was parallel to the development sequence when English is acquired as L1.

Lonna Dickerson (1974) sheds considerable light on some of the reasons why contrastive analysis may be so limited in predicting the shape of segmental IL phonology. Dickerson studied the IL phonologies of Japanese university students learning English as a second language. Her analysis is different from any of the preceding ones in that it takes into account the effect of phonological variation in both the NL and IL on the process of acquisition of the TL. Her central claim is that the acquisition of a L2 phonology proceeds by the movement of variations within the environments of variable word classes. In this study she makes no claim as to the directionality of the variable IL phonological system, the rate of its change, or the influence of any community of IL speakers on its development; her focus is on the mechanism whereby acquisition of the L2 proceeds. Dickerson concludes:

The learner's performance is essentially the output of a *variable system*. As such, predictions about this output which deny its source, as the CA [contrastive analysis] hypothesis does, will always be rejected.

One reason that the CA hypothesis will always be rejected is that positive and negative transfer do not work invariably but variably.

Note here that Dickerson is not absolutely rejecting the notions of positive and negative transfer in shaping an IL phonology. In fact, she clearly finds evidence for the existence of transfer in her data.

In many cases the learner's output does contain phones which are those used in the NL. Furthermore, they appear in environments which are often similar to NL environments. There is every reason to believe that these variants originate in the NL. . . .

She is simply stating that these processes operate variably *as they interact with other processes and constraints.* Wayne Dickerson suggests (personal communication) the following variable rule as a representation of Lonna's findings as to the linguistic constraints on the production of [s] and [z] by Japanese students learning English as a second language:

$$\left(\begin{bmatrix} +\text{ant} \\ +\text{cor} \\ +\text{cont} \\ +\text{str} \end{bmatrix}\right) \longrightarrow < \begin{bmatrix} +\text{ant} \\ +\text{cor} \\ +\text{cont} \\ +\text{str} \end{bmatrix} > / < [-\text{seg}] > \begin{bmatrix} +\text{syl} \\ -\text{bk} \end{bmatrix} > \begin{bmatrix} +\text{syl} \\ -\text{bk} \end{bmatrix} > \underline{\quad} \begin{bmatrix} +\text{syl} \\ +\text{high} \\ -\text{back} \end{bmatrix}$$

To break this rule down, we can say that in this Japanese learner's interlanguage, certain phonological environments are more favorable to the production of [s] and [z] than others. One of the most difficult environments is when this segment occurs initially in front of a high front vowel:

$$\emptyset \longrightarrow \begin{bmatrix} +\text{syl} \\ +\text{high} \\ -\text{back} \end{bmatrix} \qquad \text{(e.g., see, zip)}$$

Even harder for a Japanese speaker is the [s] or [z] sound in a medial position, between an initial front vowel, and a following high front vowel.:

$$\begin{bmatrix} +\text{syl} \\ -\text{back} \end{bmatrix} \longrightarrow \begin{bmatrix} +\text{syl} \\ +\text{high} \\ -\text{back} \end{bmatrix} \qquad \text{(e.g., easy, Lassie)}$$

Most difficult is the medial position between an initial central back vowel and a following high front vowel:

$$\begin{bmatrix} +\text{syl} \\ +\text{back} \end{bmatrix} \longrightarrow \begin{bmatrix} +\text{syl} \\ +\text{high} \\ -\text{back} \end{bmatrix} \qquad \text{(e.g., music, position)}$$

W. Dickerson (1977) develops this notion of sociolinguistic variation in IL phonology further, showing, in his longitudinal analysis of the IL phonology of a single Japanese learner of English as a second language, not only that the usage of phonological variants was correlated with linguistic environment for this learner, but also that progress was attained over time by the increasing approximation of the TL variants in each relevant linguistic environment. Further, he shows that nonlinguistic constraints such as the nature of the task (whether free speaking, dialogue reading, or word list reading) produce systematic style shifting in the interlingual phonology. He expresses such nonlinguistic constraints in this manner:

$$\emptyset = f(\text{Proficiency Level})(\text{Style: WL} > \text{DR} > \text{FS})$$

The similar variation observed by Nemser (1971) in learner performance on various experimental tasks could be systematically described by variable rules. Other researchers, such as Schmidt (1977), have also begun to explore the influence of sociolinguistic variation on IL phonology. For further details on the variable analysis of IL phonology, see W. Dickerson (1976), and Dickerson and Dickerson (1977).

It is this writer's opinion that some sort of variable system of phonological description will go far toward accounting for the relative importance of all the processes we have considered thus far in shaping an IL phonological system: negative transfer from the NL, L1 acquisition processes, overgeneralization, approximation, as well as certain external constraints such as inherent difficulty of the TL system, or, as we shall see next, even psychological constraints.

The phonological environments described by Dickerson as "favorable" to the production of a TL sound might be favorable due to transfer effects—i.e., the existence or nonexistence of those environments in the NL—or to more universal effects. As Johansson points out, some aspects of the TL (Swedish higher vowels and some long and back vowels) seemed to be inherently more difficult, and certain processes seemed to operate equally for all learners, such as the tendency of the articulators toward a neutral rest position. Tarone's research (1972, 1976) explores another area of hypothesized universal physiological constraint, which relates to the constraints on the syllable structure of IL. A language transfer hypothesis would maintain that the syllable structure of the NL would be transferred in the learner's attempt to produce the TL. So, if the NL contains only syllables of a vowel-consonant (VC) type, such as [ab], [ik], and so on, the CA hypothesis would predict a tendency for the L2 learner to transform the TL syllables into VC types. Another hypothesis as to the processes shaping IL syllable structure would be that L1 learning processes are reactivated. So, different syllables of the TL would be simplified by the L2 learner in the same way that they are by the L1 learner. In order to understand this position, it may be helpful to consider a theoretical paper by D. K. Oller (1974) in which he compares the process of consonant cluster simplification used in L1 acquisition and L2 acquisition. His conclusions are limited in that his data on L2 acquisition are gleaned from anecdotal comments in the literature of the 1960s. However, they are interesting. According to Oller, epenthesis (vowel insertion) is a characteristic strategy of L2 learners. However, in L1 acquisition of phonology, learners under three years of age usually simplify by reducing or deleting difficult sounds, e.g.:

(a) cluster reduction: blue → bue
(b) final consonant deletion: big → bi
(c) weak syllable deletion: banana → nana

But Oller's understanding of the L2 literature is that L2 learners operate quite differently:

(a) epenthesis is used rather than cluster reduction: tree → təree
(b) epenthesis is used rather than final consonant deletion: big → bigu
(c) weak syllable deletion was reportedly uncommon

Thus epenthesis seems to have been a favored strategy for L2 learners, while consonant deletion was favored for L1 learners. This epenthesis could be a result of transfer from the NL. Tarone supports another hypothesis, however, arguing that the simple open CV syllable may be a universal articulatory and perceptual unit such that the articulators tend to operate in basic CV programs in all languages. Different languages elaborate on this basic program in various ways, adding different combinations of permissible initial and/or final consonants. However, researchers such as Kozhevnikov and Chistovich (1965) have shown that in stressful situations of various kinds, speakers tend to revert to the simple CV pattern of pronunciation in their NL—i.e., they stutter. Tarone's (1976) research shows in L2 learners a similar tendency to revert to a CV syllable pattern in IL. She analyzed the spontaneous speech of six students learning English as a second language—two native speakers each of Cantonese, Korean, and Portuguese. These adult subjects were asked to describe a series of pictures. While the dominant process influencing the IL syllable structure seemed to be transfer from the NL, the preference for the CV syllable clearly operated as a process independent of the transfer process. Subjects would simplify TL consonant clusters which occurred also in their NL, reducing them to simpler CV patterns. Second language learners used *both* epenthesis *and* consonant deletion to accomplish this CV patterning.

Thus, one of the universal constraints which may shape phonological environments favorable or unfavorable to the production of TL-like sounds may be the physiological constraint of the articulators' tendency to operate in CV-like, close-open patterns.

Celce-Murcia's (1977) observations of a child learning English and French simultaneously have revealed another process which is clearly operating to shape IL phonologies—a process not clearly predictable by either contrastive analysis or error analysis—the process of avoidance. Celce-Murcia analyzed the spontaneous speech of the learner and observed that her daughter consistently attempted to avoid what were for her physiologically difficult forms. Living in a bilingual home, the child tended to prefer those lexical items which were easiest to pronounce, and thus mixed languages. For instance, she had a great deal of difficulty with fricatives, and therefore consistently used the lexical item "couteau" and avoided "knife." And, rather than say "football," she created a new word, "piedball," and insisted on using it for a long time. Here again, there are clearly some physiological constraints—in this case, developmental ones—which activate a process—in this case, a process of avoidance—to shape a learner's IL phonology.

The only other study on IL phonology I know of which relates to the issue of the processes shaping IL phonology is Backman's (1977) study on intonation in interlanguage. It describes the interlanguages of eight Spanish-speaking university students learning English. The data were collected by asking the subjects to listen to English dialogues on tape (the dialogues were not made up by the experimenter, but were dramatizations of earlier conversations which had really occurred) and then to repeat them on tape. Backman found that 78 percent of the learners' utterances had inappropriate intonation. The learners generally used a smaller overall range of pitch: smaller pitch rise, especially on yes-no questions and prefinal rises to stressed syllables; a higher pitch for unstressed syllables; and a movement of pitch prominence to the left in declarative statements and wh-questions. Not all of these characteristics could be accounted for in terms of transfer. Backman concludes:

The Spanish [NL] data then had explanatory power in certain respects; it did not however provide all the answers for the subjects' intonation errors.

Thus, even in the area of prosodic features, it would appear that the process of transfer from the NL is by no means the only process operative, and that an adequate theory of acquisition of L2 phonology must take other processes and constraints into account. To summarize, then, the following processes are claimed at this time to be operative in shaping IL phonology:

(1) negative transfer from NL (all studies)
(2) first language acquisition processes (Wode, Tarone)
(3) overgeneralization (Johansson)
(4) approximation (Johansson, Nemser)
(5) avoidance (Celce-Murcia)

And, the following constraints appear to be operative:

(1) the inherent difficulty of certain TL sounds and phonological contexts (Johansson)
(2) the tendency of the articulators to rest position (Johansson)
(3) the tendency of the articulators to a CV pattern (Tarone)
(4) the tendency to avoid extremes of pitch variation (Backman)
(5) emotional and social constraints (Dickerson, Schmidt)

The Dickerson studies suggest that all these processes and constraints may interact with one another in such a way that the rules of a learner's IL phonology must be considered variable. The degree of influence which these processes and constraints have on an IL phonology must be experimentally determined and incorporated into a variable rule system which can accurately describe IL phonology.

THE FOSSILIZATION OF INTERLANGUAGE PHONOLOGY

One of the central issues in the study of interlanguage phonology is that of the fossilization of IL phonologies in adult L2 learners. There are two related questions here: the first has to do with whether this fossilization is inevitable when adults learn a L2, and the second has to do with the causes of such fossilization. Researchers are divided in their answers to both questions.

First, is phonological fossilization inevitable for adult L2 learners? Scovel (1969) says yes; he maintains that no adult ever achieves perfect native pronunciation in a L2. He has labeled this the "Joseph Conrad phenomenon," in honor of the famous British author who achieved unquestioned native-like fluency in the syntax of English, his second language—yet retained a Polish accent all his life. Scovel has gone so far, in these days of inflation, as to offer a free dinner to anyone who can show him an individual who learned a L2 after puberty and who now speaks that L2 with perfect native pronunciation. As of April 1977 no one has been able to produce such an individual.

Other researchers disagree with Scovel. Hill (1970) maintains that this kind of fossilization is by no means inevitable, being the result of social and cultural factors in Western culture. She points to native peoples like the Vaupés Indians of the Amazon, and the Siane of New Guinea, who reportedly learn several L2s as adults and achieve native-like fluency. However, evidently Scovel remains unconvinced; presumably, he has not yet met one of these individuals and been able to determine the degree of acceptability of their accents. More recently, Neufeld (1977) has experimented with methods of teaching L2 pronunciation which, he maintains, are successful in helping adults to acquire native or near-native proficiency in pronunciation of new languages. (More will be said about Neufeld's technique later.) It is not known at this writing whether Scovel has had a chance to deliberate upon the nativeness of the pronunciation of Neufeld's subjects. Hence, at present, it would appear that the question of the inevitability of phonological fossilization in adults is still undecided.

The second question is related: what causes phonological fossilization to occur? There are several possible explanations. Some of them fall into a general category of physiological explanations. For example, a popular explanation among L2 learners themselves seems to be that when learners get older "their tongues get stiff"—that is, the muscles and nerves of the tongue and mouth have been practicing the same set of pronunciation habits for years. This theory might maintain that the nerves and muscles necessary for the pronunciation of new L2 pronunciation patterns have atrophied so that native-like pronunciation is impossible. I am aware of no research evidence that this sort of atrophy takes place. Another physiological explanation, originally supported by Scovel (1969), is based on Lenneberg's (1967) suggestion that "lateralization"—the completion of cerebral dominance—affects the learning of language. Somehow, with lateralization the brain loses its capacity for language learning, and this loss affects the pronunciation of the L2 more than the syntax or vocabulary of the L2. However, recently some questions have been raised about the lateralization hypothesis. Krashen (1973) reanalyzed data used by Lenneberg and also dichotic listening data, and showed that lateralization actually seems to take place much earlier —before the age of five, in fact—than the critical period for language learning, which is commonly supposed to occur at around puberty.

Another group of explanations can be grouped as pointing to psychological causes of phonological fossilization. In fact, Krashen has his own theory about the causes of fossilization. Krashen (1977) maintains, as does Rosansky (1975), that the close of the critical period is related to the onset of Piaget's stage of formal operations. In this stage of cognitive development, adolescents begin to consciously construct abstract theories about the world. Hence, they tend to *learn* L2s, that is, to abstract rules of grammar and pronunciation and consciously apply them, rather than to *acquire* L2s, that is, to activate the same unconscious processes that children do in acquiring a L1. The formal operations type of psychological explanation for phonological fossilization is being strongly pushed at present. However, to my knowledge, it does not explain the Joseph Conrad Phenomenon—that is, the learner who acquires the syntax and vocabulary of the L2 but not the pronunciation. Why should formal operations affect only the pronunciation, and not the syntax or morphology in cases such as these?

Another psychological explanation of phonological fossilization in adults is based on *psychological habit formation* and is related to the language transfer question. That is, theoreticians have claimed that language transfer has its strongest effect on the pronunciation of a second language. Though we have seen that this claim has been considerably weakened by recent research results, there has been no comparative study to determine the *relative* influence of language transfer on pronunciation as opposed to syntax or morphology of a IL. If this claim proves to be validated by such a comparative study, then we might say that it is psychological habit formation and negative transfer that for some reason selectively operate to make IL phonology singularly resistant to change.[1] An interesting experiment was done recently which was essentially based on a psychological habit formation hypothesis. Neufeld (1977) reports on a study in which he experimentally tested a new technique for teaching L2 pronunciation to adults. Essentially, he maintains, the problem is that we expose adults to inappropriate learning situations where they form inaccurate acoustic images of the target language sound patterns. Once formed, those acoustic images are set, and so are the learners' pronunciation patterns. (It is not clear from Neufeld's discussion why adults are negatively affected by malformed acoustic images and children are not.) In his experiment, Neufeld instructed 20 young adults in three non-Indo-European languages—Chinese, Japanese, and Eskimo. The students watched videotaped lessons consisting of 100 stock phrases in these languages. They were given no explicit instruction in the meaning or pronunciation of the utterances or the grammatical rules of the languages, since the purpose of the study was to force the subjects to focus on the sound patterns of the languages. For the first part of the study the subjects merely watched and listened and were prevented from speaking. Later they traced intonational contours of the utterances they heard and saw correct contours traced for them on the videotape. Later they were allowed to whisper repetitions of what they heard. Only in the last three lessons of the 18 were the subjects allowed to repeat the utterances in a normal voice; by this time it was assumed that they had received enough accurate input to have formed a correct acoustic image of the languages and were unlikely to destroy that image by their own pronunciation. Neufeld's subjects (Ss) then recorded the phrases on tape, and native speakers of the three languages judged the nativeness of the subjects' pronunciation. Almost half the Ss were judged to have native or near-native pronunciation. Clearly, this experiment needs to be expanded so that we can judge whether their pronunciation ability persists when they are using the TLs for real communication. But Neufeld's results are most interesting and indicate some future directions for research. Research on the processes underlying IL phonology indicates that language transfer is only one of several processes; hence one would surmise that this kind of psychological habit formation theory of IL phonological fossilization would be similarly limited in its explanatory power. But to the degree that transfer is an effect, the psychological habit formation theories must be accorded validity.

A third type of explanation very different from psychological habit formation uses the affective argument and focuses on the adult learners' essential lack of empathy with the native speakers and culture of the L2. Guiora et al. (1972) attempted to artificially increase the empathy levels of L2 learners by administering gradually increasing amounts of alcohol. They found that the learners' pronunciation of the TL improved up to a certain point and then, as subjects drank greater amounts of alcohol, rapidly deteriorated. Guiora et al. feel that IL pronunciation is a much more sensitive indicator of empathy than either syntax or morphology (and Dickerson's comments on the influence of speakers' mood on pronunciation might support this feeling). Since children have more fluid language ego boundaries, they are much more likely to identify with speakers of a TL than are adults, who have more rigid language ego boundaries. Essentially, adults have decided on their cultural identity and use their *accent* to identify themselves appropriately. They essentially have no motivation to change their accent when it communicates perfectly well who they are. Hill (1970) implicitly supports a similar position when she points to native tribes whose cultures highly value multilingualism and encourage this capacity in adults. Where the culture encourages adults to achieve multilingualism, they achieve it, according to Hill. However, Hill's tribespeople have not been studied by L2 acquisition researchers to determine the exact extent of their native-like proficiency. Another plausible explanation for Guiora's results is simply that muscle relaxation induced by the alcohol allowed the subjects to achieve better articulation of the TL sounds (H. D. Brown, personal communication).

However, intuitively, the socio-emotional factors would seem to be especially powerful in determining degree of proficiency in pronunciation. These factors are hard to measure unambiguously in an experimental setting, but there are many anecdotes suggesting their power. For one, there have been many observations that children are particularly susceptible to an at-times-cruel form of pressure to conform to (empathize with?) their peer group in all matters, including pronunciation. In her work on children at play in L2 learning situations, Peck (1977) has quite clearly shown that mockery of aberrant learner accents is a very common and particularly effective form of peer teaching. It is clearly the case that children mock the accents of child L2 learners directly and frequently, but that adults do *not* directly mock the accents of adult L2 learners. Could this be one of the reasons why children acquire native-like accents and adults do not? The possible implications for teaching are appalling; negative reinforcement has been most unpopular for years. Guiora's approach may have more pleasant implications for the use of socio-emotional factors in facilitating the learning process.

But here again, the causes of phonological fossilization are not clear. There seems to be persuasive evidence supporting several different forces active in causing this phenomenon. There seems to be less and less evidence for physiological sources of the problem. The formal operations argument and the psychological habit formation argument both seem to have some potential explanatory power, but are limited in important ways. The affective factors arguments, dealing with empathy and cultural identity, seem to provide some very strong directions for future research.

SUMMARY

We have seen that much productive research has taken place recently on different aspects of interlanguage phonology. Most of this research has focused on the collection of data and the analysis of this data in an attempt to determine the nature of the processes shaping interlanguage phonology, and the causes of fossilization of interlanguage phonology. While much progress has been made, there are many questions which remain to be answered:

What are the relative influences of such processes as transfer, overgeneralization, avoidance, and first language acquisition processes on the shape of IL phonology?

In viewing interlanguage as a variable system, can we account for those relative influences?

What are the physiological and social constraints on IL phonology?

Is it possible for adults to acquire a L2 without an accent? If not, why not?

In our attempts to answer questions such as these, undoubtedly we will learn much about the complex interrelationships of language, mind, body, and society in the process of second language acquisition.

NOTE

1. Adjémian (1976) suggests that the mental processes commanding muscle control may be slower to change than cognitive processes governing syntax; thus "habit formation" is not the only possible explanation here.

REFERENCES

Adjémian, C. 1976. "On the nature of interlanguage systems," *Language Learning,* 26, 297–320

Backman, N. 1977. "Intonation problems of eight Spanish-speaking adults learning English," Ph.D. dissertation, Boston University.

Brière, E. 1966. "An investigation of phonological interference," *Language,* 42, 4, 768–796.

Carroll, J., and S. Sapon. 1973. "Discriminative perception of speech sounds as a function of native language," *General Linguistics, 3,* 1957–58, 62–71; cited in Johansson, *Immigrant Swedish Phonology,* Lund, Sweden: Gleerup.

Celce-Murcia, M. 1977. "Phonological factors in vocabulary acquisition: a case study of a two-year-old English-French bilingual," *Working Papers in Bilingualism, 13,* May, 27–41.

Dickerson, L. 1974. "Internal and external patterning of phonological variability in the speech of Japanese learners of English," Ph.D. dissertation, University of Illinois.

Dickerson, L., and W. Dickerson 1977. "Interlanguage Phonology: Current Research and Future Directions," In Corder and Roulet, Eds. *The Notions of Simplification, Interlanguages and Pidgins.* Neuchatel: Faculté des Lettres.

Dickerson, W. 1976. "The Psycholinguistic Unity of Language Learning and Language Change," *Language Learning, 26,* 2, 215–231. (Also this volume.)

Dickerson, W. 1977. "Language Variation in Applied Linguistics," *ITL Review of Applied Linguistics, 35,* 43–66.

Felix, S. 1975. "Some Differences Between First and Second Language Acquisition." Paper presented at the 3rd International Symposium on Child Language, London.

Guiora, A., et al. 1972. "The effects of experimentally induced changes in ego states on pronunciation ability in a second language: an exploratory study," *Comprehensive Psychiatry, 13,* 421–428.

Hill, J. 1970. "Foreign accents, language acquisition and cerebral dominance revisited," *Language Learning, 20,* 237–248.

Johansson, F. A. 1973. *Immigrant Swedish Phonology: A Study in Multiple Contact Analysis.* Lund, Sweden: CWK Gleerup.

Kozhevnikov and Chistovich. 1965. *Speech: Articulation and Perception.* Moscow: Nauka.

Krashen, S. 1973. "Lateralization, language learning and the critical period: some new evidence," *Language Learning, 23,* 63–74.

Krashen, S. 1977. "Some issues relating to the monitor model," paper presented at the TESOL Convention, Miami Beach, FL.

Lenneberg, E. 1967. *Biological Foundations of Language.* NY: J. Wiley & Sons, Inc.

Lotz, J. et al. 1973. "The perception of English stops by speakers of English, Spanish, Hungarian, and Thai: A tape-cutting experiment," *Language and Speech, 3,* 1960, 71–77; cited in Johansson, *Immigrant Swedish Phonology.* Lund, Sweden: CWK Gleerup.

Nemser, W. 1971. *An Experimental Study of Phonological Interference in the English of Hungarians.* Bloomington, IN.: Indiana University Press.

Neufeld, G. 1977. "Language learning ability in adults: a study on the acquisition of prosodic and articulatory features," *Working Papers in Bilingualism,* 12, Jan. 45–60.

Oller, D. K. 1974. "Toward a general theory of phonological processes in first and second language learning," paper presented at the Western Conference on Linguistics, Seattle, WA.

Peck, S. 1977. "Language play in child second language acquisition," paper presented at the First Annual Second Language Acquisition Research Forum, UCLA.

Prator, C., and B. Robinett. 1972. *Manual of American English Pronunciation.* NY: Holt, Rinehart & Winston.

Rosansky, E. "The critical period for the acquisition of language: some cognitive developmental considerations," Ph.D. dissertation, Harvard University.

Schmidt, R. 1977. "Sociolinguistic variation and language transfer in phonology," *Working Papers in Bilingualism, 12,* 79–95. (Also this volume.)

Scholes, R. 1968. "Phonemic interference as a perceptual problem," *Language and Speech, 11,* 1968, 86–103; cited in Johansson, 1973.

Schumann, John. 1976. "Second language acquisition research: getting a more global look at the learner," H.D. Brown, Ed. *Papers in Second Language Acquisition,* Ann Arbor, MI: *Language Learning.*

Scovell, T. 1969. "Foreign accents, language acquisition and cerebral dominance," *Language Learning, 19,* 245–254.

Scovell, T. 1977. "The ontogeny of the ability to recognize foreign accents," First Annual Second Language Acquisition Research Forum, UCLA.

Singh, S., and J. Black. 1973. "Study of 26 intervocalic consonants as spoken and recognized by four language groups," *The Journal of the Acoustical Society of America, 39,* 1966, 372–387; cited in Johansson.

Stevens, K. L. 1973. "Crosslanguage study of vowel perception," *Language and Speech, 12,* 1969, 1–23; cited in Johansson.

Tarone, E. 1976. "Some influences on interlanguage phonology," *IRAL* and *Working Papers in Bilingualism, 8,* Feb. 87–111. (Also this volume.)

Tarone, E. 1972. "A suggested unit for interlingual identification in pronunciation," *TESOL Quarterly 6,* 4, Dec. 325–333.

Wode, H. 1976. "Developmental sequences in naturalistic second language acquisition," *Working Papers in Bilingualism, 11,* Aug. 1–31.

5

THE PSYCHOLINGUISTIC UNITY OF LANGUAGE LEARNING AND LANGUAGE CHANGE*

Wayne B. Dickerson

In the life sciences it has been said that ontogeny recapitulates phylogeny. In some fundamental way, the short-term developmental change in the token is a miniature of the long-term developmental change in the type. This paper explores the same theme: Are language learning and language change in a token-type relationship? In what way, if any, is language learning in the individual nonnative speaker like language change in the community of native speakers? Since language change is best understood in the area of phonology, this paper will compare the mechanism of a native language sound change with the acquisition of a second language phonology.

*This research was undertaken originally to explore the feasibility of extending a language change model to language learning. L. Dickerson (1974) has provided a broad-ranging, in-depth test and confirmation of the extension suggested in this paper. Because of her research, it has been possible in numerous ways to carry the original feasibility study reported here beyond her findings. I wish to express special thanks to Lonna Dickerson, Rebecca Finney, and William Pech for their helpful comments and criticisms of an earlier version of this paper.

THE MECHANISM OF A NATIVE LANGUAGE SOUND CHANGE

Sound change is not instantaneous. Rather, it happens gradually by means of a *wave mechanism.* The movement of the wave can be captured statistically in an *index score,* and it can be represented in grammatical form by a *variable rule.* Each of these points is elaborated below.

Wave Mechanism

The change of a phonological segment from one phonetic shape to another occurs in small increments along three linguistic dimensions. First, the change affects the set of words containing the particular phonological segment. Such words are referred to as a word class. Not all members of the word class are affected simultaneously; at first, only a subset is touched by change. Second, the affected subset of words takes on a phonetic shape or variant which is slightly different from the original variant but in the direction of the target variant. Third, each subset of words in which the new variant appears shares a particular phonetic environment.

As an example, let us assume that the segment being changed is (æw). (The parentheses designate this as a segment undergoing change.) The change affects word class members such as *out, crowd, growl, round.* The effect is to move the vowel of these words from the shape [aw] to the shape [əw]—from a low-front nucleus to a mid-central nucleus. The movement involves passing through the following variants: [a] → [aˆ] → [ɐ] → [e]. The set of words beginning this journey are those having in common a voiceless postvocalic environment, as in *about, mouse, south.*

The change proceeds by the progressive involvement of the three dimensions. With time, more and more words having the voiceless environment take on the [aˆ] variant. With time more and more advanced variants appear in these words. And with time, more and more environments of the word class (such as postvocalic voiced stops or fricatives) begin the movement. If we look at only the voiceless environment, Figure 5.1 provides a display of how change progresses in the above example. The lines represent the proportion of words having different variants at five different times.

The picture in Figure 5.1 is that of a swelling wave of words taking on more advanced variants in this particular environment. In fact, the word W-A-V-E is a convenient acronym for the sound change mechanism which involves words (W), variants (V), and environments (E). Elsewhere, the mechanism is called *ordered decomposition* (Labov, 1972). Over time, a word class having a single phonetic shape (e.g. [aw]) is decomposed by environment in an orderly way and reconstituted at the end of the change with a different phonetic shape (e.g. [əw]).

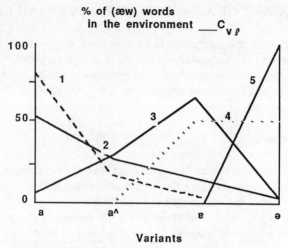

% of (æw) words in the environment __C$_{v\ell}$

100

1

5

50

3

4

2

0

a   a^   ɐ   ə

Variants

Figure 5.1 Proportion of words having four variants at five different times.

Index Score

The (æw) example used above to illustrate the wave mechanism is taken from an actual sociolinguistic case study of a thirty-five year sound change in a particular speech community (Labov 1973). The movement of the diphthong nucleus during this period is represented by lines 1–4 in Figure 5.1. (At the time the study was completed, no subject used the [ə] nucleus categorically as projected in line 5.) This graphic display is one way to represent the change. Another useful way is by means of an index score for each of the lines. By assigning a progressively greater value to the four variants (e.g. a = 0, a^ = 1, etc.), Labov constructed an index score which represented the extent to which an individual had progressed toward the [ə] nucleus. (Computations are illustrated below.) The index scores in Table 5.1 are those of four male speakers, ages 92–31, and correspond to the first four lines in Figure 5.1 (Labov, 1973, 168). The oldest member of the community sample shows the least centralization, while the youngest member shows the greatest. An index score of 300 would have meant the categorical use of [ə].

TABLE 5.1 Age and index scores of four male speakers.

Age	Centralization index score
92	10
83	52
57	111
31	211

Variable Rule

The progress of change seen in Figure 5.1 and Table 5.1 is regular and orderly, not random. Speech community members behave according to these regularities and use the patterns in interpreting the speech of their interlocutors. Thus the rule governing the change is part of the competence of speakers in this speech community and, accordingly, belongs in their grammar. A rule which captures the system underlying variable performance is called a variable rule. It is sensitive to the order of variants and environments and to the proportions of word class members affected by change (Labov, 1972, 121–5). A variable rule, then, is a third way to represent sound change. An example of such a rule is given below.

The wave mechanism of change has been found in community after community (Labov, 1966, 1971; Labov, et al., 1972; Callary, 1975). Change, of course, occurs only because individuals in the community change the language. This means that individuals are extraordinarily sensitive to word class composition, the direction of change in a word class, active and nonactive environments, subtle differences among variants, and the degree to which change has advanced in particular environments (W. Dickerson, b). In this way a change received from one generation is extended and passed on to the next generation. The question raised in the following section is this: Is the built-in wave mechanism of change operative in the individual's acquisition of a second language sound system?

THE ACQUISITION OF A SECOND LANGUAGE PHONOLOGY

In order to assess the validity of the sound change model for language acquisition, a detailed longitudinal study was made of five Japanese students learning English /ℓ/. The following sections report on this study.

Experiment Specifications

The subjects were natives of Tokyo, Japan. They had all received extensive English training (6–10 years) at home but had never before been exposed to an English-speaking community nor to native English-speaking language teachers. This study began during their first semester at the University of Illinois at which time they were enrolled in a three-hour-per-week remedial English pronunciation course. Two of the five subjects (S4 and S5) continued the course in the following semester.

The study extended over one year and involved three recordings of each subject reading prepared dialogues and work lists. The materials contained a large number of /ℓ/ words sufficiently well mixed with other words so that the focus of the reading was not discernable. The records were of high quality and yielded about 2,500 instances of the (ℓ) word class. Each instance was transcribed in fine phonetic detail and without reference to which of the three recording times it represented.

Wave Components

The first component in the wave mechanism is the changing word class, (ℓ), which consists of all English /ℓ/ words. The acquisition of English /ℓ/ represents a well-known problem of momentous proportions for Japanese learners. Bloch's description of Japanese phonology (1950) indicates the reason: laterals have, at best, only a marginal status in the language. Bloch (336) tells us that if a lateral occurs in Japanese at all, it is a rare allophone of /ř/; it is phonetically a flap [ľ] on a par with [ř], also an allophone of /ř/. In his English-Japanese contrastive analysis, Kohmoto (1960, 98–9) predicts that [ř] will be the sole substitute for English /ℓ/ "regardless of distribution and environment." In structural terms, then, the task before the Japanese learner appears to be twofold: first, to create two separate phonemes, /ℓ/ and /r/, and, second, to render the allophones of /ℓ/ consistently as unflapped laterals.

The second component in the wave mechanism is the set of variants used by the Japanese subjects to represent (ℓ). The ultimate target, of course, is the set of native unflapped laterals which may be fully voiced, devoiced, or coarticulated in appropriate environments. While control over these fine articulatory differences of native pronunciation represents the ultimate target, it also represents a target beyond what was accepted as [ℓ], namely, any unflapped lateral. In addition to [ℓ], the variants produced by the Japanese learners included those listed in Table 5.2. Unlike the (æw) example, the variants do not range along a phonetic continuum. The order of variants, then, is set up on a rough scale of articulatory approximation to the target. The variant [ℓ] is closest to the ultimate target. The [ľ] is next closest, although it is a flap. The [r] is not a flap and in this sense represents a movement in the right direction, although it is retroflexed and not a lateral. The [ř] is a retroflexed flap and has no necessary priority over [d̃], a nonretroflexed flap, except that [d̃] does not occur among all subjects, whereas [ř] does. In Table 5.2, the index values assigned to the variants increase as the variants approach the target.

The third component of the wave mechanism is the set of environments through which subjects acquire control over /ℓ/. For this study, only prevocalic (ℓ) environments were examined. As in native language change, it is impossible to know beforehand which environments will be relevant; they must be determined descriptively. A study of numerous options, including the stress patterns of adjacent vowels and the articulatory position of adjacent consonants, revealed that the height of adjacent vowels was one crucial variable in the environment of (ℓ). If no vowel preceded (ℓ), other variables were relevant. These included

TABLE 5.2 Variants produced by Japanese speakers

Variant	Index value	Description
[l]	4	Voiced lateral
[l̃]	3	Voiced lateral flap
[r]	2	Voiced retroflexed semiconsonant
[r̃]	1	Voiced retroflexed flap
[d̃]	0	Voiced flap

the presence of silence [Ø] or a consonant [C] in the position preceding (ℓ). Taking these variables into account, nine specific environments were studied as listed in Figure 5.2 with examples. Terms in square brackets refer to vowels with the particular height feature given.

Environment	Designation	Example
Ø # ℓ $\begin{bmatrix} +\text{high} \\ -\text{low} \end{bmatrix}$	C	look
Ø # ℓ $\begin{bmatrix} -\text{high} \\ -\text{low} \end{bmatrix}$	B	let
Ø # ℓ $\begin{bmatrix} -\text{high} \\ +\text{low} \end{bmatrix}$	A	lab
$\begin{bmatrix} +\text{high} \\ -\text{low} \end{bmatrix}$ ℓ $\begin{bmatrix} +\text{high} \\ -\text{low} \end{bmatrix}$	F	hilly
$\begin{bmatrix} +\text{high} \\ -\text{low} \end{bmatrix}$ ℓ $\begin{bmatrix} -\text{high} \end{bmatrix}$	E	pillow
$\begin{bmatrix} -\text{high} \end{bmatrix}$ ℓ $\begin{bmatrix} +\text{high} \\ -\text{low} \end{bmatrix}$	E	valley
$\begin{bmatrix} -\text{high} \end{bmatrix}$ ℓ $\begin{bmatrix} -\text{high} \end{bmatrix}$	D	yellow
# C ℓ $\begin{bmatrix} +\text{high} \\ -\text{low} \end{bmatrix}$	I	clean
# C ℓ $\begin{bmatrix} -\text{high} \\ -\text{low} \end{bmatrix}$	H	blow
# C ℓ $\begin{bmatrix} -\text{high} \\ +\text{low} \end{bmatrix}$	G	flap

Figure 5.2 Environments for control over ℓ.

Wave Motion

To this point, we have discussed the sound change mechanism and we have outlined an analogical extension of the wave components as they apply to Japanese learners of English /ℓ/. If the wave mechanism underlies their acquisition behavior, we would expect to see in that behavior a wave motion of progressively more words taking on progressively more advanced variants in a progressively greater number of environments. This expectation is fulfilled in the case of every subject. As an illustration, a full display of data for Subject 1 (S1) is provided in Figure 5.3. Unshaded bars represent Test One (T1), solid bars, T2, and shaded bars, T3. The proportion of words having a particular variant at one test time is indicated by the height of the bars.

In environments A-C, we see the wave motion in two respects. First, in C and B, there is a progressive movement of words toward the target end of the graphs from test time to test time. In A, S1 attained the categorical use of [ℓ] at T1 and maintained that usage during the year. Second, variants remote from the target were given up through time. In C, the subject abandoned the

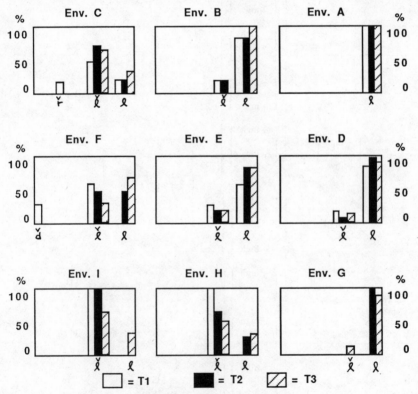

Figure 5.3 Data for Subject 1 in nine environments on three tests.

92

[řׂ] variant at T2; in B, the subject relinquished the [̌ℓ] variant at T3 to produce categorical [ℓ]. The same general picture is seen in environments D-F: The proportion of words with leftmost variants decreases, while the proportion of words with rightmost variants increases.

In environments G-I, the wave motion is apparent in all three interlocking respects. First, words move toward the target, except for a small regression at T3 in G. Second, a new variant is acquired in H at T2 and in I at T3. Third, new environments get involved in the movement. At T1, H and I are nonvariable. But at T2, H becomes variable, and at T3, I also begins to move.

The patterns observed in the data of S1 are repeated for the other four subjects. It is therefore possible to group the subjects in order to provide a composite picture of their behavior with respect to each of the three sets of environments. To do this, an index score was first computed for each environment of each subject at each test time. For a particular environment, each instance of a variant was multiplied by its index value (given in Table 5.2 above). All products were summed and divided by the value of all the instances of (ℓ) had they all been [ℓ] (4 × total number of instances). The quotient was multiplied by 100. Then, the index scores of the five subjects were averaged. The results are displayed in Figure 5.4. The lines correspond to the environments as ordered to the right of each graph. (At T1 there was an insufficient amount of data in environment G on which to base an index score for any of the subjects.)

There are two outstanding features in these graphs: the upward slope of lines and the stratification of lines. These two features point to pervasive order which governs the acquisition of /ℓ/. First, the upward slope of each line represents either an increasing number of words in a variant category or a movement to a more advanced variant, or both. That is, progress was made by means of the wave mechanism.

Second, the stratification of lines is remarkable. On the one hand, the performance of each subject was continuously changing, sometimes radically, during the one-year study. Yet there are no overlapping lines; all subjects maintained the same order of environments through time. On the other hand, the stratification reveals much about the factors defining the environments. First, the lines in Figure 5.4 show most strikingly the perfect ranking within the sets A-B-C, D-E-F, and G-H-I. The height of the vowel following (ℓ) accounts for the ranking. Low vowels in each set promote progress, while high vowels dramatically restrain it. Mid vowels have an intermediate effect favoring the target variant. Second, the environments are perfectly ranked across the sets: A-D-G, B-E-H, and C-F-I, as seen by looking at any one test time. This finding reveals that in the position preceding (ℓ), silence promotes progress, while the consonant powerfully restrains it. Vowels stand in the middle but favor the target. The effect of the two opposing forces (prelateral silence and consonant) is so strong that, for most subjects, the index scores for A-B-C, as a set, are entirely above the index scores for G-H-I, as a set.

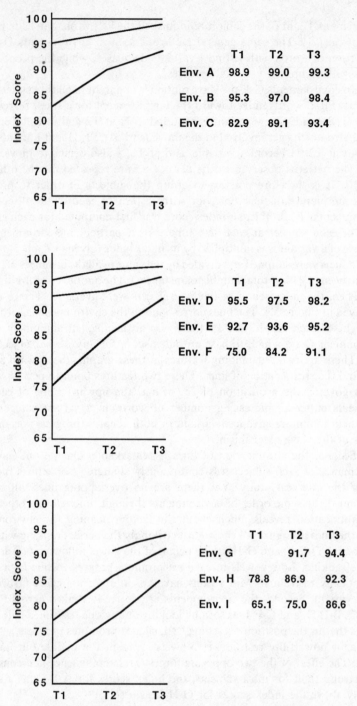

Figure 5.4 Mean index scores of the five subjects on the three tests.

Wave Rules

The variable performance of each subject reflects a profound order controlling the acquisition process—a rule-governed order. Rule-governed order underlying language behavior is typically referred to as a grammar. In this case, the grammar is that of Japanese-English. It is not a grammar of obligatory rules, nor of optional rules. Obligatory rules produce categorical behavior, while optional rules yield random variation. Rather, this grammar consists mainly of variable rules which capture the patterned (vs. random) variation which each subject exhibits at any one time and across time as Japanese-English becomes less Japanese-like and more English-like. In this section, the variable rule illustrated recasts these regularities in formal grammatical terms.

In broad outline, variable rules are expressed in the conventional manner of generative grammar, and in this case, of generative phonology. In detail, however, this study employs the notational devices developed by Labov and other sociolinguists. The variable rule describing the acquisition of English /ℓ/ is presented in Figure 5.5. The features [high] and [low] refer only to vowel segments.

The input to the rule in Figure 5.5 is the (ℓ) word class of Japanese-English. The output is the target variant which is enclosed in angle brackets to indicate variability, i.e., sometimes [ℓ] is produced, and sometimes another variant. Governing the output are factors (constraints) in the environment which act to facilitate or to hinder rule operation and thereby determine the proportion of [ℓ] in the output. The above discussion of wave motion has identified the factors relevant to the acquisition of /ℓ/ and the relative effect of these factors on progress toward the target. Specifically, the factors preceding (ℓ) are the most powerful and those following (ℓ), the least powerful. In both positions, the factors are ranked. To specify in a variable rule the relative importance and effect of environmental factors or constraints, two conventions are followed. First, the constraints are prefixed with lower case Greek letters such that alpha, α, designates the strongest constraint. Second, the presence of a constraint favors the rule while its absence restrains the rule. (The scores in Figure 5.4 could be used to determine the probability contribution to rule operation of each constraint (Cedergren and Sankoff, 1973). In this way, the

$$(\ell) \rightarrow <[\ell]> / \left\{ \begin{array}{ll} \alpha & [-\text{cns}] \\ \beta & [+\text{\O}] \\ \gamma & [-\text{high}] \end{array} \right\} \underline{\quad\quad} \left\{ \begin{array}{ll} \delta & \begin{bmatrix} -\text{high} \\ +\text{low} \end{bmatrix} \\ \\ \varepsilon & \begin{bmatrix} -\text{high} \\ -\text{low} \end{bmatrix} \end{array} \right\}$$

Figure 5.5 Variable rule for the acquisition of English ℓ.

Greek notations could be eliminated in favor of a key to probability weightings —a more satisfactory representation of competence than the statistics of Figure 5.4.)

In the case of Figure 5.5, the presence of (+) of something other than a consonant ([−cns]) has the greatest (α) positive effect on the rule. The absence of [−cns], namely, a consonant, has the greatest (α) negative effect. If no consonant precedes (ℓ), then the next strongest constraint (β) which promotes rule operation is the presence of silence (+[+∅]). The absence of silence (−[+∅]) has a comparatively negative effect. If there is no silence preceding (ℓ), then a mid or low vowel (+[−high]) will favor the rule next most (γ). Its absence, namely, a high vowel (−[−high]), will impede the rule. The effect of these constraints is schematized in Figure 5.6a. Following the (ℓ), the next most powerful positive constraint (δ) is the presence (+) of a low vowel. In its absence, the presence (+) of a mid vowel will have the next most (ε) favorable effect on the rule, but the absence (−) of a mid vowel (i.e. a high vowel) will work against the rule. This series of constraints is depicted in Figure 5.6b.

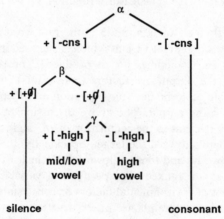

Figure 5.6a   Alpha constraint.

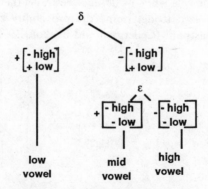

Figure 5.6b   Delta constraint.

96

When the constraints before and after (ℓ) are combined, all of the environments in Figure 5.2 are represented. In addition, the rule generates the proper order of the $\emptyset\,\ell$, V$\,\ell$, and C$\,\ell$ categories, as well as the proper ranking of vowel-height subdivisions within each category. The rule also correctly produces the subdivisions within the V$\,\ell$ category which were collapsed in environment E. In short, the rule reproduces the wave in abstract.

The wave appearance produced by the ordered linguistic constraints in Figure 5.5 is a series of adjustments in rule output. The adjustments consist of a base line level of rule operation to which are added increments according to linguistic environment. This base line reflects the learner's level of proficiency. Over time, as the learner's proficiency increases, the base line level of rule operation increases and accounts for the motion of the wave from one time to the next. Without the base line factor, the rule could not record change through time. Thus the frequency ($\emptyset$) of rule operation at any given moment is minimally a function of the learner's proficiency level; linguistic adjustments start at this level. This fact, expressed in the following rule, is part of the variable rule.

$$\emptyset = \text{f(Proficiency Level)}$$

(Other controlling factors such as style in the $\emptyset$-statement are discussed in W. Dickerson, a.) For the specific output levels used at each test time, the index scores in Figure 4 are appended to the rule.

LANGUAGE LEARNING AND LANGUAGE CHANGE

The wave phenomenon reported here is not unique to Japanese learners nor to the (ℓ) word class. It has been found in other word classes (L. Dickerson, 1974; W. Dickerson, a) and in exploratory studies of learners from other language backgrounds. In every detail, the mechanism is like that operative in language change. The significance of this finding is discussed below.

First, the profound regularities in the Japanese data lead us to conclude that sound-system learning is not the result of random or erratic attempts at a target language model. Phonology learning is no more the product of chance than the progressive reconstitution of a word class in a sound change is the product of aimless drift. Rather, sound system learning proceeds by the gradual and systematic modification of rules in a newly developed grammar in the same way that a sound change is a comparatively slow but governed alteration of rules in a first language grammar. The variable rules in both cases are rules in *native* grammars. That is, the subjects of this particular study are native, fluent speakers of Japanese-English just as much as they are native, fluent speakers of Japanese. In short, change in either of these native systems involves a continuum of principled movement toward the target, not random movement nor jumps through a series of intermediate stages.

Second, the realization that variable performance issues from variable rules in a native grammar leads to a new perspective. The study of variable rules in phonology learning is no more an "error analysis" than the study of variable rules in language change. In the first place, all variants—target and nontarget—are treated equally in the system, hence, the neutral term "variant." In the second place, all variants are included in the analysis, not just nontarget variants. The notion of error is rejected as categorically for language learning as it is for language change. If it were an error to use nontarget variants, language learning would be as impossible as language change would be. In both language learning and language change, all of the variants are native to the respective systems, and none is an error. Thus the study presented here is not an error analysis but a variability analysis.

Third, the learner's phonological system (and undoubtedly his syntactic system as well) is a system of variable rules. It would be convenient to refer to this system as the learner's interlanguage (Selinker, 1972); however, to do so would be incautious. At present, interlanguage is defined in static terms and not as a system of variable rules. There is no provision for variability as an integral part of the system, which is to say that the notion of interlanguage incorporates no grammatical model which accommodates the nature of the language learning process. Perhaps for this reason no interlanguage rules have been written which show the dynamic character of learning through time. This paper, L. Dickerson (1974, 1975), and W. Dickerson (a) provide ample motivations for defining the interlanguage phonology as a system of variable rules. Unless the learner's interlanguage is conceived of as such a system, the system will continue to elude researchers. Although providing many useful insights into strategies and sequences of learning, they will not be able to account for the learner's variable performance in grammatical terms any better than contrastive analysis could.

Fourth, given this study, it is now more understandable why contrastive analysis as a predictive hypothesis fails to account for the learner's phonological output. (Compare Kohmoto's predictions above with the learner's actual usage as shown in Figure 5.3.) The reason is that language learning, like language change, is not controlled by a theory of positive and negative transfer. The comparison and contrast of two homogeneous systems yield a list of similarities and differences which are categorical, static predictions of positive and negative transfer by the learner. Since there is no way for a transfer-based contrastive analysis to make either noncategorical or time-sensitive predictions which are testable, the finding of synchronic variability and diachronic change shows the hypothesis to be untenable. The only way systematic heterogeneity can arise is from a variable rule. Contrastive analysis recognizes neither variable rules nor the existence of a language system other than the native and target languages. Thus, as a predictive tool, contrastive analysis fails in the area of phonology learning.

The points just highlighted have focused on the *mechanism* underlying language learning and language change. The fact that a similar mechanism underlies both processes does not imply that the mechanism is *used* in the same way by the community of native speakers and by the individual language learner. As one example, in the learner's totally changing system, variable rules are used much more extensively than in the first language system. As another example, the wave motion moves at a much faster rate in the individual learner than in the community. As a third example, while community language change regularly goes to completion, learners rarely attain the target in all environments. In fact, they slow down considerably as they approach the target (cf. the ʃ-curve of language change in Bailey 1973, 77). The slope of the converging lines in Figure 5.4 testifies to this tendency to progress more and more slowly with time. These differences in the use of the wave mechanism in no way invalidate the finding that there is no appreciable difference in the structure of the mechanism from language change to language learning.

SUMMARY

The research reported here concerns an area—phonology—which has been neglected in recent investigations of second language performance. To summarize this report, we can return to the questions raised at the outset: Is language learning in the individual nonnative speaker like language change in the community of native speakers? Specifically, are these processes rooted in the same mechanism? This variability analysis of five Japanese learners of English /ℓ/ confirms that language learning and language change involve the systematic yet untutored use of the wave mechanism for effecting phonetic change in word classes. Although the wave operates in a different language system in each case, the formal grammatical device of a variable rule captures the wave in each system. Are language learning and language change in a token-type relationship? The answer is, probably, no. Second language learning and language change are tokens of the more general type "phonological change" which no doubt also subsumes first language acquisition. From this study, we can conclude that individuals approach the learning and changing of phonology in a psycholinguistically unified way. That is, *the individual as a foreign-language learner is fundamentally like himself as a native-language changer.*

REFERENCES

Bailey, C.-J. N. 1973. *Variation and linguistic theory.* Arlington: Center for Applied Linguistics.

Bloch, B. 1950. Studies in colloquial Japanese IV: Phonemics. *Language, 26;* 86–125. Reprinted in M. Joos (Ed.), *Readings in linguistics,* 329–348. Washington, D.C.: American Council of Learned Societies.

Callary, R.E. 1975. Phonological change and the development of an urban dialect in Illinois. *Language in Society, 4;* 155–69.

Cedergren, H.J. and D. Sankoff. 1974. Variable rules: Performance as a statistical reflection of competence. *Language, 50;* 333–55.

Dickerson, L.J. 1974. Internal and external patterning of phonological variability in the speech of Japanese learners of English: Toward a theory of second-language acquisition. Doctoral dissertation, University of Illinois.

Dickerson, L.J. 1975. The learner's interlanguage as a system of variable rules. *TESOL Quarterly, 9;* 401–08.

Dickerson, W.B. (a) Extensions of variability analysis. Unpublished manuscript.

Dickerson, W.B. (b) Psycholinguistic reflections of language community variable rules. Unpublished manuscript.

Kohmoto, S. 1960. Phonemic and sub-phonemic replacement of English sounds by speakers of Japanese. Doctoral dissertation, University of Michigan.

Labov, W. 1966. *The social stratification of English in New York City.* Washington, DC: Center for Applied Linguistics.

Labov, W. 1971. Methodology. In W. O. Dingwall (Ed.), *Survey of linguistic sciences,* 412–91. Baltimore: University of Maryland.

Labov, W. 1972. The internal evolution of linguistic rules. In R. Stockwell and R. Macaulay (Eds.), *Historical linguistics and generative theory,* 101–71. Bloomington: Indiana University Press.

Labov, W., M. Yaeger, & R. Steiner. 1972. *A quantitative study of sound change in progress.* 2 vols. Philadelphia: The U. S. Regional Survey.

Labov, W. 1973. On the mechanism of linguistic change. In W. Labov (Ed.), *Sociolinguistic patterns,* 160–82. Philadelphia: University of Pennsylvania Press.

Selinker, L. 1972. Interlanguage. *International Review of Applied Linguistics, 10;* 209–31.

6

A MODEL FOR INTERLANGUAGE PHONOLOGY*

Roy C. Major

INTRODUCTION

Interlanguage phonology is influenced by a number of factors, such as age, L1 interference, style, and developmental factors. General observation as well as numerous studies indicate that puberty is the critical age after which native accent is difficult if not impossible to achieve (Scovel, 1969; Seliger, et al., 1975). However, others claim that with the optimal affective and cultural factors, native accent is possible (Hill, 1970, discussed in Tarone 1978).

Interference from L1 is discussed in almost all works on foreign accent. Although it can account for many errors, interference cannot truly predict errors or explain other errors. For example, some French speakers do not substitute [R] for English [r]; Nemser (1971) found some Hungarian immigrants produced substitutions which do not occur in native English or Hungarian ([sθ] for English [θ]).

*I would like to express my appreciation to my research assistant, Melinda Dutton, for her help in analyzing the data, and to Fred R. Eckman and James Emil Flege for their comments on an earlier version of this paper.

In addition to interference, developmental factors (similar to L1 acquisition) contribute to foreign accent. For example, developmental processes are reported in L2 speakers of Swedish (Johansson, 1973) and English (Flege and Davidian, 1985); Mulford and Hecht (1980) report interference and developmental processes can operate on the same segments.

Studies report that stylistic variation is also present in L2 phonology, e.g., Tarone (1979); L. Dickerson (1974): effects of variation in the NL and TL and their effects on acquisition; W. Dickerson (1976, 1977): variation due to linguistic environment; Beebe: variation due to the listener (1977) and formality (1980).

Other explanations involve markedness theory and perceptual considerations. Eckman (1977) and Rutherford (1982) use markedness to explain order of acquisition—e.g., why word final voiced obstruents are acquired after they are mastered in other positions. Flege (1981) claims foreign accent does not occur because of production difficulties but because of the development of inaccurate perceptual targets.

Quite commonly, L2 phonological studies identify the sources of error but they do not suggest reasons for the successive stages in acquisition.[1] Furthermore, although the studies identify the sources of foreign accent, there seems to be no adequate theory that is explicit about the interrelationship of interference, developmental processes, and style.

THE ONTOGENY MODEL

In this paper I propose a model for second language phonological acquisition that claims an interrelationship of interference and developmental factors. The proposed hypothesis is an attempt to offer an integrated view of the way the L2 learner's phonology changes over time, as well as the way it varies with style, rather than merely attempting to explain the possible sources of error of an L2 learner at one particular stage.

Chronology

I hypothesize that L2 acquisition of phonology occurs in the following manner: At the early stages of acquisition interference processes predominate and then decrease over time, while at the early stages developmental processes are very infrequent, later they increase in frequency, and then they decrease over time. This can be observed in the acquisition of English [r] of a German speaker. The first substitution is often the German [R]; later it may be replaced by a partial [r], similar to a non-syllabic front rounded vowel [ø] or [œ]; finally the speaker may correctly produce [r].

According to this hypothesis interference processes gradually decrease over time while developmental processes increase and then decrease. As learning takes place, the interference process may be replaced by a developmental process which in turn is replaced by another one which is closer to the process of the native speaker. Graphically, this relationship is represented in Figure 6.1.

This model is intended to be an abstraction of the general pattern of L2 learners rather than an exact mathematical function determined from measurements of frequencies. The crossover point, if any, and the rate of change will vary considerably from individual to individual. A poor learner may fossilize at the left end of the graph—e.g. a French speaker who permanently produces [R] for English [r]. A good learner may bypass interference and developmental processes for a given phenomenon—e.g. a learner who correctly produces English [r] on the first attempt. Counter-evidence for this model would be a speaker who from one temporal stage to the next changes, for a given phenomenon, from a developmental process to an interference process.

The operation of this model can be described in the following terms: At an early stage of acquisition, interference processes predominate at the expense of developmental processes. As acquisition proceeds, interference processes give way to developmental processes, which gradually increase and then decrease over time. The reason developmental processes do not operate with a high frequency at early stages is that interference processes prevent developmental processes from surfacing. As interference is eliminated, developmental processes can blossom. For example, a speaker of Brazilian Portuguese who is beginning to learn English typically produces an [i] after voiced stops, e.g., *dog*[i]—an interference process occurring in Portuguese phonology.[2] Later, [i] is replaced by [ə]. The developmental process of terminal devoicing, common among more advanced learners, cannot surface because of this paragoge. Thus the stages that are typical for many speakers are the following: [dɔgi] (interference) > [dɔgə] (developmental) > [dɔk] (developmental) > [dɔg].

The *Ontogeny Model* follows logically from general principles of learning theory.[3] There is considerable evidence that transfer is involved in learning; i.e.,

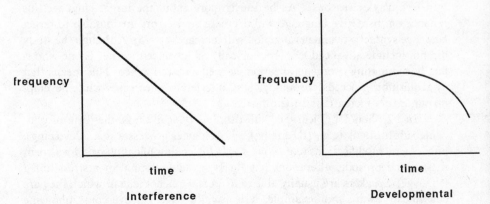

Figure 6.1 Relationship of interference and developmental processes to time

one relies on previous cognitive experience when learning new information (Schultz, 1960; Ausubel, 1963, 1967; Ausubel and Robinson, 1969; Ausubel, Novak, and Hanesian, 1978; Gagne, 1977; Travers, 1977). Ausubel, Novak, and Hanesian (1978, 165) summarize the role of transfer and its effects on creating new cognitive structures and in turn the effects of these new structures on subsequent learning:

We have just hypothesized that past experience influences, or has positive or negative effects on, new meaningful learning and retention by virtue of its impact on relevant properties of cognitive structure. If this is true, all meaningful learning necessarily involves transfer. It is impossible to conceive of any instance of such learning that is not affected in some way by existing cognitive structure. This learning experience, in turn, results in new transfer by modifying cognitive structure.

In terms of second language learning, this means that a beginning learner will transfer NL patterns to the TL because the learner has mastered very little of the TL. As he or she learns, the "existing cognitive structure" (IL system) is modified by the TL experience, creating new cognitive structures. These new cognitive structures in turn affect further modifications of the IL. That is, as the IL is increasingly affected by the TL, the IL will show increasing developmental substitutions, while the influence of pure NL transfer will decrease. This is because the IL is becoming more like the TL and substitutions will follow naturally from this system rather than from the pure NL system.[4] As the learner continues to learn and approaches TL accent, the developmental substitutions (as well as interference) will decrease. From the framework of the *Ontogeny Model* this means interference processes will decrease over time while developmental processes will first increase and then decrease.

The proposed model may apply to syntax as well. Taylor (1975) found that transfer was more common in beginning learners than for intermediate learners but overgeneralization more common for intermediate learners than for beginning learners. Using general learning theory (e.g., Ausubel's 1967 discussion of transfer), Taylor reasons: "As he learns more about the target language, his reliance on his native language will decrease, and errors attributable to target language syntactic overgeneralization will increase" (p. 75). Although the study did not include advanced learners, logically an advanced learner is one who is finally eliminating overgeneralization, as well as interference. This means that as acquisition proceeds chronologically, interference decreases while developmental errors increase and then decrease.

In L2 phonology, learners' substitutions typically take the form of phoneme substitutions (e.g., [R] for [r]), phonological processes (e.g., devoicing), phonotactic modifications (e.g., consonant cluster simplification or schwa epenthesis), and prosodic alterations (e.g., using syllable-timing for a stress-timed language). Speakers are usually able to overcome phenomena of which they are consciously aware. For example, it is usually easier to overcome phoneme substitution than substitution of phonological processes (whether developmental or interference) because phonological processes are largely unconscious. Thus many Portuguese learners of English easily master the [r] because it is immediately obvious that English /r/ is different from Portuguese /r/ (phonetically [r] or [x]). Yet these same speakers are unaware[5] that they are producing unaspirated voiceless stops in their English utterances.

Acquisition can follow discrete jumps or gradual approximations to the TL. For example, a Portuguese speaker's acquisition of English /æ/ can proceed gradually from [a] to [aˆ] to [æˇ] and finally to [æ]. Discrete jumps can be observed in the acquisition of /r/ in English for speakers with different native languages. A French, Portuguese, and Spanish speakers' first substitutions are often due to interference, i.e. [R], [x], and the trill [r̄] respectively. These substitutions may later be replaced by a slightly *r*-colored sound resembling the English [r] (e.g. [œ]), and then finally the English [r]. Similarly, an English speaker's acquisition of syllable final Portuguese /r/ (phonetically [x]) may change from [r] (interference) to deletion (an L1 developmental process) to [x] (TL pronunciation), e.g., [pɔrta] > [pɔta] > [pɔxta] *porta* 'door.'

Child vs. adult development I suggest that there is no fundamental difference in the mechanism of substitutions in children acquiring L1 and adults acquiring L2. Rather, the difference lies in the starting point of the learner. In the adult, the starting point is the native L1 system, and initially all substitutions are made with reference to this system; i.e., they take the form of interference.[6] On the other hand, the child's starting point is the native pre-language system (at the very first stage in acquisition) or the child's L1 system at a particular point in time (for those who have already begun language acquisition). Thus acquisition in the child and adult are similar because the speaker progressively approximates the target from the starting point of whatever the learner already has acquired.

This similarity between child and adult can be observed by comparing the acquisition of English /æ/ in an English speaking child and an adult speaker of Spanish. If productively the child is at a five vowel stage (usually [i, e, a, o, u]) then the substitution for /æ/ will typically be [a]. Likewise, the Spanish speaker's first substitutions will typically be [a], since Spanish has a similar five vowel system. Thus the starting points of the child and adult are the same, namely their native L1 systems, which for the adult is Spanish and for the child is also a system with five vowels. As acquisition progresses, gradual approximation to [æ] will be similar for both speakers, i.e. [a] > [aˆ] > [æˇ] > [æ].

If the *Ontogeny Model* is correct, it should be possible to predict the various stages in acquisition to the extent that it is possible in L1 acquisition. If the particular stage of a child is well described it is possible to make some reasonable predictions as to what the next stage will be like. For example, a child who produces [w] for [l] in all positions would later be expected to produce [l] prevocalically before mastering it postvocalically. Likewise, a thorough description of an adult at a particular stage (in addition to knowledge of the L1 system) should enable one to make similar predictions. These predictions should be possible for both child and adult because of universal considerations (variously called intrinsic difficulty, markedness theory, and universal order of acquisition; see Jakobson, 1940; Eckman, 1977; Rutherford, 1982). For example, universals can be used to explain why L1 and L2 learners acquire voiced obstruents in word-initial and -medial positions before they do in final position (Eckman, 1977) and why [x] is acquired before [ç] in L2 learners of Arabic.

Positive and partial transfer One difference between L2 phonological acquisition and acquisition of syntax and morphology is that in phonology positive transfer always seems to occur; i.e., if a sound or process in L1 also occurs in L2 the learner will automatically transfer it to L2 without having to go through any intermediate stages. Thus a Portuguese speaker learning English will not have any difficulty with /š/ because Portuguese also has this sound. This contrasts with the acquisition of syntax and morphology, where developmental processes often operate even when transfer would produce the correct utterance in L2. For example, speakers who use question inversion in L1 may not use the inversion in their English utterances, even when literal translation from L1 to English would produce the correct form.

Partial transfer also can operate. If L1 and L2 share a common phenomenon but in L1 it does not operate in all the environments as in L2, the learner will be able to learn the phenomenon in the L2 environments more easily than if the phenomenon did not occur at all in L1. For example, native English words have no word-initial [ž], yet English speakers seem to have no difficulty pronouncing *Zaza* as [žaža], perhaps because [ž] occurs in other positions in English. However, the fact word-initial [ŋ] is usually difficult for English speakers suggests that there are other important factors such as universal order and markedness considerations. Considerable work in this area is needed in order to specify what types of phenomena are more easily transferred than others.

Distinguishing interference from developmental processes The proposed model necessitates distinguishing interference from developmental processes. In some cases interference and developmental processes are identical. For example, in German speakers learning English, terminal devoicing could be either a developmental or interference process. Since it is a common developmental process in L1 acquisition of English and it is a process in adult native German, it would be impossible to decide if a German speaker's devoiced obstruents in English were due to interference or developmental factors.[7] However, there are other cases where developmental or interference factors can easily be distinguished. A Spanish speaker's substitution of the trill for English [r] is clearly interference since this trill substitution for [r] occurs rarely if at all in L1 acquisition of English. Another clear case is Mulford and Hecht's (1980) example of the six-year-old Icelandic boy learning English. He devoiced final stops (a developmental process) and strongly aspirated them (an interference process occurring in Icelandic). These and numerous other examples seem to indicate there are three fundamental types of substitutions: interference (processes that occur in the learner's NL but neither in the TL nor in L1 acquisition), developmental (processes that occur in L1 acquisition but do not operate in the learner's NL—e.g. devoicing in Portuguese), and processes that are ambiguous (processes that occur both in adult NL phonology and in L1 acquisition—e.g. devoicing in German).

Style

The model proposes an interrelationship of interference and developmental factors over time. I suggest that the same relationship holds for stylistic shifts: i.e., as style becomes increasingly formal, interference decreases and developmental factors increase and then decrease. This relationship is represented in Figure 6.2.

A comparison of very formal and casual styles provides evidence for this relationship. Almost every foreign language teacher will attest that L2 learners generally do better at pronouncing isolated words (e.g. minimal pairs) than they do in free speech. Many speakers are able to correctly produce sounds and words in isolation, but in running speech they slip back into L1 patterns. This suggests that in a formal style the speaker is able to suppress interference processes that will reappear in more casual speech. The reason for this seems to be that in casual speech a speaker pays less attention to form and more attention to content.[8]

The appearance of processes in L2 production are affected by both L1 processes that are stylistically conditioned as well as universal stylistic considerations involving fortition and lenition. Fortition or strengthening processes reinforce segments or sequences—e.g., insertions and lengthening. Lenition or weakening processes weaken segments and sequences and typically include ease of articulation processes, such as assimilations, reductions, and deletions. Fortition processes are much more common in formal styles than are lenition processes, which are common in more casual speech (Donegan and Stampe, 1979;

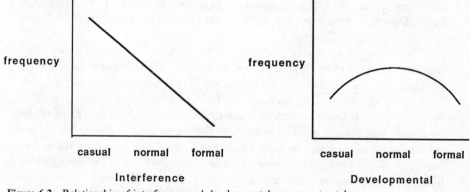

Figure 6.2   Relationship of interference and developmental processes to style

107

Lass, 1984). Thus a Portuguese speaker's pronunciation of word-final consonant clusters in English might depend on style. The operation of the two common developmental processes, schwa insertion and consonant cluster simplification (neither of which is a process in native Portuguese), might depend on the style of the speaker. The schwa insertion (e.g. [rostəs] *roasts*) would be expected more frequently in a more formal style than would consonant cluster simplification ([ros]). This is because schwa insertion is a fortition process that *insures* that the final consonants are perceived, whereas consonant cluster simplification is a lenition process.

Although an L2 learner's pronunciation is generally better in more formal tasks (such as reading word lists), this is not always the case. For example, in Portuguese stressed and pretonic /il/ and /iu/ is pronounced [iw] in normal speech, causing speakers to pronounce English *few* as [fiw] (because they interprept *few* as /fiu/ or /fil/). However, in very casual Portuguese /il/ and /iu/ becomes [yu] (Major, 1981, 1985, forthcoming). If this casual process is transferred into English the speaker would then correctly pronounce *few* as [fyu], especially in unstressed positions. The source of this variation would be transfer in both cases. The speaker's incorrect [fiw] in a normal style would be due to negative transfer while the correct [fyu] in the casual style would be a case of positive transfer. Without considering these stylistic variations in Portuguese, one might erroneously conclude that the speaker is producing the correct pronunciation in casual speech because he or she is more relaxed or because learning has taken place.

The Good Vs. the Poor Learner

According to the model, the shape of the graph is affected by rate of learning. A very good learner will progress very rapidly from left to right, and many interference processes will never surface—e.g. the learner who masters English /θ/ on the first attempt. The poor learner, however, will progress very slowly and often fossilize at the left portion of the graph (Figure 6.1). The difference between a heavy, moderate, and slight accent can also be characterized in terms of a similar graph (Figure 6.3).

The native language of one with a very strong accent can be easily identified by one who is familiar with this language. This is because interference processes predominate; i.e., the L2 utterances of this speaker sound like L1 with L2 loan words. The native language of one with a moderate accent can often be identified, but usually there are substitutions that are untypical of either language. This means some developmental processes are allowed to surface because some interference processes have been overcome. However, the native language of one with just a trace of an accent cannot often be identified by listeners. Such a learner may have successfully eliminated (nearly) all interference processes, and what remain are slight deviations from the TL due to

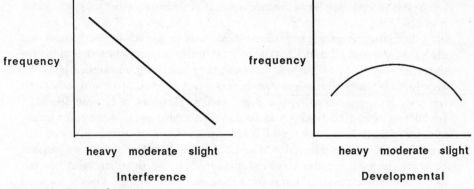

frequency   frequency

heavy   moderate   slight   heavy   moderate   slight

Interference   Developmental

Figure 6.3   Degree of accent

developmental processes occurring neither in the native utterances of L1 nor in L2.

Phonological Similarity of L1 and L2

Some researchers have claimed that interference is more likely when L1 and L2 are very similar. This characteristic follows from general learning principles. According to Brown (1980, 159): "The principle at work is common in human learning: interference can actually be greater when items to be learned are more similar to existing items than when items are entirely new and unrelated to existing items."[9]

In the framework of the *Ontogeny Model,* this means there will be more interference processes for similar phenomena and more developmental processes for phenomena that are further apart. Thus L2 phenomena which have similar counterparts in the learner's NL will be hard to learn because the learner will unconsciously analyze them as identical. In terms of the graph, a speaker may tend to fossilize at the left corner (Figure 6.1 above). On the other hand, the learner will tend to be conscious of L2 phenomena that are very different from the learner's NL. Because of this, the learner will consciously attempt to overcome the NL interference processes and in doing so will produce either developmental substitutions or the TL pronunciation. This principle can be observed in the acquisition of English /æ/ by speakers of Brazilian Portuguese. Brazilian Portuguese has /ɛ/ but no /æ/. Beginning learners typically substitute Portuguese [ɛ] for both English [ɛ] and [æ]. More advanced learners often master the [æ] but continue to substitute the slightly lower Portuguese [ɛˇ] for English [ɛ]. This may be because learners are quickly alerted to the fact that Portuguese has no /æ/ but are often unaware that the [ɛ]s of the two languages are different. It may also be because the phonetic difference between Portuguese [ɛ] and English [æ] is greater than the distance between Portuguese [ɛ] and English [ɛ]. In this second case the difference is so slight that the learner may not notice it at all.

Even though interference seems most likely for sounds or phenomena that are very similar in L1 and L2, this does not imply anything in terms of degree of foreign accent. A Portuguese speaker may produce an unrounded [š] and a very fortis [v] in his English utterances (as one does in native Portuguese), but this may be perceived as only a slight accent. However, a Korean speaker's production of English liquids may be more detectable as non-native to a native speaker of English, even though the Korean speaker is using substitutions that are neither Korean nor English. The learner has therefore *progressed* beyond pure interference, yet the accent is greater than the Brazilian who has not *progressed,* since the Brazilian is producing an unrounded [š] when a rounded [š] is characteristic of native English. If L1 and L2 are very different, a heavier accent would be expected simply because there is more to be mastered than if the languages were very similar. Whether substitutions are due to interference or developmental processes, they are still perceived by a native listener as a foreign accent.

TESTING THE MODEL

In order to thoroughly test the *Ontogeny Model,* a great number of longitudinal studies would be required. Because of the time involved in such studies, latitudinal studies could be substituted that would include comparison of a number of speakers for specific processes to see if there are any implicational relationships; e.g., does the occurrence of one process imply the occurrence of another process but not vice versa? For a given speaker, what is the relative frequency of developmental vs. interference processes as style varies? Another way to provide evidence for or against the hypothesis would be to compare a number of speakers with different degrees of accent[10] (who have a common L1) for the relative occurrence of developmental and interference factors of a given phenomenon.

Evidence from Previous Studies

Although many of the L2 phonological studies discuss the role of both interference and developmental factors, in very few of them are the data collected or presented in such a way that the relative importance of these two factors over time can be determined. One study that provides longitudinal data that can be used as evidence for the *Ontogeny Model* is Wode's 1981 work on his own German-speaking children's acquisition of English. He describes the developmental sequences of the four children (beginning at ages 3;4–7;6) for a period of approximately three years. Wode proposes that there are two fundamental types of developmental sequences: those that involve gradual approximations to the target and those that involve discrete jumps. These gradual approximations occur in the acquisition of vowels. The first substitutions for the English vowels /ʌ/ and /æ/ were [a] and [ɛ] respectively, which indicate interference from German. Wode implies that later substitutions become closer and closer to the target via gradual approximations. However, discrete jumps occurred in the acquisition of /r/, the order of which was the same for all four children [R] > [w] > [ɹ] > [r].[11] The stages for both the vowel and r substitutions are what would be predicted from the model I have proposed. The early substitutions are due to interference, which gradually yields to developmental processes, which are in turn replaced by the TL processes.

Additional evidence that interference gives way to developmental factors is provided by Flege's 1980 acoustical analysis of Saudi Arabic speakers learning English. He found that despite early interference the speakers gradually approximated the voice onset times (VOT) for English stops that were intermediate between the Arabic and English sounds. In fact, the more experienced Saudis produced stops that were closer to native English than the less experienced Saudis. These gradual approximations are typical of L1 acquisition of English; e.g., Macken and Barton (1977) found that some children gradually approximate the VOTs characteristic of native adult English.

Wode's data (1981, 228) also indicate variations due to style, although he does not specifically mention the term. For example, his daughter Birgit substituted [R] for English /r/ in her casual spontaneous speech but in the "imitation-like check-ups" she frequently used [w]. The *Ontogeny Model* claims that as style becomes more formal, interference processes decrease while developmental processes increase and then decrease. In terms of style, spontaneous speech should be considered less formal than her "check ups." Thus the model is supported by Wode's data, since the girl's spontaneous speech contained more of the [R] (interference) than did the "check-ups," where the developmental substitution of [w] was prevalent.

Another study involving [r] further supports my generalization. Dickerson and Dickerson (1977) found that Japanese speakers produced English /r/ 100 percent correctly in word lists but in free speech only 50 percent correctly. This suggests that in the word lists both developmental and interference factors had been eliminated but in free speech developmental and/or interference processes occurred.

Evidence from Brazilian English

The following is a pilot study analyzing recordings made in Brazil of the English of twelve speakers of Brazilian Portuguese. The data elicited were designed to measure the relative importance of interference and developmental factors in relation to English language proficiency and style. All twelve of the subjects were either students or teachers at Pontifícia Universidade Católica in São

Paolo, SP, Brazil. The subjects consisted of two groups: The first group were six subjects who were first-year English students and who had never travelled to an English-speaking country. The second group was composed of six subjects, five of whom were graduate students in English applied linguistics and one of whom was on the faculty. Five members of the second group had travelled or lived in an English-speaking country. Table 6.1 profiles the twelve speakers.

Phenomena investigated[12] *and procedure*   The material read by the subjects was designed to test the relative prevalence of interference and developmental substitutions for the following phenomena. The phenomena selected are typically problematic for Portuguese speakers, namely segments or phonotactic occurrences in English which do not occur in Portuguese. For the phenomena considered, /r/ and final consonant clusters and obstruents, both developmental and interference substitutions are possible.

(1) /r/

The Portuguese /r/ for the dialects of the subjects is pronounced either as a trilled [r̄] or [x] syllable-initially and as [r̄] or [r] syllable-finally. Therefore, substitutions could either be interference (native Portuguese sounds) or developmental (e.g., substitution of [w] for English /r/). Although syllable-final [r] (very similar to English [r]) is a stigmatized pronunciation in Portuguese, it sometimes does occur in the dialects of the subjects.

(2) Final consonant clusters

Since final consonant clusters do not occur in Portuguese, speakers frequently insert [i] or [ə] to break up the clusters. [i] insertion is an interference

TABLE 6.1   Subject profile

S#	sex	age	Beginners years in English-speaking country	years of English study	native state
1.	F	26	0	2	SP
2.	F	22	0	2	SP
3.	F	20	0	2	SP
4.	F	20	0	2	SP
5.	F	20	0	6	SP
6.	M	20	0	4	SP

S#	sex	age	Advanced years in English-speaking country	years of English study	native state
7.	F	32	1	7	MG
8.	F	42	3	30	SP
9.	M	39	1	17	SP
10.	F	27	0;6	16	SP
11.	F	25	0	7	PR
12.	F	32	5	10	RJ

112

process occurring in loan words, while [ə] insertion should be considered developmental since it does not occur in native Portuguese phonology, but does occur in L1 acquisition of English.

(3) Devoicing of word-final obstruents

Since /s/ is the only word- or syllable-final obstruent in Portuguese, the common developmental process of devoicing might be expected to operate in the subjects' English utterances.

(4) Paragoge

Since the only final obstruent in Portuguese is /s/, speakers often insert [i] or [ə]. [i] insertion is interference, since it occurs in loan words, e.g. *hot*[i] *dog*[i], while [ə] paragoge is developmental, since it does not occur in Portuguese but does occur in L1 acquisition of English.

Recordings were made of the subjects, who read orally from a list of sentences, a word list, and finally a short text. The subjects were first requested to read the list of sentences "normally" and then to reread this same list "as quickly as possible" and "don't worry about making any mistakes." They were then asked to read the list of words "normally" with a long pause (1–2 seconds) between each word.[13] After the word list was completed the subjects were asked to read the short text "normally." (See appendix for a list of the material used.) In terms of style, the word list can be considered the most formal, the first sentence reading intermediate,[14] and the text the most informal. Although the task of reading can be criticized for being less natural than free speech, this experiment was designed to control for as many phonological environments as possible, something that is difficult to do in free conversation. The occurrences of the various phenomena investigated, described below, were transcribed by the author and a trained research assistant who had no prior knowledge of the hypotheses of the author or the background of the subjects (other than that they were Brazilian). There was 90–95 percent agreement on the transcription between the author and the research assistant.

Results and discussion Tables 6.2–6.5 show the number of deviations from native English pronunciation and the percent deviation for the speakers.

TABLE 6.2 /r/

S	Word	Ss1	Ss2	Text	S	Word	Ss1	Ss2	Text
1	0	0	0	1 [œ]	7	0	0	0	0
2	0	0	0	0	8	0	0	0	0
3	0	0	0	1 [w]	9	0	0	0	0
4	1 [x]	0	0	1 [γ]	10	0	0	0	0
5	1 [x]	0	0	1 [x]	11	0	0	0	0
6	0	0	0	1 [w]	12	0	0	0	0
Tot	2	0	0	5	Tot	0	0	0	0
n	24	36	36	300	n	24	36	36	300
x̄	8.3%	0%	0%	1.7%	x̄	0%	0%	0%	0%

Word=word list reading; Ss1=normal reading of the sentence list; Ss2=fast reading of the sentence list; Text=reading of the text

113

TABLE 6.3 Final Consonant Clusters: Ø → [i,ə]/C(C)__C#

S	Word	Ss1	Ss2	Text	S	Word	Ss1	Ss2	Text
1	1 [ə]	2 [ə]	2 [ə]	6 [ə]	7	0	0	0	1 [ə]
2	0	0	1 [i]	3 [i]	8	0	0	0	0
			2 [ə]	1 [ə]					
3	0	3 [ə]	0	6 [ə]	9	0	0	0	0
4	1 [ə]	1 [ə]	2 [ə]	3 [ə]	10	0	0	1 [ə]	0
5	1 [ə]	2 [ə]	2 [ə]	6 [ə]	11	0	1 [ə]	1 [ə]	0
6	0	2 [ə]	1 [ə]	1 [ə]	12	0	0	0	0
Tot	3	10	10	26	Tot	0	1	2	2
n	18	18	18	36	n	18	18	18	36
x̄ [i]	0%	0%	5.6%	8.3%	x̄ [i]	0%	0%	0%	0%
[ə]	16.7%	55.6%	50%	63.9%	[ə]	0%	5.6%	11.1%	5.6%
Tot	16.7%	55.6%	55%	72.2%	Tot	0%	5.6%	11.1%	5.6%

TABLE 6.4 Terminal Devoicing: [-son] → [-voi]/__#

S	Word	Ss1	Ss2	Text	S	Word	Ss1	Ss2	Text
1	3	2	2	2	7	1	1	2	3
2	1	1	1	2	8	1	0	0	0
3	1	1	0	0	9	2	0	1	3
4	1	0	1	0	10	1	0	0	2
5	4	1	1	2	11	0	0	0	0
6	0	0	1	1	12	0	0	0	0
Tot	10	5	6	7	Tot	5	1	3	8
n	36	24	24	36	n	36	24	24	36
x̄	27.8%	20.8%	25%	19.4%	x̄	13.9%	4.2%	12.5%	22.2%

TABLE 6.5 Paragoge: Ø → [i,ə]/C__#

S	Word	Ss1	Ss2	Text	S	Word	Ss1	Ss2	Text
1	0	0	0	4 [i]	7	0	0	0	0
				1 [ə]					
2	0	0	0	4 [ə]	8	0	0	0	0
3	0	2 [i]	1 [i]	2 [i]	9	0	0	0	1 [ə]
		6 [ə]	3 [ə]	5 [ə]					
4	0	4 [ə]	1 [i]	2 [i]	10	0	0	0	0
			1 [ə]	3 [ə]					
5	0	1 [ə]	3 [ə]	1 [i]	11	0	0	1 [ə]	0
6	0	2 [ə]	0	0	12	0	0	0	1 [ə]
Tot	0	15	9	22	Tot	0	0	1	2
n	60	60	60	60	n	60	60	60	60
x̄ [i]	0%	3.3%	3.3%	15%	x̄ [i]	0%	0%	0%	0%
[ə]	0%	21.7%	11.7%	21.7%	[ə]	0%	0%	1.7%	3.3%
Tot	0%	25%	15%	36.7%	Tot	0%	0%	1.7%	3.3%

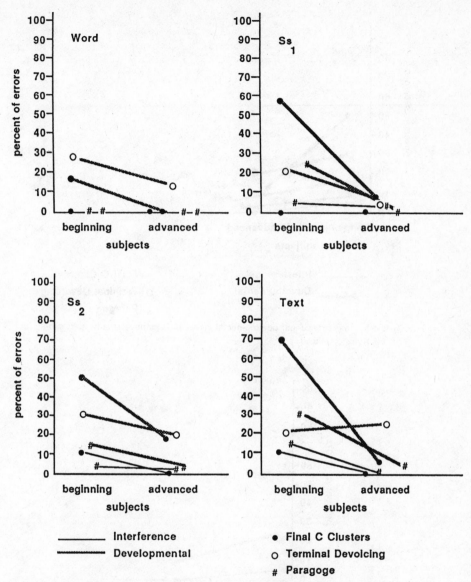

Figure 6.4 Interference and developmental errors in beginning vs. advanced subjects.

Figures 6.4–6.8 graphically depict these results (with /r/ omitted, since the total number of errors was so small). Ss1 = normal reading and Ss2 = fast reading for the sentence lists. Subjects 1–6 are the beginning speakers and 7–12 the advanced. In general, the beginning students showed a greater occurrence of both interference and developmental substitutions when compared to the advanced speakers. In addition, the number of deviations decreased as style became more formal.

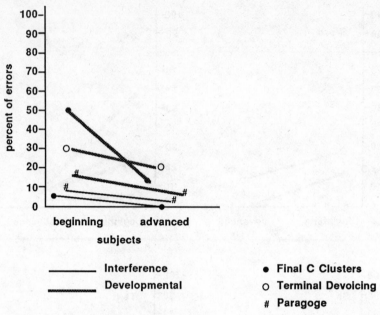

Figure 6.5 Interference and developmental errors in beginning vs. advanced subjects, all styles combined.

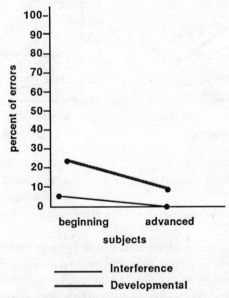

Figure 6.6 Interference and developmental errors in beginning vs. advanced subjects, all errors and styles combined.

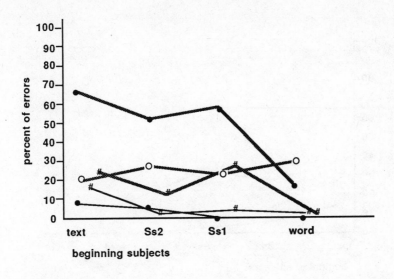

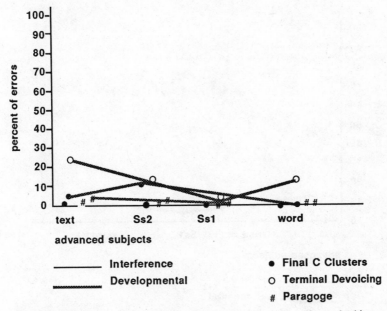

Figure 6.7 Interference and developmental errors in beginning vs. advanced subjects, according to style.

(1) /r/

The only instance of non-native substitutions were for the beginning students, who made only seven errors (Table 6.2).

Comparing styles, there are no significant differences (at 0.05 level);[15] however, the difference between the beginning and advanced groups is signifi-

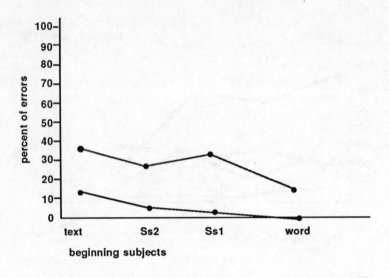

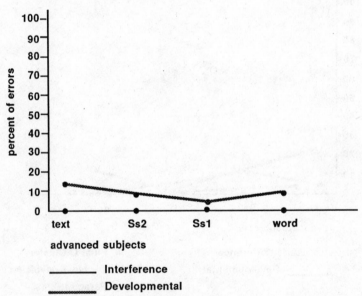

Figure 6.8 Interference and developmental errors in beginning vs. advanced subjects, according to style, all errors combined.

cant (lumping all the styles together for a given group). The relative lack of difficulty with /r/ may be due to the fact that [r] sometimes occurs in syllable-final position in the Portuguese of the speakers. It is possible that the proposed principle of partial positive transfer (discussed on p. 105–106).

118

(2) Final Consonant Clusters:

$$\emptyset \rightarrow [i,\partial]/C(C)\_\_C\#$$

The data support the hypotheses (Table 6.3), as shown in Tables 6.3–6.5 and Figures 6.4–6.8.

[i] insertion is classified as interference and [ə] insertion is developmental (discussed on p. 109). The difference between the total errors of the beginning and advanced speakers is significant. In addition, there are significant differences for the beginners' Ss1, Ss2, and text productions compared with the same styles for the advanced speakers. In the beginning learners, as style became more casual, both interference and developmental processes showed a general increase (significant between the word and text readings, grouping interference and developmental errors together). In the word list and the normal sentence reading all errors were developmental (no interference). In the fast sentence reading interference replaced some of the developmental substitutions and in the text both interference and developmental errors increased.

The advanced learners showed a similar tendency. Although the differences are not statistically significant, they do indicate a trend that supports the hypothesis. The learners had successfully overcome interference and developmental processes in a formal style, since there were no errors in the word list. In the other styles, the few errors that did occur were all developmental.

(3) Terminal Devoicing

$$[\text{-son}] \rightarrow [\text{-voi}]/\_\_\# \text{ and}$$

(4) Paragoge

$$\emptyset \rightarrow [i,\partial]/C\_\_\#$$

These two processes provide the strongest support for the hypotheses (Tables 6.4 and 6.5). [i] paragoge is interference, while [ə] paragoge and terminal devoicing are developmental (see p. 109). The differences between the beginners' productions of Ss1, Ss2, and text are significant when compared to the advanced speakers' corresponding productions.

Terminal devoicing and paragoge are in competition with one another: Paragoge preserves voicing but destroys the environment for terminal devoicing. Devoicing is a developmental process and paragoge is interference (at least [i] insertion). In the word list of the beginning learners all errors were from devoicing. As style became more casual, devoicing showed a slight decrease (although not significant), but paragoge showed a dramatic increase (significant between the word productions and the other three styles). In the advanced group, stylistic variation in paragoge is not significant. Schwa paragoge might be considered either interference or developmental. It is interference in the sense that Portuguese inserts a vowel after final obstruents but developmental in the sense that the vowel [ə] is not the one used in Portuguese paragoge—i.e., [i]. In any case the trend is clear: The prevalence of both types of paragoge in casual speech is suppressed in a more formal variety that allows the operation of the developmental process of devoicing.

The data on terminal devoicing show that, for a given group, there are no significant differences between styles. On a one-tailed test, the difference between groups is barely significant.[16] These data might seem to contradict the claim that in advanced learners developmental processes decrease. However, the advanced learners had practically eliminated paragoge in all styles (only three tokens), thus leaving a greater number of environments for devoicing to operate. On the other hand, in the beginners the prevalence of paragoge blocked many of the environments for devoicing. Since devoicing was practically the same in the text for beginning and advanced learners, this means that the beginners actually devoiced a greater percentage of the time because many of the environments had been eliminated by paragoge.[17]

Conclusion   Although the data are somewhat limited because of the small number of tokens for any given phenomenon, the trends support the *Ontogeny Model*. In general, the advanced learners showed fewer instances of interference than the beginners. Depending on the particular process and stage of development, the beginners showed either a greater or lesser occurrence of developmental processes when compared to the advanced learners. This variation is predicted by the proposed model, since developmental processes are claimed to first increase and then decrease. The claims for stylistic variation were also supported by the data.

SUMMARY

The model presented in this paper makes specific claims, in terms of chronology and style, about the interrelationship of interference and developmental factors in L2 phonological acquisition. Evidence for these generalizations was presented from various studies and from general learning theory. These claims can be summarized as follows: Interference processes first predominate and then decrease over time. However, developmental processes are at first infrequent, but later they increase and then decrease in frequency. The same pattern is also claimed to hold for stylistic variation: As style becomes more formal interference decreases, while developmental substitutions increase and then decrease.

The reason interference processes predominate at early stages of acquisition is that one relies on previous cognitive experience when learning new information (Schultz, 1960; Ausubel, Novak, and Hanesian, 1978). Thus many developmental processes cannot surface because of interference. For example, a beginning L2 learner will tend to substitute his or her native /r/ in the TL, which means that a developmental substitution cannot occur in the same token. This pattern is also true in terms of style; i.e., the more formal the style, the more a speaker can eliminate interference processes because he or she is paying more attention to form.

120

Although the model is supported from general learning theory and previous studies, further research is needed because the empirical evidence that can be used to test the claims is sketchy. In order to test these claims, research needs to rigorously control for and measure chronological and stylistic variation of interference and developmental processes.

NOTES

1. There are exceptions, e.g. Eckman (1977), Flege (1980), and Wode (1981).

2. Many of the generalizations and examples from Portuguese speakers are based on data collected from teaching EFL/ESL in Brazil for four years.

3. For considering this possibility, I am indebted to Fred R. Eckman.

4. By implication, this may also mean that continual L2 experience can not only modify the IL but it can also modify one's NL system, because of retroactive transfer. This is confirmed by widespread observations concerning immigrants whose NL utterances become increasingly non-native-like.

5. Although it is very difficult to define conscious vs. unconscious it would seem fruitful to do studies that investigate the degree of awareness one has of phenomena that occur both in the L1 and L2 and to correlate this with learnability.

6. This is not to say that all substitutions surface as interference but rather that interference is a mental operation that takes place before developmental processes can operate. In good learners the transition from interference to developmental processes takes place rapidly so that some interference substitutions never surface.

7. Beebe (1984) discusses further problems with the interference/developmental distinction. Difficulties in distinguishing interference from developmental factors are of course not unique to phonology. For example, it is impossible to tell whether a French speaker's double negative in English is due to interference (since double negatives occur in French) or negative spreading (a common developmental process).

8. However, extralinguistic factors may come into play, such as stress, which may produce poor performance even in formal styles. In this case, interference may actually be greater in formal than in casual styles.

9. For discussion of the way this principle applies to spelling, see Oller and Ziahosseiny (1970). These authors found in ESL learners that spelling was more difficult for those whose native language used the Roman alphabet than for those who did not.

10. One problem with this is that elaborating the criteria one uses for making judgments on degree of foreign accent is often very difficult. Even though a given feature might be correlated with a heavy or slight accent, it would be difficult to determine that this was a causal factor, since listeners undoubtedly make judgments based on a number of features—e.g. prosody and voice quality.

11. In Wode's phonetic transcription, [ɹ] is a "central frictionless continuant" and [r] a "target-like retroflex."

12. These and additional phenomena are discussed in Major (1984).

13. The sentence list was read first, so the subjects were unable to recognize the key words, which reappeared on the word list.

14. The interpretation of the fast readings of the sentences (S_2) is problematic because in some speakers there was no noticeable difference between the first and second reading, while in others there was a great deal of difference.

15. Because of the small sample size, the confidence limits for binomial proportions were determined in order to test significance for stylistic variation within a group of speakers. However, a one-tailed test was used to test significance between the beginners and the advanced speakers (considering all styles for each group together) because the sample size was much larger. Both tests were considered at a 0.05 level of significance.

16. However, the difference is not significant using confidence limits for binomial proportions.

17. Also note that in the advanced learners the only instances of paragoge were [ə] but not [i], indicating the speakers had successfully eliminated true interference.

APPENDIX A

Sentence List

1. It's a nice day.
2. Kim likes the cat on the right.
3. He planted the seed.
4. The thing is, butter is better than oleo.
5. The dog took the long way home.
6. The teacher doesn't like Joe.
7. You can choose it if you want to.
8. The food cost a lot of money.
9. Ted scraped the window.
10. I'll bet you don't like black coffee very well. Maybe you like tea.
11. The singer has a good voice.
12. She touched it.

APPENDIX B

Word List

1. boat	8. cat	15. ringing	22. sit	29. choose	36. goal
2. Kate	9. Bobby	16. coffee	23. cut	30. bag	37. asks
3. still	10. hit	17. spray	24. facts	31. eyes	38. cab
4. beds	11. boot	18. ice	25. Pete	32. cap	39. foot
5. Joe	12. arrive	19. sat	26. bet	33. lot	40. tell
6. sad	13. this	20. deep	27. go	34. bought	
7. thing	14. car	21. school	28. tea	35. back	

APPENDIX C

Text

The quiet street was empty. The lonesome houses seemed to stare at us as we walked down the street. I had the queerest notion that they didn't want us here. Another strange feeling was growing on me, too—the feeling of eyes somewhere, looking at me. Once I turned around quickly, but I saw nobody.

The bid iron gate and the door with the broken glass looked exactly as we had left them. We squeezed by the gate and pushed at the door. It opened slowly with an awful creak.

"Ee-ee, what a welcome," said Tracy nervously.

"If there's anybody in the house, they now know we're here, too," I said.

"Never mind the happy thoughts". Tracy's voice sounded shaky. "Let's pretend it's a treasure hunt. Where do you guess we should start looking?"

I looked down the little hall. A steep and narrow flight of stairs went up from where we stood to the first floor of the house. Ahead to the left I saw the open door of a big room that was evidently the front half of the basement. Straight on to the back, the hall opened out into another big room.

"Down here," I said and led the way. Two old laundry tubs, a little sink, and a place for a stove showed that this had been a kitchen.

"Do you know what Grandfather told me about Chinese servants in big old mansions like this?" I asked Tracy. "He said that they always lived in a little room off the kitchen."

Tracy looked around and went quickly to a door across the room. "It's here," she cried truimphantly.

REFERENCES

Ausubel, D.P. 1963. *The Psychology of Meaningful Verbal Learning.* NY: Grune and Stratton.

Ausubel, D.P. 1967. *Learning Theory and Classroom Practice.* Toronto: The Ontario Institute for Studies in Education.

Ausubel, D.P., and F.G. Robinson. 1969. *School Learning: An Introduction to Educational Psychology.* NY: Holt, Rinehart, and Winston.

Ausubel, D.P., J.D. Novak, and H. Hanesian. 1978. *Educational Psychology: A Cognitive View,* second edition. NY: Holt, Rinehart, and Winston.

Beebe, L.M. 1977. The influence of the listener on code-switching. *Language Learning, 27,* 2, 332–339.

Beebe, L.M. 1980. Sociolinguistic variation and style shifting in second language acquisition. *Language Learning, 30,* 2, 433–447. (Also this volume.)

Beebe, L.M. 1984. Discussion and critical assessment on the colloquium on interlanguage phonology. Paper presented at the annual TESOL Convention, Houston, March 7, 1984.

Brown, H. 1980. *Principles of Language Learning and Teaching.* Englewood Cliffs, NJ: Prentice-Hall.

Dickerson, L. 1974. Internal and External Patterning of Phonological Variability in the Speech of Japanese Learners of English. Ph.D. Dissertation, University of Illinois, Urbana.

Dickerson, W. 1976. The psycholinguistic unity of language learning and language change. *Language Learning, 26,* 215–231. (Also this volume.)

Dickerson, W. 1977. Language variation in applied linguistics. *ITL Review of Applied Linguistics, 35,* 43–66.

Dickerson, L., and W. Dickerson. 1977. Interlanguage phonology: current research and future directions. In S. Pitt Corder and E. Roulet (Eds.), *The Notions of Simplification, Interlanguages, and Pidgins, and their Relation to Second Language Pedagogy,* Neuchâtel: Faculté des Lettres.

Donegan, P., and D. Stampe. 1979. The study of natural phonology. In D.A. Dinnsen (Ed.), *Current Approaches to Phonological Theory,* Bloomington: Indiana University Press.

Eckman F.R. 1977. Markedness and the contrastive analysis hypothesis. *Language Learning, 27,* 2, 315–330. (Also this volume.)

Flege, J.E. 1980. Phonetic approximation in second language acquisition. *Language Learning, 30,* 1, 117–134.

Flege, J.E. 1981. The phonological basis of foreign accent: a hypothesis. *TESOL Quarterly, 15,* 4, 443–455.

Flege, J.E., and R.D. Davidian. 1984. Transfer and developmental processes in adult foreign language speech production. *Applied Psycholinguistics, 5,* 323–347.

Gagné, R.M. 1977. *The Conditions of Learning*, third edition. NY: Holt, Rinehart, and Winston.

Hill, J. 1970. Foreign accents, language acquisition and cerebral dominance revisited. *Language Learning, 20,* 237–248.

Jakobson, R. 1940. *Kindersprache, Aphasie, und Allgemeine Lautgesetze.* (Translated as *Child Language, Aphasia, and Phonological Universals.* The Hague: Mouton, 1968.)

Johansson, F.A. 1973. *Immigrant Swedish Phonology: a Study of Multiple Contact Analysis.* Lund, Sweden: CWK Gleerup.

Lass, R. 1984. *Phonology: An Introduction to Basic Concepts.* Cambridge, England: Cambridge University Press.

Macken, M.A., and D. Barton. 1977. A longitudinal study of the acquisition of the voicing contrast in American English word initial stops, as measured by VOT. *Papers and Reports on Child Language Development, 14,* 74–121.

Major, R.C. 1981. Stress-timing in Brazilian Portuguese. *Journal of Phonetics, 9,* 343–351.

Major, R.C. 1984. Interference vs. development stages in foreign accent: evidence from the English of speakers of Brazilian Portuguese. Paper presented at the annual TESOL Convention, Houston, March 9, 1984.

Major, R.C. 1985. Stress and rhythm in Brazilian Portuguese. *Language, 61,* 2, 259–282.

Major, R.C. forthcoming. Influências prosódicas na fonologia do português no Brasil. *Anais do VII Encontro Nacional de Lingüística.* Rio de Janeiro: Pontifícia Universidade Católica.

Mulford, R., and B.F. Hecht. 1980. Learning to speak without an accent: acquisition of a second-language phonology. *Papers and Reports on Child Language Development, 18,* 16–74. (Also this volume.)

Nemser, W. 1971. *An Experimental Study of Phonological Interference in the English of Hungarians.* Bloomington: Indiana University Press.

Oller, J.W., and S.M. Ziahosseiny. 1970. The contrastive analysis hypothesis and spelling errors. *Language Learning, 20,* 183–189.

Rutherford, W.E. 1982. Markedness in second language acquisition. *Language Learning, 32,* 1, 85–108.

Schultz, R.W. 1960. Problem solving behavior and transfer. *Harvard Educational Review, 30,* 61–77.

Scovel, T. 1969. Foreign accents, language acquisition, and cerebral dominance. *Language Learning, 19,* 245–253.

Seliger, H., S. Krashen, and P. Ladefoged. 1975. Maturational constraints in the acquisition of second language accent. *Language Sciences, 36,* 20–22.

Tarone, E. 1978. The phonology of interlanguage. In Jack C. Richards (Ed.), *Understanding Second and Foreign Language Learning: Issues and Approaches,* Rowley, MA: Newbury House, 15–33. (Also this volume.)

Tarone, E. 1979. Interlanguage as chameleon. *Language Learning, 29,* 181–191.

Taylor, B.P. 1975. The use of overgeneralization and transfer learning strategies by elementary and intermediate students of ESL. *Language Learning, 25,* 73–107.

Travers, R.M.W. 1977. *Essentials of Learning,* fourth edition. NY: Macmillan.

Wode, H. 1981. *Learning a Second Language, I: An Integrated View of Language Acquisition.* Tübingen: Gunter Narr Verlag.

7

ON THE NATURALNESS OF INTERLANGUAGE
PHONOLOGICAL RULES*

Fred R. Eckman

One of the more interesting hypotheses to be put forth in the field of second language acquisition in recent years is the interlanguage (IL) hypothesis (Corder, 1971; Selinker, 1972). This hypothesis states that, when acquiring a second language (TL), the learner internalizes a system of rules which may be distinct from both the target language and the native language (NL). The claim that such a system may be distinct from both the TL and the NL is of particular interest since it posits a process of "creative construction" (Dulay and Burt, 1974) in second language acquisition, rather than a process of simple transfer from the NL. Therefore, part of the interest of the IL hypothesis is that it makes

*A shorter version of this paper was presented at a UWM Linguistics Colloquium on March 18, 1980. I would like to thank the participants of this colloquium for their comments, suggestions, and discussion. In addition, I would like to express my appreciation to the following for their comments on an earlier draft of this paper: Josh Ard, Phil Connell, Dan Dinnsen, Sue Gass, Anita Hochster, Michael Mikoś, Edith Moravcsik and Jessica Wirth.

This research was supported in part by a research grant from the UWM Graduate School, whose support is hereby gratefully acknowledged.

it possible to raise a number of interesting questions concerning the nature of ILs.

The first such question which immediately comes to mind is the extent to which ILs can be said to be distinct or independent. The evidence which has been presented so far essentially argues that utterances produced by second language learners do not belong entirely to the class of TL utterances nor to the class of NL utterances and, therefore, cannot be wholly governed by a system which is a grammar of the TL or by one which is a grammar of the NL. That is, the grammar governing a learner's utterances must be, in some sense, an independent system.

While this type of evidence and argumentation is highly plausible, it is not an empirical argument. In order to show on empirical grounds that ILs are independent, one must present facts about second language utterances which necessitate the postulation of some construct as part of the IL of a given learner, where this construct is part of neither the grammar of the TL nor the grammar of the NL.

A second interesting question which is raised by the IL hypothesis is the extent to which ILs are similar to (or different from) languages which are learned as first languages. If ILs are composed only of rules transferred from the learners' NL, then such a question would lack interest. However, since it is proposed that ILs are independent systems, the possibility is open that ILs differ from first languages in significant ways.

The purpose of this paper is to present evidence from interlanguage phonology which will shed some light on each of the above questions. More specifically, evidence will be presented to show that it is necessary to postulate at least two phonological rules in the interlanguage of some English learners which are not motivated for either the TL or the NL. Such evidence argues, on empirical grounds, for the independently motivated conclusion that ILs are independent systems.

It will also be argued that, whereas one of the rules which one must postulate in the above-mentioned ILs is one which is motivated for the grammars of several languages which are acquired as a first language, the other is apparently not. This raises the question of the extent to which ILs can differ from other language systems.

EVIDENCE

Before actually presenting the facts which motivate our conclusion, it would be worthwhile to examine the type of evidence which we are proposing, and the methodology which underlies the postulation of a phonological rule. Along this line, let us consider the evidence which motivates a rule of Terminal Devoicing which has been proposed as part of the grammar of a number of first languages such as German, Russian, and Polish. We have chosen to examine a rule like Terminal Devoicing because this rule is considered to be very well motivated and because, in the grammars where this rule has been postulated, it functions as a neutralization rule. Since it is highly likely that a learner will not be able to maintain all of the phonological contrasts of the TL, at least not at the beginning stages, there is reason to believe that at least some of the rules proposed for IL phonologies will be neutralization rules. Consequently, it is necessary to specify what evidence motivates such a rule.

Therefore, following Kenstowicz and Kisseberth (1979), let us assume that the empirical criteria necessary for the postulation of a neutralization rule are those below:

1. The absence of a phonemic contrast in a particular phonological context or environment
2. The existence of a morphophonemic alternation
3. A phonemic contrast between the alternating segments in one of the alternating contexts

These criteria can be exemplified by the following data, taken from German.

a. [tak]   'day'   e. [grat]   'degree'
b. [tagə]   'days'   f. [gradə]   'degrees'
c. [dɛk]   'deck'   g. [kalp]   'calf'
d. [dɛkə]   'decks'   h. [kalbəs]   'calf's'

Although we have presented only a few forms here, they are representative of the facts in question about German. The criteria in the first list are evidenced by the data in the second in the following way. Criterion 1 is met by the fact that German has only voiceless obstruents in word-final position and therefore exhibits no voice contrast in this position. Criterion 2 is satisfied by the fact that some word-final voiceless obstruents alternate with word-medial voiced obstruents, as shown, for example, in *a* and *b*. Finally, the data in the second list meet criterion 3 by virtue of the fact that German has a voice contrast in medial position, as shown by *b* and *d*, and medial position is one of the positions which take part in the alternation.

Now, given these facts, we postulate the underlying representations shown in the list below along with a rule of Terminal Devoicing following it:

a. /tag/   e. /grad/
b. /tagə/   f. /gradə/
c. /dɛk/   g. /kalb/
d. /dɛkə/   h. /kalbəs/

Terminal Devoicing (TD)

[-sonorant] $\longrightarrow$ [-voice] / _____ #

(Word-final obstruents are voiceless)

This analysis of these facts of German is considered to be very well motivated for the following reasons: (1) The word-final voiced segments in the underlying representations are justified on the basis of the alternations and the existence of a voice contrast in medial positions, and (2) the rule of Terminal Devoicing accounts for the observed alternations and expresses a phonetically true generalization about word-final obstruents in German.

What is important in this example, for our purposes, is the nature of the evidence for both the underlying representations and the formulation of the rule. It is the observed alternations along with the medial voice contrast which motivates the postulation of word-final voiced segments underlyingly where only voiceless ones occur superficially.

The above methodology for the establishment of the existence of a neutralization rule must be contrasted with that in some of the literature on IL phonology. For example, Dickerson (1976) argues for a wave model analysis to account for the acquisition of English /l/ by a number of Japanese speakers. The purpose of Dickerson's wave model, which makes use of the variable rule below is to give a systematic account of what might otherwise be considered unsystematic performance.

$$\text{/l/} \longrightarrow \text{[l]} \; / \; \begin{bmatrix} \alpha & \text{[}-\text{cons]} \\ \beta & \text{[}+ \text{\O]} \\ \gamma & \text{[}-\text{high]} \end{bmatrix} \quad \underline{\qquad} \quad \begin{bmatrix} \delta & \begin{vmatrix} -\text{high} \\ +\text{low} \end{vmatrix} \\ \varepsilon & \begin{vmatrix} -\text{high} \\ +\text{low} \end{vmatrix} \end{bmatrix}$$

The Greek letter variables in this rule represent the environmental factors which affect the application of the rule. The alpha variable indicates the environment which has the greatest positive effect on the rule, the beta variable indicates the next greatest effect, and so on.

That Dickerson is postulating this rule as part of the IL of the speakers in question is clear from the following statement:

The input to the TD rule is the (l) word class of Japanese English. The output is the target variant which is enclosed in angle brackets to indicate variability, i.e. sometimes [l] is produced, and sometimes another variant. (Dickerson 1976, 225)

The problem with a rule like the one in Dickerson's wave model is that Dickerson presents no forms which show the necessary contrasts or alternations which would justify the postulation of the English phoneme /l/ in the underlying representation of the interlanguage forms. In the absence of such evidence, what a rule like this represents is a rule which states the relationship of the IL of the speaker in question to the grammar of English. More specifically, the rule provides a way of mapping TL forms into IL forms, which is different from an IL rule mapping underlying representations onto phonetic representations.

It is important to point out that we are not saying that a rule like the one in Dickerson's wave model could not conceivably be justified as part of the ILs of the speakers in Dickerson's study. However, in the absence of data showing the requisite contrasts and alternations, such a rule is nothing more than a statement of correspondence between the IL and TL in question, and has not been established as an IL rule.

Having considered the type of data necessary to motivate a phonological rule, we will now present some experimental data from the ILs of a number of English learners, and will consider the type of phonological rules which are motivated.

PROCEDURE

The data on which the proposed analysis is based were obtained from four students enrolled in the English as a Second Language Intensive Program at the University of Wisconsin—Milwaukee during the academic year 1978–79. These students were between the ages of eighteen and thirty. All of them had studied English in their own country before coming to Milwaukee, and all were placed in advanced-intermediate or advanced levels based on overall English proficiency. Two of the students, both males, are native speakers of Mandarin. The remainder, one female and one male, are native speakers of Colombian Spanish.

The data were obtained in three separate personal interviews where the subjects met individually with the investigator. Each interview lasted approximately one hour, during which time the subject's speech was recorded on tape. The three interviews with each subject were completed within a two-week period. The tapes were then transcribed by the investigator and independently by a research assistant. A reliability check between the two transcriptions revealed an agreement of ninety-two percent. This figure was determined by dividing the number of agreements between the investigator and research assistant by the number of agreements and disagreements.

During the interviews, different speech styles were elicited from each subject by means of a number of different tasks which he or she was to perform. The directions for each task were given both in writing and on tape, and were then followed by a practice, or warm-up, to ensure that the subject understood what he or she was to do. Each of the four tasks is described below.

The first task required that the subject listen to and repeat a list of randomly ordered words which were recorded on tape. The subject first listened to a word, immediately repeated it, then listened to another word, repeated it, and so on.

The next task was designed to elicit alternations from the subject. This was accomplished by having the subject read a word from a three-by-five card, and then produce a related form of this word. In each case, the related form was derived by the addition of one of the following morphemes: comparative, superlative, diminutive, or agentive. These forms were elicited by means of a cue written on the reverse side of the three-by-five card. Thus, for example, the subject was to read aloud the word *red,* which was typed on a card. The subject then was to flip the card over and on the reverse side would be typed, for example, *comparative,* whereupon seeing this cue, the subject was to say *redder.*

This particular exercise is designed to elicit any alternations between word-final and word-medial consonants which a subject may exhibit. Each subject was instructed in the use of the morphemes in question before the exercise and his or her understanding of the task involved was determined by means of a practice session where the task was performed on a different set of words. A similar exercise using related forms derived by adding certain prefixes such as *pre* and *re* was run to elicit any alternations between word-medial and word-initial obstruents.

Each subject was also given, as the third task, a modified cloze reading test. This consisted of a passage of approximately five hundred words with a blank in every second or third sentence. The blank was to be completed with one of the two forms which were provided adjacent to it. The purpose of the cloze test was to distract the subjects somewhat from paying close attention to their pronunciation. It was felt that, in this manner, a speech style which was less careful than reading style would be elicited.

For the final task, the subjects were asked to solve and discuss a riddle, or logical anecdote. The riddle was presented to each subject both in written form and aloud from a tape. The actual solution to the riddle was, of course, immaterial. It merely provided a common topic and impetus for conversation.

To recapitulate, data were elicited from each subject in four types of exercises. Three of the exercises were designed to elicit three distinct speech styles, and the other exercise was designed to elicit possible morphophonemic alternations. Representative forms of these data are shown in Tables 7.1 and 7.3.[1] We will now focus our attention on the analysis of these data.

ANALYSIS

Spanish

From the data in Table 7.1, we can see that both subjects 1 and 2, who are speakers of Colombian Spanish, produce a number of IL forms which have voiceless obstruents in word-final position where the corresponding TL forms have voiced obstruents. In addition to this fact, we can also see that some of the IL forms manifest alternations between word-final voiceless obstruents and word-medial voiced ones. The final fact that we need to note is that these IL forms exhibit a voice contrast word-initially, medially, and finally, since both voiced and voiceless obstruents occur in all of these positions.

These data parallel closely those discussed above for German in that the IL forms in question exhibit a voice contrast medially, and a voice alternation between some medial and final obstruents. However, the IL data depart from

130

this parallelism with German in that the IL manifests a voice contrast finally whereas German does not.

To account for the observed alternations and the medial voice contrast, we postulate the forms in Table 7.2 as underlying representations in the interlanguage of these subjects. The IL forms which exhibit voiceless segments where the corresponding TL forms have voiced segments are accounted for by assuming that the ILs in question contain a rule of Terminal Devoicing as stated above. However, there are two problems with positing a rule like the TD rule as part of these ILs.

The first problem with this rule in the present situation is that there exist forms which are counterexamples to this rule, namely, those IL forms with word-final voiced obstruents. The second problem is that, in view of these word-final voiced obstruents, the IL forms in Table 7.1 could possibly be explained by an alternative analysis.

Under this alternative, we would attempt to account for the observed alternations by postulating underlying voiceless obstruents along with a rule of Intervocalic Voicing (IV). Thus, for example, we would assume underlying forms like those below, along with a rule like the one that follows:

/fris/   'freeze'
/pɪk/   'pig'
/smuf/   'smooth'
/rɛt/   'red'

> Intervocalic Voicing (IV)
>
> [-sonorant] → [+voice] / [+syllabic] —— [+syllabic]
>
> (Obstruents are voiced between vowels)

A rule like IV is just as capable of accounting for the voice-voiceless alternations in forms like [fris] - [frizər] as is a rule like TD. Although there exist IL forms with word-medial voiceless obstruents, in contradiction to IV, there also exist IL forms with word-final voiced obstruents, in contradiction to TD. Thus, in terms of the alternations involved, both rules are equally supported.

It is possible, however, to choose between these alternative analyses on the basis of the voice contrast in word-final position. If we attempt to account for alternating forms like [rɛθ, rɛðər], 'red - redder,' by assuming an underlying form like /rɛθ/ along with a rule like IV, then we must postulate an additional rule which voices word-final obstruents to account for the fact that a speaker produces forms like [rɛd] in addition to [rɛθ] (see Table 7.1). Consequently, if we assume an analysis which postulates an intervocalic voicing rule like IV, we must postulate, in addition, a rule of final obstruent voicing.

On the other hand, if we assume underlying representations like those in Table 7.2, in which the underlying representation for alternating forms contains a word-final voiced obstruent, and if we assume a rule of terminal devoicing, then our analysis of the data requires only one rule, namely, TD.

TABLE 7.1. IL Data from Spanish Speakers

Subject	IL phonetic form	Gloss
1	[bɔp]	Bob
	[bɔbi]	Bobby
	[rɛt]	red
	[rɛðər]	redder
	[bik]	big
	[bigər ~ biɣər]	bigger
	[bref]	brave
	[brevər]	braver
	[prawt]	proud
	[prawdəst]	proudest
	[wɛt]	wet
	[wɛtər]	wetter
	[sik]	sick
	[sikəst]	sickest
	[ðə]	the
	[son]	zone
	[fʌsi]	fuzzy
	[faðər]	father
	[fris]	freeze
	[tæg]	tag
	[bɛd]	bed
	[pɪg]	pig
2	[rav]	rob
	[ravər]	robber
	[bɔp]	Bob
	[bɔbi]	Bobby
	[smuθ]	smooth
	[smuðər]	smoother
	[rɛθ ~ rɛð]	red
	[rɛðər]	redder
	[du]	do
	[riðu]	redo
	[bek]	bake
	[priβek]	prebake
	[wɛt]	wet
	[wɛtər]	wetter
	[sef]	safe
	[sefəst]	safest
	[ðə]	the
	[ðis]	this
	[pig]	pig
	[bæd]	bad
	[bɛt]	bed
	[bik ~ big ~ biɣ]	big

TABLE 7.2. Underlying Forms for Spanish Speakers

Subject	IL underlying form	Gloss
1	/bɔb/	Bob
	/bɔbi/	Bobby
	/rɛd/	red
	/rɛdər/	redder
	/big/	big
	/bigət/	bigger
	/brev/	brave
	/brevər/	braver
	/prawd/	proud
	/prawdəst/	proudest
	/wɛt/	wet
	/wɛtər/	wetter
	/sik/	sick
	/sikəst/	sickest
	/ðə/	the
	/son/	zone
	/fʌasi/	fuzzy
	/faðər/	father
	/fris/	freeze
	/tæg/	tag
	/bɛd/	bed
	/pɪg/	pig
2	/rab/	rob
	/rabər/	robber
	/bɔb/	Bob
	/bɔbi/	Bobby
	/smuð/	smooth
	/smuðər/	smoother
	/rɛd/	red
	/rɛdər/	redder
	/du/	do
	/ridu/	redo
	/bek/	bake
	/pribek/	prebake
	/wɛt/	wet
	/wɛtər/	wetter
	/sef/	safe
	/sefəst/	safest
	/ðə/	the
	/ðis/	this
	/pig/	pig
	/bæd/	bad
	/bɛd/	bed
	/big/	big

The problem presented by the IL forms which contradict this rule can be resolved if we assume that a rule like TD is an optional, or variable, rule as part of the IL in question.[2] Consequently, such a rule does not represent a phonetically-true generalization about the IL forms comparable to Terminal Devoicing as part of the grammar of German. This conclusion about the variable status of a rule like TD as part of an IL is in keeping with the generally held notion that ILs are variable, or unstable (Klein and Dittmar, 1979).

An additional reason for choosing the analysis which assumes a rule of Terminal Devoicing is that it enables us to predict the direction in which a learner tends to make errors involving voice contrasts. Inspection of the data in Table 7.1 reveals that the Spanish subjects always err in voice contrasts by substituting voiceless obstruents for voiced ones, and never the reverse. Moreover, such errors always occur in word-final position and never word-medially. These facts are readily accounted for by assuming the IL of these subjects contains a rule of terminal devoicing.

This interpretation of the facts is consistent with the widely held idea (Corder, 1967) that language-learning errors are systematic. Since the grammar of the TL does not contain a rule like TD, the systematicity in errors that one should expect from a learner who has internalized this rule as part of his or her IL is that errors should always be in the direction of substituting word-final voiceless obstruents for voiced ones, and never the opposite.

Another set of alternations observed in Table 7.1 involves some word-medial voiced spirants which alternate with either word-initial or word-final obstruents. In some cases the word-initial and final segments which participate in these alternations are stops and in other cases they are fricatives. The forms below illustrate some of these alternations.

IL forms		TL gloss	
[rɛt]	[rɛðər]	'red'	'redder'
[du]	[riðu]	'do'	'redo'
[bek]	[prißek]	'bake'	'prebake'
[pix]	[pigi]	'pig'	'piggy'

In addition to these alternations, we also note that all of the subjects exhibit a contrast between stops and fricatives in initial, medial, and final position.

Applying the same type of argumentation as in the case of Terminal Devoicing, we account for the observed alternations by postulating underlying forms with stops and deriving the spirants from a rule of Postvocalic Spirantization, formulated as below:

Postvocalic Spirantization

$$\begin{bmatrix} \text{-sonorant} \\ \text{+voice} \end{bmatrix} \longrightarrow [\text{+continuant}] \, / \, [\text{+syllabic}] \underline{\hspace{2cm}}$$

(Voiced obstruents are spirantized after vowels)

The justification for this analysis over one which postulates underlying spirants along with a rule of occlusion is essentially the same as that used for the analysis with the rule of Terminal Devoicing. More specifically, if we postulate underlying spirants along with a rule which derives intervocalic stops, we would need, in addition, a rule which derives stops word-finally. On the other hand, if we postulate a rule of spirantization, we need only one rule to account for the observed alternations, and the fact that there exist forms with postvocalic voiced stops is accounted for by assuming the spirantization rule is optional, or variable. Finally, the rule of Postvocalic Spirantization enables us to predict the direction in which the learner will make errors. Thus, all errors made in the production of stop-fricative contrasts are in the direction of substituting spirants in IL forms for corresponding stops in the TL, and never the reverse.

Mandarin

Turning now to the data in Table 7.3, which were elicited from the two Mandarin speakers, we see that the errors that these speakers make are somewhat different from those made by the Spanish speakers. More specifically, the data in Table 7.3 show that the difficulty the Mandarin speakers have with word-final voiced obstruents is reflected in the fact that they sometimes produce a schwa following what is the word-final consonant in the TL.

Given these phonetic forms, we postulate the underlying representations shown in Table 7.4, and we assume that the interlanguage of the speakers in question contains a rule of Schwa Paragoge, formulated below:

Schwa Paragoge

$$\emptyset \longrightarrow \textschwa \ / \ \begin{bmatrix} \text{-sonorant} \\ \text{+voice} \end{bmatrix} \underline{\hspace{2cm}}$$

(Add a schwa following a word-final voiced obstruent)

Thus, given an underlying representation like /tæg/'tag,' the rule of Schwa Paragoge can apply to produce [tægə]. The existence of IL forms like [tæg], without word-final schwas, is accounted for by assuming that Schwa Paragoge, like Terminal Devoicing and Postvocalic Spirantization, is an optional, or variable, rule.

An alternative to this analysis would be to postulate underlying representations with final schwas, like those in *a* below along with a rule like b, which deletes final schwas.

a. Underlying IL form   TL gloss
    /tægə/   'tag'
    /tɔbə/   'tub'
    /hizə/   'he's'

TABLE 7.3. IL Data from Mandarin Speakers

Subject	IL phonetic form	Gloss
3	[tæg ~ tægə]	tag
	[rab ~ rabə]	rob
	[hæd ~ hæsə]	had
	[hiz ~ hizə]	he's
	[smuðə]	smoother
	[rayt]	right
	[dɛk]	deck
	[zɪp]	zip
	[mɪs]	miss
	[wɛt]	wet
	[dɪfər]	differ
	[ovər]	over
	[bɪgər]	bigger
	[kɪkɪn]	kicking
	[tægɪn]	tapping
	[lebər]	label
	[lɛtər]	letter
	[blidɪn]	bleeding
	[lidə]	leader
4	[ænd ~ ændə]	and
	[hæd ~ hædə]	had
	[tɔb ~ tɔbə]	tub
	[staɒɪd ~ staɒɪdə]	started
	[fiud ~ fiudə]	filled
	[bɪg ~ bɪgə]	big
	[rɛkənayzdə]	recognized
	[ɪz ~ ɪzə]	is
	[sɛz ~ sɛzə]	says
	[wɔtə]	water
	[afə]	offer
	[lidə]	leader

b. ə → Ø $\begin{bmatrix} \text{-sonorant} \\ \text{+voice} \end{bmatrix}$ ——— #

(Delete a word-final schwa that follows a voiced obstruent)

However, such an analysis must be rejected because there exist IL forms like those listed below with superficial word-final schwas which never alternate with null.

IL form	TL gloss
[lidə]	'leader'
[ovə]	'over'

In other words, a rule which deletes word-final schwas cannot explain why the forms just above never alternate, but that other forms with word-final schwas

TABLE 7.4. Underlying forms for Mandarin speakers

Subject	IL underlying form	Gloss
3	/tæg/	tag
	/rab/	rob
	/hæd/	had
	/hiz/	he's
	/smuðə/	smoother
	/rayt/	right
	/dɛk/	deck
	/zɪp/	zip
	/mɪs/	mis
	/wɛt/	wet
	/dɪfər/	differ
	/ovər/	over
	/bɪgər/	bigger
	/kɪkɪn/	kicking
	/tæpɪn/	tapping
	/lebər/	label
	/lɛər/	letter
	/blidɪn/	bleeding
	/lidə/	leader
4	/ænd/	and
	/hæd/	had
	/tɔb/	tub
	/sta/ɒɪd/	started
	/fiud/	filled
	/bɪg/	big
	/rekənayzd/	recognized
	/ɪz/	is
	/sɛz/	says
	/wɔtə/	water
	/afə/	offer
	/lidə/	leader

(like [tægə], [tebə] etc.) do alternate. In view of these data, we opt for the analysis which postulates a rule of Schwa Paragoge.

A summary of the analyses proposed in this section is shown in Table 7.5.

DISCUSSION

Independence of the IL Rules

Given these analyses of the data, the question arises as to the relationship between these interlanguages and the respective NLs. We can ask this question from two perspectives: First, what is the relationship between a learner's IL and his or her NL; and, second, what is the relationship between a learner's IL and first languages in general?

TABLE 7.5. Summary of Native Languages, Target Language, and Resultant Interlanguages

Native languages	Target language	Interlanguages
Spanish	*English*	
No voice contrast in final position	Voice contrast in final position	Rule of Terminal Devoicing
Sonorants and some voiced and voiceless obstruents allowed in final position	Voiced and voiceless obstruents and sonorants allowed in final position	
Mandarin		
No voice contrast in final position		Rule of Schwa Paragoge
Only sonorants allowed in final position		

To answer the first question, we can show that the rules of TD and Schwa Paragoge which we have postulated are independent of the respective NLs and the TL in that these rules cannot be motivated for either of the NLs in question, or for the TL. A rule like Postvocalic Spiranticization, which is similar to a rule which is motivated for the NL, is somewhat independent of the NL because it functions differently in the IL than it does in the NL.[3]

Turning first to the rule of Postvocalic Spiranticization, it is clear that a rule which is at least similar in form is necessary for Spanish because of the existence of forms like those below:

a. [donde]   'where'   d. [laɣata]   'the cat (f.)'
b. [deðonde]   'from where'   e. [boɣa]   'vogue'
c. [gata]   'cat (f.)'   f. [laßoɣa]   'the vogue'

What is important, however, is that the rule which is motivated for the NL functions as an allophonic rule, producing voiced, spirant allophones of the corresponding stop phonemes. The rule of Postvocalic Spiranticization, on the other hand, functions as a neutralization rule, since both /d/ and /ð/ exist as phonemes in the IL. Thus, while one might argue that Postvocalic Spiranticization is structurally similar to the NL rule needed to account for the forms in *a* through *f* above, it is clear that in terms of the function of the two rules, Postvocalic Spiranticization is an independent rule.

An even stronger case can be made for the independence of Terminal Devoicing and Schwa Paragoge. Turning first to the former, it is clear that, since English has a voice contrast in initial, medial, and final position, and since English exhibits no regular voice alternations between final and medial obstruents, a rule like TD is not motivated for the TL.[4]

When we consider the facts from Spanish, it is clear that a rule of Terminal Devoicing is also not motivated for the NL. More specifically, although Spanish has no superficial voice contrast in stops in either word-medial or -final position, and has no such contrast in fricatives in word-final position, it exhibits no morphophonemic alternations which would motivate a rule of Terminal Devoicing.[5] Thus a rule like TD as part of the ILs in question must be considered to be an independent rule.

We come to the same conclusion when we consider the rule of Schwa Paragoge. First of all, in terms of the formulation of the rule, it cannot be similar to any rule in the grammar of Mandarin since Mandarin has no voice contrast in any word-position. In fact, the only voiced obstruents which Mandarin has are word-medial (Dow, 1972) and are in complementary distribution with word-initial obstruents, which are all voiceless. In word-final position, Mandarin allows only sonorant consonants and vowels. Moreover, Mandarin has no forms or alternations which would motivate a rule of word-final epenthesis, regardless of the context.

On the basis of this evidence we conclude that a rule like Schwa Paragoge could not have been transferred from the NL. Likewise, since there is no motivation for a rule like Schwa Paragoge in English, it is not the case that this rule could have been learned as a TL rule. Consequently, we conclude that Schwa Paragoge is an independent rule in the interlanguage in question.

EXPLANATION FOR THE IL RULES

The conclusion that rules like TD and Schwa Paragoge are independent IL rules does not mean that such rules have no rationale or explanation. On the contrary, it will be argued that these rules are explainable on the basis of (1) a comparison of the NLs and TL involved, and (2) principles of second language learning.

It has already been pointed out that both Mandarin and Spanish differ from English in that English has a superficial voice contrast in initial, medial, and final positions, whereas Spanish has a superficial voice contrast only initially and medially. Therefore, a speaker of one of these languages, in attempting to acquire the TL, must learn to produce a voice contrast in final position when the NL is Spanish and in all positions when the NL is Mandarin.[6]

Now it has been argued on independent grounds in Eckman (1977) that it is more difficult to acquire a voice contrast in final position than in medial position and that it is more difficult to acquire this contrast in medial position than in initial position. The principle which predicts this difficulty is the Markedness Differential Hypothesis (MDH), which is formulated as below:

Markedness Differential Hypothesis (MDH)   Those areas of the TL which will be difficult are those areas which are
1. different from the NL, and
2. relatively more marked than the NL.

The notion of *markedness* used for this hypothesis is the notion of typological markedness, which is defined below:

Markedness A phenomenon A in some language is more marked relative to some other phenomenon B if, cross-linguistically, the presence of A in a language necessarily implies the presence of B, but the presence of B does not necessarily imply the presence of A.

The relative degree of difficulty of maintaining a voice contrast in initial, medial, and final positions follows from the fact that final position is the most marked position for a voice contrast, medial position is less marked, and initial position is least marked (Dinnsen and Eckman, 1978).

Given these relative degrees of difficulty, it is reasonable to assume that a learner will acquire a voice contrast in initial position before acquiring this contrast medially, and that he or she will acquire a voice contrast medially before acquiring such a contrast finally. A situation in which a learner has acquired a voice contrast medially, but not finally, will produce forms in the IL like those in Table 1, in which the learner correctly produces the contrast medially, but errs in word-final position. The resultant alternations, as we have seen, motivate a rule like TD. Thus what explains this rule is (1) the difference in voice contrast between NL and TL, and (2) the MDH, which predicts the directionality of difficulty.

A similar argument can be constructed to explain the rule of Schwa Paragoge as part of the ILs of the Mandarin speakers. We note, first of all, that the NL lacks a voice contrast finally by virtue of the fact that only vowels and sonorant consonants can occur word-finally. Thus we can say that Mandarin has a surface phonetic constraint (SPC) against any obstruents occurring in word-final position. If we assume that such a constraint is also part of the IL,[7] and further, if we assume the underlying representations in Table 4, then we can give a plausible reason as to why Schwa Paragoge should be part of the ILs involved.

More specifically, since some of the underlying representations which are motivated for the ILs have obstruents word-finally, and since word-final obstruents are excluded by the above-mentioned SPC, some rule must apply to the underlying form. A rule of Terminal Devoicing which produces word-final voiceless obstruents is not satisfactory, because its output still violates the SPC. A rule of final consonant deletion would satisfy the SPC in some cases, but not in others where the form ended in an obstruent cluster. Moreover, a rule of final consonant deletion seems counterproductive from the point of view of the speaker. The underlying forms for the IL indicate that the learner knows that some TL forms have word-final voiced obstruents, despite the fact that these obstruents are difficult to pronounce. If, in attempting to deal with these word-final voiced obstruents, a learner internalized a rule of final voiced obstruent deletion, such a rule would drastically alter the form of the underlying representation. That is, a rule which applies to /tæg/ to produce [tæ] would neutralize the distinction between [tæg], [tæd], and [tæb]. Thus we would not expect a learner in this situation to internalize either a rule of Terminal Devoicing or Final Obstruent Deletion.

On the other hand, a rule which adds a final schwa has the following effects: (1) it always creates a form which will satisfy the SPC, and (2) it maintains the canonical form of the intended TL word. Consequently, given a TL like English, which has word-final obstruents, and given an NL like Mandarin, which has an SPC prohibiting word-final obstruents, and finally given the MDH which predicts the difficulty of word-final voice contrasts, it seems reasonable that the respective IL would contain a rule like Schwa Paragoge.

To sum up this section, we have argued that the rules of TD and Schwa Paragoge are explainable, or at least plausible, given the MDH and the nature of the respective NLs and the TL. We shall now focus our attention on whether such rules are found in the grammars of "normal" languages, that is, languages acquired as a first language.

Naturalness of the IL Rules

Having shown the independence of the rules of TD and Schwa Paragoge for the ILs in question, we now raise the issue of whether such rules are motivated for the grammars of other languages. The answer with respect to TD is a quick and straightforward affirmative. In addition to German, this rule is motivated for the grammars of Catalan, Polish, and Russian. Thus, it is clear that TD is a rule which is found in the grammars of languages which are acquired as first languages. In the case of Schwa Paragoge, however, the answer is negative. According to Sanders (1979), such a rule is not motivated for the grammar of any language which is acquired as a first language. This being the case, we must determine why such a rule should be motivated for the Mandarin-English interlanguage in question.

There are, a priori, a number of possible explanations for a rule like Schwa Paragoge being motivated as part of an IL. To cite just two, we could say that (1) first and second language acquisition are fundamentally different processes and therefore one would not expect the systems which are acquired to be similar, or (2) the rule of Schwa Paragoge can be attributed to the language contact situation. Since such language contact is not involved in first language acquisition, we would not expect a rule like Schwa Paragoge to be motivated for first languages.

On the basis of the evidence presented, a reasonable case can be made for the explanation of a rule like Schwa Paragoge on the basis of the language contact involved. Specifically, a rule like this is necessary to resolve the conflict between the underlying representations for the IL forms and the SPC. Since the motivated underlying representations contain word-final voiced obstruents which are in conflict with the SPC, a rule like Schwa Paragoge is necessary to resolve this conflict (see section under Explanations for the IL Rules). The non-occurrence of a rule like Schwa Paragoge as part of the grammar of first languages is reasonably correlated with the fact that such languages do not have both SPCs which prohibit word-final obstruents and underlying representations which contain word-final voiced obstruents. This situation can arise, however, in a second language learning situation in which the TL allows word-final voiced obstruents and the NL excludes them. Thus the non-existence of rules like Schwa Paragoge as part of the grammar of other languages can be explained.

The question of how ILs relate to other language systems has been raised in a different context by Adjémian (1976). We can see from the following passages that Adjémian takes the position that ILs are natural languages which are not significantly different from other languages.

To begin with, underlying the IL hypothesis is the unwritten assumption that IL's are linguistic systems in the same way that Natural Languages are. (By 'natural language' I mean any human language shared by a community of speakers and developed over time by a general process of evolution.) That is, IL's are natural languages. This assumption is the *sine qua non* of the IL hypothesis. (Adjémian 1976, 298)

From the position that IL's are natural languages that contain a system of rules (of some sort), it follows that they must also be subject to general constraints on the possible form of natural languages. In other words, IL's must be like "normal" languages in their structure. (p. 299)

The *"sine qua non* of the IL hypothesis" is the assumption that interlanguages are *systematic,* not that they are "linguistic systems in the same way that natural languages are." Underlying the IL hypothesis is the assumption that interlanguages are systematic enough to enable scientific description. Indeed, the notion of interlanguage loses all of its interest if ILs are beyond such description. But it does not follow from this assumption that ILs are linguistic systems in the same way as natural languages. This is true because an IL could conceivably be systematic and yet contain rules which are totally unlike those found in the grammars of natural languages.

Second, to assume, as Adjémian does, that ILs are natural languages is to assume what one should want to demonstrate. As Adjémian puts it, the question of whether ILs are like other natural languages can never be raised because the answer is assumed from the start. The issue becomes an empirical question if we attempt to describe ILs using the same framework and methodology as we use for other natural languages, and then compare IL grammars with the grammars of other languages.

Consider, as an example, the interlanguages described in this paper. We have argued that at least some IL rules, such as those of TD and Postvocalic Spiranticization, are similar to rules that are motivated for the grammars of other natural languages. But on the other hand, we have argued that a rule like Schwa Paragoge is motivated only for the grammars of interlanguages. Given this conclusion, one can say that ILs differ from other languages in a way that other languages do not differ from each other. That is, languages acquired as a first language do not vary such that the grammar of one language contains a rule of Schwa Paragoge and the others do not.

This distinction between ILs and other languages was established on the basis of empirical evidence. Now, conceivably, one could conclude on the basis of this evidence that ILs are different from other natural languages (that is, they are not natural languages), or that their grammars are not subject to the same constraints as the grammars of other languages. The position taken in this paper, however, is that such a conclusion would be unenlightening because it is possible to correlate the Schwa Paragoge rule with other facts about the NL and TL. Consequently, we can attribute such a rule to the language contact situation. In other words, it seems to be possible to predict when a learner would internalize a rule of Schwa Paragoge. The point remains, however, that if the nature of interlanguages is to remain an interesting question, it must be determined on empirical, rather than a priori, grounds.

CONCLUSION

In this paper, we have provided data and arguments for the postulation of three interlanguage phonological rules, namely, Terminal Devoicing, Postvocalic Spirantization, and Schwa Paragoge. We considered these rules from the point of view of whether they were independent of the NL and TL, and of whether they could be considered "natural." It was concluded that, although Schwa Paragoge is apparently not motivated for the grammar of any language acquired as a first language, it should not be considered an "unnatural" rule because its presence in the grammar of an interlanguage can be correlated with other facts about the NL and TL involved.

NOTES

1. The forms shown in the tables are actual utterances which are representative of the forms that occurred in all of the elicited speech styles. That is, an utterance type was not listed in the tables unless it occurred in all of the tasks which were performed.

2. If we view the TD rule as a variable rule then it must be reformulated using the variables associated with the various environments and conditions under which the rule applies. Since I did not attempt to determine the applicational conditions associated with this, or any rule discussed in this paper, the exact formulation of such rules must be left as an open question.

3. Josh Ard has pointed out to me that the independence of these rules may differ depending on the phonological theory. Thus, for example, a rule like TD would not be considered independent of the NL involved in this case by Natural Phonology, because a rule like TD is considered to be a universal process, and therefore part of the grammar of all languages. The fact that some languages do not evidence such a rule is explained by Natural Phonology by positing that universal processes are suppressed by children during the acquisition of the language if the language being acquired

contains forms which contradict the rule; that is, forms with word-final voiced obstruents, in this case. If no such contradictory forms exist, the process remains part of the grammar, that is, is not suppressed, even if there are no forms to which the process in question could apply.

If, for the sake of argument, these assumptions of Natural Phonology are granted, we could still argue for the independence of the IL in question on the basis that the IL *forms* themselves are different from those of both the NL and TL in that the IL forms exhibit alternations but the NL and TL forms do not.

4. It is assumed here that forms like *leaf-leaves, wife-wives* do not constitute a regular voice-voiceless alternation.

5. Spanish exhibits a superficial voice contrast in fricatives in forms like [axo] "garlic" and [aɣo] "I do." However, [x] and [ɣ] belong to /x/ and /g/, respectively, which differ in continuancy as well as voice. Spanish also has a superficial contrast medially between [t] and [ð], which differ in voice and continuancy on the phonetic level, but belong to /t/ and /d/, respectively. Depending on how one views these contrasts, it may be possible to conclude that Spanish has a voice contrast only in stops and only in initial position.

6. In the case of Spanish, it is reasonable to assume that initial and medial voice contrasts can be transferred from the NL, but see note 5.

7. It is clear that this constraint, at least as part of the IL in question, cannot be a true SPC since SPCs are exceptionless. I have no proposal to make in this area, and therefore will leave open the question of whether ILs can contain SPCs which have exceptions.

REFERENCES

Adjémian, C. 1976. On the nature of interlanguage systems. *Language Learning, 26,* 297–320.

Corder, S.P. 1967. The significance of learners' errors. *IRAL, 5,* 161–169.

Corder, S.P. 1971. Idiosyncratic dialects and error analysis. *IRAL, 9,* 147–159.

Dickerson, W. 1976. The psycholinguistic unity of language learning and language change. *Language Learning, 26,* 215–231. (Also this volume.)

Dinnsen, D., and F. Eckman. 1978. Some substantive universals in atomic phonology. *Lingua, 45,* 1–14.

Dow, F.D.M. 1972. *An Outline of Mandarin Phonetics.* Canberra: Australian National University Press.

Dulay, H., and M. Burt. 1974. A new perspective on the creative construction process in child second language acquisition. *Language Learning, 24,* 253–278.

Eckman, F. 1977. Markedness and the contrastive analysis hypothesis. *Language Learning, 27,* 315–330. (Also this volume.)

Kenstowicz, M., and C. Kisseberth. 1979. *Generative Phonology.* New York: Academic Press.

Klein, W., and N. Dittmar. 1979. *Developing Grammars: The Acquisition of German Syntax by Foreign Workers.* Berlin: Springer Verlag.

Sanders, G. 1979. Equational rules and rule functions in phonology. In Dinnsen, D. (Ed.), *Current Approaches to Phonological Theory.* Bloomington, Ind.: Indiana University Press.

Selinker, L. 1972. Interlanguage. *IRAL, 10,* 209–231.

Part Three

THE SEGMENT

The articles in Part Three research the acquisition of the segment. All five articles examine production difficulties, but they do so from different perspectives. Several articles rely on the perceptual acuity of the experimenters; others utilize acoustic measurements, often in combination with native speaker evaluations. The results in all cases allow the authors to formulate new hypotheses concerning the nature of L2 phonological acquisition.

The first article, by Altenberg and Vago, analyzes English L2 data provided by two native speakers of Hungarian, both of whom are at a fossilized stage of second language development. Through an examination of their output errors the authors find that while transfer is prevalent, it is not the only influence on acquisition. They determine that some errors are the result of the application of unmarked rules. Rules of this type occur neither in the NL nor the TL, but rather are natural phonological processes belonging to the learner's repertoire of innate simplification mechanisms. They also find that the rules most likely to be transferred from the NL into the interlanguage are rules that apply late in the derivation of the NL and are considered to be low-level rules.

145

Beebe, in her study, questions several widely-held myths concerning the acquisition of a new phonology by adults. Her findings are based on a comparison of data from five Asian language groups, elicited using the same instrument. By examining their pronunciation of six English phonemes, she concludes that:

1. Most errors do not result from the substitution of a L1 phoneme for a L2 phoneme.
2. Many of the phones produced were found in neither the NL nor the TL but were unique to the IL.
3. As the learner becomes more proficient, the number of phonetic variants decreases rather than increases.
4. Interlanguage phonologies are subject to the same sociolinguistic variation found in native languages.

Flege and Hillenbrand examine a number of important issues in IL phonology using both perceptual and acoustic criteria. Since it is the case that some sounds in a L2 are judged as new by the learner and others are given an interlingual identification, they attempt to determine whether a new L2 sound is produced with more accuracy than one with a direct counterpart in the L1. Previous literature has suggested that the new phone will be hardest to master. They compare the acquisition of French /u/ and /y/ by American English speakers. They find that, in fact, it is the new sound that is produced most accurately. They hypothesize that the learner's difficulty with a nearly identical phone is a perceptual one. The learner perceives the target phone as belonging to the same category as the L1 phone and thus does not attend to the acoustic differences between the two sounds. Nevertheless, these authors find phonetic approximations occurring in the production of French /t/ vs. English /t/ where bilingual speakers of French and English appear to produce these target sounds with voice onset time (VOT) values somewhere between the values for monolingual French and English speakers.

The study by Nathan, Anderson, and Budsayamongkon also utilizes acoustic measurements in the analysis of voice onset time. These authors investigate the acquisition of the VOT of English voiceless stops by native Spanish speakers. They point out that when examined from a perceptual perspective, learners tend to judge VOT values categorically, grouping together different VOT values according to the learner's L1 boundaries. They ask whether the same is true of the production of a new VOT value in the L2. Is it acquired in a gradual or all-or-none fashion? Their findings show that, as proficiency increases, the L2 VOT value gradually approximates the native speaker's. This finding is corroborated by evidence in the Flege and Hillenbrand study. Here is a case where production and perception in the acquisition of a L2 apparently diverge.

There are few studies that are concerned with the acquisition of a L2 phonology by children. The study by Hecht and Mulford is one of them. They wish to determine the extent to which either developmental or transfer processes are employed when a child learns a new phonology. Their subject is a six-year-old Icelandic boy acquiring English. The authors find evidence for the existence of both processes. Transfer, they determine, is the best predictor of the relative difficulty of a particular L2 segment, while developmental criteria best account for the phone that is substituted. In essence then, this study points out clearly that L2 phonological acquisition involves some systematic interaction between developmental and transfer strategies. This accords with the findings of several of the other studies in this volume.

8

THEORETICAL IMPLICATIONS OF AN ERROR ANALYSIS OF SECOND LANGUAGE PHONOLOGY PRODUCTION*

Evelyn P. Altenberg   Robert M. Vago

Investigators have long been intrigued by the relationship between the native language (NL) and the target language (TL) in second language phonology. Historically, the attempt to discover and explain the characteristics of second language phonology has been approached from a number of different perspectives. The contrastive analysis approach (e.g., Lado, 1957) assumes that all speakers' deviations from the target language norm are due to interference from the native language and attempts to predict where such deviations will occur. The error analysis approach (e.g., Corder, 1967) examines speakers' second language errors without any preconceived notions as to their cause. The approach proposed by Eckman, (1981), which we shall refer to as the *autonomous system analysis,* analyzes the phonology of the second language speaker as a system unto itself and then attempts to account for the characteristics of that system.

*This is a substantially revised version of a paper which appeared in *C U N Y Forum,* No. 3, 1977. A shorter version of this work was presented at the Applied Linguistics Winter Conference, Columbia University, February 13, 1981. We wish to thank Cindy Greenberg for valuable comments and suggestions.

This paper presents an error analysis of the second language (English) speech of two native speakers of Hungarian. The analysis and discussion will address four related issues of second language phonology.

It has long been acknowledged that transfer exists in adult second language phonology. Indeed, this fact must be obvious once it is recognized that listeners can discriminate, say, a French accent from a Chinese accent in English. This discrimination would not be possible if speakers did not consistently incorporate some characteristics of their native language into the production of their second language. However, it is not necessarily true that all aspects of native language phonology transfer to the target language. Our first goal will be a consideration of the constraints on transfer in second language phonology.

Second, the data presented here will allow an investigation of those factors other than transfer (see, for example, Richards and Sampson, 1974, and Tarone, 1978) which are involved in the target language production of our subjects.

Third, a description of the factors contributing to second language phonology will enable us to define "foreign accent" and to begin to clarify more strictly the notion of a "better" or "worse" foreign accent.

Our final goal is to compare the error analysis approach and its findings with the autonomous system analysis approach. It will be argued that each approach provides unique information and that both need to be used together in order to provide the most insight into second language phonology.

METHOD

Subjects

Our subjects were two native speakers of Hungarian who spoke English as a second language. Subject A was 56, female, and had had no formal education in the United States. Subject B was 29, male, and had had eight years of higher education in the United States, including a doctorate. Both subjects had lived in the United States for 12 years at the time of the study and were not actively involved in improving their second language skills. We can assume, then, that much of their phonology had become fossilized.

Materials and Procedure

Since we were interested in investigating second language production, our goal was to elicit a variety of sounds in different contexts. Subjects were asked to read a passage (see Appendix A) taken from Fairbanks (1940). This passage was selected because it has a wide variety of sounds in different phonological environments. While we recognize the limitations of using a formal reading style (e.g., Tarone, 1979), this method was chosen for two reasons: (a) Subjects would be unable to use avoidance as a strategy (Schachter, 1974) and (b) the pronunciation of words would be elicited within the context of a series of related sentences, rather than in isolation.

The readings were tape-recorded, subsequently transcribed into broad phonetic notation, and compared to educated New York American English pronunciation. A set of rules mapping American English (AE) onto Hungarian-accented English (HE) was then written for each speaker.

RESULTS

The transcriptions of the passages as read by subjects A and B are presented in Appendixes B and C, respectively. In the appendixes, each sentence is indexed for ease of reference. The analysis reported here includes only the most obvious mapping rules. The transcriptions in the appendixes exclude information on intonation, vocalic length, aspiration, and similar precise phonetic detail, although some of these are mentioned in the text when necessary to the analysis. Stress is indicated only when it is placed incorrectly (e.g., [hórizon], subject A's S3) or when it is extra heavy (e.g., [kansíderɛd], subject A's S11).

The mapping rules reveal four types of errors: transfer errors, errors due to the application of unmarked rules, spelling pronunciation errors, and idiosyncratic pronunciation errors. Each type of error will be described in turn.

Transfer Errors

The facts and analysis of the Hungarian sound system used here are taken from Vago (1980). There are two groups of mapping rules which can be described as being due to transfer from Hungarian. The first type is called *phonetic transfer:* A sound which occurs in Hungarian is substituted for an English sound which does not occur in Hungarian.

Subject A employed extensive, consistent, and pervasive phonetic transfer. The following generalizations can be noted:

Consonants		Vowels	
AE	HE	AE	HE
C^h →	C	I →	i
w →	v^1	U →	u
θ →	t	æ →	ε
ð →	d^2		
retroflex → trill			

The above errors are attributed to transfer: None of the AE sounds occurs in Hungarian, while all of the HE sounds do.

In addition, both AE[ɔ] and [ʌ] were substituted in Subject A's speech, either by HE [ɒ] or [a]:[3]

150

a. AE [ʌ] → HE [ɒ]
   sunlight [sɒnlayt] (S1)
   one [wɒn] (S5)
   other [ɒdör] (S12)
   was [vɒs] (S13)
   sun's [sɒnts] (S13)
   of [ɒv] ~ [ɒf] (S16–S19)
   result [rizɒlt] (S18)
b. AE [ʌ] → HE [a]
   colors [kalörs] (S2)
   one [wan] (S4)
   but [bat] (S5, S14)
   something [samtiŋg] (S6)
   some [sam] (S8)
   was [vaz] (S9, S10)
   considered [kansidɛrɛd] (S11)
   considerably [kansidɛrebl] (S16)
   upon [apn] (S16), [apon] (S18)
   colored [kalörɛd] (S16)
   observed [apsörvɛd] (S17)
   number [nambɛr] (S17)
c. AE [ɔ] → HE [ɒ]
   water [wɒtɛr] (S16)
   falls [fɒls] (S18)
d. AE [ɔ] → HE [a]
   long [laŋg] (S3)
   war [var] (S10)

The choice between HE [ɒ] and [a] does not appear to be rule governed. Note in particular the variant pronunciations of *one* ([wɒn] (S5) ~ [wan] (S4)) and *was* ([vɒs] (S13) ~ [vaz] (S9, S10)). Hungarian has [ɒ] and [a], but lacks [ɔ] and [ʌ].

AE [ə] was consistently pronounced as [ö] in stressed and post-stressed positions; Hungarian lacks the vowel [ə], e.g., *the* [dö] (S0, S1, S2, etc.), *colors* [kalörs] (S2), *miracle* [mirökl] (S8), *other* [ɒdör] (S12), *colored* [kalörɛd] (S16), *first* [först] (S18). In prestressed positions AE [ə] was pronounced as a weak, short [a], here symbolized as [ă], e.g., *above* [ăbōuv] (S3), *considered* [kănsidɛrɛd] (S11), *considerable* [kănsidɛrébl̩] (S16).

Similar substitutions occurred in subject B's speech, but the substitutions were less consistent. AE [ð] was pronounced as [d], aspirated consonants were deaspirated, and retroflexed *r* was trilled sporadically, rather than generally. For instance, subject B had a retroflexed *r* in the words *raindrops* (S1), *air* (S1), *considered* (S11), but a trilled *r* in the words *rainbow* (S1), *form* (S1), *apparently* (S3). The choice between [ð] and [d] for AE [ð] was apparently unpredictable. Thus, in the phrase *of the,* the definite article was pronounced with [ð] in S13 and S18, and with [d] in S6, S16, S18; for other examples, see Appendix C. Aspiration was likewise vacillating, although neither aspiration nor trilling is indicated in the transcriptions in Appendixes B and C.

We may say then that the above substitutions were optional in subject B's speech. There were also two general and consistent sets of substitutions. AE [æ] was pronounced with higher tongue position, between [æ] and [ɛ]; the symbol [æ] is used here for this pronunciation. Further, AE [ɔ] was pronounced with a lower tongue body, as [ɒ]. All of the above sound substitutions are attributed to phonetic transfer: Hungarian lacks [ð], retroflexed *r*, aspirated consonants, [æ], and [ɔ]; instead, it has [d], trilled *r*, unaspirated consonants, [ɛ], and [ɒ].

The second type of interference can be called *phonological transfer:* A phonological rule of Hungarian is applied to English. We found one example of phonological transfer in our data: Subject A frequently, but not always, applied the Hungarian voicing assimilation rule to English.

The Hungarian voicing assimilation rule assimilates an obstruent in voicing to a following obstruent. This voicing assimilation process takes place within a word as well as between words:

Hungarian Regressive Voicing Assimilation

$$[\text{-son}] \longrightarrow [\propto \text{voi}]/ \underline{\hspace{1.5cm}} (\#) \begin{bmatrix} \text{-son} \\ \propto \text{voi} \end{bmatrix}$$

Subject A applied the Hungarian voicing assimilation rule in the following pronunciations of the English data:

a. according to [ɛkordiŋk tu] (S4)
   boiling pot [boyliŋk pat] (S4)
   beyond his [biyont hiz] (S6)
   looking for [lukiŋk for] (S6)
   have tried [hɛf trayt] (S12)
b. observed [apsörvɛd] (S17)

In each of the examples in *a* above, the last obstruent consonant of the first word is devoiced in anticipation of the initial voiceless obstruent of the next word. The assimilation of a voiceless obstruent to a following voiced obstruent is evident in *about the* [aboud dö] (S15). In *b* above, the obstruent *b* is devoiced to [p] before the following obstruent [s]. The [s] pronunciation is probably due to the spelling (see the discussion on spelling pronunciation below).

It might be argued that the voiceless velar stop [k] in the words ending in -*ing* in 4*a* above is inserted by rule. This putative rule would insert, following the velar nasal [ŋ], the voiceless velar stop [k] before a word beginning with a voiceless obstruent, and the voiced velar stop [g] before a word beginning with a voiced obstruent (as in [samtiŋg biyont], subject A's S6). Note, however, that this analysis would not account for the examples [biyont hiz], [hɛf trayt], and [apsörvɛd]. In these examples the Hungarian voicing assimilation rule applies uncontroversially. Thus positing the insertion rule in addition to the voicing assimilation rule would be superfluous.

The phonotactic effect of the Hungarian Regressive Voicing Assimilation rule is that in Hungarian, obstruent clusters must either be voiced or voiceless. The same is true in English, where, as is well known, the plural, third-person singular present tense and past tense suffixes, among others, are voiced ([z] or [d]) if a voiced sound precedes and voiceless ([s] or [t]) if a voiceless sound precedes. These generalizations are captured by the following rule, assuming the base form of the suffixes to be /z/ and /d/:

English Progressive Voicing Assimilation
$$C \longrightarrow [\text{-voi}]/[\text{-voi}] + \underline{\qquad} \#$$

The English Progressive Voicing Assimilation rule conflicts with the Hungarian Regressive Voicing Assimilation rule. Subject A resolved this conflict in favor of the native language rule. This can be seen in words like *finds* [faynts] (S5), *friends* [frɛnts] (S6), *gods* [gats] (S10, S11), and *depends* [dɛpɛnts] (S16), where *d* became devoiced rather than *s* voiced.

Subject B applied his native language voicing assimilation rule in only one instance: In *floods* [flʌts] (S9), *d* was devoiced before *s*.

Unmarked Rule Application

Our results also indicate that there exists a class of mapping rules which cannot be explained as interference from the native language. These rules are part of neither the NL nor the TL and they all describe common, or "natural," phonological processes. We will term these rules *unmarked*. We will discuss three unmarked processes which were exhibited by our subjects: word-final devoicing, affrication, and stressed-vowel lengthening.

Subject A occasionally devoiced a word-final obstruent even if the next word began with a voiced sound. Thus, we find examples like *band increases* (S16) and *end of* (S6), where the last consonant of the first word is phonetically voiceless. This process is not obligatory—cf., for example, *something beyond* (S6), where *g* is voiced. The converse, i.e., word-final voicing before a following voiceless sound, is not found.

Subject B also devoiced word-final obstruents optionally, but only before pause. Thus, in *colors* (S2), *end* (S4), *ways* (S7), *floods* (S9), and *increases* (S16) the final obstruent was phonetically voiceless, but in *formed* (S15) and *bows* (S17) the final obstruent was voiced; each of these words occurred in sentence-final position. Final devoicing in the word *end* cannot be explained as spelling pronunciation; the others perhaps can, although, as will be noted later, spelling pronunciation is otherwise not characteristic of subject B's data.

The preceding examples cannot be explained as phonological transfer: Hungarian (like English) has no word-final obstruent devoicing rule. Rather, devoicing is explained by markedness principles: Voiceless obstruents are less marked in word-final position and before pause.

Subject A affricated the dental (alveolar) fricative *s* in word-final position following the dental (alveolar) nasal *n,* as in *sun's* [sɒnts] (S13) and *difference* [dɪffɛrɛnts] (S16). Again, this is due to a natural assimilation process, rather than to transfer (Hungarian lacks the affrication process): The closure at the dental (alveolar) region is maintained during the articulation of the post-nasal homorganic consonant.

It may further be noted that both subjects generally lengthened vowels under stress. Vocalic stress and length often co-occur in languages, although not in Hungarian, where stress and vocalic length are independent of each other.

The above suggests that second language speakers can apply rules not only from their native languages, but also from their "innate" conception of linguistic structure as regards pronunciation. We hypothesize that such rules are drawn from a universal set.

Spelling Pronunciation Errors

A third group of mapping rules can best be described as examples of *spelling pronunciation.* Since Hungarian spelling is phonetic in character, it is particularly natural that some Hungarian speakers should look to English spelling to aid them in pronunciation. Only subject A showed evidence of spelling pronunciation. We will consider four sets of examples.

Subject A generally pronounced the grammatical morpheme *-ed* "past tense" in its orthographic shape. This morpheme was pronounced as [ɛd] in all of its occurrences (*explained* (S7), *considered* (S11), *passed* (S11), *caused* (S13), *formed* (S15), *observed* (S17), *mixed* (S18), save one: *Used* (S10) was pronounced as [yust]. The pronunciation of *used* apparently was memorized, perhaps due to the relative frequency of the expression *used to,* the context in which *used* occurred.

The examples cited above are those where AE has either [t] or [d]. The past participle *-ed* was also pronounced as [ɛd] in *colored* (S16). In *accepted* (S8) and *complicated* (S15) the past tense and past participle suffixes were pronounced correctly with a vowel, albeit [ɛ] for AE [ə]. Likewise, *tried* (S12) was pronounced as [trayt], correctly, except of course for the final consonant.

The plural and third-person singular present tense morphemes were pronounced as [s] in the following words, where the voiceless pronunciation of *-s* is italicized (the following word is also given):

Plural *-s*	Third Person Singular Present *-s*
color*s.* These (S2)	end*s* apparently (S3)
centurie*s* men (S7)	find*s* it (S5)
Hebrew*s* it (S9)	cause*s* the (S14)
flood*s.* The (S9)	increase*s* as (S16)
sun'*s* rays by (S13)[4]	fall*s* upon (S18)
idea*s* about (S15)	
bow*s.* If (S17)	

The voiceless quality of -s cannot be attributed to voicing assimilation in the above contexts: Neither English nor Hungarian devoices s before a voiced obstruent, sonorant consonant, or vowel. Spelling pronunciation seems to be the most plausible explanation.

Word-final devoicing is also a possible explanation, although less plausibly, since the voiceless pronunciation of morphemes spelled with s is a general characteristic of subject A's speech.

A third category of spelling pronunciation was exhibited with certain common function words, such as *is, of, as*. In each of the following examples, the function words are given in the contexts in which they occurred:

a. *of*
   of white [of vayt] (S2)
   of a [of ǎ] (S3); [ɒf ɒ] (S17)
   of gold [of gold] (S4)
   of the [of dö] (S6)
   of bows [ɒf bōus] (S17)
   of bow [ɒf bōu] (S19)
b. *is*
   is a [is ǎ] (S2); [is a] (S19)
   is not [is nat] (S14)
c. *as*
   as a [ɛs a] (S8)
   as the [ɛs dö] (S16)

In other instances, the function words were pronounced correctly, most likely because of the application of the Hungarian Regressive Voicing Assimilation rule (phonological transfer), e.g., *of the* [ɒv dö] (S13, S16, S18), *of gold* [ov gold] (S6), *as a* [iz a] (S11).

The fourth category of spelling pronunciation involved geminate consonants. In some words geminate consonants were pronounced long (indicated in transcriptions with double consonants), in others short. The total set of orthographically geminate consonants in the data is listed below. The geminates in *a* were pronounced long, those in *b* short:

a. passage [péssiȷ] (S0)
   passed [péssɛd] (S11)
   difference [díffɛrɛnts] (S16)
   effect [éffɛkt] (S17)
   abnormally [abnormélli] (S18)
   yellow [yéllōu] (S18, S19)
b. apparently [ǎpɛréntli] (S3)
   according to [ɛkórdiŋk] (S4)
   foretell [fórtɛl] (S10)
   falls [fɒls] (S18)
   common [kamón] (S19)
   little [lítl] (S19)

For purposes of illustration, the placement of stress is indicated in the data above. Apparently, the pronunciation of geminate consonants was influenced by the position of stress. The proper generalization seems to be that geminate consonants were pronounced long immediately after a stressed vowel.

Since Hungarian contains phonetically geminate consonants, the long pronunciation of geminate consonants can also be due to phonetic transfer. The dependency of gemination on the placement of stress may be a natural phenomenon. In the pronunciation of *falls* [fáls] and *little* [lítl] phonological transfer seems to have occurred: The Hungarian rule of degemination, which shortens geminate consonants next to another consonant (e.g., /ott#volt/ → [otvolt], 'he was there,' /ing#gomb/ → [iŋgomb], 'shirt button'), seems to have applied.

Idiosyncratic Pronunciation Errors

In subject A's speech, but not in subject B's, examples occurred which could not be characterized as due to transfer, unmarked rule application, or spelling pronunciation. These pronunciations were inconsistent, though quite extensive. We can classify them as *idiosyncratic pronunciations,* although most of them can be explained rather reasonably. We suspect that most of these errors can be attributed to the process of reading aloud.

One type of idiosyncratic pronunciation can best be explained as confusion with other morphophonemically or phonetically related words. Below we list a number of such pronunciations together with the related words which we believe to be the source of the confusion:

Idiosyncratic pronunciation	Related word
like [laykt] (S1)	liked
physical [fizišn̩] (S8)	physician
token [tekɛn] (S9)	taken
imagine [imič] (S10)	image[5]
as [iz] (S11)	is
found [faynd] (S14)	find
considerably [kansidɛrebl̩] (S16)	considerable
width [vayd] (S16)	wide

Another type of idiosyncratic pronunciation can be explained as the overgeneralization of a phonetic variant of an orthographic symbol. Thus in *bridge* [brayt] (S11) and *since* [sayn] (S14), the [ay] variant of orthographic *i* (cf. *like*) was probably extended. Similarly, in *universal* [yunivɛrzal] (S9) the [z] pronunciation of written *s* (cf. *muse*) was overgeneralized.

A still different kind of idiosyncratic pronunciation occurred when the last syllable of the polysyllabic words *phenomenon* and *increases* was omitted: [fɛnomɛn] (S12) and [iŋkreys] (S16). This may be a kind of simplification due to dissimilation. In the pronunciation of *phenomenon,* a sequence of two *n*'s was avoided. The word *increases* was followed by the word *as* in the data. Again, a sequence of similar sounding syllables was shortened. In the same sentence (S16), the word *increases* also occurred sentence-finally, but in that case syllable reduction did not take place: cf. [iŋkreysɛs].

Other pronunciations were due to hesitation and uncertainty. In *primary* [priméri] (S17), the speaker trilled the *r* a few times, hesitating, perhaps stalling for time, not quite knowing what the right pronunciation was; note the incorrect stress placement. The word *beyond* was pronounced both as [biyant] (S3) and [biyont] (S6); the latter form probably was influenced by the spelling.

A final set of pronunciations was highly idiosyncratic in nature, although many of these are perhaps amenable to phonological explanation. Thus, in *light* [laykt] (S2) and *thought* [tɒukst] (S13) the voiceless pronunciation of written *g* can be explained as due to the Hungarian Voicing Assimilation rule. Intrusive *s* was also present in the alternate pronunciation of *light* as [laykst] (S18); it is not clear why *s* appeared in [tɒukst] and [laykst]. In *since then* [sayn dɛn] (S14), the sibilant was not pronounced; consonant cluster reduction may be the answer here. The word *beautiful* was pronounced as [byutifor] (S2); one liquid was substituted for another one. The word *rainbow* was repeatedly pronounced with a final nasal: [reynbon]. The appearance of the final nasal may be due to the nasal component of the word *rain,* the first member of the compound *rainbow.* Finally, *upon* [ápn̩] (S16) can be explained as follows: Stress shifted to the initial syllable, the unstressed second syllable vowel was syncopated, and the word-final postconsonant sonorant consonant was syllabified as part of a general strategy (see the data in Appendix B).

DISCUSSION

Language Transfer

The present analysis confirms the existence of phonetic (sound) transfer and indicates that phonological rules can also transfer to the TL. We would now like to address the issue of what constraints there might be on phonetic and phonological transfer, i.e., which NL sounds and rules are immune to transfer, and why.

As regards phonological transfer, we have seen strong evidence for the transfer of the Hungarian Voicing Assimilation rule. We have also discussed the possibility of the Hungarian rule of degemination playing a role in the pronunciation of geminate consonants in English. What unites these rules is the fact that they are "low level" rules (called "phonetic rules" in Vago, 1980), applying late in phonological derivations. Other low level rules were not transferred to HE, due to the fact that the English data contained no context for their application.[6]

Note in particular that none of the "higher level" rules of Hungarian was transferred to English. Perhaps the best known and most central higher level rule of Hungarian is vowel harmony. Our subjects showed no tendency whatsoever to harmonize disharmonic English words. For Hungarian speakers, disharmonic words are those that contain back vowels together with rounded front vowels; harmonic words are those that have only front vowels, only back vowels, or back vowels and unrounded front (neutral) vowels. Note, for example, subject A's pronunciation of *other* as [ɒdör] (S12).

It appears that phonological transfer is constrained such that only the low level rules of an NL may be transferred to a TL. This constraint on phonological transfer is consistent with the claim made in Rubach (1980) and Rubach (1984) that only automatic context-sensitive postcyclic rules may cause interference. (The Hungarian Voicing Assimilation and Degemination rules are of this type.)

An explanation of this constraint on phonological transfer is possible if we consider the nature of low level rules in languages. These rules simplify pronunciation, and as such, form a subset of what we have called natural rules. Thus, in the final analysis, phonological transfer and unmarked rule application may be the same phenomenon. That is, phonological transfer may be a language-specific instantiation of unmarked rule application.

An analogous issue can be raised with respect to phonetic transfer: Why do Hungarian speakers substitute one sound rather than another for an English sound?

The answer lies in the phonetic and acoustic characteristics of the speech sounds: The substituting sound is one of the closest, if not the closest, articulatory or acoustic equivalents of the substituted sound. Usually, phonetic similarity plays the dominant role. However, in the case of AE [ə] → HE [ö], the substitution is best explained in acoustic terms. Which of two phonetically equidistant sounds is selected for substitution by second language speakers is an important issue, but one which lies outside the scope of the present study.

Unmarked Rule Application

The presence of (unmarked) rules which are not part of the grammar of either English or Hungarian provides additional evidence for the currently held notion that all TL errors are not due to NL transfer. Unmarked rule application thus provides evidence against the strong version of the Contrastive Analysis Hypothesis, according to which all errors are due to NL transfer (see Wardhaugh, 1970, for discussion).

As we have noted, some of the errors which we have attributed to NL transfer, such as voicing assimilation, may turn out to be due to unmarked rule application. In order to make the strongest possible claim about unmarked rule application in this study, we have attributed to transfer all errors that could possibly be due to transfer.

Eckman (1977) revises the Contrastive Analysis Hypothesis by proposing

158

the Markedness Differential Hypothesis (MDH). He defines his proposed principle and the notion of typological markedness which it uses as follows (Eckman, 1981, 211):

a. Markedness Differential Hypothesis (MDH)
   Those areas of the TL which will be difficult are those areas which are
   1. different from the NL, and
   2. relatively more marked than the NL.
b. Markedness
   A phenomenon A in some language is more marked relative to some other phenomenon B if, cross-linguistically, the presence of A in a language necessarily implies the presence of B, but the presence of B does not necessarily imply the presence of A.

The essence of the MDH is that second language learners will have difficulty with precisely those areas which are more marked in the TL than in the NL. Thus English speakers learning German have no difficulty learning the German final devoicing rule because, as Eckman (1977) claims, German is less marked than English with respect to the voiced-voiceless obstruent contrast in word-final position.

Our findings are not wholly consistent with the claims of the MDH. This principle does not explain why Hungarian speakers produce English words with final devoiced obstruents, delete d between consonants, and affricate s in word-final position following a homorganic nasal consonant: English cannot be construed as more marked in these areas than Hungarian. Furthermore, it does not follow from the MDH that Hungarian speakers should apply their NL voicing assimilation rule instead of the voicing assimilation rule of English: The English progressive assimilation rule is not any more marked than the Hungarian regressive assimilation rule. In general, the MDH is not able to predict difficulties in those areas where a subordinate markedness relationship cannot be established between the NL and the TL. Yet, as we have seen, difficulties do exist in these circumstances.

In those cases where it is possible to establish that the TL is more or less marked than the NL, there are two ways in which the MDH can be falsified: There is difficulty where the TL is less marked, or no difficulty is found where the TL is more marked. In our study we did not encounter the former situation. If we accept the proposition that, at least for Hungarian speakers, words with harmonic vowels are less marked than words with disharmonic vowels, then it may be possible to argue for the latter situation. That is, the fact that our subjects had no difficulty whatsoever with the English disharmonic words is in contradiction to the MDH, which claims that Hungarian speakers *should* have difficulty with the more marked English disharmonic words.

In sum, while relative degree of markedness may be a necessary condition for phonological transfer, it cannot be a sufficient condition. Thus the MDH, as presently stated, cannot fully account for the available facts of second language phonology.

Foreign Accent

The four general categories of mapping rules we discovered define, in part, what a "foreign accent" is, at least as far as reading style is concerned. Can we draw conclusions as to what constitutes a "better" or "worse" foreign accent? To answer this question, we contrasted the number and types of mapping rules for each of our two subjects. We found that subject A used more widespread sound substitutions than subject B, that A substituted more sounds obligatorily, that A employed phonological transfer more extensively, that A utilized more articulatory/acoustic simplifications (unmarked rules), and that spelling pronunciation and idiosyncratic pronunciation were characteristic of A's speech but not B's. We then had 56 Queens College undergraduate students listen to the tape recordings of subjects A and B. Forty-nine students selected subject B as the more native sounding speaker. Thus the specific differences we noted between the speech of subject A and the speech of subject B contribute to native speakers' perception of subject A's speech as being less native-like than subject B's. We hypothesize that further investigation of the number and type of mapping rules of second language speakers will lead to a more precise characterization of the notion "degree of foreign accent."

Error Analysis Versus Autonomous System Analysis

It is important to note that we have analyzed the Hungarian speakers' pronunciation of English as a series of mapping rules going from American English to Hungarian-accented English—i.e., taking American English to be in some sense underlying. Eckman (1981) correctly points out that this kind of error analysis cannot make direct claims about what a speaker's interlanguage rules are. In order to ascertain the interlanguage rules of a speaker, it is necessary to analyze his or her interlanguage as a complete system unto itself, just as a linguist analyzes a particular language as a complete system, without assuming that some other language is underlying.

The autonomous system analysis approach and the error analysis approach have their own strengths and weaknesses. For example, the autonomous system analysis approach can tell us about the rules which generate correct second language utterances, which the error analysis approach cannot do. (". . . a correct L2 utterance can be based on an incorrect rule," [Jordens, 1980, 196]). On the other hand, the error analysis approach can relate the interlanguage to the target language and to the native language, something the autonomous system analysis approach alone cannot do. Thus the error analysis approach can investigate the constraints on transfer from the NL to the TL. It can indicate that speakers are, for example, consistently substituting [t] for target language [θ]. If [θ] never appears in second language speech, then an autonomous system analysis simply reveals the absence of [θ] but fails to indicate that [θ] appears in the TL. That is, the autonomous system analysis does not directly connect the interlanguage with the TL, nor does it indicate the ways in which speakers modify the TL.

Since the (nonperformance) errors which speakers make must be due to the application of interlanguage rules, it is not surprising that the information provided by the error analysis and the autonomous system analysis approaches should often mirror one another. Both this study and Eckman (1981) conclude that speakers have independent rules which are not part of either the native or the target language, and, in fact, both studies find evidence for the same rule, word-final devoicing. It is important to realize, however, that the error analysis approach used here and the autonomous system analysis approach used by Eckman are not identical, and that both approaches need to be used together.

CONCLUSION

In this paper we investigated errors made by two native speakers of Hungarian in reading an English passage. The errors were classified into four categories: those due to transfer, the application of unmarked rules, spelling pronunciations, and idiosyncratic pronunciations.

Native language transfer was found to be restricted to phonetic (sound) transfer and the transfer of low level phonological rules. The second category of errors was due to the application of unmarked rules, which were independent of the native language and target language grammars. Since low level rules in languages tend to be unmarked, rule transfer may be a special case of the application of unmarked rules. We also found evidence for spelling pronunciations and idiosyncratic pronunciations. These errors were less systematic, although many of them could be readily explained.

A gross measure of the quantity of each of the four factors in second language speech was seen to contribute to native speakers' perceptions of degree of foreign accent.

Finally, the error analysis approach was contrasted with the autonomous system analysis approach. It was argued that both approaches provide unique information and must be used together in order to arrive at a more complete understanding of second language phonology.

NOTES

1. [w], however, appeared in the pronunciation of the word *one:* [wan] (S4) ~ [wɒn] (S5) ~ [u͡ɒn] (S19). The speaker seemed to struggle with this word.

2. Idiosyncratically, it appears, [z] was substituted for AE [ð] in the pronouns *they* [zey] (S1), *there* [ze] (S4) ~ [zɛr] (S9), *their* [zer] (S11). But cf. *this* [dis] (S3) ~ [diz] (S19), *that* [dɛt] (S9) ~ [dat] (S10, S13, S14), *then* [dɛn] (S14), as well as *other* [ɒdör] (S12).

3. The symbol [a] refers to a low unrounded back vowel, and [ɒ] to a low rounded back vowel.

4. The possessive morpheme -*s* was also pronounced as [s].

5. The influence of the related word *image* is more apparent when we take stress placement into account: [ímič], with initial stress and word-final devoicing.

6. See the Appendix in Vago (1980) for a complete list of the low-level (phonetic) rules of Hungarian.

APPENDIX A

The Rainbow Passage (from Fairbanks 1940)

S0   The rainbow passage.
S1   When the sunlight strikes raindrops in the air, they act like a prism and form a rainbow.
S2   The rainbow is a division of white light into many beautiful colors.
S3   These take the shape of a long round arch, with its path high above, and its two ends apparently beyond the horizon.
S4   There is, according to legend, a boiling pot of gold at one end.
S5   People look but no one ever finds it.
S6   When a man looks for something beyond his reach, his friends say he is looking for the pot of gold at the end of the rainbow.
S7   Throughout the centuries men have explained the rainbow in various ways.
S8   Some have accepted it as a miracle without physical explanation.
S9   To the Hebrews it was a token that there would be no more universal floods.
S10   The Greeks used to imagine that it was a sign from the gods to foretell war or heavy rain.
S11   The Norsemen considered the rainbow as a bridge over which the gods passed from earth to their home in the sky.
S12   Other men have tried to explain the phenomenon physically.
S13   Aristotle thought that the rainbow was caused by reflections of the sun's rays by the rain.
S14   Since then physicists have found that it is not reflection but refraction by the raindrops which causes the rainbow.
S15   Many complicated ideas about the rainbow have been formed.
S16   The difference in the rainbow depends considerably upon the size of the water drops, and the width of the colored band increases as the size of the drops increases.
S17   The actual primary rainbow observed is said to be the effect of superposition of a number of bows.
S18   If the red of the second bow falls upon the green of the first, the result is to give a bow with an abnormally wide yellow band, since red and green lights, when mixed, form yellow.
S19   This is a very common type of bow, one showing mainly red and yellow, with little or no green or blue.

APPENDIX B

Subject A's Data

S0   dö reynbon pɛssij
S1   vɛn dö sɒnlayt strayks reyndraps in dö eyr, zey ɛkt laykt a prism ɛnt form a reynbou.
S2   dö reynbou is ǎ divizjn of vayt laykt intou mɛni byutifor kalörs.

162

S3   dis teyk dö šeyp of ǎ laŋg raund ɛrč, vid its pɛt hay ǎbōuv ɛnd its tu ɛnts ǎpɛréntli biyant dö hórizon.

S4   ze is, ɛkordiŋk tu lɛgénd, ǎ boyliŋk pat of gold ɛt wan ɛnt.

S5   pipl luk, bat no wɒn ɛvɛr faynts it.

S6   vɛn ǎ mɛn luks for samtiŋg biyont hiz rič, his frɛnts sey his lukiŋk for dö pat ov gold ɛt dö ɛnt of dö reynbōu.

S7   truāut dö sɛnturis mɛn hɛv ɛksplenɛd dö reynbōu in vɛrios veys.

S8   sam hɛv ɛksɛptɛd it is, it ɛs a mirökl, vitot fizišṇ ɛksp . . .

S9   tu dö hibrus it vaz ǎ tekɛn dɛt zɛr vud bi no mor yunivɛrzal flōuds.

S10   dö griks yuzt tu ímič dat it vaz a sayn for, from dö gats tu fórtɛl var or hɛvi reyn.

S11   dö norsmɛn kǎnsídɛrɛd dö reynbon iz a brayt ovɛr vič dö gats pɛssɛd from ɛrt tu zer hom in dö skay.

S12   ɒdör mɛn hɛf trayt tu ɛkspleyn dö fɛnomɛn psi . . .

S13   aristótḷ tōukst dat dö reynbon vɒs kɒusɛd bay rɛflɛkšṇ ɒv dö sɒnts reys bay dö reyn.

S14   sayn dɛn psi . . . fizisists hɛf faynd dat it is nat rɛflɛkšṇ bat rɛfrɛkšṇ bay dö reyndraps vič kɒuzɛs dö reynbōu.

S15   mɛni kampliketɛd aydeas abōud dö reynbōun hɛv bin formɛd.

S16   dö diffɛrɛnts in dö reynbon di . . . dɛpɛnts kǎnsidɛrébḷ ápṇ dö sayz ɒv dö vɒtɛr draps ɛn dö vayd ɒv dö kalörɛd, kalör . . . bɛnt iŋkreys ɛs dö sayz ɒv dö drɒps iŋkreysɛs.

S17   dö ɛktuɛl priméri reynbon apsörvɛd is sɛd tu bi dö éffɛkt ɒf superpozíšn ɒf a nambɛr ɒf bōus.

S18   iv dö rɛd ɒv dö sɛkond bōu fɒls apon dö grin ɒv dö först, dö rizɒlt is tu giv a bōu vit ɛn abnormélli vayd yɛllōu bɛnd, sayns rɛd ɛn grin laykst, vɛn miksɛd, form yɛllōu.

S19   diz is a vɛri kamón tayp ɒf bōu, ūɒn šoiŋk meynli rɛd ɛnd yɛllōu, vit litḷ or no grin or blu.

APPENDIX C

Subject B's Data

S0   də reynbow pǽsəj

S1   wɛn də sʌnlayt strayks reyndrɒps In dI eyr, dey ǽkt layk ey prizm̩ ǽnd form e reynbow.

S2   ðə reynbow Iz ə dIvIžṇ ʌv wayt layt IntU mǽnI byUDIfəl kɒlörs.

S3   ðiyz tek də šeyp ʌv ey lɒŋg rɒwnd ɒrč, wIð Its pǽθ hay ɛbɒv, ǽnd Its tu ɛndz ɛpǽrɛntlI bIyand di horayzṇ.

S4   ðɛr Iz, ɛkordiŋg tu lɛǰənd, e boylIŋg pat ʌv gold ɛt wɒn ɛnt.

S5   piypl lUk bʌt no wɒn ɛvər fayndz It.

S6   wɛn e mǽn lUks for sʌmθIŋg biyɒn hIz riyč, hIs frɛnts sey hI Iz lUkIŋg for də paD ʌv gold ǽt di ɛnd ʌv də reynbow.

S7   θruwɒwt də sɛnčərIs mɛn hǽv ɛkspleyn də vǽriyəs weys.

S8   sʌm hǽv ǽksɛptɛd It ǽz ey mIrǽkl̩.wIðɒwt fIzəkl̩ ɛkspləneyšǎn.

S9   tu də hIbruz It wɒz e towkən ðǽt ðɛr wUd biy now mor yUnIvərsəl flʌts.

S10   ðə griyks yust tə Imǽǰən ðǽt It wʌz ey sayn frʌm ðə gadz tu fortɛl wor or hɛviy reyn.

S11   ðə norsmɛn konsIdərd də reynbow ǽz ey brIǰ ovɛr wIč də gadz pǽst frʌm ərθ tu ðɛyr hom In də skay.

S12   ɒðɛr mɛn hɛv trayd tu ɛkspleyn də fInamɛnon fIzIkliy.

S13   ɒrIstatḷ θɒt ðǽt də reynbow wɒs kɒzd bay rIflɛkšənz ʌv ðə sʌnz reyz bay də reyn.

S14   sIns ðɛn fIzIsIsts hǽv fɒwnd ðǽt It Iz nɒt rIflɛkšən bʌt riyfrǽkšən bay də reyndraps wIč kɒzəz də reynbow.

S15   mɛniy kɒmplIkeytəd aydiyəz əbawt də reynbow hǽv biyn formd.

S16   ðə dIfərəns In də reynbow dipɛns konsIdərəbliy ɒpɒn də sayz ʌv də wɒtər drɒps, ǽnd də wItθ ʌv di kɒlərd bǽnd Iŋkriysəz ǽz ðə sayz ʌv də draps Iŋkriysəs.

S17   di ækčUl praymərI reynbow ɒbzərvd Is sɛd tu biy di ifækt ʌv sUpərpozIšn ʌv e nʌmbər
      ʌv bowz.
S18   If ðə rɛd ʌv ðə sɛkənd bow fɒlz ʌpɒn də griyn ʌv də fərst, də rIzʌlt Is tu gIv e bow wIð
      æn æbnorməliy wayd yɛlǫw bænd, sIns rɛd ænd griyn layts, wɛn mIkst, form yɛlow.
S19   dIs Iz e vɛrI kɒmən tayp ʌv bow, wɒn šowIŋg meynliy rɛd ænd yɛlow, wIð lItḷ or now griyn
      or bluw.

REFERENCES

Corder, S.P. 1967. The significance of learners' errors. *International review of applied linguistics, 5;*
    161–70.
Eckman, F.R. 1977. Markedness and the contrastive analysis hypothesis. *Language learning, 27;*
    315–30.
Eckman, F.R. 1981. On the naturalness of interlanguage phonological rules. *Language learning, 31;*
    195–216. (Also this volume.)
Fairbanks G. 1940. *Voice and articulation drillbook.* 2d ed. NY: Harper and Row.
Jordens, P. 1980. Interlanguage research: Interpretation or explanation. *Language learning, 30;*
    195–207.
Lado, R. 1957. *Linguistics across cultures.* Ann Arbor: University of Michigan Press.
Richards, J.C. and G.P. Sampson. 1974. The study of learner English. In Jack C. Richards (Ed.),
    Error analysis, 3–18. London: Longman.
Rubach, J. 1980. Rule ordering in phonological interference. Paper read at Conference on Contras-
    tive Projects, Charzykowy, Poland.
Rubach, J. 1984. Rule typology and phonological interference. In S. Eliasson (Ed.), *Theoretical
    issues in contrastive phonology.* Heidelberg: Julius Groos Verlag.
Schachter, J. 1974. An error in error analysis. *Language learning, 24;* 205–14.
Tarone, E. 1978. The phonology of interlanguage. In Jack C. Richards (Ed.), *Understanding second
    and foreign language learning,* 15–33. Rowley, MA.: Newbury House.
Tarone, E. 1979. Interlanguage as chameleon. *Language learning, 29;* 181–91.
Vago, R.M. 1980. *The sound pattern of Hungarian.* Washington, DC: Georgetown University Press.
Wardhaugh, R. 1970. The contrastive analysis hypothesis. *TESOL quarterly, 4;* 123–30.

9

MYTHS ABOUT INTERLANGUAGE PHONOLOGY*

Leslie M. Beebe

BACKGROUND

Despite a great deal of research during the past decade on the nature of second language learners' phonology, most current textbooks in English as a Second Language (ESL) either ignore the teaching of pronunciation or rely primarily on old stand-bys—minimal pairs—to teach non-native learners to pronounce English accurately. There is, of course, some disagreement as to whether accurate pronunciation is worth teaching. Some, like Scovel (1969), believe perfect native pronunciation in a second language is impossible for adults past puberty to attain. Although pronunciation is not unimportant, this group believes that

*Paper presented at the National TESOL Convention, San Francisco, 1980. This research was funded by a grant from the Spencer Foundation and sponsored by Teachers College, Columbia University. An NIE grant from the Institute for Urban and Minority Education provided additional research funds. I gratefully acknowledge this financial support. Furthermore, I would like to thank Robert Oprandy, Angela Sercaini, Moira Chimombo, and Susan Feldman for their research assistance and express my appreciation to Dr. Edmund W. Gordon and Dr. Joshua Fishman for their valuable comments and support.

perfection will never be achieved by adults. Others believe that pronunciation is simply not important; they maintain the philosophy that pronunciation only matters when it interferes with communication. Still others (e.g., Beebe 1978) believe that pronunciation always affects what we communicate and how well we communicate it, and that it should therefore be taught seriously to adults as well as children.

Most ESL teachers, whatever their point of view, make some effort to teach pronunciation. What is regrettable, however, is that the effort is frequently limited to drilling with minimal pairs. Minimal pairs and similar exercises are artificial drills designed to improve one's ability to make phonemic contrasts. Contrastive analysis predicts the problem areas. The research on interlanguage phonology presented in this paper, however, suggests that there is a minimal value to the use of minimal pairs.

Even pronunciation practice integrated into communicative situations, if it is aimed solely at correct phonemic distinctions, is ill-founded when used for non-beginners. In sum, then, the teaching of pronunciation seems to have lagged behind the teaching of other skills in part because many have seen it as an exercise in futility, and in part because many have based their teaching practices on myths about interlanguage phonology.

Before looking at these myths, let us first examine the concept of interlanguage. The term interlanguage was proposed by Selinker (1969) and then elaborated in Selinker (1972) to account for the unique utterances of second language learners. Selinker posits the existence of a separate linguistic system which results from a learner's attempts to produce a target language (TL) norm. This linguistic system he calls interlanguage (IL). Corder (1971) calls interlanguages a class of idiosyncratic dialects and suggests the alternative name transitional dialect for interlanguage in order to emphasize the unstable nature of such a dialect. He would schematize these dialects as transitional between the native language (NL) and the target language (TL), but partially overlapping with each of them. See Figure 9.1. Nemser (1971 a) calls these dialects approximative systems. Regardless of terminology, the contribution of these researchers has been to establish the notion of a separate linguistic system which is a dynamic continuum (Corder, 1977).

Selinker's interlanguage hypothesis claims that there are five psycholinguistic processes central to second language learning: language transfer (nega-

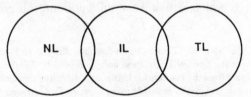

Figure 9.1 Corder's (1971) notion of idiosyncratic dialect or interlanguage (IL) in relation to the native language (NL) and the target language (TL).

tive transfer being otherwise known as interference), transfer of training, learning strategies, communication strategies, and overgeneralization of TL structures (Selinker, 1972). These processes are the basis for error analysis. A great deal of controversy has ensued about the extent to which interlanguage is influenced by language transfer, as opposed to other processes which are developmental. Dulay and Burt (1973) reported on data elicited from 145 Spanish-speaking children by means of the Bilingual Syntax Measure. They found that 85 percent of the 388 syntactic errors identified were developmental, whereas only 3 percent were attributable to interference. This finding was a devastating blow to the contrastive analysis hypothesis, which claims that student errors stem from first language interference and that systematic comparison of the first language (L1) with the second language (L2) will allow us to predict these errors. (In its weaker version, the contrastive analysis hypothesis merely states that we can "account for" the errors. See Wardhaugh (1975) for a discussion of the two versions of the contrastive analysis hypothesis.) Schachter (1974) introduced evidence of avoidance behavior predictable by contrastive analysis and Kleinmann (1977) corroborated this claim. Still, studies continue to provide evidence that the causes of syntactic errors lie primarily in developmental processes. One popular view, amidst the controversy, has been that while interference is minimal in syntactic development, it is rampant in phonological development. Scovel (1976) made this claim, and Felix (1980) suggested that the influence of L1 structure was much stronger in phonology than on the morphophonemic level.

Although the fact that there are distinct, recognizable, foreign accents suggests that Scovel and Felix are correct, empirical data reported here on the pronunciation problems of twenty-five Asian adults learning English as a second language in New York City show that very few pronunciation errors result from direct L1 transfer. Even though the problem areas are correctly predicted by contrastive analysis, the exact variants used for English targets are seldom found in L1. Ultimately, what is needed is to predict what variants will be used under specific conditions. This goal may be reached via further study of developmental stages in addition to a more sophisticated contrastive analysis. The data from this study suggest, however, that neither endeavor will be sufficient by itself. In addition, we must examine interlanguage phonology from the perspective of a variation model.

THE STUDY

This study discusses the pronunciation difficulties of twenty-five Asian adults learning ESL who are native speakers of Japanese, Mandarin, Korean, Thai, or Indonesian. Nine Thais working in New York City were originally studied. They were selected from three socioeconomic levels (based on categories established by Beebe (1974)). Data were gathered from tape-recorded interviews consisting of communicative speech, passages read aloud, and single word listing. Only the formal listing data are reported here. They are compared with the listing data of sixteen foreign students at the American Language Program (ALP) of Columbia University. Of the sixteen students, four were from Japan, four from Taiwan, four from Korea, and four from Indonesia. Within each language group, two were of low-intermediate proficiency, and two were of low-advanced proficiency, according to the ALP placement examination. The initial sounds /r/, /l/, /i/, /ɪ/, /s/, and /θ/ were investigated. In addition, the /r/ and /l/ were examined in word-final position, after an initial consonant, and before a final consonant. Thai subjects were tested only on the /r/ vs. /l/ contrast.

A number of myths about interlanguage phonology are exposed by the data collected. On the whole, these data are in accordance with the research on interlanguage done by Selinker, Corder, Richards, Nemser, and others, and they generally fit the patterns described in an excellent classifactory article by Tarone (1978), "The phonology of interlanguage." One advantage of the present paper is that it provides data which are comparable (elicited by the same instrument) for five different language groups. Most data-based studies are founded on data from one native language group (e.g., L. Dickerson, 1974). The data concur with recent studies which demonstrate multiple processes, not just language transfer, at work. The goals of this paper are to

(1) present these data,
(2) discuss their theoretical implications, and
(3) point out that current pronunciation teaching practices are predicated on myths about the nature of interlanguage phonology.

The empirical data collected show that most pronunciation errors do *not* involve confusion of two phonemes. Popular belief seems to be to the contrary, but this is a myth, at least for the learners investigated in this study. It may be that beginners have difficulty with phonemic contrasts, but this study, coupled with a great deal of other detailed phonetic work and informal observation, has convinced me that phonemic contrasts are a very minor problem for intermediate and advanced learners. Phonetic inaccuracy, compared with a TL norm, is extensive. The phonetic deviance is heard by the teacher/listener as a phonemic error.

In an airport novelties shop, I recently saw a sign which captures this basic problem in human communication. The sign read: "I know you think you understand what I am trying to say, but what you said I was trying to say is not what I meant." The sign has a more poignant stab of humor when applied to ESL learners. They have the added difficulty of not being sure whether what they meant to say was what they actually said. They have to rely on someone for feedback, and there are some inherent problems in doing this.

Native listeners will very often assign the sounds they hear to the nearest phoneme in the target language, their own native tongue. Yet this may not be the phoneme that the learner intended. A personal anecdote of a lunch I had more than ten years ago may illustrate this point. I was with an exceptionally bright Japanese doctoral student at Mark's Restaurant in Ann Arbor, which was the only delicatessen in town at that time. As my friend was reading the sandwich board, she asked, "Leslie, what's sarami?" (At that time, it was important for a linguist to know the word 'salami' because it kept cropping up as tranformational grammarians quoted George Lakoff's famous example of the English instrumental, "Seymour used a knife to cut the salami.") I'm sure if I had corrected my friend, saying, "It's salami, not sarami," she would have felt, "But that's what I meant!" and probably also, "That's what I said!" At that time, I would have analyzed her error as one of interference. It is difficult to find reliable data on [r] and [l] in Japanese, but scholars seem to agree that Japanese has only one phoneme where English has two, and if forced to name that phoneme, scholars prefer to call it an /r/, which is commonly a flap, but also very frequently a variant somewhere between English [r] and [l]. This means that ESL teachers are likely to have a great deal of difficulty in determining what Japanese students intend to say and what they have actually said. What I heard as /sarami/ may or may not have contained an /r/. If it did contain an [r] sound, it was very likely intended to be an /l/. In other words, I would hypothesize differently today than I did way back then. Now, I think it is very likely that the word was pronounced with an interlanguage variant for /l/ that had some r-like properties. I have come to this position not by ideology but through examining large amounts of empirical data.

Throughout the present study, error rates in pronunciation were high, but there were only minimal levels of phonemic substitution. Virtually all errors were phonetic. The English contrasts, /r/ vs. /l/, /s/ vs. /θ/, and /i/ vs. /ɪ/, are all popularly believed to be difficult for Japanese, Chinese, Koreans, Indonesians, and Thais. Nilsen and Nilsen (1973) claim that minimal pairs are needed to teach these distinctions to all five of the above-mentioned groups of Asians. Nevertheless, in the listed words containing TL /l/, the following low rates were found for substitution of an r-variant for /l/:

Japanese	4%
Chinese	2%
Koreans	4%
Indonesians	0%
Thais	11%

The ALP students (i.e., all subjects except the Thais) displayed an average substitution rate of 3 percent although their total error rate was 46 percent. Three-quarters of the errors were *phonetic* deviations from English /l/, not phonemic confusions that could be corrected by minimal pair drill. The rate of substitution for Thais was high (11 percent) because sociolinguistic rules in Thai (to be discussed later) led to hypercorrections with formal *r*-variants.

When the TL norm was English /r/, there was only a 7 percent substitution rate of *l*-sounds:

Japanese	4%
Chinese	4%
Koreans	17%
Indonesians	2%
Thais	9%

The ALP students were tested on four additional TL norms: /s/, /θ/, /i/, and /ɪ/. They consistently displayed low rates of phonemic substitution, as seen in Table 9.1.

In sum, most pronunciation errors do *not* involve substitution of one phoneme for another. They do not involve confusion of phonemes at all. More frequently, they involve phonetic approximation or overgeneralization of a target sound (cf. Nemser 1971 b, Johansson 1973). For example, 91 percent of the errors on /s/ were simply approximations of English /s/, and 43 percent of the errors on /i/ were approximations of /i/.

A second myth about interlanguage phonology that adversely affects our teaching practices is that pronunciation errors involve transfer of a native language variant. This is simply not true in a large number of cases. Many variants in interlanguage are "original"; that is, they cannot be found in either the NL or TL (English). Tarone (1978) discusses several processes other than interference which result in errors. Some lead to interlanguage (i.e., "original") variants.

It is extremely difficult to ascertain whether variants exist in the NL unless one is a native speaker of that language. Although this author has had some training in four of the five Asian languages studied here, she is fluent in only one, Thai. It has been necessary to rely on linguistic references for the other four languages. In the case of Thai, variation in /r/ in the native language has been studied in detail (Beebe, 1974).

TABLE 9.1. Percentage of Errors on TL Norms Made by Sixteen Adult Asian ESL Students

Rates of pronunciation errors	Target language norm			
	s	θ	i	ɪ
Rate of error due to phonemic substitution	9	6	8	14
Total rate of error	23	39	73	74

There are two main types of errors in the present study which lead to "original" variants: approximations and composites. Approximations are discussed by Tarone (1978). Composites may be considered akin to approximations, but they are termed differently here to emphasize the distinction that they involve *sequential* production of two variants, not just coloring of one. In some cases, composites appear to be a sequential merger of an L1 and an L2 sound.

Composites, or sequential mergers, found in these data were most common in the speech of the Chinese students. They produced:

sθ ⎱	for English /s/
θs ⎰	
rl	for English /l/
rl ⎱	for English /r/
lr ⎰	

The Japanese produced:

θs	for English /s/
rl ⎱	for English /l/
wl ⎰	

Indonesians occasionally produced [tθ] for English /θ/, but the claim that this is a sequence is difficult to maintain. It may be affrication of an English fricative.

As for approximation, there were many examples in the data. For instance, Thais produced five different approximations of English /r/, none of which was ever heard by this researcher during four years of research on variation in the Thai consonant system (Beebe, 1974). In addition to meeting the English norm for /r/, Thais produced a variety which was too closed and retroflexed, one which was too open, two different fricatives, and a lateralized variant. The open variety resembles an *r*-variant used by New Yorkers and could be an example of natural acquisition of a native dialectal variant. The other *r*-sounds, however, are clearly original interlanguage variants, not to be found in either the NL or the TL. If transfer had been the strategy, the English /r/ would have been produced as a flap or trill.

Another clear example of approximation was a retroflexed *l*-variant for English /l/. This was definitely not due to transfer, and it was not the result of linguistic environment, as, for example, in the pronunciation of *used car lot*.

The Chinese also resorted to approximation of English /r/, not having an exact, or even a particularly close, counterpart in their dialect. Six variants emerged, including a flapped variety, a trill, a fricative, a lateralized variant, an [lr] sequence, and the open variant used by the Thais which was insufficiently retroflexed.

A third popular belief about interlanguage phonology is that after the initial stages of formal training, the learner's phonetic repertoire expands. Corder (1977) objects to what he describes as Selinker's view that the interlanguage continuum involves only a restructuring of the learner's linguistic system at the same level of complexity. Corder claims that the interlanguage continuum is "a dynamic, goal-oriented language system of increasing complexity" (1977, 13). I am not sure that either point of view is exclusively correct. Babies learning English as their native language babble and experiment with lots of sounds before *narrowing down* their repertoire to fit the sounds of adult English. Children simultaneously acquiring two languages seem to develop a mixed code in early stages before they sort out two separate systems (Leopold, 1954). It would appear that the progression toward bilingualism involves some increased complexity, some simple restructuring, and some decreased complexity.

In the present study, no firm claims can be made about the size of the phonetic repertoire expanding or shrinking. For one reason, this study is cross-sectional, not longitudinal. The progression can be inferred, however, by comparing data from learners at increasing levels of proficiency, but this, too, is difficult since there were no true beginners in the study. Still, there seems to be a trend toward a shrinking repertoire of phonetic variants in the comparison between low-intermediate and low-advanced students. Despite the fact that the differences were not statistically significant, the trend seems to be worthy of further investigation since the number of tokens, the number of subjects, and the difference between proficiency levels in this study were small. What appears to be happening may be schematized as in Figure 9.2. During early stages, learners may not be aware of phonetic differences. With training, they may add to their phonetic repertoire, and a large number of approximations may occur as they advance to the intermediate level. Finally, however, as they progress to an advanced level of proficiency, they will realize TL norms more frequently and eliminate some of the approximations they formerly relied on. Longitudinal studies are needed to discover whether this pattern of an expanding and then shrinking phonetic repertoire really exists.

The data for this study do confirm, however, that there is more phonemic confusion (neutralization of phonemic contrasts) among the students of lower proficiency level. Interestingly, also, the range of sounds (i.e., the phonetic distance between variants) was greater for the low-intermediate students than for the more advanced learners. In sum, I believe that ESL learners tend to start out with a relatively small range of sounds for a difficult TL sound. Transfer

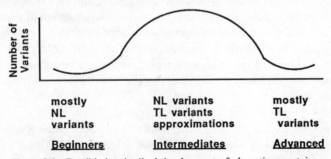

Figure 9.2 Possible longitudinal development of phonetic repertoire.

172

of an NL variant is most likely at this stage. As the learner advances in the early stages, there is a proliferation of variants used. Many approximations occur. Eventually, the number of approximations tapers off, and the phonetic distance between the remaining ones for one target narrows down. Finally, this process leads to near-native speech or fixed use of a small number of interlanguage variants (i.e., fossilization).

The fourth and final myth about interlanguage phonology that I would like to discuss concerns sociolinguistic variations. There seems to be a tacit assumption that interlanguage is not subject to sociolinguistic variation in the same way that native languages are. This popular assumption persists despite explicit evidence to the contrary (e.g., Adjémian, 1976, Tarone, 1979, Beebe, 1980). In fact, an interlanguage is a natural language, and it varies like any other natural language with the sociolinguistic setting. Patterned variation according to social setting is extremely intricate and complex. Knowledge that this is so may lead us to expect that control of social variation is acquired late, but this is simply not the case. Although many subtleties of English may be missed by ESL learners in early stages, there is still style shifting and variation from the early stages.

In these data, there is clear evidence that Thais of various proficiency levels style-shifted between interview conversation and formal word listing. This occurred due to the transfer of the social value of a sound from their native language. In Thai, the variants for initial /r/ carry strong social meaning. The teaching and usage of the 'correct' initial /r/ has been in vogue in Thailand since a decree of Rama II. (The present king is Rama IX.) The initial /r/ is properly a flapped [ř] in careful speech, and a trilled [r̃] in very formal speech. In everyday conversation, Thais use [l] for /r/ at least 95 percent of the time (Beebe, 1974). Yet the ability to use a flap or a trill in the required contexts is an effective indicator of one's social position. Prescriptive phonology is so deeply ingrained in Thai speakers that they apply it when learning English as a second language, especially in formal contexts, such as single word listing. Thais produced English /r/ correctly 48 percent of the time during an interview conversation, but only 9% of the time in the listing task. This shift was due to the fact that in formal listing, they transferred socially appropriate trilled and flapped r's from their native language. (The shift was statistically significant on a t-test; $p < .05$.) In the case of final /r/, where there is no social meaning attached to the sound in Thai, the expected shift toward higher accuracy occurred in the listing task ($p < .01$). In this environment, there were no "correct" Thai variants interfering.

THEORETICAL SIGNIFICANCE OF THE FINDINGS

The existence of four competing variants in a single environment, and a single style, for a single speaker, suggests that there is a high level of inherent variation in interlanguages, just as there is in native languages. Creative construction theory posits a learner who tests out his or her hypotheses. This theory seems inadequate by itself to explain the data showing four competing variants for one environment. It would have to claim that a learner has four competing hypotheses, or that the learner has a tremendous lack of motor control. Neither explanation seems very likely.

I believe this is a question of variation in performance, not of competing hypotheses being tested out. The variation may stem partly from a lack of motor control, but it is too systematic to be wholly explainable on this basis. It must stem, at least in part, from knowledge of sociolinguistic rules. The variation must be explained by a variationist model of performance, not a model of ideal competence.

Despite recent claims (e.g., Schmidt, 1977, Schachter, 1974) that a more sophisticated contrastive analysis is needed (and my complete agreement with this claim), I believe that contrastive analysis, no matter how refined, will ultimately fail to account for all the variation in interlanguage phonology. Similarly, the creative construction hypothesis only gives us part of the picture. Contrastive analysis helps us account for some of the variation. It accounts for problem areas in phonology fairly successfully. A sophisticated contrastive analysis (one which takes into account social variation in the NL, form and function, typological characteristics of the NL, and avoidance) is better than a simple version. Still, contrastive analysis does not account for all the variation in, say, the example of initial English /r/ for Thai speakers. Thais sometimes used TL variants, sometimes NL variants. In some cases, the NL variant was socially appropriate; in other cases, it was not. Contrastive analysis predicts difficulty for Thais with initial /r/, but it does not explain the variation that occurs. Interlanguage, being a natural language, will be subject to patterned, rule-governed processes, but it will also contain inherent variation that cannot be explained. As in the study of first language performance, a variation model is needed to explain patterned fluctuations in a social context. Beyond that, some unexplained variation will remain.

REFERENCES

Adjémian, C. 1976. On the nature of interlanguage systems. *Language Learning, 26,* 297–320.

Beebe, L.M. 1974. *Socially conditioned variation in Bangkok Thai.* Ph. D. dissertation. University of Michigan, Ann Arbor.

Beebe, L.M. 1978. Teaching pronunciation (why we should be). *Idiom, 9,* 2–3.

Beebe, L.M. 1980. Sociolinguistic variation and style shifting in second language acquisition. *Language Learning, 30,* 433–441. (Also this volume.)

Corder, S.P. 1971. Idiosyncratic dialects and error analysis. *IRAL, 9,* 147–160. (Reprinted in Schumann and Stenson (1974, 100–113).)

Corder, S.P. 1971. Language continua and the interlanguage hypothesis. In S. P. Corder and E. Roulet (Eds.), *The notions of simplification, interlanguages, and pidgins, and their relation to second language pedagogy.* Geneva: Librairie Droz, 11–17.

Dickerson, L. 1974. *Internal and external patterning of phonological variability in the speech of Japanese learners of English.* Ph. D. dissertation. University of Illinois.

Dulay, H.C., and M.K. Burt. 1973. Should we teach children syntax? *Language Learning, 23,* 245–258.

Felix, S. 1980. Interference, interlanguage, and related issues. In S. Felix (Ed.), *Second language development: Trends and issues,* 93–107. Tübingen: Gunter Narr Verlag, 93–107.

Johansson, F.A. 1973. *Immigrant Swedish phonology: A study in multiple contact analysis.* Lund: CWK Gleerup.

Kleinmann, H.H. 1977. Avoidance behavior in adult second language acquisition. *Language Learning, 27,* 93–107.

Leopold, W.F. 1954. A child's learning of two languages. *Georgetown University Round Table on Languages and Linguistics, 7,* 19–30. Reprinted in E. Hatch (Ed.), 1978. *Second language acquisition: A book of readings,* 24–32. Rowley, MA: Newbury House Publishers, 24–32.

Nemser, W. 1971a. Approximative systems of foreign language learners. *IRAL, 9,* 115–123.

Nemser, W. 1971b. *An experimental study of phonological interference in the English of Hungarians.* Bloomington, IN: Indiana University Press.

Nilsen, D.L.F. and A.P. Nielsen. 1973. *Pronunciation contrasts in English.* New York: Regents Publishing Company.

Schachter, J. 1974. An error in error analysis. *Language Learning, 24,* 205–214.

Schmidt, R. 1977. Sociolinguistic variation and language transfer in phonology. *Working Papers on Bilingualism, 12,* 79–95.

Schumann, J.H., and N. Stenson. (Eds.). 1974. *New frontiers in second language learning.* Rowley, MA: Newbury House Publishers.

Scovel, T.S. 1969. Foreign accents, language acquisition and cerebral dominance. *Language Learning, 19,* 245–254.

Scovel, T.S. 1976. Contrastive analysis is alive and well and living in phonology. Paper presented at the Tenth Annual National TESOL Convention, New York.

Selinker, L. 1969. Language transfer. *General Linguistics, 9,* 67–92.

Selinker, L. 1972. Interlanguage. *IRAL,* 10, 209–231 Reprinted in J.C. Richards (Ed.), *Error analysis: Perspectives on second language acquisition.* London: Longman, 31–54.

Tarone, E. 1978. The phonology of interlanguage. In J.C. Richards (Ed.), *Understanding second and foreign language learning: Issues and approaches.* Rowley, MA: Newbury House Publishers, 15–32. (Also this volume.)

Tarone, E. 1979. Interlanguage as chameleon. *Language Learning, 29,* 181–191.

Wardhaugh, R. 1974. The contrastive analysis hypothesis. In Schumann and Stenson (1974, 11–19).

175

10

LIMITS ON PHONETIC ACCURACY IN FOREIGN LANGUAGE SPEECH PRODUCTION

James Emil Flege   James Hillenbrand

INTRODUCTION

Most adults who learn a foreign language speak with an "accent" which derives in part from phonological and phonetic differences between their native language (L1) and the target foreign language (L2). This raises the question of the extent to which humans are capable of learning new speech patterns, or modifying existing ones, once L1 has been thoroughly acquired. This study examined factors that might limit the accuracy with which adult learners produce the phones (speech sounds) found in a foreign language.

Researchers (e.g., Lado, 1957) have frequently observed that L2 learners tend to produce the words of a foreign language with phones that can be heard in the phonetic surface of L1. Weinreich (1953) hypothesized that this resulted from the "interlingual identification" of L1 and L2 phones. Valdman (1976, p. 38) observed that:

. . . the articulatory habits of the foreign language partially overlap those of the native language.
. . . The student must learn to make new responses to stimuli which are interpreted as identical to

176

native language stimuli. For instance, French and English /s/ differ with regard to place of articulation. The former is a dental, and the latter is an alveolar. The partial similarities he perceives in the acoustic signal of French /s/ will lead an English speaker to respond with the alveolar rather than the dental sound.

This represents the hypothesis that when an L2 phone is "identified" with an L1 phone, the L1 phone will be used in place of it (i.e., be "substituted" for it). Such interlingual identification appears to depend on the auditory, and perhaps articulatory, similarity of L1 and L2 phones. However, empirical research has yet to: (1) objectively quantify the degree of phonetic similarity between phones found in two languages, (2) demonstrate which specific phones in L1 and L2 are "identified" with one another, or (3) determine whether the interlingual identification of L1 and L2 phones will cease as the learner becomes familiar with the phonetic differences that may distinguish L1 and L2 phones.

Some L2 phones have a direct counterpart in L1 with which they can be identified. To a first approximation, this includes L1 and L2 phones that are transcribed using the same IPA symbol. For example, instances of /t/ occurring in French and English words are likely to be regarded by the L2 learner as being different realizations of the same category because of their overall phonetic similarity. The interlingual identification of such pairs might be expected to occur even when acoustic differences that may distinguish the L1 and L2 phones are auditorily detectable (see Flege, 1984a). Judging acoustically different phones to be members of the same category is a fundamental aspect of human speech perception.

Other L2 phones bear less obvious resemblance to phones in L1 and may therefore not be regarded as the realization of any L1 category. For native English speakers, this may include phones such as the front-rounded vowel /y/ of French, the clicks of Southern Bantu languages, and the pharyngeal fricatives of Semitic languages. We will refer to such phones as "new," although it should be apparent that any phone encountered in a foreign language—no matter how exotic—is likely to bear some degree of articulatory and acoustic similarity to phones found in the learner's L1.

One aim of this study was to determine whether L2 learners produce "new" L2 phones more accurately than L2 phones which have a counterpart in L1. Valdman (1976) hypothesized that new L2 phones are learned more easily than L2 phones which have an L1 counterpart because they evade interlingual identification and thus tend not to be produced with previously established patterns of segmental articulation (cf. Koutsoudas and Koutsoudas, 1962). Koo (1972) suggested that talkers do not actually need to "learn" new L2 phones since they can be produced by recombining the features of L1 phones. This implies that new L2 phones and those which have a direct counterpart in L1 will be produced with equal accuracy.

Several previous studies have reported data bearing on this issue (Brière,

1966; Politzer and Weiss, 1969; Johansson, 1973; Walz, 1979; Flege and Port, 1981), but none has specifically tested the hypothesis that new L2 phones are produced more accurately than those with a direct counterpart in L1.[1] Taken as a whole, they suggest that L2 learners produce new L2 phones *less* well than L2 phones with an L1 counterpart. However the evidence which now exists is insufficient to confirm or disconfirm the hypothesis. Most of the previous studies examined the speech production of talkers with little or no knowledge of the foreign language from which the L2 phones were taken; most examined mimicry rather than spontaneous speech production; and most relied solely on phonetic transcription, often by non-native speakers.

We applied perceptual and acoustic criteria to the French syllables /tu/ ('tous') and /ty/ ('tu') to objectively examine adults' production of L2 phones.[2] English /u/ appears to be produced with significantly lower $F2$ values than its French counterpart.[3] French /y/, on the other hand, is a "new" phone that has no direct counterpart in English. Contrastive analysis (e.g., Le Bras, 1981) predicts that L2 learners will replace a new L2 phone with a "close" L1 phone, but offers no satisfactory method for determining which L1 phone is *closest* to the new L2 phone.[4] If a new L2 phone is consistently replaced by a single L1 phone the possibility exists that the L2 phone has been identified with that L1 phone. American speakers of French often realize French /y/ as an /u/-quality vowel (Gaudin, 1953; Walz, 1979). If both the /y/ and /u/ of French is identified with English /u/, native English speakers might appear to produce French /u/ more accurately than French /y/ since, in that case, they would be likely to "substitute" English /u/ for both vowels. Another possibility is that native English speakers do not identify French /y/ with any vowel category of English and therefore learn to produce French /y/ without reference to speech patterns established for the articulation of English. If so, French /y/ may be produced more accurately than French /u/, at least if adults remain capable of learning to produce new phones.

It seems likely that the amount of French language experience will affect the production of French /u/ and /y/ by native English speakers. Previous studies have focused on speech timing in L2 production. Relatively experienced L2 learners have been observed to produce L2 phones with more nativelike temporal properties than relatively inexperienced L2 learners (see Flege, 1984b). A nonauthentic pronunciation of vowels leads to foreign accent (Elsendoorn, 1983) but no study, to our knowledge, has specifically examined the effect of experience on learners' production of L2 vowels. Thus another aim of this study was to determine whether experienced American speakers of French produce French vowels more accurately than less experienced Americans and, if so, whether experience equally effects production of /y/ and /u/.

Most previous L2 research has emphasized the difficulty of establishing new motor plans for L2 phones, or the difficulty in modifying pre-existing ones. The final aim of this study was to test the hypothesis that an important cause of foreign accent is the development by L2 learners of inaccurate *perceptual* targets for L2 phones.[5] Flege (1981, 1984b) hypothesized that interlingual identification leads the L2 learner to merge the phonetic properties of L1 and L2 phones that have been identified as belonging to the same category. According to this hypothesis, learners' perceptual target for L2 phones may evolve as a function of experience with L2 (see Caramazza et al., 1973; Williams, 1980), but their perceptual target for L2 phones may never match those of L2 native speakers because of interlingual identification. Flege's (1984b) model leads to the prediction that, with sufficient experience, L2 learners will produce stop consonants differently in L2 than L1 (if the L1 and L2 stops differ phonetically), but will never perfectly match native speakers of L2. For example, if English learners judge that the /t/ of English and French belong to the same category, it is predicted they will persist in producing French /t/ with relatively long (English-like) VOT values because their perceptual target for French /t/ will merge the properties of French /t/ (including its short-lag VOT values) and English /t/ (with its long-lag VOT values).

Existing studies support the general prediction that L2 learners will be only partially successful in producing L2 phones. Studies have shown that learners whose L1 realizes /p,t,k/ with short-lag VOT values produce English /p,t,k/ with VOT values that are longer than those characteristic of L1, but are nevertheless too short by English phonetic standards (Port and Mitleb, 1980; Flege and Port, 1981; Caramazza et al., 1973; Williams, 1980; cf. Flege and Hammond, 1982). However, to our knowledge no study has examined the production of short-lag stops in a target foreign language by learners whose L1 realizes /p,t,k/ with *long-lag* VOT values. Kewley-Port and Preston (1974) hypothesized that short-lag stops are less difficult to produce than long-lag stops. It is therefore possible that native English speakers may succeed better in producing the short-lag stops of French (Caramazza and Yeni-Komshian, 1974) than native French speakers produce the *long-lag* stops of English. If Americans accurately produce French /t/ with the short-lag VOT values typical of French monolinguals, it would disconfirm the hypothesis that interlingual identification creates an absolute upper limit on the extent to which L2 learners approximate the phonetic norms of a target foreign language.

Flege's (1984b) model should apply to vowel production as well as to the VOT dimension in stop consonants. Native English speakers are likely to identify French /u/ with English /u/, despite the fact that the spectral acoustic differences distinguishing these vowels are auditorily detectable (Flege, 1984a). As a result, English learners of French may develop a perceptual target for French /u/ differing from that of French monolinguals because they merge the phonetic properties of French and English /u/. If so, they will at best produce French /u/ with formant values intermediate to the values observed for French and English monolinguals. Should the production of French /u/ by English speakers of French be observed to match that of French monolinguals, it would seriously undermine the importance of interlingual identification as a factor limiting adults' success in producing L2 phones.

One other aspect of the present data will serve to test the importance of interlingual identification. Previous studies (e.g., Flege and Port, 1981) show that the phonetic characteristics of L1 phones are often maintained in L2 speech production. To the best of our knowledge, no previous study has tested the effect of L2 learning on L1 speech production. If identifying an L2 phone with a phone in L1 affects the perceptual target developed for the L2 phone, it should also affect the perceptual target previously established for the L1 phone.[6] Flege (1981, 1984b) hypothesized that when learners identify an L2 phone with a phone in L1 they will eventually begin producing the L1 phone so that it resembles the counterpart phone in L2. For example, a native French speaker who identifies English /t/ with the /t/ of French should eventually begin producing French /t/ with VOT values that exceed the short-lag VOT values typical of French monolinguals. A failure to note an L2 effect on L1 speech production would also tend to undermine the importance of interlingual identification.

Our study is divided into three parts. In Experiment 1 listeners label the French syllables /tu/ and /ty/ produced by native French and English talkers. If new L2 phones are produced more accurately than L2 phones which have a direct counterpart in L1, the /ty/ produced by native English speakers should be correctly labeled more often than /tu/. If experience leads to increased L2 production accuracy, the syllables produced by relatively experienced English speakers of French should be correctly labeled more often than syllables produced by less experienced native English speakers. The effect of experience is further explored in experiment 2, which examines the identifiability of /ty/ and /tu/ in a paired-comparison task.

Finally, we report acoustic measures of VOT and formants 1–3 in the /tu/ and /ty/ syllables that were perceptually tested in Experiments 1 and 2. The predicted effect of interlingual identification is that French–English bilinguals and English–French bilinguals will produce the /t/ occurring in French words with VOT values that are intermediate to those observed for monolingual speakers of English and French. Further, native English speakers of French are predicted to produce French /u/ and with $F2$ values intermediate to those observed for French and English monolinguals.

EXPERIMENT 1

This experiment examined the accuracy with which native and non-native talkers produced the French syllables /tu/ and /ty/. Accuracy was assessed by computing the frequency with which French-speaking listeners correctly identified (i.e., as intended) these syllables. We examined production of /tu/ and /ty/ in three different speaking tasks to ensure a representative sampling of

French speech production. To examine the effect of linguistic experience, we compared two groups of native English speakers who differed in overall French language experience.

Methods

Talkers   Three groups of talkers differing in language background and experience were recruited from a university community for the present study. Each group consisted of seven adult talkers with self-reported normal hearing. The native French-speaking group, designated group NF, consisted of six French women and one Belgian woman with a mean age of 38 years. These talkers had lived an average of 12.2 years in an English-speaking environment (principally Chicago), and four were married to native English speakers.

There were two groups of native English speakers who spoke French as a second language, all women from the Midwest. The talkers in one group, designated group NE-1, consisted of undergraduate students with a mean age of 22 years who had spent the previous academic year in Paris. A more experienced group of native English speakers, designated group NE-2, consisted of women with a mean age of 32 years who held advanced degrees in French and were teaching French at an American university. Talkers in this group had all spent several periods of time in France, the total averaging 1.3 years. One was married to a native French speaker. Talkers in the two American groups, like the native French speakers, were using English as their primary language at the time of the study.

Talkers in both native English-speaking groups began to study French in junior or senior high school between the ages of 11 and 17 years. However, none of them appears to have acquired French as a functional second language prior to about age 20. A language background questionnaire indicated that, compared to talkers in group NE-1, those in group NE-2 had substantially more formal instruction in French language and literature, rated their own production and comprehension of French somewhat higher, and used French somewhat more often on a daily basis in the period immediately preceding the experiment.

No attempt was made to objectively assess the French-speaking proficiency of the two American groups, for the intent was simply to constitute two extreme groups differing in overall experience. There was a clear difference between the two groups in terms of the length of time they had used French to communicate. For talkers in NE-1 this was effectively less than a year, since none of them had used French on a regular basis since their return from Paris 6 months previously. The talkers in group NE-2, on the other hand, had used French on a fairly regular basis for an average of about 10 years. Thus it seems reasonable to refer to the talkers in group NE-1 as "inexperienced" and those in group NE-2 as the relatively "experienced" speakers of French.

Speech materials　The following two sets of phrases were used in counter-balanced order to elicit production of the French syllables /tu/ and /ty/ by the native speakers of French and English:

Tous les prêtres	Tu les montres
Tous les éveques	Tu les opposes
Tous les soldats	Tu les observes
Tous les marins	Tu les renvoies
Tous les médecins	Tu les obtiens
Tous les dentistes	Tu les informes
Tous les gendarmes	Tu les regardes.

Note that the utterance-initial syllable (/tu/ or /ty/) in both phrase sets was held constant. The sound following the initial syllable (/l/) was held constant across the two phrase sets to make possible a direct comparison between /tu/ and /ty/. The final word in each phrase tended to receive contrastive stress because it varied across phrases.

The two sets of phrases were produced in three progressively more demanding speaking tasks. The first task was simply to read the test phrases found in one set, each preceded by the phrase number and a pause. The next task was to generate an original sentence, initiating each with one of the phrases that had just been produced in isolation. Production was cued by the same written list of seven phrases used in the phrase production task.

The final task was to produce a story based on the seven phrases. The principal requirement was that the story include a complete sentence initiated by each of the seven phrases in the set. The talkers were given a set of cards, each bearing one of the phrases to be used. They were to arrange the cards on the table before them in order to outline their intended story. Talkers were permitted as much time as necessary to silently rehearse. They were permitted to intersperse additional sentences not initiated by one of the test phrases in the story, as needed. The talkers were not required to say the number of the phrase before initiating each utterance, as in the previous two speaking tasks. However, they were told to pause before each sentence to ensure that the syllable of interest (/tu/ or /ty/) occurred in absolute utterance-initial position in the story task as it had in the phrase and sentence tasks.

The three speaking tasks were modeled using a set of seven English phrases. The talkers then practiced the speaking tasks using these English phrases. All but one talker, who was replaced, was able to perform the three speaking tasks satisfactorily. The story produced in the third task was highly natural and spontaneous in the authors' estimation, despite the fact that the talkers were required to pause before each sentence.

The speech material was recorded (Sony model TCD5M) in a sound-treated room with the experimenter seated about 5 ft from the talker. An electret condensor microphone (Nakamichi model CM-300) was positioned about 6 in.

from the talker's mouth. To counteract the tendency for talkers to hyperarticulate in the presence of a microphone (Labov, 1972), talkers were told that the experiment examined language creativity. Debriefing afterwards revealed that none of the talkers were aware the experiment actually focused on pronunciation, and none attached special significance to the fact that a single syllable (/tu/ or /ty/) recurred at the beginning of each phrase.

Stimuli A total of 252 syllables were edited from the speech material for perceptual analysis (3 groups × 7 talkers × 2 syllable types × 2 replicate productions × 3 speaking tasks). Phrases #4 and #5 from the two phrase sets were digitized at a 10-kHz sampling rate with 12-bit amplitude resolution. The /tu/ and /ty/ syllables initiating these phrases were then isolated using the segmentation criteria illustrated in Figure 10.1. The left cursor was placed about 3 ms to the left of the sharp increase in waveform energy signaling the release of constriction of /t/. The right cursor was placed at the zero crossing that was judged to best demarcate the end of the "vowel" (/u/ or /y/) and the beginning of the following "consonant" (/l/).

Segmentation was based on changes in waveform shape and intensity, together with a perceptual appraisal. Segmentation was based on perceptual appraisal alone in the 5 percent–10 percent of syllables in which no discontinuity was visually evident in the waveform. Successive glottal periods were eliminated one at a time from the right of the syllable until "/l/ coloring" was no longer perceptible. The average duration of vowels edited in this way was 48.8 ms (s.d. = 16) for group NF, 44.8 ms (s.d. = 15) for group NE-1, and 51.1 ms (s.d. = 20) for group NE-2.

Subjects The subjects were seven female native speakers of French with a mean age of 38 years. Six had served as talkers about 3 months before the experiment. Debriefing after the experiment indicated that none of these subjects were aware that some of their own syllables had been included among the stimuli presented.

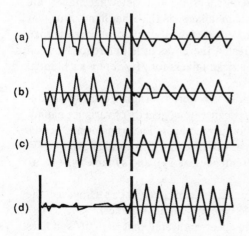

(a)

(b)

(c)

(d)

Figure 10.1 Panels (a)–(c) illustrate the point in the acoustic waveform of three different /tu/ syllables where /u/ was segmented from the following /l/ sound on the basis of changes in waveform shape and amplitude. The criterion used for the measurement of VOT is illustrated for a /tu/ syllable in (d).

Procedures The /tu/ and /ty/ syllables were stored on a high-speed mass storage device for later on-line presentation to listeners in a two-alternative forced-choice test. The syllables were blocked on speaking task (phrases, sentences, story) according to the phrase (#4 or #5) in which they had been produced. Within a block, each syllable was presented five times. This yielded a total of six blocks, each containing 210 stimuli (21 talkers × 2 syllables types × 5 repetitions). The stimuli within each block were digitally normalized for overall rms intensity.

The task was to label each stimulus as 'tu' (/ty/) or 'tous' (/tu/). The subjects were informed that the syllables had been edited from longer stretches of speech, and that an unspecified number of the talkers were not native speakers of French.

The percentage of times each subject correctly identified the /ty/ and /tu/ syllables was computed separately for each of the three speaker groups (NF, NE-1, NE-2) in each of the three speaking tasks (phrase, sentence, story). The maximum number of correct identifications of /ty/ and /tu/ was 70 (7 talkers × 2 replicate productions × 5 presentations). In addition, the percentage of times /tu/ and /ty/ syllables produced by each of the 21 talkers were correctly identified was computed separately for each speaking task. The maximum number of correct identifications was again 70 (7 listeners × 2 replicate productions × 5 presentations).

Results

Syllables produced by the native speakers of French (NF) were correctly identified more often (about 95 percent of the time) than syllables produced by either the experienced Americans (about 75 percent correct) or the inexperienced Americans (about 60 percent). The /tu/ syllables produced by the native French and experienced Americans were correctly identified at a somewhat higher rate than /ty/. For the inexperienced American talkers, on the other hand, /tu/ was correctly identified at a substantially lower rate (about 45 percent correct) than /ty/ (about 70 percent correct). As a result, there was little difference between the experienced and inexperienced American talkers for /ty/, but a substantial difference between these two groups for /tu/.

The percent correct identification scores were transformed using an arcsine transformation (Kirk, 1968, p. 66) because homogeneity of variance cannot be assumed when an analysis is based on percentages. The transformed scores were submitted to a three-way analysis of variance in which speaker group (NF, NE-1, NE-2), speaking task (phrases, sentences, story), and syllable type (/tu/ or /ty/) were all repeated measures.

The effect of speaking task was not significant ($p < 0.01$). However, the interaction of speaker group × syllable type was highly significant [$F(2,12) = 51.27, p < 0.001$]. Tests of simple main effects indicated that the /tu/ syllables produced by talkers in the native French (NF) and experienced American (NE-2) groups were correctly identified more often than /ty/ syllables, whereas the /tu/ syllables produced by the inexperienced Americans (group NE-1) were correctly identified *less* often than /ty/ syllables ($p < 0.01$).

Tests of simple main effects also indicated that the effect of speaker group was significant for both the /tu/ and /ty/ syllables. *Post-hoc* tests (Tukey's HSD, alpha = 0.01) revealed that the /tu/ syllables produced by the native French talkers (NF) were correctly identified more frequently than the /tu/ syllables produced by the experienced American talkers (NE-2) who, in turn, produced /tu/ syllables that were correctly identified more often than those of the inexperienced Americans (NE-1). *Post-hoc* tests revealed that for /ty/, on the other hand, syllables produced by the native French talkers (NF) were correctly identified more frequently than syllables produced by talkers in the two American speaker groups (NE-1, NE-2), but that there was no difference between the two American groups.

The mean percent correct identification scores for syllables produced by individual talkers in the three speaker groups are presented in Table 10.1. In this table data have been collapsed across the seven subjects (i.e., listeners) and three speaking conditions. The data for individual talkers were analyzed in a mixed design analysis of variance in which speaker group was a between-group factor, and speaking task and syllable type were repeated measures.

In this analysis the effect of speaker group was again significant [$F(2,18) = 20.2, p < 0.001$]. *Post-hoc* tests revealed that the native French talkers (NF) produced syllables that were identified more correctly than those of the experienced Americans (NE-2) who, in turn, produced more identifiable syllables than the inexperienced Americans (NE-1) ($p < 0.01$).

TABLE 10.1. The percentage of times /tu/ and /ty/ syllables produced by native speakers of French (NF), experienced American speakers of French (NE-2), and inexperienced American speakers of French (NE-1) were correctly identified. Each score is based on a total of 210 forced-choice identifications (7 listeners $\times$ 2 replicate productions $\times$ 3 speaking tasks $\times$ 5 presentations).

| | Speaker group | | | | | |
| | NF | | NE-2 | | NE-1 | |
Talker	/tu/	/ty/	/tu/	/ty/	/tu/	/ty/
1	99.5	95.1	92.3	82.8	40.3	61.3
2	99.5	91.5	89.0	66.1	89.5	3.8
3	98.5	97.5	35.8	84.1	41.2	94.1
4	97.1	99.0	99.0	93.8	24.3	79.0
5	99.0	89.5	80.7	30.1	23.6	69.0
6	94.7	90.5	99.0	46.5	44.5	97.2
7	98.0	92.6	84.3	97.0	50.2	87.1
$\bar{x}$	98.0	93.7	82.9	71.5	44.8	70.2
s.d.	(1.70)	(3.61)	(21.9)	(25.1)	(22.1)	(32.0)

The interaction between speaker group × syllable type was not significant as it was in the "listener" analysis [$F(2,18) = 2.11, p = 0.145$]. Only six of seven native French talkers, and five of seven experienced Americans produced a more identifiable /tu/ than /ty/. Only six of the seven inexperienced Americans showed the opposite pattern, producing a more identifiable /ty/ than /tu/.

The effect of speaking task did not reach significance [$F(2,36) = 2.43$], but the interaction between speaking task and syllable type did [$F(2,36) = 9.04$, $p < 0.001$]. The syllable /tu/ tended to be correctly identified more often than /ty/ in the phrase and sentence tasks, whereas the reverse was true in the story task. However, tests of simple main effects indicated that this interaction was of marginal importance. There was no significant effect of syllable type (/tu/ versus /ty/) in any of the three speaking tasks, and the effect of speaking task was not significant for either the /tu/ or the /ty/ syllables ($p < 0.01$).

Discussion

It is not surprising that listeners correctly identified more French syllables produced by French than American talkers. What is somewhat surprising is the extent to which correct identification rates differed between the experienced and inexperienced American grups. Listeners were able to correctly identify more of the /tu/ syllables produced by the experienced than inexperienced Americans, although there was no difference in the identifiability of /ty/ syllables produced by the two groups of Americans. This suggests that L2 learners' ability to produce a syllable containing a "new" vowel (i.e., /ty/) does not benefit from additional L2 experience, whereas the ability to produce a syllable with a vowel that has a counterpart in L1 (i.e., /tu/) does show an effect of additional experience.[7]

An examination of syllables produced by individual talkers did not support this conclusion regarding the effect of experience on the accuracy of /tu/ and /ty/ production. The interaction of speaker group × syllable type did not reach significance in the "talker" analysis because 4 of 21 talkers failed to conform to the general pattern evident in the "listener" analysis. There was no overall difference in the correct identification of /tu/ and /ty/ because the experienced talkers tended to produce /tu/ better than /ty/, whereas the inexperienced talkers tended to produce /ty/ better than /tu/. Thus the data do not support the hypothesis that a new L2 vowel which has no direct counterpart in L1 (e.g., /y/) will be produced more successfully than a vowel which does have such a counterpart (e.g., /u/).

Only two of the seven experienced Americans, and two of the seven inexperienced Americans produced /ty/ syllables that were correctly identified 93 percent of the time, the mean for the native French speakers. Since the experienced Americans had been speaking French for about 10 years, this suggests that few American learners will match native French speakers in the ability to produce French /y/.

Their failure to do so may be the result of developing an incorrect articulatory strategy. Students in American schools are explicitly taught to produce French /y/ by placing the tongue in a configuration suitable for English /i/ and rounding the lips, as for English /u/. The experience of the first author in teaching beginning-level French classes is that this strategy results in a reasonable approximation to French /y/. Borden et al. (1981) noted that native English speakers unfamiliar with French were able to produce a recognizable /y/ on their first imitation trial.

If Americans produce French /y/ by recombining the articulatory features used for English vowels, it might explain their initial success in producing /y/ as well as their continued deviation from the phonetic norms of French. To produce French /y/ authentically, it may be necessary for the English learner to position the tongue differently for French /y/ than for English /i/. Delattre (1951) indicates that French /y/ and /i/ are not distinguished primarily by lip rounding, but along a dimension he defines in terms of the anterior-posterior position of the tongue dorsum.

Supporting this are data presented by Linker (1982), which indicate little difference in upper and lower lip protrusion between French /i/ and /y/, little difference in the area of the mouth orifice, and little difference in the ratio of the horizontal to the vertical opening of the mouth during production of these vowels. Analogous data have been reported for Dutch vowels. Based on acoustic analysis, EMG data, and analysis by articulatory synthesis, Raphael et al. (1979) concluded that spectral differences between Dutch /i/ and /y/ were due to more than just a difference in lip rounding. It appeared that the maximum tongue constriction was somewhat greater and more anterior in the production of /i/ than /y/.

The use of lip rounding appropriate for English /u/ in producing French /y/ might also result in differences between English and French native speakers. According to Linker (1982), French /y/ is produced with somewhat greater protrusion of the upper and lower lips than English /u/, and has a substantially larger orifice size (3.53 sq cm compared to 0.23 sq cm). Since increasing the ratio of the mouth orifice relative to the length of the oral cavity importantly affects $F2$ (Stevens and House, 1955), the use of lip rounding appropriate for English vowels in producing French /y/ may result in a difference between native and non-native speakers, even assuming that the tongue configuration is correct.

The inexperienced Americans' /u/ was misidentified as /y/ more than half the time. This is about what we would expect if they were producing French 'tous' with an unmodified English /u/. Debrock and Forrez (1976) report average $F2$ values of 987 and 2188 Hz for the /u/ and /y/ produced by monolingual French-speaking women. As part of a larger study (Flege, 1987) the American talkers in this study produced English /u/ in a phonetic context comparable to the one in which French /u/ was produced here (i.e., in phrases like 'two little boys'). The average frequency of $F2$ in their English /u/ was intermediate to that for French /u/ and /y/ (1673 Hz).

The poor production of French /u/ by many of the inexperienced Americans might also have stemmed from a lack of awareness of the linguistic distinction between the /u/ and /y/ categories of French. If so, these talkers may have developed a perceptual target for French /u/ that embraced the /u/ and /y/ categories produced by native French speakers.

EXPERIMENT 2

Experiment 1 indicated that French /ty/ syllables produced by native speakers of American English were misidentified (as /tu/) about 30 percent of the time. The /tu/ syllables produced by experienced Americans were misidentified (as /ty/) an average of 17 percent of the time, as against 55 percent for Americans who were less experienced in French. This suggests that the relatively experienced Americans produced a perceptually more effective contrast between the French vowels /y/ and /u/ than the less experienced talkers as the result of their greater experience. Experiment 2 directly assessed this vowel contrast using a paired-comparison task.

Methods

Subjects Investigations of L1 acquisition suggest that adult listeners may overlook a distinction between two phones produced by children because of the tendency for speech to be perceived categorically (Monnin and Huntington, 1974; Macken and Barton, 1980; Maxwell and Weismer, 1982; cf. Locke, 1983). This can occur in instances where the child produces a reliable acoustic distinction between phones that represent a within-category phonetic difference for adult listeners.

The subjects chosen for this experiment were native English speakers. Native English speakers might be expected to be more sensitive to acoustic distinction(s) between /u/ and /y/ produced by other native English speakers than native speakers of French. There were six male and six female native English speakers with a mean age of 31 years. Each subject had studied French for at least 4 years in school. Five held advanced degrees in French and taught French, and nine had lived in a French-speaking environment for at least 3 months. Nine of the 12 had some training in phonetics, and all had normal hearing according to self-report.

Stimuli and procedures The same 256 tokens of /ty/ and /tu/ used in experiment 1 were presented to subjects in a two-interval forced-choice task. Subjects were told they would hear one token of /tu/ and one token of /ty/ on each trial. Their task was to determine which member of the pair was most likely to be /ty/. No feedback, familiarization, or training was given.

The stimuli were blocked according to the speaking task (phrase, sentence, story) and phrase (#4 or #5) from which they had been edited. Within a block, each talker's production of /tu/ and /ty/ was presented four times, twice with intended /ty/ as the first member of the pair, and twice with /ty/ in the second position. This provided a total of 84 paired comparisons per block (21 talkers × 4 presentations).

The six blocks of stimuli (2 replicate pairs of 'tu/tous' × 3 speaking tasks) were normalized for overall rms intensity and randomized separately for each subject. The order of blocks was counterbalanced across subjects. Stimulus presentation and response collection were run under the control of a laboratory computer (PDP 11/34). The interstimulus interval was set at 1 s. Presentation of each succeeding trial was triggered by the previous response, with a minimum intertrial interval of 1 s. The experiment lasted about 30 min, with a short break after the first three blocks.

The percentage of times the /ty/ syllables produced by each of the 21 talkers (3 groups × 7 groups) was correctly chosen was computed. The maximum number of correct identifications for each of the three speaking tasks was 96 (2 "tous/tu" pairs × 4 presentations × 12 listeners). In addition, the percentage of times the 12 subjects (i.e., listeners) correctly chose intended /ty/ was calculated separately for each of the three speaker groups (NF, NE-1, NE-2) in each of the three speaking tasks (phrase, sentence, story). These percent correct identification scores were based on a maximum of 56 possible correct judgments (2 'tu/tous' pairs × 4 presentations × 7 talkers).

Results and Discussion

Table 10.2 presents the percentage of times the /ty/ syllables produced by the seven talkers in the three groups were correctly chosen. The data have been averaged over the three speaking tasks. The /ty/ syllables produced by the

TABLE 10.2. The mean percentage of times the /ty/ syllables produced by native speakers of French (NF), experienced English speakers of French (NE-2), and inexperienced English speakers of French (NE-1) were correctly chosen in a paired-comparison task. An asterisk signifies that the /ty/ syllable produced by a talker was correctly chosen at a greater than chance rate ($p < 0.01$).

| Group | Talker | | | | | | | |
	1	2	3	4	5	6	7	$\bar{x}$
NF	87*	96*	90*	95*	90*	90*	88*	90%
NE-2	90*	73*	52	90*	47	83*	95*	75%
NE-1	52	46	82*	55	52	85*	70*	63%

native French speakers (NF) were correctly chosen about 90 percent of the time. Listeners correctly chose 75 percent of the /ty/ syllables produced by the experienced Americans (NE-2), as against only 63 percent of the syllables produced by the inexperienced Americans (NE-1).

After arcsine transformation, the percent correct identification scores were submitted to a mixed design analysis of variance in which speaker group was a between-group factor and speaking task was a repeated measure. The effect of speaking task was not significant [$F(2,36) = 0.18$]. The effect of speaker group did reach significance [$F(2,18) = 6.65, p < 0.01$]. *Post-hoc* tests revealed that native speakers of French (NF) produced a more effective contrast between /tu/ and /ty/ than the experienced American talkers (NE-2) who, in turn, produced a better contrast than the inexperienced American talkers (NE-1) ($p < 0.01$). An examination of data for individual talkers indicated that listeners correctly chose /ty/ at better than chance levels for all seven native French talkers, but for only five of the seven experienced American talkers, and only three of the seven inexperienced Americans ($p < 0.01$ by the binomial probability test; Siegel, 1956).

Speaker group and speaking task served as repeated measures in a "listener" analysis of the same data. This analysis produced the same results as the "talker" analysis: no effect of speaking task, but a significant effect of speaker group [$F(2,22) = 41.33, p < 0.001$]. *Post-hoc* tests (Tukey's HSD, alpha = 0.01) again indicated that the native speakers of French produced a more effective contrast between /tu/ and /ty/ than the experienced American talkers (NE-2) who, in turn, produced a more effective contrast than the inexperienced American talkers (NE-1).

These findings demonstrate the importance of experience for production of a potentially confusable pair of foreign language vowels such as /u/ and /y/. Our perceptual evaluation indicated that although the experienced American talkers did not produce as effective a perceptual contrast between /ty/ and /tu/ as native speakers of French, they were nonetheless better at doing so than relatively less-experienced Americans.

This experiment also demonstrated that native speakers of English with some experience in French are able to effectively discriminate the /u/ and /y/ produced by native speakers of French. In experiment 1, native French-speaking subjects correctly identified the /y/ produced by native French speakers about 93 percent of the time. In this experiment, native English-speaking subjects correctly chose the /y/ produced by native French speakers about 90 percent of the time.

The American subjects' success in discriminating /u/ and /y/ does not necessarily demonstrate, however, that their perception of French /y/ and /u/ matches that of native speakers of French. It is possible they discriminated /y/ and /u/ on a purely auditory basis. It is also possible they were familiar enough with the phonetic properties of French /u/ and /y/ to discriminate these vowels phonetically, but without having precisely the same "prototype" or "perceptual target" as French native speakers.

ACOUSTIC ANALYSIS

The two perceptual experiments indicated that native speakers of English produced /tu/ and /ty/ less effectively than native speakers of French. In this section we acoustically examine the syllables presented in the perceptual experiments to determine how native and non-native speakers' production of those syllables may have differed.

Based on the perceptual results, we expected to find that the native French speakers produced a substantial spectral difference between /y/ and /u/, whereas the native English speakers—especially the inexperienced ones—produced a much smaller spectral distinction. The results of experiment 1 did not support the hypothesis that new phones (such as /y/) are produced more accurately than L2 phones with a close counterpart in L1 (such as /u/). This leads us to expect that, when measured acoustically, the difference between the French and American talkers will be the same for /y/ and /u/.

The perceptual experiments did not assess the accuracy with which French /t/ was produced. The acoustic analysis of /t/ in this section will permit us to test a hypothesis concerning why L2 learners ordinarily do not match native speakers of the foreign language being learned (Flege, 1981, 1984b). If L2 learners merge the phonetic properties of L1 and L2 phones judged to be equivalent (e.g., the /t/ of French and English) we expect to observe two phenomena. First, American talkers—even experienced ones—should produce French /t/ with VOT values that are longer than the short-lag values commonly observed for French monolinguals (about 20 ms, Caramazza and Yeni-Komshian, 1974), despite the fact that it may be less difficult to produce stops with short-lag than long-lag VOT values (Kewley-Port and Preston, 1974). Second, the French talkers should also produce French /t/ with longer VOT values than monolingual French speakers because of their massive exposure to the stops of English.

Methods

The 252 exemplars of /tu/ and /ty/ examined in experiments 1 and 2 were low-pass filtered at 4 kHz (Krohn-Hite model 3343) before being digitized at a sampling rate of 10 kHz with 12-bit amplitude resolution. As illustrated in Fig. 10.1, voice-onset time (VOT) was measured from the display of a graphics terminal (Tektronix model 4010) by setting a cursor at the beginning of the noise burst signaling stop release, and at the first upward-going zero crossing of the waveform, signaling onset of phonation.

The center frequencies of formants 1–3 in the vowels of /tu/ and /ty/ were estimated by means of linear predictive coding (LPC) analysis. Using an oscillographic display of the speech waveforms, a 256-point (25.6-ms) Hamming window was positioned so that its left tail coincided with the positive peak of the first pitch period in the approximately 50-ms periodic portion of syllables.

Twelve linear prediction coefficients were calculated. Formant frequency values were then determined by picking amplitude peaks from the smoothed spectra using algorithms developed by Markel and Gray (1976).

The aperiodic portion (i.e., "VOT interval") of the syllables examined varied from about 30 to 80 ms. This means that some of the vowel measurements, especially those made of syllables with a very short VOT interval, may reflect the formant frequencies of consonant transitions into the "vowel" rather than just the "steady-state" portion of "vowels." However, since VOT did not differ across the three speaker groups (see Results), this should not invalidate between-group comparisons.

Results

VOT   Table 10.3 presents the VOT of /t/ in /ty/ and /tu/ syllables produced by talkers in the three speaker groups. These mean values represent the average of three speaking conditions and two replicate productions of both syllables. The VOT /tu/ and /ty/ was somewhat longer for the inexperienced Americans (63 ms) than for either the experienced Americans (50 ms) or native speakers of French (54 ms).

The VOT values measured in /tu/ and /ty/ syllables produced by each talker in the three speaking tasks were submitted to a mixed design analysis of variance in which speaker group (NF, NE-1, NE-2) was the between-group factor, and speaking task (phrase, sentence, story) and syllable type (/tu/, /ty/) were repeated measures. There were no significant interactions. Neither the effect of speaking task nor syllable type reached significance. The experienced Americans (NE-2) more nearly approximated the phonetic norms of French than the inexperienced Americans (NE-1). Although their VOT for /t/ averaged 13 ms shorter than that of the experienced Americans, the effect of speaker group also failed to reach significance ($p < 0.01$).

The data for individual subjects presented in Table 10.4 are highly consistent with the grouped means presented in Table 10.3. The most important point to note is that none of the talkers, including the native speakers of French,

TABLE 10.3. The mean duration, in ms, of the VOT in /tu/ and /ty/ syllables produced by native speakers of French (NF), experienced English speakers of French (NE-2), and inexperienced English speakers of French (NE-1). Each mean is based on 42 observations (7 talkers × 2 replicate productions × 3 speaking tasks); standard deviations are in parentheses.

| | /tu/ | | | /ty/ | | |
	NF	NE-2	NE-1	NF	NE-2	NE-1
mean	49.6	44.8	62.2	57.1	54.9	64.3
s.d.	(14)	(13)	(15)	(15)	(17)	(23)

TABLE 10.4. The mean VOT, in ms, of the /t/ in /tu/ and /ty/ syllables produced by native speakers of French (NF), experienced English speakers of French (NE-2), and inexperienced English speakers of French (NE-1). Each mean is based on 12 observations (2 syllable types × 2 replicate productions × 3 speaking tasks).

Talker	NF	Speaker group NE-2	NE-1
1	61.8(17)	38.8(12)	55.2(11)
2	62.3(13)	45.4(12)	49.1(15)
3	60.5 (7)	40.9(11)	76.8(10)
4	52.1(14)	61.0(16)	46.4(10)
5	39.8(10)	55.2(12)	80.0(27)
6	57.0(17)	56.8(23)	57.4(16)
7	38.3 (6)	47.9 (9)	74.3(10)

produced /t/ with an average VOT value of less than 35 ms. Thus, *none* of the talkers in this study closely resembled monolingual native speakers of French.

Vowel formant data The mean frequency values of formants 1–3 in the /y/ and /u/ vowels are presented in Table 10.5. These data have been averaged across the three speaking tasks and two replicate productions of each vowel by the seven talkers in each group. It is apparent that there was little difference between the groups for /y/. For /u/, there seems to be a between-group difference for $F3$, and an even larger difference for $F2$.

The frequency with which the 252 /ty/ and /tu/ syllables were identified as /ty/ in experiment 1 was correlated with the mean formant frequency values measured for those syllables. This analysis revealed that variations in $F2$ accounted for 62 percent of the variance in the mean identification scores, as against only 9 percent for $F3$ and 1 percent for $F1$. Therefore, only $F2$ differences will be further discussed.

A closer examination of the $F2$ data revealed clear differences between the American and French talkers, as well as a difference between the experienced

TABLE 10.5. The mean frequency, in Hz, of formants 1-3 in the /u/ and /y/ vowels produced by native speakers of French (NF), experienced English speakers of French (NE-2), and inexperienced English speakers of French (NE-1). Each mean is based on 42 observations (7 talkers × 2 replicate productions × 3 speaking tasks); standard deviations are in parentheses.

	NF	/tu/ NE-2	NE-1		NF	/ty/ NE-2	NE-1
$F1$	283(45)	262(22)	266(40)	$F1$	260(35)	247(24)	265(51)
$F2$	1387(211)	1593(267)	1909(193)	$F2$	2102(139)	2006(297)	2012(254)
$F3$	2521(279)	2624(186)	2875(229)	$F3$	2779(387)	2725(402)	2840(212)

and inexperienced Americans. When the 84 /u/ and /y/ vowels produced by talkers in each of three groups were plotted in an $F1$–$F2$ space, there was practically no overlap in $F2$ values between the /y/ and /u/ vowels produced by the native French speakers, some overlap for vowels produced by the experienced Americans, and almost complete overlap in $F2$ for the /y/ and /u/ produced by the inexperienced Americans.

The $F2$ difference between /u/ and /y/ averaged 715 Hz for vowels produced by the native speakers of French (NF). The $F2$ difference between /y/ and /u/ was much smaller for the non-native speakers, averaging 413 Hz for the experienced Americans (NE-2), and only 103 Hz for the inexperienced Americans (NE-1).

A second finding was that the American talkers more closely matched the French talkers in producing /y/ than /u/. The formant values measured for /u/ and /y/ were submitted to a mixed design analysis of variance in which speaker group was the between-subjects factor, and vowel (/u/ or /y/) and speaking tasks (phrase, sentence, story) were repeated measures. There was a significant vowel $\times$ speaker group interaction [$F = (2,18) = 11.84$; $p < 0.001$]. Tests of simple main effects revealed that the effect of speaker group was not significant for /y/ in any of the three speaking conditions, but that it was significant for /u/ in all three speaking tasks ($p < 0.01$). In each case, the French talkers produced /u/ with lower $F2$ values than the experienced Americans who, in turn, produced /u/ with lower $F2$ values than the inexperienced American speakers of French ($p > 0.01$). Tests of simple main effects also revealed that the French (NF) and experienced American talkers (NE-2) produced /y/ with significantly higher $F2$ values than /u/ in all three speaking tasks, whereas the inexperienced Americans (NE-1) did not ($p < 0.01$).

As expected from the perceptual experiments, the effect of speaking task did not reach significance.

Discussion

VOT The most striking characteristic of the VOT data is that the French talkers, who were proficient speakers of English, produced French /t/ with VOT values that substantially exceeded the approximately 20-ms VOT values commonly observed in the speech of French monolinguals (Caramazza and Yeni-Komshian, 1974). This confirms the prediction (Flege, 1981, 1984b) that L2 learning will affect the production of phones in L1. This prediction follows from the hypothesis that the perceptual target for an L1 phone—and eventually the motor plan used to realize it—changes as the foreign language learner is exposed to that phone's acoustically different counterpart in L2. More specifically, French speakers of English are hypothesized to merge the phonetic properties of French and English /t/ as the result of judging these acoustically different phones to be realizations of the same phonetic category (i.e., as the result of interlingual identifications).

194

This hypothesis receives additional support from data reported by Caramazza et al. (1973). In that study, French speakers of English labeled stops in a VOT continuum differently than monolingual speakers of French. They also produced French stops with somewhat longer (English-like) VOT values than monolingual speakers of French. Unlike subjects in the Caramazza et al. (1973) study, the French talkers in this study all learned English as adults. At the time of the study they had lived for about 10 years in an English-speaking environment, and were using English as their primary language. This may explain why learning English seems to have affected our French talkers' production of French stops to a much greater extent than it did for French talkers in the Caramazza et al. (1973) study.

Another predicted effect of interlingual identification is that English learners of French will develop a perceptual target for French /t/ which merges the phonetic properties of French and English /t/, and that this will lead them, in turn, to "overshoot" the short-lag VOT values appropriate for French /t/. As predicted, the American talkers produced /t/ with substantially longer VOT values than monolingual French speakers. Not even those who were very experienced in French produced French /t/ with an average VOT value of less than 35 ms. Of the 168 American-produced stops examined, only seven had a VOT value of less than 30 ms (cf. Flege, 1980). This seems to confirm the prediction that, because of interlingual identification, adult learners of a foreign language will never succeed in producing L2 stops with complete accuracy when stops in their native language differ substantially in VOT from those in L2.[8]

Vowel formant data The most important finding regarding vowel production was that the American talkers matched the French talkers in producing /y/ but not /u/. This supports the hypothesis that "new" L2 phones are produced more accurately than L2 phones which have a direct counterpart in the native language.

The French talkers produced /y/ with a mean $F2$ frequency of 2102 Hz. This represents a somewhat lower mean frequency than reported previously by Debrock and Forrez (1976) for five French monolingual women (2188 Hz). The experienced Americans produced /y/ with a mean $F2$ frequency of 2006 Hz, as against 2012 Hz for the inexperienced Americans. The small differences between the three groups in $F2$ for /y/ were not significant, although listeners correctly identified about 20 percent more of the /ty/ syllables produced by the French than American talkers in experiment 1. This suggests that the small between-group $F2$ differences we noted were perceptually relevant or, more likely, that some acoustic dimension(s) other than just $F2$ served to cue the identity of /y/.

The French talkers produced French /u/ with a substantially higher mean $F2$ value (1387 Hz) than previously reported for monolingual French speakers (987 Hz) by Debrock and Forrez (1976). This suggests that learning English influenced their production of French /u/, just as it influenced their production of French /t/. We hypothesize that the French speakers of English produced French /u/ with higher (more English-like) $F2$ values because they judged the

/u/ of English and French to be equivalent. By the same reasoning, the seeming lack of an L2 effect on /y/ may follow from their *not* judging French /y/ to be equivalent to an English vowel. This should be further tested in a study comparing the French vowel production of monolingual native speakers of French to that of French talkers who also speak English.

Many of our American talkers failed to produce a perceptually effective contrast between French /y/ and /u/ largely because they failed to accurately produce /u/. The French talkers produced /u/ with a mean $F2$ of 1387 Hz, compared to 1593 Hz for the experienced Americans, and 1909 Hz for the inexperienced Americans. The $F2$ value for French /u/ produced by the inexperienced Americans is somewhat surprising in view of the fact that adult L2 learners, at least those who are reasonably proficient in the foreign language, generally "approximate" the phonetic norms of a foreign language. In another study (Flege, 1987) the inexperienced American talkers produced English /u/ with a mean $F2$ value of 1675 Hz. We would therefore have expected them to produce French /u/ with somewhat lower (more French-like) $F2$ values, rather than with $F2$ values that were actually higher (less French-like) than that of their English /u/.

An explanation for this finding is not immediately apparent from the data of this study. In experiment 2 we found that four of seven inexperienced Americans did not produce a perceptually reliable contrast between /u/ and /y/. The acoustic analysis revealed that this group of talkers did not produce a reliable $F2$ contrast between /u/ and /y/. One possibility is that at least some of the inexperienced Americans were not perceptually aware of the linguistic distinction between the French /u/ and /y/ categories.

Another possibility is that they were generally aware of the existence of this vowel distinction, but mistakenly thought that the word 'tous' contains /y/ rather than /u/. A number of studies have shown that adult L2 learners sometimes replace an L2 phone which has a direct counterpart in L1 (e.g., /u/) with a new L2 phone (such as /y/) they have recently learned (see Flege, 1984b). This phenomenon may represent a form of overcompensation to the difficulty inherent in mastering the new sound system of a foreign language.

Both acoustic and perceptual criteria demonstrated that the experienced American talkers were aware of the linguistic distinction between French /y/ and /u/. Despite this, they produced French /u/ with a mean $F2$ frequency that was only slightly lower and thus more French-like (1593 Hz) than the $F2$ in their English /u/ (1670 Hz, Flege, 1987). Thus even after many years of experience speaking French they seem to have done little to modify their production of /u/ in the direction of French phonetic norms.

GENERAL DISCUSSION

The first conclusion to be drawn from this study is that adult native speakers of English may produce new phones in a foreign language (such as French /y/)

196

more accurately than L2 phones which have a clear counterpart in the native language (such as French /u/). Listeners' identification of vowels in Experiment 1 revealed a tendency for inexperienced American speakers of French to produce the new vowel /y/ more accurately than /u/. This suggested that new L2 phones may be learned more rapidly than L2 phones which have a clear counterpart in L1. However, the reverse tendency was noted for more experienced American speakers of French and, as a result, the overall difference in the rate at which /u/ and /y/ were correctly identified was not significant.

An acoustic analysis of $F2$ nonetheless revealed that /y/ was produced more accurately than /u/. The American talkers did not differ from the French talkers in producing the new vowel /y/, whereas they produced /u/ with significantly higher $F2$ values than the French talkers. The inexperienced American talkers produced French /u/ with $F2$ values equaling their French /y/, suggesting they may have confused these two vowel categories. The experienced American, on the other hand, produced French /u/ with $F2$ values that closely corresponded to the $F2$ measured in their production of English /u/ in another study.

The second conclusion to be drawn from this study is that experience enables adult learners of a foreign language to produce L2 phones with greater accuracy. Acoustic and perceptual analyses revealed that experienced American speakers of French produced a more effective contrast between French /u/ and /y/ than less experienced Americans in three different speaking tasks.[9] They also produced French /t/ with somewhat shorter (more French-like) VOT values than the less-experienced Americans. These findings are consistent with the results of previous studies of foreign language speech production (e.g., Flege and Port, 1981; Port and Mitleb, 1980; Williams, 1980).

The observation that L2 learners sometimes approximate the phonetic norms of a foreign language leaves us with the intriguing question of why they seldom if ever match L2 native speakers in producing L2 phones that differ phonetically from their counterpart in L1. Many researchers (e.g., Scovel, 1969) have suggested that the ability of humans to learn new patterns of pronunciation diminishes near the end of childhood for neurophysiological reasons. We feel an alternate hypothesis worthy of further investigation is that previous phonetic experience impedes the formation of accurate perceptual targets for phones in L2 (Flege, 1981, 1984b). More specifically, we hypothesize that phones which closely resemble one another, such as the /t/ of French and English, mutually influence one another because language learners judge them to be acoustically different realizations of the same category.

This hypothesis is supported by the VOT data. The native French talkers in this study produced the /t/ in French words with VOT values that were intermediate to the short-lag and long-lag values typically observed for French and English, respectively. We hypothesize that the French talkers identified the prevocalic /t/ occurring in English words with the /t/ of French. We further hypothesize that, as a result, their perceptual target for French /t/ represented a merger of the phonetic properties of French and English /t/.

Similarly, we hypothesize that the American speakers of French judged the /t/ of French and English as being different realizations of the same category. If the American talkers developed a perceptual target for French /t/ that merged the phonetic properties of French and English /t/, it means they were probably attempting to produce a stop with VOT values intermediate to those of monolingual speakers of French and English. We observed that although the Americans approximated the short-lag phonetic norm for French /t/, they—like the native French talkers—also produced French /t/ with VOT values that were intermediate to those of French and English monolinguals.

Previous research in L1 and L2 speech learning indicates that talkers' production of the VOT dimension eventually conforms to perception of the VOT dimension in stop consonants (see, e.g., Zlatin and Koenigsknect, 1976; Williams, 1980). If accuracy in speech production is limited by the accuracy of the perceptual target that is developed during speech learning, native English speakers may *never* match native speakers of French unless they manage to develop two distinct perceptual targets, one for the /t/ of French and one for the /t/ of English. However, speech perception data reported by Caramazza et al. (1973) indicate that although French speakers of English labeled stops differently than French monolinguals, they did not label a French /t/ differently than an English /t/ (but cf. Elman et al., 1977).

The hypothesis that English speakers will never produce /t/ with complete accuracy is further supported by the observation that even Americans talkers who held advanced degrees in French, had lived for more than a year in France, and had spoken French for more than 10 years did not produce French /t/ with the short-lag VOT values observed for monolingual speakers of French.

The acoustic measurements made of French vowels are also consistent with the hypothesized role of interlingual identification. We found that the Americans were able to accurately produce /y/ but not /u/. The "new" vowel /y/ does not have a direct counterpart in English, as does French /u/. As a result, it may not have been "identified" with any vowel in English, and thus escaped the limiting effect of previous phonetic experience.

The American talkers were much less successful in producing French /u/, a vowel which does have a clear counterpart in English. The inexperienced Americans seem to have produced French /u/ as if it were /y/. Their relatively poor production of /u/ may have resulted from a failure to perceptually differentiate the /y/ and /u/ vowel categories of French. The experienced Americans produced French /u/ much like the /u/ of English. This suggests that American learners of French may never accurately produce French /u/.[10]

This raises the question of why the American talkers seem to have approximated the VOT norm of French for /t/ but not /u/. We speculate that this is due to the nature of interlingual identification. There seems to be only a single phone in English (/t/) with which French /t/ will be identified. However, our acoustic evidence suggests that the inexperienced American talkers may have judged both the /u/ and /y/ of French to be equivalent to English /u/.

198

We alluded above to the possibility that the experienced Americans may have produced the French word 'tous' with the /u/ of English. An alternative hypothesis is that the perceptual target they developed for French /u/ represented a merger of the phonetic properties of the /u/ of French and English. Why their French /u/ much more closely resembled the /u/ of English than French, rather than falling at a point that is more nearly intermediate to the /u/ of French and English, is unclear. Perhaps their phonetic learning was slowed by the necessity of first distinguishing the /y/ and /u/ categories of French.

In summary, the results presented here indicate that adult learners of a foreign language do not always produce foreign language words with phones occurring in their native language. Both groups of American talkers produced the new vowel /y/ with relatively great accuracy. Both groups of Americans produced French /t/ with VOT values that were shorter than typical for English. This indicates that existing articulatory motor plans can be modified, and new ones established. Limits on the extent to which L2 learners approximate native speakers' pronunciation of an L2 phone which has an acoustically different counterpart in L1 may stem not from an inability to learn new forms of pronunciation, but from the interlingual identification of L1 and L2 phones. Judging acoustically different phones as belonging to the same phonetic category seems to underlie the process of speech perception. The continued operation of this perceptual process in L2 learning may lead to inaccurate perceptual targets for L2 phones which, in turn, limits the accuracy of L2 speech production.

We observed several differences between native and non-native speakers of French. The interpretation of these results was based on inferences concerning talkers' "perceptual targets" for L1 and L2 phones (see footnote 5). A great deal of further research is clearly needed to test these inferences. It will be important in future studies of L2 production to demonstrate which specific phones in the native and target language are judged to be equivalent (i.e., "identified" with one another), and to determine the extent to which the perceptual targets for L2 phones evolve as a function of experience with the foreign language.

NOTES

1. The accuracy with which a learner produces the sounds of a foreign language can be objectively assessed in a variety of ways: (1) through the use of rating scale judgments by native speakers of the target language, (2) by calculating the frequency with which L2 phones are correctly identified, and (3) through acoustic analyses. This last method depends on a comparison of specific acoustic dimensions of an L2 phone produced by non-native speakers to the average value of that dimension in the speech of monolingual speakers of the target language.

2. We examined the production of 'tous' and 'tu' in order to minimize the effect of differences in word familiarity. Studies of both L1 acquisition (e.g., Barton, 1980) and L2 learning (see Flege, 1984b) indicate that word familiarity may affect the extent to which phones are correctly produced. 'Tu' and 'tous' are among the first French words learned by non-native speakers owing to their high frequency of occurrence. 'Tu' is the second person singular pronoun meaning 'you'; 'tous' is an adjective meaning 'all.'

3. Cross-language auditory comparisons suggest that French /u/ is more "tense" or "peripheral" in the vowel space than its English counterpart (Delattre, 1953; Adamczewski and Keen, 1973; Valdman, 1976). If /u/ is articulated with a relatively more posterior tongue position in French than English, one would expect it to be produced with lower $F2$ values than English /u/ (see Lindblom and Sundberg, 1971). The comparison of French and English /u/ is complicated by the fact that English /u/ is produced more variably than its French counterpart, probably because there is no adjacent high vowel category in English (i.e., /y/) with which it risks being perceptually confused (Stevens, 1983). The results of several studies suggest that the second formant frequency ($F2$) of /u/ is about the same (700–900 Hz) in French and English (Paterson and Barney, 1952; Delattre, 1951; Debrock and Forrez, 1976; Riordan, 1977). However, other studies indicate that English /u/ is produced with considerably higher (1000–1900 Hz) $F2$ values than those reported for French /u/, especially in conversational speech (Stevens and House, 1963; Shockey, 1974; Labov, 1981). Thus if Americans produce French words with an English /u/, we expect them to produce French /u/ with higher $F2$ values than monolingual speakers of French.

4. If cross-language similarity judgments for vowels are based primarily on the position of the tongue and the resulting acoustic spectrum, it seems reasonable to think that listeners will judge French /y/ to be closer to English /i/ than to English /u/. If degree of lip rounding is important to similarity judgments, French /y/ might be judged to be closer to English /u/ than /i/. Americans seldom if ever realize French /y/ as an /i/-quality vowel (Walz, 1979), although speakers of certain West African languages are said to do so (N. Spector, 1983). Instead, they typically realize French /y/ as an /u/-quality (Walz, 1979), and at times produce French /u/ with an /y/-quality vowel (Gaudin, 1953). Evidence from speech production thus suggests that lip rounding might be more important to similarity judgments than the configuration of the tongue, Jakobson et al. (1952) note, on the other hand, that similarity judgments may depend as much on the *system* of phonological contrasts in the listener's native language as on the physical properties of phones found in L1 and L2. If so, no physical dimension, or combination of dimensions, may uniquely determine which L1 phone is judged to be "closest" to a new L2 phone.

5. In this article we use the term "perceptual target" as a convenient cover term. Phoneticians have long debated what constitutes the "target" or "goal" for various phones, but what talkers aim to achieve in producing a phone is still unclear. It might be an "auditory" effect, the tactile and/or kinesthetic feedback associated with particular configurations of the speech articulators, or some combination of all three that varies according to phone or phone class. Research in recent years (e.g., Summerfield, 1979, 1983) suggests that a phonetic "target" or "goal" is not specified in terms of a modality-specific code, but is more abstract in nature. An alternative term we might have used here is "mental representation," for we conceive of a "perceptual target" as representing the talker's notion of how a phone "ought" to be produced. Another term we might have used is "prototype," for we consider the perceptual target to include all phonetic information, including language-specific and subcategorical information, pertinent to the production of a phone.

6. Results reported by Elman et al. (1977) suggest that highly proficient bilinguals may have coexistent perceptual targets for counterpart phones in L1 and L2 (see Weinreich, 1953, 1963), but other previous studies suggest that bilinguals generally have a single perceptual target for counterpart phones in their two languages. This important issue invites further research.

7. The dynamic spectral properties of the transition into the steady-state portion of syllables may have contributed to the identification of /tu/ and /ty/. However, the identifiability of the periodic portion ("vowel") in /tu/ and /ty/ syllables probably provides a good assessment of talkers ability to produce /u/ and /y/. French- and English-speaking listeners are known to identify the vowels in French CV syllables (e.g., /tu/ and /ty/) as accurately as isolated French vowels (Gottfried, 1979, 1984).

8. One reason for caution in accepting the conclusion that L2 learners never match native speakers of a target foreign language in producing stop consonants is that the American talkers in this study were not using French as their primary language at the time of the study. This conclusion should be further tested by examining the production of French by Americans who have spent a considerable period of time in a French-speaking environment and are using French as their primary language at the time of the study.

9. Sociolinguists (e.g., Labov, 1972) have noted that variations in "attention to speech," as manipulated through the use of different speaking tasks, may affect native language speech production. Tasks that allow talkers to "pay attention" to their speech sometimes result in more "correct" productions of sounds (i.e., a more frequent production of variants found in the prestige dialect of the talkers' native language). In this study we observed that varying speaking task had no effect on L2 speech production. Acoustic and perceptual analyses revealed that American talkers produced the French syllables /tu/ and /ty/ with equal accuracy when reading a list of phrases, generating complete sentences from those phrases, and producing a series of sentences that were linked together in a spontaneous story. It seems reasonable to think that the manipulation of speaking tasks used in this study was sufficient to affect general vigilance or "attention to speech." We are forced to conclude that "attention to speech" has little effect on adults' production of L2 phones. We hasten to add, however, that no external measure was taken to demonstrate that general attention or vigilance changed across the three speaking tasks. It remains possible that "attention to speech" did *not* change as a function of speaking task, or that a manipulation of speaking task will influence the accuracy of L2 phones produced by learners who are not yet proficient in L2. Even the least experienced American talker in this study had spent nearly a year in France and was capable of the very demanding "story" speaking task in their foreign language. Weismer and Cariski (1983) suggest that the benefit of rehearsal for skilled motor control may be greatest in the early stages of acquisition, when cognitive factors are presumed to be relatively important. In the case of L2 learning, attention to speech might cease to influence production beyond the time learners establish a motor plan for producing L2 phones. Although somewhat uncertain, our negative findings in regard to the effect of speaking task is of some methodological importance for future studies of L2 speech production. It is simple to have talkers read phrase lists. Our results suggest that such a speech sample may provide a reasonable estimate of learners' production of L2 phones in other, more natural, speaking tasks.

10. We can think of an important reason for tempering the conclusion that new L2 phones are produced better than L2 phones with cognates in L1. We considered the vowels in just two French words. The vowels in 'tous' and 'tu' might be unrepresentative of the way American talkers produce /u/ and /y/ in other words. The American talkers are likely to have learned 'tous' and 'tu' very early. As a result, these words might exemplify a nonoptimal approximation to the phonetic norms of French for /y/ and /u/ that remained "frozen" after later, more accurate, productions of these vowels were learned in other French words.

REFERENCES

Adamczewski, H., and D. Keen. 1973. *Phonétique et phonologie de l'anglais contemporain.* Paris: Armand Colin.

Barton, D. 1980. Phonemic perception in children. In G. Yeni-Komshian, J. Kavanagh, & C. Ferguson (Eds.), *Child phonology,* 2:97–116. NY: Academic Press.

Bordon, G., K. Harris, H. Fitch, & H. Yoshioka. 1981. Producing relatively unfamiliar speech gestures: A synthesis of perceptual targets and production rules. Haskins Laboratories Status Report on Speech Research.

Brière, E. 1966. An investigation of phonological interference. *Language,* 42; 769–96.

Caramazza, A., and G. Yeni-Komshian. 1974. Voice onset time in two French dialects. *Journal of Phonetics, 2;* 239–245.

Caramazza, A., G. Yeni-Komshian, E. Zurif, & E. Carbone. 1973. The acquisition of a new phonological contrast: The case of stop consonants in French-English bilinguals. *Journal Acoustical Society of America, 54;* 421–28.

Debrock, M., and G. Forrez. 1976. Analyse mathématique des voyelles orales du néerlandais and du français, methode et résultats. *Revue de Phonétique Appliquée, 37;* 27–73.

Delattre, P. 1951. The physicological interpretation of sound spectrograms. *Publications of the Modern Language Association, 66;* 864–75.

Delattre, P. 1953. Les modes phonétiques du français. *French Review 27;* 59–63.

Elman, J., R. Diehl, & S. Buchwald. 1977. Perceptual switching in bilinguals. *Journal of the Acoustical Society of America, 62;* 971–74.

Elsendoorn, B. 1983. Quality and quantity in English by Dutchmen: Two parameters inducing double Dutch. In M. van den Broecke, V. van Heuven, & W. Zonneveld (Eds.), *Sound structures, studies for Antonie Cohen,* 53–69. The Netherlands: Dordrecht Foris.

Flege, J. 1980. Phonetic approximation in second language acquisition. *Language Learning, 30;* 117–34.

Flege, J. 1981. The phonological basis of foreign accent: A hypothesis. *TESOL Quarterly, 15;* 443–45.

Flege, J. 1984a. The detection of French accent by American listeners. *Journal Acoustical Society of America. 76;* 692–707.

Flege, J. 1984b. The production and perception of foreign languages. In H. Winitz (Ed.), *Human communication and its disorders, I.* Norwood Ablex. To appear.

Flege, J. 1987. The production of "new" and "similar" phrases in a foreign language: Evidence for the effect of equivalence classification. *Journal of Phonetics, 15.* 1.

Flege, J. and R. Hammond. 1982. Mimicry of non-distinctive phonetic differences between language varieties. *Studies in Second Language Acquisition, 5;* 1–17.

Flege, J., and R. Port. 1981. Cross-language phonetic interference: Arabic to English. *Language and Speech, 24,* 125–46.

Gaudin, L. 1953. Common mistakes in pronunciation. *French Review 26,* 451–60.

Gottfried, T. 1979. Identification of French vowels. In J. Wolf and D. Klatt (Eds), *Speech communication papers,* pp. 29–32. New York: Acoustical Society of America.

Gottfried, T. 1984. Effects of consonant context on the perception of French vowels. *Journal of Phonetics.*

Jakobson, R., G. Fant, & M. Halle. 1952/1963. *Preliminaries to speech analysis.* Cambridge, MA: MIT.

Johansson, F. 1973. *Immigrant Swedish phonology.* Sweden: CWK Gleerup, Lund.

Kewley-Port, D., and M. Preston. 1974. Early apical stop production. *Journal of Phonetics 2;* 195–210.

Kirk, R. 1968. *Experimental design: Procedures for the behavioral sciences.* Belmont, CA: Brooks-Cole.

Koo, J. 1972. Language universals and the acquisition of an unfamiliar sound. *International Review of Applied Linguistics, 10;* 145–52.

Koutsoudas, A., and O. Koutsoudas. 1962. A contrastive analysis of the segmental phones of Greek and English. *Language Learning, 12;* 211–30.

Labov, W. 1972. *Sociolinguistic patterns.* Philadelphia: University of Pennsylvania.

Labov, W. 1981. Resolving the neogrammarian controversy. *Language, 57;* 267–309.

Lado, R. 1957. *Linguistics across cultures: Applied linguistics for language teachers.* Ann Arbor: University of Michigan.

Le Bras, J. 1981. Utilisation de la reconnaissance automatique de la parole pour l'apprentissage des languages. Unpublished Ph.D. thesis. Université de Rennes II, France.

Lindblom, B., and J. Sundberg. 1971. Acoustical consequences of lip, tongue, jaw, and larynx movements. *Journal of the Acoustical Society of America, 50;* 1166–79.

Linker, W. 1982. Articulatory and acoustic correlates of labial activity in vowels: A cross-language study. In *Working papers in phonetics,* vol. 56, Department of Linguistics, University of California, Los Angeles.

Locke, J. 1983. *Phonological acquisition and change.* New York: Academic Press.

Macken, M., and D. Barton. 1980. The acquisition of the voicing contrast in English: A study of voice onset time in work-initial stop consonants. *Journal Acoustical Society of America, 7;* 41–74.

Markel, J., and A. Grey. 1976. *Linear prediction of speech.* New York: Springer.

Maxwell, E. and G. Weismer. 1982. The contribution of phonological, acoustic, and perceptual techniques to the characterization of a misarticulating child's voice contrast for stops. *Applied Psycholinguistics, 3;* 29–43.

Monnin, L., and D. Huntington. 1974. The relationship of articulatory defects to speech-sound identification. *Journal of Speech and Hearing Research, 7;* 352–66.

Peterson, G., and H. Barney. 1952. Control methods used in a study of the vowels. *Journal Acoustical Society of America, 24;* 175–84.

Politzer, R., and L. Weiss. 1969. Development aspects of auditory discrimination, echo response, and recall. *Modern Language Journal 53;* 75–85.

Port, R., and F. Mitleb. 1980. Phonetic and phonological manifestations of the voicing contrast in Arabic-accented English. In *Research in phonetics, vol. 1,* 137–66. Department of Linguistics, Indiana University.

Raphael, L., F. Bell-Berti, R. Collier, & T. Baer. 1979. Tongue position in rounded and unrounded front vowel pairs. *Language and Speech, 22;* 37–48.

Riordan, C. 1977. Control of vocal-tract length in speech. *Journal of the Acoustical Society of America, 62;* 998–1002.

Scovel, T. 1969. Foreign accent, language acquisition, and cerebral dominance. *Language Learning, 19;* 245–54.

Shockey, L. 1974. Phonetic and phonological properties of connected speech. In *Working papers in linguistics, vol. 17,* Department of Linguistics, Ohio State University.

Siegel, S. 1956. *Nonparametric statistics for the behavioral sciences.* New York: McGraw-Hill.

Spector, N. 1983. Personal communication.

Stevens, K. 1983. Design features of speech sound systems. In P. MacNeilage (Ed.), *The production of speech,* 247–63. New York: Springer.

Stevens, K., and A. House. 1955. Development of a quantitative description of vowel articulation. *Journal of the Acoustical Society of America, 27;* 484–93.

Stevens, K., and A. House. 1963. Perturbation of vowel articulations by consonantal context: An acoustical study. *Journal of Speech and Hearing Research, 6;* 111–28.

Summerfield, Q. 1979. Use of visual information for phonetic perception. *Phonetica, 36;* 314–31.

Summerfield, Q. 1983. Audio-visual speech perception, lip reading, and artificial stimulation. In M. Lutman & M. Haggard (Eds.), *Hearing science and hearing disorders,* 131–38. London: Academic Press.

Valdman, A. 1976. *Introduction to French phonology and morphology.* Rowley, MA.: Newbury House Publishers.

Walz, J. 1979. *The early acquisition of second language phonology.* Hamburg: Helmut Baske.

Weinreich, U. 1953/1963. *Languages in contact, findings and problems.* The Hague: Mouton.

Weismer, G., and D. Cariski. 1983. On speakers' ability to control speech mechanism output: Theoretical and clinical implications. In N. Lass (Ed.), *Speech and language: Advances in basic research and practice, vol. 10.* New York: Academic Press.

Williams, L. 1980. Phonetic variations as a function of second-language learning. In G. Yeni-Komshian, J. Kavanagh, & C. Ferguson (Eds.), *Child phonology, vol. 2, perception,* 185–216. New York: Academic.

Zlatin, M., and R. Koenigsknect. 1976. Development of the voicing contrast: A comparison of voice onset time in stop perception and production. *Journal of Speech and Hearing Research, 19;* 93–111.

11

ON THE ACQUISITION OF ASPIRATION*

Geoffrey S. Nathan   Warren Anderson   Budsaba Budsayamongkon

INTRODUCTION

Although it does not involve a contrast between phonemes, the presence or absence of aspiration in voiceless stops is a source of perceived foreign accent whenever a speaker of a language that lacks aspiration attempts to learn a language that has it and vice versa. A great deal has been written on the perception of aspiration by native speakers of languages with it, of languages without it, by infants, and even by such animals as rhesus monkeys and chinchillas. Almost no research, however, has been done on the acquisition of aspiration from the point of view of production. This paper is an instrumental study of the way adults acquire aspirated voiceless stops when their native language lacks them.

In an extensive array of papers, Abramson and Lisker (1964, 1970, 1970, 1977) argue that voiced stops, voiceless unaspirated stops, and voiceless as-

*This is a revision of a paper delivered at the Second Language Research Forum in Los Angeles, California on November 12, 1983.

pirated stops can be ranged along a continuum that they have called voice onset time (VOT). VOT refers to the interval (measured in milliseconds) between the release of the articulators (the opening of the lips; the dropping of the tongue, etc.) and the beginning of regular vocal cord pulses. If the pulses substantially precede release (conventionally expressed in minus milliseconds) the sound is said to be voiced (Figure 11.1 part *a*). (A common value is −70 msec.) If the pulses begin simultaneously with the release or a very short time thereafter (in the realm of 0−+20 msec for labials) the sound is a voiceless unaspirated one.

Aspiration will (presumably) be acquired gradually, but gradualness can come in two varieties. One is that speakers gradually stretch their VOT, slowly learning to produce greater and greater delays in the onset of voicing. Over time, then, the average length of VOT will increase as the individual stops get longer and longer delays. If we were to do a cross-sectional study we would be likely to find a clear range of individuals, some with relatively long VOT, some with relatively short VOT, and some with intermediate levels.

However, it is also possible that aspiration is an all-or-none affair. That is, for any individual sound, the speaker either produces long VOT or short. What would increase over time, then, would be the proportion of long to short VOT. At the beginning stages, most, if not all, voiceless stops would have a short lag, while someone with a good accent would be making most stops with a long VOT.

Essentially then, the question is whether aspiration is a matter of degree or a binary distinction with the *proportion* of minus to plus varying over time.

There is considerable reason to expect that we would find the latter. Perception of VOT is one of the most heavily studied of all speech perception tasks. The reason for this is that perception of VOT is one of the two paradigm cases of what has come to be called categorical perception. It has been known since the fifties (cf., Liberman, et al., 1957, 1958, 1961) that when people are presented with synthetic speech stimuli in which VOT is gradually varied from 0 to +100 msec, subjects behave as if they hear a sudden shift from voiced to voiceless at a particular point. In the case, for example, of labials, those stops with VOT of less than +30 msec are uniformly perceived as voiced while those with VOT greater than +30 msec are uniformly perceived as voiceless. That is, a difference of 20 msec between 0 and +20 is not perceived as the same jump

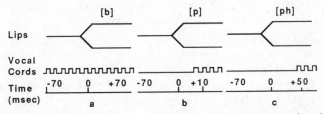

Figure 11.1 Voice onset time diagrams for fully voiced, voiceless unaspirated, and voiceless aspirated labial stops

as a difference of the identical 20 msec between $+20$ and $+40$. This effect is not only true for speakers of English but also for speakers of Thai (Lisker and Abramson, Abramson and Lisker, 1970). In fact it is even true for neonates (Eimas, et al., 1971) and even for non-humans—in particular, rhesus monkeys (Waters and Wilson, 1976) and chinchillas (Kuhl and Miller, 1975).

On the other hand, other speech sounds, notably vowels, do not show this categorical behavior in perception. What we do not know is how *production* works, and it is production that we are studying. Is *production* acquired gradually or categorically? We studied this simply by getting native speakers of Spanish with varying degrees of facility in English to say words with the requisite sounds. In order to get something approaching normal (as opposed to carefully monitored) speech, the subjects were required to repeat a list of words they heard over headphones, words that were spoken at a fairly rapid rate. They were thus, we hope, uninfluenced by the spelling, and, because of the speed at which they were required to respond, they were producing relatively unreflective speech.

As a control, subjects were also asked to say selected Spanish words presented in the same manner. Although plentiful material exists on normal VOT for Spanish stops we decided to investigate our subjects as a check on the reliability of our measurement procedures. As we expected, most subjects' voiceless stops fell well within the normal range reported for Spanish (Lisker and Abramson, 1964).

A hint of what we might have expected is found in the work of Macken (1980) and Macken and Barton (1980a,b). They studied the acquisition of aspiration and voicing contrasts by children learning English and Spanish as first languages. They found that English children go through three stages: one in which all stops are produced as voiceless unaspirated, one where the adult aspirated stops are made, and an intermediate stage where the children consistently *produce* a VOT contrast, but a contrast that falls within the region normally perceived by adults as unaspirated. That is, children apparently *do* slowly stretch their VOT until it reaches adult levels, but adults *hear* this stretching as an all-or-none affair because of their own categorical perception.

The data on Spanish children was somewhat less clear because for Spanish it is unclear whether the voiced (i.e., voicing lead) stops are in fact stops rather than fricatives. Their children had no trouble distinguishing kinds of stops, but they made the distinction consistently one of fricative vs stop rather than one of VOT. There is an extensive literature on the correct nature of the Spanish voiced-voiceless contrast in stops, but it is beyond the scope of this study.

Since we are examining the voiceless end of the continuum this will not be a problem. As we will see, our subjects had no trouble with VOT in target voiced stops, which they pronounced with long voicing leads (on the order of -70 to -100 msec), but they also had trouble producing stops rather than fricatives.

THE EXPERIMENT

Method

A list of 60 monosyllabic English words was selected, comprising minimal pairs illustrating initial stop voice contrasts. Many of the pairs are from Nilsen and Nilsen (1973). An additional 60 monosyllables were selected from among the 1,000 commonest English words. These 120 monosyllables were then randomized and recorded by the first author on TDK SA-90 tape using a JVC KD-D55 cassette recorder and a Shure Model 5655 microphone. The words were spoken at an average rate of 1.5 sec/word.

A similar tape containing selected Spanish words (not exclusively monosyllabic) was recorded by an educated native speaker of Chilean Spanish who had been recommended to us as not possessing particularly strong regional characteristics in her Spanish.

The stimulus tape thus prepared was presented to the subjects over Realistic (Koss) Pro II headphones played on a Realistic SC-17 cassette recorder. The subjects were told they would hear a list of English words that they were to repeat as soon as they heard them. The subjects' responses were recorded in the same way as the stimulus tape. A randomly selected subset (five) of the subjects were then asked to repeat the task while listening to the Spanish stimulus tape.

The resulting utterances were then analyzed on a Kay 6061B Sonagraph. VOT was measured in the following manner: A vertical line was drawn at the point where upper frequency noise began. Another was drawn at the onset of regular vertical striations of the first formant. Then the distance between the lines was measured in mm. and later converted to msec. at the conversion factor 1 mm = 7.5 msec. (Although more sophisticated methods of measuring VOT exist, our laboratory does not have the equipment necessary for it.)

The mean VOT for each point of articulation was then calculated for each speaker, and analysis of variance was calculated between speakers and within speakers between English and Spanish data.

Subjects

The production subjects fall into two classes. The first class are graduate students in the master's degree program in English as a Second Language at Southern Illinois University (SIU) from Colombia, Costa Rica, and Chile, and have lived in the United States over a period ranging from one to ten years. Their English ability is quite high, and, although not classified as completely bilingual they would rate at least a 3.5 on the Foreign Service Institute (FSI) scale. The second group of subjects are students at The Center for English as a Second Language (CESL), SIU's intensive pre-college English program. Although they were ranked at different levels within the CESL program, as will be seen, these levels did not correlate with their ability to aspirate. This is probably because levels are generally determined by writing ability and oral comprehension. The CESL subjects reported varying degrees of exposure to English in their home countries. Since many of them were vague in their answers to this question and since there may have been sociological reasons for misreporting these figures, this variable has been ignored.

Results

After measuring VOT for each token for every speaker, we calculated mean VOT per speaker for each point of articulation. Lisker and Abramson and others have found that length of VOT varies inversely with frontness, independently of language. That is, in all languages, mean VOT lag is shortest for labials, longest for velars, and at an intermediate level for alveolars. For this reason we separated the three points of articulation. We then ranked speakers by mean VOT for each point of articulation. This can be seen in Figure 11.2 parts *a, b,* and *c,* representing labial, alveolar, and velar, respectively. The speakers can be ranged along a linear function such that their mean VOTs range from clearly above to clearly below the aspirated range. There is no evidence that VOT clustered at one end or the other. Rather, speakers are evenly distributed along the VOT continuum in each case. We calculated a linear regression for each English VOT curve and found that /p/, /t/, and /k/ approximated a straight line with correlations of .95, .97, and .99.

These numbers, which represent 5 percent, 3 percent, and 1 percent deviations from an absolutely straight line, are clear indications that aspiration is acquired gradually, since this means that individual speakers are completely evenly spread out across the range of VOT produced, rather than bunching up at either end.

However, such a graph does not indicate whether the gradualness is caused by the fact that these are averages or whether people are actually producing intermediate levels of VOT. Averaging differing proportions of high and low VOT *could* produce the same smooth line as averaging gradually increasing VOT. That is, although those with high and low averages are presumably consistently producing one or the other, those in the middle might either be producing roughly 50 percent long and 50 percent short lags *or* they might be producing most stops with roughly half the correct VOT value. Fortunately, there is a relatively simple statistical test we can do to study this. For each speaker, we calculated the standard deviation value for VOT. This is a measure of whether the numbers making up the average value are all close to the average or whether they are scattered across the range.

If intermediate speakers were producing equal numbers of high and low VOT, they ought to have large standard deviations, while those with positions at either extreme would be more consistent and therefore would have low

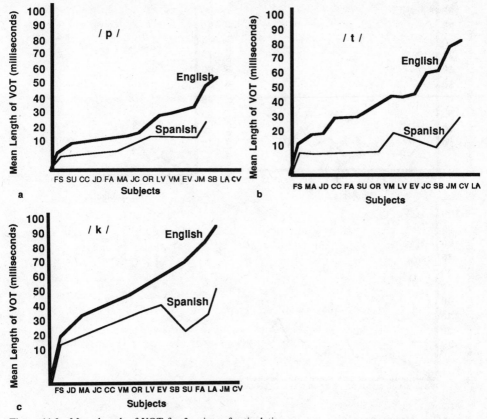

Figure 11.2 Mean length of VOT for 3 points of articulation

standard deviations. A graph of s.d. (standard deviation) would then be hill-shaped.

On the other hand, if intermediate speakers were consistently making stops with intermediate levels of VOT, a graph of s.d. should show a relatively constant level of s.d. In figures 11.3 parts *a, b,* and *c,* we can see that the graph is not hill-shaped. Instead we can detect only a very slight increase in s.d. Thus the second hypothesis is upheld, namely that production of VOT is not categorical but gradual.

The smooth increase in VOT exhibited by our subjects at each point of articulation contained an additional, somewhat disturbing fact. Although, generally speaking, the two or three shortest and longest lag speakers remained constant, there was considerable variation among the rest, and rank order correlation coefficients among speakers worked out as follows:

/p/:/t/   .88
/t/:/k/   .74
/p/:/k/   .65

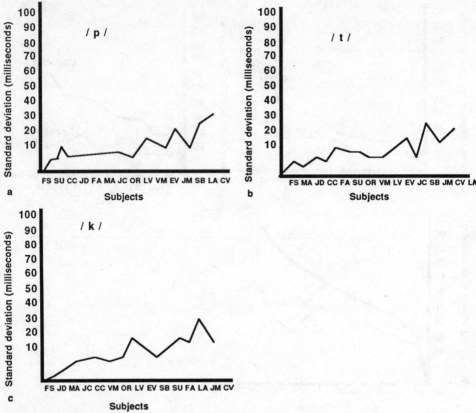

Figure 11.3   Mean standard deviation for VOT means

This finding strikes us as a little odd, but apparently ability to produce aspirated labial stops does not necessarily correlate strongly with ability to produce aspirated velar stops.

The lower curves on each of Figures 11.1 parts *a, b,* and *c* are mean VOT for Spanish stops. In each case there is a significant difference from the English curves. ANOVA run on English vs Spanish for every speaker shows a significant difference at the $p < .05$ level.

Discussion

We can tentatively suggest on the basis of this experiment, therefore, that, at least for speakers of Spanish, English-like aspiration is not an all-or-none affair. It must be acquired gradually, in the sense that speakers of Spanish must learn to delay gradually the onset of voicing relative to the release of the consonant. Obviously the next task is a longitudinal study, with all the problems inherent in such a project. There are several other questions that remain to be studied. What happens to voiced stops? English voiced stops, at least initially, are actually voiceless. Do Spanish speakers also shorten the voice onset lead of their *voiced* stops to approximate the short *lag* of English?

Another question concerns what happens in other languages. Our next project will be a replication of this study with speakers of Bahasa Malaysia, also a language with unaspirated voiceless stops.

At this point, however, it seems that the situation is very much as was suggested to me by James McCawley (personal communication) in a quote with which I close: "Very good, Mr. Gonzales. Another 10 msec. and you'll have it."

REFERENCES

Abramson, A. 1977. Laryngeal timing in consonant distinctions. *Phonetica, 34,* 295–303.

Abramson, A., and L. Lisker. 1970. Discriminability along the voicing continuum: cross-language tests. In Hala, et al., 569–573.

Bailey, P.J., and M.P. Haggard. 1980. Perception. Production relations in the voicing contrast for intial stops in 3-year-olds. *Phonetica, 37,* 377–396.

Eimas, P.D., E.R. Siqueland, P. Jusczyk, and J. Vigorito. 1971. Speech perception in infants. *Science, 171,* 303–306.

Elman, J., R. Diehl, and S. Buchwald. 1977. Perceptual switching in bilinguals. *Journal of the Acoustical Society of America, 62,* 4, 971–974.

Hala, B., M. Romportl, and P. Janota. 1970. *Proceedings of the Sixth International Congress of Phonetic Sciences.* Munich: Hueber.

Kuhl, P.K., and J.D. Miller. 1975. Speech perception by the chinchilla: voiced-voiceless distinction in alveolar plosive consonants. *Science, 190,* 69–72.

Liberman, A., F.S. Cooper, D.P. Shankweiler, and M. Studdert-Kennedy. 1967. Perception of the speech code. *Psychological Review, 74,* 6, 431–461.

Liberman, A.M., P.C. Delattre, and F.S. Cooper. 1958. Some cues for the distinction between voiced and voiceless stops in initial position. *Language and Speech, 1,* 3, 153–167.

Liberman, A., K.S. Harris, H.S. Hoffman, and B.C. Griffith. 1957. The discrimination of speech sounds within and across speech boundaries. *Journal of Experimental Psychology, 54,* 358–368.

Liberman, A.M., K.S. Harris, J.A. Kinney, and H. Lane. 1961. The discrimination of relative onset time of the components of certain speech and non-speech patterns. *Journal of Experimental Psychology, 61,* 5, 379–388.

Lisker, L., and A. Abramson. 1964. A cross-language study of voicing in initial stops: acoustical measurements. *Word, 20,* 384–422.

Lisker, L., and A. Abramson. 1970. The voicing dimension: some experiments in comparative phonetics. In Hala, et al., 563–567.

Macken, M. 1980. Aspects of the acquisition of stop systems: a cross-linguistic perspective, In Yeni-Komshian, et al., 143–168.

Macken, M., and D. Barton. 1980. The acquisition of the voicing contrast in English. *Journal of Child Language, 7,* 41–74.

Macken, M., and D. Barton. 1980. The acquisition of the voicing contrast in Spanish. *Journal of Child Language, 7,* 433–458.

Morse, P.A., and C.T. 1975. Snowdon. An investigation of categorical speech discrimination by rhesus monkeys. *Perception and Psychophysics, 17,* 9–16.

Nilsen, D., and A.P. Nilsen. 1973. *Pronunciation contrasts in English.* NY: Regents.

Pickett, J.M. 1980. *The sounds of speech communication.* Baltimore: University Park Press.

Pisoni, D., and J.H. Lazarus. 1974. Categorical and non-categorical modes of speech perception along the voicing continuum. *Journal of the Acoustical Society of America, 55,* 2, 328–333.

Stevens, K. 1977. Physics of laryngeal behavior and larynx modes. *Phonetica, 34,* 264–279.

Strange, W., and J.J. Jenkins. 1978. The role of linguistic experience in the perception of speech. In Walk and Pick, 125–170.

Walk, R., and H. Pick, Jr. 1978. *Perception and experience.* NY: Plenum.

Waters, R.S., and W.A. Wilson. 1976. Speech perception by rhesus monkeys: the voicing distinction in synthesized labial and velar stop consonants. *Perception and Psychophysics, 19,* 285–289.

Yeni-Komshian, G., J.F. Kavanaugh, and C. Ferguson. 1980. *Child Phonology,* Volume 1: *Production.* NY: Academic Press.

12

THE ACQUISITION OF A SECOND LANGUAGE PHONOLOGY: INTERACTION OF TRANSFER AND DEVELOPMENTAL FACTORS*

Barbara Frant Hecht   Randa Mulford

Informal observation suggests that children master a second language phonology, that is, they learn to speak without an accent, with relative ease and great speed. Despite ever-increasing interest in parallels between first and second language acquisition, however, children's acquisition of second language phonology is poorly understood. While there are detailed case studies of phonological development in children raised bilingually (Gregoire, 1947; Leopold, 1939–49; Major, 1977; Vogel, 1975), much of our knowledge of phonological development in second language learners is derived from anecdotal reports. In other domains of second language development, for example morphology and

*An earlier version of this paper was presented at the Fourth Annual Boston University Conference on Language Development, September 14, 1979, and appeared as a working paper in *Papers and Reports in Child Language Development,* 1980, *18,* 61–74. Throughout its preparation we benefited greatly from discussions with Charles Ferguson; Marilyn Vihman, Eve Clark, Lise Menn, and Rebecca LaBrum also made valuable comments on earlier versions. We especially want to add a hearty "Takk" to Steinar and his parents—their patience and cooperation made this study possible.

syntax, researchers have been particularly interested in the influence of the first language on the acquisition of subsequent languages (Dulay, Burt, and Krashen, 1982; McLaughlin, 1978). At least two viewpoints have been proposed concerning the relative importance of (1) developmental processes common to both first and second languages and (2) transfer from the first language.

The first viewpoint (hereafter, the Developmental Position) is that acquisition of a given language by second language learners closely parallels its acquisition by first language learners. Language transfer is considered a minor factor. As McLaughlin (1978, p. 206) states: "There is a unity of process that characterizes all language acquisition, whether first or second language, and . . . this unity of process reflects the use of similar strategies of language acquisition." Many recent studies support this position. For example, research on the second language acquisition of questions (Ravem, 1974), negation (Milon, 1974), grammatical morphemes (Dulay and Burt, 1975), and word order (Ervin-Tripp, 1974) has demonstrated similar developmental sequences for first and second language acquisition of a given language. However, developmental factors alone do not provide a complete account of second language, or L2, development. Certain discrepancies have also been demonstrated between the first and second language development of negation (Cancino, Rosansky, & Schumann, 1978; Wode, 1976), questions (Cancino et al., 1978), and grammatical morphemes (Hakuta, 1976).

An alternative viewpoint (hereafter, the Transfer Position) is that first language knowledge affects the acquisition of a new linguistic system, and many of the difficulties faced and solutions attempted during second language development can be predicted by a contrastive analysis of the two systems. Although recent empirical evidence from the second language acquisition of syntax and morphology provides little evidence for a strong version of this hypothesis (as set forth, for example, by Lado, 1957), transfer does seem to be an important factor when certain structural similarities hold between the first and second languages and in some learning environments (Ervin-Tripp, 1974; Wode, 1976).

In the domain of phonology, the Developmental Position predicts that the rank order of difficulty of segments, the role of word position, and particular error types will be similar for first and second language learners of any given language. Conversely, the Transfer Position predicts that the relative difficulty of phonemes and allophones, the importance of word position for allophonic variation, and any sound substitutions which appear will be traceable to the influence of the first language. Anecdotal evidence suggests that transfer may be a more important factor in phonology than in other domains (Dulay, Burt, & Krashen, 1982; Dulay, Hernández-Chávez, & Burt, 1978), but the relative contributions of transfer and developmental factors are not yet understood.

In the present study, we address these issues by first examining in detail the initial stages of an Icelandic child's development of English fricative and affricate segments. We provide evidence from this child's acquisition of a second language, or L2, phonology in support of a stance taken by Wode (1976) and by Ferguson and Debose (1977)—that neither developmental factors nor transfer factors alone lead to a complete explanation of a second language acquisition. We discuss the systematic interaction of these two factors, then briefly consider how our findings apply to other classes of sounds in the child's acquisition of English phonology. Finally, we raise some methodological questions which demand attention in further research.

A COMPARISON OF ENGLISH AND ICELANDIC FRICATIVES AND AFFRICATES

We have chosen to focus on the development of the fricative and affricate system for two reasons: (1) There is a substantial literature on children's native acquisition of English fricatives (Edwards, 1979; Farwell, 1977; Ferguson, 1975; Ingram, 1975; Moskowitz, 1975; Olmsted, 1971). (2) There are clear contrasts between the fricative systems of English and Icelandic. These are summarized in Table 12.1.

TABLE 12.1. Comparison of Icelandic and English Fricative and Affricate Systems

	Icelandic (L1)			English (L2)		
	Initial	Medial	Final	Initial	Medial	Final
/f/	[f] faðir 'father'	[f] kaffi 'coffee'	[f] eff 'F'	[f] fat	[f] shuffle	[f] half
/v/	[ɣ] vera 'to be'	[ɣ] hafa 'to have'	[ɣ̩] nef 'nose'	[v] vat	[v] shovel	[v] have
/s/	[s] sofa 'to sleep'	[s] lesa 'to read'	[s] is 'ice'	[s] sue	[s] fussy	[s] race
/z/				[z] zoo	[z] fuzzy	[z] raise
/θ/	[θ] þetta 'that'	[ð] eða 'or'	[ð̩] bað 'bath'	[θ] thigh	[θ] ether	[θ] teeth
/ð/				[ð] thy	[ð] either	[ð] teethe
/ʃ/				[ʃ] sheep	[ʃ] fishin'	[ʃ] mash
/ʒ/					[ʒ] fission	[ʒ] garage
/tʃ/				[tʃ] cheap	[tʃ] lecher	[tʃ] match
/dʒ/				[dʒ] jeep	[dʒ] ledger	[dʒ] Madge

An asterisk indicates weaker, less forceful pronunciation than corresponding English phone.

There are five phonemes of English which are not found at all in Icelandic: /z/, /ʃ/, /ʒ/, /tʃ/, /dʒ/. In addition, the two languages have contrasting allophonic distributions of interdental fricatives; in Icelandic, there is only one interdental, which we will call *eth* /ð/, whose allophones depend on word position. Initially, it is voiceless as in 'þak' [θakʰ] 'roof'. Medially, it is voiced, as in 'eða' [ɛða] 'or', while finally it is half-voiced as in 'bað' [baḍ] 'bath' or 'hvað' [kvaḍ] 'what'. English, in contrast, has two distinct interdental phonemes, /ð/ and /θ/, whose voicing can be contrasted in all word positions. Compare voiceless *thigh* and voiced *thy,* voiceless *ether* and voiced *either,* and voiceless *teeth* and voiced *teethe.* An Icelander acquiring English must, therefore, learn to distinguish and produce the two phonemes rather than one. Another adjustment that must be made is a more forceful pronunciation of the sound /v/, which is generally "less energetic" (Einarsson 1945, p. 22) in Icelandic than in English. This weaker quality is indicated by the asterisk under the Icelandic [v̪] in Table 12.1.

METHOD

Subject

The subject, Steinar, was a six-year-old native speaker of Icelandic who had been in the United States ten weeks at the time observations began. He and his parents lived in the Boston area, where his parents attended graduate school. Based on parental report, his Icelandic pronunciation was completely fluent and his phonological acquisition had proceeded normally; his mother had just begun to teach him to read in Icelandic before they arrived. Steinar had no exposure to English prior to coming to the Boston area. Four weeks after this study began, he entered first grade at a local school, but at no point was he given specific language instruction in English. His parents, both Icelanders, spoke fluent, accented English, and, while living in the United States, they spoke to him in English and Icelandic. Steinar had no siblings and had few regular contacts with other Icelandic children or adults during the period of this investigation.

Procedure

From the tenth week after his arrival, Steinar was tape recorded for approximately one hour weekly over a period of eight months in naturalistic interactions with one of the investigators (RM), a native English speaker who had no conversational knowledge of Icelandic at the time. Eight sessions, from the first fourteen weeks of taping, were analyzed. The recorded conversations were transcribed orthographically and then every word that contained at least one fricative or affricate segment was transcribed phonetically using the International Phonetic Alphabet with some modifications for child speech developed by the Stanford Child Phonology Project (Bush, Edwards, Stoel, Macken, & Peterson, 1973). The resulting corpus for phonological analysis consisted of more than 4,300 phonetically transcribed fricative and affricate segments. The two investigators independently transcribed every fricative and affricate segment in the eight sessions. Initial agreement between the two transcriptions was better than 95%. Of the transcribed segments that did not initially agree, all but ten were resolved upon retranscription. Those ten segments were omitted from further analysis.

RESULTS AND DISCUSSION

For sessions 1 through 5 (the first five recording sessions), we noted all the relevant segments in each of three word positions (initial, medial, and final) and their phonetic environments. By the end of the first five weeks, it was clear that some segments were giving Steinar little difficulty. We therefore eliminated from further detailed analysis any sound that, in a given word position, had at least thirty tokens across the five sessions and was produced correctly at least 85 percent of the time.[1] Those eliminated were /s/ and /f/ in all positions and initial /θ/ and /ð/.

Three sessions beyond week 5 were analyzed—those at weeks 6, 10, and 14. We expected to find more changes at monthly than at weekly intervals for the sounds Steinar had not yet mastered. By session 10 it was apparent that /ʃ/, although still relatively rare, was pronounced with very high accuracy in all positions—72/74 tokens correct overall. Of those segments analyzed beyond the tenth week, only medial /ð/ improved enough by the last session to consider it no longer problematic.

To summarize, the sounds that Steinar found easiest to produce were: /s/ in all positions, /f/ in all positions, initial /θ/, and initial /ð/, followed by /ʃ/ in all positions and then medial /ð/. Still troublesome or very infrequent through week 14 were /z/, /v/, /ʒ/, /tʃ/, and /dʒ/ in all positions, and medial and final /θ/. Table 12.2 shows the segments studied and the week at which Steinar reached our criteria for acquisition.

Order of Difficulty

How does Steinar's treatment of these sounds bear on the relative roles of developmental and transfer processes in the acquisition of a nonnative phonology? One obvious way to assess this is to examine the order of segment difficulty predicted by each and see which order best fits the data.

Relative difficulty predicted by the Transfer Position is straightforward.

TABLE 12.2. Rate of Acquisition of Fricatives and Affricates

Segment	Week at which criteria reached		
	Word-initial	Word-medial	Word-final
/s/	5	5	5
/z/	—[a]	—	—
/f/	5	5	5
/v/	—[a]	—	—
/θ/	5	—	—[a]
/ð/	5	14	—[b]
/ʃ/	10	10	10
/ʒ/	—[c]	—[b]	—[a]
/tʃ/	—[a]	—[a]	—[a]
/dʒ/	—	—[a]	—[a]

Criteria for acquisition were (1) at least 30 tokens in 5 sessions and (2) 85% correct production in 5 sessions.

[a] Rare segment, cannot determine whether criteria were reached.

[b] No tokens were produced in corpus.

[c] Does not occur in initial position in English.

Those allophones common to English and Icelandic (see Table 12.1) should be the easiest. Two other classes of sounds—the completely new segments and those involving some phonetic or allophonic adjustment of Icelandic phonemes —should be more difficult, although there appears to be no a priori reason to order these two classes with respect to each other.

An order of difficulty based on what is known about English first language (L1) fricative acquisition is harder to specify since existing studies generally emphasize substitution types and variation both within and across individual children. However, Olmsted's (1971) cross sectional study presents a developmental sequence that has not been contradicted by evidence from more recent studies (as summarized in Ferguson, 1975). Although it does not include the affricates, Olmsted's study does have the particular advantage over more recent studies of providing a developmental sequence that takes word position into account. We have collapsed Olmsted's six stages of development into three groups to make them comparable to the three classes of sounds which fall out of the contrastive analysis of English and Icelandic.

If the developmental hypothesis best accounts for L2 phonological acquisition, Steinar should have the most difficulty correctly producing those fricatives that first language learners acquire last and the least difficulty with those fricatives that first language learners acquire first. In Figure 12.1 we show the percentage of correct productions (by session) of all fricatives in the groups predicted to be the easiest, of moderate difficulty, and the most difficult. The percentage correct remains relatively constant across the five sessions. Notice that in *no* session do the percentages correct for the three groups order as predicted by the developmental hypothesis. There is little difference (and most

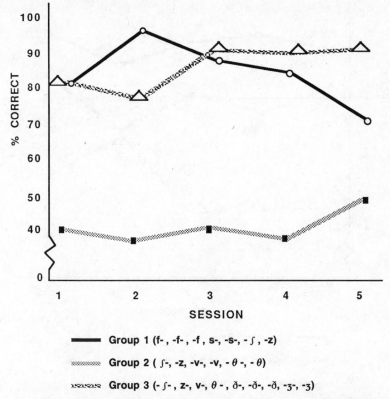

Figure 12.1 Percentage of correct productions of fricatives per session, grouped by ease of acquisition as predicted by the developmental hypothesis. Group 1 fricatives are predicted to be the easiest, Group 2 to be of moderate difficulty, Group 3 the most difficult. (Grouping based on Olmsted, 1971.)

of it in the wrong direction) between the ease of production of sounds predicted to be the easiest and the most difficult. And, the segments that should have been of moderate difficulty were much more difficult than the other two.

Figure 12.2 shows the percentage of correct productions (by session) of fricatives grouped according to the transfer hypothesis. Correct production of fricatives grouped this way also remained relatively constant across the five sessions, with the exception possibly of session 4 for new segments. However, fricatives grouped according to this hypothesis do tend to order as predicted. Fricatives common to L1 and L2 are, in fact, the easiest for Steinar to produce. He produced them correctly in more than 85 percent of all productions for all sessions. Although we had no clear grounds for predicting relative difficulty of new segments and those requiring allophonic adjustments, the new segments were consistently more difficult. The Transfer Position is thus supported by Steinar's English pronunciations, while the Developmental Position does not appear to be supported.

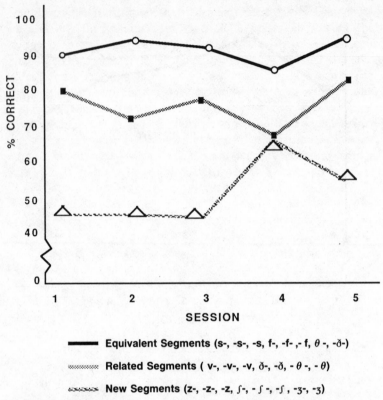

Figure 12.2 Percentage of correct productions of fricatives per session, grouped by ease of acquisition as predicted by the transfer hypothesis. Equivalent segments, the same in L1 and L2, are predicted to be the easiest; related segments, requiring allophonic/phonetic adjustment, and new segments, present in L2 but not in L1, are predicted to be more difficult.

Sound Substitutions and Phonological Processes

Another way of comparing the two hypotheses is to examine the phonological processes that govern segment substitutions in those sounds not correctly pronounced. A phonological process, in current analyses, is a phonetically systematic relationship between the speech sound the child attempts and the substituted speech sound the child actually produces (see Edwards, 1979; Macken and Ferguson, 1981). For example, when a child substitutes a voiceless [p] for a voiced [b], the process involved is *devoicing*.

We examined Steinar's erroneous productions of fricatives and affricates and classified these according to phonological process. The most common processes in Steinar's productions were: devoicing (e.g., substituting [f] for [v]), looser closure (e.g., substituting [ʃ] for [tʃ]), tighter closure (e.g., substituting [t] for [s]), deletion (e.g., saying [fɩ] for the word 'fish'), palatalization (e.g., substituting [ʃ] for [s]), voicing (e.g., substituting [z] for [s]), and labialization (e.g., substituting [b] for [d]).

For each session we tallied the number of errors attributable to each process in initial, medial, and final word positions. Table 12.3 shows the errors attributable to each process as a percentage of the total errors per session (e.g., in session 1, 40 percent of all errors involved final devoicing). Only those processes that accounted for at least 5 percent of the total errors in a given session are included. As Table 12.3 indicates, the most prevalent processes across all sessions were final devoicing and initial tighter closure. Final looser closure gained prominence in later sessions. These are all common processes in L1 fricative acquisition (Edwards, 1979).

For some segments, the Transfer and Developmental Positions predict that different processes would apply, resulting in different substitutes, while for other segments the predictions are not readily distinguishable. One of the clearest examples of conflicting predictions concerns initial /ð/. In Icelandic, only

TABLE 12.3. Most common phonological processes operating in substitutions for L2 fricatives, broken down by word position: I (initial), M (medial), F (final). Figures are percentages of total errors per session.

Processes		Session							
		1	2	3	4	5	6	10	14
Devoicing	I	7.0	4.8	1.7	—	1.8	—	0.9	—
	M	1.3	0.8	13.3^a	—	2.7	1.6	1.7	2.7
	F	40.0	49.6	41.3	50.8	53.0	74.6	65.5	71.0
Looser closure	I	1.3	0.8	5.0	3.4	0.9	—	0.9	—
	M	13.0	7.2	4.0	—	2.7	4.8	2.6	2.7
	F	0.6	—	6.6	5.1	7.2	7.9	5.2	8.7
Tighter closure	I	9.5	10.4	5.8	10.2	9.0	4.8	6.9	
	M	4.4	2.4	2.2	—	0.9	1.6	0.9	
	F	1.9	0.8	0.4	1.7	5.4	6.3	1.7	
Deletion	I	—	—						—
	M	0.6	3.2		11.8				0.5
	F	7.6	2.4		—				7.7
Palatalization	I	1.3			—				
	M	—							
	F	5.1			10.2				
Voicing	I		1.6		—				
	M		—		—			4.3	
	F		4.8		5.1			2.6	
Labialization	I		6.4						
	M		1.6						
	F		—						

Columns may not add to 100 percent because more than one process may apply in an error, and processes accounting for less than 5 percent of the errors are not included.
^{a}All due to one lexical item.

a voiceless interdental fricative may occur initially (Table 12.1); according to the Transfer Position, Steinar should substitute this voiceless variant for /ð/ in the early stages of learning English. For example, he might pronounce 'thy' [ðaʸ] as if it were the word 'thigh' [θaʸ]. Conversely, English developmental fricative studies (e.g., Edwards, 1979) show a high proportion of substitutes for initial /ð/ involving tighter closure (e.g., stopping it to [d]) and very few substitutes (3 percent) of similar fricatives like [θ]. Where Steinar made pronunciation errors of initial /ð/, substitutes of tighter closure predominated, as predicted by the Developmental Position. Devoicing, especially to [θ], was rare. Overall, however, his production of the initial /ð/ segment was quite good. This ease of production can also be accounted for in terms of general processes noted in first language development. Several investigators (Ferguson, 1975; Ingram, 1975; and Stampe, 1973) have shown that the voicing of fricatives in initial position is a common first language process, and it is one that Steinar might be exploiting in his early productions of /ð/.

Another class of sounds for which the two hypotheses make different predictions are the novel affricates and fricatives. Here, the developmental predictions can account for virtually all of Steinar's substitutions in terms of processes common among first language learners, while the transfer predictions, that phonetically similar segments from Icelandic will "fill in" for new English sounds, are only partially adequate. Table 12.4 provides some examples of substitutes for two novel sounds, [dʒ] and [tʃ]. When confronting /dʒ/, Steinar occasionally produced [d], which is an Icelandic phone, as in [dus] for 'juice'. [d] could also arise, however, from application of a common L1 process, depalatalization, to the target affricate. Similarly, both transfer and developmental processes could account for the substitution of [t] for [tʃ]. In the more telling cases, Steinar substituted sounds nonexistent in his native language, as [ʒ] for /dʒ/ in [ɛnʒɩn] for 'engine' or [ʃ] for /tʃ/ in [ʃiːs] for 'cheese.' These substitutions cannot be accounted for by transfer. However, the process of affricate weakening reported by Edwards (1979) for first language learners would account for this type of substitution. For new affricates, then, the data subsumed under the transfer hypothesis are a subset of those that can be explained by developmental processes.

TABLE 12.4. Substitutes for New Segments

	Transfer from Icelandic	English L1 process
dʒ → d	yes	yes
juice → [dus]		
tʃ → t	yes	yes
ouch → [awt]		
dʒ → ʒ	no	yes
engine → [ɛnʒɩn]		
tʃ → ʃ	no	yes
cheese → [ʃiːs]		

There are many cases, though, where the two hypotheses make the same prediction. One example is the devoicing of final /z/. In Icelandic, only its voiceless counterpart, /s/, is found. According to the Transfer Position, /s/ should appear in place of final /z/. This substitution would also be predicted by the Developmental Position since final devoicing is also prevalent in children acquiring English as a first language. Steinar did devoice final /z/ frequently, in some 54 percent of all its occurrences in our data, and showed no improvement from the first to the fourteenth week. A third factor which may have contributed to the high rate of devoicing of final /z/ is that it is an acceptable American English pronunciation in some phonetic contexts and speech styles (e.g., in rapid speech and sentence final position). To assess the relative importance of these three factors, we would need a better picture of the prevalence of final devoicing of /z/ in the English most commonly modeled to Steinar.

Thus far we have presented examples from our data predicted by one or both hypotheses. Our data suggest that *transfer* from L1 is the major factor determining the difficulty of segments, while *developmental processes* provide a more complete account of the actual substitutions Steinar made. Yet the two factors may not always operate independently in a developing phonology.

If we allow interaction between transfer and developmental processes, we may be able to explain why some substitutes persist while others do not. We would like to suggest a model in which those substitutes predicted by both transfer and developmental processes are the ones most likely to appear and to persist. This is, in fact, what we find in the case of final /z/. Devoicing of final /z/ may be a persistent and pervasive process in Steinar's phonology precisely because it has more than one possible source.[2]

Our final example is of a phenomenon that neither transfer nor developmental factors alone would have led us to expect. The transfer hypothesis was an excellent overall predictor of those sounds which Steinar produced most accurately. However, one segment from this set did not fit the pattern, medial /ð/. This segment posed no problem for Steinar in Icelandic. In English it was distorted nearly beyond recognition. This apparent anomaly became less puzzling when we noticed that Steinar had occasion to use medial /ð/ only in the environment directly preceding syllabic /r/, as in 'other' or 'father'. The American retroflexed /r/ was a totally new segment for him and one that challenged all his articulatory skills. In his early attempts to pronounce words with syllabic /r/, the /r/ itself was often produced quite adequately. The preceding /ð/, however, suffered the consequences. Our suspicion that syllabic /r/ was at fault here was confirmed by Steinar's treatment of many other consonants in the same environment. These consonants were not problematic in most positions. But in early occurrences of words like 'water', 'monster', 'eraser', 'sugar', 'hunters', and 'paper', the consonant or consonant cluster before /r/ seldom resembled its target.

This sort of "trade-off" between two presumably distinct elements in the child's developing phonology (i.e., medial /ð/ and syllabic /r/) has also been reported in the literature on first language development (e.g., Ferguson and

Farwell, 1975; Garnica and Edwards, 1977). In short, Steinar's difficulty in pronouncing medial /ð/ can be traced to the combined effects of native language interference with the production of syllabic /r/ and a subsequent phonological tradeoff that affected the production of preceding segments.

This analysis of the fricative and affricative data suggests interaction at many levels. We observed behavior predicted by both transfer and developmental processes in language acquisition. The Transfer Position is best supported when we consider the relative difficulty of segments. The Developmental Position is also upheld. It allows the most complete account of the phonological substitutions in Steinar's early attempts to produce fricatives and affricates.

The Role of Transfer in Nonfricative Segments

The pattern of interaction suggested by this study is based only on the data from fricatives and affricates. Although we did not carry out quantitative analyses of other aspects of Steinar's emerging English phonology, it is our impression that interference from Icelandic may prove to be a more important factor in accounting for substitutions for other classes of segments. Consider the following examples of substitute types that might best be accounted for by transfer from Icelandic rather than by L1 developmental processes:

1. Final oral stop consonants. In the early sessions final stops were typically devoiced and heavily aspirated, as are final stops in Icelandic (Einarsson, 1945, p. 23). Although final devoicing is an L1 developmental process, final aspiration is not a process that has been noted among children learning English as a first language.

    Examples: (a) /g/ became aspirated [kʰ] in final position but remained voiced and unaspirated medially, as in 'big' [bɪkʰ] versus 'biggest' [bɪgəst]. (b) /d/ became aspirated [tʰ] in final position, as in 'bread' [bɹɛtʰ] or 'and' [æntʰ]. (c) /k/ is aspirated in final position, as in 'like' [laykʰ].

2. Final velar nasal [ŋ]. A velar stop was frequently inserted after final [ŋ]. This corresponds to a phonotactic rule of Icelandic; velar nasals may not appear word-finally (see Einarsson, 1945, pp. 18–19). Steinar produced both voiced and voiceless stop intrusions in this position:

'going'	[gowɪŋk]	'sitting'	[sɪtɪŋg]
'coming'	[kʰʌmɪŋk]	'sleeping'	[slipɪŋg]

3. Liquids. Steinar replaced the English /r/ (written phonetically as [ɹ]) with a trilled /r/ (written phonetically as [r]).

'clarinet'	[klarɪnɛt]	'broke'	[brokʰ]
'nearer'	[niɛrə]	'room'	[rⓊm]
'water'	[wɔtr]		

    The English velar allophone of /l/ was often produced as a clear apical lateral, the only variety of /l/ in Icelandic:

'small'	[smɔlˆ]	'apples'	[aplˆɪz]
'little'	[l ˆɪtüˆ]	'twelve'	[twɛlˆy]

224

4. Vowels. Overall, vowels retained traces of an Icelandic "accent" longer than other classes of segments, even as long as one year after observations began. English diphthongs were usually rendered as pure vowels and vowels were generally produced slightly higher than their English targets.

We would like to propose that the role of interference in determining substitute types may be more or less evident in different parts of the second language learner's developing phonology. Our data suggest a continuum roughly like that shown in Table 12.5.

More systematic analyses of nonfricative data and of data from a larger number of language-learners will be necessary to substantiate this tentative proposal. The relationship between the two L1 and L2 phonologies will presumably affect the ordering of segment classes along this continuum.

Variation as a Methodological Concern

There are three sources of variation in our data which do not affect the major findings of this study, but which should be explored in future studies in order to present a more complete account of the acquisition of an L2 phonology. They are: variation among English models, individual variation, and variability due to rapid, connected speech.

Model variability We mentioned variability of the L2 model in our earlier discussion of devoicing of final /z/, and pointed out that the amount of final devoicing in Steinar's English might partially reflect the particular dialect he was learning. Not only are there no normative data on the amount of final devoicing found in the speech of English-speaking six-year-olds, but it is apparent that even if such data existed, they would not necessarily give an accurate picture of the speech actually modeled to Steinar. Certain speech patterns that Steinar developed were not modeled to him in the variety of Standard American English of the adult investigator, nor in the accented speech of his parents. Such phenomena as insertion of /r/ at the end of [ɑ]-final words, initial stopping of /ð/, and deletion of /r/ in certain environments were observed in later sessions. For example, 'idea' [aydiaɹ], 'there' [dɛɹ], 'these' [diz], 'carefully' [kʰɛəfəli], and 'car' [kʰaɤ] are all typical Boston pronunciations he could have heard from

TABLE 12.5. Hypothesized role of transfer and L1 developmental processes in major classes of phonological segments

Transfer processes predominate			L1 developmental processes predominate
Vowels	Liquids	Stops	Affricates and fricatives

225

school friends. Peer speech would have to be described in order to assess its possible influence on Steinar's pronunciations. In addition, his other main sources of English (e.g., his schoolteacher, adult "playmates," and parents) would have to be documented. The more completely the range of variability can be described in each of the L2 models the second language learner hears, the better we can evaluate the potential influence of modeled forms on the variability of the child's own speech patterns.

Individual variation Any direct attempt to compare the development of English phonology in first and second language learners is complicated by the extensive individual variation found within and among children learning the phonology of their first language. Edwards (1979), for example, has shown that her subjects acquiring English as a native language vary both in the order in which they acquire different fricative and affricate segments and in the extent to which they rely on different phonological processes in their productions. She does not find an invariant course of development common to all the children she studied, although she does suggest some general tendencies supported by data from the subjects as a group. A further characteristic of first language development—the variability inherent in any one child's phonological productions (see, for example, Ferguson and Farwell, 1975; Menn, 1979; Scollon, 1976) —must also be kept in mind when trying to compare L1 and L2 development. Some of the variability observed in the speech of a child learning a second language may well result from the same forces that produce variable pronunciations during the course of first language development, for example spontaneous production versus imitation, conflicting or changing phonological rules, and the influence of particular lexical items. The role of such forces has yet to be assessed in L2 production.

Rate of speech Rapid, connected speech is an additional source of variability in our data which makes it difficult to compare Steinar's English phonological development directly with that of young first language learners. His acquisition of English syntax proceeded at an impressive pace, so that by the third session (twelfth week of exposure to English) he often produced utterances exceeding twelve words in length. His connected speech in spontaneous conversations contrasts sharply with the carefully elicited single-word utterances that have comprised the data for most first language phonology studies. As Steinar's facility with English grammar improved, he also spoke more and more rapidly. This resulted in what looked like no improvement or even worse productions of some segments. "Mistakes" due to lack of knowledge about English phonology in Steinar's early speech may have given way to "mistakes" resulting from rapid speech phenomena common among fluent English speakers. Although Steinar in fact became a more competent English speaker, a simple error analysis might not give that impression. As a supplement to naturalistic speech data, eliciting one-word utterances from second language learners would allow better comparability of L1 and L2 studies, with the further benefit that more tokens for segments occurring rarely in the child's spontaneous speech can be collected.

CONCLUSION

This investigation of the naturalistic acquisition of a second language phonology has revealed the following:

1. Neither the Transfer Position nor the Developmental Position alone provides an adequate explanation of L2 phonological development.

2. This development is best accounted for by a systematic interaction between general processes of phonological development and transfer from L1. Transfer best predicts the order of difficulty of English fricatives and affricates, while the developmental hypothesis best predicts sound substitutions for difficult segments.

3. The pattern of interaction between transfer from L1 and developmental processes that we noted for fricatives and affricates may be somewhat different for other types of phonological segments.

4. Variability—in language models, among different language learners, and in an individual child's production—is a complicating factor for any detailed analysis of phonological development. We suggest several ways of taking these types of variability into account in future studies of L2 phonological acquisition.

Learning to speak without an accent may look like child's play, but, in fact, it is a complex process which we are just beginning to understand.

NOTES

1. Because of the variability inherent in language development and use (see under "Discussion, Variation as a methodological concern"), 100 percent correct production would be an unrealistic expectation. Moreover, there is no generally accepted criterion of phonological acquisition. When we examined our data, 85 percent seemed to be a natural cutoff point, since most items were produced with greater than 90 percent or less than 80 percent accuracy.

2. In some cases the persistence of a substitute cannot be explained by a simple cumulative model. For example, Steinar consistently devoiced medial /z/ in the word 'thousand' long after medial /z/ was correctly produced in other words. Although one might initially expect such a substitution (since Icelandic has an [s], but no [z]), why should devoicing persist in just this word? In this case the persistence of a medial [s] can be traced to an Icelandic cognate (þúsund [θusØnt^h]). Transfer may be more heavily weighted in the case of cognates and an interaction model could be modified to assign such weightings.

REFERENCES

Bush, C., M. Edwards, C. Stoel, M. Macken, & J. Peterson. 1973. On specifying a system for transcribing consonants in child language. Mimeo, Stanford Child Phonology Project, Stanford University.

Cancino, H., E.J. Rosansky, & J. H. Schumann. 1978. The acquisition of English negatives and interrogatives by native Spanish speakers. In E. Hatch (Ed.), *Second language acquisition: A book of readings.* Rowley, MA.: Newbury House.

Dulay, H.C., and M.K. Burt. 1975. Creative construction in second language learning and teaching. In M. Burt and H. Dulay (Eds.), *New directions in second language learning, teaching, and bilingual education.* Washington, DC: TESOL.

Dulay, H.C., M.K. Burt, & S. Krashen. 1982. *Language two.* NY: Oxford University Press.

Dulay, H.C., E. Hernández-Chávez, & M.K. Burt. 1978. The process of becoming bilingual. In S. Singh and J. Lynch (Eds.), *Diagnostic procedures in hearing, speech, and language.* Baltimore: University Park Press.

Edwards, M.L. 1979. Patterns and processes in fricative acquisition: Longitudinal evidence from six English-learning children. Unpublished Ph.D. dissertation, Stanford University.

Einarsson, S. 1945. *Icelandic.* Baltimore: Johns Hopkins University Press.

Ervin-Tripp, S. 1974. Is second language learning like the first? *TESOL Quarterly, 8,* 111–127.

Farwell, C.B. 1977. Some strategies in the early production of fricatives. *Papers and Reports on Child Language Development, 12,* 97–104.

Ferguson, C.A. 1975. Fricatives in child language acquisition. *Proceedings of the Eleventh International Congress of Linguistics.* Bologna-Florence, 647–664.

Ferguson, C.A., and C.E. Debose. 1977. Simplified registers, broken language, and pidginization. In A. Valdman (Ed.), *Pidgin and Creole linguistics.* Bloomington: Indiana University Press.

Ferguson, C.A., and C.B. Farwell. 1975. Words and sounds in early language acquisition. *Language, 22,* 88–122.

Garnica, O.K., and M.L. Edwards. 1977. Phonological variation in children's speech: The trade-off phenomenon. *Ohio State Working Papers in Linguistics, 22,* 81–87.

Gregoire, A. 1947. *L'apprentissage du langage.* Paris: Droz (2 vols.).

Hakuta, K. 1976. A case study of a Japanese child learning English as a second language. *Language Learning, 26,* 321–351.

Ingram, D.I. 1975. The acquisition of fricatives and affricates in normal and linguistically deviant children. In A. Caramazza & E. Zurif (Eds.), *The acquisition and breakdown of language.* Baltimore: Johns Hopkins University Press.

Lado, R. 1957. *Linguistics across cultures.* Ann Arbor: University of Michigan Press.

Leopold, W.F. 1939–49. *Speech development of a bilingual child: A linguist's record.* Evanston, IL.: Northwestern University (4 vols.).

Macken, M.A., and C.A. Ferguson. 1981. Phonological universals in language acquisition. In H. Winitz (Ed.), *Native language and foreign language acquisition.* Annuals of the New York Academy of Sciences, Volume 379. (Also this volume.)

Major, R.C. 1977. Phonological differentiation of a bilingual child. *Ohio State University Working Papers in Linguistics, 22,* 88–122.

McLaughlin, B. 1978. *Second language acquisition in childhood.* Hillsdale, NJ: Erlbaum.

Menn, L. 1979. Transition and variation in child phonology: Modeling a developing system. Paper presented at the Ninth International Congress of Phonetic Sciences, Copenhagen.

Milon, J.P. 1974. The development of negation in English by a second language learner. *TESOL Quarterly, 8,* 137–143.

Moskowitz, B.A. 1975. The acquisition of fricatives: A study in phonetics and phonology. *Journal of Phonetics, 3,* 141–150.

Olmsted, D.L. 1971. *Out of the mouth of babes.* The Hague: Mouton.

Ravem, R. 1974. The development of wh-questions in first and second language learners. In J. C. Richards (Ed.), *Error analysis: Perspectives on second language acquisition.* London: Longmans.

Scollon, R. 1976. *Conversations with a one-year old: A case study of the developmental foundation of syntax.* Honolulu: University Press of Hawaii.

Stampe, D. 1973. A dissertation on natural phonology. Unpublished Ph.D. dissertation, University of Chicago.

Vogel, I. 1975. One system or two: An analysis of a two-year-old Romanian-English bilingual's phonology. *Papers and Reports on Child Language Development, 9,* 43–62.

Wode, H. 1976. Developmental sequences in naturalistic L2 acquisition. *Working Papers in Bilingualism, 11,* 1–31.

Part Four

THE SYLLABLE

In the past, the notion of the syllable was generally excluded from many generative phonological analyses. Recently, however, researchers in phonological theory have recognized that the syllable is indeed an important constituent in phonological organization, and now L2 researchers have begun to incorporate the syllable into their analyses. For example, there have been a number of recent studies investigating the influence of the L1 syllable structure on the formation of an IL phonology. Much of the work is an outgrowth of the syllable-based analysis developed by Kahn (1976). Part Four focuses on these studies. A central concern in most of the articles is the extent to which transfer and universal simplification processes contribute to the shape of the resulting IL rules.

Tarone's article is one of the earliest attempts to determine how IL syllable structure differs from that of the TL. In studying this question she looks at which of three processes have had the most effect on the IL syllable: language transfer, reactivated first language acquisition processes, and universal processes. (Although Tarone does not discuss this issue, it may be the case that most first language acquisition processes belong to the set of universal processes of simplification.) Tarone's inquiry is based on IL English data produced by speakers of Cantonese, Portuguese, and Korean. Although most of the attested errors are attributable to L1 transfer, she found a number that were not. Tarone determines that there is a universal tendency among learners to prefer an open CV syllable pattern, even in cases where it is not predicted by transfer criteria. These findings reflect the use of unmarked rules discussed in the Altenberg and Vago study in the previous section.

The study by Sato is a continuation of Tarone's investigation. Sato asks if there will still be a preference for the open syllable in the IL in cases where the NL prefers a closed syllable in its own phonological structure. In other words, which process is more heavily weighted in the L2 acquisition of the syllable, transfer or universal simplification? Sato chooses Vietnamese learners of English to research this issue. Vietnamese, it appears, prefers the CVC syllable. Contrary to Tarone's findings, Sato's subjects favored the closed CVC syllable in their IL productions. Her data do not support the hypothesis that learners tend toward open syllables as a universal simplification process. Neither she nor Tarone discuss whether the learner's proficiency level may have an effect on the choice of IL strategy, however. This could contribute to differences in their data.

Broselow, in her first article, "An Investigation of Transfer in Second Language Phonology," believes that a revision of the Contrastive Analysis Hypothesis (CAH) must begin with a specification of the error types that are expected to result from native language transfer. She specifically examines learner difficulties at word junctures in the target language. The study utilizes American English as the source language and Egyptian Arabic as the L2. After presenting a careful analysis of the syllable structure of the two languages, Broselow determines that the problems the learners are having with TL word boundaries result from the application of English syllable structure rules to the processing of the new language. She concludes that syllable structure restrictions are particularly susceptible to transfer. However, Broselow agrees with Eckman, Altenberg and Vago, and Tarone that principles of markedness interact with transfer phenomena in determining the form of the interlanguage system.

Anderson's research is an attempt to test the validity of the Markedness Differential Hypothesis (MDH) for the acquisition of the L2 syllable. She collects data from speakers of Mandarin and Amoy Chinese and of Egyptian Arabic learning English. Her results show that the MDH is generally a good predictor of the subjects' syllable simplification strategies. However, when there is a conflict in the predictions made by markedness criteria and by transfer, the MDH is inapplicable, since both of these processes contribute to its definition. Her data reveal that the unmarked, universally simpler structures were more easily acquired than the more marked ones in cases where transfer predicts the opposite. These findings could have resulted from the fact that certain deletions that occur frequently in L1 developmental data and that are independent of the MDH also occurred frequently in her data. Nevertheless, overall, the MDH made more accurate predictions than an analysis based solely on transfer.

Broselow's second article dealing with the prediction of epenthesis errors

230

is an attempt to delineate the factors that allow prediction not just of the learner's problem areas but of the actual choice of resolution. She believes that previous failures to do so may be due to inadequate knowledge of the NL grammar rather than to a shortcoming in the theory of contrastive analysis. Broselow examines the acquisition of initial consonant clusters in English by speakers of two languages that lack them. The type of epenthesis employed by each native language group is entirely predictable using contrastive criteria, if a particular theoretical approach to syllable structure is adhered to. The results indicate that transfer may be operating in a nonobvious fashion, discernable only upon the application of a more sophisticated linguistic analysis.

The study by Karimi is a reply to Broselow. Karimi observes that native-speaking Farsi learners of English employ similar cluster simplification strategies in their English IL, as do native speakers of Egyptian Arabic—one of the two NLs of the Broselow study. Yet there are no Farsi native language rules of epenthesis that can be said to underlie the IL strategy. In Farsi impermissible clusters are resolved internally through consonant deletion, not epenthesis. In addition, Broselow accounts for some of the English IL strategies employed by Egyptian Arabic speakers through an appeal to universal principles of markedness. Karimi shows that the same universals are invalid for the Farsi speakers' IL data. Her conclusion is that the linguistic analysis of syllable structure offered by Broselow is inadequate for a prediction of the IL strategies used by learners from every native language background.

REFERENCES

Kahn, D. 1976. *Syllable-Based Generalizations in English Phonology.* (M.I.T. doctoral dissertation.) NY: Garland Publishing Company, 1980.

13

SOME INFLUENCES ON THE SYLLABLE STRUCTURE OF INTERLANGUAGE PHONOLOGY*

Elaine E. Tarone

INTRODUCTION

One area of second language acquisition which research has largely overlooked until recently has been the area of phonology. Most recent studies have centered upon the acquisition of morphemes, the auxiliary and a few higher-order structures (cf. Hatch, 1978, for an overview of this research to date). I know of very few studies which have attempted to systematically gather performance data on the structure of the learners' interlanguage phonology.[1] A great many papers have been written in the past which claim to predict performance in interlanguage (IL) pronunciation by presenting contrastive analyses of the phonologies of English and various other languages—but of these, only a handful have gone on to present systematically-gathered and analyzed performance data to test these predictions.[2]

*A preliminary version of this paper, entitled "Some Influences on Interlanguage Phonology," appeared in *Working Papers in Bilingualism,* 8, February 1976, by permission of the editors of IRAL. Thanks are due to D.K. Oller, Larry Selinker, and Amy Sheldon for comments on preliminary versions of this paper.

NEEDED RESEARCH IN INTERLANGUAGE PHONOLOGY

The study of interlanguage phonology may focus upon a great many variables. Several of the areas in which research is needed are listed below.[3]

Data Base

First, there is need for interlanguage researchers to begin accumulating a base of phonological data, collected and transcribed systematically. Such a common data base is essential in establishing the basic facts which must be accounted for by any theory of interlanguage phonology. The analysis of such a data base might profitably concentrate upon either segmental features (such as the "substitution" of individual speech sounds for others, or the systematic modifications of individual target language sounds in interlanguage), or suprasegmental features such as stress, rhythm, intonation and syllabification in interlanguage.

Causes of Phonological Fossilization

An issue of primary psychological interest is the question of why it is that pronunciation often remains problematic even for advanced learners of the second language (Scovel, 1969). Indeed, adult learners often report that matters of "accent" may continue to mark them as non-native speakers long after fine points of syntax, semantics, or even style have been mastered. What is the cause of this phenomenal "fossilization" of phonology?

One possible explanation might be some kind of physiological habit formation. After all, the muscles of the tongue and mouth region have been practicing the production of one set of sound patterns for years, and it may be (as learners often insist) that the nerves and muscles needed to produce another set of sound patterns have atrophied so far as to prohibit accurate pronunciation of the second language. Such a physiological explanation need not be limited to muscles and nerves at the periphery—perhaps some neural functions in the central nervous processes have atrophied somehow—perhaps along the lines of Lenneberg's (1967) suggestion of lateralization of the cortical function, the "flexibility" of the brain has diminished with age and this lack of flexibility has affected pronunciation of the second language more than the syntax and semantics. (See Scovel [1969] for a discussion of the possible effects of lateralization on interlanguage phonology.) Krashen and Harshman (1972) and Krashen (1973) raise questions about the physiological hypothesis, however, reanalyzing data used by Lenneberg, and dichotic listening data, and claiming that lateralization seems to take place long before the end of the "critical period" for language learning.[4]

Krashen (1977) supports a hypothesis which falls into the second group of explanations for the fossilization of phonology—the "psychological" explanations. Krashen suggests that the close of the critical period is related to the onset

233

of Inhelder and Piaget's stage of formal operations; Krashen suggests that this stage, in which adolescents begin to consciously construct abstract theories about the world, may inhibit "natural" language acquisition, including the acquisition of phonology. Another "psychological" hypothesis attempting to explain the fossilization of phonology in particular, is one based in psychological habit formation. It is becoming common for researchers to claim that language transfer probably has its strongest effect in the area of pronunciation. If this is true (though it has by no means been clearly demonstrated to date), and if language transfer is evidence for habit formation (some serious questions may be raised about this claim as well), then perhaps we might lay the cause of the difficulty of second language pronunciation at the door of psychological habit formation. That is, it may be that a learner's speech perception and production have become permanently influenced by the first language phonology so that s/he has become psychologically unable to perceive or produce a new phonology with any great facility. This type of psychological habit formation would not result from physiological causes, but rather would derive from the subject's psychological inability to alter the criteria used to categorize speech sounds.

A third type of explanation would stress the learner's underlying lack of empathy with the native speakers of the second language. Considerable work has been done by sociolinguists such as Labov[5] showing that patterns of pronunciation tend to be adopted when the speaker identifies with a particular social group. Guiora et al (1972) have claimed that when empathy with native speakers of a second language is artificially induced, the pronunciation of the second language improves. Guiora feels that interlanguage pronunciation is a sensitive indicator of empathy, or the degree to which the language learner identifies with the speakers of the second language. Does the lack of empathy lead to a fossilized phonology?

It should be the function of research into interlanguage phonology to attempt to resolve this issue of the cause of phonological fossilization.

Processes Shaping Interlanguage Phonology

Another issue for research to deal with—one which has already been touched upon—is the relative importance of language transfer processes, first language acquisition processes, and other processes in shaping the interlanguage phonology. Several questions need to be investigated:

1. How does language transfer from the first language affect the interlanguage phonology and cause it to deviate from the target language? Which aspects of the interlanguage phonology are most influenced by the first language?
2. Are first language acquisition processes reactivated in learning to pronounce the target language? To what extent does the second-language learner behave like the first-language learner in the acquisition of phonology?
3. Are there other processes traceable neither to language transfer nor to the reactivation of first-language acquisition processes, which influence the shape of the interlanguage phonology?

Variability and Instability in Interlanguage Phonology

We know from work in sociolinguistics that pronunciation seems to be extremely sensitive to social situation; L. Dickerson (1975) and W. Dickerson (1977) have shown that this kind of *variability* exists in the interlanguage of the second-language learner as well as the native language. They have begun to isolate the factors which influence this variability of interlanguage phonology. Similar work needs to be done in investigating the *instability* of interlanguage phonology *over time*. Of special interest is the issue of the influence of the classroom situation upon interlanguage phonology, and the extent of carry-over of certain patterns of pronunciation from the classroom to other situations.

PILOT STUDY ON THE SYLLABLE STRUCTURE OF INTERLANGUAGE

Focus of the Study

There are, then, a great many variables to study in the area of interlanguage phonology. No one study can begin to answer all these questions. This paper describes a pilot study which (1) focusses on the syllable structure of the interlanguage, in an attempt to determine how it differs from the syllable structure of the target language, and which (2) begins to identify some of the processes which may shape that interlanguage syllable structure.

Theoretical Background of the Study

In spite of the absence of empirical data, there have been some speculations as to the nature of the processes which might influence interlanguage phonology. Three separate influences on the shape of the interlanguage syllable structure might be suggested: language transfer, reactivated first language acquisition processes, and universal processes of various kinds.

The language transfer hypothesis would suggest that the learner would simply use the syllable structure from the first language in his or her attempt to communicate meaningfully in the target language. Thus, if the hypothetical first language contains only syllables consisting of a vowel-consonant (VC) type, this hypothesis would predict that the learner would tend to transform the target language syllables into VC types.

The second hypothesis would suggest that the second-language learner would tend to do what the first language learner does with syllable structure. That is, difficult syllables would be simplified by the second language learner in the same way that they are by the first language learner. The nature of this hypothesis is best understood by considering the work of D.K. Oller (1974). Oller believes that second language learners do *not* reactivate first language acquisition processes in the acquisition of their target language phonology; rather, he has suggested that the processes which shape the interlanguage phonology are quite different from those which shape phonology in first language acquisition. Oller makes this claim on the basis of an examination of the literature which does exist on the phonologies of second language learners—a literature which is very sparse and unsystematically-reported, unfortunately. Oller points to such phenomena as the reportedly characteristic epenthesis in the speech of second language learners as evidence for his claim. He maintains that in first language acquisition of phonology, it is most characteristic for learners under 36 months of age to simplify by reducing or deleting difficult sounds, as:

a) cluster reduction:
      e.g., blue ⟶ bue
b) final consonant deletion:
      e.g., big ⟶ bi
c) weak syllable deletion:
      e.g., banana ⟶ nana

However, in the data reported in the literature on second-language acquisition, second language learners appeared to use a very different strategy to pronounce difficult sounds:

a) instead of cluster reduction, second language learners reportedly used vowel insertion (epenthesis) much more frequently:
      e.g., tree ⟶ təree
b) instead of final consonant deletion, second language learners more commonly favored vowel addition (epenthesis):
      e.g., big ⟶ bigu
c) and where first language learners deleted weak syllables, this phenomenon was reported to be very uncommon among second language learners. (Oller, 1974)

The literature examined by Oller apparently gave no indication of the strength of this reported tendency to epenthesize, nor of the existence of any strong tendency among second language learners to delete consonants in the way that first language learners reportedly do. Oller emphasizes the need for a systematically-described empirical data base on interlanguage phonology; he feels that such a data base would show that the processes shaping interlanguage phonology *were* different from those shaping first language phonology.

If it is true that epenthesis is a common strategy in second language learners' acquisition of phonology, there may be two alternative explanations for it: it may result from language transfer, or it may be the result of an alternative process.

This third suggested influence on the shape of interlanguage syllable structure is a possible universal preference for the open (CV) syllable. Tarone (1972) has argued that the simple open syllable may be a universal articulatory and perceptual unit; that is, that the articulators tend to operate in basic CV programs in all languages, and the various languages simply elaborate upon this program by adding various combinations of initial and final consonants. In stressful situations of various kinds, speakers have been shown to revert to very simple CV patterns of pronunciation in their native languages (see, for example, Kozhevnikov and Chistovich, 1965). In learning another language, then, it would seem to be possible that any learner, regardless of first language background, might tend to break difficult sound combinations into simple CV patterns, using the kind of epenthesis described by D.K. Oller above.

In order to determine whether the reported tendency towards epenthesis is a result of language transfer, or of a process of movement towards a universal open syllable, we will have to examine attempts by speakers of a variety of first languages to learn the phonology of the same target language—in this case, English. Many languages, such as Cantonese, have a fairly simple CV syllable structure, so that (based on predictions of contrastive analysis) one might expect Cantonese speakers learning English to break difficult sound combinations into CV syllable units as a result of language transfer. It would be hard, studying subjects whose first language was Cantonese, to find instances of syllable simplification in the interlanguage which could clearly be demonstrated to originate from causes other than transfer. However, speakers whose native languages have some of the *same,* relatively complex syllable structures as those appearing in the target language, and who *still* attempt to break those structures into simpler open syllables as they speak the interlanguage, would provide clear evidence that some process other than language transfer was operating. In such cases, one might claim that a universal process of simplification towards an open or CV syllable was being evidenced.

The Syllable Structures of the Three Native Languages in the Study[6]

Native speakers of three different languages were studied in this pilot project: Cantonese, Portuguese and Korean. A word about the syllable structures of these three languages may be helpful. Cantonese and Portuguese are both considered to be more or less "open-syllable" languages; that is, the syllabic structure of both languages is fairly simple, with most syllables being of a consonant-vowel, or CV, variety. In Cantonese, "closed" syllables which may end in one of a limited number of consonants may occur; these may be used to test our hypothesis. Consonant clusters in Cantonese occur primarily as syllables occur together, across syllable boundaries. In Portuguese, similarly, there is a limited number of permissible final consonants, but a somewhat larger number of consonant clusters permitted within a syllable. While Korean is also considered to be primarily an open-syllable language, it contains a much more complicated syllable structure, especially in its final consonant structure, than either Cantonese or Portuguese. Note that where Cantonese and Portuguese speakers make syllable structure errors in English, it will be very difficult to trace the source of these errors to anything other than language transfer. This is because, in order to show that interlanguage syllable structure errors do *not* result from language transfer, it is necessary to demonstrate clearly that the *same* sequence of vowels and consonants exists in the native language and the target language, and that the learner still makes syllable structure errors in trying to produce that sequence in the target language. A comparison of Cantonese and English, or Portuguese and English, shows that the number of such identical sequences of vowels and consonants in both languages is not large. A comparison of Korean and English, however, shows much more similarity of syllable structure, and thus provides much more opportunity for the researcher to separate out the relative influences of language transfer, and any universal CV simplification process which may exist. Unfortunately, native speakers of languages with more complex syllable structures were simply not available to the researcher at the time of this study; stronger evidence for the hypothesis might be found with such subjects.

Procedure and Subjects

In this pilot study, six speakers were recorded as they described orally a sequence of pictures, narrating a story in the process. Each speaker was shown the same series of pictures. Previous experience with this method of data elicitation had shown it to be fairly effective in eliciting the same general English lexical items and grammatical structures from all subjects. (A possibly more orderly method might have been to ask each subject to read the same passage into a tape recorder; however, this procedure might have confounded the data with "reading pronunciation.") Two of the subjects were Cantonese speakers from Hong Kong, two were Portuguese speakers from Brazil and two were native speakers of Korean. All the subjects were between 19 and 30 years of age.

Each subject's narration of the story was transcribed using a standard IPA (International Phonetic Alphabet) transcription with diacritics where needed to note deviation from a Standard American English transcription. (All six transcriptions are included in Appendix A.) Next, a score was obtained for each subject. This score noted the number of errors in syllable structure made by each subject. An error in syllable structure was categorized as (1) epenthesis, (2) consonant deletion, and (3) insertion of glottal stops. The score did *not* include the substitution of one consonant for another consonant, or of one vowel for another vowel, since such substitutions do *not* substantially alter the syllable structure.[7]

Results and Discussion

In Table 13.1, we see that about 20 percent of all the syllables attempted by each subject contained some sort of syllable structure error.

TABLE 13.1. Overall Percentage of Syllable Structure Errors

	Approximate # syllables attempted	# Syllable structure errors	Approximate % errors
Korean # 1	72	15	21%
Korean # 2	70	15	21%
Cantonese # 1	129	25	19%
Cantonese # 2	148	36	24%
Portuguese # 1	112	23	21%
Portuguese # 2	144	23	16%

In examining the overall use of the strategies of epenthesis and consonant deletion, displayed in Table 13.2, it is immediately apparent that the subjects did *not* rely heavily on epenthesis as a strategy in altering syllable structure, as D.K. Oller's sources had suggested they might. Rather, the subjects used *both* epenthesis *and* consonant deletion. This would seem to indicate that, insofar as consonant deletion is a strategy used in the acquisition of first language phonology, it may be possible that first language acquisition processes *are* in fact reactivated to a certain extent in the acquisition of second language phonology. However, if such a reactivation does take place, it does not seem to operate with great force. The two strategies of consonant deletion and epenthesis seem to affect the syllable structure with approximately equal force for most of the subjects. Different subjects do seem to prefer different strategies, however; the critical variable in their choice of strategies appears to be their native language background. In Table 13.2 we can see that Cantonese and Korean speakers preferred consonant deletion as a strategy, while the Portuguese speakers decidedly favored epenthesis as a strategy in simplifying syllable structure.

Table 13.3 shows each subject's performance in terms of the strategies used in simplifying either final consonants or consonants or consonant clusters. It is clear from Table 13.3 that most consonant deletion and epenthesis took place in the subjects' production of final consonants rather than of non-final consonant clusters. Where non-final consonant clusters *were* simplified, the

TABLE 13.2. Overall Preferred Strategies for Syllable Simplification

	Consonant deletion	Epenthesis
Korean # 1	71%	29%
Korean # 2	80%	20%
Cantonese # 1	68%	32%
Cantonese # 2	62%	38%
Portuguese # 1	20%	80%
Portuguese # 2	20%	80%

TABLE 13.3. Strategies Preferred in Simplification of Final Consonants or Consonant Clusters

	Final consonants		Consonant clusters	
	Deletion	Epenthesis	Deletion	Epenthesis
Korean # 1	10 (59%)	4 (24%)	2 (12%)	1 (5%)
Korean # 2	10 (67%)	3 (20%)	2 (13%)	0
Cantonese # 1	10 (40%)	8 (32%)	7 (28%)	0
Cantonese # 2	13 (45%)	11 (38%)	5 (17%)	0
Portuguese # 1	2 (11%)	11 (58%)	2 (11%)	4 (20%)
Portuguese # 2	0	8 (80%)	2 (20%)	0

subjects almost always used consonant deletion as a strategy; both consonant deletion and epenthesis were used in simplifying final consonants.

In the analysis of the data, all the errors, or points of deviation, between interlanguage and target language syllable structure, were crossclassified as to whether their origin could be reliably traced to language transfer or not. So, for example, the Korean speaker's

[kəlas]   for   [klæs]

was classified as an error originating in language transfer, since Korean does not have any [kl] clusters. However, the same speaker's rendition of

[sku:]   for   [skuəl]

was classified as non-transfer in origin. Since Korean has a word [kuəl] (meaning "ninth month"), [sku:] is not likely to have been caused by language transfer from Korean. In many cases, it was hard to tell whether an error was the result of language transfer or not. For example, the same speaker produced

[tɛ̃]   for   [ðɛn]

where the final [-n] was omitted from the word "then." Korean does have syllables which end with a final [-n], so one might be inclined to exclude language transfer as a cause of this error. However, further investigation shows that Korean has no *words* which end in [-n]. In cases like this, the error was called a language transfer error. Since one of the purposes of this study was to isolate clear cases of syllable structure errors in the interlanguage which clearly could not be caused by language transfer, whenever there was any doubt in the investigator's mind about the origins of any particular error, that error was classified as "language transfer" rather than "non-transfer."

It can be seen in Table 13.4 that the majority of errors in syllable structure made by the subjects were attributed to the influence of language transfer. But for each learner, there was a number of such errors which did *not* seem to be

TABLE 13.4. Processes Underlying Interlanguage Syllable Structure
Errors

	# Errors	# Errors due to language transfer	Non-transfer errors
Korean # 1	17	9 (53%)	8 (47%)
Korean # 2	15	11 (73%)	4 (27%)
Cantonese # 1	25	19 (77%)	6 (23%)
Cantonese # 2	29	21 (73%)	8 (27%)
Portuguese # 1	19	16 (84%)	3 (16%)
Portuguese # 2	10	9 (90%)	1 (10%)

due to language transfer. Forty-seven percent of Korean Speaker # 1's syllable structure errors could not be accounted for solely in terms of language transfer; this learner had the largest percentage of such "non-transfer" errors. For Portuguese Speaker # 2, who had the smallest percentage of such errors, only 10 percent were clear cases of non-transfer errors.

Table 13.5 contains an exhaustive list of all the syllable structure errors made by these learners which, in the investigator's judgment, could not be the result of language transfer. These non-transfer errors are listed together with permissible syllable sequences from the respective learners' native languages which contain the same (or nearly the same) sequence of vowels and consonants as the sequence in English which the learner failed to produce correctly. The examples of epenthesis, consonant deletion and glottal stop insertion shown in Table 13.5 seem to be difficult to account for in terms of language transfer, if the information contained therein regarding the learners' native language syllable structure is correct. Neither can those examples be accounted for entirely in terms of the reactivation of first language acquisition processes, since epenthesis is clearly one of the strategies used by these learners, and as D.K. Oller has claimed, epenthesis is not a first language acquisition strategy. Note that in every case, the result of consonant deletion and epenthesis is to "simplify" the second language syllable structure—that is, to modify it towards a basic consonant-vowel pattern. Since the consistent result of this pattern of epenthesis and consonant deletion is to modify the syllable structure towards a basic CV pattern, it is suggested here that pattern may be a result of a universal preference for the open syllable, and for the CV syllable in particular. Such a preference may combine with other processes, such as language transfer, to produce an even stronger preference for the open syllable in the interlanguages of some learners; but clearly, the preference for the CV syllable seems in this study to be a process which operates independently of language transfer.

In examining glottal stop insertions, it was found that in *every* instance the glottal stop was inserted at word boundaries—usually when the first word ended with a vowel, and the next word began with a vowel. The result of this insertion was usually to change the syllable structure to a consonant-vowel

241

TABLE 13.5. Syllable Structure Errors Apparently Not Due to Language Transfer

Subject	Target sequence	IL sequence	Permissible NL sequence	Strategy
Korean No. 1	sɪtsʌmples	sɪː sʌmples	kɪts'ɑ	Deletion
	hoːl	hoː	koːl	Deletion
	sɑlðə	sɑːə	sɑldzidɑ	Deletion
	gɔn	gɔ̄	kɑn	Deletion
	gɔn	gɔ̄	kɑn	Deletion
	sæk	sæke	sæk	Epenthesis
	lɑikðədɔg	lɑikədɔ̣g'	kəktɑ	Epenthesis
	ɔɪnsæk	ə'ɪnsɛk'	tsuye ɪt	Insertion
Korean No. 2	ɑut	ɑuː	ut	Deletion
	skuəl	skuː	kuəl	Deletion
	hoːl	hoː	koːl	Deletion
	gowɔkɪŋ	gɔ'wɔkɪŋ	oɑtɑ w	Insertion
Cantonese No. 1	dʒon	dʒɔ̄ː	dzon	Deletion
	bʌtʃi	bəʃi	mɑtɛɔɪ	Deletion
	blæŋkət	blæŋkətʂ̣	kɑt	Epenthesis
	gɛrʂ̣t	gɛrʂ̣tʂ̣	kɑt	Epenthesis
	ədʒæm	ə'dʒæm	sɛː tsi	Insertion
	nowɑi	no'wɑi	ŋoʰwɑː	Insertion
Cantonese No. 2	ɑutəv	ɑuəv	ut	Deletion
	sæk	sætʂ̣	[sæk] [tsæt]	Epenthesis
	sæk	sǣt'ə	[sæk] [tsæt]	Epenthesis
	sæk	sɛtʂ̣	[sæk] [tsæt]	Epenthesis
	tuit	tuʔit'	tɛɑu iːu	Insertion
	sætn̩	sæt'ʔʂ̣n	teŋiɑt iɑnwɑi	Insertion
	ðiʌðə˞	ţiʔʌtə˞	lɑi ɑː	Insertion
	ɑə˞itɪŋ	ɑə˞ʔitɪŋ	kɑ iɑtko	Insertion
Portuguese No. 1	blæŋkət	bæŋkʂ̣tʂ̣	problemɑ	Epenthesis
	bægwəz	bægʂ̣wʌs	iguɑl	Epenthesis
	pleswɛə˞	plesʂ̣wɛə˞	sueño	Epenthesis
Portuguese No. 2	lɑsθri	lɑstʂ̣dʂ̣tri	eʃtrɑɲo	Epenthesis

pattern. It seems likely that the insertion of glottal stops may be the result of an attempt to produce lexical items as separate units in the speech stream—possibly as a consequence of transfer of training, or of the learners' greater familiarity with written English than with spoken English (see Tarone, 1972) —and possibly in interaction with the hypothesized preference for the open syllable.

Summary

In summary, then, the data accumulated in this preliminary study supports the following findings:

242

(a) the syllable structure of the interlanguage is often markedly different from that of the target language;

(b) in the syllable structure of the interlanguage examined in this study, both epenthesis and consonant deletion seemed to be used as strategies for syllable simplification, with the first language background of the learner seeming to be related to a preference for one strategy over the other;

(c) the dominant process influencing the syllable structure of the interlanguage phonology appeared to be language transfer;

(d) a preference for the open (CV) syllable seemed to operate as a process independent of language transfer in influencing the syllable structure of the interlanguage phonology; and

(e) glottal stop insertion appeared only between words, possibly as a result of an attempt to produce lexical items as separate units in the speech stream.

NOTES

1. For a summary of this research on interlanguage phonology, particularly as it has occurred in the United States, see Tarone (1978). In addition, Eliasson (1976) summarizes some European work in this area.

2. Among these empirical studies are Brière (1966), and Nemser (1971). Johansson's (1973) multiple contact analysis is one of the most thorough of these empirical studies, contrasting nine different languages with Swedish, and examining data from 180 learners of Swedish.

3. I am endebted for some of these ideas to the participants in John Schumann's session on phonology at the University of Michigan's Sixth Annual Conference on Applied Linguistics at Ann Arbor.

4. The term "critical period" is used to describe an age range during which it is possible to learn a second language easily; after that period, it is suggested that the second language cannot be learned with the facility supposedly characteristic of children.

5. Labov (1972), for example, shows that an adolescent's degree of inclusion in a particular peer group is highly correlated with the phonological patterns evidenced in that adolescent's speech.

6. Information on the syllable structures of the S.s native languages was obtained for Cantonese, from Chao (1947); for Korean, from Cho (1967); and for Portuguese, from a native-speaker informant. A more rigorous replication of this study should combine reference to contrastive analyses with information from native-speaker informants.

7. In Table 13.2 and 13.3, certain syllables which are usually simplified in American English were not counted. Most notable syllables excluded from the counts are the expressions: 'an' ', as in 'you an' I,' and 'and, uh,' as in 'I saw Joan and, uh, Tom.'

APPENDIX A: TRANSCRIPTIONS OF SIX SUBJECTS LEARNING ESL

Korean No. 1

αiθιŋ:kɔ̌ʃi:mes:æmɪtʃɔ̌ . . . ţɛn:pʊtṇəsæke . . .
ðɛn:ɔ̌ . . . ʃigo . . . ʔɑuʔ . . . ţɛ̃ʃiwɔʔ . . . ţɛ̃ʃidrɔp' . . . ʃidrɔp' . . .
əʃisɪ:sʌmples: . . . ɔ̌nɔ̌kɔ̌lɑsɔ:sʌmples . . .
αiɪlidonowʌrɪʃiduiŋ . . . ţɛn . . . ʔə . . . ʃi . . .
pʊtṇəʔɪnsɛk'tɔ̌tʃɛk'ţəsɛʔ . . . ʔɔ̌zɔ̌ho: . . .
ţɔ̌sɑ:ɔ̌sæmɪtʃɔ̌gɔ̌ . . . ɔlgɔ̌ . . . zədɔ̌ɡʔit' . . .
lʊkslɑikɔ̌dɔɡ'fʌn . . .

243

Korean No. 2

ʃime:əsæemɪtʃɪ . . . ʃimekɪŋ . . . əsæemɪʔ . . . æn:ʃipʊrɪn: . . .
pepə˞bæɪ . . . æn:ʃiteḳ'ɑu: . . . ŋʃiyoʔwɔkɪŋno . . .
αiθɪŋt̯ē . . . ʃigosʌmə̯̈sku:ə˞sʌmðɪŋ . . . æn:ʃi . . .
ʔn:ʃidrɔpʔ . . . sæems: . . . so . . . ʃi . . . ʃipʊrɪnəbæ: . . .
t̯ə:pepə˞hæs: . . . ʔə . . . ho: . . . so . . . ʃi . . . s3pɪʔm . . . s . . . ʔm̩ . . .
o: . . . ʃisi: . . . ʔə̄hosæ̈:ʔɪʃisæ̈wɪtʃɪ: . . . dɔʔ . . .
dɔ: g̈'it . . . h3sæ̈wɪtʃə̯̈ . . .

Cantonese No. 1

t̯ə̯̈g3ɣznemɪs . . . dʒō: . . . ʔæn: . . . ʃiʐgoɪŋ . . .
ʔə:tuhævə̯̈pɪʔŋɪk' . . . æn: . . . f3sʔəvʔɔ: . . . ʃiə̯̈pʔ . . .
pɪpɛə˞s:əʔdʒæm:sæ̈wɪtʃə̯̈ . . . æn: . . . ʃipʊʔsɪʔɪnə̯̈bæ:k . . .
ʔə̯̈m . . . ʃibɪɪŋ:z . . . ʔəm . . . sæ̈mɪʃ . . . ʔænəʔ . . . blæŋkə̯̈t̯ə̯̈ . . .
wɪθh3αnə̯̈weɪ: . . . æn: . . .
sʌdŋli . . . ʃi . . . dɪɔps . . . t̯əsæ̈wɪtʃə̯̈ . . . bəʃidʌzə̯̈noðæʔ . . .
æn: . . . wɛ̄ʃi . . . ɪɪtʃəz:ðə̯̈ples'ə̯̈ . . . wɛə˞ʃi . . . pɪænstuhævə̯̈
pɪʔŋɪkə̯̈ . . . ʃiə̯̈spɪɛʔ . . . spɪɛʔs:t̯ə̯̈bɪæŋkə̯̈ts . . .
ʔαn . . . ʔαnə̯̈gɪαū: . . . ænt̯ē . . . ʃiteksαurə̯̈sæ̈wɪtʃə̯̈ . . .
bʌʔ . . . ʃidɪskʌvə˞t̯æt̯ʔəsæ̈wɪtʃʃwəzgɔ̄:ŋ . . .
æn . . . ʃidə̯̈zŋoʔwαi: . . . æn . . . ðærə̯̈zbkʌz . . . ʔəm: . . .
ʃidɪɔpsɪtʔαnə̯̈weɪ:ən . . . t̯ə̯̈dɔʔ . . . dɔgʔz . . . gɛʔ . . . gɛrə̯̈t̯ə̯̈ . . .

Cantonese No. 2

ʔəg3:ɪsə: . . . fɪsɪŋh3to:s . . . wɪf . . . dʒæm . . .
ænαifɪŋə:ʃiɪstrαintu:hæfəpɪʔnɪʔt' . . . ænhig' . . . ænhihæʔ . . .
ʔænhihæʔ . . . ænə̯̈ʃihæsʔɛvɪfɪŋ . . . ɪɛdiænə . . . ʃiwə . . .
ʃiwəsohæpiə̯̈n: . . . gɛtɪŋʔαʊəvt̯ə̯̈dɔə . . . æn: . . . ʃiwαso: . . .
sʔʃʔ . . . (unintelligible) ʃiwɔkə̯̈lɔŋt̯əɪo:æn: . . . ə̯̈ŋʃidɪdə̯̈no . . .
ɛə . . . t̯ə . . . t̯əsæʔwəs' . . . wəs' . . . ʔə̯̈ . . . ə̄ʃ . . .
ʃidɪ:ŋ:otɪsəʔ . . . notɪst̯æt̯ə̯̈sæ̈t'ə: . . . wɛs'bɪokænə̯̈t̯ə
sæ̈wɪtʃə̯̈kemαʊt . . . ænə: . . . hi . . . higotutt̯əbitʃænə̯̈pe:wɪfəsæn
. . . æn: . . . αftə:wαijʃi:fɛlt'hæʔhʌŋgɪiʔænʃiwαnts . . .
ʃiwʌnətuʔitʔsʌmsæ̈wɪtʃə̯̈ . . . ænə: . . . ʃitʊkαutəsætʔə̯̈ɔ̄n: . . .
ʃifαuŋαut̯æt̯isɛt̯ə̯̈ . . . wəsbɪokə̯̈ . . . ænə: . . .
æ ənʃiwəs:ə̯̈n . . . ʃiwəsə̯̈nαʔʃʊə˞wɛə˞ . . . wɛə˞ʃilɔst̯ə̯̈sæ̈wɪtʃə̯̈z . . .
æn: . . . ænαnt̯iʔʌt̯ə˞hænə: . . . t̯idɔ-sαə˞ʔitɪŋ: . . . h3sæ̈wɪtʃə̯̈z . . .

Portuguese No. 1

ðig3ə̯̈l . . . pɪkʌp . . . æ:bɔn: . . . æn: . . . pɪipɛə˞dəhiz: . . . ə . . .
fudfɔə˞ . . . h3fudfɔə˞ . . . ə:pikənik . . . ə: . . . hwɛn . . . ʔhi . . .
wʌzgoiŋtuðəpɪkənik . . . ʃi: . . . lαst̯ə̯̈ . . . h3s . . . sαndəwɪʃ . . .
æn: . . . ʃi . . . ʃidʌsəntə̯̈n . . . noəbαut'ɪt . . . æn: . . . hwɛ̄:s . . .

244

ʃi . . . ərɑivtŝ̞ðəplesŝ̞ʔwɛᴧ . . . ʃiwɑntugo . . . ʔə . . . ʃi . . . pʊtə . . .
ʔə . . . bæŋkŝ̞tŝ̞ . . . ðəflɔᴧ . . . ænpıipɛᴧtuit' . . . bʌt' . . . hwɛ̃hi . . .
gɛtŝ̞h3:bæg . . . ʃi . . . ʔɛː . . . notŝ̞ðæt . . . h3bægŝ̞wʌs: . . . bŝ̞ıokən: . . .
ænðætʃilostŝ̞ . . . h3 . . . sænwıʃ' . . . ænʃiː . . . bikemzvɛᴧs . . . oː . . .
sᴧpıɑizdŝ̞ . . . ænə . . . ðəf3sθıŋ . . . ðəkemztuh3mɑin:əzðæt . . .
sʌmdɔgz . . . wʌ:zitıŋ . . . h3fud . . .

Portuguese No. 2

suziʔwʌzŝ̞gʊdə . . . vɛıivɛıigʊdəg3l . . . ʃi . . . ʃilɑik' . . .
ʃilɑikʔit' . . . vɛıimʌtʃ'bikʌzʃizfæt . . . ʃizʌɛritæt . . .
ændəː . . . wʌndeiʃi . . . wʌndeʃipıipɛᴧmɛnisænwıʃ . . .
fɔıgotŝ̞ðskul . . . sndiː . . . hwɛntŝ̞bigin . . . ʔəː . . . hwɛ̃hwɛ̃
hwɛ̃nŝ̞bigın . . . tuwɔk' . . . ınzıː . . . hwɛnŝ̞bigıntuwɔkŝ̞ . . .
ınðəfɔıst' . . . ʔəʔıʔıntigɑıdən . . . ınti . . .
ıntʔıntigɑıdən . . . ʃiʃilɑstŝ̞dŝ̞tıi . . . tsænwıʃ . . . oi . . .
ʃigotŝ̞dihɑuzə . . . ænəbigınvɛıvɛıihʌŋgıi . . . vɛıivɛıi
hʌŋgıi . . . ænŝ̞ʃicıɑivɛıimʌtʃ' . . . bʌt' . . . vn̩ . . . ʃŝ̞ . . .
əbʌtʔə . . . ʃicıɑivɛıivɛıimʌtʃ'bʌtəti . . . tŝ̞ . . . ʃihævŝ̞ . . .
ti̩ː . . . dɔgz:zistıitŝ̞dɔgz . . . hævŝ̞tiyɑıdən . . .
itŝ̞ti̩lʌntʃ . . . ænipænsvɛıivɛıiwɛl . . .

APPENDIX B: GLOSS OF TRANSCRIPTIONS OF SIX SUBJECTS

Korean No. 1

I thinka she ma(kes) sammitcha . . . then put 'n a sackay . . . then uh . . . she go . . . ou(t)
. . . the(n) she wa(lk) . . . the(n) she drop . . . she drop?
uh she si(ts) someplace . . . in a c/ə/lass or someplace . . . I really don' know what is she
doing . . . then . . . uh . . . she . . . out 'n a in sack to check the sa(ck) . . . is a ho(le) . . .
the sa . . . uh sammitcha go(ne) . . . all go(ne) . . . the dog eat . . . looks like a dog fun . . .

Korean No. 2

She ma(kes) a sammitchy . . . she making . . . a sammi(tch) . . . an' she put in . . .
paper ba(g) . . . an' she take ou(t) . . . 'n she go walking, no?
I thin(k) the(n) . . . she go somea schoo(l) or something . . . an' she . . . 'n she drop . . .
sams . . . so . . . she . . . she put in a ba(g) . . . the paper has . . . a . . . ho(le) . . . so . . .
she . . . surpr . . . um . . . s . . . m . . . oh . . . she see . . . a ho(le) sa, i, sa(nd)witchy . . . do(g) . . .
. . . dog eat . . . her sa(nd)witcha . . .

Cantonese No. 1

The girl's name is . . . Joa(n) . . . an' . . . she's going . . . uh to have a pi(c)nic . . .
an' firs(t) of a(ll) . . . she uhp . . . p(r)epares a jam sa(nd)witcha . . . an' . . . she puts

245

i(t) in a bag . . . um . . . she brings . . . um . . . samish . . . an' a . . . blanketa . . .
with her n (th)e way . . . an' . . .
suddenly . . . she . . . drops . . . the sa(nd)witcha . . . bu(t) she doesn't know tha(t)
an' . . . whe(n) she . . . reaches the place uh . . . where she . . . prans to have a pi(c)nica
. . . she uh sprea . . . sorea /ʔ/s the brankets . . .
on . . . on (th)e grou(nd) . . . an' the(n). . . . she takes out a sa(nd)witcha . . . bu(t) . . .
she discover(s) that (th)e sa(nd)witcha was gone . . .
an' . . . she doesn' know why . . . an' . . . that is b'cause . . . 'um . . . she drops it on
(th)e way an' . . . the do(g) . . . dogs . . . ge . . . get ita . . .

Cantonese No. 2

A gir(l) is uh . . . fixing her toas(t) . . . wif . . . jam . . . an' I thin(k) uh she is
trvin' to have a pi(c)nic . . . an' he g . . . an' he ha . . . an' he ha' . . . an' uh she has
everything . . . ready an' uh . . . she wa . . . she was so happy an' . . . geting ou(t) of
the doo(r) . . . an' . . . she was so . . . s, sh . . . (unintelligible) she walk along the
roa(d) an' . . . 'mshe didn' know uh . . . the . . . the sa(ck) was . . . was . . . uh . . . uh,
sh . . .
she di(dn't) noticea . . . notice that (th)e sack uh. . . . was broken a(nd) the sa(nd)witcha
came out . . . an' uh. . . . he . . . he go to the beach an' uh p(l)ay wif (th)a san(d) . . .
an'. . . . afte(r) while she felt ha, hungry an' she wants . . .
she wanted to eat some sa(nd)witcha . . . an' uh . . . she took out (th)a sacka an'
she found ou(t) tha(t) the sacka . . . was brokea . . . an' uh . . .
a, an' she wasn' . . . she wasa no(t) sure where . . . where she los(t) (th)e sa(nd)witches . . .
an' . . . an' on the other han(d)a . . . the do(g)s are eating . . . her sa(nd)witches

Portuguese No. 1

The girl . . . pick up . . . aah, bun . . . an' prepareda his . . . uh . . . food for . . . her
food for . . . a picanic . . . uh . . . when . . . he . . . was going to the picanic . . . she . . .
losta . . . her s . . . sandawish . . . an' . . . she . . . she doesn'ta n . . . know about it . . .
an' . . . whe(n) s . . . she . . . arrive to the placea where . . . she want to go . . . uh . . .
she . . . puta uh . . . b(l)anketa . . . the floor . . . an' prepare to eat . . . but . . . whe(n)
he geta her bag . . . she . . . eh . . . notea that . . . her baga was . . . baroken . . . an' that
she losta . . . her . . . sanwish . . . an' she . . . becames ver's . . . oh . . . surpriseda . . .
an' uh . . . the firs' thing . . . tha(t) cames to her min(d) is that some dogs . . . was eating
. . . food.

Portuguese No. 2

Susie was a gooda . . . very very gooda girl . . . she . . . she like . . . she like eat . . . very
much because she's fat . . . she's very fat . . . and uh . . . one day she . . . one day she prepare
many sanwish . . . for go to the school . . . and, ee . . . when the begin . . . uh . . . whe,
whe . . . when (sh)e begin . . . to walk . . . in the . . . when (sh)e begin to walka . . .
in the forest . . . uh, i, in the garden . . . in the . . .
int, in the garden . . . she, she losta the t(h)ree . . . sanwish . . . oh . . . she go to the

housea . . . an' a begin very very hungry . . . very very hungry . . . an' ah she cry very
much . . . but . . . m . . . ya . . . uh but uh . . . she cry very very much but uh ti . . .
the . . . she havea . . . the . . . dogs the streeta dogs . . . have i(n) the garden . . .
eata the lunch . . . an' (h)e pan(t)s very very well . . .

REFERENCES

Brière, E. 1966. An investigation of phonological interference. *Language, 42,* 4: 768–96.
Chao, Yuen Ren. 1947. *Cantonese primer.* Cambridge, MA.: Harvard University Press.
Cho, Seung-Bog. 1967. *A phonological study of Korean.* Uppsala, Sweden: Acta Universitatis Upsaliensis.
Dickerson, L. 1975. The learner's interlanguage as a variable system. Paper presented at the Ninth Annual TESOL Convention, Los Angeles, California.
Dickerson, W. 1977. Language variation in applied linguistics. *ITL Review of Applied Linguistics, 35,* 43–66.
Eliasson, S. 1976. Theoretical problems in Scandinavian contrastive phonology. In John Weinstock (Ed.), *The Nordic languages and modern linguistics.* Austin, TX: University of Texas.
Guiora, A.Z., *et al.* 1972. The effects of experimentally induced changes in ego stages on pronunciation ability in a second language: An exploratory study. *Comprehensive Psychiatry, 13,* 421–28.
Hatch, E. 1978. Acquisition of syntax in a second language. In Jack Richards (Ed.), *Understanding second and foreign language learning.* Rowley, MA.: Newbury House.
Johansson, F.A. 1973. *Immigrant Swedish phonology.* Lund, Sweden: CWK Gleerup.
Kozhevnikov & Chistovich (Eds.), 1965. *Speech: Articulation and perception.* Moscow: Nauka. Translation: JPRS: 30, 543, pub. Joint Publications Research Service, Washington, D.C.
Krashen, S. 1973. Lateralization, language learning, and the critical period: Some new evidence. *Language Learning, 23,* 63–74.
Krashen, S. 1977. Some issues relating to the monitor model. Paper presented at the Eleventh Annual TESOL Convention, Miami, Florida.
Krashen, S. & R. Harshman. 1972. Lateralization and the critical period. *Working Papers in Phonetics* (UCLA), *23;* 13–21.
Labov, W. 1972. The linguistic consequences of being a lame. *Language in the inner city: Studies in the black English vernacular.* Philadelphia: University of Pennsylvania Press.
Lenneberg, E.H. 1967. *Biological foundations of language.* New York: John Wiley and Sons, Inc.
Nemser, W. 1971. *An experimental study of phonological interference in the English of Hungarians.* Bloomington: Indiana University Press.
Oller, D.K. 1974. Toward a general theory of phonological processes in first and second language learning. Unpublished paper presented at the Western Conference on Linguistics, Seattle, Washington.
Scovel, T. 1969. Foreign accents, language acquisition, and cerebral dominance. *Language Learning, 19,* 245–54.
Tarone, E. 1972. A suggested unit for interlingual identification in pronunciation. *TESOL Quarterly, 6,4,* 325–31.
Tarone, E. 1978. The phonology of interlanguage. In Jack Richards (Ed.), *Understanding second and foreign language learning.* Rowley, MA.: Newbury House. (Also this volume.)
Tarone, E. 1984. The role of the syllable in interlanguage phonology. In Stig Eliasson (Ed.), *Theoretical issues in contrastive phonology.* Heidelberg: Julias Groos Verlag.

14

PHONOLOGICAL PROCESSES IN SECOND LANGUAGE ACQUISITION: ANOTHER LOOK AT INTERLANGUAGE SYLLABLE STRUCTURE*

Charlene J. Sato

INTRODUCTION

To date, most research on phonological aspects of second language acquisition (SLA) has been conducted within the framework of contrastive analysis. Considerably less cross-linguistic work has been done to identify universal developmental processes. Yet, as Tarone (1978, 1980) has argued, theorists must consider work of this latter kind, carried out on a variety of source and target languages, if they are to derive an explanatory account of SL phonology. The present study uses data on syllable structure in the ILs of two Vietnamese children acquiring English in order to test some previous claims concerning L1 transfer and universal phonological processes in IL development.

*This is the revised version of a paper presented at the 17th Annual TESOL Convention, March 15–20, 1983, Toronto, Ontario, Canada. I would like to acknowledge helpful comments from Elaine Tarone, Edith Moravcsik, Craig Chaudron, Diane Larsen-Freeman, and two anonymous reviewers for *Language Learning*.

INTERLANGUAGE SYLLABLE STRUCTURE

Some of Tarone's own work (1976, 1980) has focused on the relative influence of three processes on IL phonological development—namely, the reactivation of first language (L1) acquisition processes in SLA, L1 transfer, and universal processes. In an earlier paper summarizing available data on the phonological systems of second language learners, Oller (1974) had argued against assigning a primary role to the reactivation of L1 acquisition processes in IL development. Oller presented as evidence the observation that vowel epenthesis occurred frequently in SLA data but not in L1 acquisition data.

In an attempt to bring empirical evidence to bear on this issue, Tarone (1976, 1980) conducted a pilot study of IL syllable structure with data from six adult learners of English, two each from three L1 backgrounds: Cantonese, Brazilian Portuguese, and Korean. The study was primarily concerned with (1) the nature of IL syllable structure and (2) the relative influence of L1 syllable structure transfer and universal processes of simplification towards the open (consonant vowel or CV) syllable.

It was Tarone's (1980; 143) contention that the dominance of processes other than L1 transfer could be demonstrated by showing that

the *same* [italics in original] sequence of vowels and consonants exists in the native language and the target language, and that the learner still makes syllable structure errors in trying to produce that sequence in the target language.

Since Cantonese and Brazilian Portuguese, both characterized as CV languages, do not share a large proportion of identical segment sequences with English, it was argued that syllable structure errors in English made by speakers of these L1s would be difficult to attribute to anything other than transfer. Korean, on the other hand, provided a good test case because of the larger set of segment sequences shared with English and its more complex syllable structure, as compared to Cantonese and Brazilian Portuguese. The Korean data, in other words, were expected to yield the crucial evidence for or against the hypothesized universal preference for CV syllable structure.

Tarone's data consisted of a sample of speech elicited from each learner on a story narration task involving picture stimuli. Errors in syllable structure —categorized as vowel epenthesis, consonant deletion, and glottal stop insertion —were noted for an average of only 20 percent of the total number of syllables attempted by each learner.

Contrary to Oller's claim that epenthesis occurs frequently in second language speech, only the Portuguese speakers demonstrated a strong tendency to epenthesize. The four Cantonese and Korean speakers relied primarily on consonant deletion and glottal stop insertion in modifying English syllable structure. Thus the findings did not support the hypothesized prevalence of epenthesis in learners' speech or Oller's argument against the reactivation of L1 acquisition processes in L2 phonological production.

Through a closer inspection of the findings, Tarone determined that the majority of all errors were attributable to L1 transfer. However, a number of *non*-transfer errors were observed, ranging from 10 percent (one token) for a Portuguese speaker to 47 percent (eight tokens) for a Korean speaker. Tarone (1980, 148) pointed out that in every case the effect of syllable modification was "to 'simplify' the second language syllable structure—that is, to modify it towards a basic consonant-vowel pattern." She went on to suggest that the pattern might derive from a universal preference for the open syllable. Finally, while noting that language transfer may combine with this universal process to strengthen the open-syllable preference in some learners' ILs, Tarone (ibid.) took the position that this preference could also "operate independently of transfer."

To summarize, Tarone's study provided clear evidence of marked differences between IL and target language syllable structure, of learners' reliance on both epenthesis and consonant deletion strategies, and of the predominance of L1 transfer as a force shaping IL syllable structure. However, while the tendency to simplify toward CV structure is apparent in those few tokens *not* attributed to transfer, the bulk of the data showed L1 transfer to be the main influence on the IL production of Tarone's subjects. On the basis of these data, is it valid, therefore, to claim a universal preference for the CV syllable?

CLUSTER INVENTORIES VS. CLUSTER POSITION

In other work on IL syllable structure, Greenberg (1983) provided some evidence that L1 transfer occurs, not only as a result of contrasts between L1 and L2 consonant cluster inventories, but also because of differences in preferred cluster position—syllable-initial (SI) or syllable-final (SF)—in the L1 and L2.

The Greenberg study involved three native speakers each of Turkish, Greek, and Japanese, the choice of these L1s being motivated by their difference from each other and from English in terms of syllable structure. As reported by Greenberg, Turkish does not allow syllable-initial clusters except in borrowings, Greek does not allow syllable-*final* clusters, and Japanese allows neither. Greenberg predicted that such facts would be reflected in the learners' IL production.

The subjects, described as intermediate-level ESL learners, performed two tasks, a picture description and a naming task involving flashcard pictures. The data excluded syllable structure modifications apparently due to performance constraints and those considered ambiguous with respect to such constraints and genuine modifications. Because of this reduction of the corpus, Greenberg obtained only a 3 percent average error rate for her subjects, as compared to the 20 percent error rate reported by Tarone.

With respect to syllable modification strategies, both consonant deletion and epenthesis occurred, with the former preferred by the Japanese and Greek learners and the latter, by the Turkish learners. It was not the case, however, that all three speakers of each language group showed a preference for the same strategy.

L1 transfer was clearly demonstrated for cluster position. The three Turkish speakers produced the highest error rate for clusters in SI position. The Greeks did so for SF clusters, and the Japanese also for SF clusters. Greenberg thus concluded that L1-to-L2 contrasts in permissible cluster positions affected syllable structure in IL production.

While a larger sample of data from beginning rather than intermediate learners would provide stronger support for this conclusion, the tendency discovered in Greenberg's study for cluster position to influence IL syllable structure appears genuine. The present study seeks to corroborate, then, the finding that L1 transfer manifests itself not only in terms of contrasts in L1 and L2 consonant cluster inventories but also in terms of cluster position preferences.

VIETNAMESE SYLLABLE STRUCTURE

Vietnamese is described as a monosyllabic tone language (see, e.g., Nguyễn 1967, Du'o'ng and Gage 1975, and Thompson 1965), monosyllabic because a large proportion of its words consists of single syllables, and tonal, because pitch variations signal meaning differences for otherwise homophonous words.

Syllables in Vietnamese can take the following shapes:

V	VC	CwV
CV	CVC	CwVC

(where V = vowel or diphthong, C = consonant, and w = /w/). While syllable onsets are reported by Nguyễn (1967) to be optional, Thompson (1959, 466) seems to disagree:

In one sense, the onset is an optional element; but since the option consists of the occurrence or absence of /ʔ/ and since all syllables without onset have alternates with the onset /ʔ/, it is more economical to consider the presence of an onset as constant.

As for syllable-final (SF) position, only eight of the 22 consonants in Vietnamese can occur as codas: /p, t, k, m, n, ŋ, w, and y/ (Nguyễn 1967). These are either unreleased or coarticulated. Finally, the language allows consonant clusters (CCs) only in syllable-initial (SI) position, with all 14 possible CCs taking /w/ as a second member. CCs are not permitted syllable-finally.

It is difficult, on the basis of the available literature on Vietnamese syllable structure, to determine the language's preferred syllable type. However, evidence can be presented to support the claim that the closed—CVC—syllable is preferred. An examination of Nguyễn's (1967) inventory of phonemic syllables in Saigon Vietnamese reveals that, of 4467 phonemic syllables, 3437 (76.9 percent) end in consonants. Further, it is noted by Thompson (1959, 461) that all syllables with low level tone end in a weakly articulated glottal stop. In Nguyễn's inventory, low level tone syllables amount to 17 percent (758 tokens) of the total. Of these, 4.5 percent (199 tokens) are identified as open syllables. Applying Thompson's observation to Nguyễn's inventory yields a total proportion of closed syllables of 81.4 percent, when the 4.5 percent of supposedly "open" syllables ending in glottal stops are added to the 76.9 percent which end in consonants. In light of this (admittedly limited) evidence, it can be tentatively proposed that Vietnamese prefers the closed syllable.

With respect to the hypothesized universal preference for the open syllable, then, Vietnamese constitutes an interesting test case, since a transfer hypothesis would predict a preference for the closed syllable. The question posed in this study is whether an open syllable preference can be identified in Vietnamese-English IL.

A transfer hypothesis would also predict a dispreference for SF as opposed to SI CCs, since the L1 does not allow SF CCs. In other words, English SF CCs should undergo more restructuring in Vietnamese-English IL than SI ones, with this restructuring being manifested as complete absence of a cluster, reduction of a cluster by one segment, reduction of a cluster through vowel epenthesis, or as a feature change in one or more members of a cluster.

Finally, an examination of these restructuring processes will make possible an empirical evaluation of Oller's claim that vowel epenthesis characterizes L2 speech.

METHODOLOGY

Subjects

The learners in this study are brothers, Tai and Thanh, who were about ten and twelve years old upon arrival in the United States. Boat refugees who were somehow separated from their family during their departure from South Vietnam, they were placed in a Malaysian refugee camp for two months before their relocation to Philadelphia, Pennsylvania. Since their arrival, they have lived with American foster parents.

Tai and Thanh are enrolled in a local public school in a predominantly black working- to middle-class community outside Philadelphia. They were placed in classes according to their apparent ages upon arrival, Tai in a mixed third and fourth grade class and Thanh in the sixth grade. Neither has received English as a Second Language instruction since there are no ESL classes or teachers available in their school.

Although these learners began attending school a few weeks after arrival, they and their teachers report that they remained quiet and uncomprehending for much of the spring 1981 school term. Because of a prolonged teachers' strike the following fall, the boys did not return to school until November, 1981, roughly a month after data collection for this study began.

As for their education in Vietnam, both attended school regularly, although it is not clear what grade levels they had reached when they left the country. While Thanh is literate in Vietnamese, Tai was not upon arrival and has therefore been receiving some tutoring in Vietnamese reading and writing once a week. Neither learner had any English instruction before leaving Vietnam.

Data Collection

The data for this study were collected through weekly audiotaping of visits between the learners and me, primarily in the home context. The children's foster mother was present during most of these visits, and other occasional participants included their foster father, their peers, family friends, and friends of the researcher.

Corpus

The data for the analysis of syllable structure consist exclusively of spontaneous speech from unstructured informal conversation sampled at three points during the ten-month study. These points are identified as Time 1, 2, and 3. The Time 1 data are taken from weeks 2 and 3, the Time 2 data from weeks 19 and 20, and the Time 3 data from weeks 36 and 37. Limitation of the corpus to spontaneous speech was motivated by the need to control for possible task variation.

Analysis

All the speech in each sample was transcribed using the International Phonetic Alphabet for the learners' speech and English orthography for their native English-speaking interlocutors' speech. The data from the learners were then analyzed as follows:

1. All words containing syllable-initial and syllable-final consonant clusters were recorded.
2. Each cluster was then coded for
   a. Target language form
   b. Articulatory feature change (i.e., retention of a cluster but with some change in place or manner of articulation). Examples:

English		Interlanguage	Process
[θri]	'three'	[tri]	Stopping
[juzd]	'used'	[just]	Devoicing

c. Consonant cluster reduction: deletion of part of the cluster. Examples:

    English   Interlanguage

    [fʏst]   'first'   [fʏt]

    [groʷ] 'grow'   [goʷ]

d. Consonant cluster reduction: vowel epenthesis. Examples:

    English   Interlanguage

    [pleis] 'place'   [pəleis]

    [skeit] 'skate'   [ɛskeit]

e. Consonant cluster deletion (i.e., total deletion). Examples:

    English   Interlanguage

    [læst] 'last'   [læ]

    [nɛkst] 'next'   [nɛʔ]

3. The number of tokens in each category was then tallied and percentages obtained for syllable-initial and -final positions.

Results

Looking first at Tai's overall production of consonant clusters (CCs) in Table 14.1, a 15 percent increase is observable between Time 1 and Time 2 in target production of CCs—from 28 percent to 43 percent. Less of an increase occurs between Times 2 and 3, from 43 percent to 49 percent. Of importance is the finding that by Time 3, just about half of all CCs are target forms.

An examination of syllable-initial (SI) and syllable-final (SF) CC distribution, however, provides a different picture. Tables 14.2 and 14.3 contain the relevant figures. It is evident that SI rather than SF CCs are produced more frequently in target form. As shown in Table 14.2, even at Time 1 target SI clusters amount to over half (52 percent) of the total. This figure increases to 92 percent at Time 2, then decreases slightly at Time 3.

SF clusters, on the other hand, reveal a reverse trend, as shown in Table 14.3. Most of the SF CCs are non-target forms, in the proportions: 85 percent at Time 1, 91 percent at Time 2, and 81 percent at Time 3. There is, in fact, a slight decrease in non-target forms at Time 3.

The overall increase in the target production of CCs displayed in Table 14.1 seems to be the result of conflicting trends in SI and SF CC production,

TABLE 14.1. Tai's Target and Non-Target Production of Consonant Clusters: Syllable-Initial and Syllable-Final

	Sample					
	Time 1		Time 2		Time 3	
Prod.	#	%[a]	#	%	#	%
Target	21	28	70	43	106	49
Non-Target	53	72	92	57	112	51
Total	74	100	162	100	218	100

[a]In this and all other tables, percentages are rounded off to the nearest whole number.

TABLE 14.2. Tai's Target and Non-Target Production of Syllable-Initial
Consonant Clusters

	Sample					
	Time 1		Time 2		Time 3	
Prod.	#	%	#	%	#	%
Target	14	52	61	92	84	82
Non-Target	13	48	5	8	18	18
Total	27	100	66	100	102	100

TABLE 14.3. Tai's Target and Non-Target Production of Syllable-Final Consonant
Clusters

	Sample					
	Time 1		Time 2		Time 3	
Prod.	#	%	#	%	#	%
Target	7	15	9	9	22	19
Non-Target	40	85	87	91	94	81
Total	47	100	96	100	116	100

with target forms being achieved for most SI clusters and with non-target forms
being characteristic of SF clusters over Times 1, 2, and 3.

With respect to particular processes of syllable modification in Tai's IL,
the findings for initial clusters are as given in Table 14.4. In SI position, 62
percent of the cluster modifications at Time 1 is attributable to Cluster Reduction (deletion of one member) and 38 percent to Feature Change. A reversal
occurs at Time 2 and is maintained at Time 3, where movement toward target
formation is apparent since Feature Change processes predominate, accounting
for 80 percent and 78 percent, respectively, of the SI clusters produced.

It should be recalled that most of Tai's SI clusters are target forms. Table
14.4 shows that even those clusters considered non-target are only slightly
modified; i.e., they involve Feature Changes rather than more radical restructuring. Moreover, there are no instances of Cluster Deletion in initial position.

TABLE 14.4. Tai's Syllable-Initial Cluster Modification

	Sample					
	Time 1		Time 2		Time 3	
Process	#	%	#	%	#	%
Feature Change	5	38	4	80	14	78
Cluster Reduction	8	62	1	20	4	22
Cluster Deletion	0	0	0	0	0	0
Total	13	100	5	100	18	100

As for the occurrence of these processes in SF clusters, shown in Table 14.5, the predominant modification strategy is Cluster Reduction (deletion of one member), followed by Cluster Deletion. No instances of Feature Change appear at either Time 1 or 2, and there are only 3 (3 percent) at Time 3. In other words, more radical restructuring is observed for SF than SI clusters.

Finally, it is important to note that only two instances of vowel epenthesis occur in Tai's data. One involves *prothesis,* the insertion of a vowel syllable-initially in the word 'skating': /ɛskeitɪn/. The other is insertion of a schwa in a proper noun, 'Dwight': /dəwait/.

The results obtained for Thanh yield roughly the same patterns. Table 14.6 shows that Thanh gradually increases his production of target clusters (both initial and final) by 10 percent between Times 1 and 2 and again between Times 2 and 3.

When SI and SF cluster production are examined separately, differences related to syllable position appear in the proportions of target forms produced. As revealed in Table 14.7, even at Time 1, the majority of SI clusters—67 percent—are target forms. This increases to 88 percent at Time 2 and decreases slightly to 86 percent at Time 3.

A striking contrast between initial and final clusters emerges when figures for the latter are examined. In Table 14.8, non-target forms amount to 94 percent at Time 1 and 98 percent at Time 2. As in Tai's case, the percentage of non-target production decreases at Time 3 for Thanh (to 79 percent). In terms of *target* production, the finding is that SF clusters increase from a mere 2

TABLE 14.5. Tai's Syllable-Final Cluster Modification

	Sample					
	Time 1		Time 2		Time 3	
Process	#	%	#	%	#	%
Feature Change	0	0	0	0	3	3
Cluster Reduction	33	83	83	95	80	85
Cluster Deletion	7	17	4	5	11	12
Total	40	100	87	100	94	100

TABLE 14.6. Thanh's Target and Non-Target Production of Consonant Clusters: Syllable-Initial and Syllable-Final

	Sample					
	Time 1		Time 2		Time 3	
Prod.	#	%	#	%	#	%
Target	21	27	58	37	68	47
Non-Target	58	73	97	63	77	53
Total	79	100	155	100	145	100

TABLE 14.7. Thanh's Target and Non-Target Production of Syllable-Initial Consonant Clusters

	Sample					
	Time 1		Time 2		Time 3	
Prod.	#	%	#	%	#	%
Target	18	67	56	88	50	86
Non-Target	9	33	8	12	8	14
Total	27	100	64	100	58	100

TABLE 14.8. Thanh's Target and Non-Target Production of Syllable-Final Consonant Clusters

	Sample					
	Time 1		Time 2		Time 3	
Prod.	#	%	#	%	#	%
Target	3	6	2	2	18	21
Non-Target	49	94	89	98	69	79
Total	52	100	91	100	87	100

percent at Time 2 to 21 percent at Time 3. In short, the persistence of larger proportions of non-target forms in SF but not SI position is evident for Thanh as well as Tai.

Turning to Tables 14.9 and 14.10 for a closer look at syllable structure processes, one can make the following observations. The few tokens of non-target forms produced in initial position—nine for Time 1 and eight for Times 2 and 3—are largely the result of Feature Changes at Time 1 (89 percent), Cluster Reduction (62 percent) at Time 2, and both (50 percent each) at Time 3. No instances of Cluster Deletion occur in any sample. Again, there is a difference between the learners; in Tai's case, Feature Change processes predominate at Times 2 and 3.

Table 14.10 shows that for SF clusters, Cluster Reduction accounts for most of the tokens at all three times in the proportions of 76 percent, 76 percent,

TABLE 14.9. Thanh's Syllable-Initial Cluster Modification

	Sample					
	Time 1		Time 2		Time 3	
Process	#	%	#	%	#	%
Feature Change	8	89	3	38	4	50
Cluster Reduction	1	11	5	62	4	50
Cluster Deletion	0	0	0	0	0	0
Total	9	100	8	100	8	100

TABLE 14.10. Thanh's Syllable-Final Cluster Modification

Process	Sample					
	Time 1		Time 2		Time 3	
	#	%	#	%	#	%
Feature Change	3	6	2	2	1	1
Cluster Reduction	37	76	68	76	58	83
Cluster Deletion	9	18	19	21	11	16
Total	49	100	89	99	70	100

and 83 percent. Cluster Deletion increases slightly from 18 percent at Time 1 to 21 percent at Time 2 and then decreases to 16 percent at Time 3. Very few cases of Feature Change occur at Times 1 and 2, and only one appears at Time 3. Finally, as for vowel epenthesis, no instances of this type of cluster modification can be found in Thanh's data.

DISCUSSION

It was hypothesized that, because of L1 transfer, Vietnamese-English IL would show a preference for closed rather than open syllables in the modification of English syllable-final (SF) consonant clusters (CCs). This hypothesis was confirmed. Analysis revealed, for both learners, that modification of syllables containing CCs more frequently yielded closed rather than open syllables. Specifically, it was shown that cluster reduction by one segment was favored over other processes: cluster deletion, vowel epenthesis, and feature change. These results cannot, therefore, be viewed as support for the alternate hypothesis of a universal preference for the open syllable.

Secondly, L1 transfer was clearly demonstrated in terms of the effect of syllable position on IL cluster production. Both learners had much more difficulty with SF than SI clusters, confirming Greenberg's (1983) earlier findings. This interpretation derives, not only from the relative frequencies of non-target clusters in SF vs. SI position, but also from the observed tendency toward more radical restructuring of coda than onset clusters.

A problematic aspect of the learners' production of target SI clusters warrants mention here. A decrease in target production of SI CCs was observed from Time 2 to Time 3 for both learners, the percentage for Tai dropping from 92 percent to 82 percent and that for Thanh from 88 percent to 86 percent. It is not clear why this occurred. Because all the samples were matched for task —spontaneous conversation among the two subjects and the researcher in the home setting—it is doubtful that task variation is at issue. A more likely possibility is that a larger number of more difficult consonant clusters were attempted by the learners, Tai in particular, at Time 2 than at Time 3.

The third major result of this study has been the disconfirmation of the hypothesized primacy of vowel epenthesis as a syllable modification process in all ILs. The virtual absence of epenthesis in the Vietnamese-English IL data examined here suggests that this phonological process is strongly influenced by constraints on syllable structure in the first language.

A different interpretation of the first two findings presented above has been proposed by Tarone (personal communication). She argues that, because Vietnamese seems to prefer the (C)VC—i.e., optional consonant-vowel-consonant—syllable, Vietnamese learners of English should have more difficulty with SI than SF CCs in English. This transfer hypothesis, she notes, makes a prediction contrasting with one made by the "universals" hypothesis, which would predict that SI position is universally less difficult than SF position. Confirmation of the latter hypothesis is claimed by Tarone because the learners in this study found initial position less difficult than final position. However, a closer look at the hypotheses being tested renders this claim problematic.

It should be recalled that, although one source (Nguyễn 1967) characterizes onsets in Vietnamese syllables as optional, another (Thompson, 1959) considers them obligatory. If they are optional, a prediction about learners' production of target clusters would still need to be further specified in terms of *cluster* constraints in the L1. Similarly, if onsets are obligatory, a transfer hypothesis would have to take into account whether clusters are allowed in initial position in Vietnamese. Thus the fact that the learners in this study were found to have more difficulty with initial as opposed to final clusters can be predicted from the fact that Vietnamese allows final but not initial clusters.

It is important to distinguish the hypothesis specifying relative strength of SI vs. SF position from that tested in this study, which predicts that second language learners will "tend to break difficult sound combinations into simple CV patterns" (Tarone, 1980, 142). Assuming that a "tendency" is identified on the basis of relative frequencies, the occurrence of a small proportion of open rather than closed syllables as a result of cluster modification does not constitute adequate evidence of a tendency. On the contrary, when between 75 percent and 85 percent of modified clusters yield closed syllables, it seems preferable to acknowledge a tendency away from open syllables. Accordingly, the hypothesized universal preference for the CV syllable is said to be disconfirmed.

The thrust of the present argument is not a denial of the important and pervasive role played by universal processes in IL development. Rather, it is the relative influence of these processes over others that is being examined. In the case of Vietnamese-English IL, the evidence seems to fall on the side of the transfer argument with respect to the restructuring of L2 consonant clusters. With more comprehensive analyses of IL phonology—i.e., studies that take into account such features as stress, rhythm, and intonation, may come evidence of the ultimately more powerful influence of universal principles of the structure of natural languages in particular domains of IL phonology.

CONCLUSION

Longitudinal data from two Vietnamese learners of English were examined in this study to provide insights into IL syllable structure. As in previous research by Tarone (1980, 148), first language transfer emerged as "the dominant process influencing syllable structure in interlanguage phonology." Specifically, the present study showed that L1 transfer is reflected in Vietnamese-English IL as (1) a preference for the closed syllable in the modification of English syllable-final consonant clusters; (2) greater difficulty in the production of final than initial clusters; and (3) negligible use of epenthesis as a syllable modification strategy. These results were interpreted as evidence against the hypothesized universal preference for the CV syllable and the hypothesized prevalence of epenthesis as a syllable modification strategy in IL speech.

REFERENCES

Du'o'ng-Thanh-Bình and W. Gage. 1975. *Vietnamese-English Phrasebook with Useful Word List (for English Speakers)*. Washington, DC: Center for Applied Linguistics.

Greenberg, C. 1983. Syllable structure in second language acquisition. *CUNY Forum, 9,* 41–64.

Nguyễn-Dang-Liêm. 1967. Phonemic syllable repertory in Vietnamese. Papers in South East Asian Linguistics No. 1, 11–18 (+ Tables 5–24). Linguistic Circle of Canberra Publications, Series A, No. 9.

Oller, D.K. 1974. Toward a general theory of phonological processes in first and second language learning. Unpublished paper presented at the Western Conference on Linguistics, Seattle, WA.

Tarone, E. 1976. Some influences on interlanguage phonology. *Working Papers in Bilingualism, 8,* 87–111.

Tarone, E. 1978. The phonology of interlanguage. In J. Richards (Ed.), *Understanding Second and Foreign Language Learning.* Rowley, MA: Newbury House. (Also this volume.)

Tarone, E. 1980. Some influences on the syllable structure of interlanguage phonology. *International Review of Applied Linguistics, 28,* 2, 139–152. (Also this volume.)

Thompson, L. 1959. Saigon phonemics. *Language, 35,* 454–476.

Thompson, L. 1965. *A Vietnamese Grammar.* Seattle: University of Washington Press.

15

AN INVESTIGATION OF TRANSFER IN SECOND LANGUAGE PHONOLOGY*

Ellen Broselow

INTRODUCTION

One of the crucial questions in second language acquisition research concerns the role played by interference from native language rules and patterns in accounting for learners' errors in the target language. When language learning was viewed as a process of acquiring a set of habits, it was generally assumed that the patterns of the first language would be carried over into the second. Attempts to account for learners' errors in this framework led to the formulation of the Contrastive Analysis Hypothesis, the proponents of which claimed that all errors in second language learning could be predicted from a comparison

*A first draft of this paper was written in 1979. Since that time, a good deal of work has been done on many of the issues the paper deals with. Rather than attempt to incorporate various alternative analyses in the text, I have simply mentioned relevant recent work where appropriate. I am indebted to various people for discussion of the paper, and most particularly to Fayssal Abdallah and Ali Farghally for confirmation of the data. All errors are of course my own.

of the structure of the native language and the target language. Differences between the two would, it was believed, result in transfer from the first language to the second (Stockwell and Bowen, 1965, Wardhaugh, 1970). One would expect to find negative transfer operating in cases in which, for example, the native language had a rule which the target language lacked. Thus a German speaker learning English might devoice final obstruents in English in accord with the rules of German phonology.

More recent research has shown, however, that in many cases in which the Contrastive Analysis Hypothesis predicts the occurrence of errors, language learners in fact experience no difficulty, while many errors which do occur cannot be attributed to the effects of interference from the native language (Dulay and Burt, 1975; Richards, 1975). These discoveries have led to a revision of the Contrastive Analysis Hypothesis; it is now generally believed that differences between the native language and the target language may be used not to predict but to explain the nature of some subset of actually occurring errors. This weaker version of the hypothesis is clearly less interesting than the original, since it lacks predictive power and is therefore unfalsifiable. But it is clear that interference is one factor in accounting for learners' errors, although only one of several. Therefore the attempt to predict where native language-target language differences will result in error need not be abandoned. What is needed is a revised version of the original Contrastive Analysis Hypothesis, one which would define the subset of errors which are caused by transfer and which would predict just what sorts of native language-target language differences will cause language learners to make errors.

The first step in revising the Contrastive Analysis Hypothesis is an investigation of the sorts of errors which can be shown to result from native language interference. This paper provides an analysis of one such case. This case is particularly interesting since it deals with a type of error which has not been systematically explored in the literature: the production and perception of word juncture in the target language. It is argued below that word juncture phenomena—for example, the differences between *a name* and *an aim* in English—are a function of syllable structure; the rules determining the syllable structure of a language will account for the phonetic effects associated with word juncture in that language. This study focuses specifically on the problems with the perception and production of word juncture which native speakers of American English invariably encounter when studying the Egyptian dialect of Arabic. The errors of these learners are shown to be a result of language transfer of a sort not previously discussed—an attempt to apply the syllable structure rules of the native language both in processing and in producing strings of the target language. Then other cases illustrating the effects of differences between syllable structures in the native and target languages are discussed, and hypotheses are advanced concerning transfer as a factor in producing errors in interlanguage phonology.

262

TRANSFER FROM ENGLISH TO ARABIC

Common Errors

The two sorts of errors made by English speakers studying Egyptian Arabic involve the segmenting of a phonetic string into words. The first type of error involves strings consisting of a word which ends in a consonant followed by a word which begins with a vowel; English-speaking students tend to perceive the word-final consonant as part of the second word. Thus the string *miš ana* 'not I' will often be heard incorrectly as consisting of two non-existent words **mi šana,* and the typical pronunciation of this string by the English speaker will also be criticized as non-native by Egyptians. The second class of errors involves strings such as *ʔilkursi gdiid*[1] 'the chair is new', consisting of a word ending in a vowel followed by a word beginning in two consonants; here the learner hears the string as **ʔilkursig diid,* associating the first consonant of the second word with the word preceding it. These mistakes occur even when the second word begins with a consonant cluster which can begin a word in English, such as *sm; binti smiina* 'a fat girl' is heard as **bintis miina.* Furthermore, these misperceptions occur no matter how familiar the language learner is with the words of the string.[2] The pervasiveness of this problem is evidenced by the fact that all the texts designed to teach Egyptian Arabic to Americans mention word juncture as something the student must contend with. Thus Lehn and Abboud (1965, 5) consistently mark word linkage to assist students in pronunciation and comprehension: "The sequence of /ʔilkursi/ and /gidiid/ occurs as /ʔilkursi-gdiid/, pronounced as if the words were /ʔilkursig/ and /diid/. The hyphen is used to show this type of linkage."

It is generally recognized that this word linkage is an effect of Egyptian Arabic syllable structure. According to Abdel-Massih (1974, 21),

> In most cases word and syllable boundaries do not coincide. If we look at /ʔilgumla gdiida/ 'the sentence is new' in terms of syllable and word boundaries, we get #ʔil-gum-la/ /g-dii-da#. The most difficult part for a non-native speaker is the last syllable of the first word and the first [segment] of the last word, which he hears as /lag/. At the beginning this is difficult to produce and recognize. . . .

Mitchell (1962, 62) makes it clear that however difficult it may be to acquire, this ability to link words is an essential component of native speaker competence:

> The ability to link in one syllable . . . the end of one word and the beginning of the next is absolutely essential to the attainment of fluency in the language . . .

Thus word juncture is a real and striking problem for English speakers learning Egyptian Arabic. In the following sections I will show that the facts of word

263

juncture in each language can be accounted for by independently motivated syllable structure rules. A comparison of the rules describing Egyptian Arabic syllable structure with those describing English syllabification will reveal that the English speaker attempts to pronounce and to analyze the Arabic strings according to the rules of his or her native language.

Egyptian Arabic Syllable Structure

The question of exactly what sort of syllable structure a language has is not a simple one; speakers often do not have clear intuitions about what constitutes a syllable, or where to put syllable boundaries within an utterance. Fortunately, however, researchers in Egyptian Arabic have available to them a diagnostic tool, the phenomenon of 'emphasis'—the term traditionally used to describe pharyngealization. Egyptian Arabic has pairs of words distinguished only by the presence or absence of emphasis, such as the following, where an emphatic sound is represented by an upper case letter:

tiin   'figs'
TIIN   'mud'

baat   'he spent the night'
BAAT   'armpit'

Any utterance which is pronounced with emphatic articulation contains one of the emphatic phonemes *T, D, S, Z, L* or *R;* the occurrence of emphasis, then, is conditioned by the presence of these phonemes. What is important for our purposes is the fact that the domain of emphasis is the syllable: any syllable which contains an emphatic phoneme will have emphatic articulation in each of its segments.[3] Thus we find such alternations as the following:

LATIIF / LATIIfa 'pleasant masc./fem.' F/f
FASL/FASlu 'class/his class' L/l

The *F* of *LATIIF* and the *L* of *FASL* are emphatic because they share a syllable with an emphatic phoneme (*T* in the first case, *S* in the second). With the addition of a vowel suffix, however, the distribution of emphasis changes. This can be accounted for by the assumption that the syllable structure of these words is as in Figure 15.1. Each syllable is represented by a tree connecting each segment of that syllable; the emphatic phonemes are italicized.

$$LA\ TIIF \qquad LA\ TIIfa \qquad FASL \qquad FASlu$$
$$S\ \ S \qquad\quad S\ \ SS \qquad\quad S \qquad\quad S\ \ S$$

A similar alternation is evidenced by the following:

RAAgil / RAGleen 'man/men' g/G

(The loss of the *i* and the shortening of *aa* are the result of general rules of the language; for a detailed discussion of these rules, see Broselow, 1976). Here the syllable structure is presumably as in Figure 15.2.

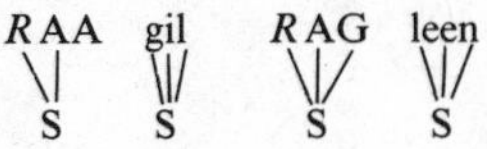

Figure 15.2

The distribution of emphasis can be accounted for, then, by the following rule:

Egyptian Arabic Syllable Rule: Each syllable must begin with one and only one consonant.

This rule is a fairly natural one; consonant-initial syllables are universally preferred. What is interesting about Egyptian Arabic is that this rule operates regardless of the division of consonants and vowels into words. Thus the distribution of emphasis within a word is affected by the words which precede or follow it:

FADDAL 'he preferred'
FADDAl ilwalad 'he preferred the boy'

Here when a vowel follows *l*, *l* becomes a member of the next syllable, obeying the injunction that a syllable must begin with a consonant. Therefore *l* is no longer subject to the influence of the emphatic phoneme *D*. Similarly, we find

kitiir 'many'
DAKATRA Ktiir 'many doctors'

When *kitiir* follows a vowel, *i* is lost by a rule which deletes *i* in the environment VC_CV, and the *k* joins the syllable of the vowel before it. It is then affected by the emphatic *R* of *DAKATRA*.

Thus the rule that a syllable must begin with one and only one consonant is followed without regard for word boundaries. Evidence that this rule has an effect on word juncture is pı vided by the following strings, which are pronounced exactly alike, because they have the same syllable structures:

FADDAl ilwalad   'he preferred the boy'
(?idda) FADDA lilwalad   ('he gave) silver to the boy'

It is now clear that the sorts of phrases which give trouble to English-speaking students of Arabic are those which involve syllable linkage across words,[4] as shown in Figure 15.3 below.

Figure 15.3

In the next section the reasons for this are explored. It will be shown that while English also allows cross-word linkage of syllables, it does not allow quite the same sorts of linkage which are found in Egyptian Arabic.

English Syllable Structure

It is a well-known fact that there is often a difference in the pronunciation of strings which consist of identical segments but differ in the placement of word boundaries. Lehiste (1960) has studied the acoustic differences between the members of the following pairs:

it sprays / it's praise
keep sticking / keeps ticking
gray day / grade A
a name / an aim

In other sorts of strings, however, word juncture seems to have no effect on pronunciation:

get a board / get aboard
a pall / appall
hock it / Hockett

This phenomenon, referred to as "blending," has been recognized in the literature on teaching English; Prator and Robinett (1972; 34) write that "a person who did not know any English would find it hard to tell where one word ended and another began. The blending of the two words of *read it* is as close as that between the two syllables of *reading.*" It will be argued below that a careful analysis of English syllable structure will account for the differences between the forms in the first set above and the identity between the forms in the second. The pairs which are pronounced differently will be shown to have different syllable structures, while those which are pronounced alike will be shown to have the same syllable structures.

The analysis of English syllable structure presented here is adapted from Kahn (1976). For the purpose of clarity, consonant clusters are ignored; thus the version of the syllable structure rules presented here is a greatly simplified one. Kahn gives a number of different arguments for his analysis of syllable structure in English, involving the dependence of various phonological processes on syllable structure. The reader is referred to the original for detailed arguments in favor of this theory.

The cases in which word juncture has no phonological effect in a string are as follows:

a. VCV́ = V#CV́ (but not VC#V́)
    apall = a pall (≠ up all, as in up all the stairs)
b. VCV̆ = VC#V̆ (but not V#CV̆)
    atom = at Amanda's (≠ a tomato)

V́ = stressed vowel, V̆ = unstressed vowel, # = word boundary

If it is correct that word juncture is a function of syllable structure, then *appall* and *a pall* must have identical syllable structures. A reasonable structure for both is the following, Figure 15.4:

appall   a pall

[əpɔl]   [əpɔl]
 | \\/ | \\/
 S S   S S   **Figure 15.4**

The rule below will derive these structures:

Rule I: Within a word,
   a. attach a consonant to the vowel on its right
   b. attach a 'left-over' consonant to the vowel on its left
   c. all consonants at the end of a word are attached to the nearest vowel within the word.

Rule Ia will attach the *p* of *appall* to the second vowel; Ib will attach the *l* to the second vowel.

Independent motivation for Rule I is found in the area of aspiration of voiceless stops. These stops are generally aspirated in two environments:

a. within a word: between two vowels, but only when the second vowel is stressed: $at^{h}ómic$ vs. *atŏm*
b. word-initially: before either a stressed or an unstressed vowel: $t^{h}ómcat, t^{h}ŏmato$

These two environments can be described simply if the syllable structure provided by Rule I is assumed; then only the following rule is needed:

Voiceless stops are aspirated when they are syllable-initial.

A stop which begins a word will always be syllable-initial, regardless of the stress of the following vowel.

The question which now arises is why the *t* of *atom* is unaspirated; this *t* is phonetically a flap *(D)*. Kahn suggests (as have Bailey, 1973; Anderson and Jones, 1974; Hooper, 1977, and others) that the *t* of *atom* is actually ambisyllabic, a member of both the first and the second syllables of the word. This accounts for the difficulty speakers have in dividing words such as *atom* into discrete syllables. To account for the structure of *atom,* the following rule is needed:

Rule II: within a word, a consonant which is connected to an unstressed vowel on its right must also be connected to the vowel on its left.

This gives Figure 15.5:

atŏm   atómic
|\\|/ | \|
S S   S S

by I, II   by I only   **Figure 15.5**

The rule for the flapping of *t* can then be written as follows:

t becomes D when it is ambisyllabic

Still to be accounted for is the flapping of *t* at ends of words in certain environments; for example the *t* of *at Amanda's* is *D* in connected speech. Notice here that word-final *t* is flapped in a slightly different environment than *t* within a word; even before a stressed vowel, a *t* may become *D*.

at Annie's   [æDǽniyz]

Thus any final *t* before a vowel is ambisyllabic. Recall that Rule I will give the following structure for *at Amanda's* and *at Annie's,* as in Figure 15.6.

at Amanda's   at Annie's
\| | \| |
S S   S S   **Figure 15.6**

The ambisyllabicity of the *t* in these structures can be accounted for by a rule connecting *t* with the next vowel:

Rule III: When a word beginning with a vowel is preceded by a word ending with a consonant, connect the word-final consonant to the word-initial vowel.

$$C\#V \longrightarrow C\#V$$
| \|
S   S   S

This rule will produce the structures, as in Figure 15.7.

at Amanda's   at Annie's
\|\| |/ \|
S S   S S   **Figure 15.7**

This allows for the preservation of the generalization that t becomes D when it is ambisyllabic, and provides an explanation of the similarity in pronunciation of *atom* and *at Am(anda's)*, *reading* and *read it*. These rules together account for the word juncture facts discussed above:

$$\text{a. V}\#\text{C\'V} = \text{VC\'V}$$
$$\text{b. VC}\#\text{V̌} = \text{VCV̌}$$

Only Rule I can apply to forms having the structure shown in a, giving them identical structures; forms with the structure of b will also receive the same syllable structures, albeit by different routes, as in Figure 15.8.

a tómcat	atómic	hock ĭt	Hockĕtt	
I |I	I |I	I/|I	I/|I	
S S	S S	S S	S S	
by I	by I	by I, III	by I, II	**Figure 15.8**

Strings which are pronounced differently, however, will receive different syllable structures, as in Figure 15.9.

an aim	a name	
I/|I	I |I	
S S	S S	
by I, III	by I	**Figure 15.9**

Explanation of Learner Errors

Given these rules of English syllabification, it is now possible to explain the English speaker's problems in perceiving and producing Egyptian Arabic word juncture. It has been argued that English allows cross-word linkage of syllables, but of only one type, that of *hock it*, in which the k is a member both of the syllable of its own word and of the syllable containing the first vowel of the following word. The cross-word linkages of Egyptian Arabic, however, are not of this type. This can be seen by comparing the syllable structure of the Egyptian Arabic phrases with the syllable structure which would be assigned to these phrases by the English rules, as shown in Figure 15.10.

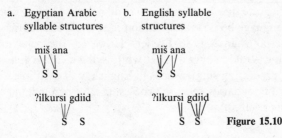

a. Egyptian Arabic   b. English syllable
    syllable structures   structures

Figure 15.10

The righthand column accurately represents the way in which English-speaking students tend to pronounce the Egyptian phrases (a pronunciation which is perceived as a lack of fluency by native speakers). Therefore the pronunciation errors of the American learners can be seen as simply a result of assigning syllable structure to the target language phrases according to the rules of the native language. The perception problem is also directly explainable as a result of language transfer. The English speaker seems to hear the syllable structure correctly—or, more precisely, to hear the acoustic correlates of syllable structure, such as differences in the length of syllable-initial consonants and consonants which are not syllable-initial. These differences are analyzed as indications of syllable structure; thus the strings are heard as they are represented in *a*. The problem arises in factoring the strings into words. In English, word boundaries are always accompanied by syllable boundaries, except in cases where Rule III has applied—in *hock it,* for example, where *k* is a member of two syllables simultaneously. Thus a consonant can be a member of a syllable in another word, but it must also belong to a syllable in its own word. The English speakers, hearing *mi-š a-na,* in which *š* belongs only to a syllable in the second word, must assume therefore that *š* cannot be part of the first word. Similarly, hearing */ʔil-kur-si g-diid/,* in which *g* belongs only to the final syllable of *ʔilkursi,* the student will assume that *g* must be a part of the word *ʔilkursi.* Interestingly enough, this problem in perception seems to persist long after the production of these strings has been mastered.

These findings bear on fundamental questions in the area of language processing. It is argued above that English speakers' misperceptions of Arabic strings result from their interpreting the syllable structure of these strings in accord with the dictates governing the relationship between word structure and syllable structure in English; thus syllabification plays an important role in speech processing. This finding is consistent with work by Mehler, Dommergues, Frauenfelder, and Segui (1981), which demonstrates that French speakers appear to use knowledge of French syllable structure in processing French sequences; reaction time of subjects to a target sequence was faster when the target corresponded to the first syllable of a word than when the target sequence was distributed through the first two syllables. However, later work by Cutler, Mehler, Norris, and Segui (1983) suggests that English speakers, in contrast to French speakers, do not make use of syllable structure. English speakers did not show a significant difference in reaction time to single-syllable vs. double-syllable target strings, whether these strings were English or French. The authors conclude that English speakers do not use a syllabification strategy in processing language because the location of syllable boundaries in English is so much less clear than it is in French. However, the behavior of English speakers learning Arabic suggests that while syllabification may not be especially useful in processing single words in English, it *is* used in determining the position of word boundaries, even in processing a foreign language (with sometimes disastrous results).[5]

OTHER CASES OF TRANSFER OF SYLLABLE STRUCTURES

Restriction on Syllable Structure

It was argued in the preceding sections that syllable structure plays a crucial role in the production and perception of language and that transfer of syllable structure rules from the native language to the target language may be a source of learners' errors; certain errors of English speakers learning Arabic were explained as a result of such transfer. Another sort of transfer related to syllable structure has been documented by Brière, Campbell, and Soemarmo (1968). Their study concerns the production of word-initial ž and ŋ by language learners whose first language is English. Since English has neither ž nor ŋ in word-initial position, the Contrastive Analysis Hypothesis would at first glance seem to predict that speakers will find the production of each of these sounds at the beginning of a word equally difficult. But in fact, English speakers have little trouble learning to produce word-initial ž, and a great deal of trouble with word-initial ŋ. The authors argue that this difference can be traced to the fact that English allows ž—but not ŋ—to begin a syllable, just so long as the syllable is not the first in a word. Thus learning to produce word-initial ž is simply a matter of learning to relax the prohibition against a syllable with initial ž beginning a word. Learning to produce word-initial ŋ, however, involves the mastery of an entirely new syllable structure. This study shows, then, that the role of the syllable must be taken into account in serious attempts to test the Contrastive Analysis Hypothesis; the syllable plays a role in positive transfer, as well as in negative transfer, as in the case of Egyptian Arabic word juncture.

Vowel Insertion

When the target language has syllable structures which do not occur in the native language, speakers may take action to force the target language structures into conformity with native language restrictions. A common means of dealing with differences between first and second language syllable structures is insertion of a vowel to transform the target language syllables into shapes which are acceptable in the first language. This phenomenon is often observed in the speech of Spanish speakers, who tend to insert a vowel before English words which begin with s followed by another consonant, since syllables beginning with this combination of elements are not permitted in Spanish. The tendency to force foreign strings to conform to Spanish syllable structure constraints is illustrated by such words as Spanish *esnob,* meaning 'snob'. Speakers of Egyptian Arabic make similar sorts of errors, described in Broselow (1983). Syllables in Egyptian Arabic must begin with one and only one consonant, and English words beginning with consonant clusters are often pronounced by Egyptians with an epenthesized vowel; 'plastic', for example, is pronounced [bilastik], with a vowel inserted to produce a syllable structure which is acceptable in Egyptian Arabic. (Note also the substitution of *b* for *p,* which does not occur as a phoneme of Arabic.)

THE SYLLABLE STRUCTURE TRANSFER HYPOTHESIS

Thus, three types of transfer of native language syllable structures to the target language are well-documented: word juncture errors resulting from application of native language syllabification rules to target language strings; ability to produce the sounds of the target language in a particular position in a syllable dependent on whether those sounds occur in that position in syllables of the native language; application of vowel insertion to bring target language syllables into line with native language restrictions on syllable structure. These facts bear out the predictions of the Contrastive Analysis Hypothesis that differences between native language and target language structures will result in errors. More specifically, the following hypothesis can be proposed:

Syllable Structure Transfer Hypothesis: When the target language permits syllable structures which are not permitted in the native language, learners will make errors which involve altering these structures to those which would be permitted in the native language.

This hypothesis accounts for the cases discussed above. In the case of word juncture in Arabic, the sorts of structures illustrated by *mi-š #a-na* 'not I' and *ilkur-si #g-diid* 'the chair is new' would be impossible in English because of the position of word boundaries with respect to syllable structure. English speakers hearing these strings in a sense alter the position of word boundaries to conform to English dictates on the relationship between word structure and syllable structure (i.e. they "hear" the word boundaries where they are not). In pronouncing these strings, English speakers alter the syllable structure in accord with the position of the word boundaries. In the other cases discussed above, language learners actually alter the consonant-vowel makeup of the string to produce syllable structures which would be permissible in the native language; thus [esnob] for 'snob' by Spanish speakers, [bilastik] for 'plastic' by Arabic speakers, and [enkomo] for 'Nkomo' ([ŋkomo]) by English speakers.

An interesting test of this hypothesis involves word juncture phenomena in the speech of Egyptian speakers learning English. The Contrastive Analysis Hypothesis predicts that transfer should occur whenever the native language and the target language differ: Arabic speakers should, if the strong version of this hypothesis is correct, attempt to apply the syllable structure assignment rules of Arabic to English strings. Thus the following sorts of errors would be expected to occur among speakers of Egyptian Arabic learning English:

this ink	pronounced as	the sink
the sink	heard as	this ink
the snail	pronounced as	this nail
this nail	heard as	the snail

The Egyptian Arabic rules requiring that each syllable begin with one and only one consonant would assign similar syllable structures to these strings in Figure 15.11.

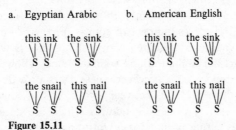

Figure 15.11

Arabic speakers' treatment of initial consonant clusters was discussed above. Their treatment of the other sorts of problematic structures, illustrated by *this ink,* is interesting. The incorrect pronunciation of these strings predicted above does not seem to occur. In fact, rather than doing excessive "blending" —linking of syllables across word boundaries—Arabic learners, like other learners of English, tend not to blend at all; their speech is often characterized by rather stilted-sounding word-by-word articulation. Thus the common syllabification of *this ink* by Arabic speakers is neither that shown in Figure 15.12 in *a,* according to English syllabification rules, nor that of *b,* according to Egyptian Arabic rules, but rather that in *c.*

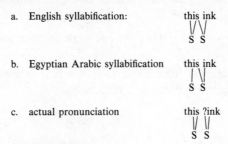

Figure 15.12

In Figure 15.12 a glottal stop has been introduced before the word-initial vowel of *ink.* The effect is to eliminate the necessity for any cross-word syllabic linkage while still maintaining the Egyptian Arabic prohibition against syllables beginning in a vowel. These facts appear at first glance to contradict the Contrastive Analysis Hypothesis, since one would expect the Arabic speakers to apply their native language syllabification rules to the target language strings. But some additional facts of Arabic reveal that speakers are in this case simply making use of another native language process. When a word beginning with a vowel stands at the beginning of a phrase in Egyptian Arabic, speakers always insert a glottal stop before the vowel; for example, *ana* 'I' is pronounced [ʔana] in isolation or sentence-initially. This process of glottal stop insertion may also be employed within phrases. Thus while the normal pronunciation of *miš ana* 'not I' involves moving the *š* to the syllable of the vowel following it, in extremely slow and deliberate speech this phrase may be pronounced [miš ʔana]. Glottal stop insertion, then, is another means available in Egyptian Arabic for ensuring that syllables always begin with one and only one consonant.

These facts are interesting on two counts. First, they provide additional support for the hypothesis presented above, that speakers will have difficulty with syllable structure configurations which are not allowed in their native languages. More importantly, however, these facts provide a case in which language learners have a choice between two means of converting the target language syllable structures into structures which are acceptable by native language standards: either by moving a word-final consonant into the syllable of a following vowel, or by inserting a glottal stop. In either case the resulting syllable structure will conform to the native language specifications that each syllable begin with one and only one consonant and that no consonant be ambisyllabic. The Arabic speakers' choice of glottal stop insertion, with the result that cross-word syllable linkage is minimized, seems to be governed by universal principles. Syllabification on the domain of the word, with insertion of a glottal stop before an initial vowel, is allowed, at least in slow speech, in every language of the world. Cross-word syllabification, however, is in many languages restricted to rapid speech, if it is permitted at all. Thus, the alternative chosen by Arabic learners—syllabification on the word—is more natural or less marked sort of syllable structure, where markedness is defined as follows:

A structure A is marked with respect to a structure B if no language has B unless it also has A.

Any language which has the syllable structure in *a* of Figure 15.13 will also permit the less marked syllable structure in *b*.

a. . . . V C # V   . . . (as in miš ana)
         S   S   S S

b. . . . V C # C V . . . (as in miš ?ana)
         S   S   S S   **Figure 15.13**

When confronted with a target language syllable structure which is not acceptable in their native language, Arabic learners convert it to the less marked structure in *b*, using the universally available device of glottal stop insertion.[6]

These facts suggest that some notion of relative markedness must be incorporated into the Contrastive Analysis Hypothesis. This point has been made by other researchers as well. Tarone (1976) presents evidence that while many syllable structure related errors can be accounted for as a result of transfer, many cannot; language learners often simplify syllable structure in the target language (by deletion of one or more consonants or epenthesis of vowels) even when the target language word has a syllable structure which is permitted in the native language. She cites, for example, such errors as a Korean speaker's pronunciation of *school* as [sku:], even though Korean has a word containing final *l* after *u:* [kuel] 'ninth month'. These sorts of non-transfer errors, Tarone argues, are a result of a universal tendency to prefer the unmarked syllable structure CV in stressful situations; learning and using a second language tends to be associated with stress, and therefore precipitates the retreat to CV syllables.

Additional arguments for including the notion of markedness in contrastive analysis are made by Eckman (1977). While Eckman offers interesting syntactic evidence for the operation of markedness principles in second language learning, his arguments from phonology are less convincing, precisely because he fails to take the role of the syllable into account. Eckman argues that the relative ease with which English speakers learn to produce word-initial *ž* in a foreign language follows from a universal principle that maintenance of a contrast in voicing is least marked in word-initial position and most highly marked in word-final position. Since English speakers have word-initial *š*, the voiceless counterpart of *ž*, in their native language, it is easy for them to produce word-initial *ž*, because it involves maintaining a voicing contrast in word-initial position, where such a contrast is least marked. But as discussed above, an alternative explanation of the ease with which English speakers learn to produce word-initial *ž* is provided by contrastive analysis, once it is recognized that English does contain *ž* in syllable-initial position, and that producing word-initial *ž* is simply a matter of removing the restriction on where in a word syllables beginning with *ž* may occur.

CONCLUSIONS

This paper has presented evidence in support of the following hypotheses:

a. Transfer does play a role in second language acquisition, at least in the area of phonology.
b. Syllable structure restrictions are particularly susceptible to transfer.
c. Universal principles of markedness play a role in learners' errors; for example, language learners show a preference for less marked (more 'natural') syllable structures.

These findings represent a step in the direction of a revised Contrastive Analysis Hypothesis, one which will predict which sorts of differences between the native language and the target language will result in learner difficulties. But many questions remain. One question which must be addressed is why syllabification rules in particular are so often transferred; this is part of the broader question of what sorts of phenomena tend to participate in transfer. I propose as a preliminary hypothesis that those aspects of a phonology which are generally considered "surface," "low-level," or "phonetic" rules and constraints are those which are most likely to be transferred to the target language. The class of "low-level" phenomena include phonotactic constraints—for example, the stipulation that no English syllable may begin with ŋ—and allophonic rules, generally exceptionless and not conditioned by the presence of particular morphemes or grammatical configurations; the aspiration of syllable-initial voiceless stops in English is one example of such a rule. Those rules which one would not expect to contribute to learner errors are rules which apply only in certain lexically marked classes of forms or which rely on grammatical or morphological information in their structural descriptions. Thus for example one would not expect to find English speakers making errors such as mispronouncing the plural of Spanish *dios* 'god', which is [dioses], as [*diozes], even though English has a rule converting word-final voiceless fricatives to their voiced counterparts in the plural: *house* [haws] but *houses* [hawzɨz], *bath* [bæθ] but *baths* [bæðz], *knive* [nayf] but *knives* [nayvz]. The reason this rule would not be expected to participate in transfer is that it is conditioned by morphological information—the rule applies only in the plural—and it applies only to a lexically marked class of forms. The rule does not make predictions about possible surface forms of English, since there are many words which have just the configuration of elements which the rule is designed to destroy *(buses, kisses)*.

Thus phonetic rules, particularly rules involving syllable structure, appear to play a role in both the production and the perception of second language strings. The recognition of the role of these rules in second language acquisition makes possible an account of many learner errors as a result of transfer.

NOTES

1. A sequence of two identical short vowels represents a single long vowel. The word-initial cluster in *gdiid* results from a rule of vowel deletion (see Broselow 1979 for details).

2. The author can testify to the reality of this problem, having wasted a good deal of time combing Arabic-English dictionaries for nonexistent words as a result of having misanalyzed the word structure of familiar Arabic phrases.

3. The converse, that any syllable which is emphatic contains an emphatic phoneme, is not true; emphasis may spread beyond the syllable containing the primary emphatic segment. When it does, however, it still appears to encompass entire syllables (but see Ghazeli, 1977).

4. Here and below only the relevant aspects of syllable structure are indicated.

5. Numerous alternative analyses of English syllable structure have been offered since Kahn's. These will not be discussed here, since any theory which recognizes an effect of word boundaries on English syllable structure is consistent with the hypothesis of this paper.

6. The insertion of a glottal stop at the beginnings of English words by language learners of various native language backgrounds is attested in Tarone 1976.

REFERENCES

Abdel-Massih, E. (1974) *Introduction to Egyptian Arabic.* Ann Arbor: University of Michigan Press.

Al-Ani, S. (1970) *Arabic Phonology: An Acoustic and Physiological Investigation.* The Hague: Mouton.

Ali, L. and R.G. Daniloff. (1972) "A contrastive cinefluorographic investigation of the articulation of emphatic-non-emphatic cognate consonants," *Studia Linguistica, 26,* 81–105.

Anderson, J. and C. Jones. (1974) "Three theses concerning phonological representations," *Journal of Linguistics, 10,* 1–26.

Bailey, C. (1973) "Gradience in English syllables and a revised concept of unmarked syllables," unpublished ms.

Brière, E., R. Campbell, and N. Soemarmo. (1968) "A need for the syllable in contrastive analysis," *Journal of Verbal Learning and Verbal Behavior, 7,* 384–389.

Broselow, E. (1976) The Phonology of Egyptian Arabic. Ph.D. dissertation, University of Massachusetts at Amherst.

Broselow, E. (1979) "Cairene Arabic syllable structure," *Linguistic Analysis 5,* 345–382.

Broselow, E. (1983) "Nonobvious transfer: on predicting epenthesis errors," in L. Selinker and S. Gass, eds., *Language Transfer in Language Learning,* 269–280. Rowley, MA: Newbury House. (Also this volume.)

Cutler, A., J. Mehler, D. Norris, and J. Segui (1983) "A language-specific comprehension strategy," *Nature, 304,* 159–160.

Dulay, H. and M. Burt. (1975) "Creative construction in second language learning and teaching," in *On TESOL '75: New Directions in Second Language Learning, Teaching and Bilingual Education.* Washington, D.C.: TESOL, 21–32.

Eckman, F. (1977) "Markedness and the contrastive analysis hypothesis," *Language Learning, 27,* 315–330. (Also this volume.)

Gass, S. (1980) "An investigation of syntactic transfer in adult L2 learners," In R. Scarcella and S. Krashen, eds., *Research in Second Language Acquisition.* Rowley, MA: Newbury House.

Ghazeli, S. (1977) Back Consonants and Backing Coarticulation in Arabic. Ph.D. dissertation, University of Texas at Austin.

Harrell, R. (1957) *The Phonology of Colloquial Egyptian Arabic.* New York: ACLS.

Hooper, J. (1977) Syllabic and non-syllabic issues in phonology. Preliminary version, paper prepared for the Symposium on segment organization and the syllable. Boulder, Colorado.

Ioup, G. and A. Kruse. (1977) "Interference versus structural complexity as a predictor of second language clause acquisition," in C. Henning (Ed.), *Proceedings of the Second Language Research Forum.* Los Angeles.

Kahn, D. (1976) "Syllable-based generalizations in English," distributed by the Indiana University Linguistics Club.

Lehiste, I. (1960) *An Acoustic-Phonetic Study of Internal Open Juncture.* New York: S. Karger.

Lehn, W. (1963) "Emphasis in Cairo Arabic," *Language, 39,* 29–39.

Lehn, W. and P. Abboud. (1965) *Beginning Cairo Arabic.* Austin: University of Texas Press.

Lehn, W. and W. Slager. (1959) "A contrastive study of Egyptian Arabic and American English: the segmental phonemes," *Language Learning, 9,* 25–33.

Liberman, M. and J. Pierrehumbert. (1982) "Intonational invariance under changes in pitch range and length," ms. Bell Laboratories.

Mehler, J., J. Dommergues, U. Fravenfelder, and J. Segui. (1981) "The syllable's roles in speech segmentation," *Journal of Verbal Learning and Verbal Behavior, 20,* 298–305.

Mitchell, T. (1956) *An Introduction to Colloquial Egyptian Arabic.* London: Oxford University Press.

Mitchell, T. (1962) *Colloquial Arabic.* London: The English Universities Press Ltd.

Prator, C. and B. Robinett. (1972) *Manual of American English Pronunciation.* New York: Holt, Rinehart and Winston.

Richards, J. (1974) "A non-contrastive approach to error analysis," in Richards (Ed.), *Error Analysis*. London: Longman.

Schachter, J. (1974) "An error in error analysis," *Language Learning, 24,* 205–214.

Scott, M. and R. Tucker. (1974) "Error analysis and English language strategies of Arab students," *Language Learning, 24,* 69–97.

Stockwell, R. and J. Bowen. (1965) *The Sounds of English and Spanish.* Chicago: University of Chicago Press.

Tarone, E. (1976) "Some influences on interlanguage phonology," *Working Papers in Bilingualism, 8,* 87–111. (Also this volume.)

Wardhaugh, R. (1970) "The contrastive analysis hypothesis," *TESOL Quarterly, 4,* 123–130.

16

THE MARKEDNESS DIFFERENTIAL HYPOTHESIS AND SYLLABLE STRUCTURE DIFFICULTY*

Janet I. Anderson

One of the questions second language (L2) researchers have been concerned with is why certain target language (TL) forms are more difficult to acquire than others. Several theories of L2 learning difficulty have been proposed. Among the most notable and testable are the Contrastive Analysis Hypothesis, the Language Universals Hypothesis, and the Markedness Differential Hypothesis.

The Contrastive Analysis Hypothesis (Lado, 1957) predicts that forms in the TL that contrast with equivalent forms in the native language (NL) will be difficult to learn, while forms that are similar will be easy to learn. Also, the kinds of contrast (i.e., convergent, divergent, or new) that exist between NL and TL structures are sometimes considered in the analysis.

The Universals Hypothesis, on the other hand, does not take into account

*This is a revised version of a paper presented at the Conference on the Uses of Phonology, Carbondale, 1983. The research reported in the paper was funded by a grant from Iowa State University. Thanks are extended to Kenneth Koehler for his help with the statistical analysis, to Dan Flickinger for the phonetic transcription, and to Horabail Venkatagiri and Clyde Thogmartin for their help in spot-checking the phonetic transcriptions. My gratitude also goes to Marilyn Dale for typing the paper.

279

NL structure; instead, it bases its predictions of difficulty on universality. The least expected or least universal forms across the languages of the world are considered to be the most difficult for L2 learners to acquire, while the most expected or natural forms are considered to be the easiest, independent of native language transfer.

The Markedness Differential Hypothesis takes into account both NL transfer and language universals (Eckman, 1977). The hypothesis states that forms in the TL that differ from and are more *marked* than NL forms will be difficult to learn, and that the relative degree of difficulty will correspond to the relative degree of markedness. The aspects of the target language that are different but *unmarked* will not be difficult to learn. In this view, a phenomenon A in some language is considered to be more marked than a phenomenon B, "if the presence of A in a language implies the presence of B, but the presence of B does not imply the presence of A." (Eckman, 1977, 320). To illustrate this notion of markedness, Eckman uses the example of *voiced* versus *voiceless* stops. There are languages, such as Korean, that have only voiceless stops, and there are languages, such as English, that have both voiced and voiceless stops. However, there are no languages that have only voiced stops. Thus voiced stops always imply the presence of voiceless stops and are thus said to be more marked (or less natural) than voiceless ones. The hypothesis, then, would predict that a voiceless stop would be easier for the L2 learner to acquire than its voiced counterpart, if neither occurred in the NL of the learner.

An aspect of L2 performance that is of special interest in examining these hypotheses is L2 syllabification. Because languages often vary in syllable structure complexity from languages, such as Hawaiian, which allow only "open" consonant-vowel (CV) syllables, to languages like English or Russian, which allow complex onsets and codas, it is possible to make predictions about the relative difficulty of L2 syllables based on contrastive analysis and to compare the performance of language learners from diverse language backgrounds.

It is also possible to make predictions of syllable difficulty based on language universals. Research on the syllable has shown that the most universal syllable type is the open CV syllable and that, in any given language, syllables with consonant clusters always imply the presence of more simple syllable types. Thus the longer the cluster, the more marked it is considered to be. The research has also shown that consonant clusters occur less frequently across languages in syllable-final position (Greenberg, 1978). Thus final clusters can be considered more marked (or less universal) than initial clusters, although they are not considered "marked" in the strictest sense of the word (see discussion of Eckman above). Predictions of L2 learning difficulty can be made based on these facts.

RESEARCH ON L2 SYLLABIFICATION

Research studies on L2 syllabification have generally examined L2 syllable structure errors in light of the contrastive analysis hypothesis. Broselow (1984) argues that native language transfer is a valid means of predicting the second language learner's syllable structure errors. She states that when learning Egyptian Arabic, American English (AE) speakers tend to use English syllabification rules to perceive and produce Arabic utterances. Presenting examples of errors made by AE learners of Arabic, she shows that they tend to create syllable boundaries in Arabic that conform to English syllable structure. She also shows how Egyptian Arabic speakers tend to use their native language syllabification rules when speaking English. The Egyptian Arabic speaker tends to simplify clusters in English through epenthesis, a rule widely used to simplify consonant clusters in Egyptian Arabic.

Tarone's 1976 study on L2 syllabification presents a somewhat different picture. She analyzed utterances produced by six ESL learners—two native speakers each of Cantonese, Korean, and Portuguese—and tabulated and categorized all of the syllable simplification errors. Her findings revealed that although native language transfer was a dominant factor in determining where syllable simplification would occur, she also found cases of simplification that could not be explained by transfer. For example, in attempting to pronounce *blanket,* one of the Portuguese subjects simplified the initial cluster by deleting the /l/ even though a /bl/ sequence occurs in Portuguese, as in *problema* 'problem.' She found several such examples of open syllables occurring independent of language transfer. This led her to raise the question of whether there was a preference or tendency for L2 learners to use the universal open syllable under the pressure of communication.

Anderson (1983) extended the research on L2 syllabification to two other language groups to more clearly delineate the extent to which the L2 learner's syllabification performance could be explained by the contrastive analysis hypothesis. The native languages of the two groups she investigated—Chinese and Egyptian Arabic—contrast with each other and with English in the types of syllables they allow. While Chinese is a predominantly open syllable language, Egyptian Arabic allows clusters of two consonants in word-final position. American English (AE), on the other hand, allows consonant clusters in both initial and final position. Predictions of difficulty were made based on these contrasts. Although some of her predictions were confirmed, she also discovered some parallels between universals of syllable structure and certain patterns of error in her data.

Although Tarone's and Anderson's data both showed evidence of language universals as well as native language transfer, neither study systematically investigated Eckman's (1977) Markedness Differential Hypothesis (MDH), which takes into account both factors. Thus it is the purpose of this paper to test the MDH using some of the data from Anderson's 1983 study. In the 1983 study, all of Anderson's predictions were based on contrastive analysis. In the present paper, predictions will be made only on the basis of the MDH. Because the MDH predicts the relative *frequency* of error, not the *kinds* of error that are likely to occur, predictions concerning types of simplification errors (i.e., epenthesis versus deletion) will not be made. Nevertheless, the kinds of errors found will be examined in light of native language transfer and other factors.

SYLLABLE STRUCTURE OF ENGLISH, ARABIC AND CHINESE

The languages under consideration in this study are American English (AE), Colloquial Egyptian Arabic (CEA), Mandarin Chinese (MC), and Amoy Chinese (AC).

In AE syllables, consonant clusters occur in both word-initial and word-final position: Clusters of up to three consonants are allowed in initial position, and clusters of up to four consonants are allowed in final position. Thus it is theoretically possible for as many as seven consonants to occur in a sequence at word boundaries (Bowen, 1975).

The syllable structure of CEA is not as complex as that of AE. No more than one consonant can occur in syllable-initial position, and no more than two consonants can occur in a cluster in syllable-final position before a pause. However, there are conditions that determine syllable boundaries so that if a syllable ending in two consonants is followed by a syllable beginning with a vowel, the last consonant of the first syllable is reassigned to the second syllable. In cases where a syllable ending in two consonants is closely followed by a syllable beginning with a consonant other than a glottal stop, the vowel /i/ is inserted after the second consonant. This epenthesis rule is used widely in CEA to simplify clusters (Broselow, 1976). The combinations of CEA consonants in final clusters are almost unlimited, and many of the CEA final clusters of two members have AE equivalents (Harrell, 1957).

The syllable structures of MC and AE contrast with each other markedly. Although MC allows complex syllable peaks, consisting of as many as three vowels, it does not allow any consonant clusters, either initially or finally, and the sequences that occur are highly restricted. Further, there are only three consonants that can occur in syllable-final positions: /n, ŋ, ɹ/ (Cheng 1973). The syllable structure of AC is also very simple. Like MC, it does not allow clusters either initially or finally. However, AC allows a few more consonants to occur as single consonants in syllable-final position: /m, n, ŋ, p, t, k/ (Sung, 1973).

MDH PREDICTIONS

As noted above, the MDH predicts that TL structures that are more marked than corresponding NL structures will be difficult to learn and that the relative degree of difficulty will correspond to the relative degree of markedness. It further predicts that areas that differ but are unmarked will not be difficult (Eckman, 1977). In the following discussion MDH predictions of difficulty will be made concerning the length of the clusters and their positions in syllables.

Length

Since longer clusters are more marked than shorter ones, and since neither CEA nor the Chinese dialects, MC and AC, allow clusters as long as those found in English, MDH predicts that the relative difficulty (i.e. relative frequency of error) of English consonant clusters for each group will correspond to the length of the cluster: The longer the cluster the more difficult it will be. Since a cluster can also be considered marked or unmarked according to its position in the syllable, comparisons of difficulty according to length will be made when position is held constant.

Position

Since final clusters are more marked than initial ones, and since neither MC nor AC allows consonant clusters either initially or finally, the MDH predicts that final clusters will be more difficult for the Chinese group than initial clusters, when length is held constant.

A difference in difficulty between initial and final clusters cannot be predicted for the Arabic group because in CEA, the determinants of difficulty implicit in MDH predictions—native language transfer and markedness—cancel each other out. CEA allows consonant clusters only in final position, the marked position in the syllable, but the MDH does not predict whether native language transfer or markedness will predominate. That is, will English consonant clusters be easier for the Arabic group when they occur in final position (because they are allowed in that position in CEA) or will they be easier in initial position (because initial position is less marked than final position)? Since the MDH does not specify which of the two factors will prevail, no difference in difficulty between initial and final clusters will be predicted for the Arabic group.

METHOD

Subjects

The CEA group consisted of twenty native speakers of CEA, all of whom were natives of Egypt. The Chinese group consisted of twenty natives of Taiwan, all of whom spoke MC, the official language of Taiwan. However, ten of these individuals spoke AC as their native language. In the CEA group, there were seventeen men and three women; in the Chinese group there were sixteen men and four women. The age range in the CEA group was twenty-six to forty-two; the age range in the Chinese group was twenty-three to thirty-nine. All of the individuals were graduate students in the United States when the study was conducted. Thirty-seven were enrolled at Iowa State University, two at Kansas State University, and one at the University of Kansas. The length of time they had been in the United States varied from five to sixty months, but there was an equal number of subjects from the Arabic and Chinese groups in each of the following time periods: 0–12 months—4; 13–24 months—7; 25–36 months—4; 36–48 months—5.

In order to determine whether the Arabic and Chinese groups were equal regarding English language proficiency, the *Michigan Test of Aural Comprehension* was given. It was felt that this test was appropriate because it is a standardized test of English language proficiency which tests for knowledge and comprehension of the spoken language. The mean score for the Arabic group was 79.9 and for the Chinese group 81.5. A t-test revealed no significant difference between the 2 groups (t = .56; df = 38; p = .58). Thus it was assumed that the Arabic and Chinese groups did not differ from each other in general English language proficiency.

Procedures

Each subject was interviewed individually and asked to talk about a holiday in his or her home country. This topic was chosen because it had proven to be a good topic for eliciting spontaneous speech in earlier studies on pronunciation (Suter, 1976). It was felt that eliciting spontaneous speech rather than administering an articulation test would produce speech samples more akin to performance in a real communicative situation. The subjects were allowed several minutes to organize their thoughts before speaking. They were encouraged to speak naturally, and every attempt was made to create a relaxed, supportive environment. Three minutes of spontaneous speech from each subject were recorded on a Uher tape recorder at 7½ inches per second. The tapes were transcribed phonetically in narrow transcription using the IPA system of notation. In order to avoid bias, the transcriber, a linguist trained in phonetic transcription, was not informed of the objectives of the study. Sound spectrograms were taken of some of the clusters and sequences and were checked against the phonetic transcriptions. The agreement was found to be very high.

In analyzing the speech samples, 125 words of running text in each of the 40 phonetic transcripts were examined for simplification errors. If a cluster or sequence was not simplified, it received a score of 1, regardless of substitution errors, which were not tabulated because they were not relevant to the research questions. If the cluster or sequence showed 1 or more simplification errors, it received a score of 0.

The standard against which the L2 learners' performance was measured was formal, unsimplified, standard American English rather than casual speech.

RESULTS AND DISCUSSION

Length

Both the Arabic and Chinese groups performed better, although not always significantly so, on shorter forms than on longer ones when position was held constant. The Arabic group mean percentage score on single initial consonants was 100 percent and on initial clusters of 2 members 92.9 ($p < .00001$). Initial clusters of 3 members occurred too infrequently in the data to be used for comparison. The Arabic group mean percentage score on single final consonants was 98.4, and on final clusters of 2 members 82.6 ($p < .00001$). The Arabic mean percentage score on final clusters of 3 members was 69.4 ($p = .06$). These differences are illustrated in Table 16.1.[1]

The Chinese group showed the same pattern of accuracy according to length. The Chinese group mean percentage score on single initial consonants was 99.2; on initial clusters of 2 consonants 89.6 ($p < .00001$). The number of occurrences of initial clusters of 3 consonants was too small for a comparison to be made between clusters of 2 and 3 members. The Chinese group mean percentage score on single final consonants was 79.7 and on final clusters of 2 members 50.2 ($p < .00001$). The group mean score on final clusters of 3 consonants was 26.3 ($p = .006$). These differences are illustrated in Table 16.2.

These results support the predictions made by the markedness differential hypothesis on the relative difficulty of clusters according to length. As predicted, as the forms increased in length, and thus in markedness, they increased in difficulty for both the Arabic and Chinese groups.

Position

The Chinese group performed significantly better on forms in initial position than on forms in final position. The group mean percentage score on initial

TABLE 16.1. Arabic Group Mean Percentage Scores and Chi Square Values on Consonants and Consonant Clusters According to Length

	Shorter form			Longer form			
Type	Number of occurrences	Percentage correct	Type	Number of occurrences	Percentage correct	X^2 value (df = 1)	P value
IC	1233	100	ICC	141	92.9	87.74	< .00001
FC	856	98.4	FCC	293	82.6	101.72	< .00001
FCC	293	82.6	FCCC	36	69.4	3.62	.057ns

IC = Initial Single Consonant; ICC = Initial Consonant Cluster of 2 members; FC = Final Single Consonant; FCC = Final Cluster of 2 Consonants; FCCC = Final Cluster of 3 Consonants

TABLE 16.2. Chinese Group Mean Percentage Scores and Chi Square Values of Consonants and Consonant Clusters According to Length

	Shorter form			Longer form			
Type	Number of occurrences	Percentage correct	Type	Number of occurrences	Percentage correct	X^2 value (df = 1)	P value
IC	1172	99.2	ICC	96	89.6	69.27	< .00001
FC	885	79.7	FCC	249	50.2	86.0	< .00001
FCC	249	50.2	FCCC	38	26.3	7.55	.006

IC = Initial Single Consonant; ICC = Initial Consonant Cluster of 2 members; FC = Final Single Consonant; FCC = Final Cluster of 2 Consonants; FCCC = Final Cluster of 3 Consonants

single consonants was 99.4, and on final single consonants, 79.7 (p < .00001). The mean score on clusters of 2 consonants in initial position was 89.6, and in final position, 50.2 (p < .00001). These differences are illustrated in Table 16.3. Thus, for the Chinese group, the results on position uphold the predictions made by MDH, which predicted that forms in initial position would be simplified less often than forms in final position, the universally weaker syllable position.

Although no difference in difficulty was predicted between initial versus final forms for the Arabic group, final forms were nonetheless found to be more difficult than initial ones (see Table 16.4). The group mean percentage score on initial single consonants was 100% and on final single consonants, 98.4 (p <

TABLE 16.3. Chinese Group Mean Percentage Scores and Chi Square Values on Consonants and Consonant Clusters According to Position

	Initial position			Final position			
Type	Number of occurrences	Percentage correct	Type	Number of occurrences	Percentage correct	X^2 value (df = 1)	P value
IC	1172	99.4	FC	885	79.7	237.8	< .00001
ICC	96	89.6	FCC	249	50.2	45.2	< .00001

IC = Single Initial Consonant; ICC = Initial Cluster of 2 Consonants; FC = Single Final Consonant; FCC = Final Cluster of 2 Consonants

TABLE 16.4. Arabic Group Mean Percentage Scores and Chi Square Values on Consonants and Consonant Clusters According to Position

	Initial position			Final Position			
Type	Number of occurrences	Percentage correct	Type	Number of occurrences	Percentage correct	X^2 value (df = 1)	P value
IC	1233	100	FC	856	98.4	20.23	< .001
ICC	141	92.9	FCC	293	82.6	8.38	.0038

IC = Single Initial Consonant; ICC = Initial Cluster of 2 Consonants; FC = Single Final Consonant; FCC = Final Cluster of 2 Consonants

.001). The score on initial clusters of 2 consonants was 92.9 and on final clusters of 2 consonants, 82.6 (p = .0038). Most of the final consonant clusters simplified (-st, -nt, -zd, -nd) had equivalents in CEA, indicating a preference for a more simple syllable, independent of language transfer.

When examining second language acquisition data, comparisons of performance among diverse language groups can often be revealing. Although the MDH made no specific predictions concerning group differences, the Arabic and Chinese data on position and length were nevertheless compared. (See Table 16.5.) It was found that although both the Arabic and Chinese groups demonstrated the same relative accuracy in their performance on the forms investigated, the absolute frequency of errors on certain clusters was dramatically higher for the Chinese group than for the Arabic group. This was especially noticeable on final clusters. On final clusters of 2 members, for example, the Arabic group mean percentage score was 82.6, while the mean score for the Chinese group was 50.2 (p < .00001).

This dramatic difference in performance between the two groups was not apparent on initial clusters of 2 members. The Arabic group mean percentage score on this type of cluster was 92.9, and the Chinese mean score was 89.6 (p = .37,ns). This pattern of error—the small difference between groups on initial clusters and the large difference on final clusters—can be understood in light of the MDH. Since initial position in the syllable is unmarked, it is unsurprising that both groups would perform well on initial clusters. Final clusters, on the other hand, are more marked and thus present learning difficulty when the native language does not also allow final clusters. Since CEA allows final clusters of 2 members while MC and AC do not, it is not surprising that the Arabic group performed dramatically better on these marked forms than the Chinese group.

The above discussion is concerned only with the accuracy rate of the forms investigated, not with the types of errors that occurred, because the MDH is concerned only with relative difficulty, not with sources of error. Nevertheless, an error analysis was done in order to throw more light on the factors that influenced the learners' performance. It was found that, to simplify syllables, both groups generally used deletion more often than epenthesis, although the Arabic group used epenthesis more often in initial clusters and medial sequences

TABLE 16.5. Group Mean Percentage Scores and Chi Square Values on Initial and Final Clusters for Arabic and Chinese Groups

| Cluster type | Arabic group | | Chinese group | | X^2 value (df = 1) | P value |
	Number of occurrences	Percentage correct	Number of occurrences	Percentage correct		
ICC	141	92.9	96	89.6	0.82	.37 ns
FCC	293	82.6	249	50.2	64.6	< .00001

ICC = Initial Cluster of 2 members; FCC = Final Cluster of 2 members (see Tables 16.6 and 16.7). In addition, both groups tended to delete many of the same consonants, although the number of deletion errors was much greater for the Chinese group. The consonants most often deleted by both groups were /t, d, ɹ/. The /t, d/ were most often deleted in word final position in consonant clusters, and the /ɹ/ was most often deleted post-vocalically in word-medial sequences and final clusters.

For the Arabic group, the patterns of error can be only partially explained by native language transfer, which would have predicted that epenthesis would be the dominant simplification strategy, since epenthesis is used widely in CEA to simplify clusters and sequences formed through the morphology of the language. However, as noted above, the dominant simplification strategy was deletion, although epenthesis was used somewhat more often in initial and medial position (see Table 16.6). Nor could the deletion of /t, d, ɹ/ be explained by native language transfer since CEA allows these consonants in medial sequences and final clusters.

Since epenthesis does not occur at all and since deletion does not occur widely in either dialect of Chinese, contrastive analysis cannot predict which simplification process would be the dominant one for the Chinese group. Thus the fact that deletion occurred more frequently than epenthesis cannot be explained by native language transfer (see Table 16.7). Nor can native language transfer explain why /t, d, ɹ/ were the consonants most often deleted since /t/ is allowed syllable finally in Amoy and /ɹ/ is allowed syllable-finally in Mandarin. Thus factors other than native language transfer need to be explored.

A review of research studies in first language acquisition shows some similarities between the syllable simplification strategies of children acquiring English as their first language and those of the L2 learners investigated in this study. The dominant simplification strategy used by children is deletion, and they tend to delete some of the same consonants. Hodson's 1975 study on the misarticulations of 60 normal four-year-old children acquiring American English as their first language showed that alveolar consonants in word-final position were either inadequately articulated or omitted completely. Compton's summary (1976) of the more deviant patterns of 20 children with phonological disorders showed that final alveolar consonants are much more likely to be deleted than other consonants. He also found that /ɹ/ and /l/ were often deleted in consonant clusters.

However, while there appear to be certain parallels between L1 simplification processes and the L2 simplification processes uncovered in this study, the overlap is by no means complete. There are certain syllable simplification processes used by children in acquiring the first language that the L2 learners in this study did not use. For example, the initial /sC-/ cluster in the word *step* would be simplified by first language learners as [tʰɛp], but the second language learners in the present study never simplified initial /sC-/ clusters by deleting the /s/. The Arabic speakers tended to simplify such clusters through epenthesis, inserting a vowel before the first consonant. Thus while L1 and L2 syllabifi-

TABLE 16.6. Classification of Simplification Errors in Clusters and Sequences for Arabic Group

		Number of occurrences clus/seq	Percentage correct	Percentage deletion errors	Percentage epenthesis errors	Percentage compound errors	Percentage metathesis errors
Initial Cluster	CC	141	92.9	0	7.1	0	0
Final Consonant	C	856	98.4	1.4	0.2	0	0
Final Cluster	CC	293	82.6	14.7	2.7	0	0
Final Cluster	CCC	36	69.4	16.7	11.1	2.8	0
Word-Medial Seq.	CC	197	91.4	3.0	5.1	0	0.5
Word-Medial Seq.	CCC	36	80.6	2.8	16.7	0	0
Word-Boundary Seq.	CC	171	86.5	12.9	0.6	0	0
Word-Boundary Seq.	CCC	64	67.2	29.7	3.1	0	0

TABLE 16.7. Classification of Simplification Errors in Clusters and Sequences for Chinese Group

		Number of occurrences clus/seq	Percentage correct	Percentage deletion errors	Percentage epenthesis errors	Percentage compound errors	Percentage metathesis errors
Initial Cluster	CC	96	89.6	10.4	0	0	0
Final Consonant	C	885	79.7	20.2	0.1	0	0
Final Cluster	CC	249	50.2	46.2	2.0	1.6	0
Final Cluster	CCC	38	26.3	68.4	5.3	0	0
Word-Medial Seq.	CC	195	75.4	24.6	0	0	0
Word-Medial Seq.	CCC	48	54.2	41.7	4.2	0	0
Word-Boundary Seq.	CC	108	56.5	33.3	8.3	1.9	0
Word-Boundary Seq.	CCC	49	4.1	59.2	32.7	4.1	0

cation processes may overlap to some extent, the two processes are by no means identical.

SUMMARY AND CONCLUSIONS

The results of this study have shown that the MDH is a fairly good predictor of the syllabification performance of the Arabic and Chinese ESL learners investigated. As predicted, the marked longer clusters were more difficult than the unmarked shorter ones for both groups, and for the Chinese group, the marked final clusters were more difficult than the unmarked initial ones.

In addition, certain similarities and differences in performance between groups were explained in light of the MDH. Both groups performed very well on unmarked forms, whether they were new or not. They performed differently on marked forms, when they were new to only one group. This pattern of performance is consistent with the MDH.

However, one of the MDH predictions was incorrect. For the Arabic group, no difference in performance had been predicted between the marked final clusters and the unmarked initial ones because the two determinants implicit in the MDH—native language transfer and markedness—had made the opposite predictions and thus cancelled each other out. Thus no differences in difficulty were predicted. Yet the results showed that unmarked forms (initial clusters) were easier, indicating that the universal factor implicit in the hypothesis overruled the transfer factor. Thus the MDH may have to be modified to make a stronger statement about the power of its universals determinant.

Nevertheless, the predictions of relative difficulty made by the MDH proved to be more accurate than the contrastive analysis predictions made in Anderson's 1983 paper on syllabification. This is because the MDH accepts that native language transfer *by itself* is insufficient to explain L2 learning difficulty. There are problems inherent in the target language, independent of language transfer, that present difficulties to the ESL learner, and it seems that these difficulties can be understood in light of language universals. The MDH is more tenable than contrastive analysis because it takes into account both of these factors.

In addition, the error analysis showed that native language transfer by itself was insufficient to explain the patterns of error that occurred. Some of the errors were better understood in light of first language acquisition processes.

Thus it seems that, at least for the two groups investigated, L2 syllabification performance—error types as well as relative accuracy—cannot be understood in light of native language transfer alone. In the case of relative difficulty, the MDH proved to be a more accurate predictor of performance than NL transfer. In the case of the types of errors that occurred, first language acquisition processes offered a better explanation for some of the errors than contrastive analysis by itself.

290

NOTE

1. The chi square test is sensitive to the number of observations in the categories being tested. Some of the lower chi square values reported in this study may have been due in part to the relatively low number of observations in some of the categories.

REFERENCES

Anderson, J.I. (1983) Syllable simplification in the speech of second language learners. *The Interlanguage Studies Bulletin 3*, 4–36.

Bowen, J.D. (1975) *Patterns of English Pronunciation*. Rowley, MA: Newbury House.

Broselow, E. (1976) *The Phonology of Egyptian Arabic*. Doctoral dissertation, University of Massachusetts.

Broselow, E. (1984) An investigation of transfer in second language phonology. *IRAL 22*, 253–269. (Also this volume.)

Cheng, C-C. (1973) *A Synchronic Phonology of Mandarin Chinese*. The Hague: Mouton.

Compton, A.J. (1976) Generative studies of children's phonological disorders: Clinical ramifications. In D.M. Morehead, and A.E. Morehead (Eds.) *Normal and Deficient Child Language*. Baltimore: University Park Press, 92–93.

Eckman, F.R. (1977) Markedness and the contrastive analysis hypothesis. *Language Learning 27*, 315–330. (Also this volume.)

Greenberg, J.H. (1978) Some generalizations concerning initial and final consonant clusters. In J.H. Greenberg, (Ed.), *Universals of Human Language*, II. Palo Alto, CA: Stanford University Press.

Harrell, R.S. (1957) *The Phonology of Colloquial Egyptian Arabic*. NY: American Council of Learned Societies.

Hodson, B.W. (1975) *Aspects of Phonological Performance in Four-year-olds*. Doctoral dissertation, University of Illinois, Urbana.

Lado, R. (1957) *Linguistics Across Cultures*. Ann Arbor: University of Michigan Press.

Sung, M.M.Y. (1973) A study of literary and colloquial amoy Chinese. *Journal of Chinese Linguistics 1*, 414–436.

Suter, R.W. (1976). Predictors of pronunciation accuracy in second language learning. *Language Learning 26*, 233–253.

Tarone, E. (1976) Some influences on interlanguage phonology. *Working Papers on Bilingualism 8*, 87–111. (Also this volume.)

17

NON-OBVIOUS TRANSFER:
ON PREDICTING EPENTHESIS ERRORS*

Ellen Broselow

Disenchantment with the strong form of the contrastive analysis hypothesis stemmed in part from the fact that while researchers could often predict which aspects of the second language would present problems for language learners of a particular first language background, it was often impossible to predict what the language learners would do to resolve these problems. Many errors could be explained after the fact as a result of differences between the native language and the target language, but the form of the errors could not be predicted with any regularity. While it is certain that many factors other than transfer from the first language are involved in phonological errors made by language learners, the failure to predict errors from an examination of the linguistic systems of the first and second languages by no means constitutes sufficient grounds for abandoning the contrastive analysis hypothesis altogether. Our inability to predict the occurrence and nature of many errors may well stem from inadequacies in our understanding of native speaker comeptence rather than from the failure of

*I would like to offer thanks to Ali Al-Bayati, Mushira Eid, Greg Iverson, Mohammed Jiyad, John McCarthy, Abdel-Rachman Sayed, Ahmed Shabana, and the many people at the University of Texas Intensive English Program who assisted me in this project.

the contrastive analysis hypothesis itself, and it is likely that a more sophisticated linguistic theory may in fact allow us to predict many of the systematic phonological errors made by speakers of a second language. In this chapter I examine the adequacy of two linguistic theories in predicting one type of learners' errors, the epenthesis of vowels into initial consonant clusters. I show that while standard generative theory makes no predictions about where and when epenthesis will occur, an extension of this theory makes very specific predictions. The fact that these predictions are borne out provides strong support both for a particular theory of phonology and for the hypothesis that language transfer plays a significant role in the acquisition of a second languge.

ERRORS INVOLVING CONSONANT CLUSTERS

The problem I am concerned with is the pronunciation of English words beginning in consonant clusters by speakers of two dialects of Arabic. I have argued elsewhere (Broselow, 1984) that errors involving consonant clusters generally occur when these clusters must be analyzed as belonging to syllable structures which are not permitted in the native language, and that the mispronunciation of the clusters represents an attempt by the language learner to bring second language forms into conformity with first language restrictions defining possible syllables. In English, for example, no syllable may begin with a nasal followed by a consonant. When clusters consisting of nasal plus consonant occur between vowels in foreign words, they do not create problems for English speakers, since the word may be analyzed as consisting of permissible syllables, for example, (u) (gan) (da) for *Uganda.* But when such a cluster is word-initial, there is no way to analyze the syllable containing it as a possible English syllable, and so the cluster is often modified. The wide variety of ways in which such clusters may be modified in English is illustrated below:

	English	*Native*	
a.	[ɛnkomo]	[ŋkomo]	'Nkomo'
b.	[n+krumə]	[ŋkruma]	'Nkrumah'
c.	[t‿itsi]	[tsitsi]	'tsetse (fly)'
d.	[‿nam]	[pʰnam]	'Phnom (Penh)'
e.	[swɛps]	[šwɛps]	'Schweppes'
f.	[šri]	[sri]	'Sri (Lanka)'
g.	[gotzbadɛ]	[ɣotbzadɛ]	'Ghotbzade'

In *a* and *b,* the technique used to create a syllable structure which conforms to English restrictions is to insert a vowel, either before the cluster as in *a* or inside the cluster as in *b.* Another possibility is to delete one of the consonants (the second in *c,* the first in *d*), and still another is to change one of the consonants: In *e, š* is changed to *s* to avoid the proscribed sequence *šw,*[1] while in 1f, *s* is changed to *š* to transform the un-English sequence *sr* into the permitted *šr* into the permitted *šr* (as in *shriek*). And finally, the order of the consonants may be changed, as it is in *g;* since no English syllable may end in *tb* or begin in *bz,* this cluster cannot be divided into permissible syllables, many speakers simply reverse the order of the consonants to create the permitted syllable-final cluster *tz.* [2]

It is apparently not possible to predict which of these means of resolving the conflict between first and second language syllable structures will be employed by speakers of English. It would be interesting, then, if speakers of other languages consistently chose only one of these methods of transforming foreign language strings to fit native language patterns, and if different methods were associated with speakers of different native language backgrounds, since this would suggest that the choice of a method of resolving the conflict between first and second language syllable structures is influenced by factors in the native language. In this paper I examine consistent patterns of errors in the speech of Arabic learners of English. I argue that their systematic choice of one means of resolving the conflict between first and second language syllable structures is a result of the transfer of a native language rule.

ERRORS BY ARABIC LEARNERS OF ENGLISH

The errors I discuss here were made by native speakers of two dialects of Arabic: Iraqi Arabic (the dialect of Baghdad and environs) and Egyptian Arabic (the dialect of Cairo and lower Egypt in general). The errors were collected in various ways: (1) by recording errors I have heard in conversation with speakers of these dialects over the course of several years; (2) by asking linguists who were native speakers of these dialects to record errors made by their compatriots; (3) by asking teachers who had taught English to Egyptian and Iraqi students what sorts of errors their students had made consistently; (4) by searching the literature on second language learning for discussions of errors by speakers of these dialects and of the treatment of borrowed words (which seem to be treated in just the same way as new vocabulary in the second language); and (5) by asking two speakers of each dialect to read a word list and read and answer questions on various passages. ·

These methods revealed interesting differences in the treatment of initial consonant clusters by members of the two dialect groups, and a surprising uniformity within dialect groups. The forms below show typical errors made by Egyptians:[3]

Errors by Egyptian speakers

a. [filoor] 'floor'
b. [bilastik] 'plastic'
c. [θirii] 'three'
d. [tiransilet] 'translate'
e. [silayd] 'slide'
f. [firɛd] 'Fred'

Speakers of this dialect tend to insert an [i] between the first and second consonants of an initial two-consonant cluster (except in one class of clusters, three-
consonant clusters, below). Speakers of Iraqi Arabic, on the other hand, tend
to make fewer errors involving initial two-consonant sequences, but when such
errors do occur, they reveal a different pattern—insertion of *i* **before** the initial
cluster, as illustrated below:

Errors by Iraqi speakers
a. [ifloor]   'floor'
b. [ibleen]   'plane'
c. [isnoo]   'snow'
d. [iθrii]   'three'
e. [istadi]   'study'
f. [ifrεd]   'Fred'

(These words were pronounced with a glottal stop before the *i* when they
occurred utterance-initially, in accord with a general rule of Arabic phonology
inserting glottal stop before a syllable-initial vowel.)

The fact that Iraqi speakers have on the whole less difficulty in producing
initial clusters than Egyptian speakers do may clearly be attributed to positive
transfer: while Egyptian Arabic words may begin with only one consonant, Iraqi
words may and often do begin with consonant clusters, as the list below illustrates; as the list also shows, *i* may optionally be inserted before initial clusters,
giving the alternate forms shown here:

Iraqi initial clusters
a. qmaaš   ~   iqmaaš   'cloth'
b. θneen   ~   iθneen   'two'
c. člaab   ~   ičlaab   'dogs'

Thus the insertion of *i* before initial clusters by Iraqis appears to be a clear case
of transfer of a phonological rule from the first language to the second. The
explanation of the Egyptian errors, however, is much less obvious. The mispronunciation of these forms by Egyptian speakers is to be expected, since their
first language does not permit syllable-initial consonant clusters, and the insertion of a vowel between the two members of the cluster served to bring the
English word into conformity with Egyptian syllable structure constraints. But
the interesting question of why Egyptian speakers consistently choose this
means of resolving the conflict rather than one of the other means available, such
as insertion of a vowel *before* the cluster, remains to be answered. This cannot
be accounted for by invoking a native language rule inserting vowels into initial
clusters, since there is no reason to assume that native language forms contain
initial clusters at all; thus there is no motivation for postulating a rule of initial
epenthesis on the basis of the facts of the native langauge. And in fact, the one
set of cases which might be used to motivate a rule inserting a vowel in the
vicinity of initial clusters would actually lead one to expect that Egyptian

speakers would treat initial clusters as Iraqi speakers do. These cases are the imperative forms, which are generally equivalent to the imperfect stem of the verb, minus the subject-marking prefix:

Egyptian imperfects and imperatives
yikallim 'he speaks'   yišiil 'he carries'
tikallim 'she speaks'   tišiil 'she carries'
kallim   'speak!'   šiil   'carry!'

When the imperfect stem begins with two consonants, the imperative is preceded by *i*.[4]

Egyptian imperfects and imperatives
yiktib 'he writes'
tiktib 'she writes'
iktib 'write!'

Thus the rule inserting *i* in imperative forms, if transferred to the second language, should give [ifloor], [iblastik] instead of the attested Egyptian pronunciations [filoor] and [bilastik]. These forms, then, clearly do not result from transfer of the rule affecting imperatives.

Thus the Egyptian errors appear to pose a serious problem for the hypothesis that both the Egyptian errors and the Iraqi errors are a result of language transfer. However, a closer examination of the facts provides convincing evidence that the Egyptian errors, like the Iraqi ones, do in fact result from the transfer of a productive phonological rule of the native language.

EPENTHESIS IN THREE-CONSONANT CLUSTERS

Both Iraqi Arabic and Egyptian Arabic have rules inserting a vowel into medial three-consonant clusters. As shown below, the rules of the two dialects differ in one respect: In Iraqi, the vowel is inserted after the first of three consonants, while in Egyptian, the vowel is inserted after the second of three consonants:

a. Iraqi epenthesis

    kitaba (kitab+a)   'he wrote it/him'
    kitabta (kitab+t+a)   'I wrote it/him'
    kitabla (kitab+l+a)   'he wrote to it/him'
    kitab*i*tla (kitab+t+l+a) 'I wrote to it/him'

b. Egyptian epenthesis

    katabu (katab+u)   'he wrote it/him'
    katabtu (katab+t+u)   'I wrote it/him'
    katablu (katab+l+u)   'he wrote to it/him'
    katabt*i*lu (katab+t+l+u) 'I wrote to it/him'

These rules of epenthesis are quite general and productive, leading to the attested errors shown below:

a. Iraqi error: chil*i*dren   'children'
b. Egyptian error: child*i*ren   'children'

The epenthesis rules, then, can be represented as below:

$$\text{a. Iraqi:} \qquad \emptyset \longrightarrow i \; / \; C\_CC$$
$$\text{b. Egyptian:} \qquad \emptyset \longrightarrow i \; / \; CC\_C$$

As written here—the proper formulation in a standard, segmentally based generative framework—these rules make no predictions concerning the treatment of initial consonant clusters in these dialects. But an alternative view of the rules as rules referring specifically to syllable structure will predict just the error patterns discussed in the preceding section.

The analysis of epenthesis I present here depends on the notion that epenthesis is actually a rule bringing underlying forms into conformity with restrictions on possible surface syllable structures: When a form contains consonants which cannot be analyzed as grouping into sequences of acceptable syllables, epenthesis applies to create permitted syllables. An analysis of epenthesis in these two dialects as syllable-based was first offered in Broselow (1980), and a reanalysis was presented in Selkirk (1980); the analysis presented here incorporates most of the suggestions made by Selkirk. In this analysis, a string is first analyzed into permissible syllables. As stated in the list below, both dialects allow only syllables consisting of consonant-vowel or consonant-vowel-consonant, except at the beginning or end of an utterance; Iraqi optionally allows syllables beginning in two consonants phrase-initially, while Egyptian allows syllables ending in two consonants phrase-finally:

a. Iraqi syllables
    CV
    CVC
    occasionally CCV(C) (only phrase-initially)
b. Egyptian syllables
    CV
    CVC
    CVCC (only phrase-finally)

Thus if we divide the forms below, for example, into the syllable types shown above, we find that some consonants cannot be included in any of the permitted syllables without creating a violation of the restriction that syllables within an utterance begin and end with no more than one consonant:

a. Iraqi
   (ki) (tab) t (la)
   (čil) d (ren)

b. Egyptian
   (ka) (tab) t (lu)
   (čil) d (ren)

To account for the position of the epenthetic vowel in these dialects, we need only assume that in Iraqi a vowel is inserted to the left of a "leftover" (nonsyllabified) consonant, creating a closed syllable, while in Egyptian a vowel is inserted to the right of the nonsyllabified consonant, creating an open syllable. These rules may be written as below:

a. Iraqi epenthesis
   C → iC, where C is not included in any syllable

b. Egyptian epenthesis
   C → Ci, where C is not included in any syllable

The dashes in the examples below show where this formulation of the rule predicts that vowels will appear in various words:

a. Iraqi
   (ki) (tab) (__t) (la)
   (čil) (__d) (ren)

b. Egyptian
   (ka) (tab) (t __) (lu)
   (čil) (d __) (ren)

In fact, this is just where vowels do appear in these words.[5] This analysis, then, is motivated on the grounds that it captures the similarities between the two types of epenthesis in Iraqi, epenthesis into three-consonant clusters and epenthesis affecting initial clusters when the option of creating a two-consonant cluster at the beginning of a phrase is not chosen.[6] The analysis also captures nicely the similarities between the Egyptian and the Iraqi epenthesis rules. These reasons would be sufficient to argue for adoption of the syllable-based analysis; it can therefore be seen as an additional and unexpected virtue of the analysis that it also makes just the right predictions concerning the appearance of epenthetic vowels in the pronunciation of words in the second language. The treatment of initial clusters in the speech of Egyptians follows automatically from the view of the first-language epenthesis rule as syllable-based; although no initial clusters arise in the first language, the statement of medial epenthesis given in the Iraqi and Egyptian epenthesis rules above automatically predicts that if initial clusters arose they would be treated as they in fact are treated by Egyptian foreign-language learners:

a. Iraqi: (＿ f) (loor)
b. Egyptian: (f ＿) (loor)

If the analysis of epenthesis as a syllable-based process is accepted, then, it allows us to see the differing treatment of second language clusters by speakers of these two Arabic dialects as a result of the transfer of first language rules. If epenthesis is a way of dealing with impermissible syllable structures which arise in the native language as a result of the concatenation of morphemes, it makes sense that the same process will be used to facilitate the pronunciation of second language forms which are defined as impermissible by the native language syllable structure constraints. It is to be expected as well that the rules which are transferred are the general and productive rules of epenthesis rather than morphologically restricted processes such as the rule affecting imperative forms in Egyptian Arabic. This rule, discussed above under Errors by Arabic Learners of English, affects only a small class of morphemes, while the rule of medial epenthesis applies to any cluster of three consonants, regardless of the morphological or syntactic environment; even clusters which arise from the juxtaposition of words undergo the rule:

Egyptian epenthesis
a. bint   'girl'
b. nabiiha   'intelligent'
c. bint ^{i} nabiiha 'an intelligent girl'

It is not surprising, then, that Egyptian speakers use the productive epenthesis rule which inserts a vowel after an unsyllabified consonant rather than the morphologically restricted rule for imperatives to impose the first language syllable structure restrictions on second language forms.[7] This pattern of transfer is consistent with the hypothesis presented in Broselow (1984) that syllable-conditioned phenomena are particularly susceptible to transfer, while morphologically conditioned processes are generally not transferred to the language learning situation.

Epenthesis in Four-Consonant Clusters

Thus far we have considered clusters of no more than three consonants, but in fact the epenthesis rules of Egyptian and Iraqi Arabic must be expanded to handle clusters of four consonants as well. The position of an epenthetic vowel in four-consonant clusters is the same in both dialects; the vowel appears between the first two consonants and the last two:

a. Iraqi
   kitabt*i*lha (kitab+t+l+ha)   'I wrote to her'

b. Egyptian
   katabt*i*lha (katab+t+l+ha)   'I wrote to her'

299

This can be handled quite simply if we assume that when two consonants are left unsyllabified after the string has been divided into permissible syllables, a vowel is inserted between the two consonants, creating a permitted CVC syllable:

a. (ki) (tab) (t-l) (ha)
b. (ka) (tab) (t-l) (ha)

This positioning of the vowel serves to bring the string into conformity with syllable structure restrictions with the minimum possible adjustment. This more complete formulation of the rule of epenthesis, it should be noted, makes predictions concerning the treatment of initial clusters of *three* consonants in English forms. Words such as *street,* for example, should be analyzed as below, with *rit* forming the only possible syllable and *st* left unsyllabified:

(s t) (rit)

Since the epenthesis rule inserts a vowel between two unsyllabified consonants, the expected pronunciation of this form for speakers of both dialects is [sitrit]. This is precisely the pronunciation found in the speech of Iraqi learners of English.

Iraqi errors
a. [sitrit]   'street'
b. [siblaš]   'splash'
c. [sikwer]   'square'

But Egyptian speakers show a different pattern:

a. [istirit]   'street'
b. [izbilaš]   'splash'
c. [izbilendid] 'splendid'

In these forms, a vowel is inserted both before the cluster and after the second consonant.[8] This appears to be a problem for the generalizing of epenthesis to three-consonant clusters, but in fact it is a consequence not of the fact that these clusters contain three consonants but rather of the fact that all three-consonant clusters in English begin in *s* followed by a stop consonant *p, t,* or *k.* And, as was mentioned earlier, there is one class of initial two-consonant clusters which do not conform to the usual Egyptian error pattern; English initial clusters consisting of *s* plus a stop are pronounced, as illustrated below, with epenthesis inserting a vowel *before* the initial cluster:

Egyptian errors
a. [istadi]   'study'
b. [izbasyal]   'special'
c. [iski]   'ski'

These clusters contrast, then, with clusters of *s* followed by consonants other than stops, which follow the regular pattern, as illustrated below:

Egyptian errors
a. [siwetar]   'sweater'
b. [silayd]   'slide'

Thus the exceptionality of the pronounciation of initial three-consonant clusters by Egyptians is another instance of the exceptionality of initial clusters consisting of *s* plus a stop consonant.

    There are two approaches one might take in accounting for the exceptionality of *s*-stop clusters in the pronunciation of English by Egyptian speakers. It might be argued, first, that this exceptionality is a result of interference from the morphology of the first language. Egyptian Arabic has a fairly common verbal prefix of the form *ista,* and clusters consisting of *s* plus *t* might conceivably be associated with this prefix, with other *s*-stop clusters treated similarly by some principle of analogy. It is likely, however, that the explanation should be sought in the realm of phonology rather than morphology, and has to do with other exceptional properties of *s*-stop clusters. These clusters are actually exceptional in English as well: They are the only syllable-initial clusters which violate the principle that segments within a syllable tend to be arranged in terms of their sonority, with the most sonorous element—the vowel—in the middle, and with segments decreasing in sonority as they approach the margins of the syllable. The relative sonority of various classes of sounds is indicated below:

The sonority hierarchy
stops - fricatives - nasals - liquids - glides - vowels
least sonorous   most sonorous

The principle that segments which are closer to syllable margins will be less sonorous than segments which are closer to the nucleus of a syllable predicts, correctly, that there will be no initial clusters in English consisting for example of *l* followed by *s* (a liquid followed by a fricative) or *m* followed by *p* (a nasal followed by a stop). The only English clusters which violate this principle are the *s*-stop clusters, which contain a fricative preceding a stop. Thus these clusters are exceptional in violating the sonority hierarchy. (Note that clusters of *s* plus *w,* a glide, or *l,* a liquid, do not violate the sonority hierarchy, and that those are treated like other two-consonant clusters by Egyptians, as in the pronunciation [siwetar] for *sweater* and [silayd] for *slide.*)

In addition to being the only two-consonant clusters which may contain an obstruent as their second member, s-stop clusters are exceptional also in being the only initial clusters which may be followed by a third consonant:

a. s-stop consonant
    spr, spl, spy: spring, splash, spew
    str: string
    skr, ski, sky, skw: scream, sclerosis, skewer,
        square

b. other clusters
    *blw
    *sly
    *psm
    etc.

Thus we can describe the possible syllable-initial consonant clusters in English by means of the following diagram:

Position 1	Position 2
consonant s+obstruent	sonorant (glide, liquid, nasal)

If, as Selkirk (1984) argues, we consider clusters of s plus obstruent to function at some level as a single consonant, we have an extremely simple description of the restrictions on clustering within English syllables. (Selkirk points out that these clusters pattern as single consonants in syllable-final position as well.) The functioning of these consonants as a single unit may also account, then, for the reluctance of the Egyptian learners of English to break these consonants apart by inserting a vowel between them, as the transfer hypothesis predicts they should. It is significant that language learners of other backgrounds show exactly the same pattern of errors: the tendency to insert a vowel between the first two consonants of an English cluster unless that cluster consists of s followed by an obstruent. Preliminary investigation reveals similar patterns in the errors of native speakers of Sinhalese (Samarajiwa and Abeysekera, 1964), Turkish (Swift, 1963, p. 19), Persian (Yarmohammadi, 1969), and Hindi (Russ Tomlin, personal communication). Thus, while the anomalous treatment of these clusters by language learners does not follow from the contrastive analysis hypothesis, it is interesting that the only case which cannot be explained as a result of transfer from the native language involves clusters which constitute a violation of what has been proposed as a universal principle: The arrangement of segments within a syllable according to their relative sonority is the unmarked or most common case in all languages. Errors of this sort—errors which are systematic but are not attributable to transfer from the first language—may perhaps arise in just those cases in which the target language forms violate certain universal principles.[9]

CONCLUSIONS

I have argued that language transfer does play a significant role in second language acquisition: certain systematic errors can be directly attributed to the use by language learners of a phonological rule in the production of second language forms. I have also speculated on the type of rule which can be transferred—morphologically restricted rules tend not to play a role in second language learning, while general rules such as epenthesis, which function to bring phonological forms into conformity with restrictions on possible phonetic syllable structures, are the ones most likely to be transferred. Finally, I have noted one sort of error which is not attributable to language transfer and have suggested that universal principles of phonological patterning also play a role in accounting for the errors of language learners. No doubt as our knowledge of linguistic universals increases and as our understanding of the competence of native speakers of various languages becomes more sophisticated, we will be better able to explain and to predict the errors made by learners of a second language.

NOTES

1. I have heard this pronunciation in various areas of the Midwest.

2. Voicing assimilation gives [ts] or [dz] here, either of which may end a syllable in English. Epenthesis is also sometimes used to "nativize" this form, giving (got) (bi) (za) (dE).

3. Since Arabic has no [p] phoneme, this sound is often pronounced as [b] by Arabic speakers.

4. Automatic insertion of a glottal stop before a syllable-initial vowel will give the phonetic form [?iktib].

5. Since vowel-initial syllables are prohibited in the phonetic forms of these dialects, independently motivated rules will apply after epenthesis to readjust the syllable structure in the Iraqi forms, giving (ka) (ta) (bit) (la) and (či) (lid) (ren).

6. Iraqi also has a rule inserting a vowel between two word-final consonants which is of course a manifestation of exactly the same phenomenon. I have omitted discussion of this aspect of epenthesis because of space limitations, but the interested reader is referred to Selkirk's paper.

7. Further evidence that initial epenthesis is not a rule functioning, like the general epenthesis rule, just to bring forms into conformity with restrictions on syllable structure is that the rule exists even in dialects in which initial clusters are permitted; thus Gulf Arabic has *druus* "lessons" but *?idrus* "study!" My analysis differs crucially on this point from that of Selkirk, whose analysis would predict forms such as *ifloor* for Egyptian speakers.

8. Lehn and Slager (1959) say that forms like this are pronounced CiCCV, as I would predict, but I haven't found this sort of pronunciation.

9. See Tarone (1980) for discussion of the relationship between errors and linguistic universals.

REFERENCES

Broselow, E. 1980. Syllable structure in two Arabic dialects. *Studies in the Linguistic Sciences, 10,* 2, 13–24.

Broselow, E. 1984. An investigation of transfer in second language phonology. *IRAL, 22,* 253–269. (Also this volume.)

Lehn, W., and W. Slager. 1959. A contrastive study of Egyptian Arabic and American English: the segmental phonemes. *Language Learning, 2,* 23–33.

Samarajiwa, C., and R. M. Abeysekera. 1964. Some pronunciation difficulties of Sinhalese learners of English as a foreign language. *Language Learning 14,* 45–50.

Selkirk, E. 1980. Epenthesis and degenerate syllables in Cairene Arabic. *MIT Working Papers in Linguistics:* Cambridge, MA.

Selkirk, E. 1984. *Phonology and Syntax: The Relation Between Sound and Structure.* Cambridge, MA: MIT Press.

Swift, L.B. 1963. *A Reference Grammar of Modern Turkish.* vol. 19, Uralic and Altaic Series. Indiana University Publications.

Tarone, E. 1980. Some influences of the syllable structure of interlanguage phonology. *IRAL, 18,* 139–152. (Also this volume.)

Yarmohammadi, L. 1969. English consonants and learning problems for Iranians: a contrastive sketch. *TESOL Quarterly, 3,* 231–236.

18

FARSI SPEAKERS AND THE INITIAL CONSONANT CLUSTER IN ENGLISH*

Simin Karimi

INTRODUCTION

In the following project I have examined the strategy Farsi speakers employ to overcome the difficulty of pronouncing the initial consonant clusters in English. I have arrived at the conclusion that the strategy employed by Farsi speakers cannot be traced to their native language, and hence cannot be considered as a case of language interference.

Farsi syllable structure differs in many points from that in English. One of these differences is the initial cluster in English that doesn't appear in Modern Farsi.[1] The Contrastive Analysis Hypothesis would predict that the Farsi speaker would have difficulty in producing the initial cluster. It makes no prediction, however, as to what strategy would be employed when Farsi speakers attempt initial clusters in English.

*I would like to express my gratitude to Georgette Ioup (University of New Orleans) and Ellen Broselow (State University of New York), who read carefully the first version of this paper, pointed out many weaknesses, and offered helpful suggestions. I am also indebted to Steven Weinberger and Dawn Bates for their helpful comments on the earlier version of this paper.

Ellen Broselow (1983) states that "our inability to predict the occurrence and nature of many errors may well stem from inadequacies in our understanding of native speakers' competence. . . ." By analyzing the syllable structure of Egyptian Arabic, she indicates that the Egyptian speaker's strategy in handling the problem of initial consonant clusters in English can be considered as interference of the native language into their interlanguage (IL); in Egyptian Arabic a vowel is inserted to the right of the nonsyllabified consonant creating a new syllable. I will formulate this rule as in Rule 1 below, which is, according to Broselow, a productive epenthesis rule in Egyptian Arabic.:

$$\text{Rule 1} \quad \emptyset \longrightarrow \begin{bmatrix} -\text{bk} \\ +\text{hi} \end{bmatrix} / \underset{x}{\overset{C}{|}} \underline{\hspace{2cm}}$$

Rule 1 applies to the data in the list below:

(ka)   (tab)   t   (lu)
(čil)   d   (ren)

They result in the following surface forms:

ka   tab   ti   lu   'I wrote to it/him'
čil   di   ren   'children'

Broselow goes on to say that the exceptionality of forms such as

[istadi], [istop], or [iski]

is due to the fact that the consonant clusters with initial /s/ followed by a stop violate the universal sonority hierarchy. Therefore, the Egyptian epenthesis rule in this case is the sort of unmarked epenthesis provided by universal grammar.

By analyzing the syllable structure of Farsi and by comparing it to English and Egyptian syllable structure, I have tried to examine whether the same conclusion reached by Broselow holds for Farsi speakers as well; that is, if the strategy used by the Farsi speaker can also be traced to their native language.

METHOD

Informants

I had four Farsi speakers as my subjects; three females and a male. All of them had had English for from three to six years at school before coming to the United States. Subjects were similar in that they were all educated people: Subject A, besides having a Ph.D. in Literature from Iran, has a master's degree in Business Education from one of the universities in America. Subjects B and C each have an M.S. in Civil Engineering and Business Administration, respectively, from universities in this country. The last informant is a college student. The age of my informants when they moved to the United States differs considerably. Table 18.1 indicates the above information about my subjects.

Procedure

Data were gathered through three different procedures.

(i) I chose two different passages out of a book written for ESL classes. One of these passages was on women's liberation and the other one was on smoking. I added some words with initial clusters and asked the above-mentioned Farsi speakers to read them and to discuss them with an American woman. I told them that I was looking for different opinions on women's liberation and on smoking, so they were not aware of the data I was attempting to elicit. Finally, I gave them a list of words with initial clusters to read. At this point they knew, of course, what was going on, even though they still didn't know what specific kind of structures I was examining. I taped the discussion and the readings, and my informants were aware of the taping.

(ii) I gave another reading test, including words and phrases crucial to my analysis to two informants. The subjects for this activity were Informant A from my previous test and an eighteen-year-old boy who is a college student and has been in the United States for five years.

(iii) The rest of my data were gathered from other discussions and previous experience.

Results

The data from the word list gave the fewest number of errors (by "error" I mean the insertion of a vowel to avoid the initial consonant cluster). The paragraph reading indicated more errors, while the discussion, which was a controversial one, revealed the most errors. All my subjects used the same method in order to avoid the initial consonant cluster in English—that is, the errors revealed the same kind of strategy employed by all of them.

TABLE 18.1 Subject Characteristics

Informant	Age	Sex	Formal education	Age when moved to USA
A	55	F	Ph.D.	48
B	34	M	M.S.	24
C	27	F	M.S.	17
D	19	F	College Student	12

SYLLABLE STRUCTURE OF FARSI[2]

The structure of the syllable in Farsi could be illustrated as follows:

(C) V (C (C))

There is, however, some disagreement on this structure since some Farsi phonologists (Samareh, 1977, among others) claim that the obligatory syllable structure is CV, since every initial vowel is preceded by an invisible glottal stop.

Examples for different syllable structures in Farsi are:

V	= u	(or ?u)	'he, she'
CV	= bâ		'with'
VC	= ân		'that'
CVC	= sar		'head'
CVCC	= râst		'right'

Farsi, similar to English, maximizes the onset, with the maximum number of onset consonants being one consonant in Farsi. Syllabification, based on Kahn's rules,[3] will be illustrated as in Figure 18.1.

Farsi lacks structures at the surface containing 3-consonant clusters (CCC); the following rule applies in normal speech:

$$\text{Rule 2} \quad C \longrightarrow \emptyset \ / \ C \underline{\hspace{2cm}} C^4$$

Examples:

xâst # ke	→ xâs ke	'wanted that'
sabr # kon	→ sab kon	'be patient'
fekr # kon	→ fekkon	'think do = think'
češm + dâšt	→ češ dâšt	'expectation'
roft + gar	→ rof gar	'someone who cleans the streets'

Farsi speakers use, therefore, consonant deletion in order to avoid nonpermissible clusters in the language.[5]

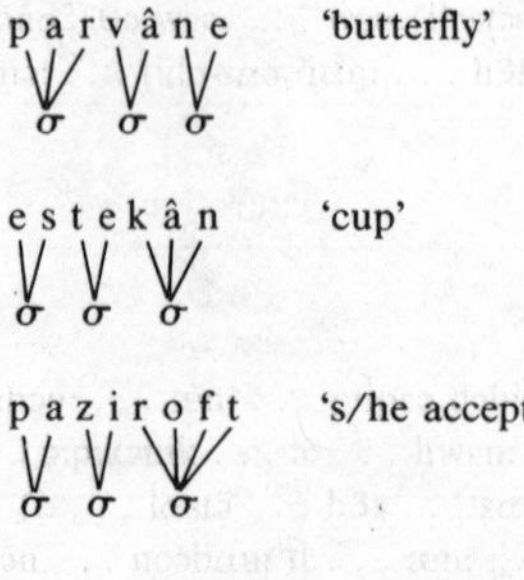

Figure 18.1

Kahn's "normal speech rules"[6] don't apply in Farsi, since there is no ambisyllabic segment in this language. His "connected speech" rule, however, applies in a different way, as shown below:

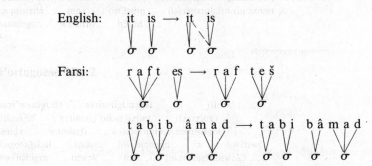

English: it is → it is

Farsi: r a f t es → r a f t e š

t a b i b â m a d → t a b i b â m a d

These forms, however, can be derived from the principle that Farsi maximizes onsets.[7]

FARSI SPEAKERS' SOLUTION TO THE PROBLEM OF CONSONANT CLUSTERS IN ENGLISH

Initial Cluster

The Farsi speaker handles the difficulty of initial clusters in three different ways:
In the case of # $C_1 C_2$, where $C_1 \neq S$, the following epenthesis rule applies:

$$\text{Rule 3} \quad \emptyset \rightarrow V \ / \ C \underset{x}{\rule{1.5cm}{0.4pt}} C$$

where x indicates that the consonant is not syllabified—that is, the consonant doesn't belong to any syllable.

Examples:

stop + liquid
proved → p[u]roved
progressive → p[o]rogressive
drink → d[i]rink

fricative + liquid
Fred → F[e]red
three → th[i]ree

The vowel insertion rule is not necessarily a copying rule:

proud → p[e]roud
plastic → p[e]lastic

309

In the case of # SC the following epenthesis rule applies:

$$\text{Rule 4} \quad \emptyset \longrightarrow \begin{bmatrix} + \text{ syll} \\ - \text{ high} \\ - \text{ low} \\ - \text{ back} \end{bmatrix} \bigg/ \underline{\hspace{2cm}} \begin{array}{cc} S & C \\ | & | \\ x & \sigma \end{array}$$

where S includes both /s/ and /š/.

Examples:

s + stop
struggle $\longrightarrow$ [e]struggle
statistic $\longrightarrow$ [e]statistic

The same rule applies when the Farsi speaker tries to handle the following initial consonant clusters in German:

štrasse $\longrightarrow$ [e]šterasse 'street'
špigel $\longrightarrow$ [e]špigel 'mirror'

Furthermore, the rule is not different for initial /s/ followed by a liquid or nasal:

slide $\longrightarrow$ [e]slide
snow $\longrightarrow$ [e]snow
smoke $\longrightarrow$ [e]smoke
sleep $\longrightarrow$ [e]sleep

In the case of $\#SC_1C_2$, Rules 3 and 4 apply:

street $\xrightarrow{\text{R4}}$ [e]street $\xrightarrow{\text{R3}}$ est[i]reet

spring $\xrightarrow{\text{R4}}$ [e]spring $\xrightarrow{\text{R3}}$ esp[i]ring

As Rule 4 indicates, Farsi speakers treat the initial SC in a manner different from the way they do other kinds of initial clusters. It has to be mentioned, though, that Farsi allows initial [s], as the following examples reveal:

sirus 'a name'
setâre 'star'
sabad 'basket'
surâx 'hole'
sorx 'red'
sâde 'simple'

The application of Rule 3 to initial SC, therefore, wouldn't violate the syllable structure of the NL of Farsi speakers.

In the case of # SG, where the initial /s/ is followed by a glide, Rules 5 and 6 will apply:

Rule 5 $\begin{bmatrix} - \text{cons} \\ - \text{syll} \end{bmatrix} \longrightarrow [+ \text{syll}] \;/\; \# \; S \; \underline{\hspace{2cm}}$

Rule 6 $\emptyset \longrightarrow \begin{Bmatrix} ? \\ y \end{Bmatrix} \;/\; V \; \underline{\hspace{1.5cm}} \; V$

Examples:

sweet $\longrightarrow$ s u ? i t   or   s u y i t

sweat $\longrightarrow$ s u ? e t

swim $\longrightarrow$ s u ? i m   or   s u y i m

Rule 5 seems to be a rule of the IL, while Rule 6 is a productive rule in Farsi; vowel clustering is not permitted in Farsi. Therefore, glides or glottal stops will be inserted in order to avoid the structure VV (sequences of two vowels).

Examples:

bačče # e $\longrightarrow$ bačče y e   "child of"

xâne # e $\longrightarrow$ xâne y e   "house of"

In the case of syllables where a nasal or liquid is the nucleus of the syllable, the Rule 7 applies:

Rule 7 $\emptyset \longrightarrow \begin{bmatrix} + \text{syll} \\ - \text{back} \\ - \text{high} \\ - \text{low} \end{bmatrix} \Big/ \; C \; \underline{\hspace{2cm}} \; \begin{bmatrix} + \text{cons} \\ + \text{son} \end{bmatrix}$

people $\longrightarrow$ [p^{h}ip^{h}el]

trouble $\longrightarrow$ [t^{h}erabel]

DIFFERENCES BETWEEN FARSI AND EGYPTIAN STRATEGIES

The following table, Table 18.2, summarizes the differences between Farsi and Egyptian strategies of cluster reduction. In the case of Egyptian Arabic, numbers 1–4 on Table 18.2 include rules of the interlanguage (IL). That is, these rules belong to the English grammar of the Egyptian speaker, while number 5 consists of a rule belonging to the grammar of her native language. In the case of Farsi, however, all epenthesis rules belong to IL (the English grammar of Farsi speakers), and only the Consonant Deletion Rule (CDR) in 4 and 5 is a productive rule of NL. As the table shows, all Egyptian IL rules (except for the rule in number 2) can be considered instances of the NL rule in number 5, while this doesn't hold for the epenthesis rule of Farsi speakers.

TABLE 18.2 Egyptian and Farsi Strategies of Cluster Reduction

		Egyptian	Farsi
1	# C_1C_2, if $C_1 \neq S$	$\emptyset \rightarrow V / C—C$ Fred → F[i]red floor → f[i]loor	$\emptyset \rightarrow V / C—C$ (The same rule as Egyptian) Fred → F[e]red floor → f[e]loor
2	# C_1C_2, if $C_1 = S$ and $C_2 =$ stop	$\emptyset \rightarrow V / —CC$ street → [i]stireet study → [i]study	$\emptyset \rightarrow V / —CC$ (The same rule as Egyptian) street → [e]stireet study → [e]study
3	# C_1C_2, if $C_1 = S$ and $C_2 =$ nasal or liquid	$\emptyset \rightarrow V / C—C$ slide → s[i]lide	$\emptyset \rightarrow V / —CC$ slide → [e]slide
4	CCC	$\emptyset \rightarrow V / CC—C$ children → child[i]ren	$\emptyset \rightarrow V / CC—C^8$ children → child[e]ren or $C \rightarrow \emptyset / C—C$ česm dâšt → češdâšt children → chilren
5	CC CC	$\emptyset \rightarrow V / CC—CC$ (ka) (tab) t l (ha) → ka tab til ha	$C \rightarrow \emptyset / C—C$ $\emptyset \rightarrow V / C—C$ esmart geranmother

Number 5 in Table 18.2 needs some explanations considering the rules of Farsi speakers:

```
                smart  grandmother
1. C Deletion                Ø
2. Epenthesis   e            e
                esmart geranmother
```

The Consonant Deletion Rule (CDR), an NL rule of Farsi speakers, deletes /d/ in "grandmother" to avoid a nonpermissible consonant cluster. The epenthesis rules (rules included in numbers 1–5 of the chart) insert vowels preceding the initial /s/ of "smart" and following /g/ of "grandmother" to avoid initial consonant clusters (order-relevant, since otherwise the epenthesis rule would block the CDR from applying in examples such as "first snow".

Furthermore, the Farsi rule of normal speech, which syllabifies the last consonant of the word (or morpheme) with the initial vowel of the next word, doesn't apply in the IL of my informants, as shown in Figure 18.2.

/s/ in "first" is not deleted, since it is preceded by /r/ (see note 4). /t/ is deleted, since it is followed by a consonant (Rule 2) before the vowel insertion.

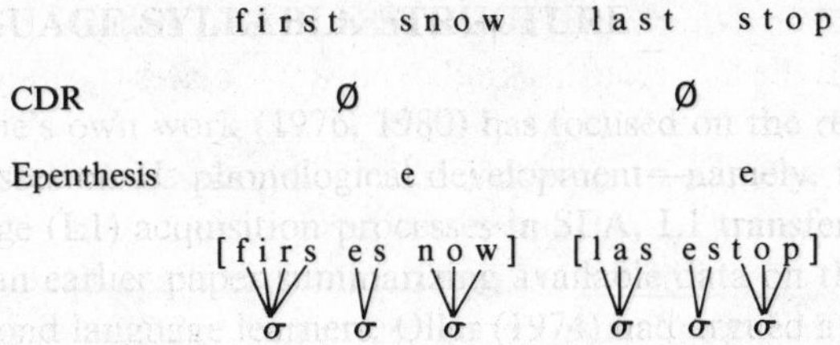

first   snow   last   stop

CDR   Ø   Ø

Epenthesis   e   e

[f i r s e s n o w]   [l a s e s t o p]
  σ   σ   σ   σ   σ   σ

Figure 18.2

In neither case is the last consonant of the first word resyllabified with the next vowel (which is the inserted vowel). If we had resyllabification, we would have:

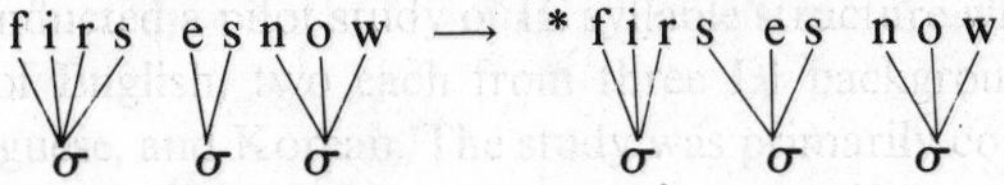

f i r s e s n o w → *f i r s e s n o w
  σ   σ   σ   σ   σ   σ

This would be similar to the following example, which has undergone the resyllabification rule in the native language:

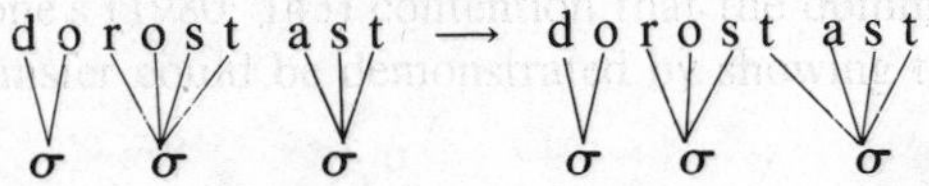

d o r o s t a s t → d o r o s t a s t
  σ   σ   σ   σ   σ   σ

The implications of this fact are: (a) that the resyllabification rule of NL doesn't hold in the corresponding IL, and (b) that the syllabification rule applies before CDR and the epenthesis rule, which violates the transparency of the syllabification rule.[9]

DISCUSSION

Broselow's hypothesis (1983) indicates that ". . . language transfer plays a significant role in the acquisition of a second language." She also states that the nontransferred rules, such as the Egyptian epenthesis rule in her discussion, can be considered as the sort of unmarked rules provided by the universal grammar. My data, however, contradicts her hypothesis in two ways:

Epenthesis is not a rule in Modern Farsi; L1 Farsi speakers use consonant deletion rather than the vowel insertion rule in order to avoid impermissible consonant clusters. Therefore, epenthesis cannot be considered as being transferred from the native language into the target language. The only case where L1 Farsi speakers use epenthesis is in the case of borrowed elements:

class   → [k e l â s]
statistic → [e s t a t i s t i c]
ski   → [e s k i]

Broselow claims that vowel insertion before S + stop clusters by Egyptian speakers is due to the fact that this kind of cluster violates the universal sonority hierarchy, which states as follows (Figure 18.3):

"Stop" violates the sonority hierarchy, whereas "snow" doesn't, because /t/ is not very sonorant; in particular, it is less sonorant than /s/, but in "stop" it appears in a position which is more sonorant than the position of /s/. On the other hand, /n/ in "snow" is more sonorant than /s/. Therefore, the sonority hierarchy is not violated in this case. Farsi speakers, however, use the same pattern for both structures.

It is interesting to mention that all initial consonant clusters that existed in Middle Farsi had been broken up by an epenthesis rule before the time of Modern Farsi. This holds also for clusters starting with /s/ and /š/:

	Mid. F		Mod. F	
	g r i y e n d	→	g e r y a n d	'(they) cry'
	x r o s	→	x u r u s	'rooster'
	f r o : d	→	f o r u d	'down'
Also:				
	s t a d	→	s e t a d	'took'
	s p u r d a n	→	s e p o r d a n	'give'
	š k a s t	→	š e k a s t	'broke'
	s r i š k	→	s e r i š k	'drop'
	š m â h	→	š o m â	'you'

However, since all Farsi speakers use the same strategy in handling the initial cluster, there might be some undiscovered relation between this strategy and the native language.[10] On the other hand, there are speakers of other languages who handle this in the same way as Farsi speakers do. Spanish speakers insert a vowel before /s/: [e]school, [e]sport. That is, the vowel insertion rule inserts a vowel before the initial /s/, and it is indifferent to the quality of the following consonant. There might be the possibility that the initial closed syllable with final /s/ ([estop], [esnow]) is less marked than those with final stops or fricatives other than /s/ ([*eproud], [*efred]); that is, V/s/ is less marked than $V \begin{Bmatrix} \text{stop} \\ \text{fricative, other than } /s/ \end{Bmatrix}$. It is interesting to note that Farsi speakers overcome comparatively soon the initial clusters that don't start with /s/, whereas even very advanced speakers tend to insert a vowel before /s/ in normal speech.

CONCLUSION

The strategy employed by Farsi speakers as well as the treatment of the initial /s/ cannot be traced to their native language, as shown by various examples.

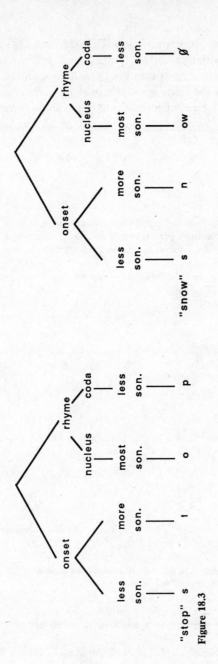

Figure 18.3

315

On the other hand, all Farsi speakers use the same strategy in avoiding the initial consonant cluster, and, in addition, they all use a different strategy in handling initial /s/. These facts suggest that the hypothesis mentioned above, including the assumption that the Farsi speaker's strategy is an instance of interference from her NL, calls for better insight into the syllable structure of Farsi, more careful research on the exceptionality of /s/, and better understanding of the structure of IL in general.

NOTES

1. Old and Middle Farsi had initial consonant clusters.

2. As far as I know, there is no reference on syllable structure of Farsi in the framework of Generative Phonology. I have tried to analyze Farsi syllable structure on the basis of Kahn's model (1976).

3. Kahn's first and second syllabification rules are as follows:

Rule I: $[+ \text{syll}] \longrightarrow [+ \text{syll}]$

Rule II:

(a) $C_1 \ldots C_n \, V \longrightarrow C_1 \ldots C_i C_{i+1} \ldots C_n \, V$

where $C_i + 1 \ldots C_n$ is a member of the set of permissible initial clusters but $C_i C_{i+1} \ldots C_n$ is not.

(b) $V \, C_1 \ldots C_n \longrightarrow V \, C_1 \ldots C_i \, C_{i+1} \ldots C_n$

where $C_1 \ldots C_i$ is a member of the set of permissible final clusters but $C_1 \ldots C_i C_{i+1}$ is not.

4. There is an exception to this rule: if the first consonant is /r/, then the second consonant will not be deleted; that is, Rule 1 will apply vacuously:

šarm kon	$\longrightarrow$ šarm kon	'be ashamed'
xarj kard	$\longrightarrow$ xarj kard	'spend money'

5. It must be mentioned that [st] in [xâst], [br] in [sabr], [šm] in [čašm], [ft] in [roft], and [kr] in [fekr] are possible final clusters in Farsi as the following examples indicate:

mâst 'yogurt'; hast 'is'; kebr 'haughtiness'; jabr 'algebra'; pašm 'wool'; xašm 'anger'; joft 'pair'; moft 'parasitic'; makr 'deceit'; šokr 'thanks'

6. Kahn's III, IV, and V syllabification rules are as follows:

Rule III (normal speech only)

$$\text{in } [-\text{cons}]\ C\ C_0 \begin{bmatrix} V \\ -\text{stress} \end{bmatrix} \quad \text{associate C and } s_1$$

(with association lines to s_1 and s_2)

Rule IV (normal speech only)

$$\text{in } C\ C_0 \begin{bmatrix} V \\ -\text{stress} \end{bmatrix} \quad \text{associate C and } s_2$$

(with association lines to s_1 and s_2)

Rule V (connected speech only)

$$\text{in } C\ V \text{ associate C and } s$$

(with association lines to s)

Rule V applies across words while the domain of the other rules is only the word.

7. This was pointed out to me by Dawn Bates.

8. Three of my informants pronounced "children" as [čilderen], with vowel insertion. The pronunciation of the last informant, similar to my own pronunciation, was [čil ren], with consonant deletion. Reason: If the Farsi speaker interprets this word as one morpheme, she will break up the consonant cluster by a vowel:

$$\text{č i l d r e n} \longrightarrow \text{č i l d e r e n}$$
$$\sigma \quad x \quad \sigma \qquad\qquad \sigma \quad \sigma \quad \sigma$$

Rule 3 has applied in this case.
If she interprets it as two morphemes, then she will delete the second consonant:

$$\text{c i l d + r e n}$$
$$\downarrow$$
$$\emptyset$$

Rule 2 has applied in this case.

9. The transparency of the syllabification rule requires that this rule follow all other rules such as the Epenthesis and Consonant Deletion Rule.

10. This was pointed out by Professor Georgette Ioup. I agree with her, even though I have not found any explanation to support this assumption.

REFERENCES

Broselow, E. 1983. Non-Obvious Transfer: On Predicting Epenthesis Errors. In S. Gass and L. Selinker (Eds.), *Language Transfer in Language Learning*. Rowley, MA: Newbury House. (Also this volume.)

Hyman, L.M. 1975. *Phonology, Theory and Analysis.* NY: Holt, Rinehart and Winston.

Kahn, D. 1976. *Syllable-Based Generalization in English.* Indiana University Linguistics Club.

Lado, R. 1957. *Linguistics Across Cultures.* Ann Arbor: The University of Michigan Press.

Samareh, Y. 1977. *The Arrangement of Segmental Phonemes in Farsi.* Tehran, Iran: Tehran University Press.

Part Five

SUPRASEGMENTALS

Research on the acquisition of suprasegmentals is a recent development in studies of L2 phonology. Part Five contains three articles that have begun to define the nature of this process.

The article by Neufeld deals with adult acquisition of prosodic contours in a language whose structure is completely unknown to the learner. Neufeld investigates whether adults can acquire a native-like accent in a new language without reference to its grammatical structure or lexical meaning. English speaking subjects are given unlimited exposure to a short passage of either Japanese or Chinese that they are asked to master phonologically. When their final productions are evaluated by native speakers, they are judged to be native-like. This article has implications for an optimal time frame for the introduction of the new phonological system into a beginning language course.

Ioup and Tansomboon compare the acquisition of tone by children and adults learning Thai. They determine that tone is one of the first aspects of the target grammar to be mastered by children, regardless of whether Thai is their first or second language, and one of the last to be mastered by adults, having eluded even the most proficient learners. They propose that the dichotomy is due to different cognitive processing strategies employed by children and adults

319

and that only the child's approach is amenable to the complete acquisition of a new intonation system.

The article by Broselow, Hurtig, and Ringen asks whether transfer at the phonological level is confined to the production of the target language—that is, if it is only the learner's motor skills that cannot be adapted to the new language. They would like to determine the role of the native language in the perception of the target phonology. Their investigation focuses on the second language acquisition of tone. Subjects are adult native speakers of English acquiring Mandarin Chinese. Results show that English speakers transfer their knowledge of the native language phrasal intonation system to their perception of lexical tone in the target language. The authors conclude that transfer affects the learner's perception as well as production of the target phonological system.

19

ON THE ACQUISITION OF PROSODIC AND ARTICULATORY FEATURES IN ADULT LANGUAGE LEARNING

Gerald G. Neufeld

This paper reports on a study in which twenty young adults were tested for their ability to accurately reproduce the articulatory and prosodic features of three non-Indo-European languages in which they had received instruction. The first of two basic goals of this research was to partially test, at the purely phonetic level, the "critical period for language learning" hypothesis (Lenneberg, 1967). The second aim was to see if students could acquire the linguistic features associated with "native-like accent" with no reference to grammar or lexical meaning. Both questions are considered, with special attention to theoretical problems, and to what the results of our study imply for future research.

Prior to the late fifties, many specialists in foreign language learning considered modern language aptitude as a normally distributed variable (Kaulfers, 1930; Harding, 1958; Salomon, 1954). The exhaustive efforts of Carroll and Pimsleur to quantify this ability, and to provide a reliable measure for predicting success in the classroom, clearly reflect this position. (Carroll, 1958; Pimsleur, Stockwell, and Comfrey, 1962). There were others, of course, who held that learning of any kind was less a question of talent than it was a problem of drive and reinforcement contingencies. (Lane, 1964; Skinner 1968a, 1968b). Though some work in language aptitude continued, interest in this area dropped off rapidly because of two new and compelling hypotheses. While entirely different in origin and scope Chomsky's "language acquisition device" and Penfield's concept of "cerebral dominance" were compatible in that they sought to explain language learning in terms of "nature," as opposed to "nurture" (Chomsky, 1957; Penfield, 1959; Penfield, 1965). Lenneberg (1967) relates the two hypotheses when he argues convincingly for a "critical period" in language learning; he claims that species specific innate linguistic capacity weakens progressively with the onset of puberty. He attributes this phenomenon to "cerebral dominance" or lateralization of the speech centres in the brain (Scovel, 1969).

Although a number of interesting studies point to maturational constraints as the explanation for the adult's inability to match the child in learning another language, others suggest that purely biological factors may not suffice to account for adult performance (Asher and Garcia, 1969; Seliger, Krashen & Ladefoged, 1975). Neufeld maintains that the hypothesis does not clarify what happens with adults who do manage to achieve nativelike proficiency (Neufeld, 1974 and 1978). He also rejects as an oversimplification Selinker's claim that the "5 percent" who are successful employ a different set of psycholinguistic strategies than the remaining 95 percent (Selinker, 1972). At a more practical level, Burstall found that students in England who had begun French early in school did not fare significantly better than older students who started French in secondary school (Burstall, 1975). Finally, the remarkable progress of Genie, who began her first language as an adolescent, casts further doubt on the validity of the "critical period" hypothesis (Curtiss et al, 1974; Fromkin et al, 1974).

Since there is adequate evidence that at least some adults can attain nativelike proficiency in another language, it seems reasonable to approach the question of learning ability from a somewhat more positive point of view. It is conceivable that the differences between adults and children may not lie in innate ability, but rather in their psychological disposition toward the target language and culture. There may also be some disparity between the two age groups with respect to language learning strategies (Gardner, 1975; Dumas, Selinker & Swain, 1973).

The research described in the present paper does not consider the "equal ability" hypothesis in its entirety. Indeed, it seemed to the author that this complex question was not amenable to a comprehensive study with a conventional control-experimental design. In addition to the numerous contingent variables at non-linguistic levels, a large-scale study would require a means by which the experimenter could accurately measure how much attention each student devoted to learning vocabulary, phonological and syntactic rules, prosody, and articulatory habits.

Furthermore, a true test of the hypothesis would necessarily involve both children and adults in carefully controlled language learning situations, a formidable undertaking at best. To reduce the variables to manageable proportions, a less ambitious "micro" design was used, where the focus was upon exclusively phonetic material. If adult students' performance could be shown to be close to native articulation and intonation, the design could later be expanded to include rule-governed levels as well as lexical meaning.

The underlying assumption of the project was that adults retain the potential for acquiring nativelike proficiency in a new language (Neufeld, 1975). The problem was how to access this potential and how to sufficiently motivate our students to exploit it. None of the well-known language teaching techniques seemed appropriate since their orientation and sequencing of new material were not compatible with our criteria.

Because of our special interest in the acquisition of phonetic skills, we needed an approach which would highlight articulatory and prosodic features. Another concern was that our students be thoroughly introduced or sensitized to the sound patterns of the target language *before* attempting to reproduce them (Postovsky, 1974). We also had to be sure that none of the participants in our study enjoyed a linguistic advantage because of previous knowledge or exposure to the target language. A more complex problem was whether we could successfully teach university students to produce native-like utterances without ever telling them the meanings of the words they used and without ever presenting grammatical cues. How long could we expect to maintain their interest and motivation when the language learning situation was contrived to this extent?

PROCEDURES

One eighteen-hour program for individualized instruction was videotaped for Chinese, another for Japanese, and a third for Eskimo. We chose three non-Indo-European languages in order to reduce the chance that subjects (Ss) would have to be rejected because of prior contact with the languages. The format for each program was identical. The one-hour lessons were divided into two twenty-five-minute segments with a ten-minute break after the first segment. All instructions were in English and recorded by a native speaker. The remaining material was in the target language and read by a native speaker of that language. (More specific details about the teaching materials prepared for the study are available from the author.) As can be seen in the schedule below, the first three lessons required no audible production whatsoever. By delaying oral production, we hoped to minimize contamination of the "acoustic image imprint" (Neufeld, 1977). We intended, at first, to systematize the presentation of new sounds by commencing with phonemes which approximated the sound patterns of English. While feasible for Japanese, the task proved all but impossible for Chinese and Eskimo. In retrospect, such sequencing would have unnecessarily complicated an already highly artificial language learning situation. The procedure we finally adopted was to tabulate the relative frequency of specific phonemes in differing linguistic environments as they occurred in the spontaneous speech of each of our three instructors and to observe these frequencies when drafting the core material. (Samples of one thousand running words each were used for this purpose.)

Phase one Lessons 1–3 contained variations of 100 stock phrases specially prepared for the program. Utterances ranged in length from one to eight syllables. In the instructions which preceded each twenty-five-minute segment, the need to listen carefully was emphasized. Ss were actively discouraged from orally producing what they heard by means which will be discussed later. Phase One constituted what we referred to as the "initial imprinting stage."

Phase two While the first three lessons required only attentive listening, Phase Two (Lessons 4–12) involved three types of exercises in which non-verbal responses were elicited. The first was designed to sensitize Ss to the intonational contours of the target language. In the first segment of Lesson 4, an utterance was followed by a visual display of a piece of chalk which traced a rising and falling line, corresponding to the general rise and fall of intonation in the statement. This line intersected a horizontal centre line which represented the mid-point in the range. Figure 1 illustrates the procedure, first with the Chinese word "ma," which has a rising then falling pitch, and second, with the Japanese phrase "arigato gozaimas." In the remaining five segments, Ss were required to trace new utterances in the manner already described.

The second exercise, introduced in Lesson 7, emphasized the cadence, or rhythmic contours, of the language. Broken lines varying in length were traced by S, to correspond to *perceived* stress and duration of utterances of four to ten syllables. Figure 19.2 shows a typical pattern traced by Ss for many of the utterances in Eskimo.

Lessons 7–9 consisted of practice on both cadential and intonational contours, along with a few simple listening passages.

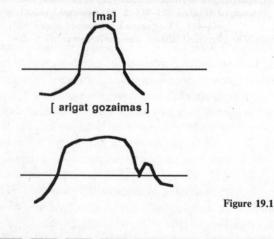

[ma]

[arigat gozaimas]

Figure 19.1

Figure 19.2

The third exercise in Phase Two was a conventional auditory discrimination procedure where Ss were asked to distinguish between phonemes in minimal pair contexts. Periodic reviews of earlier material were also included in these lessons (10–12).

Phase three The last six lessons were divided into two groups. Beginning with Lesson 13, Ss heard material which they imitated at a devoiced or whisper level. Utterances were increased in length with each lesson. Short review exercises covering previous material were also included. Lessons 16–18 called for oral imitation of model utterances with instructions for self-correction. As in earlier phases, these utterances increased in length as lessons progressed.

Subjects

We contacted more than 100 English-speaking students at the University of Ottawa who had participated in several of our earlier studies; these studies were not related in any way to this project. Because of the fifty-four hours required of Ss to complete the three language programs, only forty agreed to take part. To obtain a more or less representative sample of the student population, we selected twenty-five of the forty, based upon their performance on several measures used in previous research. We had data for the *Otis* test of verbal intelligence (form B), the *Minnesota Multiprofile Personality Inventory,* the *Modern Language Aptitude Test* of Carroll and Sapon, and Pimsleur's *Language Aptitude Battery.* Twenty completed the series, twelve females and eight males, ranging in age from nineteen to twenty-two years. All were told that they had been specially chosen because of their unusually high scores on the language aptitude tests which we had administered the year before. Although many expressed surprise at being considered excellent language learning prospects, they appeared willing to accept our word. Our intent was to heighten their interest, if possible, and to increase their desire to learn; in actual fact, the aptitude scores indicated a wide range of ability rather than overall high potential. When compared with published norms, our group did score slightly higher than average university students.

Method

The project assistant contacted each of our twenty-five Ss to schedule the four weekly sessions. They were told that they were to be involved in a novel experiment intended to prove that adults can achieve nativelike proficiency in another language, despite prevailing opinion to the contrary. The assistant informed them that they would receive full reports of the goals and results of the study upon the completion of the project. We considered this important since many of the students who had served as Ss in our previous work had contacted us with enthusiastic comments or further questions after reading accounts of the studies in which they had taken part. No other information was given to Ss at this time, except to say that all pertinent details would be covered in the first lesson. Twelve students were scheduled for the September trimester and the remaining thirteen for the January to April session. Ss were instructed individually.

Ss were seated at a small console where they were given a pair of close-fitting headphones which were to be used for each lesson. Attached to these headphones was a sensitive and inconspicuous microphone positioned immediately in front of S's mouth. Before beginning the videotaped program, the project assistant carefully adjusted the microphone amplifier, which activated a buzzer whenever any extraneous sound was detected. A different level was necessary for each S because of varying respiratory noise. The amplifier was then switched to the automatic sequencing equipment. The first twenty-five-minute segment was then started.

Ss were told that the task expected of them was not especially difficult, but that it would require their closest attention. As they already knew, the instructions continued, they were to learn to make native-like utterances in a new language. Since the aim was to see how well they could acquire the native-like "accent" of this language, they were not expected to learn either meanings of sounds or grammatical rules. The instructions went on to point out that presentation of meaning and formal rules would seriously distract them from attending to the sound patterns and musical qualities of the language. They were told that it was vitally important to refrain from imitating the new sounds they were to hear until requested to do so. First, they would be unable to hear what they said because of the specially designed headphones, and second, such attempts would make the listening task more difficult for them. Ss were then informed that, to help them to remain silent, they would hear a buzzer through their headphones every time they made a sound. The microphone amplifier was then turned on. Ss were asked to give their first name aloud; the buzzer sounded the moment they began to speak. They were then directed to whisper their name, at which point the buzzer again sounded. This technique caused much amusement but functioned nevertheless as an excellent inhibitor. The instructions terminated by re-emphasizing the need to listen carefully to the material in the new language, and to listen only. The language was never explicitly named in the program, although Ss normally identified it correctly by the end of the first session. Each of the six possible orders for the three language programs was used for the first six Ss, after which the ordering was recommenced.

Except for the initial instructions, Lessons 2 and 3 proceeded in the same way as Lesson 1, where only listening was required. We could devise no unobtrusive way of monitoring how attentive Ss were during this phase. Some listened with their eyes fixed on the video screen before them, while others appeared to be concentrating with eyes partially or entirely closed. Inadvertent noises which triggered the buzzer from time to time probably had a salutary effect.

For Lessons 4–6, Ss were given pencil and paper which they were to use for tracing intonational contours. Immediately following the instructions, an utterance was presented auditorily, then repeated, while in a visual display, a piece of chalk simultaneously traced the intonational pattern. This procedure was repeated several times with different utterances to illustrate what Ss were expected to do. They were then told to listen very carefully to the following utterance and attempt to trace the pattern in the manner of the preceding examples. The project assistant was prepared to stop the equipment if further explanation was required. The utterance was heard three times, then given again with the correct visually displayed contour, against which Ss could compare their versions. The scratch pad was collected after each session.

The same procedure was observed for Lessons 7–9, where both intonational and cadential contours were involved. To compensate for anticipated boredom or impatience, we kept Ss busy with exercises which varied in length, complexity and order.

In the auditory discrimination exercises in Lessons 10–12, Ss indicated their responses by depressing one of two keys located on the console in front of them. For 50 percent of Ss, the right-hand key was designated for "no difference" responses and the left-hand key for "different." The reverse order was used for the remaining 50 percent. The project assistant tabulated correct or incorrect responses by marking the colour of the light (red or green) which flashed on the monitor panel as either of the keys was depressed. Because of the interspersed review material, pads and pencils were again provided.

Beginning with Lesson 13, Ss were expected, for the first time, to imitate what they heard. The responses were to be no louder than an audible whisper. The gain control on the microphone amplifier was readjusted to prevent the buzzer from sounding with devoiced utterances. The signal was fed back into the headphones to permit Ss to monitor their responses. In the second segment of these three lessons, Ss were instructed to refrain from speaking when reviewing material from Phase Two.

The final three lessons were similar to Lessons 13–15, except for the absence of review exercises. The instructions in Lesson 16 called for oral imitation in a normal voice; the buzzer was switched off at this point. The stimulus utterance was played twice, after which Ss were requested to repeat precisely what they heard. The model was again presented twice to allow for self-correction. As in Lessons 13–15, the first utterances presented were very short, increasing to eight syllable units in Lesson 18. Ss' responses throughout Phase Three were tape-recorded for later analysis.

When the first program had been completed, Ss were told that they had done even better than we had expected. We hoped, in this way, to sustain their interest, which was already at a surprisingly high level. In fact, the project assistant had no way of judging how well Ss had actually performed. Appointments for the next program were then confirmed. The assistant explained that the following session would be like the very first except with a different language.

Testing

Had we been interested in the acquisition of lexical meaning or of combinatorial rules, we could have used any number of well-known procedures to test for proficiency; standardized tests for our three language programs were, of course, not available. As already explained, our aim was to teach exclusively phonetic material where it is difficult to objectively assess performance. Although instrumental analysis was a possibility, we opted for native-speaking judges. We did so because of the complexities involved in measuring intonation, which is a composite of change in pitch, stress, and duration. Even if we had had the sophisticated computerized equipment devised by Léon and his colleagues at the University of Toronto, proficiency testing would have been long and costly.

Native-speaking judges who had experience teaching their first language seemed a more reasonable alternative. With the kind assistance of the Chinese and Japanese embassies in Ottawa, we were successful in locating three judges for each of these languages who more or less met our criteria. For Eskimo, we had considerable difficulty in finding even two native speakers who had any teaching experience whatsoever. The situation was further complicated by the dialectal differences of the two Eskimo speakers, one coming from Inuvik and the other from northern Québec.

Judges were interviewed individually, at which time they were told that our study consisted of detecting linguistic interference resulting from learning English as a second language. The assistant responsible for this phase of the project explained that they were to hear tape-recorded speech samples of twenty persons, some of whom, as recent arrivals, might not yet have learned English. (Judges actually heard 21 samples, one of which was the tape-recorded version of the native speaking instructor for the program. Assessments for these control samples all rated "unmistakably native" were not included in the analysis of the data.) Still others, it was explained, might be fluent speakers with detectable traces of interference. In addition, judges were told that the design of the experiment required that an unspecified number of non-native speakers be included in the twenty samples. The judges were then shown the five-point scale which they were to use when assessing each speech sample. This scale reads as follows:

1. Heavily accented with nearly all English-like sounds.
2. Noticeably foreign with many English-like sounds.
3. Near-native with frequent English-like sounds.
4. Appears native with occasional English-like sounds.
5. Unmistakably native with no signs of interference.

Judges were reminded that, although improbable, many or conceivably all the samples they were to hear might be non-native. The assistant further explained that the success of this study depended upon their ability to make subtle distinc-

328

tions which should be neither over- nor under-estimates of the extent of interference.

The final section of Lesson 18 consisted of ten statements of four- to eight-syllable units each, which Ss repeated in the normal manner. Only the fifth attempt for each statement was retained for evaluation purposes.

The scores for each S were calculated, first, by averaging the three independent ratings, and second, by computing the average between this figure and the collective rating given for each S in the second assessment where all three judges were assembled. Scores assigned in the second assessment were determined by majority opinion.

RESULTS AND DISCUSSION

Unfortunately, we were unable to analyze Ss' performance in Eskimo; because our two judges were frequently so far apart in their evaluations, we could not confidently average the two scores.

In the following table, Table 19.1, composite scores for each S in Japanese and Chinese are listed, along with means and standard deviations in parentheses which have been corrected for bias.

Judges for the Japanese program differed little in their independent assess-

TABLE 19.1 Composite Scores with Means and Standard Deviations for Japanese and Chinese

Subject number	Japanese	Chinese
4	5	4
8	5	5
23	5	4
2	4	3
5	4	4
12	4	4
15	4	3
16	4	4
17	4	4
1	3	3
21	3	3
10	3	4
11	3	3
19	3	3
20	3	3
6	2	2
22	2	3
14	2	2
25	2	1
7	1	2
	Mean, 3.30 (1.12)	Mean, 3.20 (0.95)

ments, $r_{tt} = 0.92$. Although there was some last minute disagreement about the meaning of "2" versus "3" on the five-point scale, overall differences between assessors were not statistically significant, $F(2,58) = 0.99$, $p > .05$. In general, the scale was functional and sufficiently sensitive to enable judges to distinguish good from poor performance. Ss were found to differ significantly in terms of their degree of mastery of the prosodic and articulatory features of Japanese, $F(2,58) = 12.24$, $p < .001$. Of particular interest were the ratings for nine of our Ss, three of whom obtained a score of five or "unmistakably native" and six of whom appeared to be native with traces of linguistic interference, based upon their ability to imitate ten high-frequency statements. We were concerned that, despite our instructions, judges might have been over-generous in their evaluations. When recontacted individually and informed that they had heard only non-native speakers, all three judges expressed surprise and disbelief.

We would have pursued this matter further had Ss' performance in the Chinese program differed markedly from their progress in Japanese. On independent assessments the three judges for Chinese scored Ss in almost an identical manner, $r_{tt} = 0.95$. Discrepancies were not statistically significant, $F(2,58) = 1.21$, $p > .05$. Our backup procedure with group assessments closely paralleled initial ratings, $r = 0.97$. As was the case in the Japanese program, Ss' performance varied significantly between excellent and poor, $F(2,58) = 19.44$, $p < .001$. Our experience in assessing performance in Japanese enabled us to be more precise in our instructions for scoring proficiency in Chinese. That only one of twenty Ss was viewed as "unmistakably native" may have been a reflection of our remark to judges that we were not necessarily looking for high scores. We were reticent to be too specific in our instructions about degree of nativeness for fear of biasing the judges.

The composite scores shown in the table clearly demonstrate consistency of performance in both programs, $r = 0.82$. We were curious to know whether Ss found one language to be more difficult than the other. It will be recalled that Programs I, II and III were presented in six different configurations. Statistical analyses yielded no significant differences between results obtained for Programs I and II, $t(1,19) = 0.69$, $p > .05$. Nor did the order in which programs were presented appear to have any influence on Ss' performance, $F(1,39) = 1.96$, $p > .05$. We had expected Ss to be better with succeeding programs, primarily because of their increasing ability to perform the various exercises in the lessons. The only reason we could find to explain the absence of differences was the ease with which Ss mastered the tracing task in their initial program. Accordingly, one would expect learning effects to have dropped off rapidly after the first few lessons.

What had we shown, and how could we account for overall performance? After eighteen hours of contact time, nine Ss managed to convince three native speakers that Japanese was their first language; six others qualified as near-native. Only five had performed in the manner one would normally expect after such a short period of instruction. Similarly, Ss mastered the prosodic and articulatory features of Chinese, to the extent that eight out of twenty were judged to be native speakers (4 and 5 on the scale). Of considerable interest to us was Ss' ability to pass for native speakers in two "exotic" languages without ever having been presented with syntactic or semantic cues. Because of the results of a much earlier pilot study where French was the target language, we were concerned that Ss might become bored or impatient with material they could neither analyze nor even repeat aloud. We were relieved to find that our revised approach all but eliminated such reactions.

In other words, young adults appear able to acquire native or near-native proficiency in the sound patterns of new languages. It is not yet clear whether persons who have acquired these skills in this manner will be able to utilize their knowledge when constructing meaningful and structurally acceptable statements. Although some of our Ss obtained above average scores on language aptitude batteries, these tests did not prove to be especially good predictors of success. With the *Modern Language Aptitude Test,* we obtained a correlation coefficient of $r=0.42$. Even with the Sound Discrimination sub-test of the *Language Aptitude Battery,* only a slightly higher value was observed, $r=0.45$. Scores on measures in some of our earlier studies led us to conclude that our sample was more or less typical of the university student population. It seems difficult, therefore, to explain our results in terms of a wide range normally distributed foreign language learning ability. Needless to say, the "critical period" hypothesis does little to account for the data.

There are some important questions which remain unanswered. Although the languages we used were real, the learning situation was very unusual. Ss did well with purely phonetic material. Could they have achieved this proficiency if they had been required to process additional information, in order to derive meaning and combinatorial rules? If presented first with phonetic material like ours, followed by vocabulary and grammar, could students retain their mastery of prosodic and articulatory features in a formal language learning situation? If we were to replicate this experiment with adolescents or adults in everyday classroom contexts, could we duplicate our data?

Stated another way, all we have demonstrated is that highly motivated university students, accustomed to the routine and paraphernalia of psychological experimentation, can acquire nativelike proficiency in the sound patterns of another language in an artificial learning situation. Our findings are compelling from a theoretical standpoint, for we seem to have found the means to tap ability which is believed by many to be virtually non-existent in most adults. If these results can be duplicated, and the scope of the design enlarged to include additional parameters, our study may have practical significance as well. Answers to questions such as how our data can be used to improve current teaching techniques, are unavailable at present. It would be premature, for instance, to say that adults should now be encouraged to place more importance on the acquisition of phonetic skills. We have not even touched on the problem of whether such skills are prerequisites for functional communication. It is hoped that renewed interest in adult language learning ability will prompt researchers to pursue issues like these which, to date, have played only a very minor role in our search for sound theories on second-language acquisition and communication.

REFERENCES

Asher, J., and R. Garcia. 1969. The optimal age to learn a foreign language. *Modern Language Journal, 53,* 334–41.

Burstall, C. 1975. French in the primary school: The British experiment. *Canadian Modern Language Review, 31,* 5:388–402.

Carroll, J.B. 1958. A factor analysis of two foreign language aptitude batteries. *Journal of General Psychology, 59,* 3–19.

Chomsky, N. 1957. *Syntactic structures.* The Hague: Mouton.

Curtiss, S., V. Fromkin, S. Krashen, D. Rigler, & M. Rigler. 1974. The linguistic development of Genie. *Language, 50,* 528–554.

Dumas, G., L. Selinker, & M. Swain. 1973. L'apprentissage du Français langue seconde en classe d'immersion dans un milieu Torontois. *Working Papers on Bilingualism,* 1.

Fromkin, V., S. Krashen, S. Curtiss, D. Rigler, & M. Rigler. 1974. The development of language in Genie: A case of language acquisition beyond the "Critical Period." *Brain and Language, 1.*

Gardner, R.C. 1975. Social factors in second language acquisition and binguality. Proceedings of the Canada Council's Conference on *The individual language and society.*

Harding, F.D., Jr. 1930. Tests as selectors of language students. *Modern Language Journal, 42,* 120–122.

Kaulfers, W.V. 1958. Why prognosis in the languages. *Modern Language Journal, 14,* 296–301.

Lane, H. 1964. Programmed learning of a second language. *International Review of Applied Linguistics, 2,* 4:249–301.

Lenneberg, E.H. 1967. *Biological foundations of language.* New York: Wiley.

Neufeld, G. 1974. Foreign language aptitude: An enduring problem. In G. Rondeau (Ed.), *Some aspects of Canadian applied linguistics.* Centre Educatif et Culturel Inc.

Neufeld, G. 1975. The case for case studies. Proceedings of the Canada Council's Conference on *The individual, language and society.*

Neufeld, G. 1977. Language learning ability in adults: A study on the acquisition of prosodic and articulatory features. *Working Papers on Bilingualism, 12.*

Neufeld, G. 1978. A theoretical perspective on the nature of linguistic aptitude. *International Review of Applied Linguistics, 16,* 15–25.

Penfield, W. 1959. *Speech and brain mechanisms.* Princeton: Princeton University Press.

Penfield, W. 1965. Conditioning the uncommitted cortex for language learning. *Brain, 88,* 787–798.

Pimsleur, P., R. Stockwell, & A.L. Comfrey. 1962. Foreign language learning ability. *Journal of Educational Psychology, 53* 15–26.

Postovsky, V. 1974. Effects of delay in oral practice at the beginning of second language learning. *Modern Language Journal, 58,* 229–239.

Salomon, E. 1954. A generation of prognosis testing, *Modern Language Journal, 38,* 299–303.

Scovel, T. 1969. Foreign accents, learning acquisition and cerebral dominance. *Language Learning, 19.*

Seliger, H.W., S. Krashen, & P. Ladefoged. 1975. Maturational constraints in the acquisition of second language accent. *Language Sciences, 36,* 20–22.

Selinker, L. 1972. Interlanguage. *International Review of Applied Linguistics, 10,* 209–231.

Skinner, B.F. 1957. *Verbal behavior.* NY: Appleton Century-Crofts.

Skinner, B.F. 1968. *The technology of teaching.* NY: Appleton Century-Crofts.

20

THE ACQUISITION OF TONE:
A MATURATIONAL PERSPECTIVE*

Georgette Ioup   Amara Tansomboon

INTRODUCTION

In this paper we will address the question of age differences in second language acquisition. We will investigate specifically the ability to acquire a language tonal system as compared to other structural aspects of language. Data is obtained from Thai learners of various ages and analyzed in terms of error rate. It is observed that native-like production of tone appears very early in the language of the child but has eluded even the most proficient adult learners of Thai. This appears to contrast greatly with certain syntactic patterns of the language. An attempt is made to account for the differences through an exploration of cognitive maturational factors that may underlie the process of language acquisition.

Many researchers have noted a contrast in the adult's ability to acquire a second language syntax and phonology. They observe that a near-native

*We wish to thank Robert Bley-Vroman, John Kingston, Peter MacNeilage, and Harvey Sussman for reading an earlier draft of this paper and providing very helpful comments.

fluency in syntax seems much more attainable for the adult learner than a native-like pronunciation. Lenneberg (1967) stated that although adults can communicate in a foreign language, foreign accents cannot be overcome easily after puberty. One of the first L2 researchers to attempt to account for this difference was Scovel (1969). He discusses the case of Joseph Conrad, who acquired English as a young adult. Although Conrad became a major English writer, his pronunciation of English never lost its characteristic non-native accent.

A study by Ioup (1984) found that in judging the accents of adult L2 learners, linguistically trained speakers of English were able to group together learners belonging to the same first language background using only phonological information; however, they were unable to do so on the basis of syntactic cues. This study led to the conclusion that a foreign accent, as characterized by the presence of interference errors in the interlingual system, is found predominantly at the level of phonology in the adult learner.

In laboratory experiments studying the adult's ability to discriminate synthetic speech cues, it was found that adults could distinguish only those stops or liquids that were identified as different phonemes in their native languages. When the native language did not contain the particular contrast presented, subjects were unable to make the discriminations. The same stimulus pairs presented as non-speech comparisons evoked highly accurate judgments, regardless of their phonemic status in the native language (Abramson and Liberman, 1970; Miyawaki, Strange, Verbrugge, Liberman, Jenkins, and Fujimura, 1975).

Children, on the other hand, seem not to experience difficulty mastering an L2 phonology. Differences have been found experimentally between the adult's capabilities in L2 phonology and the child's. Oyama (1976) tested adult Italian immigrants with varied ages of arrival (from 6 to 20) and variations in length of stay (from 5 to 18 years). Native-like phonological ability was correlated negatively with the age of arrival, but not significantly correlated with the number of years in the United States. Native-like pronunciation was found in the earliest-arriving subjects, with accents developing as age of arrival increased.

This observed difference has been accounted for in several ways. The earliest explanation was based on neurological factors. Lenneberg (1967) posited a critical period for language acquisition that terminated at puberty, due, he believed, to the completion of hemispheric lateralization and the end of cerebral plasticity. He did not extend the critical-period hypothesis to an explanation of the adult's diminished capacities in second language acquisition, especially in phonology. This was done by Scovel (1969), who believed that neurological maturation was responsible for adult L2 performance, including the discrepancy between the expected achievement in syntax and phonology. This phenomenon was claimed to be related to the fact that phonological output is dependent on a neurophysiological mechanism. Scovel gives no evidence to support this view.

Krashen (1973) dismisses the neurological explanation by arguing that language lateralization is complete by age five and therefore cannot be responsible for the end of the critical period at puberty. Biological determinants, then, should not be used to explain the accent-free pronunciation of older children. Krashen's conclusions are based mainly on two considerations: a reexamination of the lesion data that gave rise to the critical period hypothesis, which he finds consistent with a lateralization-by-five hypothesis, and a reanalysis of results from dichotic listening studies, which provide most of his evidence. He demonstrates that the right-ear advantage for language stimuli increases until the age of five, at which point children begin to perform like adults. There is a problem using the results of dichotic listening studies to support a hypothesis concerning the completion of language lateralization. The studies considered test only the perception of monosyllables. Their results do not reflect the organization of the complex linguistic system of the five-year-old. The realization that the five-year-old can process monosyllables like an adult gives no information on the organization within the brain of the sophisticated linguistic mechanisms that comprise the five-year-old's grammar. Krashen himself notes later that if the dichotic stimuli are increased to the complexity of only two digits, children beyond the age of five cease to perform like adults (Krashen, 1975; 1982). Other problems with the lateralization-by-five hypothesis are discussed in Schnitzer (1978). He suggests that one should look for different maturational developments to explain the foreign accents that appear in adult second language acquisition.

The trend in L2 research, however, has been to turn away from neurological explanations for the age differences found in pronunciation ability and to develop instead explanations based on socio-affective variables. Among the first to do so was Guiora and his associates (1975). They also observe that children can acquire with ease all aspects of a foreign language; however, beyond puberty pronunciation skills tend to be reduced while the capacity to acquire the grammar and lexicon is not. They suggest that the sound system, as opposed to other aspects of language, is tied intimately to self-identification and is thus incapable of being altered to adapt to a different phonological structure. Support for their hypothesis is drawn from a study on the effects of alcohol ingestion on pronunciation. An indirect association is made between the findings of this study and the construct of ego permeability, suggesting that certain amounts of alcohol ingestion induce a flexible psychic state. However, no evidence is presented to indicate that the correlation they find between alcohol level and pronunciation ability is indeed the result of an uninhibited language ego and not some other factor, such as, say, muscle relaxation.

Schumann (1975) also suggests that affective factors provide a better explanation of unsuccessful adult second language acquisition, but he cannot account for the discrepancy between achievement in phonology and syntax. He finds Guiora et al's proposal intuitively appealing but essentially unsubstantiated. More recently Krashen (1982) argues that age differences are primarily the result of social and psychological changes related to puberty; namely, that the affective filter component of his language acquisition model is strengthened at this point. However, why it should have such a pronounced effect on phonology is left unexplained.

A different socially-based explanation is proposed within a discourse analysis account of L2 acquisition. Peck (1978) concludes from her data on native-non-native interactions that children learning a second language engage in more sound play when interacting with other children than they do when interacting with adults. The focus on and manipulation of sounds that characterizes child-child discourse could be one reason children gain a better command of the phonology. However, it is difficult to sort out cause and effect with this explanation. Furthermore, we have no insights into the source of the child's need to engage in sound play and the reason for its disappearance over time.

Since explanations of maturational differences based on social interaction seem uninsightful or lack empirical support, we would like to return to an explanation related to biological maturation. We will explore the feasibility of constructing a new cognitive account of the developmental variability found in phonology. Data to support our inquiry come from a study of the first and second language acquisition of tone in Thai by children and adults.

METHOD

The study was designed to compare the facility of tone acquisition in relation to the acquisition of certain more segmental aspects of language. The structures of Thai selected for this study were those predicted by contrastive and developmental considerations to be problematic for native speakers of English. The structural description of Thai is drawn from Hass (1964).

Thai has five phonemic tones, of which three are level and two are contoured. They are described in Table 20.1. For speakers of a nontonal language like English, the acquisition of tone is predicted to be difficult. The stop consonant system manifests three voice onset times that are phonemically relevant. Stops may be voiced, voiceless and unaspirated, or voiceless and aspirated. The stop consonants are shown in Table 20.2. A contrastive theory predicts that English speakers whose native language contains only two phonemically relevant voice onset times will have difficulty mastering a three-way contrast.

TABLE 20.1. Thai Tonal System

Tones	Symbol	Examples	
mid	(unmarked)	[na]	'field'
low	`	[nà]	'custard apple'
falling	^	[nâ]	'face'
high	´	[ná]	'aunt'
rising	ˇ	[nǎ]	'thick'

TABLE 20.2. Thai Stop Consonants

	Bilabial	Alveolar	Palatal	Velar
voiced	b	d		-g
voiceless unaspirated	p-	t-	c-	k-
voiceless aspirated	p^h-	t^h-	c^h-	k^h-

Certain syntactic aspects of the language are predicted to be difficult for either contrastive or developmental reasons. Contrastive differences appear in the word order relationship of the noun phrase head with its modifiers. In English an adjective without a complement precedes the head, while one with a complement follows it. For example:

A big old brown house
A man proud of his family

In Thai all attributes follow the noun no matter how simple or complex the adjective phrase is:

sŷ:a   tu:a   dæ:ŋ
blouse   classifier   red
'the red blouse'

A second aspect of Thai predicted to be difficult, but for developmental reasons, is the classifier system. A classifier is obligatory when the noun is modified by a quantifier or certain determiners. It is optional in other noun phrase configurations.

mæ:w   să:m   tu:a
cat   three   classifier
'Three cats'

There are approximately 200 classifiers in standard Thai, the choice being determined arbitrarily by the head noun. The frequency of use for each classifier is unequal. A few are more general and occur more often. [?an] is used for most inanimate objects, [tu:a] for most animals and [k^{h}on] for human beings. These three classifiers tend to be overgeneralized in both the speech of learners and that of nonstandard speakers.

Subjects

Subjects for the study were selected by both criteria of age and degree of Thai proficiency. They were grouped into four categories, as follows:

337

Group I: child first language learners of Thai
Group II: child second language learners of Thai
Group III: adult beginning learners of Thai
Group IV: adult advanced learners of Thai

There were eight subjects in the study, two for each group. All subjects were living in Seattle, Washington, at the time of the study.

Group I consisted of two girls, ages 3;2 and 5;4, who were acquiring Thai as a first language. Both were both in Thailand and had acquired Thai monolingually. At the beginning of the study the younger subject had been in America only three weeks. Her acquisition of Thai was not yet complete. The five-year-old subject had arrived in the United States one year prior to the study, at which time her control of Thai phonology was fairly complete and her syntax was quite well developed. After a year of exposure to English at daycare, she began to lose some of her Thai. Even though it continued to be her dominant language at the time of the study, she was experiencing difficulty with it. The data obtained from this subject give evidence of language loss as well as acquisition.

Group II consisted of two female subjects who were born in the United States. The first one, age 4;3, is a native-born American who speaks English as a native language. She lived in Thailand with her family between the ages of 3;2 and 4;0. At that time she began acquiring Thai through exposure to peers and a Thai housekeeper. She continued in the acquisition of Thai upon return to the States through communication with her father and Thai family friends. Her acquisition of Thai is not complete.

The second child, age 7;1, is Thai but spent her early years with American babysitters, from whom she acquired English as a first language. She also is acquiring Thai from her parents, but it is definitely the nondominant language. Her Thai speech shows considerable English influence, and she frequently switches to English when confronted with difficulty.

All four children are from the same socioeconomic background, with parents who are professionals. The dialect of Thai they speak is Standard (Bangkok) Thai.

Group III consisted of two English-speaking adult subjects, one male and one female, who were in their second quarter of elementary Thai at the University of Washington. Neither of them had previous familarity with a tone language.

Group IV consisted of two older male subjects who began the study of Thai after the age of twenty. They both had extensive formal instruction in Thai and had each lived many years in Thailand as missionaries, where they were doing linguistic research. Their control of Thai is very advanced, which we attested through observations of their fluency and accuracy.

The testing was carried out by a native speaker of Thai who was a graduate student in linguistics at the University of Washington.

Procedures

The investigator met with the subjects individually once a week over a three-month period for a total of twelve sessions. Each session lasted a minimum of forty minutes. All the interviews were taped. The interviews were conducted in Thai and consisted of relaxed informal conversation as well as playing sessions with the children. Material from the taped sessions provided information on all four constructs tested.

In addition to the taped conversations, data were elicited through two tests, a picture identification task and a humming task. The tests were designed to assess subjects' productive and receptive command of tone. The picture identification task consisted of fifteen sets of pictures. Each set depicted a Thai paradigm representing the five different Thai tones on the same segmental syllable. The words chosen were simple ones, likely to be acquired by even the youngest subjects. When a paradigm lacked a lexical item for a given tone, a new Thai word was created and represented by a cartoon drawing. Thus each set contained an entry for all five tones. Subjects were first given a training session to insure that they were familiar with all the Thai lexical items and to teach the meaning associated with the created words. The training and the testing were conducted for each set individually, with only one or two sets tested at each interview session.

The test itself consisted of a recognition and a production component. Receptive control of tonal distinctions was tested by requiring subjects to match the correct picture with the stimulus word. The stimuli were presented randomly, with one of the five words selected arbitrarily for repetition in order to minimize deductive guessing. Productive control of tone was assessed by requiring subjects to name pictures that were randomly presented. Responses were scored as correct or incorrect at the time of the testing. This test was a measure of subjects' phonemic command of tone.

The humming task was adapted from a technique developed by Van Lancker and Fromkin (1973). Its intent was to discern whether tone functioned differently when utilized as melodic pitch rather than as a linguistic contrast. Subjects were asked to imitate a given sentence by humming the prosodic contours, ignoring all segmental information. Van Lancker and Fromkin reported that pitch alone yielded different dichotic listening results from pitch functioning in linguistically meaningful contexts. The responses were taped for later evaluation.

The evaluation was conducted by three native speakers of Thai, one of which was the investigator. All were graduate students at the University of Washington and had some familarity with phonetics. Five-minute samples from data toward the end of each conversational interview were selected. Judges were asked to listen to the taped samples and to the humming test in order to assess the degree of control of the constructs under investigation. Correct-incorrect judgments were required for the aspiration distinction and the two syntactic constructs. The data on tone were evaluated on a three-point scale, as follows:

Level 1:   phonemically and phonetically incorrect
Level 2:   phonemically correct but with phonetic deviation
Level 3:   indistinguishable from native speakers

The judges rated tone acquisition on both the taped conversations and the humming test.

RESULTS

The three judges concurred completely on their evaluations of the phonemic accuracy of tones, the stop consonant distinctions, and the two grammatical constructs. In evaluating the phonetic quality of the tones they agreed on 93 percent of their judgments. On all measures, the results for both subjects in the same group revealed no essential differences. Therefore, scores were totalled within each group, and a mean number of correct responses per group was obtained for each category. The results are presented in Table 20.3. Scores for the categories of tone reflect the number of level 2 ratings for the phonemic aspects and the number of level 3 responses for the phonetic aspects. The Ns in each group were too small to allow statistical analysis. However, the results for each group show enough variation to provide interesting comparisons without such measures. The totals for subjects in Group I are given separately, because they provide data on both language acquisition and language loss.

As can be seen from the figures in Table 20.3, the order of difficulty for the children and adults is by and large in reverse. The adult subjects in Groups 3 and 4 had the most difficulty with tone accuracy, especially the phonetic aspects of pronunciation. Aspirated stops and correct classifier choice presented some difficulty, while word order within the noun phrase seems to have been mastered. The children, on the other hand, performed consistently better on tone production, both phonemically and phonetically, than on the syntactic structures tested. The one exception is the three-year-old subject in Group I, who appears to have also acquired the rules for noun phrase word order. The

TABLE 20.3. Mean Percentage of Accurate Responses for Each Group

	Phonemic tone	Phonetic tone	Hums	Asp.	Class.	Noun-attr.
Group I	99%	95%	100%	45%	32%	80%
3-year-old	100%	90%	100%	43%	23%	97%
5-year-old	98%	100%	100%	46%	40%	63%
Group II	96%	55%	100%	54%	19%	22%
Group III	58%	3%	97%	78%	70%	95%
Group IV	95%	8%	99%	97%	94%	100%

child acquirers found the phonemic control of aspiration more difficult than the phonemic control of tone. The reverse is true of the adult acquirers exemplified by Group III. In general, the adults experienced the most difficulty with the phonetic contours of tone. This was true of even the very advanced group, who had near-native control of the other aspects of the language. The phonetic quality of their tone production appeared no better than that of the beginning adults. They spoke with a marked foreign accent which resulted from the fossilized development of their prosodic contours. If we compare the children in Group II, who are learning Thai as a second language, with the adults in Group III, who are in the elementary stages of Thai acquisition, we observe that the children have acquired the phonemic contrasts of tone, find the contrasts in voice onset times more difficult, and have little command of either of the syntactic constructs, the classifier system, or the noun phrase word order. The adults do far better with the classifier, word order, and stop contrasts. Their most problematic aspect of Thai is tone production, both phonemic and phonetic. It is interesting that the humming test produced native-like responses for all groups, even those who had not yet mastered tone production. The implications of this will be discussed later in the paper.

It is of interest, at this point, to compare the two first language learners of Group I, the one who is in the process of acquiring Thai and the other who is in the process of losing it. It appears that the first acquired aspects of the language are the last lost. This pattern has been observed in other studies of language loss. The five-year-old subject's control of tone is 100 percent correct in all aspects. Her aspiration production is only 46 percent accurate. This child, who previously had perfect control of phonology, is now losing some segmental distinctions, something that makes her speech sound foreign. However, her tones are still accurate in every respect. Her control of the noun-attribute word order is decreasing. It is uncertain whether the problems with the classifier system reflect language loss or incomplete mastery.

The three-year-old subject has not yet acquired the vowel and consonant system of Thai, with the result that her speech is often incomprehensible, yet her facility in the phonemic control of tone is 100 percent accurate, in both production and perception. The following are examples of her phonological errors.

L1 Form	Target Form	Gloss
[côːj dôːj]	[cʰûːaj dûːaj]	'help'
[pɔ̂ːma: jǽːw]	[pʰɔ̂ːma: lǽːw]	'Daddy has come'

DISCUSSION

The results of this study indicate that tone is one of the earliest aspects of Thai to be acquired by children, regardless of whether the language is their first or second, and one of the latest to be acquired by adults. Other studies on the acquisition of tone language have also found that the tonal system is acquired very early by the young child, well before the segmental system. (For a review, see Li and Thompson, 1978.) It appears, then, that the aspects of grammar that younger and older learners find easiest to master are different.

There are some interesting implications that follow from this finding. For example, a theory of age differences based on affective variables has no obvious explanation for the reason certain aspects of phonology, namely ones classified as suprasegmental, should be among the earliest-acquired features of the language by children but remain problematic for even very proficient adult learners. Such a difference does not seem to follow naturally from the learner's degree of motivation or ability to integrate socially. It seems more likely to be a function of the types of cognitive processes involved in acquiring different modes of information and of the way these processes are utilized by children and adults. It is from this perspective that we would like to explore the development of a more insightful explanation of age differences in the ability to acquire phonological competence.

At this point it will be useful to examine the characteristics of tone that determine the way in which it will be processed cognitively. Tone is normally classified as a suprasegmental feature of the phonology because tones occur in conjunction with phonological segments and are typically defined over a syllable. Tones, like other phonemic segments, are lexically associated with particular words. To identify a lexical item one must be aware of its tone just as one must know its segmental composition. The most salient feature of a tone is its *pitch,* defined acoustically as its fundamental frequency. Also important in identifying a particular tone is the *dynamic contour,* or the degree of movement of the fundamental frequency over time. (Abramson, 1976; Gandour, 1978). Tone must be distinguished from other prosodic aspects of language, such as intonation. Tone is phonemic, being bound to a particular word, whereas intonation is freely applied to longer stretches of speech.

There have been many studies on the lateral processing of pitch in the brain. When pitch is presented independent of language it is claimed to be processed by the right hemisphere (Kimura, 1964; Curry, 1967; Darwin, 1968), bilaterally (Shankweller and Studdert-Kennedy, 1967; Darwin, 1968; Bogan and Gordon, 1971) and even subcortically (Curry, 1968). It has been shown through dichotic listening techniques that the same pitch discrimination stimuli will shift ear advantage from left to right when subjects incorporate the pitch information into language. Spellacy and Blumstein (1970) presented vowels embedded in words and melodies. With the former, they observed a right-ear advantage (REA), suggesting left hemisphere processing, but with the latter a left-ear advantage (LEA) was produced, suggesting that the stimuli were processed primarily through the right hemisphere. A study relevant to our research was carried out by Van Lancker and Fromkin (1973). Using dichotic listening techniques, they measured native Thai speakers' perception of tone in a linguistic context and as hummed melodies. When the tones functioned to distinguish

Thai words, a significant REA was obtained, but there was no significant ear advantage for the hummed tones. English speakers with no knowledge of Thai were tested on the same tasks. For these subjects tone embedded in words gave the same ear preference as the hummed tones. No significant ear advantage was found for either. These results lead the authors to conclude that when pitch becomes part of the linguistic system to the extent that it is incorporated as a phonemic distinction, it will be lateralized to the left hemisphere in the same way as most other grammatical aspects of language.

In normal language use prosodic features of speech like sentential intonation contours have been shown to be lateralized to the right hemisphere. This is illustrated through the observation of aphasic speech resulting from left hemisphere trauma, where such intonation contours are seldom disturbed. (Jakobson, 1941; Danly, de Villiers, & Cooper, 1979; Cooper, Danly, & Hamby, 1979), and through a study of the prosodic disruption resulting from certain right hemisphere lesions (Weintraub, Mesulam, & Kramer, 1981; Danly, Shapiro, & Gardner, 1982; Tomkins and Mateer, 1985; Shapiro and Danly, 1985). Evidence also comes from dichotic listening experiments that obtain consistent left-ear advantage for intonation, indicating that the right hemisphere plays a major role in the propositional use of intonational contours (Blumstein and Cooper, 1974).

The lateralization of function to the left or right hemisphere is thought to be a result of the different modes of information processing associated with each hemisphere. The left, or major, hemisphere has been associated with propositional, analytical, and relational thought, while the right, or minor, hemisphere is related to appositional, gestalt, and holistic reasoning (Bogen, 1969; Bever 1975, 1980). It has been argued that the earliest developing cognitive processes in children are those typically associated with the right hemisphere (Seth, 1973; Crowell, Jones, Kapunai, & Nakagawa, 1973). Support for this comes from the fact that speaker and face recognition are two of the earliest cognitive functions to appear in the infant (DeCasper and Fifer, 1978; Fantz, 1958; Fagan, 1976; Young-Browne, Rosenfield, & Horowitz, 1977). Speaker and face recognition have been shown to be right hemisphere functions in the adult (DeRenzi and Spinnler, 1966; Warrington & James, 1967; Benton and Van Allen, 1968; DeRenzi, 1968, for face recognition; Matsumoto, Hiki, Sone, and Nimura, 1973; Bricker and Pruzansky, 1973; Van Lancker and Canter, 1982, for speaker recognition). In addition, those aspects of language associated with the right hemisphere have been observed to be the first acquired by the young child. Many studies of child language acquisition have noted that the intonational contours of a language appear well before the phonemic contrasts (Lewis, 1951; Leopold, 1953; Weir, 1966; Peters, 1974).

It seems reasonable, then, to hypothesize that the child acquiring linguistic tone first perceives and processes it as part of the prosodic system of language, analyzing the input data relevant to tones using gestalt or holistic cognitive strategies. This would allow the child to internalize the acoustic correlates of tone that define it at the phonetic level before he or she has complete grasp of the phonemic contrasts represented by the tones. When the phonetic quality of the tones becomes well integrated into the communicative system, their contrastive values become the main focus in the child's emerging grammar, and the processing of the tonal system becomes more and more a left hemisphere function. It would be interesting to test this hypothesis experimentally.

In general, adults acquiring a new language seem to have great difficulty with those aspects associated with the right hemisphere, such as prosody and intonation. Data from Ioup (1984) indicate that the foreign accents of the subjects were most easily identified by their foreign-like intonation contours and non-native vowel coloring. Very few phonemic substitution errors were observed. Assal, Zander, Kremin, and Buttet (1976) report that patients with right hemisphere lesions were significantly more impaired than left hemisphere cases in discriminating among foreign accents. Anecdotal data from learners and language teachers alike support the claim that the prosodic system of the language is the last to be mastered, that it tends to become fossilized in advanced learners, and characterizes them as having a foreign accent even though other aspects of pronunciation present no problem. The findings of the present study lead to the same conclusion. We believe that adults learning a new language rely on the linguistic hemisphere for processing all aspects of the language system even those better processed by the minor right hemisphere. The humming data in our study indicate that adults are as capable as children at reproducing the tones in a phonetically correct manner. Their difficulty in doing so occurs only with the tones functioning within the linguistic system. One might speculate that the adults are using a different cognitive system, located in a different area of the brain to produce the tones as hums. This would accord with the shift in ear advantage found in the studies cited above which result when the stimuli were divorced from linguistic contexts (Spellacy and Blumstein, 1970; Van Lancker and Fromkin, 1973), and with the studies on speech perception which give different results for the same stimuli in speech and nonspeech situations (Abramson and Lisker, 1970; Miyawaki, et al., 1975).

It is interesting to note that adults do not normally have difficulty acquiring new information requiring gestalt analysis. They can learn to recognize new faces and new voices as well as, or even better than, any child.[1] It is only when they must process new linguistic data that adults seem to have difficulty applying holistic techniques to acquisition tasks. If the same material is perceived as extralinguistic, adults are very capable of internalizing it. Goldberg and Costa (1981) have argued convincingly that when new descriptive systems are integrated into preexisting codes, they are processed with greater facility by the left hemisphere. However, when there is no relevant descriptive system immediately available in the cognitive repertoire, the right hemisphere's participation is most essential for initial orientation. This suggests that adults may be processing tone in relation to their preexisting linguistic framework via the left hemisphere, while children, who approach tone in the absence of any related cognitive network, employ right hemisphere strategies of analysis. If our hypothesis is correct, it could be validated experimentally. One could measure the cortical AER (average evoked response) to tonal input to children at various stages of tone acquisition and compare it to that of adults under similar circumstances.

There is an important study by Neufeld (1978) which supports this view of the adult's approach to the acquisition of phonology. Neufeld investigated the adult's ability to acquire a native-like pronunciation in a completely new language. English speaking subjects were tested on their ability to pronounce stimulus strings in Chinese and Japanese. Subjects were given no information on the linguistic structure or lexical content of the material they heard. They were told only to mimic, as closely as possible, the pronunciation of a short passage of speech. They were allowed as much practice as they wished and could monitor their feedback with the aid of various machines. Subjects, as rated by native speaking judges, achieved unusual degrees of phonetic accuracy, after very limited exposure. In this experiment subjects' success could be the result of the mode of information processing employed. The subjects were quite likely approaching the input stimuli as melodic contours rather than linguistic data. They would therefore be utilizing gestalt cognitive strategies associated with the right hemisphere. If the same data had been analyzed from a linguistic perspective, it most certainly would have been assimilated in a different way, giving rise to different results.

In summary, then, the inability of the adult subjects in our study to achieve native-like control of Thai tone, even after years of fluency in the language, is attributed to the adults' need to process all linguistic data using analytic strategies associated with the major left hemisphere, because language is situated in that hemisphere. The reliance on analytic procedures may make the adult more proficient than the child at acquiring certain aspects of language in the short run, but it will impede, at every stage of language learning, his or her acquisition of components of language that seem to require holistic analysis for internalization and will lead ultimately to a foreign accent.

It has been argued by Bogen et al (1972) that some adults are better than others at utilizing holistic strategies for cognitive processing. If this is the case, it could account for some of the individual variation adults exhibit in their ability to acquire native-like pronunciation. Those adults who apply holistic approaches to cognitive problem solving activity more freely should be better at L2 phonological acquisition. One criticism of previous hypotheses based on cognitive or neurological correlates, raised by Neufeld (1979), is that they do not explain individual variation. Neufeld contends that hypotheses defined in terms of maturational constraints cannot, nor do they even attempt to, account for the adults who are capable of attaining a near-native proficiency in a second language. We hypothesize that it is the degree to which individuals normally rely on different modes of cognitive activity that will determine the degree of facility in certain aspects of phonological acquisition. One could certainly test whether those adults who have a better accent in a foreign language are also those who excel on tests said to measure holistic processing.

A new cognitively based model of second language acquisition has recently been proposed by Felix (1985); however, it does not offer a ready explanation for our findings. Felix argues, as well, that cognitive processing differences account for the maturational variability found in language acquisition. According to his Competing Cognitive Systems Model, adults and children have access to the same language acquisition device, referred to as language specific cognitive structures, or the LSC-system. This system is the one that Chomsky (1968) has argued is innate and chiefly responsible for child language acquisition. Adults fail to achieve native-like control of a new language not because of their inability to apply active LSC-structures to the learning task but because they have a competing problem-solving cognitive system, or PSC-system. This mechanism appears around puberty with the advent of formal operations. It is the system used for general problem-solving needs by the adult. With the aid of PSC-structures the adult is able to gain knowledge about the new language but not the ability to use it creatively. The latter is achieved only through application of LSC-structures to the language input data. It is argued that adults are not as successful at language acquisition as children not because of some diminished capacity in the functional ability of the LSC-system but because there is a second system competing with it for the processing of input data. This model is appealing in many respects and merits further investigation; however, as stated above, it does not seem to provide an explanation for the results of the present study. It does not explain why the competition between the PSC- and LSC-systems should cause suprasegmental features of the phonology to be more difficult for the adult to acquire than segmental features while the reverse is true for children who are not faced with competing cognitive systems.

CONCLUSION

This study has attempted to augment our understanding of the factors that distinguish child from adult language acquisition. It investigated the acquisition of four constructs in Thai by children and adults to compare their degree of facility with these measures at various stages of learning. We wished to ascertain from a relational perspective the level of difficulty of each of the constructs for the children and adults. Our aim was to determine whether children and adults acquire different aspects of grammar with the same relative ease. The study involved both phonological and syntactic measures.

We found that adults were experiencing most difficulty with the tonal system, while the children had acquired it best of the constructs tested. In order to explain our results we examined the prevailing hypotheses on maturational differences and found them inadequate. None seemed to offer any explanation for the reason certain aspects of the grammar should be relatively easy for children to acquire but difficult for adults. We proposed a cognitively based explanation that focused on maturational differences in the use of cognitive strategies to process language input data.

NOTES

1. We are indebted to Robert Bley-Vroman for this observation.

REFERENCES

Abramson, A. 1976. Static and dynamic acoustic cues in distinctive tones. *Haskins Laboratories Status Report on Speech Research,* SR-47, 121–127. New Haven, CN: Haskins Laboratories.

Abramson, A., and L. Lisker. 1970. Discriminating along the voicing continuum. *Proceedings of the 6th International Congress of Phonetic Sciences.* Prague: Academia.

Assal, G., E. Zander, H. Kremin, and J. Buttet. 1976. Discrimination des joix lors des lesions du cortex cerebral. *Archieves Suisse de Neurologie, Neurochirugie et de Psychiatric, 119,* 2, 307–315.

Benton, A., and M. Van Allan. 1968. Impairment in facial recognition in patients with cerebral disease. *Cortex, 4,* 344–358.

Bever, T. 1975. Cerebral asymmetries in humans are due to the differentiation of two incompatable processes: Holistic and analytic. In D. Aaronson and R. Rieber (Eds.), *Developmental Psycholinguistics and Communicative Disorders,* NY: Academy of Sciences.

Bever, T. 1980. Broca and Lashley were right: Cerebral dominance is an accident of growth. In D. Caplan (Ed.), *Biological Studies of Mental Processes.* Cambridge, MA: MIT Press.

Blumstein, S., and W. Cooper. 1974. Hemispheric processing of intonation contours. *Cortex, 10,* 146–158.

Bogen, J. 1969. The other side of the brain, II: An appositional mind. *Bulletin of the Los Angeles Neurological Societies, 34,* 135–162.

Bogen, J., and H. Gordon. 1971. Musical tests for functional lateralization with intracarotid amobarbital. *Nature, 230,* 5295; 524–525.

Bogen, J., R. DeZure, W. Tenhouten, and J. Marsh. 1972. The other side of the brain, IV: The A/P ratio. *Bulletin of the Los Angeles Neurological Society, 37,* 49–61.

Bricker, P., and S. Pruzansky. 1976. Speaker recognition. In N. Lass (Ed.), *Contemporary Issues in Experimental Phonetics.* NY: Academic Press.

Chomsky, N. 1968. *Language and Mind.* New York: Harcourt Brace Jovanovich.

Cooper, W., M. Danly, and S. Hamby. 1979. Fundamental frequency (Fo) attributes in the speech of Wernicke's aphasics. In J. Wolf and D. Klatt (Eds.), *Speech Communication Papers Presented at the 97th Meeting of the Acoustical Society of America.* NY: Acoustical Society of America.

Crowell, D., J. Jones, L. Kapunai, and J. Nakagawa. 1973. Unilateral cortical activity in newborn humans. *Science, 180,* 205–208.

Curry, F. 1967. A comparison of left-handed and right-handed subjects on verbal and non-verbal dichotic listening tasks. *Cortex, 3,* 343–352.

Curry, F. 1968. A comparison of the performances of a right hemispherectomized subject and 25 normals on four dichotic listening tasks. *Cortex, 4,* 144–153.

347

Danly, M., J. deVilliers, and W. Cooper. 1979. The control of speech prosody in Broca's aphasia. In J. Wolf and D. Klatt (Eds.), *Speech Communication Papers Presented at the 97th Meeting of the Acoustical Society of America.* NY: Acoustical Society of America.

Danly, M., B. Shapiro and H. Gardner. 1982. Dysprosody in right brain damaged patients: Linguistic and emotional components. Paper presented at the Academy of Aphasia, New Paltz, NY.

Darwin, C. 1969. *Auditory Perception and Cerebral Dominance.* University of Cambridge dissertation.

De Casper, A., and W.P. Fifer. 1980. Of human bonding: newborns prefer their mother's voices. *Science, 208,* 1174–1176.

DeRenzi, E. 1968. Nonverbal memory and hemispheric site of lesion. *Neuropsychologia, 6,* 181–189.

DeRenzi, E., and H. Spinner. 1966. Facial recognition in brain-damaged patients. *Neurology, 16,* 145–152.

Fagan, J.F. 1976. Infants' recognition of individual features of faces. *Child Development, 47,* 627–638.

Fantz, R.L. 1958. Pattern vision in young infants. *The Psychological Record, 8,* 43–47.

Felix, S. 1985. More evidence on competing cognitive structures. *Journal of Second Language Acquisition Research, 1,* 47–72.

Foldi, N., M. Cicone, and H. Gardner. 1983. Pragmatic aspects of communication in brain-damaged patients. In S. Segalowitz (Ed.), *Language Function and Brain Organization,* New York: Academic Press.

Gandour, J. 1978. The perception of tone. In V. Fromkin (Ed.), *Tone: A Linguistic Survey,* NY: Academic Press.

Goldberg, E., and L. Costa. 1981. Hemispheric differences in the acquisition and use of descriptive systems. *Brain and Language, 14,* 144–173.

Guiora, A., M. Paluszny, B. Beit-Hallahmi, J. Catford, R. Cooley, and C. Dull. 1975. Language and person—studies in language behavior. *Language Learning, 25,* 43–62.

Hass, M. 1964. *Thai-English Student's Dictionary.* Stanford, CA: Stanford University Press.

Ioup, G. 1984. Is there a structural foreign accent? A comparison of syntactic and phonological errors in second language acquisition. *Language Learning, 34,* 1–18.

Jakobson, R. 1941. *Child Language, Aphasia and Phonological Universals.* The Hague: Mouton.

Kimura, D. 1964. Left-right differences in the perception of melodies. *Quarterly Journal of Experimental Psychology, 17,* 355–358.

Krashen, S. 1973. Lateralization, language learning, and the critical period. *Language Learning, 23,* 63–74.

Krashen, S. 1975. The development of cerebral dominance and language learning: More new evidence. In D. Dato (Ed.), *Developmental Psycholinguistics: Theory and Application.* Washington, DC: Georgetown University Press, 179–192.

Krashen, S. 1982. Accounting for child-adult differences in second language rate and attainment. In S. Krashen, R. Scarcella, and M. Long (Eds.), *Child-Adult Differences in Second Language Acquisition.* Rowley, MA: Newbury House.

Lenneberg, E. 1967. *Biological Foundations of Language.* NY: John Wiley & Sons.

Leopold, W. 1953. Patterning in children's language. *Language Learning, 5,* 1–14.

Lewis, M. 1951. *Infant Speech.* New York: Humanities Press.

Li, C., and S. Thompson. 1978. The acquisition of tone. In V. Fromkin (Ed.), *Tone: A Linguistic Survey.* NY: Academic Press.

Lieberman, P. 1968. *Intonation, Perception and Language.* Cambridge, MA: MIT Press.

Matsumoto, H., S. Hiki, T. Sone, and T. Nimura. 1973. Multidimensional representation of personal quality and its acoustic correlates. *IEEE Transactions on Audio and Electroacoustics AV, 21,* 428–436.

Miyawaki, K., W. Strange, R. Verbrugge, A. Liberman, J. Jenkins, and O. Fujimura. 1975. An effect of linguistic experience: The discrimination of [r] and [l] by native speakers of Japanese and English. *Perception and Psychophysics, 18,* 331–340.

Neufeld, G. 1978. On the acquisition of prosodic and articulatory features in adult language learning. *Canadian Modern Language Review, 34,* 163–174. (Also this volume.)

Neufeld, G. 1979. Towards a theory of language learning ability. *Language Learning, 29,* 227–242.

Oyama, S. 1976. A sensitive period for the acquisition of a nonnative phonological system. *Journal of Psycholinguistic Research, 5,* 261–285.

Peck, S. 1978. Child-child discourse in second language acquisition. In E. Hatch (Ed.), *Second Language Acquisition,* Rowley, MA: Newbury House.

Peters, A. 1974. The beginning of speech. *Stanford Papers and Reports on Child Language Developments, 8,* 26–32.

Schnitzer, M. 1978. Cerebral lateralization and plasticity: Their relevance to language acquisition. In M. Paradis (Ed.), *Aspects of Bilingualism.* Columbia, SC: Hornbeam.

Schumann, J. 1975. Affective factors and the problem of age in second language acquisition. *Language Learning, 25,* 209–236.

Scovel, T. 1969. Foreign accents, language acquisition, and cerebral dominance. *Language Learning, 19,* 245–254.

Seth, G. 1973. Eye-hand coordination and handedness: A developmental study of visio-motor behavior in infancy. *British Journal of Educational Psychology, 43,* 35–49.

Shankweiler, D., and M. Studdert-Kennedy. 1967. Identification of consonants and vowels presented to left and right ears. *Quarterly Journal of Experimental Psychology, 19,* 59–63.

Spellacy, F., and S. Blumstein. 1970. The influence of language set in ear preference. *Cortex, 6,* 430–439.

Tomkins, C., and C. Mateer. 1985. Right hemisphere appreciation of prosodic and linguistic indications of implicit attitude. *Brain and Language, 24,* 185–203.

Van Lancker, D., and G. Canter. 1982. Impairment of voice and face recognition in patients with hemispheric damage. Paper presented at a meeting of BABBLE held at Niagara Falls, NY.

Van Lancker, D., and V. Fromkin. 1973. Hemispheric specialization for pitch and tone: Evidence from Thai. *Journal of Phonetics, 1,* 101–109.

Warrington, E., and M. James. 1967. An experimental investigation of facial recognition in patients with unilateral cerebral lesions. *Cortex, 3,* 317–326.

Weintraub, S., M. Mesulam, and L. Kramer. 1981. Disturbances in prosody: A right hemisphere contribution to language. *Archives of Neurology, 38,* 742–744.

Weir, R. 1966. Some questions on the child's learning of phonology. In F. Smith and G. Miller (Eds.), *The Genesis of Language,* Cambridge, MA: MIT Press.

Young-Browne, G., H.M. Rosenfield, and F.D. Horowitz. 1977. Infant discrimination of facial expression. *Child Development, 48,* 555–562

21

THE PERCEPTION OF SECOND LANGUAGE PROSODY*

Ellen Broselow   Richard R. Hurtig   Catherine Ringen

INTRODUCTION

The question of the extent to which transfer from a first language affects the learning of subsequent languages continues to be a perplexing one. In recent years, researchers have questioned the importance of transfer, suggesting that if transfer operates at all in second language acquisition, it is a factor only in the acquisition of phonology, not of syntax (Richards, 1974; Dulay and Burt, 1974), and that even in the acquisition of second language phonology, transfer may play a role in the production of second language strings but not in the

*An earlier version of this paper was presented at the Tenth International Congress of Phonetic Sciences at Utrecht, The Netherlands, in August 1983. We wish to express our thanks to Carol Binder, Jack Gandour, David Jung, Kee Ho Kim, Jocelyn Liu, James Tai, Ingo Titze, Andrea Tyler, Robert Wachal, Yuen-Mei Yin, and Hsio-Ching Yuan for their assistance and suggestions. We would also like to thank Pat Colsher and William Cooper for providing the fundamental frequency plots in Figure 21.2. That work was performed in Cooper's lab and was supported by NIH NS20071.

perception of the second language (Neufeld, 1980). If this is in fact the case, it suggests that transfer is a rather limited phenomenon, involving the transfer of motor skills rather than of linguistic competence.

It is the contention of this paper that transfer does play a role—in fact, a significant role—in the perception of a second language, and that what we might call "perceptual transfer" is an extremely interesting phenomenon, both because it makes certain aspects of the learning of a second language comprehensible, and because it reveals something of the speaker's knowledge of his or her native language grammar. The phenomenon investigated in this paper is the perception of tone in sequences of Mandarin Chinese syllables by native speakers of English. The paper discusses the pattern of responses of English speakers presented with the task of identifying Mandarin tone sequences. We argue that the initially mysterious response pattern of English subjects becomes comprehensible when the Mandarin tonal system is compared with the corresponding system in the subjects' native language—that is, when Mandarin tone is compared with English sentence intonation. While pitch functions very differently in Mandarin and in English, English speakers' perception of Mandarin tone appears to be strongly influenced by their knowledge of the function of pitch in the intonation system of English.

The paper discusses two types of evidence that transfer plays a role in the perception of Chinese tone by English speakers. The first involves an examination of the relative ease with which each of the four Mandarin tones is perceived in different positions in strings of two and three syllables. Only one of the Mandarin tones exhibits any significant positional effect (aside from effects that are attributable to acoustic variations in the tones themselves), and this tone is the only one that is markedly similar in its acoustic properties to a common English intonation contour. This tone is perceived significantly better when it occurs in the position in which it is normally found in English sentences (namely, in final position). Thus this tone is more easily perceived when it occurs in the position in which subjects are accustomed to hearing it in their native language, and it is more difficult to perceive when it occurs in an unfamiliar context. The second type of evidence of transfer involves the sorts of errors that English speakers make when they misidentify the Mandarin tone that is phonetically equivalent to an English intonation contour. Again, this misidentification appears to be affected by the position in the string of the contour, and the pattern of misidentification suggests that English speakers tend to analyze this tonal contour in terms of English intonation. This analysis leads to a particular error pattern that can be understood by assuming that speakers analyze only part of the tonal contour as having lexical significance; the rest of the contour is presumably dismissed as part of the sentence intonation pattern. In both these cases, we argue, the performance of the English speakers is what we would expect if we assume that they are perceiving the second language strings in terms of their native language phonological system.

METHOD

To examine the ability of English speakers to identify Mandarin tones, we presented a tape made by a female Mandarin speaker from Taiwan to 50 students in an introductory linguistics course at the University of Iowa. All these students were native speakers of English and none had studied a tone language. The tape consisted of both training and identification tasks. The four lexical tones of Mandarin Chinese were first introduced with the syllable *ti,* and this syllable was produced three times using each tone. Following this very brief training, the subjects were directed to identify the tones of individually presented syllables. The order of the tones was randomized, with each tone appearing three times. The procedure was then repeated with a different syllable *(ma).* The subjects were then asked to identify tones presented in series of two and three syllables (a total of 56 syllables in doublets and 72 syllables in triplets). In the doublets and triplets, each tone occurred the same number of times in each position and with each of the other tones. In the doublets, each tone was also paired with itself. A single example was presented prior to each set of identification trials (6 for singlets and triplets, 7 for doublets), and subjects were given feedback after the presentation of singlets and doublets. No other training was given. Two native speakers of Mandarin were asked to identify the tone on the tape as a control. Their judgements coincided exactly with those of the speaker who had made the tape.

Mandarin Tones

The tape provided no acoustic description of the four tones, identifying them only as first, second, third, or fourth tone. The traditional representation of these tones is presented in Figure 21.1.

The numerical descriptions presented in Figure 21.1 assume a fundamental frequency range exending from a high point of five to a low point of one. The first one, the only level tone of the series, is spoken on the highest pitch and neither rises nor falls. The second tone begins in the middle range and rises. The third and fourth tones both involve falling contours. The third tone begins quite low and falls to the lowest point of the register, where it is often associated with laryngealization. In absolute final position it also contains a rise, indicated by the parenthesized four. The fourth tone also falls, but it begins at a much higher point and falls much more sharply than the third tone.

Pitch in Mandarin is phonemic; changing the pitch of a syllable can change its meaning. Thus the tone of a Mandarin word must be part of its lexical entry. Pitch is used quite differently in English, however, where the pitch pattern of a string may be used to convey such things as the emotional state of the speaker or whether the string is intended to be a question or a statement. However, the Mandarin fourth tone is acoustically quite similar to a common

352

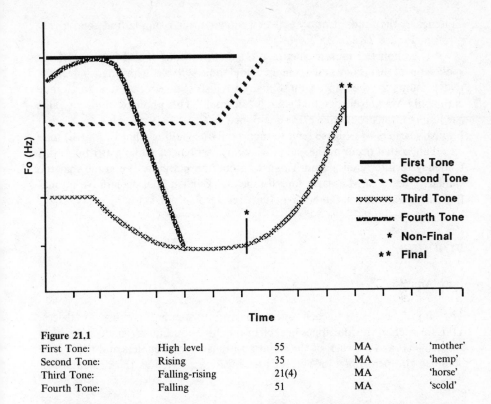

Figure 21.1

First Tone:	High level	55	MA	'mother'
Second Tone:	Rising	35	MA	'hemp'
Third Tone:	Falling-rising	21(4)	MA	'horse'
Fourth Tone:	Falling	51	MA	'scold'

English intonational contour. The unmarked pattern for declaratives in English, traditionally called "rising-falling," involves a rising pitch on the so-called "tonic" syllable—the rightmost pitch-accented syllable—followed by a fall on all material following the tonic syllable. This contour is represented below:

My name is Mary.

When the tonic syllable of a sentence is also the last syllable of that sentence, then both the high pitch generally associated with the tonic syllable and the fall associated with material following the tonic syllable are realized on that single syllable, as below:

My name is John.

This rising-falling contour is also typical of single-word utterances spoken as declaratives, as in *a,* and of the final item in a series, as in *b:*

a. What's your name? John.
b. I invited Susan, Mary, and John.

353

Tracings of the fundamental frequency showing this rising-falling contour are given in Figure 21.2.

The phonetic similarity between the pitch contour of a Mandarin syllable spoken on a fourth tone and a sentence-final tonic syllable in an English declarative accounts for the impression of many English speakers that the fourth tone is the only Mandarin tone that sounds "normal." This phonetic similarity also accounts for the production error mentioned by Chiang (1979), who reports that English learners of Chinese tend to incorrectly use falling (that is, fourth) tone on syllables that occur at the end of Mandarin sentences. Chiang attributes this tendency to interference from English intonation patterns. We argue that the similarity between Mandarin fourth tone and English final declarative intonation also accounts for the error pattern revealed in our study.

RESULTS

Data Analysis

The subjects' response to each tone were cast into standard confusion matrices. Thus for each of the four tones in each of the three conditions (singlets, doublets and triplets) and for each of the serial positions in the doublets and triplets we obtained the percentage of correct identification as well as the percentage of

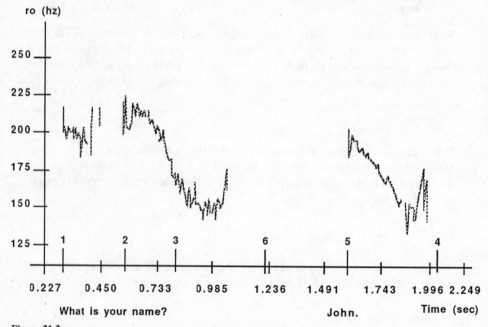

Figure 21.2

misidentification. From these data we computed the index of detectability
(d') and response bias (β):

$$d' = z(X|\overline{X}) - z(X|X)$$
$$\beta = f(X|X)/f(X|\overline{X})$$

We utilized the statistic proposed by Gourevitch and Galanter (1967) to assess
the significance of the differences that we obtained in the detectability of the
tones.

Relative Detectability of Mandarin Tones

If fourth tone is the only Mandarin tone readily perceived in terms of English
intonation patterns, we might expect it to be perceived differently from the other
three tones of Mandarin. An examination of the relative detectability of the four
tones in different positions does reveal some interesting differences between the
perception of fourth tone and the perception of the other tones. As Table 21.1
shows, in a task involving the perception of single tones, fourth tone is the most
easily perceived tone. Its index of detectability (d' = 3.44) is significantly
different from that of all the other tones, (p < .02). This is shown graphically in
Figure 21.3.

Thus the fourth tone appears to be the easiest tone for English speakers
to identify—a property we might ascribe to its combination of a very high
beginning point and very steep fall. This result is consistent with the results of
the various studies of perception of Mandarin tone reviewed in Gandour (1978).
These studies confirm that both native speakers and learners of Mandarin find
tones one and four easiest to identify, while tones two and three, which are
acoustically most alike, are most often confused. All these studies investigated
the perception of tones in single syllables, and their findings suggest that the
perceptibility of a tone is a direct consequence of its acoustic properties. However, when we examine the percent of correct responses for longer strings, a
simple account of detectability only in terms of acoustic properties is not main-
tainable.

As Table 21.2 shows, detection of the fourth tone declines dramatically
in nonfinal position. In fact, fourth tone in the middle position of a triplet

TABLE 21.1. Single Tones

	% Correct	d'
Tone 1:	81%	2.44
Tone 2:	67%	1.72
Tone 3:	78%	2.18
Tone 4:	94%	3.44

TABLE 21.2. Percent Correct Responses: Strings of Two and Three Syllables

	Position				
	1	2	1	2	3
Tone 1:	70%	69%	65%	52%	61%
Tone 2:	55%	47%	47%	48%	40%
Tone 3:	49%	71%	41%	47%	61%
Tone 4:	31%	79%	49%	28%	77%

actually has, at 28 percent, the lowest percent correct score of any tone. Note that while the percent of correct responses declines for all tones in longer strings, the pattern of correct responses for tone four is very different from that of tones one and two. First and second tones show no dramatic positional difference in the percent correct responses in two- and three-syllable strings; as Table 21.3 shows, the indices of detectability of these tones in different positions are fairly close, and the differences between them are not statistically significant. Only tones three and four show a significant difference in detectability between different positions ($p < .01$). For both these tones, detectability in final position—that is, the second position in two-syllable strings and the third position in three-syllable strings—is significantly greater than detectability in nonfinal positions. This is illustrated graphically in Figure 21.3.

The greater detectability of third tone in final vs. non-final position has a straightforward explanation in the facts of Mandarin. The third tone is really produced differently in final position; an examination of narrow band sonagrams and Fo tracings of our tape confirmed that the third tone has a marked rise in final position that is generally absent in non-final positions, as indicated in Figure 21.1. Speakers of Mandarin have of course learned to ignore this allophonic variation in the third tone, but our subjects, whose training exposed them only to the final variant of third tone, predictably have difficulty in recognizing the non-final variant.

No such explanation is available, however, for the positional differences in the detection of the fourth tone, which has essentially the same acoustic properties in all positions, yet is identified correctly far more often in final than

TABLE 21.3. D': Strings of Two and Three Syllables

	Position				
	1	2	1	2	3
Tone 1:	1.71	1.91	1.47	1.13	1.56
Tone 2:	.81	.92	.60	.45	.70
Tone 3:	.85	1.63	.85	.76	1.36
Tone 4:	.98	2.46	1.31	.83	2.02

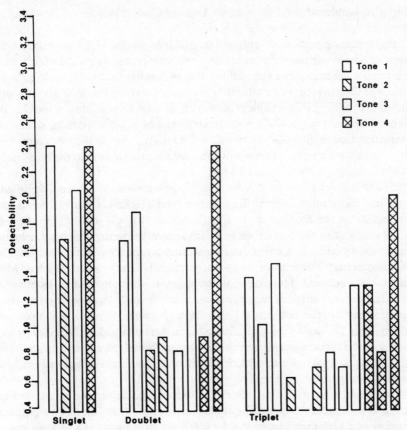

Figure 21.3

in non-final position. This effect, we argue, is a result of interference from English intonation. The contour of the fourth tone is a familiar one, since it corresponds to the fall at the end of declaratives in English. When the fall occurs in final position, then, it is easily recognized as something the listener is accustomed to hearing. In non-final position, however, fourth tone sounds as odd to an English speaker as would an English phoneme occurring in a position in which it does not normally occur in English, such as word-initial velar nasal or word-initial *t* followed by *l*. The relative ease of detectability of the fourth tone in final and non-final positions, then, appears to be a clear result of transfer from the native language. The relative ease of detectability of the fourth tone in string-final position is a result of positive transfer: a familiar item occurring in a familiar position is easy to hear. The difficulty of hearing the fourth tone in non-final position, on the other hand, is a result of negative transfer; the high falling pitch contour normally does not occur in non-final position in English strings.

357

The Misidentification of the Fourth Tone in Final Position

In the preceding section we argued that English speakers are better at identifying the fourth tone in final than in non-final position because in this position the fourth tone corresponds to something that is familiar to them from their native language. We now turn our attention to the pattern of errors that appears when the fourth tone is misidentified. A wealth of anecdotal evidence testifies to a rather surprising pattern of errors: In strings of Mandarin syllables, students of Mandarin tend to identify the fourth (high falling) tone as the first (high level) tone,[1] although the fourth tone and the first tone are otherwise the most distinguished tones.

The answer to the question of why fourth tone should be misidentified as first tone more often in final than in non-final position is fairly obvious once we recall that the contour of the fourth tone is virtually identical to the pitch contour found at the end of an English declarative sentence with a sentence-final tonic syllable. In English, the high pitch on the tonic syllable is linguistically significant; the location of this high pitch indicates which element of the sentence is focussed. Thus the English speaker is accustomed to listening for the high portion of the rising-falling contour, since its location carries semantic information. The fall that follows the high pitch, however, is simply what comes after the tonic syllable. English speakers who identify a final fourth tone as a first tone are apparently dismissing the fall at the end of the string as redundant—part of the sentence contour rather than associated with any particular syllable.

Thus the identification of falling tone as high level tone at the end of a string is interpretable as a consequence of transfer from the native language: English speakers may ignore the final fall because they analyze it as the fall normally associated with the end of a declarative. They identify the starting point of the fall as the portion of the tone contour that is lexically significant —that is, associated with the fourth-tone syllable itself rather than with the sentence contour. This error pattern bears in an interesting way on a controversy in linguistic theory: the question of whether pitch contours are to be represented on the underlying level in terms of contours, such as rising and falling, or whether these surface contours are actually, at a deeper level of analysis, a series of level pitches, such as high and low. A number of convincing analyses of contour tones in terms of level pitches have been offered (for example, Goldsmith, 1976). Analyses of English intonation contours in terms of level pitches have been proposed by Pike (1945), Trager and Smith (1951), among others, and most recently by Liberman (1978) and Pierrehumbert (1980). In all these analyses, the phonetic pitch contours of English intonation represent the surface realization of an underlying pattern of level pitches, with pitch changes merely the necessary transitions from one level pitch to the next.

Given this analysis of English intonation, along with the assumption that English speakers tend to analyze the strings of Mandarin tones in terms of their native language system, the identification of a final falling tone as a high level tone by English speakers makes perfect sense. The fourth tone begins at the highest point of the register but falls immediately to the bottom of the pitch range, while the first tone is a sustained high tone. Thus what the fourth and first tones have in common is their starting points. If the fall characteristic of the ends of English declaratives is, at a deeper level of analysis, composed of two level pitches, a high pitch followed by a low pitch, it is not at all surprising that English speakers should exhibit a tendency to identify the high falling tone as a high level tone in final position. English speakers hearing the Mandarin fourth tone in final position disregard the fall, analyzing it as the surface reflex of a low tone associated with the sentence boundary—that is, an effect of the intonation contour of the sentence—and identify what remains when this sentence contour is stripped away as a high tone. The final fall is apparently decomposed into a high tone, associated with the final syllable, and a low tone, associated with the sentence boundary, and therefore irrelevant to the pitch of the syllable itself. Thus an analysis of the pitch contours of English intonation as the surface realization of an underlying series of level pitches is entirely consistent with the error of identifying final fourth tone as first tone. Confirmation of the assumption that English speakers tend to analyze foreign language pitch phenomena in terms of level pitches is provided by a recent study (Gandour, 1983), which showed that English speakers given the task of rating the dissimilarity of pairs of tones relied far more on the dimension of tone height than on a dimension of direction of change. It should be noted that the alternative theory of English intonation, which posits pitch contours such as rise and fall as underlying units of representation, contributes nothing to our understanding of the identification of final fourth tone as first tone, since this theory offers no explanation for the reason it should be the starting point of the falling contour that is identified as the portion associated with the final syllable, or why a contour tone should be misidentified as a level tone.

Although our subjects made few errors on fourth tone in final position, an examination of the pattern of the response bias (see Figure 21.4) reveals a pattern consistent with the anecdotal evidence that English speakers learning Mandarin Chinese tend to identify fourth tone as the first tone in final position. As predicted, the difference in the response bias between final and nonfinal position as shown in Table 21.4 was greatest for first tone; note also the complementary decrease in β for fourth tone in final position.

CONCLUSION

We have argued that transfer from the intonational system of English accounts for two aspects of English speakers' perception of Mandarin Chinese tones. First, we found that subjects in this study found the fourth tone significantly easier to perceive when it occurred in a position in which the phonetically

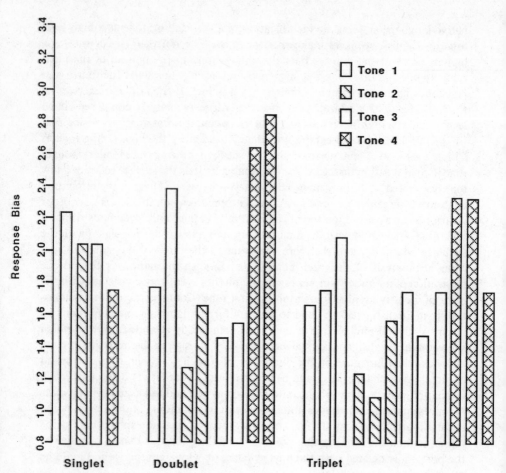

Figure 21.4

similar English pitch contour appears, and that it is significantly more difficult to perceive when it occurred in a position in which it would be anomalous in English. The fourth tone is both the only tone that is markedly similar to an English intonational contour and the only tone that shows a significant posi-

TABLE 21.4. Response Bias ß

| | Position | | | | |
	1	2	1	2	3
Tone 1:	1.74	2.39	1.66	1.79	2.18
Tone 2:	1.25	1.64	1.26	1.13	1.53
Tone 3:	1.47	1.54	1.74	1.42	1.72
Tone 4:	2.64	2.81	2.27	2.28	1.73

360

tional effect. We argued that these two facts can be related once the effect of language transfer is taken into account. Second, we have shown that the response bias is consistent with the anecdotal evidence that a final fourth tone is likely to be heard as a first tone. We can understand the identification of a final fourth tone as a first tone in terms of transfer by assuming that the English speaker analyzes the fourth tone as composed, like the English rising-falling intonation contour, of a redundant fall associated with the sentence boundary preceded by a high tone associated with the syllable itself. Thus the concept of transfer provides an explanation of an otherwise puzzling array of facts (i.e. the positional variation in the detectability of the fourth tone) and it suggests a means of testing the predictions of competing linguistic theories.

NOTE

1. This phenomenon was noticed by one of the authors in several phonetics classes in which students were taught to identify Mandarin tones. The persistence of this error was confirmed by teachers and by English-speaking learners of Mandarin. We are indebted to Susan Schmerling for the report that the entire phonetics class in which she was a student made this error on a final exam.

REFERENCES

Chiang, T. 1979. "Some Interferences of English Intonations with Chinese Tones," *IRAL, 17,* 245–250.
Dulay, H., and M. Burt. 1974. "Errors and Strategies in Child Second Language Acquisition," *TESOL Quarterly, 8,* 129–136.
Gandour, J. 1977. "Counterfeit Tones in the Speech of Southern Thai Bidialectals," *Lingua, 41,* 125–143.
Gandour, J. 1978. "The Perception of Tone," in V. Fromkin (Ed.), *Tone: A Linguistic Survey.* New York: Academic Press.
Gandour, J. 1983. "Tone Perception in Far Eastern Languages," *Journal of Phonetics, 11,* 149–175.
Gandour, J., and R. Harshman. 1978. "Crosslanguage Differences in Tone Perception: A Multidimensional Scaling Investigation," *Language and Speech, 21,* 1–33.
Goldsmith, J. 1976. "An Overview of Autosegmental Phonology," *Linguistic Analysis, 2,* 23–68.
Gourevitch, V., and E. Galanter. 1967. "A Significance Test for One Parameter Isosensitivity Functions," *Psychometrika, 32,* 1, 25–33.
Kiriloff, C. 1969. "On the Auditory Perception of Tones in Mandarin," *Phonetica, 20,* 63–67.
Neufeld, G. 1980. "On the Adult's Ability to Acquire Phonology," *TESOL Quarterly, 14,* 285–298.
Pierrehumbert, J. 1980. *The Phonology and Phonetics of English Intonation.* Doctoral dissertation, MIT.
Pike, K. 1945. *The Intonation of American English.* Ann Arbor: University of Michigan Press.
Richards, J. 1974. "A Non-Contrastive Approach to Error Analysis," in J. Richards (Ed.), *Error Analysis.* London: Longman.
Selkirk, E. 1984. *Phonology and Syntax: The Relation Between Sound and Structure.* Cambridge, MA: MIT Press.
Trager, G., and H. Smith. 1951. *Outline of English Structure.* Norman, OK: Battenburg Press. (Revised edition 1957, Washington: American Council of Learned Societies.)
Tseng, Chiu-Yu. 1981. *An Acoustic-Phonetic Study of Tones in Mandarin Chinese.* Doctoral dissertation, Brown University.

Part Six

VARIATION

Another relatively new area of investigation in IL phonological research is the study of variability and the sources of it. The variability may result from several different factors: sociolinguistic variation, anxiety, level of formality, style shifting, etc. The articles in Part Six discuss variation in IL phonology from many different perspectives.

Schmidt focuses on the relationship between sociolinguistic variation and language transfer in L2 phonological acquisition. He observes that a traditional contrastive comparison can offer no explanation for the Egyptian Arabic speaker's substitution of /s,z/ for /θ,ð/ in the course of acquiring English. However, if the sociolinguistic patterns that characterize the use of colloquial and formal Arabic are well understood, then an explanation of the substitution errors in terms of sociolinguistic transfer becomes available. It would be interesting to attempt an extension of Schmidt's analysis to other dialects of Arabic where many of the same sociolinguistic variables hold but where the substitution patterns in English may be different.

Beebe approaches sociolinguistic variation in IL phonology from a different perspective. Her objective is to demonstrate that a learner's interlanguage exhibits style shifting and sociolinguistic variation in a fashion similar to that found in natural language. Data is collected from nine Thai learners of English. She determines that when a construct in the native phonology is strongly marked for social value, style shifting occurs in the interlanguage according to what would be a socially appropriate speech form in the native context. She also finds that conscious monitoring increases in more formal contexts, giving rise to additional style shifting.

Stølen's study investigates the relative influence of anxiety and formality on L2 when both interact in the learning situation. Here the target language is Danish and the native language is English. She wishes to determine which of the two variables has the greatest impact on L2 phonological productions, and with what consequences. She observes that in an earlier study she conducted, high anxiety appeared to facilitate the subject's performance in syntax. The study of phonological performance involves two testing situations: testing in a classroom setting, where anxiety was moderately high but where the situation was quite informal, and testing in the language laboratory, where anxiety was almost nonexistent yet the speech context was formal, with heavy focus on form. Results from this study indicate that higher anxiety does not promote improved pronunciation. On the other hand, when the testing situation involves low anxiety coupled with a highly formal context, the subject's phonological performance improves. So while high anxiety seems to greatly affect syntactic fluency, it is formality that plays the larger role in influencing phonological performance.

Weinberger, in his study, also looks at the level of formality in his analysis of syllable simplification strategies. He points out that speakers of certain L1s such as Mandarin appear to employ two distinct methods to simplify L2 syllables: vowel epenthesis and consonant deletion. While previous studies have shown that test formality may account for some variation in the overall amount of syllable simplification, Weinberger is concerned with the effect of various data elicitation tasks on the variability *between* these two simplification strategies. The results obtained from testing Mandarin L1 speakers on three different elicitation tasks indicate that formality is not as crucial as linguistic context in the choice of simplification strategy. Weinberger suggests that the epenthesis/deletion differential may be due to the notion of recoverability, and he further speculates that L2 proficiency may affect the overall ratio between these two simplification strategies.

22

SOCIOLINGUISTIC VARIATION AND LANGUAGE TRANSFER IN PHONOLOGY

Richard W. Schmidt

INTRODUCTION

Exaggerated claims for the predictive power of contrastive analysis are no longer fashionable. On the contrary, virtually all researchers in the field would agree that not all second language errors have their source in the learner's native language, and many would agree that "a majority of students' deviations or 'errors' are attributable to intralanguage interference rather than to mother tongue interference" (Scott and Tucker, 1974, 70).

Recent studies of second language acquisition have tended to imply that contrastive analysis may be most predictive at the level of phonology, yet even in this area considerable skepticism remains. This may be due at least partly to the failure of contrastive analyses to provide reliable or complete predictions:

For although a differential description of English and French for example, may indeed point out the fact that a French learner of English may have difficulty pronouncing the interdental sounds of *thin* and *then* because of their absence from the French phoneme inventory, it cannot predict as well as can the experienced teacher which way a given learner or group of learners will handle the difficulty. In point of fact, different learners with the same native language do make different mistakes; the above interdental sounds, for example, are rendered sometimes as /s,z/, sometimes as /t,d/. But this information is supplied, not by an *a priori* comparison of English and French, but by the observations of language teachers. (Mackey, 1966, 8–9)

It is also true, as Tarone (1976) points out, that while many papers have been written claiming to predict performance on the basis of contrastive analysis, few of these have presented systematically gathered and analyzed data to validate the predictions made. Tarone calls for a systematically gathered data base against which various theories of interlanguage phonology could be tested, including the relative importance of language transfer from the native language, the reactivation of first language acquisition processes (the extent to which the second language learner behaves like the first language learner), and—possibly —other processes traceable neither to language transfer nor to the re-activation of first language processes and strategies (Tarone, 1976, 91).

The purposes of this paper are, first, to demonstrate that a careful contrastive analysis can indeed predict some facts about interlanguage phonology in a rather precise manner and, second, to argue that at least for certain types of foreign language (FL) learning problems a more sophisticated type of contrastive analysis than that generally used or assumed must be developed. The FL learning problem to be examined here is the substitution of /s,z/ for English /θ,ð/ by native speakers of Egyptian Arabic. The refinement required in the contrastive analysis is the recognition that neither the target language (English) nor the native language (Arabic) can usefully be described as a self-contained, homogeneous, and static system, used by idealized speaker-hearers in a homogeneous speech community. In the case of Arabic, it may not even be very useful to talk about two such self-contained systems, i.e. colloquial and classical Arabic, in terms of the diglossia model (Ferguson, 1959).

BACKGROUND OF THE PRESENT STUDY

The FL Learning Problem

Teachers of English to native speakers of Egyptian Arabic are well aware of the fact that the majority of their students will have difficulties with English /θ/ and /ð/ and will often substitute /s/ and /z/, respectively. This fact has been noted by innumerable observers and generally has been accounted for in contrastive analyses of English and Egyptian Arabic by the observation that the English interdental fricatives have no counterparts in colloquial Cairo Arabic. The problem is therefore seen as a basic phonemic error of the type in which the target language has a phoneme unmatched in the phonemic inventory of the native language (Todaro, 1970).

The problem with the explanation provided by this type of contrastive analysis is that classical Arabic *does* have the interdental fricatives /θ/ and

/ð/ (as well as a third, emphatic interdental /ð̣/). It ought to be the case, therefore, that students who are literate in Arabic and who have been exposed to Classical Arabic will have little or no difficulty with these English fricatives. But as Todaro and others have pointed out, this is simply not the case (Todaro, 1970, 32). Lehn and Slager observe that even if the student has been exposed to the /θ,ð/ sounds of classical Arabic, in English "he has usually substituted /s,z/ while labouring under the illusion that he was saying something else" (Lehn and Slager, 1959, 28).

In other words, given two types of learners, illiterate and literate, one must claim that both groups exhibit phonological transfer from colloquial Arabic only. This is a totally *ad hoc* explanation, unfortunately, since there may be other mistakes made by literate learners for which interference must be claimed to originate in the classical rather than the colloquial variety of the native language (Kaplan, 1967; Richards, 1973, 124–7). These facts are an embarrassment to a theory of contrastive analysis that claims to predict learners' errors. A comparison of classical and colloquial Arabic and English also fails to explain the fact that while colloquial Egyptian Arabic has both sibilant and stop reflexes for the etymological (classical) interdentals, only sibilant substitutions have been reported in the English of these speakers.

One is tempted to look for other explanations. Since the English interdental fricatives cause problems for learners who speak many different native languages (French, Russian, Japanese, Spanish, etc.), an explanation in terms of inherent difficulty, independent of the learner's native language, is attractive. In discussing the phonology of Erica, a two-year-old native speaker of American English, Moskowitz (1970) has suggested that production problems with the interdentals and other fricatives are primarily due to lack of sufficient motor control—an inability to maintain the articulators in as finely adjusted position as is required. Menyuk (1968), following many other observers, reports that /θ,ð/ are the sounds mastered last and substituted most frequently by English native speakers and further reports that it is the distinctive features $\pm$ continuant (the feature which differentiates /θ,ð/ from /t,d/) $\pm$ strident (differentiating /θ,ð/ from /s,z/) that are the features last mastered by native speakers of English.

However, in the present case, it is this writer's opinion that an explanation based on general developmental processes is less satisfactory than an explanation based on direct interference from the native language. The identification of the source of Egyptian students' difficulties with English *th*-words is suggested by Harrell's observation that "for the Egyptian, /θ/ and /ð/ are merely supercareful stylistic variants of /s/ and /z/ in certain words" (Harrell, 1960, 69). This brief statement requires explanation. The remainder of this paper will deal with the historical origins of the relevant fricative-stop-sibilant alternations in Egyptian Arabic, the ways in which these segments function synchronically as sociolinguistic variables, and the degree of similarity between student performance in Arabic and in English with respect to these variables.

Historical Background

Two diachronic changes have affected the classical Arabic fricatives /θ,ð,ð̣/ in the development of the Egyptian dialect. An early historical rule merged these three segments with the stop series /t,d,d̲/:

Classical Arabic		Egyptian colloquial Arabic
'thick'	θaxi:n	tixi:n
'more'	ʔakθar	ʔaktar
'wolf'	ði²b	di:b
'back'	ð̣ahr	d̲ahr

At some point in time, this sound change ceased to operate. Words that were then borrowed (or re-borrowed) from the classical into the colloquial lexicon instead underwent a new sound change, merging the interdentals /θ,ð/ with the sibilants /s,z/ and creating a new emphatic sibilant /z̲/ as the reflex of /ð̣/:

Classical Arabic		Egyptian colloquial Arabic
'to act'	maθθal	massil
'to mention'	ðakar	zakar
'great'	ʕað̣i:m	ʕaz̲i:m

Although it is impossible to date either of these rules precisely, there is no doubt about their relative chronology. Birkeland (1952) points out that the change from interdental fricatives to stops is common to Lower and Upper Egypt and so must be presumed to have taken place as soon as a distinctive Egyptian Arabic dialect was being formed. The beginning date of the interdental fricative to sibilant change cannot be pinpointed with any precision, but Birkeland gives some evidence ordering the change between the two rules known to have operated after the 14th century.

For contemporary colloquial Egyptian Arabic, Robertson (1970, 147) has observed that "there seems to be no rule as yet for determining which sound will prevail in a given word." This is true in the sense that there are no phonological or other linguistic conditioning factors involved; both the first and the second diachronic changes were unconditioned. What is equally true, however, and important for the present discussion, is that the change from interdental fricatives to stops is no longer operating in Egypt. Words that have not been in the colloquial vocabulary for a long time—including newly coined technical terminology, some older words that are generally acquired by native speakers only through formal education or formal channels, retaining their character as learned words, and foreign borrowings—cannot now be colloquialized with stops. Since this rule is no longer productive, there is no reason to predict any transfer effect from it to a foreign language. The change of fricatives to sibilants remains a productive rule in Egypt, on the other hand, and *any* classical Arabic word with /θ,ð,ḏ/ may be colloquialized with /s,z,z̧/; e.g. /mumaθθil/ ~ /mumassil/, 'actor', but not */mumattil/; /θawra/ ~ /sawra/, 'revolution', but not */tawra/.

Synchronic sociolinguistic variation

As a result of the two historical sound changes discussed above, there are in contemporary Egyptian Arabic numerous lexical triplets with interdental fricative, sibilant and stop variants, e.g., /θa:liθ/ ~ /sa:lis/ ~ /ta:lit/, 'third'. Both linguists and native speakers tend to identify such variants with different linguistic systems (i.e., classical and colloquial) and to assign the alternations to code switching, code mixing, or free variation. The important fact to note, however, is that such switching and mixing is orderly rather than random, and the variation is not really free. These alternations constitute, in Labov's terms, a sociolinguistic variable—"one which is correlated with some non-linguistic variable of the social context: of the speaker, the addressee, the audience, the setting, etc." (Labov, 1970, 192).

I have investigated the stylistic use of interdental fricative, sibilant, and stop pronunciations in lexical items with potential interdentals (hereafter referred to as the Arabic TH-variable) among 16 university students and 12 working class males with secondary education or less in Cairo (Schmidt, 1974). In each of four discrete styles—relatively informal interview speech, formal interview style, reading passages, and reading word lists—a distinctive distribution pattern appeared.

As Table 22.1 shows, different pronunciations of the Arabic TH-variable predominated in different styles. Interdental fricatives accounted for slightly more than half of all realizations of the TH-variable when reading from word lists, but in no other style. Sibilants predominated when reading from texts. Stops did not occur at all in the reading styles but prevailed in the relatively casual parts of the oral interview. Stop and sibilant pronunciations were about equal in the more formal parts of the interview.

The same general pattern—an increase in sibilant pronunciation in the middle of the stylistic continuum and increases in fricative and stop pronuncia-

TABLE 22.1: Pronunciation of the Arabic TH-variable in Various Styles—All Informants (Schmidt, 1974, 95)

	Informal interview speech	Formal interview speech	Reading passage	Reading word lists
Interdental fricatives	—	4%	39%	56%
Sibilants	22%	45%	61%	44%
Stops	78%	51%	—	—

tions at the formal and informal ends, respectively—held for both informant groups. There was, however, a striking difference between the two socioeconomic groups studied. While all the university students produced at least some instances of interdental pronunciations, seven of the twelve working-class informants produced no interdentals at all. Those working-class informants who did produce some instances of the classical interdentals did so less than half as frequently as the mean for the university group. The Arabic TH-variable thus appears to be a highly developed sociolinguistic marker, an indicator that co-varies along at least the two dimensions of style and socioeconomic class.

Something should be said here about the subjective reactions of native speakers to the varying pronunciations of words containing the TH-variable. Stop pronunciations of words with etymological interdentals are universally identified by native speakers as colloquial and therefore "incorrect" when used in any context that normatively calls for the use of classical Arabic. The status of sibilant variants is much more complex, and whether or not /s,z,z/ are considered "correct" pronunciation of Arabic ث, ذ, ظ depends on both the critic and a finer definition of the speech situation (cf. Kaye, 1970). If a student reciting from the Koran reads using sibilant pronunciations, he will be forcefully corrected by his Arabic teacher. However, a television newscaster who alternates between interdental and sibilant pronunciations will occasion no comment. His variable behavior in that context (still formal and still normatively requiring "classical" Arabic) will be neither censured nor even noticed.

VARIABILITY AND LANGUAGE TRANSFER

Hypotheses

In the light of the foregoing discussion, two hypotheses are suggested regarding the pronunciation of *th*-words in English by native speakers of Egyptian Arabic:

(1) Native speakers of Egyptian Arabic learning English as a FL will alternate interdental and sibilant (but not stop) pronunciation of *th*-words along the dimension of style (formal-informal), in English as in Arabic.

(2) Within a given style level, the frequency with which a given speaker substitutes sibilants in English *th*-words will reflect his performance in Arabic at an equivalent style level.

Subjects and Procedure[1]

Subjects for the present experiment consisted of 34 native speakers of Arabic, all male, all students of English at the time the study was carried out. Twenty-two of the subjects were first- and second-year students in Egyptian public (government) secondary schools. Their ages ranged between 15 and 17 years.

370

In each of the four schools from which these students were drawn, Arabic is the primary language of instruction, and English is the major foreign language taught. Since English instruction is begun at the preparatory (junior high) level in Egypt, each of these Ss had already completed three or four years of study of English at the time of the study. The remaining twelve Ss were adult learners (24–40 years) enrolled in beginning and lower intermediate level English classes at the Division of Public Service of the American University in Cairo. These Ss comprised a socially and educationally more heterogeneous group than the secondary students but were judged by teachers familiar with both groups to be roughly equivalent to the secondary students in terms of overall English proficiency.

Each S was interviewed separately, on school grounds, by his regular English teacher and was asked to read aloud the following:

a) a reading passage of about 150 words in Arabic
b) a reading passage of approximately the same length in English
c) a list of 20 Arabic words, all containing either /θ/ or /ð/
d) a list of 10 minimal pairs in Arabic contrasting /θ/:/s/ and /ð/:/z/
e) a list of 20 English words, all containing either /θ/ or /ð/
f) a list of 10 English minimal pairs for /θ/:/s/ and /ð/:/z/

The reading passages in both English and Arabic were chosen on the basis of appropriateness of level for the student subjects. Natural texts were altered slightly (a) to increase the occurrences of /θ/ and /ð/ and (b) to reduce excessive repetition of a few specific lexical items with these fricatives in English (e.g. *the, there*) and Arabic (e.g. /ha:ða/, 'this'). The Arabic reading passage had a total of ten potential occurrences of /θ/ (10 types, 10 tokens), and thirteen potential occurrences of /ð/ (10 types, 13 tokens), The English passage had a total of twelve potential occurrences of /θ/ (11 types, 12 tokens) and eighteen potential occurrences of /ð/ (11 types, 18 tokens). As far as possible the test materials were constructed using words that the teachers judged to be familiar to the students.

Ss were told that their teachers wanted to compare their reading levels in Arabic and English. They were of course not told about the particular phonological contrast of interest, but since the presentation of the first minimal pair list was assumed (and intended) to make the students aware of this specific interest, no word lists were presented to the subjects until both reading passages were completed. Within the two major groups of tasks, reading passages and reading word lists (including minimal pairs), the order of presentation (Arabic-English or English-Arabic) was randomly varied.

All Ss were tape-recorded while reading. From these tapes, scores were computed initially for the number of instances of /θ/ and /ð/ separately in each of the three parts of the test for each of the two languages. Subsequent analysis showed no significant differences on the voiced-voiceless dimension, so only

371

figures for /θ/ and /ð/ summed are presented in the following section. Realizations of classical Arabic /ð̣/ were not observed in this study. The frequency of this phoneme in Arabic is low, and since there is no English counterpart of this Arabic segment there is no place in English where one could look to find interference from the Arabic alternations.

Since the number of occurrences of the TH-variable in the English reading passage was greater than the number of such occurrences in the Arabic reading passage, percentage scores were used for this analysis. For the word lists and minimal pairs lists only raw scores were used.

Results and Discussion

In the English test battery, four Ss pronounced all *th*-words correctly, using /θ,ð/ in every case. One of these Ss used /θ,ð/ consistently in the Arabic part of the test as well. One S produced only sibilant pronunciations in both languages. All other Ss alternated between /θ,ð/ and /s,z/ in both English and Arabic. As expected, there were no occurrences of /t,d/ pronunciations in either language, with the single exception of one S who read /talati:n/ ('thirty') rather than the expected /θalaθi:n or /salasi:n/ in the Arabic reading passage.

The hypothesis that Ss would vary their pronunciations of *th*-words stylistically in the two languages was confirmed, although the patterns found were *not* identical. As can be seen from Table 22.2, Ss increased the frequency of *th*-pronunciations in both languages when moving from the most informal style used here, the reading passage, to the two more formal styles of word lists and minimal pairs.

In Arabic, Ss increased the frequency of interdental pronunciations gradually in successively more formal reading styles. For Arabic, the differences when moving from the reading passage to the word list and when moving from the word list to the list of minimal pairs are both statistically significant (by t-test, significant at the 1 percent level of confidence). However, it is apparent from the table that the English test did not elicit completely parallel behavior. The increase from reading passage to word list is less in English than in Arabic (though still significant at the 1 percent level), and there was no increase at all when moving from reading word lists to reading minimal pairs in English.

TABLE 22.2: Realizations of the TH-variable in
English and Arabic—All Subjects

	% of interdental pronunciations		
	Reading passage	Word list	Minimal pairs
Arabic	33%	64%	77%
English	54%	73%	73%

At least two facts need to be explained here: the higher base point (reading passage) for English than for Arabic, and the absence of measurable differences in performance in word lists as opposed to minimal pairs. In the first case, there are at least two possibilities. The English reading passage might not have been sufficiently equivalent to the Arabic passage to get comparable results, or some or all of the Ss may actually perform less variably in English than in Arabic, although still not in control of a categorical interdental-sibilant contrast. The latter seems the more plausible explanation and is discussed further at the end of this section.

The lack of increase in *th*-pronunciations when reading minimal pairs, on the other hand, may well be the result of the instrument used. As noted above, the English test was constructed attempting to use only words familiar to the students. For the reading passage and word list this was possible, but familiarity could not be ensured for the minimal pairs list. Minimal pairs such as *then:Zen*, the latter almost certainly unfamiliar to Ss, were eliminated from consideration, but some items included, such as *seething: seizing* or *breeze:breathe* (the latter pronounced by several Ss as /breθ/ an incorrect pronunciation scored as correct in this case, since only the interdental-sibilant alternation was at issue) proved also to be unfamiliar. It is suspected that the effectiveness of minimal pairs testing as a device to draw attention strongly to the contrasts being tested was neutralized in this case by the attention focused by Ss on the meanings of unfamiliar lexical items.

The hypothesis that, within a given style level, the frequency with which a given S would substitute sibilants for interdentals in English *th*-words would reflect his or her alternations in Arabic was strongly supported. As can be seen from Table 22.3, performance scores for English *th*-words correlated highly with scores on the Arabic TH-variable for both subject groups at each style level measured.

While the correlations reported in Table 22.3 permit rejection at a high level of confidence of the null hypothesis that pronunciation of English *th*-words is not related to performance on the Arabic TH-variable, such correlations do not, strictly speaking, prove a causal relationship, i.e. language transfer *from*

TABLE 22.3: Pearson Product-Moment Correlations for English and Arabic TH-variable in Various Styles

	r (correlation coefficient) for:		
	12 Adults	22 Secondary students	Total all S's
Reading passages	.6977*	.7913**	.7348**
Word lists	.6863*	.6968**	.6897**
Minimal pairs	.7225**	.6952**	.7015**
Total battery	.7687**	.8436**	.8499**

*p < .01   **p < .005   (one-tailed)

Arabic *to* English. The theoretical possibility that English performance has caused the Arabic performance is in the present case highly implausible. The third possible interpretation, that some unmeasured variable lies behind both the Arabic and the English interdental-sibilant alternations, is not implausible, however, since as reported earlier performance on the Arabic TH-variable was shown in a previous study to be a function of socioeconomic class and education.

The present experiment was not designed to include detailed information on the socioeconomic status of Ss. However, several ex post facto analyses have been performed on the data to discover possible differences among subject groups.

It was suspected that there might well be measurable differences between the secondary students and the adult learners used as Ss. These two subject groups differ in several ways, including age and educational experience as well as exposure to different teaching methods, materials, and teacher-models. However, t-tests carried out on the means of these two groups at each style level revealed no significant differences in either English or Arabic.

A closer examination of the secondary students, on the other hand, indicated that these Ss could be broken into two groups that exhibited quite different behavior. Of the 22 secondary Ss, six were drawn from a terminal secondary school program that trains elementary school teachers for public schools. By reputation at least, such teacher training schools enroll students of lower socioeconomic background and offer poorer quality instruction than do the full-curriculum college preparatory secondary schools. The remaining 16 secondary Ss were students in regular, non-terminal secondary schools and are at least potentially future university students.

As shown in Table 22.4, there were striking differences between these two groups of secondary students. In all six test contexts, the means for the non-terminal secondary Ss are higher than those of the terminal secondary Ss. In spite of the fact that the number of Ss in the terminal group is very small, differences in the means for the reading passage and word lists in both languages were significant at the 5 percent level of confidence or better.

TABLE 22.4 Mean Scores for the TH-variable in English and Arabic for Two Groups of Secondary Students

		6 Ss Terminal secondary	16 Ss Non-terminal secondary	t-value
Arabic	Reading passage	8.66	45.63	2.369*
	Word list	43.33	70.62	1.747*
	Minimal pairs	68.33	78.75	.704
English	Reading passage	19.66	60.25	3.243**
	Word list	40.00	86.25	5.087**
	Minimal pairs	53.33	79.38	1.615

df = 20   *p < .05   **p < .01   (one-tailed)

Something might be said also about the performance of these two groups with regard to the minimal pairs list, particularly in English. It was speculated above that the identical means for all Ss (secondary and adult combined) for the English minimal pairs list might have been due to the inclusion of unfamiliar words that distracted Ss from the phonological contrasts at issue. From Table 22.4, we see that the two secondary groups behaved quite differently in this regard; the terminal secondary Ss did tend to increase the frequencies of interdental pronunciations of English *th*-words when reading minimal pairs, while the non-terminal students tended to *decrease* interdental pronunciation. This suggests the further speculation (no more than that) that the university preparatory students were more distracted by and concerned about the meanings of unfamiliar words, while the terminal students were able to concentrate on simply reading aloud in as acceptable a manner as possible, with little regard for meaning.

One final aspect of the data collected in the present experiment might be discussed, not because firm conclusions can be drawn but because of the importance of questions that need to be answered by future research. One needs to ask how it is that the kind of phonological interference from native language to FL demonstrated here for relatively low proficiency FL learners persists for some very advanced second language speakers, while other such learners quite successfully develop disjunctive phonologies for the two languages. The data here may offer no answers in terms of the strategies that such successful learners use, but do provide evidence that some of the Ss in this experiment are moving in that direction. A comparison of individual subject scores for the total English battery versus the total Arabic battery reveals no S whose total score (interdental realizations of the TH-variable) in Arabic exceeds his English scores by as much as ten percentage points. On the other hand, six of the twelve adult Ss and six of the 16 non-terminal secondary Ss (but none of the terminal secondary S's) did have total English *th*-scores exceeding their Arabic scores by ten or more percentage points. While continuing to exhibit *th*-variability in both languages and continuing to express this variability along the dimension of style, these Ss are apparently moving towards a categorical system for English. Two Ss, both non-terminal secondary students, appear to have almost achieved the goal of disjunctive phonologies for the two languages: The total English interdental scores for those students were 90 percent and 88 percent; their total Arabic *th*-scores were 51 percent and 19 percent, respectively.

CONCLUSIONS

The study reported here has investigated a very limited area of interlanguage phonology in order to support the claim that a careful, sociolinguistically oriented, contrastive analysis can predict some FL errors—i.e. that a better case can be made for language transfer than for explanations independent of native language. The data support the following conclusions with regard to the specific phonological variable investigated:

First, the common observation that native speakers of Egyptian Arabic frequently substitute sibilants in English *th-*words, regardless of whether or not they have been exposed to classical Arabic, was confirmed. The explanation offered is that the traditional dichotomy between classical and colloquial Arabic is misleading in this respect, and alternation among interdental and sibilant pronunciations of Arabic *th-*words is normal and acceptable in most speech contexts that normatively require "classical" Arabic.

Second, the observation that Egyptians do not substitute stops in English *th-*words was also confirmed. The explanation offered here is that while colloquial stops do often alternate with classical interdentals, this is the result of a historical sound change that is no longer productive.

Third, the hypothesis that Ss would alternate interdental and sibilant pronunciations of the TH-variable stylistically in the two languages was confirmed. However, an English minimal pairs list did not elicit the expected increase in standard interdental pronunciations. It was suggested that this unexpected result might have been due to the inclusion of unfamiliar words in the English minimal pairs list, which may have distracted some (but not all) Ss from the phonological contrast at issue.

Fourth, the hypothesis that, within styles and across the stylistic spectrum, Ss' substitutions of sibilants for interdentals in English would correlate highly with their performance in Arabic was supported.

Fifth, previous research showing that performance on the Arabic TH-variable is an indicator of social class and educational background was at least partially supported by the differences in performance in the two languages by terminal and non-terminal secondary students.

Besides predicting the occurrence and distribution of second language errors in pronunciation in a more precise manner than conventional analyses contrasting native and target languages as static systems, the present investigation may have something to say about the relative persistence of phonological interference in even advanced second language learners. The patterning of the Arabic TH-variable has a number of properties that allow it to be classified as a "stable sociolinguistic variable" (Labov, 1970). Labov has suggested that one of the striking characteristics of such stable sociolinguistic variables is that while there is general awareness that one variant is "correct," individual members of the speech community are unaware that they shift in the way they do, nor do they know that others shift in the same manner. This is certainly true in the present case. An educated native speaker of Egyptian Arabic is typically skeptical when told that literate native speakers often substitute /s,z/ for /θ,ð/ when reading Arabic and incensed if told that he himself makes such substitutions. These substitutions are made well below the level of conscious awareness.

There is finally at least one implication for teaching English to native speakers of Egyptian Arabic. A rather common device used by teachers of English who are themselves native speakers of Arabic is to stress the identity of English *th* with orthographic Arabic ث (θ) and ذ (ð), rather than س (s) or ز (z). In the light of the present analysis, this seems misguided. For although there are minimal pairs showing that Arabic /θ,ð/ and /s,z/ are phonemically contrastive in careful speech, the fact remains that any printed ث may be read aloud as /s/ and any ذ as /z/. Identification of English *th* with the Arabic variable *th* is precisely what must be avoided.

NOTES

1. Salah Abdel Khalek Gawad, Abdel Mottaleb Abdel Aaty, Abbas Mohamed Shalaby, and Mona Zaklama Fahmy, students in TEFL 503 (Psychological factors in language learning) at the American University in Cairo, assisted in the design, administration, and scoring of the experimental materials used in this study.

REFERENCES

Birkeland, H. 1952. *Growth and Structure of the Egyptian Arabic Dialect.* Oslo: Avhandlinger utg. av Det Norske Videnskape-Acad.

Ferguson, C.A. 1959. Diglossia. *Word 15,* 325–340.

Harrell, R.S. 1960. A linguistic analysis of Egyptian radio Arabic. In C.A. Ferguson (Ed.), *Contributions to Arabic Linguistics.* Cambridge, MA: Harvard Middle Eastern Monograph Series No 3.

Kaplan, R. 1967. Contrastive rhetoric and the teaching of composition. *TESOL Quarterly 1,* 4; 10–16.

Kaye, A. 1970. Modern standard Arabic and the colloquials. *Lingua 24,* 374–391.

Labov, W. 1970. The study of language in its social context. *Studium Generale 23,* 66–84. Reprinted in J.A. Fishman (Ed.), *Advances in the Sociology of Language,* Vol. I. 152–216. The Hague: Mouton.

Lehn, W., and W.R. Slager. 1959. A contrastive study of Egyptian Arabic and American English: the segmental phonemes. *Language Learning 9,* 25–33.

Mackey, W.F. 1966. Language didactics and applied linguistics. *English Language Teaching, 20,* 197–206. Reprinted in J.W. Oller and J.C. Richards, *Focus on the Learner: Pragmatic Perspectives for the Language Teacher.* Rowley, MA: Newbury House.

Menyuk, P. 1968. The role of distinctive features in children's acquisition of phonology. *Journal of Speech and Hearing Research 11,* 138–146.

Moskowitz, A.I. 1970. The two-year-old stage in the acquisition of English phonology. *Language 46,* 426–441.

Richards, J.C. 1973. Error analysis and second language strategies. In J.W. Oller and J.C. Richards (Eds.), *Focus on the Learner: Pragmatic Perspectives for the Language Teacher.* Rowley, MA: Newbury House.

Robertson, A.M. 1970. Classical Arabic and colloquial Cairene: An historical linguistic analysis. Unpublished doctoral dissertation. University of Utah.

Scott, M.S., and G.R. Tucker. 1974. Error analysis and English language strategies of Arab students. *Language Learning 24,* 69–97.

Schmidt, R.W. 1974. Sociostylistic variation on spoken Egyptian Arabic: A re-examination of the concept of diglossia. Unpublished doctoral dissertation. Brown University.

Tarone, E.E. 1976. Some influences on interlanguage phonology. *Working Papers on Bilingualism.* Ontario Institute for Studies in Education, 8, 87–111. (Also this volume.)

Todaro, M. 1970. A contrastive analysis of the segmental phonologies of American English and Cairo Arabic. Unpublished doctoral dissertation. University of Texas.

23

SOCIOLINGUISTIC VARIATION AND STYLE SHIFTING IN SECOND LANGUAGE ACQUISITION*

Leslie M. Beebe

One of the most neglected areas of inquiry in the field of second language acquisition (henceforth SLA) is sociolinguistic variation. Labov (1966) convinced linguistic researchers that we could not continue to place our undivided attention on the abstract, ideal competence of native speakers, but that in order to understand the greater picture, we would have to focus as well on their actual, variable performance. Although many linguists continued to investigate only the idealized, invariant rules of native-speaker competence, most were convinced of the legitimacy of sociolinguistic research and the necessity of investigating sociolinguistic variation in language performance. There was some carryover to the field of second language acquisition and second language performance. Both Adjémian (1976) and Tarone (1979) have insisted that an interlanguage (IL) is

*The data discussed in this paper were collected under a grant from the Spencer Foundation with the sponsorship of Teachers College, Columbia University. The research was subsequently funded by an NIE grant awarded by the Institute for Urban and Minority Education. I gratefully acknowledge the support of these institutions. I would also like to thank Robert Oprandy, a doctoral student at Teachers College, who as research assistant conducted the interviews and phonetically transcribed the data.

like a first language in that it is a natural language. A natural language, unlike an artificial computer language, is, by definition, variable.

As Tarone (1979) points out in her article "Interlanguage as Chameleon," SLA researchers have responded to the challenge of proving that interlanguage has the same type of style shifting (according to experimental task) as is found in native language (NL) research (e.g., Dickerson, 1975, Dickerson and Dickerson, 1977; LoCoco, 1976, Wong-Fillmore, et al., 1979). However, for the most part, sociolinguistic variation has been ignored by SLA researchers. While this is not as detrimental as claiming it does not exist, the decade of the 70s was characterized by an unfortunate disregard for sociolinguistic variation in IL. The onset of the 1980s presents a renewed challenge to SLA researchers to investigate sociolinguistic variation. Several important questions, hitherto virtually unexplored, are discussed in this paper.

RESEARCH QUESTIONS

First of all, this paper examines the claim made by Tarone (1979) that IL is progressively more permeable in increasingly more formal situations to the superordinate rule system—that is, the target language (TL). In this research, the claim would be that in listing data, pronunciation more closely approximates native English than in interview conversation because of the fact that the formal reading of words has been permeated by the superordinate target language (English) system. Second, the paper explores the question posed by Tarone (1979): Can the NL as well as the TL act as a superordinate rule system and thereby permeate the IL? In other words, this study asks: Is IL characterized in formal situations by a high level of both correct TL variants and transferred NL variants? A third set of questions posed here involves the nature of the sounds transferred from the NL. In a shift toward a formal style, if there is a great deal of transfer from the NL, does this transfer follow rules of sociolinguistic appropriateness in the NL? Is there perhaps more permeation by the NL in environments where the NL sounds carry social value? Finally, this paper examines the question of whether the Monitor specifically and monitoring in general are used on a sliding scale or an "on-off" basis. (Throughout, I observe Krashen's convention of using the term "*M*onitor" to refer to conscious application of grammatical rules, and "*m*onitoring" to refer to attention paid to speech.)

METHODOLOGY

The data used to investigate these claims and questions are a subsample of data from a study in progress of phonological variation in the speech of twenty-five Asian subjects living in New York. The subsample consists of nine adult Thais. The nine subjects are classified into three social classes, based on the findings of an occupational prestige survey conducted in Thailand (Beebe, 1974). There are three subjects in each social class. The three in the upper social level are doctors or professors at a medical school (the occupation of professor has a high prestige in Thailand relative to its status in the United States). The three in the middle social level are nurses; the three in the lowest social level are dishwashers or food vendors. All subjects are native speakers of Bangkok Thai. They range in age from twenty-five to forty years, with a mean age of thirty-one. Only one subject, a nurse, does not fall into the twenty-five to thirty-three age range. Without this subject, the mean age of the group is twenty-nine.

There are approximately equal numbers of male and female subjects in the study: five females and four males. Unfortunately, it was impossible to find available and qualifying female subjects in the lowest occupational group and male subjects in the middle level group. This situation reflects sex-based occupational preferences. The unequal distribution of males and females in this study is not considered to be particularly problematic, however, since sex was *not* a factor in a sociolinguistic study of variation on R in Thai[1] (Beebe, 1974).

As for the method of data collection, all interviews were tape-recorded on a Uher 4000. The interviews were approximately one hour in length. All were conducted fully in English by a twenty-nine-year-old male graduate student who is a native speaker of American English and a second language speaker of Thai. The same person phonetically transcribed and scored the data.

Interviews were conducted in one sitting at Columbia University. They consisted of a conversation, the reading of a passage, the reading of a list of twenty-five isolated words selected from the passage, and a listening perception test, in that order. The data presented here are taken solely from the conversation and the single word listing task. These two parts of the interview were intended to demonstrate style shifting by eliciting a sharp contrast in styles.

Though not the same as spontaneous speech, an interview conversation is a speech event which has its own rules and produces a characteristic style (Wolfson, 1976). Reading a list of words is a strictly experimental task which produces another, more formal, less regular style (Labov, 1966, 1972). Contrasting these two speech events, we can demonstrate style shifting (by definition a sociolinguistic phenomenon) while keeping constant social factors such as topic, setting, and listener. These social factors normally vary in "free" conversation. This is not a problem if we are studying one individual, but it does prevent us from making comparisons in cross-sectional studies.

There are drawbacks in using interview settings and artificial tasks to collect sociolinguistic data. However, there are also serious problems in gathering totally unselfconscious speech (Labov's "Observer's Paradox," 1969). The data in this study are not claimed to be unselfconscious, spontaneous, everyday, or vernacular conversation. They are, however, natural in the sense that Wolfson (1976, p. 208) suggests; that is, they are "appropriate to the occasion." They are appropriate to the interview—a normal speech event in our society.

The questions in the interview conversation dealt with (1) getting the ingredients in this country to make one's own native food, (2) "scary" experiences while living in New York, (3) embarrassing incidents that occurred as a result of the interviewee's being a newcomer to this culture. Although the interviewer asked each subject about each topic in the same way initially and in the same order (given here), there was a good deal of unregulated conversation involved in simply responding and getting the subject to elaborate. No attempt was made to elicit specific words or sounds. The number of tokens for each phonological variable varied with the speaker.

The listing task was more uniform. Subjects were asked to read a list of twenty-five words containing an /r/ or an /l/ in single initial, single final, initial cluster, or final cluster position. The words were selected from the passage they had read on the basis of containing /r/ or /l/ in representative syllable positions and environments. (For the list of words, see Appendix A.) Five of the words contained single initial /r/; two contained single final /r/. Thus there were fewer tokens in general in the listing task than in the interview conversation.

FINDINGS AND ANALYSIS

The raw data on the use of initial and final R in the two styles are presented in Table 23.1. Analysis of these data suggests that Tarone (1979) may be correct in some instances in claiming that IL is progressively more permeable in increasingly more formal situations to the superordinate rule system of the TL. For example, final R was pronounced correctly by the Thais significantly more often in the listing task than in the conversation. They pronounced it correctly 72 percent of the time in listing, but only 35 percent of the time in conversation. The TL (English) permeated the formal listing style. (See Table 23.2)

On the other hand, the findings from the Thai data on initial R indicate that although the IL is more permeable in a formal context, the superordinate rule system that is permeating it is the NL. That is, phonetic interference is rampant in initial R listing. Consequently, although Thais pronounced 48 percent of the initial R's correctly in conversation, they pronounced only 9 percent of them correctly in listing (Table 23.2).

It is impossible to do a reliable error analysis of final R. Final R does not exist in Thai, the NL; therefore, any non-TL variant used in the IL could be attributed (in the broadest sense) to interference. However, these IL variants may, in fact, be approximations of the TL norm. In the case of non-native speakers living in New York, the problem is even more complicated since New York City is known for its "r-less dialects"—i.e., the dropping of postvocalic R. The /ø/ and /ə/ IL variants for English R that Thais produce can be analyzed in several different ways. One view might be that the variants are naturally acquired New York English. Another view is that they are due to NL interference. Still another view is that Thais are transferring a pattern of using /ø/ and /ə/ that they have adopted for loanwords with postvocalic R. Finally,

TABLE 23.1 Number and Percentage of Tokens for Each IL Variant of the R Variable in Two Different Speech Styles

IL variant		Conversation #	Conversation %	Listing #	Listing %
Initial R					
ɹ	TL variant (correct)	30	38.5	4	8.9
ɹ'		40	51.3	5	11.1
ɻ		2	2.6		
ɭ	new variants	3	3.8	15	33.3
wɹ'				1	2.2
ɾ				2	4.4
ḻ				1	2.2
ḻ				3	6.7
ř	NL variants (interference)	3	3.8	3	6.7
r̃				11	24.4
	Totals:	78	100%	45	99.9%
Final R					
ɹ	TL variants[a]	9	4.6		
ɹ'	(correct)	72	36.5	13	72.2
ø	possible NL	65	33	3	16.7
ə	interference	49	24.9	2	11.1
w	new variant	2	1.1		
	Totals:	197	100.1%	18	100%

[a]In final position, both /ɹ/ and /ɹ'/ are considered correct. See Appendix B.

some would say these are new variants, not interference, because Thais pronounce /n/ for the final letter "r" in Thai words, and interference theory would therefore predict /n/ substitution for English final R in IL. We cannot claim to have a definite answer. Given the ethnic diversity of the New York population at large and the sociolinguistic variation within single groups of New Yorkers on postvocalic R, we cannot even determine the exact nature of the input available for natural acquisition. We simply know it is variable.

Table 23.3 gives a complete error analysis for the initial R. A major reason for the low accuracy rates on this variable in listing is interference from Thai. Substitution of Thai /ɣ̃/, /ř/, and /ḻ/ for American /ɹ/ accounts for 39.4

TABLE 23.2 Accuracy Rates[a] Reflecting Style Shifting of Nine Thai ESL Speakers on Pronunciation of R

Phonological variable	Speech style	
	Conversation	Listing
Initial R	48	9 (permeated by formal NL variants, nonexistent in English)
Final R	35	72 (permeated by TL variants)

Initial R: $t8 = 2.93$; $p < .02$ (SD = .397)
Final R: $t8 = -5.31$; $p < .001$ (SD = .211)

[a]Accuracy rates are measured in percents. The percents in this table are based on mean proportions (i.e., the mean of the individual proportions for the nine subjects). In Table 23.1, however, each percentage represents a total group score (i.e., a percentage that is based on one aggregate proportion). Therefore, mean percentages for accuracy rates may differ from aggregate percentages for correct TL variants in Table 23.1.

TABLE 23.3 Percentage of Error Due to Interference and Creation of New IL Variants for R Variable

	Speech style	
Cause of error	Conversation	Listing
Initial R	6.2	39.4
Interference		
[ř], [ɾ], [l̪]		
New Variants	93.8	60.6
[ɹ'], [wɹ'], [ɻ], [ɹ̠], [ɽ], [l̪]		
Final R[a]		

Interference: $t8 = 2.73$; $p < .05$ (SD = .373)

[a]Final R does not exist in the NL (Thai). Therefore, the distinction between NL interference and TL approximation (new variants) cannot be maintained.

percent of the error. (See Appendix B for a phonetic description of all R variants.) An even greater reason for the low accuracy on initial R in listing, however, is the creation of new variants which do not exist in either Thai or English. These new variants (/ɹ'/, wɹ'/, /ɻ/, /ɹ̠/, /ɽ/, and /l̪/) comprise 60.6 percent of the error. Interference accounts for 39.4 percent of the error in initial R listing data but only 6.2 percent of the error in the conversation data. This shows that there is more negative transfer for initial R in the listing data than in the conversation. That is, interference prevails in the more formal context. The formal situation is the one where there is permeability by the NL.

At this point, there is some evidence to examine Tarone's questions. The data support the view that the IL becomes more permeable in the formal context and show that it is sometimes permeated by the TL, as in the case of the final R, and sometimes permeated by the NL, as in the case of the initial R. The important question may therefore be: What factors determine which system acts as the superordinate rule system that permeates the IL in formal contexts?

383

The data here suggest that the social value of the sounds in the NL may be an important factor in determining whether the NL acts as the superordinate system. Schmidt (1977) has demonstrated that sociolinguistic patterns may be transferred from the NL to the TL. In his study, Egyptian Arabic was the NL and English was the TL. In the Thai data here, there is additional evidence that a sociolinguistic pattern may be transferred. There is also clear evidence that the social value of R sounds plays a role in the degree to which Thai permeates English IL in a formal context.

The evidence that a sociolinguistic pattern is being transferred in these data comes from the fact that Thais use /l/ for R an average of 95 percent of the time in informal contexts. The majority of Thais in truly spontaneous situations seem to use /l/ for R 100 percent of the time, but the most casual settings have never been tape-recorded and analyzed. In careful speech, Thais use flapped /ř/, which they consider to be correct R. In formal settings, they attempt to use trilled /r̃/ (Beebe, 1974). In the English data from Thais in this study, we find that the proper flapped /ř/ is used 3.8 percent of the time in conversation, but 6.7 percent of the time in listing. The most formal R, the trilled /r̃/, is never once used in conversation, but it occurs 24.4 percent of the time in the formal listing task. This is clear evidence that a formal Thai variant is being transferred in a sociolinguistically formal setting. The variation in the use of trilled /r̃/ demonstrates both style shifting and transfer of a socially appropriate variant based on NL rules.

The evidence that the social value attached to a variable affects the degree to which the NL permeates the IL in a formal context is a separate argument. It stems in part from the fact that within the listing data, the trilled /r̃/ appears only in initial position, the same position where it could occur in Thai. It is also based on the fact that initial position is more permeated by NL variants than final position. It is initial position R variants in Thai that have a highly conscious, learned social meaning. The teaching and usage of the "correct" initial R has been in vogue in Thailand since a decree of Rama II. (The present king is Rama IX.) Final position for R, being nonexistent except in loanwords, has no social value for Thais other than demonstrating their knowledge of English, and then even fluent speakers of English regularly omit R at the end of English words borrowed in Thai. Final R has a 72 percent accuracy rate in the English listing task because it is permeated by the TL superordinate rule system. Initial position has a 9 percent accuracy rate because it is permeated by the NL superordinate rule system. It is suggested here that the social importance attached to the phonetic value of initial R influences the degree to which Thai permeates English IL in this formal context. It may also be that the lack of social value attached to final R variants affects the minimal influence of the NL in this context despite the formal situation. After all, if interference were a stable influence, the lack of final R in Thai would probably have led to a high percentage of /ø/ or /ə/ for final R. That did occur in the conversation data, but there was a style shift in the formal listing for final R which involved adopting the TL (English) as the superordinate rule system.

Another area which this paper set out to explore was the question of whether monitoring and the conscious Monitor (Krashen, 1978) operate on a sliding scale or an "on-off" basis. Tarone (1979) and Krashen (personal communication) have both suggested that monitoring (attention to speech) is on a continuum. I would like to claim that Monitoring (conscious application of grammatical rules) also operates on a continuum. Although Monitoring is "on-off" at the level of the individual token, it is sliding if viewed within the context of a conversation, an interview task, or a speech act. This continuum is impossible to demonstrate. Tarone (1979) suggests that verification of a monitoring continuum is impossible because we have been so lax in reporting the data-gathering situations we have used. While it is true that most studies are vague in their descriptions of sociolinguistic setting and that this may be a critical barrier in the study of monitoring, it is not the major block to proving that the Monitor operates on a continuum. The primary obstacle here lies in the discrepancy between knowing the conditions necessary for the abstract theoretical construct, the Monitor, to operate, and knowing not only that the Monitor does exist but also that, given optimal conditions in a particular situation, it did operate. In other words, we can only argue that the prerequisite conditions for the Monitor (e.g., time, focus on form, and knowledge of the rule) were present and that TL accuracy was or was not achieved. We are not really proving that the Monitor operated, let alone that it operated on a continuous sliding scale of various degrees versus an absolute situation of operating or not operating. This bind is in the nature of the research we are doing. It does not render useless the act of looking at evidence for the operation of the Monitor.

In the data collected for this study, there is some evidence to support the claim that the conscious Monitor (assumed to exist) operates on a continuous sliding scale and not on an "on-off" basis. It should be stated that current Monitor Theory is in agreement with this claim (Krashen, personal communication). In a recent article, Krashen (1978, p. 177) states that "editing (i.e., conscious Monitoring) results in variable performance, that is, we see different types and amounts of errors under different conditions." Still, this article sounds as if individuals are either Monitoring or not Monitoring at a given time, and that by personality and background, the individuals are either underusers, overusers, or optimal users of the Monitor. Krashen's interest in variation is one of classifying individual cases, whereas Tarone's and mine is one of looking for sociolinguistically conditioned patterns along a continuum for whole groups of subjects.

The findings of the present study suggest that Monitoring occurred on a sliding scale. The most convincing evidence is the data showing that there is a much higher rate of correct final Rs in the listing data than during the interview conversation. Other possible evidence is that on the listing task, where there were optimal Monitor conditions (time, focus on form, and knowledge of the rule), there was more hypercorrection by lower-middle-class subjects than during the conversation. That is, Thais of this group hypercorrected initial L to an r-sound 6 percent of the time in the conversation but hypercorrected it 13 percent of the time during listing. Presumably, if data from truly spontaneous speech were available, there would be no hypercorrection. Finally, the data showing that Thais use more correct variants from their native language, Thai, on initial R in the formal listing task could be used as evidence that the use of the Monitor is on a sliding scale.

The disturbing part of interpreting evidence for a Monitor continuum is that one questions what information is available for Monitoring. If hypercorrection is evidence of Monitoring, then misinformation or incorrect learning can be used to edit. If social norms from the NL continue to surface under Monitor conditions, one might wonder whether, according to Monitor theory, these elements would be "interference" or whether some strongly stigmatized areas of speech which are consciously learned in the NL are tapped by providing optimal Monitor conditions in the TL, and they become, misguidedly but perhaps temporarily, part of the editing rules that constitute the Monitor. Somewhere in SLA theory, we must account for socially motivated editing, with conscious rules both from the NL and from the TL.

CONCLUSION

The data presented here have indicated that the Thais' style shifting toward the NL in a formal context involves transfer of a socially appropriate variant from the NL. This happens in the case where there is sociolinguistic variation in Thai, the initial R. In the case where there is no variation in Thai, the final R, the subjects' IL became more permeated by the TL rules. In both cases, IL became more permeable in formal situations. And, overall, it appeared that conscious Monitoring increased in the formal context to enhance the degree of style shifting.

In sum, the findings of this study provide empirical evidence (though somewhat limited) in support of several broad generalizations about the nature of interlanguage phonology:

1. Style shifting occurs in all natural languages, including interlanguages.
2. IL becomes more permeable to a superordinate rule system in formal situations.
3. Either the NL or the TL may act as the superordinate rule system.
4. If there is strong, conscious social value attached to an area of the NL phonology, this knowledge can become part of the Monitor in the TL.
5. The conscious Monitor operates on a sliding scale within the context of a conversation, interview task, or speech act.

At this point, the evidence is insufficient to warrant accepting these generalizations as "fact." Still, there is value in making an explicit list of the potential claims in their strongest forms. It is, of course, necessary to consider them tentative until they are verified through research in a variety of spontaneous and experimental settings and in situations involving different native languages.

NOTE

1. Capital letters are used as names for phonological variables. These names should not be confused with phonemes, allophones, or any type of actual phonetic variant. They are symbols for socially conditioned variables and do not have a single phonetic realization, but rather a continuum of phonetic realizations. For example, the name R represents a phonological variable in Thai which may be realized phonetically as a flap, a trill, or a lateral continuant. The choice of actual phonetic variant is socially conditioned, and even when it sounds like /l/, speakers report that they are trying to pronounce an "r." When nonnative speakers use English R, they produce a variety of sounds. Some of these sounds, e.g., /l/, sound like allophones of the English phoneme /l/. Still, if the sound is an attempted realization of an intended /r/, it is considered to be a variant of the R variable. Labov (1966, 1972) used the convention of parentheses to mark a phonological variable. Capital letters used here are conceptually identical but seem perceptually more distinct from transcription for phonemes, allophones, and lower case letters. Although some linguists believe that phonemic symbols are sufficient for use here, I concur with Labov in positing a distinct symbol. This avoids confusion stemming from the principle in classical phonemics that an allophone can belong to one and only one phoneme. In the study of socially conditioned variants, whether in a natively spoken language or an interlanguage, phonetic variants are frequently found to belong to more than one target or phonological variable. The use of a distinct symbol for this intended target, or "phonological variable," maintains precision.

APPENDIX A

Word List

bolt	rip	freeze	school	rode
carp	black	work	late	prop
pal	rent	beer	plume	far
croak	call	load	rob	help
leave	last	room	hurt	lots

APPENDIX B

Key to the IL Phonetic Variants of R

ɹ   a retroflex continuant; considered correct (native) in initial or final position in American English; not native to Thai (but occasionally borrowed as an initial)

ɹ'   a more open, less retroflex, continuant; considered correct (native New York English) in final position, but incorrect in initial position; not native to Thai

ɹ̥   a voiceless retroflex continuant; initial position IL variant

ʐ   a retroflex, post-alveolar fricative; initial position IL variant

wɹ'   an /ɹ'/ preceded by the English labio-velar continuant /w/; initial position IL variant

r   a rolled fricative; initial position IL variant

ɭ   a retroflex, post-alveolar lateral; initial position IL variant

l   an apico-alveolar or denti-alveolar clear lateral with a flap-like quality due to tense articulation and more sudden release than American /l/; initial IL variant transferred from Thai

ř   an apico-alveolar flap; initial position IL variant transferred from Thai

r̄   an apico-alveolar trill; initial position IL variant transferred from Thai
ø   a zero sound for post-vocalic R; final position IL variant either transferred from Thai or acquired from an "r-less" dialect of English; usually accompanied by vowel lengthening on the immediately preceding vowel
ə   a mid-central vowel; final position IL variant either transferred from the Thai rendition of loanwords or acquired from an "r-less" dialect of English
w   a labio-velar continuant; final position IL variant

REFERENCES

Adjémian, C. 1976. On the nature of interlanguage systems. *Language Learning 26,* 297–320.

Beebe, L.M. 1974. Socially conditioned variation in Bangkok Thai. Ph.D. Dissertation, University of Michigan.

Dickerson, L. 1975. The learner's interlanguage as a system of variable rules. *TESOL Quarterly 9,* 401–407.

Dickerson, L., and W. Dickerson. 1977. Interlanguage phonology: Current research and future directions. In Corder, S.P., and E. Roulet (Eds.), *The Notions of Simplification, Interlanguages and Pidgins and Their Relation to Second Language Pedagogy.* Neufchâtel; Faculté des Lettres, and Genève: Librairie Droz.

Krashen, S. 1978. Individual variation in the use of the monitor. In Ritchie, W. (Ed.), *Second Language Acquisition Research: Issues and Implications.* NY: Academic Press.

Labov, W. 1966. *The Social Stratification of English in New York City.* Washington, DC: Center for Applied Linguistics.

Labov, W. 1969. The study of language in its social context. *Studium Generale 23,* 30–87.

Labov, W. 1972. *Sociolinguistic Patterns.* Philadelphia: University of Pennsylvania Press.

LoCoco, V. 1976. A comparison of three methods for the collection of second language data: free composition, translation and picture description. *Working Papers on Bilingualism 8,* 59–86.

Schmidt, R.W. 1977. Sociolinguistic variation and language transfer in phonology. *Working Papers on Bilingualism 12,* 79–95 (Also in this volume).

Tarone, E. 1979. Interlanguage as chameleon. *Language Learning 29,* 181–191.

Wolfson, N. 1976. Speech events and natural speech: Some implications for sociolinguistic methodology. *Language in Society 5,* 189–209.

Wong-Fillmore, L., R. Cathcart, and M. Strong. 1979. The social and linguistic behavior of good language learners. Paper presented at the Thirteenth National TESOL Convention, Boston.

24

THE EFFECT OF AFFECT ON INTERLANGUAGE PHONOLOGY

Marianne Stølen

INTRODUCTION

The purpose of this study is to investigate one subject's speech production as it varies along the dimensions of anxiety and formality. Two important issues are raised in this connection: (1) which of the two variables has the major impact on the subject's second language pronunciation? and (2) what types of effects are brought about?

A number of studies (Nemser, 1971; Dickerson, 1977; Tarone, 1978, 1979; Beebe, 1980a) have looked at the interaction of formality of speech situation and level of language performance. Other studies (Spielberger, 1966; Verma and Nijhawan, 1976; Scovel, 1978) have considered the effect of affect on the learning of skills. Because situational constraints and anxiety arousal may both be present as conditioning factors of a given speech situation, it would be of value to tease out the relative role played by each.

RESEARCH ON SITUATION

Viewing interlanguage as a variable whose rule system is akin to that of a natural language, Tarone (1979) discusses its "chameleon" nature: ". . . in its use in human interaction, it varies with the subtlest shifts of situation, just as the chameleon changes color as its surroundings change" (p. 181).

Clearly, as indicated by Tarone (ibid.), a precise definition of speech situation is a prerequisite for research on situationally induced style-shifting of interlanguage. What, then, constitutes a formal context as opposed to its informal counterpart? Tarone uses Labov's methodological axiom on formality as a valid criterion for defining a given context: "When a speaker is systematically observed, a formal context is thereby defined, and the speaker pays more than the minimum attention to speech" (p. 186). In other words, style-shifting in a speaker's second language is here defined by the degree of attention paid to speech production—the less attention paid, the closer to the informal style or the vernacular of interlanguage.

The casual speech, typical of subjects interacting with family members in a home setting, Tarone characterizes as equivalent to the vernacular of interlanguage. Even with the presence of a researcher and/or tape-recorder, it is possible to devise situations in which the subjects focus on the message conveyed rather than on the code. As Tarone (ibid.) points out, researchers in the field of sociolinguistics have for years been able to collect spontaneous data by employing a variety of methods that divert the subject's attention from being observed and/or recorded.

Even alcohol has been used as a means of facilitating language performance in a second language speech situation. Guiora, et al. (1975), found evidence for their prediction that a small amount of alcohol would enhance the pronunciation ability of the subjects of their study. The experiment was based on the theory that a relaxation of the ego boundary of the second language learner is required before the subject is able to shed native pronunciation habits: Because pronunciation is "at the core of the language ego" (p. 45), it follows that successful L2 speakers must acquire a new language identity during their performance.

Because situational elements impose constraints on a given subject's language production, it is unsurprising that a number of researchers (Gatbonton, 1975; Felix, 1977 [a summary of these findings in Tarone, 1979]) find a noticeable difference in the character of the data obtained in different situations. In his study, Felix found much less invasion from the rule system of the target language in the spontaneous speech of family interactions than in the speech produced in formal settings. This and similar studies leads Tarone (1979) to conclude that formal situations induce speech that is much less regular than that of informal situations: IL in formal situations seems to be more permeable to invasion from both target language norm and native language norm; hence the instability of its nature.

The instability of interlanguage pronunciation in formal situations is evidenced in a study by Beebe (1980 b). Thai speakers' reading of a list of words containing initial [r] and/or final [r] showed clear interference of the target language, English, whereas their speech production in a less formal interview setting gave evidence of less permeation of the target language norm.

RESEARCH ON ANXIETY

As pointed out by Scovel (1978), studies of the relationship between affective variables and language performance are abundant. Unfortunately, the research has yielded results that are both contradictory and confusing.

Scovel believes Chastain (1975, 160) comes close to describing the crux of the problem of this research when he states that "perhaps some concern about a task is a plus while too much anxiety can produce negative results." In other words, anxiety may have facilitating or debilitating effects on a subject's performance, the nature of the influence depending on a number of factors, extrinsic and/or intrinsic to the performer.

Affective arousal is normally measured in three ways: by conducting physiological tests of the subject's blood pressure, heart beat, etc.; by observing the behavior of the subject; and/or by having the subject self-report on his or her condition.

Of the three measuring techniques, the physiological testing has proved especially applicable for correlating emotional states and athletic achievement. It seems that, in the area of demanding physical activities, high affective arousal (HA) has an adverse effect on the performance.

Articulatory skills and athletic ability are related in many ways, as pointed out by Scovel (ibid.). In other words, physiological measures of emotional arousal might be linked to success or failure in this aspect of language performance.

Behavioral tests have been used extensively as a means of evaluating the impact of emotional arousal on academic performance.

Scovel (ibid.) refers to a study by Verma and Nijhawan (1976) which examines the impact of anxiety on the academic performance of subjects with either high or low IQ. Their findings indicate that "higher states of anxiety facilitate at upper levels of intelligence whereas they are associated with poorer performance at lower IQ levels" (p. 161).

This study is supported by Spielberger (1966) and Gaudry and Fitzgerald (1971), the latter study investigating the effect of affect on the performance of various tasks by seventh-grade children. A slightly higher than normal performance was observed in high IQ children under conditions of high anxiety while the low IQ children performed at lower than normal levels under the same conditions.

In summary, research on the relationship between affect and learning performance has focused on the variables of intelligence, nature of skill(s) performed, difficulty of task, and stage of learning, all of which may play a part in determining whether emotional arousal will facilitate or debilitate a subject's performance in a given area.

STUDY I

In the first part of a study of the second language skills of a sixty-four-year-old native American subject, a female university student of first-year Danish, her performance in syntax and phonology was related to the level of anxiety arousal in four different testing situations, as shown in Table 24.1.

The nature of the speech production was unique in the sense that in all four situations the subject was producing the memorized lines of her part of a play—a dramatized version of a Hans Christian Andersen fairy-tale. Her approximately sixteen lines had been fully internalized at the time of the first tape-recording in the first situation. In all four situations, a tape-recorder was placed unobtrusively, outside the subject's visual field so as not to interfere with her involvement in the playing of her role. In all tests there was an audience, although, as will be seen from Table 24.1, the size and character of her audience varied. I shall claim that, in the Labovian sense, the subject was paying very little attention to her production of speech per se—her attention was focused on recall of crucial key words, on observing and responding to verbal and non-verbal cues coming from her co-players, etc. In other words, the playing rather than the speaking was her main concern.

Using the Labov criterion of formality of situation, we can say that all four situations had a low level of formality. The other variable, level of emotional arousal, is indicated in the other column. Based on my observation of her behavior before and during the four different performances of the play, her physical condition (flushed cheeks, etc.) and her self-report, I was able to give the following rating of her anxiety level in the four situations: *low* during an ordinary rehearsal in the classroom, *medium* during the dress rehearsal on the stage with peers as audience, *very high* during the real performance on a stage for an audience of people, many of whom were total strangers, and *very low* during the after-the-event performance in the class more than a week later.

A third variable, intelligence, was also included as a conditioning element in the study: I had been the subject's teacher in Danish for four months when

TABLE 24.1

	Anxiety level
Situation 1. Rehearsal in the classroom	Low
Situation 2. Dress rehearsal on the stage	Medium
Situation 3. Performance on a real stage, in front of an audience of appr. 150 people	Very high
Situation 4. "Aftermath"—performance in the classroom	Very low

the study took place. During this period I had had occasion to evaluate her written and oral work and her performance on exams. In addition, her involvement in extracurricular activities connected with the play production was included in my observation. Her competence in all of these areas clearly evidenced a high intelligence.

FINDINGS OF THE STUDY

Syntax

An interesting observation was made in this aspect of the study. Under extreme pressure—i.e. in the high-anxiety situation of the staging of the real play, the subject had certain slips of memory in regard to her lines, yet was able to communicate adequately with her co-players by producing "filler lines" of her own that, in all cases, followed the rules of Danish syntax. In other words, for this subject, a student with a high IQ, high anxiety (HA) facilitated performance in syntax.

Phonology

In the other aspect of investigation, the subject showed no variation in her pronunciation of the words I had selected for consideration. She mastered the words equally well—i.e. made no errors, whether performing under conditions of high or low anxiety arousal. A possible reason for the lack of variation may be found in the nature of the data. Because the selected words formed part of a relatively small corpus of memorized lines, problematic aspects of pronunciation had been the focal point of many sessions of individual language laboratory work and of in-class work. In other words, the pronunciation rules of the relatively few focal words had been fully internalized and "habitualized."

In the sub-area of prosody, an improvement in performance was observed in the HA situation. The subject gave extra emphasis to the focal points of her lines, hence both rhythm and intonation were improved under conditions in which she was conscious of the need to be heard even by people in the back rows.

In order to investigate phonological variation in the subject's speech production related to the variables of anxiety and situation, data of a less unique nature were obviously needed.

STUDY II

In this study, the subject, whose anxiety arousal had facilitated her performance in syntax and prosody, was observed in three different testing situations of varying degrees of anxiety and formality, the focus this time being on her mastery of an aspect of the Danish sound system: her application of the distribution rules for the Danish phoneme /l/.

Distribution Rules for /l/ in English and Danish

In English, /l/ has two realizations at surface level: the alveolar allophone, the clear [l], which occurs in front of vowels and [y], and the velarized allophone, the dark [ɫ]; found before consonants, in final parts of syllables, and when the lateral is syllabic. The rule is exemplified in the following words: 'Lee' and 'stallion' pronounced with clear [l], 'film' and 'will' pronounced with the dark [ɫ].

In Danish, the rule governing the realization of /l/ states that the allophones will be the alveolar sound, the clear [l], regardless of phonological environment. In other words, [l] in Danish such words as *le, film,* and *vil* will in all cases be pronounced palatalized.

Contrastive Analysis Predictions: Positive Transfer

The strong version of CA predicts that the English native speaker will have positive transfer to the target language, Danish, in cases where the phonological environment for clear [l] is the same in the two languages. Transfer of the clear [l] of 'Lee' would therefore cause no error in the Danish word 'le.'

Negative Transfer

Transfer of the dark [ɫ] can be predicted in positions where the English speaker would find this allophonic variant in his or her own language. In other words, negative transfer would cause errors in such words as *vil* and *film.*

At the underlying level, the two languages have the same form. At surface level, however, the allophonic realization of /l/ differs. The English speaker of Danish thus faces the problem of having one allophonic variant in all environments instead of the "usual" two.

To the predictions of negative transfer in cases such as those outlined above, I shall add the following:

1. Negative transfer would be most noticeable in cognate words.
2. Negative transfer would typically take place in words unfamiliar to the subject.
3. As was the case in the areas of syntax and prosody, anxiety arousal would have a facilitating effect on the subject's performance in phonology.
4. The variable of anxiety would be a more powerful determining factor than that of formality. Thus, in a formal task, in which Beebe would predict more permeation of the target rule system and therefore a closer approximation to the target language than in the informal task, I would predict no improvement of pronunciation skills, my hypothesis being that the level of emotional arousal of the subject would be too low for the subject to perform well in this type of task.

394

Procedure

Materials Four different types of testing materials were designed to be used at two different locations (the classroom and the language laboratory) on three different locations.

Studies I and II are connected in two important ways:

a) The same subject participated in both studies over a period of approximately three months.
b) Four words from Study I containing the feature under investigation, (/l/), were incorporated in the materials of tests 1–4, thus giving the researcher a comparative tool with which to work. (See the Appendix for a complete list of the words of the materials of the two studies.) In addition other words were used in which the distribution rules for the Danish /l/ would be operating, the aim being to incorporate sufficient items in the materials to allow the researcher to make valid judgments about the subject's command of the aspect of phonology under consideration.

Testing situations The anxiety and formality levels of the four tests are described in Table 24.2.

Test I The setting here was the classroom. The subject was asked to participate in a role-play situation—i.e. interact with three other students in a mock panel discussion I designed. The situation was that of a simulated PTA (Parent-Teacher Association) meeting called by the teacher of a class of third-graders in order to discuss the problem of smoking. Background materials included a problem statement, role descriptions for each participant, and a handout suggesting ways in which to interrupt and argue effectively. No prior rehearsal of the role-play had taken place. The students had prepared their respective roles at home using the appropriate materials. They had been told not to write out their roles but instead to prepare key words that could be used during the actual performance. The nature of this type of interaction requires that the participants continually adjust their performance to the response(s) coming from the other participants—a typical feature of real-life communication. In other words, in spite of the artificial classroom setting, we were as close as possible to spontaneous speech, and I would therefore characterize Situation I as informal. Observations of the subject's behavior and physical condition combined with her self-report indicated a medium level of anxiety.

Test II This testing also took place in the classroom. The subject was asked to interact with three other students in a "memory game." A short story

TABLE 24.2

	Anxiety level	Formality level
Test 1.	medium	informal
Test 2.	low-medium	informal
Test 3.	very low	formal
Test 4.	very low	formal

of approximately five lines was read aloud by me to the subject. She in turn would relate it to the next student in line (waiting outside the door), who would retell it to the third student, and so on. The purpose of this type of task was to have the subject produce speech somewhat more structured than in the previous testing situation. This type of task "forces" the subject to focus her attention on certain crucial items of the story, normally the content words. It is possible for the designer of the test to construct a story whose key words will contain the features under consideration. Given the nature of the present study, I deliberately incorporated the words, *Ole, gammel, vil,* and *altid,* four items found in Study I. In addition other content words were used in which the distribution rules for /l/ could be observed. Because the subject's attention was focused on getting the essence of the message across rather than on producing correct speech, I would characterize this situation as informal. The level of anxiety in my subject was slightly lower than that observed in the role-play situation.

Tests III and IV   The language laboratory provided the setting for both tests. Test III was a cloze test. I deliberately designed this test in such a manner that the blanks would be filled with words not selected for observation. In other words, I tried to divert my subject's attention from the area of research. Having filled the blanks, she made a tape-recording of the passage. She was allowed to erase and re-record as she saw fit. The anxiety level for this test I evaluated as very low, the nature of the task formal. The emphasis here was clearly on correct production of the TL forms, the subject having ample time for "conscious editing" of her output (see Krashen 1978).

During the same recording period, the subject was asked to record eleven words from a word list, the items on the list illustrating important aspects of the rules governing the distribution of /l/. The anxiety level of test IV was the same as that of the previous task, the nature of the task also falling in the category of formal.

Findings

The words, *vil, altid, gammel,* and *Ole* were produced with no errors in all situations where they occurred. This was unsurprising, since the words had been used numerous times in previous work. They had become part of the subject's basic (error-free) vocabulary.

Another finding, relating to the HA hypothesis, concerns positive transfer. The words *'lidt'* and *'landet,'* both of which contain the clear [l] variant, were pronounced correctly in all cases in which they occurred. Following the distribution rules for the English /l/, they should be clear. The positive transfer hypothesis was thus borne out in the case of this study.

In Table 24.3 is a list of the subject's correctly and incorrectly produced basic stock of words. Items carrying positive transfer are not included in this

TABLE 24.3. Basic Stock of Words that Might be Conditioned by Negative Transfer

Situation I:	The following were correct:	*altid, vil*
(role-play)	The following were incorrect:	*gammel, aldrig, til*
Situation II:	The following were correct:	*altid, gammel*
(memory game)	The following were incorrect:	*til, aldrig*
Situation III:	The following were correct:	*vil, altid, gammel*
(cloze test)	The following was incorrect:	*aldrig*
Situation IV:	The following were correct:	*vil, altid, gammel, aldrig, til*
(word list)		

section. In other words, there were no errors in the basic stock of words in Situation IV.

From the results, the following can be concluded: the error-free basic stock of words was so well internalized that no cases of regression took place. With regard to the words that were incorrect in some situations, correct in others, the following can be concluded: the word *gammel* is given the correct pronunciation in the second situation (a little below medium anxiety) but is incorrect in Situation I, with slightly more anxiety. In both cases the task was informal. This observation seems to point to the fact that increase in anxiety arousal does not have a facilitating effect on the subject's performance.

A similar tendency can be observed in the word *aldrig,* maybe an even more noticeable trend: A highly formal situation with low level of anxiety improved the subject's performance. Again, the hypothesis of a correlation between HA and improved performance seems not to apply to phonology.

The hypothesis of negative transfer taking place in cognate words was not borne out in the case of *vil,* but, as I observed earlier on, *vil* already seemed to be part of the learner's correct vocabulary. *Til,* however, was given an incorrect pronunciation in the first two situations. The hypothesis of similar form having an impact on transfer processes was thus borne out, as shown in Table 24.4 below:

TABLE 24.4. The Unusual Stock of Words

Situation I:	Correct:	
(role-play)	Incorrect:	*spildte, forældre, skikkelse*
Situation II:	Correct:	*forældre*[a]
(memory game)	Incorrect:	*spildte, skikkelse*
Situation III:	Correct:	*skikkelse, forældre*
(cloze test)	Incorrect:	*spildte*
Situation IV:	Correct:	*skikkelse, forældre*
(word list)	Incorrect:	*spildte*

[a]*forældre* was possibly an approximation rather than correct pronunciation. The subject had asked me what the word meant. She therefore heard me pronounce it twice.

397

A trend similar to that of the subject's performance on basic vocabulary can be observed in the area of "unusual" words: The more formal the situation and the less the amount of anxiety arousal in the subject, the better her performance in phonology. Again, Beebe's hypothesis seems to be borne out in this study.

As predicted, unfamiliar words did cause problems for the subject. She was unable to pronounce *skikkelse* correctly in the first two situations. In Situation III, possibly because of conscious editing, she was able to produce the correct form. The word *spildte,* not a word belonging to the everyday stock of words, was incorrect in all four situations. The hypothesis of unfamiliar words causing problems seems to have been borne out.

In conclusion, level of formality of task rather than level of anxiety seemed to be the important conditioning factor in the present study: An experimental setting (the reading of a word list) showed positive correlation with high level of performance. Increase in anxiety arousal, on the other hand, did not seem to have a facilitating effect on the subject's production of sound segments.

This finding, then, is in opposition to findings on syntax and the prosodic features of rhythm and emphasis in an earlier study of the language performance of the same subject. Here we observed a positive correlation between high level of anxiety and high level of fluency. Because the conditioning elements were the same in all four testing situations, the factor "level of formality" was not a significant variable.

To get as complete a picture as possible of the subject's performance in phonology, prosody, and syntax, this variable should be incorporated in a complementary study. The focus of this study would then be on the subject's performance in the latter two areas, at various levels of formality and anxiety.

REFERENCES

Beebe, L.M. 1980a. Sociolinguistic variation and style shifting in second language acquisition. *Language Learning 30,* 433–447. (Also this volume.)

Beebe, L.M. 1980b. Myths about interlanguage phonology. Paper presented at the National TESOL Convention, San Francisco. (Also this volume.)

Chastain, K. 1975. Affective and ability factors in second language acquisition. *Languagr Learning 25,* 153–161.

Davidsen-Nielsen, N. 1971. *Engelsk Fonetik.* Copenhagen: Gyldendalske Boghandel.

Dickerson, L., and W. Dickerson. 1977. *Interlanguage phonology: current research and future directions.* In S.P. Corder and E. Roulet (Eds.), The notions of simplification, interlanguages and pidgins and their relation to second language pedagogy. Neufchâtel: Faculté des Lettres, and Genéve: Librairie Droz.

Felix, S. 1977. How reliable are experimental data? Paper presented at the Eleventh Annual TESOL Convention, Miami, FL.

Gatbonton, E. 1975. Systematic variations in second language speech: A sociolinguistic study. Ph.D. Dissertation, McGill University.

Gaudry, E., and D. Fitzgerald. 1971. *Test anxiety, intelligence, and academic achievement.* In E. Gaudry and C. Spielberger (Eds.), Anxiety and Educational Achievement. Sydney: John Wiley and Sons.

Guiora, A.Z., M. Paluszny, B. Beit-Halbhmi, F.C. Catford, R.E. Cooley, C. Yoder Dull. 1975. Language and person: studies in language behavior. *Language Learning 25,* 43–61.

Krashen, S.P. 1978. The monitor model for second language acquisition. In R.C. Gingrass (Ed.), *Second Language Acquisition and Foreign Language Teaching.* Arlington, VA: Center for Applied Linguistics.

Nemser, W. 1971. *An Experimental Study of Phonological Interference in the English of Hungarians.* Bloomington, IN: Indiana University Press.

Scovel, T. 1978. The effect of affect on foreign language learning: A review of the anxiety research. *Language Learning 28,* 129–42.

Spielberger, C. (ed.) 1966. *Anxiety and Behavior.* NY: Academic Press.

Tarone, E. 1978. The phonology of interlanguage. In F.C. Richards (Ed.), *Understanding Second and Foreign Language Learning: Issues and Approaches.* Rowley, MA: Newbury House. (Also this volume.)

Tarone, E. 1979. Interlanguage as chameleon. *Language Learning 29,* 181–191.

Verma, P., and H. Nijhawan. 1976. The effect of anxiety, reinforcement, and intelligence on the learning of a difficult task. *Journal of Experimental Child Psychology 22,* 302–308.

APPENDIX

Testing Materials 1

Study I

The following words occurred in the testing situations:
ole gammel vil altid

Study II

In Situation I, the following words occurred:
Basic stock of words: *vil, altid, aldrig, ole, til*
Unusual stock of words: *spildte, skikkelse, forældre*

In Situation II, the following words occurred:
Basic stock of words: *vil, altid, ole, gammel, til, landet, lidt, aldrig*
Unusual stock of words: *spildte, forældre, skikkelse*

In Situation III, the following words occurred:
Basic stock of words: *vil, altid, gammel, aldrig*
Unusual stock of words: *spildte, forædre, skikkelse*

In Situation IV, the following words occurred:
Basic stock of words: *vil, landet, altid, gammel, lidt, til, ole, aldrig*
Unusual stock of words: *skikkelse, forældre, spildte*

Testing Materials 2

II memory game

(the words forming the focus of our attention have been written in capital letters)
Ude påLANDET boede der en mand, der hed OLE. Han boede pa en GAMMEL gård sammen med sine FORÆLDRE. OLE havde en sjov SKIKKELSE, og han var også LIDT klodset. Han SPILDTE ALTID kaffe på bordet. "Pokkers osse!" sagde han. "Hvorfor ka' jeg ALDRIG passe på?"
VIL du fortælle historien videre TIL den der står udenfor døren?

III cloze-test

Jeg VIL mægtig . . . . .ha' at du ska' besøge mig . . . . .dag. Mine FORÆLDRE har et . . . . .hus, så du ka' ALTID . . . . .hos mig. Der er ALDRIG for mange . . . . i mit hus. Her boede en gang en GAMMEL mand. Han havde en . . . . .SKIKKELSE, og han var . . . . .klodset. Han SPILDTE . . . . . .kaffe på bordet.

IV word list

vil	gammel
skikkelse	spildte
aldrig	lidt
landet	ole
forældre	til
altid	

25

THE INFLUENCE OF LINGUISTIC CONTEXT ON SYLLABLE SIMPLIFICATION*

Steven H. Weinberger

It is a well-known fact that native speakers of languages without word-final obstruent consonants may display some production difficulty in their attempt to pronounce target language items that contain these final obstruents. Indeed, the strong version of the Contrastive Analysis Hypothesis (CAH) explicitly predicts this production difficulty (Lado, 1957). Nevertheless, even a research program like the CAH is unable to predict just how these non-native target language learners will resolve the difficulty. This question can be divided into at least two subparts: (1) what strategies are available and used by these speakers in dealing with word-final obstruents? and (2) will there be any systematic variability—that is, will the choice or frequency of strategy be conditioned by some set of factors like native language syllable structure, certain developmental considerations, type of testing situation, etc.?

*This is a revised version of a paper delivered at the Washington Association for the Education of Speakers of Other Languages, Seattle, Washington, 1983.

I would like to thank Georgette Ioup and Ellen Kaisse for their helpful comments and criticisms.

401

With regard to the first of the two inquiries, a review of the recent literature reveals that there exist at least two syllable simplification strategies that second language (L2) learners utilize when dealing with word-final obstruents: deletion and epenthesis (Anderson, this volume; Eckman 1981a, 1981b; Major, this volume; Tarone, 1980). If we adopt Tarone's (1980) suggestion that there is a universal L2 preference for the canonical consonant-vowel (CV) syllable, then deletion and epenthesis will serve the same purpose by attempting to open the problematic closed target syllables. For example, a closed CVC syllable will become CVØ by deletion, while the same target CVC syllable will become CVCV by final vowel epenthesis.

Certainly the study of universal processes and the interest in variation in L2 research have overshadowed the earlier contrastive analyses, but the predictive nature of the CAH continues to appeal to many L2 investigators. It is just this ability to predict learners' errors that is salvaged in Eckman's (1977) Markedness Differential Hypothesis (MDH). The MDH actually enriches the CAH to a point where the degree of difficulty in syllable simplification can now be predicted. Utilizing the notion of typological markedness, the MDH is able to make certain predictions based upon the target language and native language syllable type. For example, it is generally assumed that the CV syllable is the optimal syllable (Jakobson and Halle, 1956; Hooper, 1976). All languages contain such syllables. Moreover, if a language contains more "complex" (or more marked) syllable types, the most complex type will always imply the presence of a less complex type (Greenberg, 1965). So a language containing syllables of the type CVCC will necessarily contain CVC syllables as well as CV syllables. The reverse is not true. Therefore, assuming for the moment that a learner's native language has only CV syllables and the target language contains CV, CVC, CVCC, and CVCCC syllables, the MDH will not only predict difficulty with the different syllable types (a prediction also made by the CAH), but it will also predict that the most difficulty will be found with CVCCC syllables, followed with decreasing difficulty by CVCC and CVC syllables. Clearly, then, it seems as if the degree to which syllable simplification strategies as a whole operate should be dependent upon the structure of the target item. Nevertheless, it is our goal to provide some principled account of the relative employment of deletion and epenthesis as individual strategies, and of the fact that both the MDH and the CAH fail to predict when each strategy is used.

An examination of the second part of the two-part question posed above will certainly be more involved and complex than the relatively straightforward inquiry that merely seeks to identify the possible syllable simplification strategies. The complex nature of the second inquiry can certainly be compounded by the outcome of the first. That is, if a given L2 learner does in fact exhibit both epenthesis and deletion strategies, then not only must we account for the overall frequency of syllable simplification (i.e., deletion and epenthesis), but we must also explain the individual strategy frequencies (i.e., deletion vs. epenthesis).

This paper will investigate the phenomenon of syllable simplification in L2 learning. If variation is found to occur, an attempt will be made to identify the underlying factors responsible for such variation.

There is no doubt that the type of elicitation task or testing situation affects interlanguage phonological performance. Perhaps this type of variable influences the degree and choice of syllable simplification. Much work has been done along the lines of task formality. Tarone (1979) points out that an interlanguage may be viewed as a continuum of styles that is defined by the amount of attention paid to speech. She adopts Labov's ideas concerning superordinate and subordinate language varieties—specifically, the notion that, in formal speech situations, the subordinate system (interlanguage) is more permeable to the superordinate system (target language). We should therefore expect more errors in informal speech situations. Here again, just as the MDH is limited in its ability to predict only overall L2 difficulty with respect to the degree of syllable structure markedness, this formal-informal style continuum hypothesis only points out that the formality of the task is inversely related to the frequency of simplification errors. It makes no claim regarding the differential use of the two strategies: epenthesis and deletion.

Much of the reported data have shown that if a word-final syllable simplification strategy is employed, it will predominantly be one involving deletion (Anderson, this volume; Tarone, 1980). Moreover, research in this area suggests that the choice of strategy generally has some connection with the native language (NL) of the learner. So, for example, we find that Portuguese and Japanese speakers of English predominantly adopt the epenthesis strategy,[1] while native Korean and Cantonese learners most often use deletion to simplify English syllable structure (Eckman, 1981b; Tarone, 1980). If it is true that the NL determines the type of syllable simplification employed, then certainly it should be expected that Portuguese and Japanese syllable structure is quite different from Korean and Cantonese syllable structure. While Tarone does not make much distinction between Portuguese and Cantonese syllable structures, she does point out the need for a more rigorous analysis (1980, p. 143). Although it is beyond the scope of this paper, one might consider it an interesting challenge to determine the precise syllable structure template differences between these languages and see if they in fact account for the choice of strategy. But the interesting nature of such an enterprise is somewhat diminished when we consider that there remain conflicting language-internal results. For instance, Eckman's Mandarin speakers appear to exclusively utilize epenthesis (Schwa Paragoge) (1981a p. 207), while Anderson's Mandarin speakers favor the use of deletion (see this volume).

Perhaps these apparently conflicting data can be shown to be a result of some independent factors. In order to identify what is involved, it will be necessary to examine the processes of deletion and epenthesis in more detail. What should be noted is that while epenthesis and deletion both serve the same function, they nevertheless produce quite different outputs. Consider some English target language forms:

1: big
    bid
2: list
    lisp

Suppose that a language learner whose native language (NL) has no final obstru-ents employs a deletion strategy to simplify the syllable structure in Set 1 and Set 2. (We will assume here for the sake of the argument that only the final consonant in the cluster in Set 2 is deemed problematic.) The output would roughly be Set 3 and Set 4 respectively:

Set 3: big → /bi/
        bid → /bi/
Set 4: list → /lis/
        lisp → /lis/

Notice here that the resultant forms in each pair appear to be identical on the surface, with no overt avenue available to "recover" the initial target language form. In other words, the operation of final consonant deletion in these cases causes a high degree of ambiguity. If, on the other hand, the final consonants in Set 1 and Set 2 were to be simplified by a process of schwa-epenthesis, the following forms would obtain:

Set 5: big → /bigə/
        bid → /bidə/
Set 6: list → /listə/
        lisp → /lispə/.

Unlike the outputs in Set 3 and Set 4, these forms maintain their distinctiveness and hence are not ambiguous.

It is safe to assume that all natural languages contain a constraint against rampant ambiguity, particularly that resulting from homonymy of underlyingly distinct phonological forms. Furthermore, it has been proposed that the notion of recoverability (i.e., the ability to work backward from the surface form through a derivation to obtain the unique underlying representation) is highly valued by a grammar of natural language (Kaye, 1974, 1981; Hankamer, 1973). Indeed, recoverability in phonology is not only a result of the more general tendency to avoid ambiguity, it also enhances learnability—at least in L1 acqui-sition (Kaye, 1981).

As an illustration, the functional notion of recoverability is shown to operate in Ojibwa, an Algonquian language of North America. In Ojibwa, the operation of phonological rules is not necessarily governed by the theory of markedness of rule-ordering relationship but rather by the degree of recoverabil-ity that the derivation exhibits (Kaye, 1981). Kaye argues that languages do in fact exhibit derivations with marked rule-orderings, as long as they result in relatively more recoverable outputs. Basically, Ojibwa possesses the following phonological rules: (a) nasal assimilation (whereby a nasal adopts the place of articulation from the immediately following consonant) and (b) vowel syncope (where an unstressed [short] vowel is deleted). Given the underlying form /a:naki:/ 'although', two possible rule-orderings can result in two possible phonetic outputs. If nasal assimilation precedes vowel syncope, typifying a marked "counter-feeding" ordering relationship, we obtain [a:nki:].

Notice here that nasal assimilation did not apply because the syncope rule had not yet deleted the intervening unstressed vowel between /n/ and /k/. The second rule ordering, the unmarked version, actually orders the rules so that the first rule creates the required environment for the second to operate. So if nasal assimilation now follows vowel syncope, the intervening unstressed vowel is deleted first, allowing the nasal to be immediately adjacent to the consonant. Nasal assimilation is therefore allowed to take place, and the output [a:ŋki:] is obtained.

Now, given that Ojibwa has three possible underlying unstressed vowels: /i/, /o/, and /a/; and two underlying nasals: /n/ and /m/, the output from the marked ordering (counterfeeding) [a:nki:] is three-ways ambiguous:

$$/a\!:\!n \begin{bmatrix} i \\ o \\ a \end{bmatrix} ki\!:\!/.$$

The result of the unmarked rule-ordering (feeding) [a:ŋki:] is seven-ways ambiguous:

$$/a\!: \begin{bmatrix} n \\ m \end{bmatrix} \begin{bmatrix} i \\ o \\ a \end{bmatrix} ki\!:\!/.$$

Because of the principle of recoverability, it is in fact the less ambiguous form [a:nki:] that obtains in Ojibwa. According to Kaye, this notion of recoverability can be viewed as as a "global constraint on the degree of ambiguity permitted in a phonology" (1981, p. 471). Moreover, if this conception of recoverability is correct, Kaye asserts that "deletion-rules may not involve classes with more than 3 or 4 members" (1981, p. 472).

If we do in fact believe that interlanguage respects natural language constraints,[2] then we may impose the notion of recoverability along with the constraint "avoid ambiguity" onto interlanguage phonology. Additionally, syllable simplification operations like deletion and epenthesis in L2 production are assumed here to be derivations with underlying representations analogous to the intended target language (TL) forms.[3]

Returning now to the examples in Sets 3–6, we see that in the deletion examples in Sets 3 and 4, the derivations are not recoverable, since, given no other clues, the deleted elements cannot easily be inferred—hence a high degree of ambiguity. In the epenthesis examples, Set 5 and Set 6, a unique element is added, and, because there is no deletion, it is possible to work back through the derivation to reach the intended TL form. Therefore, epenthesis is shown to allow a higher degree of recoverability. If this is the case, then deletion should generally be less highly valued in an interlanguage phonology, since it not only minimizes recoverability but also maximizes ambiguity.

As demonstrated above, recoverability is enhanced when there is an insertion of a "unique" segment—that is, the segment has a transparent origin. This appears to be the case with the reported cases of glottal stop insertion in Tarone's Korean and Cantonese subjects (Tarone, 1980). In her data, every occurrence of glottal stop (insertion) appeared at a word boundary usually where one word ended in a vowel and the next word began with a vowel. Tarone attributes this insertion strategy to the tendency of maintaining a CV syllable structure—that is, the glottal stop is syllabified onto the second word.[4] Recall that Tarone's Korean and Cantonese subjects also employed consonant deletion strategies and epenthesis strategies to simplify syllables. With this in mind, these data can be interpreted to support the recoverability hypothesis. In order to maintain a CV syllable structure between words, these L2 learners chose insertion of glottal stops rather than deletion of vowels precisely because it results in recoverable (or transparent) derivations.

Broselow's (1984) data on Egyptian Arabic can also be interpreted in such a manner. Because Egyptian Arabic rules of syllabification require that each syllable begins with one and only one consonant, Arabic learners of English would presumably resyllabify a target language example like that of Figure 25.1 *a* as *a* in Figure 25.2, without affecting the *b* examples:

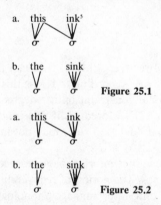

Figure 25.1

Figure 25.2

If the forms in Figure 25.2 actually obtained, example *a,* according to Broselow, would be heard and produced as *the sink.* That is, *a* and *b* would be indistinguishable. The actual pronunciation reveals that these speakers insert a glottal stop in front of the vowel in the second word in the *a* examples:

this   ?ink
 ᐯ   ᐯ
 σ   σ   **Figure 25.3**

Broselow points out that Egyptian Arabic speakers employ glottal stop insertion in their NL—specifically, in phrase-initial position and between words in slow speech. Cross-word syllabification (as in Figure 25.1) is restricted to fast speech, and, according to Broselow, is more marked than glottal stop insertion (p. 265). Therefore, she asserts that because of a markedness criterion, these Egyptian Arabic learners of English choose the simpler syllable structure (Figure 25.3), in order to obey the constraint that all syllables must begin with one and only one consonant. If one adopts the notion of recoverability, the same conclusion can be reached for different reasons. These Egyptian Arabic speakers choose glottal-stop insertion instead of cross-word syllabification precisely because the former strategy leads to recoverability and because it results in less ambiguity.

Returning now to the discussion of epenthesis and deletion strategies, recall that, if all factors are kept constant, epenthesis results in a higher degree of recoverability than does deletion. Presumably, if an interlanguage has available to it both of these syllable simplification strategies, and if the notion of recoverability is just as highly valued in an interlanguage as it is in natural languages, then epenthesis should predominate.

It can be shown from earlier empirical studies that there certainly is an interlanguage that exhibits both strategies—that of Mandarin L1 speakers of English—but the results reported by different researchers appear to conflict. As noted earlier, Eckman (1981a) reports epenthesis as the strategy employed by his Mandarin speakers, while Anderson registers a majority of deletion errors. This apparent conflict is due clearly to the reality that all factors cannot be kept constant. Looking at one such factor—the type of elicitation task—we observe that Anderson utilized informal spontaneous speech exclusively, while Eckman's study drew data from four distinct tasks, each differing in the level of formality. The tasks ranged from high formality (list reading) to low formality (riddle discussion). Perhaps, then, formality is the crucial determiner of syllable simplification strategy. Therefore, we may be able to strengthen the previously reviewed claim that formality is inversely related to the degree of overall error and hypothesize that formal tasks promote epenthesis while informal tasks promote deletion.[6]

Notice that, in most formality continua, the most formal tasks are those that deal with word-list reading of some sort, while the least formal tasks are concerned with spontaneous speech in a relaxed environment. I propose that it is not formality that determines the differential use of epenthesis and deletion; rather, it is linguistic context. Spontaneous speech tasks or story-reading tasks have built into them devices that tend to insure recoverability of the individual words. The linguistic context of these tasks reduces ambiguity. Word-list reading tasks, on the other hand, do not contain such context. Hence recoverability will be difficult and ambiguity may flourish. If recoverability is indeed an active component in interlanguage, and if epenthesis preserves recoverability, then we should observe differing proportions of epenthesis and deletion within tasks containing contextual cues as opposed to tasks free of context.

To review then, we can now formulate some specific hypotheses that deal with the three variables discussed so far: (a) degree of structural markedness of final consonant clusters, (b) task formality, and (c) linguistic context. The first two of these variables determine overall need for simplification while the third determines relative degree of epenthesis vs. deletion. The hypothesis is stated below:

Syllable Simplification Strategy Hypothesis
(i)   The degree of overall syllable simplification will increase as the final consonant cluster increases.
(ii)   The degree of overall syllable simplification will increase as the task formality decreases.
(iii)   The proportion $\dfrac{\%\ \text{epenthesis}}{\%\ \text{deletion}}$ should be greater in tasks without linguistic context than in tasks with linguistic context.

METHODOLOGY

This study examines word-final data from native speakers of Mandarin Chinese. The target language is English. A rough constrastive analysis specific to word-final syllable structure shows English to contain a marked syllable-final structure. Final C, CC, and CCC are all possible. Mandarin Chinese, on the other hand, is less marked, with the general syllable structure of $C_0^1\ V_1^3\ N_0^{17}$ where C, if an obstruent, is unvoiced, and N = /n/, /ŋ/, or /ɹ/ (a retroflex "r") (Li and Thompson, 1981; Tiee, 1969). Incidentally, Mandarin Chinese has no native language rule of vowel epenthesis.

SUBJECTS

Four subjects (two females and two males) were recruited from the intensive ESL program at the University of Washington. All were in the same placement level (high intermediate), and all obtained roughly similar scores on a University of Washington standardized test. Their ages ranged from twenty-one to thirty-one years, and each had been in the United States for about eighteen months. All had begun learning English in the People's Republic of China. They were all native speakers of the Northern dialect of Chinese (Mandarin).

PROCEDURE

The subjects were required to perform three tasks. First, in order to elicit word-final consonants and clusters, they were shown a series of three-by-five index cards with either a noun or a verb written on the front, and, on most cards, the word "plural" or "past" written on the back. The subject was asked to read aloud the word on the front—e.g. TALK, and then produce the proper form from the cue on the back of the card, (e.g. "past" = TALKED). This methodology is intended to keep script interference at a minimum. In all, fifty-six cards were presented resulting in a total of ninety-seven words. (See Appendix A for the list of words.) Next, the subjects were each asked to read a short paragraph containing many of the same clusters found in the list reading (see Appendix B). Finally, each was asked to tell the investigator a story about a frightening experience in America.

Each session was recorded on audiotape in a sound studio, and the tapescripts were transcribed into a broad phonetic form by two experienced linguists. Agreement between the two transcriptions was found to be 100 percent on all relevant clusters.

RESULTS

The calculated results deal only with word-final syllable simplification. Word-final substitution errors are not scored because they are few in number and do not affect syllable structure. There is, however, a significantly high rate of terminal devoicing and, because of the prevalence of this added strategy, it is included in the results of Table 25.1. It may be argued that final-consonant devoicing is itself a

TABLE 25.1

Epenthesis	(%)	
list	11.3	
paragraph	10.5	overall 9.9%
story	8.0	
Deletion	(%)	
list	5.5	
paragraph	13.3	overall 10.2%
story	11.8	
Devoicing	(%)	
list	72	
paragraph	58	overall 66%
story	68	

type of syllable simplification strategy, since it simplifies the feature complex of the coda. But because it does not modify the syllable structure template of the target language by promoting CV syllables, the Syllable Simplification Strategy Hypothesis will make no claims regarding final devoicing.

The process of final devoicing also acts to create ambiguity, but not the high rate of ambiguity that deletion potentially creates. Final devoicing should create only a two-way ambiguity—like that of neutralizing the distinction between *lock* and *log*. If we adopt Kaye's (1981) assertion that phonological processes may not neutralize the distinction between more than three or four segments, then we should not expect any recoverability constraint to prevent final consonant devoicing.[8]

Overall, as Table 25.1 shows, from an average of all task modalities, deletion and epenthesis occur in roughly equal proportions, 9.9 percent epenthesis vs 10.2 percent deletion. An analysis of word-final consonant cluster length from the data confirm part *i* of the Syllable Simplification Strategy hypothesis above. Although the number of CCC tokens is small in the paragraph task and nonexistent in the story-telling task, the list task shows a clear relationship between markedness and percentage of error. As the target syllable structure becomes increasingly marked, progressing from $-C$ to $-CC$, to $-CCC$, the percentage of error correspondingly increases from 2.4 percent to 9.0 percent to 43.0 percent respectively (See Table 25.2).[9]

There is no apparent relationship between cluster length and the type of strategy used. That is, the ratio between deletion and epenthesis is fairly stable within each task regardless of the cluster length. This result can be used to validate Tarone's (1980) claim that deletion and epenthesis are actually reflexes of some more general tendency to revert to a canonical CV syllable structure. Even though there may be little structural similarity between a deletion rule and an epenthesis rule, they nevertheless share a "functional unity" insofar as they produce a similar effect (Kisseberth, 1970).

Assuming that the relative formality level is greatest for the list-reading task, intermediate for the paragraph-reading task, and least formal in the story-telling task, part *ii* of the Syllable Simplification Strategy Hypothesis above predicts an inverse degree of overall epenthesis and deletion simplification errors. The results indicate, however, that for the list task, overall simplification is 16.8 percent, for the paragraph task 23.8 percent, and, for story-telling, simplification reaches 19.8 percent. These figures do not appear to be signifi-

TABLE 25.2 Syllable Simplification Error (%)

	List	Paragraph	Story	Overall
C#	2.4	8.3	5.7	5.5
CC#	9.0	36.0	44.5	29.8
CCC#	43.0	41.0	—	42.0

cantly different and do not fully support part *ii* of the Syllable Simplification Strategy Hypothesis. We have seen above that longer consonant clusters generally give rise to higher simplification rates. There is a possible answer for why the story-telling task, presumably being the most informal of the tasks, fails to produce a relatively higher simplification rate. In view of the fact that the subjects seem to be avoiding difficult consonant clusters, they are not producing words that contain them, and consequently their error rates are relatively reduced. This same avoidance phenomenon is found in children's L1 acquisition (Kiparsky and Menn, 1977; Ferguson 1978).

Turning now to part *iii* of the Syllable Simplification Strategy Hypothesis, we can determine from Table 25.1 that in the tasks that supply linguistic context, i.e. paragraph reading and story telling, the average rate of epenthesis is 9.3 percent while the average rate of deletion is 12.6 percent. The proportion of epenthesis to deletion in these two tasks is .74. In the list-reading task there is an average rate of epenthesis of 11.3 percent and a 5.5 percent rate of deletion, yielding a 2.0 proportion of epenthesis vs. deletion. Recall that the overall rate of simplification—epenthesis plus deletion—is 16.8 percent for the list task and an average of 21.8 percent in the context tasks of paragraph-reading and story-telling. While the rate of epenthesis by itself does not seem to vary to any great extent across tasks, the difference in the rates of deletion, as an independent strategy, accounts for the above proportion differentials. Since a context is not supplied in the list-reading task, there remains a potential for high ambiguity. Therefore the "avoid ambiguity" constraint is strictly enforced, resulting in a reduced rate of deletion. Clearly then, these results support the prediction of *iii* above.

DISCUSSION

In addition to the numerical/proportional analyses, a phonological analysis was done for each subject to determine the rules involved in the various simplification strategies. If the domain of these rules is limited to the word, epenthesis and deletion are shown to generally occur interconsonantally in the word list task:

Rule Paradigm 1

a. $\emptyset \longrightarrow \vartheta / C\_C_1^2 \#$

b. $C \longrightarrow \emptyset / C\_C_1^2 \#$

(e.g. [tɑpəs] 'tops', [strɛŋs] 'strengths')

In the paragraph-reading and story-telling tasks, on the other hand, deletion and epenthesis generally occur word-finally:

Rule Paradigm 2

a. $\emptyset \longrightarrow \partial / C_1^2\_\#$

b. $C \longrightarrow \emptyset / C_1^2\_\#$

(e.g. [dræftə] 'draft')

[dræf]

Even though the above analysis looks as if it may have interesting consequences, it is naive to assume a word-level domain for the paragraph- and story-telling tasks. Closer examination reveals that between-word interactions actually produce environments similar to those of Rule Paradigm 1. In other words, if the rule environments depicted in Rule Paradigm 2 occur before an adjacent consonant-initial word, the resulting environment, except for the word boundaries, is precisely the same as that of Rule Paradigm 1. Therefore the proper general environment for all of the simplification strategies is as below:

C_(##)C

Another interesting phenomenon surfaces when we examine the produced forms of the word *amidst*. In list reading it is rendered as below:

[ʌmIdəst]

In paragraph-reading and story-telling, the same word is produced as below:

Set 7

a. [ʌmIdəst]   (by epenthesis)
b. [ʌmIst]   (by deletion)
c. [ʌmIts]   (by deletion)
d. [ʌmIdsə]   (by deletion and epenthesis)

Consider also the produced alternations of the word *and:*

Set 8

a. [ænd][10]
b. [æn]   (by deletion)
c. [ændə]   (by epenthesis)
d. [ænə]   (by deletion and epenthesis)

In the *d* examples, there appears to be a definite ordering relation between (1) deletion and (2) epenthesis. For example, if we assume underlying representations analogous to the target language items, the derivations for Set 7 and Set 8 are:

/ʌmIdst/	/ænd/	
ʌmIdsØ	ænØ	deletion
[ʌmIdsə]	[ænə]	epenthesis

Since our deletion rules, Rule Paradigm 1*a* and Rule Paradigm 2*a*, require a word boundary or a consonant after the deleted item, epenthesis could not be ordered before deletion to obtain the results above. It has been proposed that phonological rule-ordering sometimes reflects the acquisition order of the rules, or rather "the synchronic order of the rules will reflect the relative chronology of their appearance in the language" (Halle, 1962, p. 66). If this is the case, then we can conclude that deletion, as an independent strategy, predates epenthesis in some developmental sequence. This fits in nicely with the belief that children display deletion strategies before and in lieu of epenthesis (Ingram, 1976, p. 32). Moreover, it is accepted that children learning their first language rarely utilize epenthesis as a syllable simplification strategy (Olmsted, 1971). Instead, they employ deletion quite extensively. On the surface, it appears as if these first language learners are violating the notion that recoverability is valued in any grammar. Indeed, many researchers report that homonymy is quite widespread among child first language acquirers, particularly in the earlier stages (Vihman, 1981; Stoel-Gammon and Cooper, 1984).

I suggest that the construct of recoverability is acquired developmentally. That is, during the period of homonymy, the child has not yet incorporated recoverability into his or her grammar. An implicit assumption here is that the child must also acquire the adult underlying representations. I speculate that the reason epenthesis rarely surfaces in child language is that the time at which recoverability is acquired corresponds to the attainment of adult-like phonetic accuracy. Therefore, the child now possessing a high level of phonetic accuracy need not simplify any syllable structures, so deletion subsides and epenthesis never gets a chance to be utilized.

Further, I propose that the reason adult language learners utilize epenthesis more than first language learners is precisely that many of the L2 learners acquire the notion of recoverability (along with TL underlying representations) well in advance of their attainment of native-like L2 phonetic proficiency. This is because adults, relative to children, seem to "fossilize" at some point short of native-like phonotactic ability. Additionally, by virtue of their advanced cognitive abilities, adults are better equipped to abide by ambiguity constraints.

Finally, I wish to suggest that the use of deletion vs. epenthesis as a syllable simplification strategy is related to L2 proficiency. This may provide another reason (in addition to the one mentioned above) Anderson's Mandarin speakers preferred deletion while Eckman's Mandarin speakers favored epenthesis. As a learner becomes more proficient, he or she not only acquires target language underlying representations but also becomes more and more cognizant of potential ambiguity. Indeed, these two abilities are related to the development of the notion of recoverability.

Perhaps, then, Anderson's Mandarin speakers used deletion more than Eckman's Mandarin speakers because they were relatively less proficient in English—they had yet to fully develop an L2 notion of recoverability. Within this framework, the Mandarin subjects in this study should be categorized with an English proficiency somewhere between Anderson's subjects and Eckman's subjects, since they generally exhibit fairly equal rates of deletion and epenthesis (see Table 25.1).

CONCLUSION

In conclusion, this study has demonstrated that the CAH, the MDH, and the formality-continuum hypothesis are adequate only on a general level in predicting syllable simplification errors. The CAH can predict only that errors will occur. The MDH and the formality-continuum hypothesis, while being able to predict the relative degrees of overall simplification, cannot make any claims concerning the relative degrees of the two different strategies discussed here.

By operationalizing the functional notion of recoverability, it has been shown that the degree of linguistic context in an elicitation task affects the ratio of epenthesis to deletion. Other factors certainly contribute to influencing this ratio, and among them are the native language syllable structure and the degree of L2 proficiency. In order to progress from a programmatic study to a fully explanatory study, these and other factors need to be examined in greater detail.

NOTES

1. The fact that Portuguese exhibits a relatively high degree of epenthesis errors may be due to transfer of a NL epenthesis rule. See Major (this volume) for a discussion of transfer vs. developmental reasons for epenthesis in Portuguese.

2. See Eckman (1981a) (and this volume) for a discussion of natural rules in L2 phonology. See also Schane (1972).

3. Eckman (1981b) points out that there is no a priori reason to assume that a L2 learner has acquired target language underlying representations. These assumptions must be based upon the learner's production alternations.

4. She also suggests that this glottal stop insertion is the result of an attempt to maintain lexical items as separate units in the speech stream.

5. In English, the /s/ in this example is considered ambisyllabic. Egyptian Arabic does not allow ambisyllabic consonants.

6. Major (this volume) independently suggests that the operation of epenthesis vs. deletion might depend upon formality. He expects more epenthesis in formal situations because this fortition process would insure the perception of final consonants.

7. Superscripts indicate the maximum number of segments and subscripts indicate the minimum number: for example, $V_1^3 = V$ or VV or VVV.

8. Eckman (1981b) also believes that the reason his Cantonese learners of English display terminal devoicing but avoid deletion strategies is to maintain the integrity of the underlying form.

9. This same type of markedness-related error progression is also found in pathological data. For example, Blumstein reports that her aphasic patients simplify consonant clusters to a greater degree than single consonants (1973, p. 60).

10. Because of the alternation in the forms for *and*, I am not at this point assuming a rule of fast or casual speech that deletes terminal /d/ when preceded by /n/. This process is to be considered here a subpart of final deletion. See Labov (1972) for a discussion of dental deletion in English.

APPENDIX A

1. has
2. splash
   splashed
3. crack
   cracks
4. scream
   screamed
5. zone
   zones
6. hosts
7. risk
   risked
8. clasps
9. judge
   judged
10. serve
    served
11. telephone
    telephoned
12. rasp
    rasps
13. wave
    waves
14. lock
    locked
15. top
    tops
16. laugh
    laughs
17. rich
18. ice cream
    ice creams
19. draft

20. rage
21. fifth
    fifths
22. raft
    rafts
23. curves
24. crib
    cribs
25. land
    lands
26. fourth
    fourthed
27. shrimp
    shrimps
28. elephant
    elephants
29. alarm
    alarmed
30. soothe
    soothed
31. bride
    brides
32. zooms
33. soap
    soaps
34. fourth
    fourths
35. catch
36. mash
    mashed
37. attack
    attacked

38. match
    matched
39. loop
    looped
40. cough
    coughs
41. house
42. wrist
    wrists
43. save
    saved
44. kite
    kites
45. watch
    watched
46. soothes
47. masks
48. flag
    flags
49. ribs
50. look
    looked
51. kissed
52. string
    strings
53. strength
    strengths
54. fifthed
55. fizz
    fizzed
56. amidst

APPENDIX B

While I was cleaning my room in my house, I started to look admidst the things scattered on the floor, under the bed that was next to the orange chair. I was home alone in the house, and I got down on my hands and knees to look for the pants and socks that I had lost on Wednesday. I missed

415

them and it was quite a search to find them amongst everything that had collected on the floor that I had been saving for the past few weeks.

Suddenly a draft came into the room and I felt frightened. Something crashed downstairs and then the doorbell buzzed. I wanted to go downstairs to find out who was there, but it was very dark and I lost my courage. All I could do was think of the worst possible fate. I clasped my hands together and hoped that the stranger downstairs would not kill me. I was in the darkness of the fourth floor, hidden in a pile of memories.

At this time I heard footsteps coming up the stairs! My lips quivered. My strength disappeared and I screamed. Then I heard somebody running away. I was saved! I talked to myself in the mirror to lift my spirits, and when I was calmed down I telephoned the police to inform them of what had happened. After that, I felt glad to be alive and went downstairs to eat something, because being frightened always makes me hungry. I prepared some eggs that had recently been hatched, and then went to sleep, never having found the pants and socks that I had been looking for.

REFERENCES

Anderson, J. (this volume.) The markedness differential hypothesis and syllable structure difficulty.

Blumstein, S. 1973. *A Phonological Investigation of Aphasic Speech.* The Hague: Mouton.

Broselow, E. 1984. An investigation of transfer in second language acquisition. *IRAL 22,* 253–269. (Also this volume.)

Eckman, F. 1977. Markedness and the contrastive analysis hypothesis. *Language Learning 27,* 315–330. (Also this volume.)

Eckman, F. 1981a. On the naturalness of interlanguage phonological rules. *Language Learning 31,* 195–216. (Also this volume.)

Eckman, F. 1981b. On predicting phonological difficulty in second language acquisition. *Studies in Second Language Acquisition 4,* 18–30.

Ferguson, C.A. 1978. Learning to pronounce: The earliest stages of phonological development in the child. In F.D. Minifie and L.L. Lloyd (Eds.), *Communicative and Cognitive Abilities—Early Behaviorial Assessment.* Baltimore: University Park Press.

Greenberg, J. 1965. Some generalizations concerning initial and final consonant sequences. *Linguistics 18,* 5–34.

Halle, M. 1962. Phonology in generative grammar. *Word 18,* 54–72.

Hankamer, J. 1973. Unacceptable ambiguity. *Linguistic Inquiry 4,* 17–68.

Hooper, J. 1976. *An Introduction to Natural Generative Phonology.* NY: Academic Press.

Ingram, D. 1976. *Phonological Disability in Children.* London: Edward Arnold.

Jacobson, R., and M. Halle. 1956. *Fundamentals of Language.* The Hague: Mouton.

Kaye, J. 1981. Opacity and recoverability in phonology. *The Canadian Journal of Linguistics 19,* 134–149.

Kaye, J. 1981. Recoverability, abstractness and phonotactic constraints. In D.L. Goyvaerts (Ed.), *Phonology in the 1980's.* Ghent: E. Story-Scientia.

Kiparsky, P., and L. Menn. 1977. On the acquisition of phonology. In J. MacNamara (Ed.), *Language Learning and Thought.* NY: Academic Press. (Also this volume.)

Kisseberth, C. 1970. On the functional unity of phonological rules. *Linguistic Inquiry 1,* 291–306.

Labov, W. 1972. The internal evolution of linguistic rules. In R. Stockwell and R. MaCaulay (Eds.), *Linguistic Change and Generative Theory.* Bloomington: Indiana University Press.

Lado, R. 1957. *Linguistics Across Cultures.* Ann Arbor: The University of Michigan Press.

Li, C.A., and S.A. Thompson. 1981. *Mandarin Chinese.* Berkeley: University of California Press.

Major, R. (this volume.) A model of interlanguage phonology.

Olmsted, D.L. 1971. *Out of the Mouth of Babes.* The Hague: Mouton.

Schane, S.A. 1972. Natural rules in phonology. In R.P. Stockwell and R.K.S. MaCaulay (Eds.), *Linguistic Change and Generative Theory.* Bloomington: Indiana University Press.

Stoel-Gammon, C., and J.A. Cooper. 1984. Patterns of early lexical and phonological development. *Journal of Child Language 11,* 247–271.

Tarone, E. 1979. Interlanguage as chameleon. *Language Learning 29,* 181–191.

Tarone, E. 1980. Some influences on the syllable structure of interlanguage phonology. *IRAL 18,* 139–152 (Also this volume).

Tiee, H.H-Y. 1969. Contrastive analysis of the monosyllable structure of American English and Mandarin Chinese. *Language Learning 19,* 1–16.

Vihman, M. 1981. Phonology and the development of the lexicon. *Journal of Child Language 8,* 239–265.

CONCLUSION

The papers presented in this volume have attempted to analyze the phenomenon of interlanguage phonology from a number of perspectives. By examining the acquisition of L2 phonology from different structural levels, such as the segmental, the suprasegmental, and the syllable, we have come to determine that the same basic principles operate throughout. The concepts of markedness, language transfer, and developmental universals are clearly evident and interact with one another within each structural level, yielding differing degrees of variation. We have also determined that it is a necessary prerequisite to explore the theoretical underpinnings of both first and second language phonological acquisition before trying to deal with the empirical findings. As was shown in almost all the articles, the acquisition of a second language phonology is not the simplistic process of overcoming language transfer as was once thought. Rather, L2 phonological acquisition is much like L2 syntactic acquisition insofar as it is a dynamic phenomenom, governed by a set of universal developmental processes that interact with transfer processes in many interesting ways.

While there remain many unsolved problems requiring much more research, we believe that the articles in this text explore many important areas and constitute a substantial advancement toward a unified theory of interlanguage phonology.

INDEX OF KEY CONCEPTS WITH DEFINITIONS

Several key concepts are discussed repeatedly throughout the volume. These are defined below followed by a list of the articles which make substantial reference to them.

rone, ch. 13; Sato, ch. 14; Broselow, ch. 15; Anderson, ch. 16; Broselow, ch. 17; Karimi, ch. 18; Weinberger, ch. 25)

Fossilization
The cessation of acquisition before the complete mastery of the grammar at a native speaker level. In the domain of phonology, fossilzation results in a foreign accent.
(Tarone, ch. 4; Major, ch. 6; Beebe, ch. 9; Tarone, ch. 13; Ioup and Tansomboon, ch. 20)

Glottal Stop Insertion
The insertion of a glottal stop in word initial position to create a less marked syllable structure.
(Tarone, ch. 13; Broselow, ch. 15)

Interlingual Identification
The process by which a second language learner judges acoustically different native and target phones to be members of the same phonemic category.
(Flege and Hillenbrand, ch. 10)

Markedness
Structures which share all features but one may be compared in terms of markedness. They may be referred to as marked and unmarked, or more marked and less marked with respect to universal grammar. The criteria used to determine the categories differ according to the definition used. Markedness is sometimes defined in terms of complexity or neutrality. The one most frequently employed in this volume is that of *typological markedness,* where A is more marked than B if the presence of A in a language implies the presence of B, but not vice versa.
(Eckman, ch. 3; Eckman, ch. 7; Altenberg and Vago, ch. 8; Broselow, ch. 15; Anderson, ch. 16; Broselow, ch. 17; Karimi, ch. 18; Weinberger, ch. 25)

Markedness Differential Hypothesis (MDH)
The prediction that the areas of the target language which differ from and are more marked than the native language will be difficult to acquire, with the rela-tive degree of difficulty corresponding to the relative degree of markedness. Target language elements which are different from the native language but are not more marked will not be difficult.
(Eckman, ch. 3; Eckman, ch. 7; Altenberg and Vago, ch. 8; Anderson, ch. 16; Weinberger, ch. 25)

Open Syllable
A syllable ending in a vowel, usually of the form CV, or V.
(Macken and Ferguson, ch. 1; Tarone, ch. 4; Tarone, ch. 13; Sato, ch. 14; Anderson, ch. 16; Weinberger, ch. 25)

Permeability
The degree to which rules from one system penetrate another rule system. In second language acquisition the interlanguage can be permeated by rules from either the target or native language.
(Beebe, ch. 23)

Phonological Universal
A cross-linguistic phonological pattern which has a high probability of occurrence, though it may admit exception. Many of these universals derive from the specific properties of the human articulatory and perceptual systems. Phonological universals are often discussed in terms of markedness.
(Macken and Ferguson, ch. 1; Kiparsky and Menn, ch. 2; Tarone, ch. 4; Major, ch. 6; Tarone, ch. 13; Sato, ch. 14; Anderson, ch. 16; Weinberger, ch. 25)

Prosody
The relative levels of stress and pitch as they occur within syllables and words, and across phrases and longer stretches of speech, giving a language its characteristic intonational contours.
(Neufeld, ch. 19; Ioup and Tansomboon, ch. 20; Broselow, Hurtig and Ringen, ch. 21; Stølen, ch. 24)

Recoverability
The ability to recover an underlying representation, no longer apparent at

the surface, by reversing the application of the rules and working back from the surface to a unique underlying representation.
(Eckman, ch. 7; Weinberger, ch. 25)

Sonority Hierarchy
The universal tendency of segments within a syllable to be arranged with the least sonorant segments on the edges and the most sonorant segments in the middle, where sonority is defined as being the most vowellike.
(Broselow, ch. 17; Karimi, ch. 18)

Stylistic Variation
Variation in the choice of structure based on the level of formality of the context. The style may range from casual to highly formal.
(Tarone, ch. 4; Schmidt, ch. 22; Beebe, ch. 23; Stølen, ch. 24; Weinberger, ch. 25)

Syllable Structure Transfer
The alteration of the target language syllable structure to allow it to conform to the syllabic patterns permitted in the native language.
(Tarone, ch. 4; Tarone, ch. 13; Sato, ch. 14; Broselow, ch. 15; Weinberger, ch. 25)

Terminal Devoicing
The phonological rule which devoices a voiced consonant in word-final position. Such rules are found in the native grammars of Polish, Russian and German, among others.
(Eckman, ch. 3; Major, ch. 6; Eckman, ch. 7; Altenberg and Vago, ch. 8; Weinberger, ch. 25)

Transfer
The imposition of the native language grammar on the structure of the target language. The influence may enhance learning–positive transfer, or impede acquisition–negative transfer. Negative transfer is often referred to as interference, and the errors which result are termed interlingual.
(Macken and Ferguson, ch. 1; Tarone, ch. 4; Dickerson, ch. 5; Major, ch. 6; Eckman, ch. 7; Altenberg and Vago, ch. 8; Beebe, ch. 9; Flege and Hillenbrand, ch. 10; Hecht and Mulford, ch. 12; Tarone, ch. 13; Sato, ch. 14; Broselow, ch. 15; Anderson, ch. 16; Broselow, ch. 17; Broselow, Hurtig and Ringen, ch. 21; Schmidt, ch. 22; Beebe, ch. 23; Stølen, ch. 24)

Variability
The differences noted in acquisition patterns either between learners of similar backgrounds or at similar stages of acquisition, or in one particular learner at various times throughout the data collection, due to the influence of paralinguistic factors.
(Macken and Ferguson, ch. 1; Tarone, ch. 4; Dickerson, ch. 5; Major, ch. 6; Beebe, ch. 9; Hecht and Mulford, ch. 12; Ioup and Tansomboon, ch. 20; Schmidt, ch. 22; Beebe, ch. 23; Stølen, ch. 24; Weinberger, ch. 25)

Variable Rule
The rule which captures the system underlying variable performance.
(Tarone, ch. 4; Dickerson, ch. 5; Eckman, ch. 7)

Voice Onset Time (VOT)
In the articulation of stop consonants, the value in milliseconds of the interval which occurs between the release of air pressure and the beginning of regular vocal cord vibration.
(Macken and Ferguson, ch. 1; Flege and Hillenbrand, ch. 10; Nathan, Anderson and Budsayamongkon, ch. 11)

LANGUAGE INDEX

The following languages, classified as L1 /L2 are substantially discussed in the text chapters noted.